MALAYA

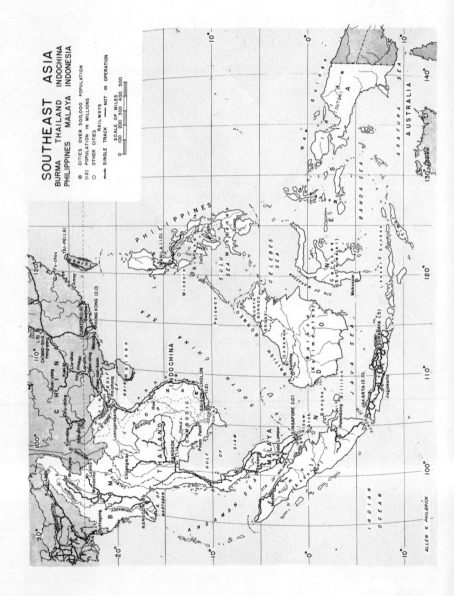

SOUTHEAST ASIA

BURMA   THAILAND   INDOCHINA
PHILIPPINES   MALAYA   INDONESIA

◉ CITIES OVER 500,000 POPULATION
(1.2) POPULATION IN MILLIONS
○ OTHER CITIES

           RAILWAYS
⎯⎯ SINGLE TRACK ---- NOT IN OPERATION

SCALE OF MILES
0 100 200 300 400 500

ALLEN K. PHILBRICK

THE AMERICAN ETHNOLOGICAL SOCIETY

Verne F. Ray, Editor

MALAYA

By
NORTON GINSBURG
and
CHESTER F. ROBERTS, JR.

with the collaboration of
Leonard Comber
Burton Stein
C. Lester Stermer
John E. Trotter

University of Washington Press
Seattle

The maps and figures in this book are based on the following
sources. Maps 1-7, 10, 17, and 19-26, as well as figure 2,
are from M. V. Del Tufo, Malaya: A Report on the 1947 Census of Population (London: Crown Agents for the Colonies,
1949). Maps 8, 9, 11, 12, and 14 are taken from selected topographic sheets, Federation of Malaya Survey Department,
Kuala Lumpur. Various Federation of Malaya government maps
and text sources were used for Maps 13 and 16. Map 15 is
derived from reports of the UNESCO Commission on Technical
Needs in Press, Film, Radio, and reports of the UNESCO
Department of Mass Communication; the base is from Goode's
Series of Outline Maps, No. 227, ed. Henry M. Leppard (Chicago: University of Chicago Press). Map 18 is after Purcell
and others, and Map 27 from The Pattern of Asia, ed. Norton Ginsburg (New York: Prentice-Hall, 1958). Figures 1
and 4 are based on information from The Economist and the
Singapore press as well as The Pattern of Asia. Figure 3 is
from Granville St. John Orde-Browne, Labour Conditions in
Ceylon, Mauritius, and Malaya (London: H. M. Stationery
Office, 1943).

U.S. AIR FORCE

Preface

ON AUGUST 31, 1957, a new state made its appearance on the
political map of Asia. The former Federation of Malaya took
its place among the several Asian nations which have acquired
their independence since the end of World War II. The process
of self-determination, which has been transforming southern
and southeastern Asia from a region of colonies and dependencies to an area of independent states, has almost run its
course.

It is fitting, therefore, that some attempt be made to examine the new Malaya in light of the systems of organization that
have characterized the old. In this analysis it has been considered necessary to include Singapore, which has functioned
traditionally as the primary city for the Federation, even
though it has retained its identity as a separate and not yet
independent political unit. Thus, Singapore and the Federation
have been considered together as an entity, and the two are
discussed under the regional name, Malaya.

This volume, then, is a kind of bench mark, an attempt to
provide a descriptive and analytical basis for understanding
a new Malaya about to embark on an unpredictable course of
independence. It takes due cognizance of the pluralistic character of Malayan society, composed as it is of three major
ethnic groups, by individual ethnographic analysis of the Malaysian, Chinese, and Indian communities. It describes and
appraises the environmental, social, economic, and political characteristics of Malaya. In addition, it analyzes some of
the key problems that face Malaya as a whole, especially
those dealing with communication among its several communities, political organization, and the prospects for balanced

v

and accelerated economic development. Not all aspects of Malayan life and environment have been dealt with; the book does not pretend to be, nor is it to be interpreted as, an encyclopedic gazetteer. The phases emphasized are those which in the authors' view are most significant in understanding the nature and potentials of what is clearly destined to be an increasingly important element in Southeast Asia's regional structure.

In the preparation of the volume the authors were hampered by limited field experience in Malaya and by the absence of a fund of scholarly research material such as results from prolonged library and field study by many workers in an area. At the time of preparation, to the authors' knowledge, only two American social scientists had done extended field work in Malaya, and the results of the considerably more intensive research of British social scientists, with the exception of Raymond and Rosemary Firth, had only begun to be available. The lack of abundant research material, and the difficulty of obtaining government documents without working in Malay itself, necessitated the use of data referring to years as far back as 1953 and 1954.

The same problem of inadequate research information applies, of course, to all Asian societies and countries. Nevertheless, much excellent material not usually available for other Southeast Asian countries is available for Malaya. Most of the area has been mapped topographically at relatively large scales, and these maps, though frequently out of date, can when thoughtfully interpreted provide valuable information about the areal organization of the country. An excellent census of population was completed in 1947. Without the demographic data extracted from this census, the monograph could not have been completed in its present form. Unfortunately, when the manuscript was being written, these data were already nearly a decade old, but it was considered wiser to work with them, qualifying them where possible, than to await publication of the next census tabulation, which might not appear until 1959 or 1960. The annual reports for the Federation and Singapore also served as valuable sources of information, although no attempt was made to duplicate in this volume the great variety of data that characterizes them and other government publications that have proved no less valuable. The detailed analysis of the Malayan economy produced by the International Bank for Reconstruction and Development was also consulted, as were

Professor Frederic Benham's materials on national income. In addition, a series of valuable studies appeared in the Malayan Journal of Tropical Geography, published by the University of Malaya, covering aspects of Malayan life which previously had been unknown or at best little understood.

The book is the result of an interdisciplinary research project originally performed in 1955-56 under contract to the Human Relations Area Files, Incorporated, of New Haven, Connecticut, by a staff of social scientists at the University of Chicago. These included geographers, historians, anthropologists, sociologists, political scientists, and specialists in the fields of communication and international relations. Out of their efforts came a series of essays covering aspects of Malayan society which together formed the basis for this publication. The interdisciplinary nature of this staff and its research is reflected in the present volume. The senior author is a geographer; the junior author is a student of international affairs.

The original drafts for Chapters 1, 3, 4, and 5 were prepared by John Trotter, geographer; for Chapters 7, 9, and 10 by Burton Stein, historian; for Chapter 8 by C. Lester Stermer, specialist in Asian international relations. In addition, Leonard Comber, F. R. A. S. , graciously made available an essay on Chinese secret societies, which was incorporated into Chapter 8. The assistance of Fred Eggan and Irving Kaplan, anthropologists at the University of Chicago, contributed significantly to the character and quality of the volume.

The authors were fortunate in having the counsel of experts whose presence at the University of Chicago made possible the consideration of aspects of the study that could not otherwise have been attempted. These included Sir Sydney Caine, then vice-chancellor of the University of Malaya and now director of the London School of Economics; P. T. Bauer of Cambridge University; Raymond Firth of the London School of Economics and visiting professor of anthropology at the University of Chicago in the winter and spring of 1956; Haji M. Eusoff, Dato Panglima Kinta and chairman of the governing board of the University of Malaya; and G. E. D. Lewis, assistant director of education for the Federation of Malaya. Thanks are also due to Isadore Falk and William Gilmartin of the International Bank of Reconstruction and Development Mission; to the British Information Service, and to the members of the governments of

the Federation and of Singapore with whom a considerable cor-
respondence was carried on.

The counsel of Verne Ray, professor of anthropology at the
University of Washington and editor of the American Ethnological Society, under whose auspices this publication appears, was indispensable. Appreciation is expressed also to
Donald Hudson, executive officer of the department of geography at the University of Washington, for the opportunity made
available to the senior author to spend the spring of 1957 on
the staff of his department, thereby facilitating the final work
on the volume.

Additional thanks are due to the Human Relations Area Files,
Incorporated, which sponsored the original project; to the
department of geography, the division of the social sciences,
and the University libraries at the University of Chicago for
research facilities; to Mrs. Zelda Hauser and Mrs. Bette
Gifford Johnson for assistance during the project period; and
to Mrs. Lois Grotewold, Miss Ann Larimore, and Miss Jac-
quelyn Beyer for their cartographic contributions.

The authors also appreciate the financial assistance of the
Social Science Research Committee, the University of Chicago,
in completing the manuscript.

The responsibility for the contents of the book itself, of
course, lies with the authors.

Norton Ginsburg
Seattle, Washington

Chester F. Roberts, Jr.
San Francisco, California

Contents

Illustrations

MAPS

xi

FIGURES

MALAYA

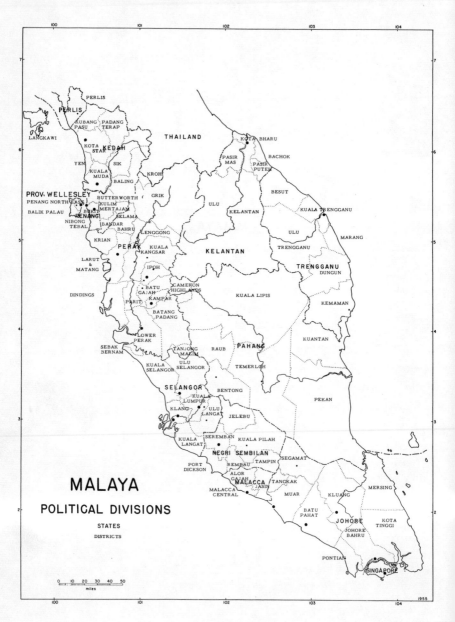

MALAYA

POLITICAL DIVISIONS

STATES

DISTRICTS

Map 1

1. The Malayan Peninsula

SOUTHWARD FROM mainland southeastern Asia an attenuated peninsula thrusts far into a region of islands and seas, insular Southeast Asia. Although continental in that it is connected by the Isthmus of Kra with the Asiatic mainland, the peninsula in other respects bears a remarkable resemblance in natural conditions, and even in patterns of human occupance, to the archipelagoes which form the Indies and the Philippines.

The northern portion of the peninsula is shared by Burma and Thailand. It consists of generally north-south-trending granitic ridges with fringing and discontinuous coastal plains, is some thirty-five miles wide at its narrowest, and is for the most part sparsely populated. The peninsula begins to widen markedly at about 7 degrees north latitude. Here it is shared by Thailand and the Federation of Malaya. From about 5 degrees, 30 minutes north, the Federation fills the peninsula southward to the island of Singapore.

Malaya,[1] therefore, occupies the southernmost direct projection of the Asiatic continent, the Malayan peninsula. It extends some five hundred miles from the Thai border in the north to the islands just south of Singapore, or roughly from 1 to 7 degrees north latitude. At its widest point, just north of center, it measures some two hundred miles from east to west, and it tapers to a width of about sixty miles near its southern tip. To the east lies the South China Sea, an arm of the Pacific Ocean; on the west the twenty-three-mile-wide Strait of Malak-

---

1. Henceforward, the word "Malaya" will be used to include both the Federation of Malaya and Singapore.

ka, an extension of the Andaman Sea and the Indian Ocean, separates Malaya from Sumatra. Thus, the peninsula is interposed between the Indian and the Pacific oceans, and this strategic fact has placed an indelible stamp on its history. The area of Malaya covers some 50,886 square miles, roughly that of the states of Alabama or New York in the United States, or of England alone, without Wales.

Malaya provides its inhabitants with a distinctive physical setting which resembles that of the archipelagoes bordering Southeast Asia. This setting consists of a peninsula set amidst nearly surrounding seas, a backbone of forest-clad mountains and hills set in swampy or marshy plains, and mantling soils, easily eroded when cleared of their forest cover. Tendencies toward soil erosion, however, are less a reflection of the intrinsic qualities of the soils than of the torrential downpours, high humidities, and uniformly high temperatures which characterize Malaya.

Surface Configuration[2]

Malaya rises above a great block of land, known as the Sunda Platform, extending southward and eastward from mainland Southeast Asia. This structure is for the most part submerged beneath the shallow southern portion of the South China Sea, the depth of which averages some 120 feet, and its shallow bordering seas, the Gulf of Thailand and the Java Sea. Most of Borneo and northern Java also rise from the submerged platform. The platform is tectonically stable and is free from geologically recent volcanic activity. In other words, the Asian continental shelf extends well into archipelagic Southeast Asia, and Malaya is the emergent western portion of the shelf, just as Borneo is an elevated eastern portion. The elevated parts of the Sunda Platform are topographically mature, with rounded mountains and hills reflecting the high rate of weathering characteristic of the equatorial regions.

Malaya itself is characterized by mountains and hills rising abruptly from flat plains of deep alluvium. Mountains form an ever-present background to the peopled plains. Maturely dis-

---

2. Much of the following discussion is based on the excellent chapters on Malaya in E. H. G. Dobby, Southeast Asia (London: University of London Press, 1950).

sected, they are not rugged, barren peaks, but are subdued to a general roundness and are covered with forest.

The mountains of Malaya are part of a series of generally north-south ranges extending through Southeast Asia and marking a break from the east-west lines of the Himalayan ranges. They are the remains of ancient mountains much older than the Himalaya, generally characterized by relatively low altitudes and rounded relief. Erosion over long periods has stripped the sedimentary cover from them, baring crystalline (largely granitic) cores and leaving the sedimentary strata outcropping at their bases as flanking foothills. Where the sedimentary strata are more resistant to weathering, precipitous relief is characteristic. The mountain ranges project southward from the Thai border, diverging from north to south. The trend is north-northeast to south-southwest in the northern portions of the country and varies to north-northwest to south-southeast in the south. The highest average elevation (between six thousand and seven thousand feet) is found in the north. Elevations diminish southward, and the ranges may be said to disappear beneath the sea.

The Central Range (actually west of center) is the longest and highest. It reaches from the Thai border to Malakka. To the west of the Central Range there are four shorter ranges, none reaching further south than northern Perak. The ranges to the east of the Central Range are discontinuous and much broken by drainage lines. In the Kelantan-Trengganu-Pahang border area the system merges with the dissected Trengganu plateau, which averages about 2,500 feet above sea level. Ranges to the south are distinguishable mainly as rows of hills in otherwise level or undulating country.

Low flat plains fringe the Malayan peninsula and are found between the mountain ranges inland. Both coastal and inland plains are the results of prolonged erosion and a rising sea level which causes rivers to deposit much of their load inland or along the immediate coast. Characteristic of these plains are marshes far inland, fresh-water swamps over wide areas of the coastal plains, and seaward fringes of brackish-water swamps. The coastal plains are from five to forty miles wide along the entire west side of the peninsula and up to twenty miles wide on the east coast. They are generally low, with elevations commonly less than three hundred feet above sea level far inland, and are either flat or of undulating relief.

Drainage

The streams of Malaya carry exceptionally large volumes of water, when compared with the size of the areas they drain, and large loads of transported material; they also experience rapid changes in volume due to the local and torrential nature of Malaya's rainfall. In general they are short. The Sungei Pahang is the longest (about 205 miles). In the upper reaches of the streams gradients are steep and currents are rapid, but the middle and lower courses are characterized by sluggish flow, meanders, swamps, and natural levees.

Two important factors influence the drainage pattern of Malaya. They are (1) the north-south trend of the ranges and (2) rising sea levels since the last glacial period.

The north-south trend of the mountain ranges produces stream courses which parallel the ranges in the valleys, while east-west tributaries drain the flanks of the slopes. This creates a trellislike drainage pattern over much of northern and central Malaya. Under certain conditions narrow defiles in the ranges have been cut by streams. Common features of rivers in such circumstances are sharp turns in their courses when they pass laterally through the defile from one valley lowland to another. The valley sections of such streams are apt to be covered by marshes resulting in part from the jamming effect within the narrows during downpours. Heavy and sudden rains, dense vegetation impeding runoff from low ground, and the difficulty of drainage in the below-stream-level areas behind natural levees along streams also contribute to the formation of inland swamps and marshes.

The effect of rising sea levels has been pronounced in forming the alluvial plains of Malaya. Stream base levels have been raised, resulting in decreased down-cutting, reduced load-carrying power, meanders, and indefinite drainage far inland. Offshore and estuarine sedimentation in shallow seas, aided by mangrove growth, has created coastal plains and shallow banks to considerable distances off some coasts. Strong ocean currents have generally restricted delta formation and encouraged extended coastal deposition, a common condition on both coasts of southern Malaya.

Vegetation

Malaya is mantled by forests which originally covered mountains, hills, and plains alike. Cleared areas in permanent cultivation are limited principally to the Kelantan delta and to a relatively narrow band along the west side of the peninsula. The forests of Malaya fall broadly within the class of tropical rain forest, though in detail there is much diversity and local variation.

Three general kinds of vegetation associations may be distinguished. They are (1) coastal, (2) lowland, and (3) upland.

Characteristic coastal vegetation types are the beach woodlands and the mangrove swamps. Neither type covers large areas (there are perhaps 450 miles of mangrove forest), but they are important because of their use by people settled within or near the areas.

Beach woodlands, dominated by the tall needle-leaved casuarina and coconut palms at the shore, and including scrub and grass on the landward side, are found along dunes and sand flats on the east coast from Trengganu southward and in various places along the west coast. This vegetation type seldom reaches more than a few hundred feet inland.

Stilt-rooted mangrove forest is found along the west coast in association with tidal flats and silting estuaries and to a lesser extent along the east coast in tidal lagoons. The mangrove, whatever the species, is capable of living in salt or brackish water and is essentially a salt-water swamp growth. It is used for charcoal, for firewood, and in tanning. Malayan settlement is sometimes situated in the mangrove forests rather than in the sandy coastal strips, which are avoided because of the prevalence of malaria and sandfly fever. On the landward side of these swamps are found various palms, including the nipa and the pandanus. The leaves of both of these are used for thatching roofs and for making woven materials.

Two prominent forest types found inland from the coastal types on the lowlands, hills, and lower mountain slopes are the fresh-water swamp forest and the lowland tropical rain forest. Fresh-water swamp forest is widespread along the entire west side and the southern half of the eastern side of Malaya on alluvial lowlands. Much of this land has been cleared and drained and put to cultivation. Swamp forest usually is not permanently under water but is subject to irregular flooding. The ground is often covered with a thick layer of peat (up to thirty feet); undergrowth is usually thick.

About 60 per cent of Malaya is covered by lowland tropical

5

rain forest found on the plains and hills and to heights of two thousand feet in the mountains. It is a two-storied evergreen tropical forest with great admixture of species and few homogeneous stands of any one species. Heavy undergrowth is not common. The family Dipterocarpaceae predominates. Much of this forest may be called secondary forest since it follows the clearing and burning carried on in shifting cultivation. Stages of vegetation regeneration range from grass to forest which is virtually indistinguishable from untouched rain forest.

At heights of from two thousand to four thousand feet the rain forest changes in character and gives way to what may be called hill forest. The principal trees of this association are <u>serava</u> and a thorny palm, <u>bertam</u>. Dipterocarps, so prominent in lowland rain forest, are not present. Hill forest is quite widespread along the slopes of the Central Range and on the ridges of the Trengganu plateau.

At elevations in excess of four thousand feet, oak and other temperate-climate trees form the forests, giving way to scrub or moss forest at the highest levels. Such areas are found mainly in eastern Perak and western Kelantan.

Climate and Weather

The climate of Malaya is tropical. The country is always under the influence of warm, moist air masses. Rainfall and humidity are high; temperatures, uniform. Strong winds are found almost exclusively in association with line squalls or isolated thunderstorms. Seasonal rhythm is definite but is related mainly to changes in prevailing wind direction.

There are four seasons: (1) the northeast monsoon, from late October or November to March, (2) the southwest monsoon, from late May or June to September, and (3) and (4) the two seasons separating the monsoons. The onset and termination of the monsoons in Malaya are not well defined and in this respect differ markedly from the monsoon prototype of India, where seasonal changes are sharply defined.

The northeast monsoon blows during the northern-hemisphere winter and represents the equator-ward movement of the trade winds. The southwest monsoon results from the northward movement and deflection to the right of the southeast trade winds as they cross the equator. The intermediate seasons are represented by the periods between the advance

6

of one of the air flows and the retreat of the other. They are periods of calm, sometimes known as doldrums.

Temperatures are markedly uniform in all seasons, and changes are small. The greatest of these occurs on the east coast when cool daytime temperatures are common during the northeast monsoon. As is characteristic of many tropical regions, yearly mean ranges in temperature are less than daily mean ranges. Daily mean ranges of 10 to 15 degrees Fahrenheit are found near the sea, and ranges of 15 to 20 degrees Fahrenheit inland. Yearly mean ranges at Penang and Singapore are 2.9 degrees and 2.7 degrees Fahrenheit, respectively.[3] (Compare with other Southeast Asian places, Figure 1.)[4] Daytime temperatures seldom exceed 90 degrees Fahrenheit and generally fall to 70 to 75 degrees during the night in the lowlands. In the highlands (four thousand to five thousand feet) the uniformity of temperatures persists, but at slightly lower levels. Both daytime and nighttime temperatures are somewhat lower than in the lowlands. Humidity is high and is quite oppressive during the day when no breeze is present. Relative humidities of 70 per cent or more are usual.

Rainfall occurs at all times during the year, but some seasonal concentration is evident (Figure 1). Along the east coast and for short distances inland the maximum rainfall occurs during the northeast monsoon. December is usually the month of greatest rainfall. Over the interior and on the west coast maximum rainfall occurs during the intermediate periods, with the greatest amounts in October and November. There is considerable variation in periods of peak rainfall from area to area. At Penang, for example, the peak period usually extends from August through November, while at Singapore the concentration is from November through January.

Annual rainfall on the peninsula is generally over 75 inches, enough for the growing of wet rice without artificial irrigation. It exceeds 125 inches on the east coast and decreases westward

---

3. I. G. John, Malayan Meterological Service, Summary of Observations, 1953 (Singapore: Government Printing Office, 1954), p. 8.

4. Figure taken from Norton Ginsburg, ed., The Pattern of Asia (New York: Prentice-Hall, 1958). Note the relative uniformity of rainfall at Singapore as compared with other Southeast Asian Stations.

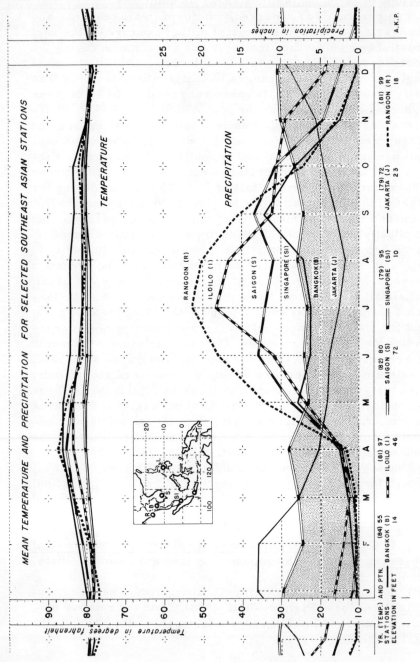

MEAN TEMPERATURE AND PRECIPITATION FOR SELECTED SOUTHEAST ASIAN STATIONS

TEMPERATURE

PRECIPITATION

Figure 1

toward the Central Range. Along the west side of Malaya the distribution of rainfall is more irregular. Annual rainfall is 90. 4 inches at Alor Star in the north. It increases southward through south Kedah and Perak (Penang, 107. 2 inches) and then decreases again through Selangor, Negri Sembilan, and Johore (Kuala Lumpur, 94 inches; Singapore, 95. 2 inches). Heaviest recorded rainfall occurs in the Larut hills near Taiping (198 inches). [5] The district around Jelebu, east of the Central Range and surrounded on all sides by mountains, is the driest part of Malaya. Average annual rainfall here is sixty-five inches.

Rainfall is largely of the instability type, occurring during storms characterized by cumulo-nimbus clouds, lightning, sudden wind shifts, and localized torrential downpours. These thunderstorms are of three types: (1) local convective storms closely related to local differential heating of the earth's surface and to orographic influences, (2) storms or line squalls associated with boundaries between air streams, and (3) "Sumatras," squalls which apparently form in the Strait of Malakka under the influence of land breezes from the west coast of Malaya. Storms are sometimes quite violent and cause considerable local damage. Sudden and large amounts of rainfall create local floods, and winds with gusts often in excess of forty miles per hour, frequently bring heavy seas to coastal areas and blow down trees and structures inland. While most of these storms last only a few minutes to a half hour, some last an hour or more. [6]

Thunderstorms are more frequent in given localities at certain seasons and at certain times during the day. The pattern of occurrence of squalls at Kota Bharu (northeast Malaya) was studied for two consecutive years. The greatest number occurred in two periods. One period with ninety-two squalls included the months from May to August. The second period, from September to October, had thirty-eight squalls in two years. In the two years during which the study was made there

---

5. Ibid.

6. I. E. M. Watts, "Line-Squalls of Malaya," The Malayan Journal of Tropical Geography, October, 1954, p. 3. Squalls are defined in this article as storms with gusts of over thirty miles per hour accompanying a marked change in wind direction.

were only fourteen squalls in the remaining six months of each
year. It is noted that the greatest frequency is during the southwest monsoon, with a secondary concentration in the fall inter-
monsoon period. Line squalls characteristically occur at
different times of the day during different seasons. The squalls
at Kota Bharu during the southwest monsoon occur mainly in the
afternoon and early evening. During September and October
they occur almost entirely in the afternoon, usually before
6:00 p. m.

In contrast, on the west coast at Malakka thunderstorms of
squall intensity occur throughout the year. The period of greatest frequency is May through August (118 in two years). The
period from November to February has the next highest frequency (42 in two years). However, the other months are not
free of squalls to the extent at Kota Bharu. During the period
of May through August in the two years of analysis, most of
the squalls occurred at Malakka in the early morning from
midnight to 6:00 a. m. In the November-to-February period
squalls were most frequent from noon until midnight.

Soils

Malayan soils have been formed under conditions of uniformly heavy rainfall. Soils with lateritic characteristics
are found over wide areas, and in a few places a true laterite "iron pan" has been formed. [7] Erosion is prevalent in

---

7. A conventional interpretation of the formation of such
soils states that laterization appears to be due to continuous
leaching by warm, heavy rainfall of surface materials low in
organic content. Under these conditions the silica in the soil
is broken into aluminum silicates and removed, leaving clays
and iron compounds. Under certain conditions (when there is
a fluctuating groundwater table) iron concretions and eventually
an iron pan appear at varying depths in the soil profile. Soils
over such an iron pan (laterite) are called laterite soils. It
should be noted that there are those who disagree with the conventional interpretation and argue that "laterization" is not a
distinctive soil-forming process. See G. F. Carter and R. L.
Pendleton, "The Humid Soil: Process and Time, " Geographical Review, October, 1956, pp. 488-507.

many areas which have been cleared for cultivation. Often the upper soil layers (horizons) have been removed. Even when erosion has been retarded, impaired soil structure and rapid deterioration of exposed soils through oxidation of organic matter are common. The result is soils of low inherent fertility.

The description of soils presented here is based principally on classification according to the parent material from which the soils have been derived. [8] In the broadest terms there are (1) soils which have weathered from the rocks over which they now lie and (2) soils that have been transported to their present position by the action of flowing water. The former include soils derived both from igneous (molten) rocks and from sedimentary (deposited by ancient seas) and metamorphosed sedimentary rocks. Transported soils are those of relatively recent coastal and inland deposition as marine or riverine solids. The character of alluvial soils depends on the source of the constituent materials, local drainage, and vegetation.

Coastal deposits form a belt of soils on both the east and west coasts of Malaya. Those on the east coast tend to be more sandy than those on the west, which are largely blue-grey to dark brown silty clays. Many of these soils are associated with extensive accumulations of peat. Relief in these areas tends to be flat or undulating, and the land is often in need of drainage before cultivation is practicable. [9] These soils are relatively fertile.

Inland alluvial soils are found on flat or undulating land of riverine deposition. There are three types of such soils: (1) silty clay loams of poor drainage, (2) reddish or yellow clay loams of good drainage, and (3) alluvial sands of excessive drainage. The first two are used extensively for rubber cultivation, but they demand good management practices.

---

8. G. Owen, "A Provisional Classification of Malayan Soils," The Journal of Soil Science, January, 1951, pp. 20-42. It must be borne in mind that no thorough soil survey has been conducted in Malaya and that heavy forest obscures the ground in many districts. Large areas remain unvisited by soil scientists.

9. E. H. G. Dobby, "The North Kedah Plain: A Study in the Environment of Pioneering for Rice Cultivation," Economic Geography, October, 1951, pp. 287-315.

Soils derived in situ from acidic igneous rock (mainly granitic) cover most of Malaya. They are composed of reddish-yellow sandy clay loams of considerable depth and variable textures. As with virtually all inland soils in Malaya, these soils are not high in plant nutrients. They show no lateritic concretions.

Residual soils of sedimentary rock origins tend to be found on undulating or rolling land. These soils are usually sandy loams, silty clays, and sandy clays or clay loams. They are all generally reddish-yellow or yellow in color. Some of the soils of these series erode severely under conditions of clean cultivation. Lateritic concretions are not unusual in some of these, and one series has a very pronounced laterite horizon.

Mineral and Power Resources[10]

Malaya is highly mineralized, and there is believed to be an abundance of mineral ores lying at or beneath its surface, although in the absence of thorough surveys the extent of these resources is difficult to assess. Only about a fifth of Malaya has been explored mineralogically by scientific means, but it appears that only four minerals--tin, coal, iron, and bauxite-- are to be found in economically workable deposits. Of these, tin clearly predominates. The output of the other metals is primarily from one or two individual mines. Copper, lead, and zinc are known to exist, and tungsten, manganese, and phosphates have been mined in the past. Although evidence for or against the existence of large mineral deposits in Malaya is limited, the discovery of such deposits is unlikely, since min-

---

10. Among the sources of information concerning Malaya's mineral resources are: United Nations, Department of Economic Affairs, Development of Mineral Resources in Asia and the Far East (Report and Documents of the ECAFE Conference on Mineral Resources Development, Tokyo, 20-30 April, 1953; Bangkok, 1953); United Nations, ECAFE, Coal and Iron Ore Resources of Asia and the Far East (Bangkok, 1952); and the report of the International Bank for Reconstruction and Development, The Economic Development of Malaya (Baltimore: Johns Hopkins University Press, 1955), Chapter 4 and Technical Reports 5 and 6.

ing is a very old industry in Malaya and was practiced by both Malays and Chinese long before the West came to play an active role. It can be assumed that large deposits of the common metals would have been discovered by this time, although the rarer metals might not fall into this category.

Tin

Tin is found in nine of the eleven major political units of the Federation. It occurs principally in the form of cassiterite, both as lode deposits and as residual or alluvial deposits. In western Malaya, tin is found in and along the Central Range in what may be termed the Malayan tin belt, which extends northward into Thailand and to a lower degree into Burma. In eastern Malaya smaller deposits are known to occur in all four eastern states (including Johore). The chief developed area is the Kinta field in Perak and a second field some forty miles south. A discontinuous zone of tin-bearing formations, either granitic or alluvial, extends from Perlis to Johore chiefly along the western slopes of the Central Range and its outliers, although tin is also found on the eastern slopes of the range.

The tin originated as concentrations in the igneous flows which form the cores of the principal mountain ranges. It is found in fractures in the granite and in the adjacent limestones and other sedimentaries chiefly at zones of contact between the sedimentaries and the granites. Other deposits have accumulated along fissures in the irregularly surfaced limestone, which have been filled by alluvium rich in cassiterite. These fissure deposits are more difficult to mine than those in alluvium nearer the surface, which are the most easily exploited and possibly the most abundant. The depths at which ores are situated also vary enormously from several feet to over one hundred feet, making the application of consistent mining methods from one area to another difficult.

The cassiterite occurs in forms ranging from sizable lumps to a fine powder. It tends to be free of common impurities, but some rarer minerals such as titanium oxides and tungsten ores are recovered from some of the tin ores.

Reserves are uncertain, and estimates vary from 750,000 to nearly 2,000,000 tons of tin metal, but these are crude guesses. The ores are reported to average about .46 tons of tin concentrate per cubic yard, although this figure varies markedly from place to place even within the same mining area. Even

13

the larger reserve estimates suggest a relatively short life to the tin deposits, but in the absence of thorough surveys, these should not be regarded too pessimistically.

Other metals

Iron-ore reserves in Malaya are estimated at about forty-six million long tons. These are located chiefly in the eastern states near the coast, although smaller deposits are known also in Perak and Kedah. The quality of the ores tends to be high, approaching 60 per cent metal, and they are chiefly magnetite and hematite. The chief deposits appear to be at Bukit Besi in Trengganu and near Ulu Rompin in southeastern Pahang. "The [Ulu Rompin] iron-ore bodies are a series of lenses and pockets with more or less N-S elongation, paralleled with the regional strike and shearing. They have generally been more resistant than the country rock and so occur on the crests of roughly parallel ridges."[11] At Bukit Besi, the ores occur in several forms, the chief of which consists of fragments of a massive ore body along the contacts between the granites and adjacent shales. The outlook appears good for further discoveries.

Bauxite deposits occur widely in southern Malaya, but the high silica content decreases their value, in terms of present technology. Reserves are small and scattered.

Low-grade manganese deposits are found in northeastern Malaya and were mined before the war for export to Japan. Tungsten ores are found in association with tin and gold ores, although the latter appear restricted to one area around Raub in western Pahang. Columbium and tantalum ores are also found in association with tin ores, chiefly in Kedah; and ilmenite (titanium ore) is also a tin-refining by-product.

Power resources

Malaya is relatively poorly endowed with power resources, and of the five major sources of inanimate energy--petroleum, natural gas, coal, water power, and wood--she possesses a clearly exploitable abundance of only one--wood.

Since most of the country is wooded, Malaya's forests

---

11. United Nations, ECAFE, Coal and Iron Ore Resources of Asia and the Far East, p. 117.

14

supply an exceptional amount of energy for fuel in homes, largely in the form of charcoal. Wood can also be used to generate steam power for small installations, and it has been used as locomotive fuel as well. However, the relative inefficiency of wood as a source of energy and the eating away of the more readily accessible stands make undesirable the use of fuelwood in place of more efficient fuels, although locally its use might be expanded.

Malaya possesses no known reserves of petroleum and natural gas, and geological formations appear unfavorable to their discovery. Coal reserves, concentrated almost entirely near Batu Arang in Selangor, have been estimated at about thirty-two million long tons, of which perhaps half may be extractable. The coal is subbituminous, and its calorific value is relatively low, ranging from 9,000 BTU to about 11,000 BTU; it is high in water content, and paradoxically is strongly liable to spontaneous combustion. The relatively low quality of the coal and the availability of petroleum from other areas in Southeast Asia have resulted in declining production at Batu Arang. Peat deposits represent a marginal potential resource as well.

Water power resources are virtually undeveloped in Malaya, only one major plant of 27,000 KW capacity being in operation at Chenderoh, north of Ipoh. Total hydroelectric potential is estimated at about 250,000 KW, but this is subject to extensive revision. Development of hydroelectric resources is made all the more difficult by seasonalities of precipitation, the frequency of torrential downpours, the shortness of the streams, the hazards of silting, and the particular characteristics of Malayan settlement and economy, which militate against integrated river basin development.

2. Past and Present

FROM THE EARLIEST TIMES the history of the Malayan peninsula has been less a Malayan history than that of the essentially foreign interests which happened to converge upon it.
The Sri Vijaya and Majapahit empires, which at one time
controlled much of what is now modern Malaya, had their
power cores in areas outside of the peninsula itself, and
the later history of the area consists of the changing relations between Portuguese, Dutch, English, Arabs, Indians,
Chinese, and Malaysians such as the Bugis, whose origins
for the most part were not on the peninsula itself but in the
adjacent East Indian archipelago. Even the Empire of Malakka,
which flourished during the fifteenth century and formed the
cornerstone for modern Malayan history, was an outpost on
the one hand of Islam and on the other of Thailand and China;
the power of the empire depended not so much on its control
of the peninsula but on its control of the Strait of Malakka.

This characteristic of Malaya's history is reflected in the
role the peninsula has played through the centuries as a pivot
around which political and social movements eddied and flowed.
It is reflected in modern times not only in the diversified composition of Malaya's sizable immigrant population but also in
the role of Singapore as the great entrepôt for southern Southeast Asia. The hackneyed phrase, "crossroads of Asia," has
been applied to Singapore and Malaya innumerable times;
though a commonplace, this phrase establishes the theme for
any survey of Malayan history.

16

Attempts to identify the aboriginal inhabitants of Malaya have been, on the whole, inconclusive. Anthropologists tend to distinguish four types of indigenous inhabitants of the Malay Peninsula and the surrounding islands--the Negrito (Semang), the Senoi, the Proto-Malays (Jakun), and the Deutero-Malays (the "Malay" of the present day). Through comparisons of physical characteristics, language, and cultures, it has been noted that the Semang of Malaya appear related to the Mincopi of the Andaman islands and the Aëtas of the Philippines; that the Senoi appear related to various hill tribesmen in Yünnan, Indochina, the Philippines, Formosa, Borneo, the Celebes, and Sumatra; that the Jakun combine a number of Mongoloid characteristics with a basic Indonesian physiognomy and culture; and that the modern Malay appears to be a synthesis of proto-Malayan, Mongoloid, and Indian strains.

Although archeological discoveries in the peninsula are not numerous, stone implements, pieces of pottery, and other objects found in a number of sites indicate the presence of human groups certainly as early as 5, 000 B. C. , while the discovery of the remains of Java man suggest a much earlier occupancy of the region by this subhuman or his immediate ancestors.

The commonly accepted hypothesis concerning early human migration and settlement, crudely stated, postulates (1) a basic Negrito population inhabiting the peninsula and the Indonesian littoral, possibly evolved from late descendants of Java man; (2) a later southward migration through the area of the more culturally developed ancestors of the Senoi, who tended to expel the Negritos from the more habitable locations, isolating them in the swamp and jungle areas; (3) a still later migration of proto-Malayan peoples from southern China, who tended to intermarry with the Senoi while at the same time restricting them to the less favorable areas of habitation, mainly the hill regions of the interior; and finally (4) the intermarriage of those Proto-Malays who settled along the coasts with Chinese and Indians who migrated to or traded in the region, resulting in the Deutero-Malay.

It appears certain that just prior to the historic period in Malay, a substantial population with a fairly well-developed culture existed on the Malay Peninsula and in the Malaysian archipelago. A large variety of tools had been developed for specific purposes; stock-breeding and rice-culture had been developed; the early Malay had begun to invent artistic techniques, had developed a rudimentary kind of animist worship, knew how to navigate by the stars on the open ocean, and maintained some sort of political and social organization through which his relations with others could be expressed. In short, the Malay entered the historic period a civilized being; the early Indian and Chinese traders who came to Malaya encountered few savages.

The Pre-European Era

Just as the prehistory of Malaya was characterized by a succession of outside influences and migrations, so too is the historic period dominated by the effects of external factors working on the people and their institutions. Indian influences from the west and Chinese from the north and east established the early pattern; the expansions of Islam and Europe mark the the later stages.

The Hindu period

Chinese chronicles report an early trade between India and China as far back as the seventh century B. C. , suggesting also the possibility of an Indian trade with the peninsula, lying as it does across the maritime route between the two countries. The dating of beads and other articles of trade found at various spots on the peninsula point to some sort of commercial exchange between the inhabitants of the region and the peoples of China, India, and even the Levant in the pre-Christian era. Ptolemy's account of the "Golden Chersonese" is seen by many scholars as a description of Malaya in those early days.

The arrival of Hindus in the Malay world was not a sudden occurrence but rather a slow process by which a few ships, arriving seasonally with the monsoon from India, instituted a small trade with the various native settlements along the Malayan coast. Apparently as the trade grew it was found expeditious for a trader to remain throughout the year in a settlement, accumulating goods in trade for shipment back to India. The immigrant trader, because of his position and role in the settlement as the source of increased wealth and potential power, was often treated by the natives as an individual of prestige, somewhat equal in rank with the local ruler. Often his trade gave the settlement increased power in its relations with other Malay settlements, which, in order to obtain his goods, found it necessary to place themselves in respectful relationship with the settlement in which he operated. This appears to have been particularly true in the relations between the coastal settlements and the inland villages. The position of the Hindu trader led, apparently, to his acceptance into the family of the local ruler through marriage. This relationship between the Hindu traders and the local ruling families usually led to the adoption by the latter of Hindu ideas of kingship and the introduction of Hinduized ceremonials in the local courts. Vestiges of these practices are apparent today in the corona-tion rites in several of the Malayan states.[1]

As the Hindu traders resident on the peninsula increased in numbers and influence, they came to demand certain serv-ices calling for the immigration of Hindu Brahmans and ar-tisans, thus further increasing the size of the Hindu commu-nities. The importation of Indian artifacts, not merely for trade but for the local use of the growing Hindu community and the Hinduized ruling elite, also increased.

These earliest Indian arrivals appear to have come largely from Bengal, Orissa, and the Coromandel coast of India; the customs and institutions which they introduced were those pre-vailing in those regions at the time. They were generally fol-lowers of Brahma, Siva, and Vishnu, or proponents of Thera-vada Buddhism. Traces of them dating back to the fourth cen-tury A. D. have been found in recent times as far east as Bor-neo and Cambodia. Pallava inscriptions have been found at several places in Province Wellesley and Kedah.

Under this early Indian influence, several of the Hinduized kingdoms of Southeast Asia were able to expand, absorbing their weaker neighbors and attaining great extent and power. Notable among these was Fu-nan, centering around the lower Mekong valley. This latter empire extended its domain through southern Thailand and down the peninsula, possibly including the coastal areas of the present states of Patani (Thailand), Kelantan, and Trengganu. Possibly under the early suzerainty of Fu-nan was the Malay kingdom of Langkasuka. Although little is known of this kingdom, it appears to have existed

---

1. For an alternative view see the discussion in D. G. E. Hall, A History of Southeast Asia (New York: St. Martin's Press, 1955), pp. 5 ff.

through the fifteenth century, some time after the decline of southern Indian influences during the previous century.

By that time a new and dynamic force had begun to stem from northern India, destined to supplant the older stream of southern Indian influence. The northern Indians replaced the Pallava alphabet with the Nagari script and introduced a form of Mahayana Buddhism and Saivism in place of Theravada Buddhism and Brahmanism. The focal point of this new Indian influence was southern Sumatra and Java. By 683 the Mahayana empire of Sri Vijaya had been established, with its capital near present-day Palembang. Sri Vijaya absorbed its neighboring states, expanding its control over southern and central Sumatra and parts of the peninsula, where one of its monarchs left an inscription at Ligor in 775, indicating a relationship with Langkasuka.

About the time that the Sri Vijayan monarch was erecting his stele at Ligor, the first of the Buddhist Sailendran dynasty was establishing hegemony over the Saivite kingdoms of central Java. For about a century the two empires, the Sailendran and Sri Vijaya, enlarged side by side. While the latter expanded northward through Sumatra and Malaya, the Sailendras exerted their efforts toward the conquest of the Mekong delta region, probably dealing a final deathblow to the ancient kingdom of Fu-nan. Although there are no records, it is probable that relations between the two powers were not without clashes. About the middle of the ninth century a Brahmanist reaction against the Buddhism of the Sailendras resulted in the overthrow of the Sailendras in Java. Apparently several of them escaped to Sumatra, however, and Sailendran monarchs are listed as monarchs of Sri Vijaya from that time.

The fall of the Java empire left Sri Vijaya supreme in the area and in a position to monopolize the sea route through the Straits of Sunda and Malakka. Its capital swiftly became the commercial center for the entire region. This dominant position naturally excited the jealousy of those states not already under Sri Vijayan domination. In the latter part of the tenth century, Sri Vijaya came under attack from Java, and only a few decades later it was overwhelmed by the newly arisen Cholla kingdom on the Coromandel coast of India, which had revived the power of the southern Indians. The Cholla conquest extended to the vassal states of Jambi and Lamuri in central and northern Sumatra, respectively, and to the colonies in Kedah, Langkasuka, Tumasik (Singapore), the Dindings, and elsewhere on the peninsula. Distance prevented the south Indian power from effectively maintaining its conquests in Sumatra and Malaya, however, and Sri Vijaya enjoyed a short period of revival.

The Cholla raids, in addition to internal decay, had weakened Sri Vijaya, and by the end of the twelfth century the vassal state of Jambi appears in the Chinese chronicles as an independent and equal, if not suzerain, power. Jambi appears to have held for a while the former Sri Vijayan dependencies of Kedah, Langkasuka, Trengganu, Kelantan, Ligor (Thailand), and Pahang. Apparently the overlord of Ligor and Kedah was able to break away from Jambi control by 1230 and was sufficiently powerful to join the Sukhodaya king of Thailand in a campaign against Ceylon. In 1275 Jambi was beset by an east Javan kingdom which seized from it certain sections of Sumatra and laid claim to Pahang, while the first Moslem inroads in northern Sumatra resulted in the independence of several small states in that area.

Finally, in the middle of the fourteenth century, the recently risen Javanese kingdom of Majapahit conquered all Sumatra, including Jambi. Palembang, the site of the Sri Vijaya capital, deteriorated into a center for Chinese pirates. Besides Sumatra, Majapahit claimed control over Johore, Langkasuka, Kelantan, Trengganu, Muara Dungan, Klang, Kedah, and Sungei Ujong (in Negri Sembilan) on the peninsula. The Majapahit rulers, however, were primarily conquerors, not colonizers, and their influence on the peoples and institutions of Malaya was minimal. Various remnants of this short period of Javanese control do, however, persist along the east coast in the form of the shadow play, kris designs, and court ritual.

Throughout the period of Hindu dominance no truly independent Malay power seems to have arisen, except possibly Langkasuka, for which there are not sufficient data for judgment, but which appears during most of its existence as a dependency of one or the other of the great powers, Fu-nan, Sri Vijaya, or Majapahit. Certainly the primary influences during the period were Hindu in origin, stemming from southern India either directly or, in the case of Majapahit, through Java. Theravada Buddhism appears to have had some influence on customs and institutions during the early Pallava period, but traces of it virtually disappeared with the advent of Mahayana influences from Sri Vijaya, returning only much later to Thailand and Cambodia.

The Indians brought a large number of Sanskrit words into the Malay language and strongly influenced the life and customs of the ruling elite. Court ceremonials and political structure in a number of the Malayan states attest to the endurance of Hinduization, as do the folk tales, plays, and legends bearing an unmistakable Indian origin. Very little of this Hindu influence appears to have seeped down to the masses, however, and in general the pattern of life among these lower classes appears to have continued much as it was before the advent of Hindu and Buddhist influence. Primitive animism remained the religion of the people; their relationship to their Hinduized kings was little different from that in the pre-Indian period.[2]

Early Chinese contacts

It is probable that the Chinese were in contact with Malaya as early as were the Indians. However, the Chinese tended to confine their interests to trade rather than to settlement or cultural infiltration, and until the nineteenth century their internal influence was small. Chinese chronicles from 100 A.D. appear to know of Langkasuka, and in 515 it is reported to have sent an envoy to China, a custom which was continued during the remainder of that century. Early Chinese travelers, mostly Buddhist monks on their way to study in India, appear to have stopped at various places on the peninsula. The kings of Sri Vijaya, too, dispatched envoys to China bearing tribute to exchange for "the advantages of trade and the imperial presents."[3] Indeed, it is largely from the Chinese chronicles that information concerning Sri Vijaya is derived. It appears, in fact, that the primary power of Sri Vijaya rested on its position as a central port of call for trading ships from India and junks from China, which found it easier to meet halfway for the exchange of goods than to make the long sea haul from one country to the other. This was indeed the functional rationale for the existence of most of the great trading empires of the region, traces of which are still to be seen in the entrepôt

2. Kenneth P. Landon, Southeast Asia, Crossroad of Religion (Haskell Lectures in Comparative Religion [Chicago: University of Chicago Press, 1948]), p. 69.
3. R. O. Winstedt, A History of Malaya (Singapore: Malayan Branch of the Royal Asiatic Society, 1935), p. 22.

trade of Singapore. A fairly large Chinese population appears to have gathered at Palembang, which, with the fall of the Sri Vijaya empire, established there a sort of pirate kingdom. One of the more important of the subsidiary trading ports of the region during the Sri Vijaya period was Tumasik (Singapore). The early history of the island is lost in myth and tradition. Tumasik appears to have been ruled by a branch of the Sailendran royal house, but this was perhaps only fiction to give an air of legitimacy to the king. By the thirteenth century it acknowledged the suzerainty of both China and Thailand. In 1349 it reportedly was attacked by the Thai and saved only by the arrival of a Chinese fleet. Two decades later the port was sacked by Majapahit raiders. Following the withdrawal of the Majapahit forces, the entire east coast of Malaya, as well as Tumasik and possibly Malakka, appears to have come under the quasi control of Thailand, though Thailand and its dependencies continued to acknowledge the suzerainty of China.

The role of China during this early period of Malaya was largely commercial and political. The wealth and power of the great commercial ports of the region stemmed primarily from their position midway along the maritime trading route between China and India. Tumasik particularly was a natural crossroads and meeting point for traders from India, Sri Vijaya, Java, Siam, Champa, and China, much like present-day Singapore. Politically, Chinese power and friendship were to the smaller states of the region a valuable counterweight to the aggressive designs of their stronger and more immediate neighbors. China could successfully fend or prevent Thai aggression into the peninsula, and Chinese protection was useful against the demands of Sri Vijaya and Majapahit. The economic necessity of the Chinese trade and respect for Chinese political power were acknowledged by most of the Southeast Asian states, for often a mere warning, threat, or command from the imperial forces in the region was sufficient to turn back a raiding party or change political alignments.

By 1400 it appears that most of modern Malaya and Singapore was divided into a number of small tribal states. Those in the northwest and along the east coast were under the suzerainty of Thailand, which itself was a titular vassal of China, while those fronting on the Strait of Malakka were probably under the hegemony of one or another of the Sumatran states, who were in turn vassals of Majapahit.

23

Islam and the Empire of Malakka

According to legend, one of the petty princes vassal to Majapahit threw off his allegiance to that empire and in return was forced to flee his country sometime in the latter part of the fourteenth century. He obtained refuge with the ruler of Tumasik, a vassal and relative to the king of Thailand. The prince, Parameswara, repaid this kindness by assassinating his benefactor and usurping his throne. He managed to rule over the island for about five years, until the dissatisfied natives, aided by Thai forces and the Patani Malays, forced him to flee northward with his followers. After stopping for a short time to found an agricultural community at the mouth of the Sungei Muar, Parameswara and his followers finally arrived at the mouth of the Malakka River. Prior to the arrival of Parameswara, Malakka appears to have been a small fishing village inhabited by a proto-Malayan people, probably under the nominal control of one of the Sumatran states. Within a relatively short period of time, Parameswara appears to have established Malakka as the leading commercial port along the Strait, as well as the capital of a fairly broad hinterland. At least three factors seem to account for the growth of the settlement: (1) its commanding position over the narrowest part of the Strait, (2) its location outside of the zones of effective Thai or Majapahit control, and (3) its early adherence to Islam.

Two narrow straits form the major maritime gateways between China and India, the Strait of Malakka and the Sunda Strait between Java and Sumatra. Majapahit commercial policies and fear of the Chinese pirates operating out of Palembang and Bangka island made the former the preferred route. Too, it was shorter and the monsoon winds allowed fast and easy voyages. Majapahit raids had broken the power of the small states along the Sumatran side of the Strait of Malakka. Parameswara, therefore, was able to make a virtual toll road of the Strait, controlling the coming and going of every craft. All ships passing through the Strait could be forced to stop at Malakka. In addition, however, Parameswara and his successors had foresight enough to make trade at Malakka attractive. Port fees were low, and there were port officials appointed from each different group of traders to deal with their own countrymen, thus avoiding intergroup antagonisms. The good harbor with its relatively safe surroundings attracted traders from all parts of the Asian world--Arabs, Indians, Javanese, Thai, and Chinese.

During its first few years of existence, Malakka acknowledged the nominal suzerainty of Thailand. A Ming dynasty chronicle relates that in 1403 the emperor of China dispatched an envoy to Malakka directly, and in return a mission was sent to China which received from the emperor a commission and seal appointing Parameswara king of Malakka and apparently releasing him from the suzerainty of Thailand. The Thai continued to retain control over Kedah and the east-coast states, while Malakka was able to establish its own control over such west-coast areas as Selangor, the states of Negri Sembilan, and northern Johore. Fortunately for Malakka, the power of Majapahit had begun to wane, and that Javanese state, occupied with internal troubles, had little time to turn its attention to the rising power of Malakka; the latter state intensified the decline of Majapahit by crippling its trade and encouraging the introduction of Islam in a move to undercut the Hindu foundations of the older empire.

By the end of the fifteenth century, Malakka had become the center of Islam for the region. Islam had first been introduced into the northern Sumatran city states of Pasai, Pedir, and Perlak by Moslem traders from India, Persia, and the Hadramaut coast of Arabia in the fourteenth century. In the course of his reign Parameswara became a convert to Islam through his marriage to a princess of Pasai. It is probable, however, that the adoption of Islam was more strongly influenced by the desire to promote trade with the Moslems, who by 1400 had virtually assumed control of the Indian Ocean. With the adoption of Islam, the older Hindu title of maharajah was discarded by the Malakka rulers for that of sultan. When the third ruler of Malakka attempted to revert to the Hindu title and theory of government, a palace revolution led by Moslem Tamils overthrew the new ruler and reinstituted Moslem power. Islam under the Malakka sultanate, however, remained, as had Hinduism and Buddhism, largely a religion of the elite; it was not until after the fall of Malakka to the Portuguese that conversion among the lower classes began in earnest.

Although Islam was a new influence in opposition to the older Hindu and Buddhist influences, it should not be supposed that it was non-Indian, for the Islam which was adopted by the Malays was not that of Arabia and Persia so much as an Indian form which had taken on many of the mystical formulations of

Indian religions.[4] Nevertheless, it was a break from the complete Indian dominance of previous centuries. India lost its pre-eminence as a sort of mother country, and the many gods of Hinduism were replaced by the concept of a single god. The Arabic alphabet replaced the Indian scripts, and Arabic words entered the Malayan language, replacing in many cases the former Sanskrit. In these and many other ways--in eating habits, in clothing, in ceremonials--did Islam replace the former Hindu and Buddhist influences.

Despite its growing power and prestige, the Sultanate of Malakka was destined to last less than one hundred years, for already the Portuguese had begun the long series of voyages which were to open up the African coast and lead to India and beyond. In 1498 Vasco da Gama landed at Calicut, and eleven years later the first Portuguese trader visited Malakka.

During the years of the Malakka sultanate, the successors of Parameswara, through the aid of the Chinese and the other Moslem states, were able to fend off the attempts of the Thai to reassert their authority, and in the process took control over Pahang, and several other small states. A member of the Malakka royal family was made Sultan of Pahang, and governors were placed over the other areas. Several large areas on the Sumatran side of the Strait were also acquired. By 1500 Malakka ruled the entire lower end of the peninsula, including the Lingga Archipelago.[5]

It is with the founding and growth of the empire of Malakka that the cornerstone of modern Malayan history appears. With Malakka, Malaya becomes an historical, political, cultural, and geographical entity, rather than a peripheral and shadowy appendix to other histories and other cultures.

---

4. R. O. Winstedt, The Malays, a Cultural History (rev. ed.; London: Routledge and Kegan Paul, Ltd., 1950), p. 37.

5. The administrative structure of the Malakka sultanate was to form the model for later Malayan state systems. At the top was the royal family, headed by the sultan. Closely associated with him were the bendahara (prime minister), temenggong (chief of police), laksamana (admiral), and the mentri (secretary). The first three of these, and particularly the bendahara, tended to become hereditary titles and positions. Thus, one may speak truthfully of a bendahara "family" or "line." In many cases the bendahara wielded greater per-

The Portuguese period

The Portuguese came to the Indian Ocean as traders attempting to break the monopoly of the Arabs in the rich spice trade of the Indies and as devout Christians intent upon conversion. By the time of their arrival Malakka had become the key to the spice trade. Nearly all spice from the Indonesian archipelago was funneled through the port of Malakka and into the hands of Moslem traders for transport to the spice markets of the Near East and Europe. It was as a trader that Diego de Sequeira visited Malakka in 1509, seeking to obtain spice and other commodities from the Far East for direct transport to Portugal and to thus circumvent the Arabic traders. The overtures of de Sequeira were rebuffed by the sultan, largely at the instigation of Gujarati traders, and it was made plain to the Portuguese that if they were to wrest control of the spice trade from the Arabs they would have to seize and control the great market at Malakka. An attack was launched, and Malakka was overpowered in 1511 and immediately converted into a Portuguese stronghold and center for Southeast Asia. With the capture of the key market, the Portuguese rapidly expanded through the archipelago as far as the Molukkas.

Despite their seizure of Malakka, the Portuguese were unable to effect any real control over the rest of the peninsula. The last sultan, Mahmud, escaped overland to Pahang

---

sonal power than the sultan, and it became almost traditional that a bendahara woman would be taken as wife by the sultan and that the male offspring of this union had the best chance of becoming the heir apparent. In this way the power of the bendahara was maintained through an intimate family relationship with the royal family. To a lesser extent the temenggongs, laksamanas, and mentris also attempted to perpetuate their family power through intermarriage with the royal line, with the bendaharas, or with one another. In time the temenggong's title became the prerogative of a branch of the bendahara family. Beneath these four great chiefs there were eight appointed governors to rule over the various provinces, and under them were sixteen smaller chiefs and thirty-two still more minor chiefs. This numerical ratio, taken from a Hindu tradition, is perpetuated in Perak.

and was able a short time later to establish a new capital at
Bintan in the Rhio (Riouw) Archipelago, from which he continued to govern over Johore, Pahang, Trengganu, and Perak.
Kelantan and Kedah continued as vassals of Thailand, and in
essence the Portuguese controlled only the small enclave immediately surrounding Malakka. From Malakka, however, they
continued to control the Strait and the seas at either end, thus
limiting the commerce of the Malays and impelling them to attack Portuguese and other shipping in the Strait in retaliation.

Portuguese insistence upon the monopolization of trade,
their practice of setting prices to quash the free market, and
their intolerance of Islam drove the Moslem traders to seek
another center outside the zone of the Portuguese maritime
patrols. Two major Moslem trading centers were established,
one at Brunei and the other in northern Sumatra, where during
the early sixteenth century grew the Kingdom of Acheh (Atjeh),
embracing the former trading ports of Perlak, Pasai, and
Pedir, the earlier centers of Islam in the region. The power
of Acheh grew rapidly, and as early as 1537 it attempted the
capture of Malakka from the Portuguese. Defeated, the Achinese turned next toward the Rhio-Johore sultanate, which had
been weakened as the result of an unsuccessful attack on Malakka. The old sultan, Mahmud, had left two heirs, one of whom
became Sultan of Perak. The other succeeded to the Rhio-
Johore throne and moved his capital back to the mainland, from
which he continued his father's policy of sniping raids on Portuguese shipping and attacks upon Malakka. A probable cause of
the Achinese attack on Johore appears to have been the lack
of discrimination on the part of the latter, who had taken to
raiding Achinese trading vessels as readily as the Portuguese
shipping. A further factor appears to have been the proselytizing zeal of the Islamic Achinese, who spread the word of
Allah throughout the archipelago and the peninsula by the medium of the sword. The conversion of the Malayan masses to
Islam is due largely to the work of these Achinese zealots.
Finally, Johore was undoubtedly jealous of the rising Achinese
power which had usurped its place as the leading native state
in the area, and it also feared its own relative decline in prestige.

For over 100 years (1537-1641) a triangular war raged between the three leading powers of the area, the Portuguese,
the Achinese, and Johore; but no one of the three was strong
enough to defeat decisively the other two, nor were any two

of them able to maintain an alliance for a long enough time to ensure the extinction of the third. Perhaps the hardest hit by this succession of wars were the Portuguese. The continual defense of Malakka made heavy extractions upon Portuguese finances, while trade, seriously disrupted by Johore piracy and by the Portuguese policy of alienating Moslem shipping at the port, failed to bring in the expected revenue. Too, Portuguese administration was characterized by a rapacity and corruption which further crippled the commercial potentialities of the port while creating further drains upon its revenues. It appears that the population of Malakka declined concomitantly with its trade and power during the years of Portuguese administration. With the arrival of a new European power in the region, the Dutch, the days of Portuguese rule over Malakka and the surrounding seas were numbered.

The influence of the Portuguese on Malayan history is difficult to assess. Cultural infusion was slight and restricted almost entirely to the immediate vicinity of Malakka. There, remnants of Portuguese colonial architecture, a greater propensity toward Catholicism, and a profusion of Portuguese family names are the primary reminders of Portuguese rule. It is perhaps possible, however, to date the political disruption of the Malay world from the fall of Malakka to the Portuguese. Not until the federation agreement of 1948 were the states of the peninsula to enjoy a unity comparable to that of the Malakka sultanate, and indeed the Federation is too new for adequate comparison. The history of the period from 1537 to 1900 is largely concerned with the slow and sporadic disintegration of the old Malakka empire.

The Dutch period

In the last decade of the sixteenth century the ships of two other European nations began to appear over the Southeast Asian horizon. In 1580 Sir Francis Drake passed through the region with his small fleet, and in 1588 Ralph Fitch, another English adventurer, stopped in his travels to spend seven weeks in Malakka. In 1600 the East India Company was chartered and the first ship sent out **traded for pepper at Acheh and Bantam.** The British were intent upon their trade more in China and India, however, than in the islands, and although British trade seriously threatened the Portuguese monopoly at times, it was not they, but the Dutch, who were to put an end to Portuguese dreams of empire.

The Dutch had been the primary distributors in Europe for the spice trade of Lisbon, and when during the Dutch war for independence from Spain Lisbon was closed the Dutch economy was threatened with collapse. As the Portuguese had wrested the monopoly of the spice trade away from the Arabs, now the Dutch attempted to reinstitute that monopoly under their own control. By 1606, Dutch raids on Portuguese shipping in the Indian Ocean had begun to shake the foundations of the latter's commerce in the region. The Dutch, based on Java, recognized the necessity of eliminating Portuguese competition in the area, and as early as 1606 made a treaty with Johore for the capture of Malakka from their common enemy. The Sultan of Johore, however, was more interested in pursuing quarrels of his own with the Sultan of Patani and the Sultan of Pahang. Disgusted, the Dutch concluded an agreement with the Achinese, who, given a free hand, attacked Johore and began an intensive effort at conquest and conversion. By 1620 they had conquered Johore, Pahang, Perak, Kedah, and the Rhio and Lingga archipelagoes, virtually liquidating the Johore holdings and the royal family. The Malays fled Achinese aggression, turning toward the east. Johore traders and vessels at this time began a fairly steady migration to Borneo, the Celebes, and the Molukkas, providing the base for the present Malay populations of those areas. With the fall of Johore, Jambi, in central Sumatra, emerged as the strongest of the Malay states. The Achinese conquest was shortlived, however, and in 1636 in Pahang a prince of the Johore house proclaimed himself king of Johore and Pahang and made a treaty with the Dutch against the Portuguese.

This time Johore kept its word, and the attack on the Portuguese stronghold began in 1640. Despite a strong defense it fell the next year, and the Dutch moved in to replace the Portuguese. Because of the new alliance between Johore and the Dutch, the Achinese refused to aid in the attack and even threatened to ally themselves with the Portuguese. With the ascendency of Dutch power in the Strait, Acheh began a steady decline. Johore had reasserted its control over Johore, Pahang, and the Rhio and Lingga archipelagoes; Kedah returned to the nominal suzerainty of Thailand along with Trengganu; the Dutch controlled the coasts of Negri Sembilan and Selangor. Only Perak remained vassal to Acheh, and even there the Dutch were shortly to undermine Achinese monopoly over the tin trade and thus weaken its political control.

The re-emergence of Johore as a political and commercial power in the region brought it into direct conflict with its old vassal, Jambi, which had usurped Johore's position after the Achinese conquest. This conflict, brought to a head over a broken marriage contract, was to bring two new powerful groups of conquerors into the already overcrowded arena, the Bugis and the Minangkabau.

The Bugis, coming from their homeland in Celebes, had settled as early as 1681 around the Klang and Selangor estuaries. A dynamic and warlike coastal people, they had gained renown as invincible sea fighters, and their use of chain armor had made them nearly as invincible on land. In Malaya they were primarily river pirates and mercenaries, ready to fight on their own or on payment from someone else.

Minangkabau settlers had crossed the Strait of Malakka from their highland homes in Sumatra to settle in Negri Sembilan at an early date. They were primarily agriculturalists joined in a number of small matriarchal states under the nominal suzerainty of Johore, the economic control of the Portuguese and Dutch, and the direct overlordship of the laksamana of Johore.

The war between Johore and Jambi broke out in 1673. Jambi at first seriously defeated Johore, driving the sultan to his death. His successor was forced to call to his aid Bugis mercenaries, while the Minangkabau of Negri Sembilan renounced their allegiance to such a weak suzerain and elected as their ruler a Minangkabau from Sumatra. With the aid of the Bugis, Jambi was finally defeated, but the throne of Johore had passed to a minor under the regency of the laksamana. This laksamana was ousted by his fellow chiefs after a short reign, and his charge, the last of the legitimate royal line of Rhio-Johore, was assassinated. Power now fell into the hands of the bendahara, who in 1699 was proclaimed successor to the throne.

By a number of the former Johore vassals, however, the bendahara was looked upon as a usurper and was toppled from the throne, retiring to his old title and position. The Minangkabau Rajah Kechil, who had led the revolt, had sought the aid of the Bugis in his venture, promising their leader the office of ruler of Johore for their aid. He had, however, attacked without their aid and reneged on his promise. Rajah Kechil ruled as sultan only four years when the disgruntled Bugis established the son of the then deceased bendahara sultan on the throne, and he in turn appointed a Bugis chief as underking of Rhio. From then on the Malay sultan was to be a puppet ruler, with the Bugis underking the real power over the domain. The Bugis, in 1700, had had one of their chiefs proclaimed as independent ruler of Selangor, and in 1740 a Bugis was created sultan of that state.

The Johore empire had shrunk to include, in reality, only Rhio, with only nominal control over the states on the peninsula. When the capital had been removed to Rhio following the assassination of the last of the old royal line, a bendahara had been left in control of Pahang, the temenggong in charge of Johore, and another member of the bendahara family in charge of Trengganu. These persons and their offspring became the rulers in their respective states and the predecessors of the present royal families.

Rajah Kechil, the Minangkabau usurper, made several other attempts to regain Rhio from Bugis domination. In 1724 the Bugis and Minangkabau found themselves supporting opposing sides in a war of succession in Kedah. War raged between the two forces throughout Kedah, Perak, and Selangor.

The Dutch slowly came to see that Bugis ravages posed an incipient threat to both their maritime control and their commercial interests in Perak and Selangor. Acheh, by 1740, had been squeezed from any effective control over its nominal vassal, Perak. The Dutch maintained forts along the coast to ensure their monopoly of tin shipments from the state; however, the Bugis dominated the war-ravaged interior, disrupting mining activities. In 1745, the Malay Sultan of Johore concluded an agreement with the Dutch behind the backs of his Bugis masters in which the Dutch were given a complete monopoly of the tin trade if they would help him regain his peninsular territories from the Bugis. The Bugis immediately recognized the threat to their ascendancy, and the next forty years were marked by a seesaw struggle between the Dutch and the Bugis, with the Malays alternately playing one against the other. In 1784 the Dutch succeeded in driving the Bugis from the capital at Rhio, all that was left of the Johore Empire, and conquered Selangor, driving its Bugis sultan to Pahang. Rhio, with Johore and Pahang, was made a Dutch dependency, with the Malay sultan a vassal. The Dutch conquest, however, had alienated the Malays, who, led by their sultan, attempted to evict their conquerors but were forced to flee. It was at this point that the British were to re-enter the political and commercial scene in Malaya, largely as a result of events half a world away.

The overriding interest of the Dutch in Southeast Asia was commerce. Dutch policy, like that of the Portuguese, was based on monopoly control of commodity shipments. Although Batavia on Java rather than Malakka became the center of Dutch activity, Malakka assumed importance in Dutch policy on two counts: (1) as a control point over shipping (all foreign shipping passing through the Strait was required to stop at Malakka to pay duties and/or dispose of their cargoes at Dutch prices, while Malakka also served as a bastion in the defense of the Dutch shipping lanes) and (2) as a gathering and transshipment point for commodities from the Malayan hinterland, particularly tin. These two functions served to determine Dutch actions in the region and the course of relations between the Dutch and the native states.

Dutch interference in native commerce resulted in innumerable petty wars, and the necessity of maintaining Dutch dominance and preventing the rise of any powerful competitor from among the native states brought into being a policy of supporting one such state against another. Acheh, Jambi, the Bugis, and Rhio all fell when their power threatened Dutch supremacy. In the case of Rhio, actual Dutch administration was extended to the area after the Dutch recognized the danger of its control by any other power. Otherwise, the weakened states were apparently allowed to keep their independence, so long as certain commercial prerogatives accrued to the Dutch. Dutch influence upon the culture of the country appears to have been even less than that of the Portuguese.

The British period

The British incursions into Southeast Asia during the early seventeenth century were followed by withdrawal to India. In the eighteenth century the East India Company, trading out of India, established trade with Burma and eventually with Kedah, which was too far north for effective Dutch control and was favorably situated for trade across the Bay of Bengal. In 1771 Francis Light, a British trader employed with the East India Company, informed his company that the Sultan of Kedah was prepared to cede most of his coast in return for aid against the Bugis of Selangor. As much as the company desired the opportunity which was offered, it was not prepared to lend military assistance to the sultan, who therefore refused to continue negotiations. By 1782, however, war in Europe with France and Holland had made the Bay of Bengal unsafe for British shipping. It became necessary to establish a base for refueling and defense of English shipping somewhere along the shipping lanes on the coast opposite India. In 1782, therefore, Light persuaded the sultan to cede the island of Penang to the company in return for an annual payment, in a trickily worded agreement which the sultan accepted as a promise of military and naval aid against his enemies. The company had little intention of entering into any war on behalf of the sultan. Penang, however, was occupied by the British before the company had ratified Light's agreement. The sultan threatened war for the recovery of Penang, but, defeated by Light and a company of Sepoys, he again agreed to relinquish the island--for a lower stipend and without the assistance clause.

Meanwhile, the Stadholder of Holland had been pushed from his position by the creation of the Batavian Republic under the auspices of revolutionary France and had sought asylum in England. In 1795 the British occupied Malakka in the name of the Stadholder to prevent its becoming a base for French operations. The days of the Dutch company were at an end; in 1798 the Batavian Republic took over its remaining assets.

At the same time the British reinstated the deposed Sultan of Rhio-Johore and his Bugis underking, removing the Dutch resident. A question arose at this time which was to plague the future course of events, concerning just what had been returned to the sultan. The Dutch, who had come to an agreement with the sultan shortly before the British took over Malakka, later claimed that they had agreed to return only the Rhio Archipelago and that Johore and Pahang remained dependencies of Malakka. The British reminded them, however, that after the British had taken Malakka the Dutch had insisted that Johore and Pahang had also been returned to the sultan and were not, therefore, subject to British-held Malakka. It is apparent that in both cases the Dutch were attempting to retain their hold on as much territory as possible, keeping it from the control of the British.

The Bugis came back to power with the British, again extending their control over Perak in 1804, only to lose it when faced by pressures from Thailand and the British at Penang.

The British gained another strip of land opposite Penang in 1800 when the Sultan of Kedah ceded what is now Province Wellesley to the East India Company. The Convention of Lon-

don, following the defeat of Napoleon in 1814 and the Stadholder's return to Holland, returned Malakka and Java to
Holland, but it was not until 1818 that the Dutch took Malakka
back. Then in 1824, by the Treaty of London, Malakka and
Dutch rights on the Malay Peninsula were traded to the British for the relinquishments of rights and properties on Sumatra.

As a result of the return of Malakka to the Dutch in 1814,
the East India Company determined to establish another trading
center along the Strait. In 1818 Thomas Raffles was commis-
sioned to inquire concerning the possibilities of establishing
such a post. Thwarted by the Dutch from settling at Rhio,
Raffles in 1819 landed at Singapore, site of the once thriving
trade center of Tumasik. Recognizing Singapore as the logical
base for British trade in the area, Raffles determined to obtain it if possible.

The nominal ruler of the area, the Sultan of Rhio-Johore,
and his underking were both under the influence of the Dutch,
who would hardly allow the relinquishing of it to their commercial rivals. Fortunately, however, the true succession to the
throne of Rhio-Johore was in doubt. Raffles turned his back
on the accepted sultan, whom he had already recognized, and
extended recognition to a rival claimant to the throne. With
the apparent consent of the underking and the temenggong,
both of whom appeared willing to accept the British as a
counterbalance to Dutch power, the rival claimant was installed
as Sultan of Johore and in return agreed to allow the East India
Company to establish itself on the island. Thus was the historic
sultanate of Rhio-Johore divided. Henceforth, one sultan was to
rule in Rhio, under Dutch protection; another in Johore, under
the English. The arrangement was formalized by the treaty of
1824 between Holland and England. At the same time Bugis
unity was sundered, with the underkings of Rhio and Lingga
separated from their brothers in Selangor. Several of the Malay
rulers in the east-coast states of Pahang and Trengganu continued to recognize the Rhio sultan as their overlord, but without much effect.

By 1824 the future political divisions of Malaya were fairly
well established. In the north, Kelantan, formerly an area
of small petty states, some vassal to Thailand and others to
Trengganu, had been united in 1730 and declared a sultanate
in 1800, although remaining nominally vassal to Thailand.
Trengganu maintained a sort of autonomy, although nominally
vassal to both Thailand and the Sultan of Rhio. Kedah had come

under the full control of Thailand. Penang and Province Wellesley were British possessions. Perak maintained an uneasy
independence, threatened alternately by Thailand and Selangor, under its own sultan, the last direct descendant of the
old Malakka royal line. In central and southern Malaya, Selangor was the stronghold of the Bugis, fighting alternately
with Kedah and with the Minangkabau of Negri Sembilan to
the south. Malakka and Singapore were in British hands. Pahang was ruled by a bendahara swearing allegiance to the Rhio
sultan. The states of Negri Sembilan were still only loosely
and uneasily united, and Johore was under the real rule of
the temenggong, though nominally under the British puppet
sultan. Singapore, Penang, and Malakka were shortly to be
brought together under the direct rule of the East India Company as the Strait Settlements.

The development of the Straits Settlements

In February, 1819, when Raffles took over Singapore, the
small population consisted of Chinese and Malays. By June,
however, the influx of Chinese, Bugis, and Malakka Malays
had raised the population to five thousand, and a year later
it had doubled. Trade increased at an even faster rate, and by
1825 the trade at Singapore was twice that of both Penang and
Malakka, despite the opposition of the Dutch, the Penang authorities, and many of the Malays. The key to the success of
Singapore lay largely in its being a free port, with trade accepted and invited from all quarters without restriction--the first
truly open port in the area since the fall of Malakka to the
Portuguese. In addition, Singapore's position and excellent
harbor made it a natural focus of shipping for the entire region. Finally, from 1824 to 1941 the entire region was under
the Pax Britannica; not until the Japanese invasion was there
any serious military threat to the settlement. By adopting
a policy diametrically opposed to that of the Portuguese and the
Dutch, the British were able to achieve political and commercial success in Malaya where the others had failed.

On the other hand, Penang, from its inception, was plagued
by poor administration. At no time did it pay its own way and
it was thus a continual drain upon the financial resources of the
East India Company. With the competition from Singapore in
1819 the prestige of Penang fell even further. Originally the
center of British administration, it lost this function when the
government was moved to Singapore in 1832. It was not until

after 1900 that Penang was to undergo a revival, due mainly to the northern extension of the railhead to Prai in Province Wellesley, the increased emphasis on tin production, and the introduction of rubber.

Malakka, once the queen port of the entire region, was destined to recede into the backwater of Malayan history. By 1835 heavy silting had ruined the harbor. Maladministration and poor judgment contributed further to its decline. In 1830 a misinterpretation of the former Dutch relations with the small Minangkabau state of Naning bordering Malakka led the British into a costly and unjust war. After conquering the small state at a considerable expenditure of personnel and funds, the British found themselves with it on their hands; unable to give it back to another of the Negri Sembilan states, they annexed it to Malakka. The remaining story of Malakka concerns its slow decline to a small port for coastal shipping.

Another portion of Malayan territory held for a short time as a part of the Straits Settlements was the Dindings, acquired from Perak by the Pangkor Treaty of 1874. Supposedly the cession was made in order that the British could control piracy in the area, although the prime rationale appears to have been pressure exerted upon the sultan by a Chinese creditor who desired English protection for his investments there. The Dindings did not fit strictly into the pattern of the Straits Settlements. It had neither a valuable harbor nor a particularly valuable hinterland. The costs of administering the settlement were consistently greater than its strategic, political, or economic value as a British possession, and in 1935 it was returned to Perak.

The primary importance of the Straits Settlements lies in their strategic position as bases for the extension of British power and control (the basis of the Pax Britannica in the region) over the Malay states and as centers for the introduction and distribution of Western institutions, concepts, and technology. Strategically the Settlements provided the British with a chain of naval bases commanding the Strait of Malakka. In the overall scheme of empire these were an important link in the larger chain of British bastions protecting the shipping lanes to the Orient, from Gibraltar to Hong Kong.

Internally the Settlements came to dominate fairly extensive hinterlands. As the inland areas developed commercially, the Settlements became their natural maritime outlets. In return the Settlements tended to become the primary bases for commercial expansion and development in their hinterlands. Singapore was related in this way to the southern part of the peninsula; Penang to Kedah, Perak, and Selangor; and Malakka, to a lesser extent, to Negri Sembilan. With commercial development came cultural change--missionaries; Western industrial techniques; the estate system; improved transportation, communication, and educational facilities; a money economy; and, due to the increasing demands for labor, large migrations of Chinese, Indians, and others.

Developments within the Malay states

The refusal of the East India Company to ratify the military aid clause in the agreement concerning the secession of Penang set the theme for British policy regarding the Malay states during most of the following century. The company, and after it the Colonial Office, which took over the Straits Settlements in 1867, was interested primarily in trade and in the protection of the Far Eastern shipping lanes. They were not interested in conquest or interference in the affairs of the native states, especially after the costly Naning incident demonstrated the financial inexpediency of such actions.

After 1824 and the division of the Johore empire into British and Dutch sections, however, affairs in the Malay states rapidly deteriorated, and the following half century was marked by violence, anarchy, and war. These troubles stemmed generally from two sources: (1) the encroaching claims of Thailand upon the northern states and (2) the machinations and intrigues of various rivals for the several thrones of the central and southern states.

The defeat of Malakka by the Portuguese and the removal of its effective control over Trengganu and other vassal states had had the effect of reviving Thai pretensions to suzerainty over these areas. Although effective Thai control was hardly ever exercised over these states, each state periodically sent a ceremonial present to their rulers as a token recognition of Thai suzerainty. The Malays resented Thai dominance, generally disregarding it and at times attempting to throw it off. In return, the Thai resented the independent attitudes of the Malay states.

The issue between Kedah and Thailand was brought to a head at the time of the British occupation of Penang. The Thai feared a loss of their vassal to the British and resented the action of the Sultan of Kedah in dealing with the British without

38

asking permission. Reverting to a policy which kept all the vassal states weak in relation to itself, Thailand in 1816 ordered Kedah to attack Perak, which it did. In 1821, under the pretext that the Sultan of Kedah had been plotting with Burma against Thailand, the Thai ordered Ligor to attack Kedah. As a result the sultan and his family were forced to flee to Penang for protection, while the Thai forces overran the state. The deposed sultan pleaded with the British for help in regaining his throne, but was refused. On the other hand, the British, afraid that Thai occupation of Kedah would threaten the safety of Province Wellesley and the trade of Penang, attempted to come to an agreement with the Thai, while virtually holding the sultan prisoner on Penang to prevent him from provoking more trouble with Thailand. During the next twenty years Kedah guerrilla forces attempted several times to retake their country from the Thai; in this effort they received the moral and sometimes the actual support of a number of the British civilians at Penang, but not the official support of the government.

In 1842, after guerrilla warfare had virtually nullified any benefit which the Thai might have had from their conquest, peace was arranged through the governor of Penang whereby Kedah was returned to the sultan, except for three small sections which were carved out of it, Setul, Perlis, and Kubang Pasu; these were placed under independent rajahs. Setul reverted to Thailand in 1909; Perlis has retained its identity, as a Malay state, since 1909; and Kubang Pasu eventually reverted to Kedah. Kedah remained a nominal vassal of Thailand. A few years later Kedah was again caught in a war with Perak over possession of Krian, but this dispute was settled by the British. From this time on, Kedah entered upon a period of peace broken only by the Japanese invasion in 1941.

In 1822 Perak, with the aid of the Sultan of Selangor, threw off the Siamese yoke, and for the following three years a seesaw battle between the Thai on the one hand and Perak and Selangor on the other threatened to lay waste the country. Faced with the threat of Siamese control over the tin-rich regions of lower Perak and Selangor, the British intervened in 1826 to gain the promise of the Thai that they would not attempt to seize either of the two Malay states. At the same time the British governor of Penang promised aid to the Sultan of Perak in the event of invasion by the Siamese or by other Malays.

The same agreement with the Thai which guaranteed the independence of Perak and Selangor provided that the British might trade in the Thai vassal states of Kelantan and Trengganu and that such trade would not be interrupted by the Thai. This clause was put to test in 1862 when the Thai attempted to depose the ruler of Trengganu and install in his place the former Sultan of Rhio-Lingga, who had been deposed by the Dutch. The British considered this act an attempt to interrupt British trade with Trengganu and demanded the return of the rightful ruler. A naval bombardment of Kuala Trengganu persuaded the Thai to accede to British demands, and thereafter the British treated with Trengganu as an independent state with only nominal ties with Thailand. Kelantan remained the acknowledged vassal of the Thai, however, until the formal independence of both Trengganu and Kelantan under British protection was recognized by Thailand in 1909.

The largely Malay-populated state of Ligor remained under Thai suzerainty to become the province of Patani, forming a Malay irredenta region. Conversely, Thai suzerainty over the northern states has resulted in considerable Thai settlement south of the present border of Kelantan, Perak, Kedah, and Perlis. This minority population tends to form cultural and racial enclaves, maintaining their own language, customs, and institutions distinct from those of the predominant Malay group. These former Thai vassal states, with Johore, were to form the Unfederated Malay States of the early twentieth century.

The wars of succession throughout the central and southern Malay states during the middle of the nineteenth century were the direct outgrowth of the division of the Johore empire between the Dutch and the British. Formerly the Rhio-Johore sultans had been determining factors in deciding succession in the states under their control, while the sultans of Selangor were seldom invested without the approval of the Bugi underkings of Rhio. With the division, however, the chains of control were severed. None of the state rulers acknowledged the British puppet sultan of Johore as their overlord, and even the British, after their first appointee died, refrained from backing any successor, leaving the rule of Johore in the hands of the temenggong. For twenty years the succession to the throne of Johore was held in abeyance, until in 1855 the indigent heir agreed, in return for a yearly allowance, to cede full sovereignty to the temenggong. For the third time the throne of Johore had been taken from the rightful heirs.

In 1857 war broke out between the Temenggong of Johore and the Temenggong of Muar. In the same year, the **bendahara** ruler of Pahang and the Sultan of Selangor died, and in 1861 the ruler of Negri Sembilan died. Ten years later, in 1871, the Sultan of Perak passed away. Between 1857 and 1871 this series of deaths left rival claimants to the various thrones and precipitated a series of disastrous internecine wars.

In Pahang the war was further complicated by the attempts of the deposed Sultan of Rhio to lay claim to the state as the legitimate heir of the Rhio-Johore empire. The Temenggong of Johore was allied to another pretender to the throne by marriage. A third claimant, Wan Ahmed, eventually won out and in 1863 succeeded to the throne. A series of sporadic battles continued, however, up to 1870.

In Selangor the growth of tin mining provided the economic impetus for a series of attempts by various factions to seize control of the country. The new ruler of Pahang, the Sultan of Johore, and the Sultan of Kedah each backed rival factions, while the British maintained their hands-off policy, much to the dismay of British and Chinese commercial powers whose investments in Selangor tin were at stake. Here the dispute was not over who should become sultan, but rather over which of the chief officers of the state should rule in the name of the ineffectual heir. In 1874 the viceroy, aided by the forces of the Pahang **bendahara**, finally gained control of the state.

In Perak trouble had long brewed between rival Chinese societies in the district of Larut. This district was under the sole control of the Mentri of Perak, who ruled it as an independent state. While the **mentri** sided with one Chinese faction, the heir apparent to the throne sided with the other faction. The situation was further complicated when the Perak chiefs refused to seat the heir on the throne at the death of his father, installing the **bendahara** instead. Supporters of the legitimate heir immediately began a series of raids upon customs stations and royal offices in retaliation.

In Negri Sembilan the death of the ruler resulted in a number of petty squabbles between the chiefs of the various Minangkabau states over the succession. Since the ruler must be elected unanimously by the chiefs of the four leading states, it was impossible to arrive at a consensus concerning the successor. The disagreements were further complicated by several boundary disputes leading to armed conflict.

These various quarrels throughout the central and southern

41

states had a considerable effect on the economic and commercial bases of the British colonies. As the British government continued in its refusal to interfere in Malay affairs, except where some injury was received by a British subject, the outcry from the trading groups in Singapore and Penang grew. One official dispatch of the period noted that only in Johore and the states under Siamese suzerainty was peace preserved.

Partly in response to the growing demands for intervention, the Colonial Office suddenly reversed its previous stand and in 1873 announced, "Her Majesty's Government find it incumbent to employ such influence as they possess with the native princes to rescue, if possible, these fertile and productive countries from the ruin which must befall them if the present disorders continue unchecked."[6]

The dispatch to the colonial governor recommended the appointment of British officers to reside in the various states with the consent of the native governments but at the expense of the colonial government. At least three factors other than pressure by the traders contributed heavily to this reversal of policy. At the time, many of the great European powers were engaged in creating colonial empires; as this posed a threat to the British, it was in their interest to block such moves by annexing territory of their own. Thai activity was increasing on the peninsula, and moves in Perak and Trengganu suggested an attempt to reassert Thai dominance over the northern states; moreover, Thailand was itself imperiled by French moves in Indochina, and if Thailand fell, the British faced the possibility of French attempts to extend their authority into the Malay states. British capital, attracted by the mineral wealth of the interior, demanded security and peaceful conditions for investment and development.

The first British move was toward Perak. There, the legitimate heir was willing to agree to any provision which would insure the return of his throne and fortunes. Through British pressure and persuasion, the Perak chiefs agreed to reverse themselves and accept the legitimate heir as sultan, who in return agreed to accept a British resident. It was by this same kind of agreement that the Dindings and the island of Pangkor were ceded.

Piracy against British shipping in the Strait of Malakka and

---

6. Cited in Winstedt, A History of Malaya, p. 233.

the murder of several citizens of Malakka led the British to intervene in Selangor. At British suggestion, the Selangor chiefs asked for the services of a resident in order to bring peace to the state.

The British intervened in Negri Sembilan in 1876, and the states were induced to accept a British collector of taxes and revenue. This office was later expended to that of a resident.

Wan Ahmed, the bendahara ruler of Pahang, had elevated himself to the rank of sultan following the death of the deposed Sultan of Rhio. His administration, however, remained corrupt, inefficient, and tyrannical. The slaying of a Chinese British subject led the colonial governor in 1888 to demand that the sultan either pay an indemnity or accept a British resident. Wan Ahmed accepted the latter course.

The treaties between Great Britain and each of the four states of Perak, Selangor, Negri Sembilan, and Pahang were substantially similar. The principal provisions were as follows:

(1) The Malay States agreed to accept British protection and to have no dealings with foreign powers except through Great Britain.
(2) Great Britain guaranteed the States protection against attack by foreign powers.
(3) The agreement provided for the appointment to the State of a British officer whose advice must be taken and followed except in matters concerning Malay religion and Malay custom.[7]

By these agreements the British raj replaced the sundered Sultanate of Rhio-Johore, and an end was put to the wars of succession. No longer would the petty chiefs struggle for power, for now all power was in British hands. Moreover, there was little need for struggle, for the British guaranteed the mutual security of each; loss of political hegemony was more than recompensed by financial gain and peaceful stability. In 1895 the four states were brought together as the Federated Malay States under the colonial governor as high commissioner.

In 1885 the governor had recognized the Temenggong of

---

7. Federation of Malaya, Annual Report, 1952 (Kuala Lumpur: Government Press, 1953), p. 322.

Johore's change in title to Sultan, and a treaty had promised British protection in case of external attack. In 1914 the sultan asked for the services of a general adviser.

By the Treaty of Bangkok in 1909, Thailand transferred to Great Britain all rights of suzerainty, protection, administration, and control over Kelantan, Trengganu, Kedah, and Perlis in return for a modification of British extraterritorial jurisdiction in Thailand and a loan to construct a rail line between Malaya and Bangkok. The four new states accepted the appointment of British advisers, despite an initial objection by Kedah. Refusing to enter into the Federated Malay States, they, with Johore, retained their independent status under British protection as the Unfederated Malay States.

Between 1909 and 1941 the history of the Malay states under British protection is concerned largely with economic, political, and social developments which will be treated more fully in other chapters. Highlights of the period are the introduction and development of rubber planting on a large scale and the increasing technical development of tin mining; the economic stimulus provided by World War I; the increasing concentration of administrative functions in the Federated States up to 1932, followed by rapid decentralization and the diminution of the federal power; increasing immigration of Chinese and Indian labor with attendant difficulties and problems; the growth of governmental social services; and the impact of new political and social theories, particularly nationalism and its more virulent counterpart, communism.

Suddenly in February, 1942, British rule was exchanged for the more rigorous and exacting three-and-one-half-year reign of the Japanese. Welcomed by some at first as an antidote to British colonialism and a return to "Asia for the Asians," it was soon discovered that despite the change the lot of the Malayan masses--Malay, Chinese, or Indian--was little better, if not a great deal worse, than that under the British. The relatively efficient British-trained civil service almost totally disintegrated; its members were interned in prison camps and replaced by Japanese military rule. The state structures were left nominally as they were under the British, but the heavy hand of the Japanese was felt throughout.

Perhaps the major effect of the Japanese occupation on the native populations was the growth of uncertainty and disillusionment concerning the efficacy of British rule. Unfortunately, growing opposition toward the Japanese did not appear to re-

44

sult in any closer ties among the various communities; rather, each tended to accuse the others of intriguing with the common enemy. Moreover, there arose a feeling that the people had been misled and duped by the British into believing in their protective guardianship, while at the first sign of danger British protection crumbled and the country was deserted and left to the mercies of the Japanese. After this sorry defeat, British prestige with the native peoples could hardly hope to regain its former status. Out of this common attitude appears to have grown a determination not to heed unquestioningly future British policy decisions.

Throughout the war the British had given considerable thought to postwar policy for Malaya. In 1945 the government issued its "White Paper" announcing the plan for the amalgamation of all the Malay states into a Malayan Union. The plan almost immediately aroused the antagonism of all classes among the Malays, who, through numerous demonstrations, rallies, meetings, and public proclamations, showed that their previous political apathy had ended. The issue was carried to London, where after considerable controversy the scheme was laid aside in favor of a more acceptable plan for a Federation of Malaya, worked out between the British and representatives of the local communities.

The Malay has discovered his political voice and the techniques of political maneuvering to attain Malay ends. Steadily increasing, too, is the political power of the Chinese and Indian communities. The political future of Malaya is no longer so much in the hands of the British as in those of the leaders of the three Asian communities. It will ultimately be determined by the degree to which they are able to adjust their differences and combine their powers toward the creation of a Malayan nation.

Besides the political conditions mentioned, the aftermath of the Japanese occupation left Malaya war-ravaged. Resources and equipment had been sadly overworked; little time or money had been devoted to repair or maintenance; rubber stands had been destroyed in large numbers; the labor force was disorganized, with a considerable segment of the Chinese population scattered and dislocated in the jungle. The creation of synthetic rubber during the war and the more recent drops in the price of tin threatened economic bankruptcy for the country. Under the Japanese administration the system of land tenure and ownership had been altered. Those who had fled before the

Japanese armies returned to find their lands in other hands. Even more crucial than the political problems faced by the returning British was the economic rehabilitation of the country. Although considerable efforts have been expended along this line, the presence of the Communist "Emergency" has prevented fully effective reconstruction in many parts of the country.

The Emergency itself has caused a heavy drain on British and Malayan resources--material, financial, and human. Although the Communist guerrilla forces appear to hold only a few small spots, their raids on tin mines and rubber estates have made serious inroads into the productive efficiency of the country. The cost of maintaining a considerable armed force throughout the area has resulted in serious financial deficits for the government each year. The dislocation and resettlement of large numbers of Chinese and Malays has created severe social and economic problems and is bringing about a considerable change in the demographic structure of the country.

These various social, economic, and political problems will be more intensively surveyed in later chapters; their solutions lie in the future.

3. Demographic Patterns

THE 5,848,910 PERSONS inhabiting the 50,886 square miles of Malaya in 1947 were almost entirely Asian. [1] They lived within the British colonial system, were administered by a relatively small number of Englishmen--scarcely 1 per cent of the population--and were organized into two political units, the Federation of Malaya and the Colony of Singapore. Although major political changes are taking place rapidly in Malaya, the major characteristics and distribution of the population are expected not to change rapidly or, in the short run, radically, and the 1947 census provides a useful bench mark from which trends may be discerned and projected.

The interplay of colonialism and immigration has been most important to the present distribution and composition of the population of Malaya. Over the past fifty to sixty years major changes have occurred which are closely related to the development of a colonial estate and mining economy in Malaya and to the function of Singapore as an entrepôt in a wider sphere of colonial and international activity and trade.

Five general characteristics of Malaya's population, each closely related to colonialism and immigration, provide a convenient setting for description and analysis. (1) People are concentrated very largely in areas that have been most actively

1. These and all subsequent population data, unless otherwise noted, are taken from M. V. Del Tufo, Malaya: A Report on the 1947 Census of Population (London: Crown Agents for the Colonies, 1949). By mid-1954, the total population of Malaya is estimated to have increased to 7,054,955.

developed under the impact of colonial development. (2) The population is a plural society comprised of three ethnic groups making up 98 per cent of the total population. (3) The role of immigration in contributing to the population has been very important in the recent past. (4) Malaya has a comparatively high degree of urbanization relative to other Southeast Asian countries. (5) Because of a number of factors, including present restrictions on immigration, the population is assuming certain characteristics indicative of a more stable society though in no sense indicative of increasing homogeneity. [2]

Distribution of Population

In Malaya high densities of population are found along much of the coast; the forested interior is sparsely peopled (Map 2). There are two major areas of population concentration. One extends from north to south along the entire west coast of the country; the other is centered on the level expanses of the Kelantan delta along the northeast coast near the Thai border.

Western population concentration

In 1947, 72 per cent of the then nearly six million inhabitants of Malaya were concentrated in a narrow band of settlement along the western coast, constituting about 25 per cent of the total land area of the country. This settlement extends in the form of contiguous districts of high densities of population (not less than one hundred persons per square mile) along the entire length of the western littoral. The degree of localization relatively near the coast is considerable. In only two places, the Kinta valley and around Kuala Lumpur, do these high-density districts generally reach more than thirty miles inland.

This coastal strip, including the two inland projections of densely peopled districts, contains the regions of maximum economic development. Here are found the most intensively mined areas and the most extensive area of rubber estates.

----

2. The use of stable in this sense is not to be confused with the demographic concept "stable population," which refers to an age-sex structure which would ensue if given natality and mortality rates prevailed indefinitely. "Stable" will not be used in this latter sense in this report.

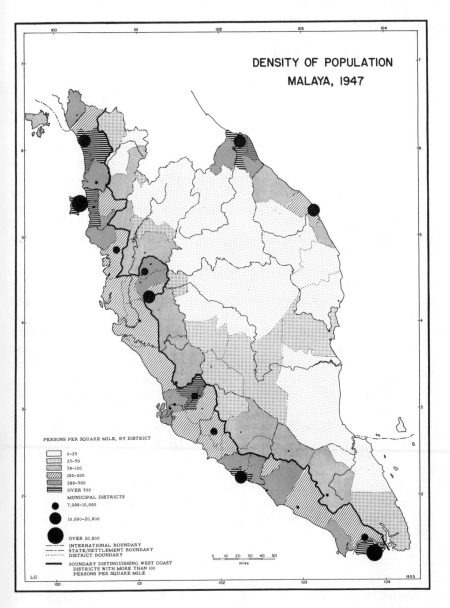

DENSITY OF POPULATION
MALAYA, 1947

PERSONS PER SQUARE MILE, BY DISTRICT

0-25
25-50
50-100
100-200
200-300
OVER 300
MUNICIPAL DISTRICTS
7,000-10,000

10,000-20,000

OVER 20,000
INTERNATIONAL BOUNDARY
STATE/SETTLEMENT BOUNDARY
DISTRICT BOUNDARY
BOUNDARY DISTINGUISHING WEST COAST
DISTRICTS WITH MORE THAN 100
PERSONS PER SQUARE MILE

0 10 20 30 40 50
miles

Map 2

The best and most used transportation facilities serve these districts. This, then, is the area of maximum colonial development in Malaya. As measured by densities, the concentration of people in the area is evident. With the exception of five districts along the northeast coast, excluding districts which are solely municipalities, all other districts in Malaya have lower densities. In contrast with an over-all density of 115 persons per square mile for all Malaya (including Singapore), the average density in this great coastal concentration is 343 persons per square mile. [3] Rural densities in excess of 150 persons per square mile are commonly found.

Virtually all of the urban dwellers in Malaya live in the cities and towns along the west coast. These districts included 1,846,041, or 90 per cent, of the 2,054,113 urbanites in 1947. Only four of the twenty-three places of more than ten thousand inhabitants were outside this area. Two of these four are excluded only because district boundaries were used to delimit the area. In reality they are part of the area in terms of function as well as proximity.

Within the bank of dense settlement along the west coast there are localities of greater concentrations of people. These groupings are associated with more intensive agricultural uses of the land, mining activities, and urban functions. There are five such population clusters, as seen in the districts with densities of population in excess of two hundred persons per square mile, centering on towns or cities in which many of the activities of a larger area are brought to focus (Map 2). (1) Foremost among these is Singapore and Singapore island, in most respects the entrance and exit of Malaya as well as a major city in Southeast Asia and world affairs. (2) In the north a second population cluster appears on Penang island, reaching northward into the rice and rubber producing areas of Kedah as well as southward into Perak. (3) A third cluster includes Kuala Lumpur, the capital of the Federation, and nearby mining and rubber areas. (4) Another population cluster is found in the Kinta valley, associated chiefly with the tin-mining there. (5) Finally, a sizable concentration of people is

---

3. The contrast is probably greater than these figures suggest. The average density for the Federation alone was 97 in 1947 and estimated to be 109 in 1953.

TABLE 1
POPULATION

Total Population

	1911	1921	1931	1947	1953 (est.)	1954 (est.)
Federation	2,339,051	2,906,691	3,787,758	4,908,086	5,705,952	5,888,578
Singapore	305,439	420,004	559,946	940,824	1,015,453	1,166,377
Malaya	2,664,490	3,326,695	4,347,704	5,848,910	6,721,405	7,054,955

Rate of Increase (per cent)

	1911-1921	1921-1931	1931-1947	1947-1953
Federation	24.3	30.3	29.6	16.2
Singapore	37.5	33.3	68.0	19.4
Malaya	25.8	30.6	34.5	16.3

found in the old rubber areas around Malakka, between Kuala Lumpur and Singapore.

The first three of these population groups each center on one of the three largest cities of Malaya (Singapore, Georgetown, and Kuala Lumpur) and together account for 30 per cent of the population of Malaya. Singapore island alone contains 16 per cent of the total population and one-third of the urban population of Malaya. Population densities in the districts immediately surrounding these cities exceed three hundred persons per square mile, while adjacent districts commonly have two to three hundred persons per square mile. Suburbanization and such intensive agricultural uses of land as market gardening exist around these larger cities. Although the actual extent of such conditions is not readily determinable without detailed field study, high population densities give some indication of them. This is especially true of Singapore island outside of the city of Singapore. In spite of areas of rubber plantation, reserved areas, and water catchments, the density per square mile is over 1,300.

Population of the interior

The west-coast concentration of population is bordered by districts of less dense population and smaller and fewer villages and towns. Many of these districts are areas of colonial-immigrant development, although less intensively so than the coastal districts. They are the frontiers, in effect, of such development, with densities of twenty-five to one hundred persons per square mile. Settlement is not continuous, and transportation routes are fewer and farther apart. The urban pop-

ulation of the area is only 3 per cent of the total urban population of Malaya. Roughly only one in seven persons is an urban
dweller.

Population concentration in the northeast

The other major concentration of population is along the
northeast coast reaching from the Thai border southward for
120 miles or so to Kuala Trengganu. This concentration consists of two population clusters, the larger on the Kelantan
delta with Kota Bharu (22, 765) as the only town of any size,
and a smaller group about the mouth of the Trengganu river
centering on Kuala Trengganu (27, 004). While this area is the
second major population concentration in Malaya, only about
7 per cent of the total population lives there, and scarcely 3
per cent of the urban population. The proportion of urban
dwellers to the total population of the area is lower than one
in eight.

Though there are few urban dwellers, this rice-growing
area has high rural densities, especially in the districts of
the Kelantan delta (Map 3). The lowest total densities in the
delta region proper are above 200 persons per square mile.
Rural densities in two districts exceed 400 persons per square
mile, one of these actually having a rural population of 650 per
square mile in an area of 273 square miles. These are the
highest rural densities in Malaya. The rural densities shown
around the larger west-coast cities must be regarded with
caution since they include an undetermined number of suburban dwellers.

Southward from Kuala Trengganu to the tip of the peninsula and westward to the districts bordering the western littoral, the east coast and the interior of Malaya are indeed
sparsely populated. Few districts have as many as fifty persons per square mile. These are areas in which settlement
is found in small clusters along the coast, the rivers, or the
few land transport routes and the remaining territory is virtually uninhabited forest.

Urbanization

Malaya's population is highly urbanized in contrast with that
of other Southeast Asian countries. In 1947, 35 per cent of the
total population were urban dwellers (Table 2). Estimates place
the urban population of Southeast Asia at something like 15 per

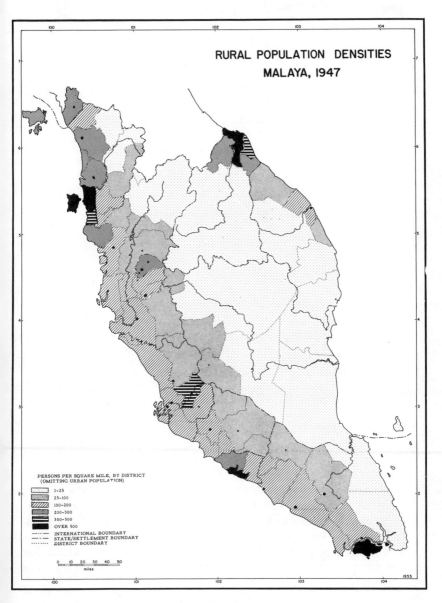

RURAL POPULATION DENSITIES
MALAYA, 1947

PERSONS PER SQUARE MILE, BY DISTRICT
(OMITTING URBAN POPULATION)

0-25
25-100
100-200
200-300
300-500
OVER 500
INTERNATIONAL BOUNDARY
STATE/SETTLEMENT BOUNDARY
DISTRICT BOUNDARY

0   10   20   30   40   50
miles

1955

Map 3

cent, while for individual countries it is as low as 10 (Indochina, Indonesia). In the Philippines about 24 per cent of the population is urban. [4]

TABLE 2
URBAN POPULATION

Total Urban Population 1947, and
Per Cent Urban of Total Population 1911-1947

	1911	1921	1931	1947	
				Total Urban Pop.	Per Cent of Total Pop.
Federation	17.2	19.1	21.1	1,301,376	26.5
Singapore	85.0	83.4	79.6	752,737	80.0
Malaya	22.7	27.7	29.5	2,054,113	35.1

Urban Population by Major Ethnic Groups 1947

	Malaysians	Chinese	Indians
Federation	274,618	811,520	179,434
Singapore	83,333	592,172	54,557
Malaya	357,951	1,403,692	233,991

Per Cent of Total Urban Population in Each Group 1947

	Malaysians	Chinese	Indians
Federation	21.1	62.4	13.8
Singapore	11.3	78.5	7.2
Malaya	17.4	68.3	11.4

Per Cent Urban of Each Group

	Malaysians	Chinese	Indians
Federation	11.3	43.1	33.8
Singapore	72.0	81.1	79.1
Malaya	14.1	53.7	39.0

The importance of one city, Singapore, in accounting for the high rate of urbanization must not be underemphasized. Although Malaya as a whole has 35 per cent of its population classified as urban dwellers, the Colony of Singapore is 80 per cent urban, while the Federation is 27 per cent urban.

Urban dwellers are concentrated to a high degree in particular areas. Five territories had 85 per cent of all urban dwellers in Malaya (Table 3). The Colony of Singapore had the highest total number (752,737) and the highest degree of urbaniza-

---

4. Norton S. Ginsburg, "The Great City in Southeast Asia," The American Journal of Sociology, March, 1955, p. 455.

TABLE 3
URBAN POPULATION BY STATES

States with Highest Absolute Numbers of Urban Residents

	Urban Population	Per Cent of Total Population of State
Singapore	752,737	80.0
Perak	281,203	29.5
Selangor	272,531	38.3
Penang	250,940	56.2
Johore	166,781	22.6
Total	1,724,192*	

States with Highest Proportion of Urban Residents to Total Population of State

	Per Cent Urban of Total Population of State
Singapore	80.0
Penang	56.2
Selangor	38.3
Perak	29.5
Malakka	26.3

*Eighty-five per cent of all urban dwellers in Malaya.

tion in terms of inhabitants (80 per cent). Perak, Selangor, and Penang each had between 250,000 and 282,000 urbanites, and Johore had the fewest of the top five states (166,781). Johore also had a low proportion of urban population to total population (22.6 per cent). Malakka, with fewer total urban dwellers, had a slightly higher proportion of urban dwellers (26.3 per cent). Penang had a 56.2 per cent urban population. No other state had a higher than 40 per cent urban population; most were far below that proportion.

The Plural Society

The population of Malaya is composed almost entirely of three major ethnic groups, which make up 98 per cent of the total population. The three groups and their proportions of the total population are the Chinese (in 1947, 44.7 per cent), the Malaysians[5] (43.5 per cent), and the Indians (10.3 per cent)

---

5. The terms "Malaysian" and "Malay" are used somewhat

(Table 4). Thus, representatives of two great peoples of Asia, the Chinese and the Indians, are found intermingled with the Malays, the most numerous people of Southeast Asia. Each ethnic group remains almost entirely distinct from the others; each is localized to a considerable extent in different parts of Malaya; and each is to varying degrees engaged in specific kinds of activity.

Ethnic group distribution

While it is true that representatives of each of the major ethnic groups are to be found in some numbers throughout Malaya, concentrations in certain areas are common.

The Chinese. --The Chinese are found primarily in the more developed districts of the countryside and in the cities and towns. They form the bulk of the urban population (62.4 per cent in the Federation and 78.5 per cent in Singapore) (Table 2). They constitute over half of the urban population in every state except Kelantan, Trengganu, and Perlis. These three states have high proportions of Malays and low proportions of urban residents. The concentration of Chinese in a few cities is even more striking (Table 11). Three cities of more than 100,000 (including Singapore) have over half of the urban Chinese and 30 per cent of all Chinese in Malaya. Ten places of 30,000 or more inhabitants have 72 per cent of the Chinese urban population. There are eight towns in Malaya with more than 35,000 inhabitants; with one exception (Johore Bahru) each has more than a 60 per cent Chinese population. Half of all the Chinese in Malaya are urban dwellers. In contrast, only about two-fifths of the Indians and one-eighth of the Malays are urbanites (Table 2).

Besides comprising more than half of the population in most of the cities and towns, the Chinese are found in considerable numbers in many rural districts (Map 4). These districts are invariably among those which are most developed by Western

---

interchangeably. More narrowly, "Malay" is used to describe Malay-speaking peoples indigenous to the Malayan peninsula, while "Malaysian" is used to indicate inclusion of indigenous "Malays" and immigrants of Indonesian and other southeast Asian origins. However, in discussing recent immigrants of peoples ethnically Malay, from Indonesia and other places of origin, the census term "Other Malaysians" is used.

TABLE 4
MAJOR ETHNIC GROUPS

	1921	1931	1947	1953 (est.)	1955 (est.)
Federation					
			Total Numbers		
Malaysians	1,568,588	1,863,872	2,427,834	2,803,863	2,967,233
Chinese	855,863	1,284,888	1,884,534	2,152,906	2,286,883
Indians	439,172	470,987	530,638	665,503	713,810
			Per Cent of Total Population		
Malaysians	54.0	49.2	49.5	49.5	49.0*
Chinese	29.4	33.9	38.4	38.5	37.8*
Indians	15.1	15.1	10.8	10.9	10.1*
Singapore					
			Total Numbers		
Malaysians	54,426	66,172	115,735	137,697	143,685
Chinese	316,877	419,564	730,133	860,509	893,004
Indians	32,342	50,860	68,978	87,224	91,029
			Per Cent of Total Population		
Malaysians	12.9	11.8	12.3	12.2	12.3
Chinese	75.2	74.9	77.6	77.2	76.6
Indians	7.7	9.1	7.3	7.3	7.8
Malaya					
			Total Numbers		
Malaysians	1,623,-14	1,930,044	2,543,569	2,941,560	
Chinese	1,171,740	1,704,452	2,614,667	3,013,415	
Indians	471,514	621,847	599,616	752,727	
			Per Cent of Total Population		
Malaysians	48.8	44.4	43.5	43.5	
Chinese	35.2	39.2	44.7	44.5	
Indians	14.2	14.3	10.3	10.2	

*Total percentage is lower than expected. Data are probably in error.
Federation of Malaya, Annual Report, 1955 (Kuala Lumpur: Government Press, 1956).

standards. Some are rubber-growing districts, but many are mining areas. Without exception these districts are located along the western littoral. Those with the heaviest concentrations of Chinese are extensions of the great population clusters in Penang, the Kinta valley, Kuala Lumpur, and Singapore.

The Malays. --Malays are primarily rural; they shun, however, estates and activities associated with a wage economy in general; only recently have they begun to move to the larger towns of Malaya. They predominate in those districts in the high-density areas of the west coast which are largely agricultural, and in general in the east and north of Malaya (Map 5).

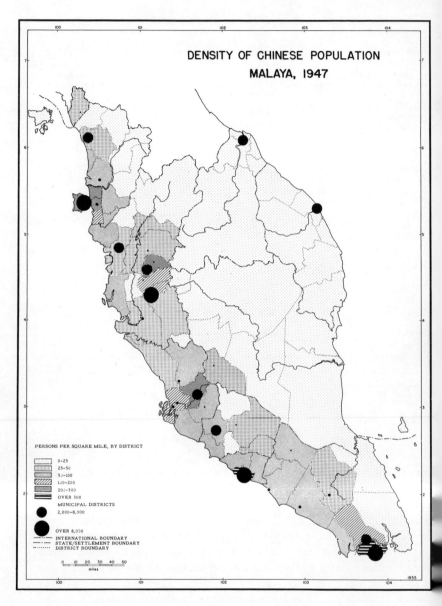

DENSITY OF CHINESE POPULATION
MALAYA, 1947

PERSONS PER SQUARE MILE, BY DISTRICT

- 0–25
- 25–50
- 50–100
- 100–200
- 200–300
- OVER 300

MUNICIPAL DISTRICTS

2,000–8,000

OVER 8,000

INTERNATIONAL BOUNDARY
STATE/SETTLEMENT BOUNDARY
DISTRICT BOUNDARY

0 10 20 30 40 50
miles

1955

Map 4

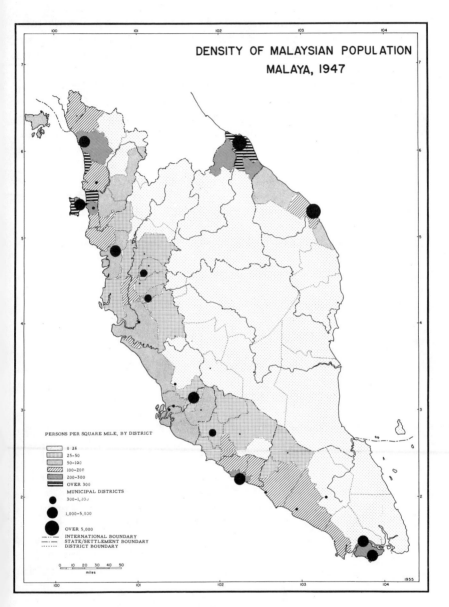

DENSITY OF MALAYSIAN POPULATION
MALAYA, 1947

PERSONS PER SQUARE MILE, BY DISTRICT

- 0 25
- 25-50
- 50-100
- 100-200
- 200-300
- OVER 300

MUNICIPAL DISTRICTS

- 300-1,000
- 1,000-5,000
- OVER 5,000

— · — INTERNATIONAL BOUNDARY
— · · — STATE/SETTLEMENT BOUNDARY
· · · · · DISTRICT BOUNDARY

0 10 20 30 40 50
miles

1955

Map 5

There are two kinds of distribution of Malays. The first consists of areas that are not only predominantly but almost exclusively Malay. Some of these have high population densities and total numbers; others have low densities and total numbers. This type of Malay settlement is found along the east coast, the interior, and the northwest coast. Along much of the west coast, where the effects of colonialism and immigration have been felt most strongly, a second type of Malay population distribution is evident. Here, the Malays are found in the rural areas, leading a Malay way of life. Around them are the cities, estates, and mining districts, with large numbers of people of other ethnic origins living entirely different kinds of lives. Here are found districts in which both total numbers and densities of Malays are high, but in which the proportion of Malays is low in relation to those of the other ethnic groups. Excluding the states of Perlis and Kedah, there are perhaps fifteen districts in the west-coast area in which Malays comprise over 50 per cent of the total population. In a few districts they amount to less than 50 per cent of the population but are about equal in numbers to the other large group, the Chinese. In these areas the Malays form the basic rural population, while the Chinese and other groups are found largely in the cities, engaged in agricultural commercial pursuits, or in retail commerce in rural areas.

As previously noted, the Malays are not urban dwellers. In 1947, 54 per cent of the Chinese and 39 per cent of the Indians, but only 14 per cent of the Malays, were found in towns (Table 2). In all Malaya the Malays represented only 17 per cent of the urban population while they constituted over two-fifths of the total population. Malays, in contrast to the Indians and Chinese, form larger proportions of the population in the towns and villages under ten thousand than they do in the towns and cities of more than ten thousand. Only two cities in Malaya with more than ten thousand inhabitants, Kuala Trengganu and Kota Bharu, have over 50 per cent Malays. These are both in the northeast. Even Alor Star in north Kedah, amid districts that are generally more than 80 per cent Malay, has a population which is 48 per cent Chinese and 14 per cent Indian.

The "Other Malaysians."--Most of the peoples now inhabiting the Malayan peninsula are immigrant peoples, though the greater part of those called Malays or Malaysians represent earlier movements and are now for convenience regarded as indigenous. The movement of Malay peoples to the peninsula has been a continuing one, however, and the most recent arrivals, roughly contemporaneous with the bulk of the Chinese and Indians, form a somewhat distinct group among the Malays of the peninsula. The "Other Malaysians," as they are termed in the census, are from many places in Southeast Asia, more specifically from Indonesia, and to a considerable extent from Sumatra. Ethnically, they are close to the peninsular Malays, especially those of the west coast. Like the Chinese and Indians, the "Other Malaysians" have been attracted to Malaya by the prospect of material improvement. They, too, have participated in the colonial economic development of Malaya, especially as estate laborers.

In 1947 there were some 309, 000 of these comparatively recent immigrants. They represented about 12 per cent of the Malaysian population and slightly more than 5 per cent of the total population. Most of the "Other Malaysians" (over 90 per cent) are found in Johore, Selangor, Perak, and Singapore. More particularly, they are found in the coastal districts of these states. They amount to at least 10 per cent of the total population in seven districts, and in the Batu Pahat district of western Johore they constitute almost as large a share of the total population as do the peninsular Malays. In one small district in northern Selangor they equal more than half of the total population of 41, 704 persons, or one-fourth of the "Other Malaysians" found in the state as a whole. Such concentrations are almost entirely in association with estate operation.

The Indians. --The Indians in Malaya form a much smaller group (just over half a million people in 1947) than either the Chinese or Malaysians. They are found in significant numbers only in the west-coast concentration of population, mainly in the north about Penang and in the bordering districts of Kedah and Perak, in Selangor and southern Perak, and in Singapore (Map 6 and Map 20). Fifty-nine per cent of the Indians in 1947 were found in these areas.

About two-fifths of the Indians of Malaya are urban dwellers, with the remainder living in the country (Table 2). Urban Indians dwell chiefly in the larger towns. In 1947 almost 80 per cent (185, 668 of a total of 233, 991) lived in towns of more than ten thousand inhabitants. Urban Indians are somewhat less concentrated in the three major cities of Malaya than are urban Chinese. Nevertheless, 45 per cent of the urban Indians lived in these three cities (Table 11). The four largest cities in Malaya had over half of the urban Indians; no other city in Ma-

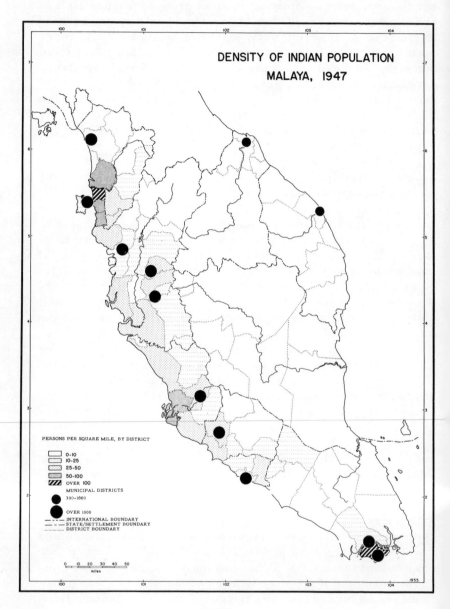

DENSITY OF INDIAN POPULATION
MALAYA, 1947

PERSONS PER SQUARE MILE, BY DISTRICT

☐	0-10
☐	10-25
☐	25-50
☐	50-100
▨	OVER 100

MUNICIPAL DISTRICTS

● 300-1000

● OVER 1000

— · — INTERNATIONAL BOUNDARY
— — — STATE/SETTLEMENT BOUNDARY
· · · · · · DISTRICT BOUNDARY

0 10 20 30 40 50
miles

1955

Map 6

laya had as many as ten thousand. Indians are not numerous in the towns and villages of less than ten thousand inhabitants in general, though they appear to be somewhat more numerous in towns of this size in Perak than elsewhere. In fact, 39 per cent of the 48,323 Indians living in such towns and villages were located in Perak.

The remaining three-fifths of the Indian population in Malaya are largely associated with the rural estate economy. Over two-thirds of the rural Indians in Malaya are estate dwellers. They are found chiefly in a central concentration extending from the southern districts of Perak through Selangor and including two northern districts of Negri Sembilan. Most are found in the coastal districts of Selangor and in southern Perak. In 1947 Selangor and two districts of southern Perak had 30 per cent of all the Indians in Malaya. These coastal districts are highly developed rubber-producing areas. Other concentrations of Indians are found in parts of Penang and in bordering districts of Perak and Kedah. Here, too, the Indians are associated especially with the cultivation of rubber. Other groups of Indians are to be found in Johore, although total estate populations of Indians do not approach those of either Perak or Selangor. It is chiefly in Selangor (eight districts) that the Indian population forms a significant proportion of the total population.

Migrations and Population Change

The great influx of immigrant peoples into Malaya followed the consolidation of the British colonial interests, the development of port cities, and the exploitation of the resources of the peninsula. Europeans came as administrators and entrepreneurs in the developing colonial economy. The labor and accompanying service population came from other Asian places, principally China, India, and the islands of the Indies.

The earlier arrivals (there were significant numbers by 1850) settled in the port cities of Singapore, Georgetown, and Malakka. Late nineteenth century developments of rubber and mining activities extended the area of immigration into the states of Perak, Selangor, Negri Sembilan, Johore, and Kedah; in short, into the entire western littoral from Kedah southward.

Early immigration

As early as 1850 there was a rapid increase in the Chinese

population in Penang. In 1851 the Chinese were about one-third as numerous as the Malays. Men outnumbered women by a ratio of 5 to 1. The Indian population was increasing rapidly at this time also. By 1881 the Indians and Chinese together outnumbered the Malays. After the turn of the century the influx of Chinese accelerated. In 1911 there were more Chinese than Malays in Penang. Since 1830 Singapore has had large numbers of Chinese in its population. By 1901 more than two-thirds of the population of the Colony of Singapore were Chinese. Here, too, the males outnumbered females (4 to 1). Since then, the proportion of Chinese has continued to grow phenomenally, and Singapore has become virtually a Chinese city.

> The Chinese population in the three Settlements grew very rapidly after the beginning of British administration. From 1820 to 1860 the numbers of Chinese on Penang Island rose from under 9,000 to over 36,000; in Singapore the numbers rose from just over 3,000 in 1823 to 28,000 in 1850 and 50,000 in 1860; the growth of the Chinese population in Malacca . . . rose from 4,000 in 1834 to 10,000 in 1860. The very great majority of the immigrants at that time were males, and it is not surprising, therefore, to find that the ratio of Chinese females to males was 1 to 3 in Malacca in 1852, 1 to 4 in Penang in 1851, and 1 to 12 in Singapore in 1850. Singapore had had the most rapid population growth of all the Settlements. [6]

By 1880 the development of the west coast was under way. Perak experienced huge influxes of both Chinese and Indians between 1891 and 1900. There apparently was a continuing movement of Indians into Perak, Selangor, Negri Sembilan, Johore, and Kedah from 1910 to 1931. Pahang has had much less immigration, and the east-coast states and Perlis have had very little.

---

6. T. E. Smith, Population Growth in Malaya: An Analysis of Recent Trends (London: Royal Institute of International Affairs, 1952), pp. 62-63.

Recent migrations

In the thirty-six years from 1911 to 1947 the population of Malaya increased from 2.5 million to 5.8 million. The influence of immigration was conspicious but was modified by sizable annual departures.

Some impression of the in-and-out movement may be obtained by looking at the migrational surplus or deficit figures for the years 1931 to 1941 (Table 5).

TABLE 5
MIGRATIONAL SURPLUSES AND DEFICITS

| Year | Total | | Balance | | | |
	Arrivals	Departures	Total	Chinese	Indians	Malaysians
1931	330,146	517,675	-187,529	-112,965	-70,555	-3,110
1932	264,738	427,716	-162,978	-97,518	-59,640	-3,996
1933	250,126	288,575	-38,449	-31,178	-7,418	304
1934	494,753	352,664	142,089	61,639	73,798	3,425
1935	548,339	423,133	125,206	90,986	36,893	-3,060
1936	525,621	442,812	82,809	75,801	9,970	-4,326
1937	760,453	493,247	267,206	180,502	89,645	-3,850
1938	465,564	434,526	31,038	53,180	-20,110	-5,748
1939	383,738	386,450	-2,712	14,339	-11,143	-8,558
1940	306,736	315,035	-8,299	3,322	-7,595	-4,852
10-year period			248,381	238,108	37,861	-20,759
1952	330,253	310,518	19,735	-13,588	21,121	8,309
1953	308,278	278,924	29,354	-6,405	25,409	8,488

It is found that the beginning and end of this period included years in which there was a net out-migration. Following the war there was an out-movement which by mid-1951 had changed to a small in-migration, which still continues. Restrictions on immigration since 1933, tightened in 1952, further limit immigration. [7]

To a considerable degree the immigrant population was transient. That is, the majority of immigrants came for only a

---

7. The immigration ordinance which went into effect in August, 1953, replaced the various immigration regulations previously applicable in both the Federation and Singapore.

relatively short period and then left Malaya. For example, while 1931 was a year of net out-migration, the number of in-migrants was 330, 146 and the number of out-migrants was 517, 675 (Table 5). In recent years there have been enlarged migrations. Arrivals and departures in both 1952 and 1953 were over or near three hundred thousand persons. [8] The balances in these years were plus nineteen thousand and plus twenty-nine thousand, respectively. The positive balances were due chiefly to the net in-migration of Indians, which exceeded twenty thousand, and of Malaysians, which exceeded eight thousand, in each of these years. In both years there was a net out-migration of Chinese.

The foreign-born population

The percentage of the population which was not born in Malaya provides a further index to the immigrant quality of the population (Table 6). Since 1931 there has been a steady decline in the proportions of foreign-born in the total population.

TABLE 6
PERCENTAGE OF POPULATION BORN IN MALAYA

		Total	Chinese	All Malaysians	Indians
1921	Federation	56.4	20.9		12.1
	Singapore	31.0	25.1		17.1
	Malaya	53.2	22.0		12.4
1931	Federation	58.9	29.9	92.0	21.4
	Singapore	39.0	35.6	72.5	17.7
	Malaya	56.3	31.2	91.3	21.1
1947	Federation	78.3	63.5	96.0	51.6
	Singapore	60.7	59.9	81.9	36.3
	Malaya	75.4	62.5	95.4	49.8

Although in 1921 nearly half of the population of Malaya was foreign-born, in 1947 78.3 per cent of the population of the Federation and 60.7 per cent of the population of Singapore

---

8. For the most part these data do not represent true immigration and emigration only, since they include every entry or departure of a Malayan resident traveling abroad. In 1953, only 7, 835 documents of entry for permanent residents were granted to aliens by the Federation.

was born in Malaya.[9] The western states of Selangor, Johore, and Negri Sembilan are the states with the largest proportions of foreign-born population. Selangor has the highest proportion of foreign-born persons (nearly 33 per cent of the total population), followed by Johore (30 per cent) and Negri Sembilan (28 per cent). The three northeastern states and Perlis have less than a 15 per cent foreign-born population. Perak, Pahang, and Penang have about one-quarter of their populations made up of foreign-born persons.

Malaya-born females continue to form a large proportion of the total female population. Federation-born males, formerly constituting less than half of the total male population (a reflection of the nature of the immigration), now form over 80 per cent of the total male population. In the last three censuses, the number of locally born females had represented more than 70 per cent of all Federation females. The same trends are apparent in Singapore, but the proportion of foreign-born persons is higher since this is a great immigrant receiving center. Higher proportions of Malaya-born males are closely connected with the growing tendency of Chinese to settle permanently in Malaya.

The recent tendency for both Indians and Chinese to settle in Malaya, as contrasted with the former large-scale in-and-out movements, is pronounced. This, however, is less true of the Indians than of the Chinese. In 1947, 63.5 per cent of the Chinese population was Malaya-born as contrasted with 30 per cent in 1931 and 21 per cent in 1921. A similar trend is apparent in Singapore. Pahang, Johore, and Negri Sembilan are states with large Chinese populations which still have under 60 per cent Malaya-born Chinese.

In 1931 only 12 per cent of the Indians in Malaya had been born there. By 1931 about 20 per cent were Malaya-born, and in 1947, 50 per cent were Malaya-born.

The "Other Malaysians" (chiefly Patani and Indonesians) now have substantial proportions of Malaya-born persons. Malaya-born "Other Malaysians" constitute 67 per cent of their total numbers. Europeans are largely foreign-born, and Eurasians are over 90 per cent Malaya-born.

---

9. In 1954 the percentage of locally born population in Singapore was estimated to have risen to 73.

General increase

The rate of growth of the population of Malaya continues to be over 2 per cent per annum in spite of a great reduction in net immigration. In 1911 the population of Malaya was about two and one-half million; in 1947, the year of the last census, it was 5, 848, 910, and in 1954 it was estimated at just over seven million (Table 1). The percentage increase from 1931 to 1947 was 34. 5; the estimated increase from 1947 to 1954 was 20. 6 per cent. This rate of growth (well over 2 per cent) is high and appears to be continuing.

The increase in population between 1931 and 1947 was due mainly to a natural increase in the Malaysian and Chinese segments of the population. In the Federation the proportion of Chinese grew from 34 to over 38 per cent of the total population. In the same period the proportion of the population which is Malaysian declined from over half to just under half, while in Malaya as a whole it is now about two-fifths of the total. The proportion of Indians in the total population declined from about 15 to about 11 per cent in both the Federation and Malaya as a whole between 1931 and 1947. The decline of the proportion of Indians was caused by an actual decline in numbers through the war period when the Indian population suffered considerably at the hands of the Japanese.

Over the years since the turn of the century--the period of the rapid development of Malaya under British rule--certain areas have advanced much more than others in both development and population growth. The rates of increase in population by territories has been generally high in Johore, Selangor, Negri Sembilan, and Singapore. Between 1911 and 1931 each of these territories for each decade grew at rates greater than 30 per cent; Johore grew more than 50 per cent in the first decade of the period and over 75 per cent in the second decade. The growth in these areas was largely the result of the development of the rubber industry. Between 1931 and 1947 Singapore grew the most (68 per cent), while Johore and Selangor continued to grow at rates in excess of 30 per cent, as did Pahang and Perlis.

In the last census period no state grew less than 20 per cent. No state has declined in population since 1921. (Trengganu declined slightly from 1911 to 1921.) Throughout the period no east-coast state has been in the upper ranges of the ranking of territories by rates of growth, and some west-coast places, such as Malakka, have not evidenced continuously high rates of growth.

68

Recent population increases

The greatest absolute increases in population on a territorial basis in the 1931-1947 period took place in Singapore, Johore, Selangor, Perak, Kedah, and Penang, in that order. Singapore increased by 380,000 and Johore by 232,000. The other states increased by more than 100,000, while Perlis had the smallest absolute increase. Perlis, however, had a rate of increase of 43 per cent (third highest in Malaya).

Analysis of increase by districts yields a more detailed picture of area differences. Out of eighty-seven districts, eighty-one had increases in the period and six had decreases (Map 7). Twelve of these districts constitute municipalities. Only five of the municipal districts showed increases of 50 per cent or less--Georgetown, Taiping, Kampar, Ipoh, and Malakka. [10] With few exceptions the other districts having large rates of increase were in or adjacent to the western population concentrations. Only two east-coast districts (other than the two municipalities) had more than 30 per cent increases. Most of the west-coast districts increased from 15 to 25 or 30 per cent. Large increases were noted in essentially frontier districts bordering the west-coast districts. Two districts in western Pahang in the interior of Malaya increased more than 50 per cent. Both were sparsely settled districts with fewer than fifty thousand inhabitants each. Densities were correspondingly low. Two districts in northern Perak showed increases of more than 50 per cent, but these districts also had very sparse populations. The Cameron Highlands had the greatest percentage increase (345 per cent) of any district in Malaya, but this represented an absolute increase of only six thousand. The other large (over 50 per cent) percentage increase occurred in four districts of Johore and on Singapore island, exclusive of Singapore municipality (which also increased more than 50 per cent but has been included in the discussion of changes in districts which are entirely municipalities). The area in Johore which showed these increases consists of a central strip north and south in the state in districts which are predominantly Chi-

---

10. This discussion of municipal district changes is not to be confused with subsequent discussion of city changes, which is not concerned with district boundaries.

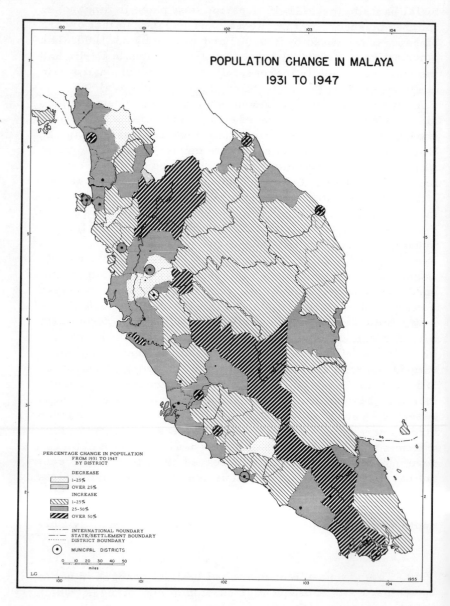

POPULATION CHANGE IN MALAYA
1931 TO 1947

PERCENTAGE CHANGE IN POPULATION
FROM 1931 TO 1947
BY DISTRICT

DECREASE

1–25%

OVER 25%

INCREASE

1–25%

25–50%

OVER 50%

———— INTERNATIONAL BOUNDARY
– – – – STATE/SETTLEMENT BOUNDARY
· · · · · DISTRICT BOUNDARY

⊙ MUNICIPAL DISTRICTS

0 10 20 30 40 50
miles

LG

1955

Map 7

nese.[11] One predominantly Malayan west-coast district also increased over 50 per cent.

The remaining districts of the west coast show wide ranges in increases and some even show declines. One heavily populated district of Kedah (density, 118 per square mile) which borders Penang showed a decline of some 12 per cent in the period. Although both Malaysian and Chinese populations declined slightly, most of the loss was in Indians, who declined some 40 per cent. Two districts in the Kinta valley area declined 9 per cent and 12 per cent, respectively. The decline was in the Chinese and Indian segments of the population; the Malaysians in both districts actually increased in numbers. Two small districts in relatively sparsely settled northern reaches of Kedah and Perak showed declines, as did a district in Negri Sembilan to a minor extent. Without further information it is impossible to account for these local changes.

Internal migration

Internal migration is of two main kinds: (1) agricultural population movement of a seasonal nature or into newly developed areas and (2) movement from rural to urban areas. It appears that great distances are not involved in these internal movements, since only small proportions of the two largest ethnic groups were enumerated outside their state of birth in 1947. Malays enumerated outside their state of birth then numbered 128,582, or about 6 per cent of the total Malaysian population. Chinese in this category numbered 109,848, or 6.8 per cent of all Chinese. Such figures can scarcely give an accurate picture of internal migration, of course, since much movement (especially rural-urban) may occur within borders, and many Chinese and others are foreign immigrants whose movements from place to place within Malaya cannot be followed.

Among Malaysian agriculturists, however, there has been a movement from Penang and Province Wellesley into southern Kedah and northern Perak, and another from southern Perak into the rice-growing areas of the northern Selangor coast. There has also been some movement from Kelantan into northern Trengganu. It is felt, however, that the internal migration of Malaya (other than rural-urban) is inconsiderable, "partic-

---

11. See also the section on the "New Villages," in Chapter 4.

ularly if it can be remembered that some of it consists of seasonal movements connected with fishing and padi cultivation or movements of a few miles across an uncontrolled boundary."[12]

A similar viewpoint has been expressed with reference to the Chinese:

> Interterritorial movement of the Malaya-born Chinese is no greater than the corresponding internal migration of the Malays. In fifty-two of the eighty-nine census districts, more than 90 per cent of the Malaya-born Chinese population were residing at the time of the 1947 census in their native State or Settlement. In only four of the census districts did the percentage fall below 80.[13]

Smith points out that this probably reflects the restricted mobility of the Chinese family in Malaya.

Perhaps the principal substantiation for the belief that there is considerable rural-urban movement is the increase in the size of the urban population as related to the total population (Table 2). The urban population increased from 29 to 35 per cent of the total population between 1931 and 1947. "The rate of increase in the general urban element has been considerable; and the larger towns, with their surrounding areas, have drawn large populations into them during the past sixteen years."[14]

This movement may well include some Malays, since the urban population of all Malaysians has grown from 10.6 to 14.1 per cent between 1931 and 1947. It seems reasonable that a large part of the urban increases can be attributed to a movement from rural to urban areas, even considering that the cities often serve as reservoirs for arriving and departing migrants.

Other Characteristics of the Population

As immigration has declined or changed in nature, and as more immigrants have settled permanently in Malaya, the

---

12. Del Tufo, Malaya, p. 87.
13. T. E. Smith, Population Growth in Malaya, p. 66.
14. Del Tufo, Malaya, p. 44.

population has come to appear more "stable." This has been true of the Malays in past censuses, but the Chinese, Indians, and "Other Malaysians" have had unmistakable immigrant ("unstable") characteristics. High proportions of males in the middle age groups, low proportions of females, low numbers of children, and low fertility rates are common to immigrant populations. The Chinese, and to a lesser extent the Indians, have begun to assume some of the characteristics of a settled population.

Age-sex structure

In spite of the unreliability of age reporting in Malaya, [15] certain factors stand out with respect to the age and sex structure of the population: (1) the past great excess of males in the 20-44 age group, though still evident, is less pronounced; (2) there has been a great increase in children under fifteen in Malaya between 1931 and 1947; and (3) the sex ratio, formerly greatly out of balance, is becoming more in balance with an increase in females.

Figure 2, showing the Malay population by age groups arranged as a pyramid, indicates that in 1931 there was a great disproportion of males of immigrant ages (20-50). The pyramid shows that by 1947 the disproportion had greatly lessened; this was true especially in the male-female ratio of Chinese and Indians. Table 7 shows that the ratio of the Indian females to males, while vastly improved, is still not as balanced as that of the Malaysians or Chinese. The Malaysians, in spite of some immigration, do not show an excess of males over females. On the contrary, there is a deficit of males in the Federation which is sufficient to result in a slight deficit for all Malaya. The Malays proper show excesses of females in all states except Selangor and Singapore. The "Other Malaysians" generally show deficits of males. It will be noted in Table 7 that Singapore shows a lower proportion of Malaysian females than that in the Federation. This deficit has actually increased from 1931 to 1947. The situation probably reflects the attractive force of Singapore for the younger unmarried

---

15. Inaccuracies derive primarily from general tendencies to state age to the nearest year ending in zero, and to systematic misstatement because true age is not known.

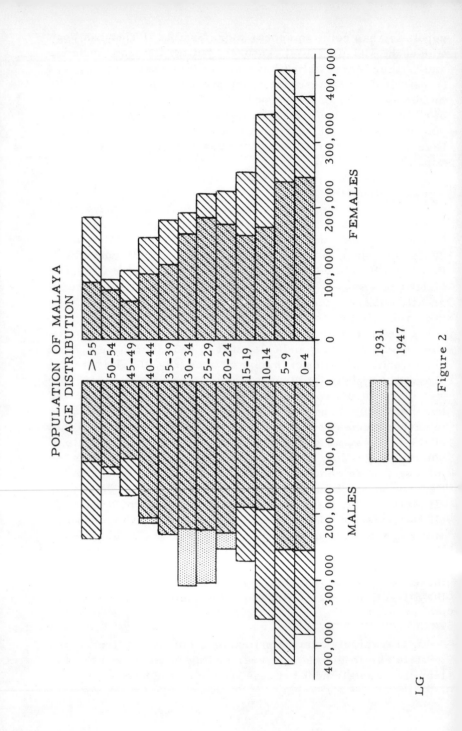

POPULATION OF MALAYA
AGE DISTRIBUTION

> 55
50–54
45–49
40–44
35–39
30–34
25–29
20–24
15–19
10–14
5–9
0–4

FEMALES

MALES

400,000   300,000   200,000   100,000   0   100,000   200,000   300,000   400,000

1931

1947

Figure 2

LG

Malays and indicates its position as a reservoir of immigrant "Other Malaysians."

TABLE 7
FEMALES PER 1,000 MALES

	1911	1921	1931	1947
Federation	592	648	703	891
Singapore	406	489	583	821
Malaya	572	628	688	879
Chinese				
Federation	215	371	486	815
Singapore	356	469	602	882
Malaya	247	384	513	833
Indians				
Federation	320	424	514	687
Singapore	204	199	186	334
Malaya	308	406	482	637
Malaysians				
Federation			973	1,010
Singapore			863	830
Malaya			969	1,001

Undoubtedly associated with the more nearly balanced sex ratio has been a great increase between 1931 and 1947 in children under fifteen years of age in Malaya. For the population as a whole there was a 68 per cent increase in the number of these children. Both the Malaysian and Indian communities increased in this respect by over 30 per cent, but the greatest increases (135 per cent) were among the Chinese.

Marriage

Another indication of relative stability among the former immigrant groups is the decrease in proportion of married females and increase in proportions of married males. All ethnic groups in Malaya have high marriage rates, with over 59 per cent of the males and 66 per cent of the females married as of 1947.

In general women in Malaya marry younger than men, as elsewhere. Malayan and Indian females marry earliest, but males do not marry in appreciable numbers until after the age of twenty. Among Malaysians only about 1 per cent remain unmarried. Greater percentages of the Chinese remain unmarried. Only the Malays have a significant divorce rate. There is a decreasing excess of married males over married females, especially among the Chinese, indicating a smaller proportion of males with wives overseas. The Malays actually have an excess of married females over married males. This is a result of polygamy only to a minor degree; it probably results from the peculiarities of Mohammedan divorce procedures which make it likely that males will report themselves as single and females report themselves as married, when in fact they are in the process of being divorced.

Some regional differences in proportions of married persons are apparent. Among Malaysians, those in the northeast tend to have higher proportions of married persons (especially among the males) than in other parts of the Federation. Singapore has a somewhat larger proportion of unmarried females than elsewhere. However, this in general is a reflection of greater numbers of females in the under-nineteen age groups. These same characteristics are markedly true of the Indians.

Reproduction and death rates

Malaya is characterized by high birth rates and low death rates, indicating a rate of high natural increase. With immigration controlled and restricted, natural increase will play an increasingly important role in the growth of the population. As in other matters, the ethnic groups evidence distinctive traits in matters relating to fertility. Both the Chinese and Indians appear to have a rate of natural increase of about 3 per cent per annum. The Malaysians have a rate of 2 per cent per annum.[16]

The crude birth rates of the three major ethnic groups now vary in the neighborhood of forty to forty-five per one thousand of the population in the Federation. In Singapore the birth rates appear to be higher, insofar as the rates may be relied upon (Table 9), although birth rates generally are lower among urban dwellers. The Chinese, for example, who dwell in large numbers in cities, had the fertility ratios noted in Table 8. "Fertility is appreciably lower in Penang and Singapore with

16. T. E. Smith, Population Growth in Malaya, pp. 59, 81, 87.

their large urban communities than in Kedah and Johore with their largely rural Chinese population."[17] This urban-rural differential is also true for the Malaysians, though less important since so few of them live in cities.

TABLE 8
FERTILITY RATIOS AMONG CHINESE WOMEN*

	Children 2-4 per 1,000 Women 20-44	Children 5-9 per 1,000 Women 20-49	Children 6-12 per 1,000 Women 25-54
Malaya	528.3	828.2	1,232.4
Seven towns with 20,000 Chinese inhabitants or more	428.1	652.2	986.4

*T. E. Smith, Population Growth in Malaya, p. 76.

Urban-rural differentials are the most conspicious differences in Chinese fertility. However, among the Malaysians it is possible to distinguish other factors. The "Other Malaysians" are most fertile, the northern Malays least fertile, and the indigenous Malays of central Malaya are intermediate. It appears that these differences are related more to different types of Malay people than to differing occupations. [18]

Death rates are highest in the rural areas (hence among the Malaysians generally) and the lowest in the urban areas. Of the three main ethnic groups it appears that the Chinese have the lowest death rates, with the Indians next and the Malaysians the highest (Table 9). In general, however, both rural and urban rates are among the lowest in Asia and, for the Chinese and Indians at least, compare favorably with those in western Europe and North America. This in no small way reflects British colonial policy and practice, but it also raises the specter of future high populations in Malaya at a time when

17. Ibid., p. 75.
18. Ibid., p. 51.

political development will be running ahead of economic progress. Until birth rates decrease, the possibility of a population explosion cannot be discounted or ignored. Fortunately, the Malayan economy is better prepared to face it than most in Asia.

TABLE 9
MALAYAN BIRTHS, DEATHS, AND NATURAL INCREASE

Year	Total Population	Malaysians	Chinese	Indians
Crude Birth Rates (per 1,000)				
Federation				
1947	43.0	41.4	44.0	49.1
1955	43.0	45.1	40.6	43.9
Singapore				
1947	45.8	48.1	46.1	44.8
1954	48.9	57.0	48.0	46.5
Crude Death Rates (per 1,000)				
Federation				
1947	19.4	24.3	14.3	15.8
1955	11.5	14.0	9.0	9.5
Singapore				
1947	13.3	17.8	12.8	12.7
1954	9.3	13.5	8.7	8.8
Rate of Natural Increase (per 1,000)				
Federation				
1947	23.6	17.1	29.7	33.3
1955	31.6	31.1	31.6	34.4

Religion

With only minor exceptions, the religions of the peoples of Malaya correspond to their ethnic origins.

No inquiry as to religion was made on this occasion, past experience having shown it to be of little value in Malaya where the entire Malay population is Muhammadan, practically every European and Eurasian is a Christian and the great majority of Chinese hold to the national religion of China which some describe as Confucian and others prefer to regard as ancestor-worship. [19]

Table 10 presents the estimated numbers in the various religions as defined in the 1947 census.

TABLE 10

MALAYA: ESTIMATED NUMBERS OF ADHERENTS TO VARIOUS RELIGIONS

Moslems	2,575,000
Chinese "National Religion"	2,560,000
Hindus	510,000
Christians	120,000
Sikhs	18,000
Pagans	35,000
Others	31,000
Total	5,849,000

The Malays are almost without exception Moslems. "Other Malaysians" are probably predominantly Moslem, but a few Balinese Hindus and some Christians are to be found. Indians are mainly Hindus with substantial proportions of Moslems, Christians, and Sikhs. The aboriginal tribes are classified as pagan by the census. [20]

There are some converts to Christianity among both the Indians and the Chinese. These Christians are proportionately more numerous in urban than in rural areas. In the heavily Malay areas some Chinese have become converted to Mohammedanism. In 1931 Chinese Moslems numbered from 1.5 per thousand Chinese to 3.6 per thousand, depending on the area.

19. Del Tufo, Malaya, p. 123.
20. Many of the data on religions presented in the 1947 census are taken from the 1931 census. See C. A. Vlieland, British Malaya: A Report of the 1931 Census (London: Malayan Information Agency, 1932).

4. Patterns of Settlements

HALF THE POPULATION of Malaya consists of peoples who have immigrated to Malaya relatively recently and their immediate descendants. These immigrant peoples--the Chinese, the Indians, and "Other Malaysians"--amounted to about 60 per cent of the population in 1947. In general they have remained distinct groups among the indigenous inhabitants, the Malays, who constitute 38 per cent of the total population.

The immigrant peoples are superimposed on the landscape evolved by the Malays or on previously unoccupied lands. Settlement patterns associated with colonialism and the immigrant peoples have supplemented Malay settlement patterns in some instances and have modified or displaced them in others.

Settlement is divisible into two broad types: (1) that of the predominantly Malay areas where the land-use pattern and settlements are those of the Malays, with varying degrees of modification by immigrant peoples and colonial influence, and (2) that of the areas of estate and mining development and of the towns and cities, which have grown as a part of colonial-immigrant activities. The latter areas are those of greatest Chinese and Indian populations. The two types of settlement may not always be discrete. Malay settlement is not confined to regions untouched by immigration or colonial development; it is found also in juxtaposition to or intermingled with estate and mining activity.

The Settlement Pattern of the Malays

The settlements of the Malays prevail in rural Malaya, es

pecially in the northwest (Kedah and Perlis) and in the northeast (Trengganu and Kelantan). In each of these areas the Malays are occupied principally as rice cultivators and to a lesser extent as fishermen. Malay settlement forms in the developed districts of western Malaya are found along with immigrant settlement forms. These are often areas of combined rice and rubber cultivation.

Malay settlements

The Malay unit of settlement is the village, or kampong, sited along or near streams or along the coast, usually in relatively narrow ribbonlike groupings. The village is primarily an agricultural or fishing village with no shops. The Malays tend to select slightly higher ground for their house sites. Former beaches and natural levees are favored coastal and riverside sites. The structures are not closely clustered but are widely dispersed. They are seldom prominent in the landscape, since the houses are invariably surrounded by a miscellany of fruit trees and gardens.

House types. --The houses of the Malays are built of timber and thatched and woven palm leaves, and are raised five or six feet above the ground on log stilts. The stilts are often set in turn on blocks of dried laterite. [1] The space below the house floor may be used to dispose of garbage and waste dropped through the house floor, to shelter livestock, or for storage of nonedible property. Stilting also provides protection from flooding on shore or other low sites, protection from wild animals, a place for smudge fires to combat insects, and an opportunity for air to circulate throughout the house.

The framework of the house is of wooden timbers; the roof is ridged and steep and covered with thatched palm leaf. The walls are usually of split bamboo. There are two main rooms, an open veranda and an enclosed multipurpose room. Cooking may be done on a platform attached to the house or in a separate building. The usual number of occupants of these houses is three or four persons. There are not many houses with fewer than three or more than five or six persons in most areas, although in Kelantan half the households contain four to six

---

1. E. H. G. Dobby, "Settlement Patterns in Malaya," Geographical Review, April, 1942, p. 218.

persons. [2] The typical house may contain two or three generations of an extended family.

The skill of the builder and the availability of materials for building cause some variation in the primary pattern. In Kelantan, for example, the cost of houses some years ago ranged from about $10 to $500. Houses may also have concrete foundations, more substantial and costly walls, carved screens, and solid teak beams. Again, variation may occur in cases of polygamous marriages, where it is expected that each wife will have her own room. Another pattern is created by those Malays who can afford to maintain a single household in two houses.

Other structures which may be present in a Malay settlement are a local mosque, a small Koranic school for boys, and small, stilted, thatched houses for grain.

Malay houses are relatively easily constructed and are movable. Thus, a man may buy a house in a settlement some distance from his own, disassemble it, move it, and reassemble it in his home settlement. There is an important market in secondhand houses.

The possessions in the house vary with the income of the family and tend also to vary regionally. The east-coast Malays are likely to have fewer household articles than those of the west since the money they can spend above subsistence is small. Household possessions may include only jars for water, cooking utensils usually made in Japan (prewar), some clothing, a tray of necessary equipment for the preparation of betel chew, the equipment used for fishing (or farming) which cannot be stored below the house, and a few mats for sitting or lying.

Areal differences in village patterns. --Within the limitations of the rather dispersed Malay village the general form is ribbonlike, though not without exception. The villages may extend along roads, trails, streams, levees, or beaches, or they may follow the contour of slightly higher elevations or the bases of hills. Four general types of village form are distinguishable:(1) ringlike arrangements around low knolls and small circular hills, in northwest and northeast Malaya; (2) parallel settlements on opposite sides of long narrow valleys,

---

2. M. V. Del Tufo, Malaya: A Report on the 1947 Census of Population (London: Crown Agents for the Colonies, 1949), p. 129.

in west-central and southern Malaya; (3) levee settlements, common in Perak and Pahang; and (4) coastal settlements, on both west- and east-coast margins. Peculiarities and variations in each category result from the disarrangement contingent upon the introduction of modern roads and from the regularity induced by planned drainage projects.

The settlements on the coastal plains of northwest and northeast Malaya are located on low tree-covered hills amid flat plains (Map 8A). The paddy fields of the rice cultivators surround these settlement islands. Where roads have been built, settlement in linear form has developed along the roads. In drained localities, especially in government developments, settlement lines the drainage ditches and canals often for considerable distances and over large areas. This pattern is widespread in western Johore; it is found also in Krian.

Throughout Malaya in the smaller valleys it is usual to find the villages aligned along the contour where the flat valley bottom is broken by the slopes of the valley sides. In Negri Sembilan settlement along the sides of long narrow valleys gives rise to a characteristic pattern (Map 8B). In these areas the valley bottoms are devoted to paddy; houses occupy the edge of the paddy land and extend to the lower slopes of the valley sides, and the intermediate slopes of the valley are in rubber. The interfluves remain forested.

Along the middle Perak and Pahang rivers settlement on the natural levees of these rivers is usual (Map 9A). The houses are situated on tree-covered levees which rise ten feet or so above the adjacent flood plain. In many places the flood-plain side of the levee has been planted in rubber trees, while the bordering portions of the plain produce rice. Swamp and forest predominate further inland.

Coastal settlement is found along both coasts of the country. On the east coast, villages are grouped on the southern side of northwest-southeast-trending ridges to obtain protection from the winds of the northeast monsoon. These settlements, usually fishing villages, are generally formless clusters without shops or roads (Map 9B). Coastal settlements on the western coast are sited along estuaries, on mud flats, and on sand bars. They have to tend a linear arrangement, but because of the width of the sand bars the houses are scattered widely.

Urbanization in the Malay areas

The towns and cities of the predominantly Malay areas of the

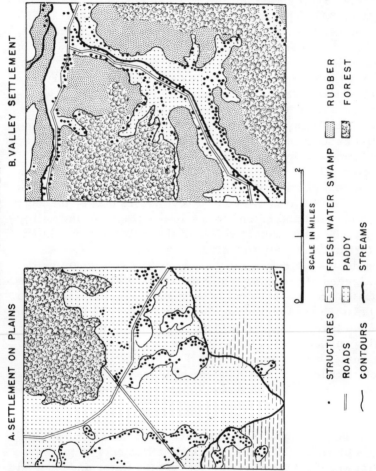

MALAY SETTLEMENT

A. SETTLEMENT ON PLAINS

B. VALLEY SETTLEMENT

SCALE IN MILES

- STRUCTURES
= ROADS
〜 CONTOURS

FRESH WATER SWAMP
PADDY
STREAMS

RUBBER
FOREST

1955

TV

Map 8

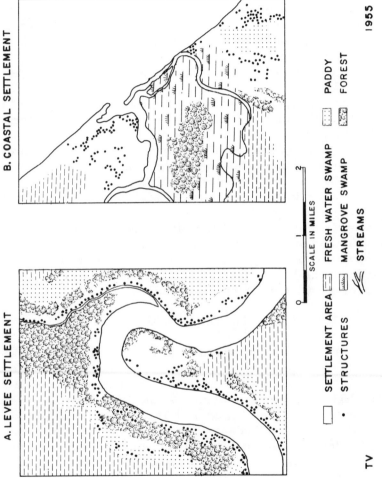

MALAY SETTLEMENT

A. LEVEE SETTLEMENT

B. COASTAL SETTLEMENT

SCALE IN MILES

0   1   2

SETTLEMENT AREA   FRESH WATER SWAMP   PADDY

STRUCTURES   MANGROVE SWAMP   FOREST

STREAMS

TV

1955

Map 9

northeast and northwest are small. Only four have more than ten thousand inhabitants. The largest city is Alor Star in Kedah with some thirty-two thousand inhabitants. The larger villages and the towns often have rectilinear arrangements of structures, but the commercial cores are commonly small, sometimes consisting of only a few Chinese shophouses. Kuantan in Pahang has a large dispersed Malay population with a few blocks of Chinese shops.

The larger cities and many of the smaller ones have large immigrant populations. There are only two cities in all Malaya with populations of more than ten thousand which have Malay majorities, Kota Bharu and Kuala Trengganu in the northeast. In 1947, 64 per cent of the population of Kota Bharu and 82 per cent of the population of Kuala Trengganu were Malay (Table 11). Each of these cities is largely Malay in character, although Chinese and their shops are also present.

The towns of Kedah and Perlis are similar to those of the west side of Malaya further south in that Malays are outnumbered by immigrant peoples. Alor Star (32,424) was only one-third Malay in 1947. In Sungei Patani ten thousand of the thirteen thousand inhabitants were non-Malay. Even Kangar in strongly Malay Perlis had Chinese and Indian inhabitants in sufficient numbers to comprise more than half of the total population of 3,970. Nothing in the rates of growth of these cities since 1921 suggests any general differences in this respect from the other cities of Malaya.

The Cities of Malaya

Immigrant (as opposed to Malay) settlement forms identify most of Malaya's cities, with their intermingled ethnic groups and close ties with the production and export of commercial products, the mining settlements, the rural estates, and most recently, the "New Villages." The larger, and many of the smaller, cities of Malaya are the result of colonial economic activities and immigration. This is reflected in their locations, their functions, and the ethnic groups composing most of their populations.

The size and function of urban places

Two hundred and twenty-nine urban places contained the 2,054,113 Malayan urban dwellers in 1947. Of these, 178 were of one thousand inhabitants or more. All but a negligible num-

TABLE 11
THE MAJOR CITIES OF MALAYA*

	Number of Persons	Per Cent Increase 1931-1947	Area (sq. mi.)	Density (per sq. mi.)	Occupied Houses	Number per Occupied House	Per Cent of Each Ethnic Group		
							Malaysians	Chinese	Indians
Singapore	679,659	52.5	31.15	21,800	57,200	11.9	6.4	79.0	7.2
Penang (Georgetown)	189,068	26.5	9.4	20,100	17,978	10.5	10.3	73.0	13.9
Kuala Lumpur	175,961	57.9	18.0	9,780	20,271	8.7	11.0	66.4	18.0
Ipoh	80,894	52.1	11.8	6,860	8,328	9.7	7.5	70.0	18.2
Malakka	54,507	43.3	4.22	12,900	5,760	9.5	12.6	74.5	7.7
Taiping	41,361	37.5	5.68	7,280	4,566	9.1	13.6	61.8	24.0
Johore Bahru	38,826	80.9	5.0	7,770	4,247	9.1	36.4	41.0	12.9
Seremban	35,274	64.4	3.54	9,960	3,737	9.4	8.6	65.0	17.6
Klang	33,506	60.2	2.67	12,500	4,565	7.3	15.2	60.5	18.0
Alor Star	32,424	74.6	2.82	11,500	4,055	8.0	36.6	47.8	13.9
Bandar Maharani	32,228	58.5	4.69	6,870	3,907	8.2	29.3	58.5	6.5
Kuala Trengganu	27,004	93.3	1.8	15,000	4,774	5.7	81.6	15.6	2.0
Bandar Penggaram	26,506	98.8	5.5	4,820	3,537	7.5	20.4	66.5	5.9
Telok Anson	23,055	57.1	1.9	12,100	2,561	9.0	19.6	60.5	16.8
Kota Bharu	22,765	53.4	1.95	11,700	3,539	6.4	63.6	30.3	4.3
Butterworth	21,255	57.0	1.92	11,700	3,992	5.3	30.3	46.0	21.2

*In fourteen of sixteen cities Chinese are the largest group. In two, Malaysians are the largest group. In three cities in which Chinese are the largest group they are less than half the total; in these cities Malaysians constitute about one-third of the total population and Indians constitute one-eighth to one-fifth.

ber of the urban population lived in settlements of more than
one thousand. In the Federation, for example, there were but
17,499 out of a total of 1,301,376 urban dwellers who lived
in urban places of less than one thousand inhabitants.

The urban settlements of Malaya are located almost entirely
within the west-coast band of denser population. As has been
mentioned, only two places of more than ten thousand were
really unconnected with this area. Of a total of 178 urban
places in Malaya in 1947, 120 were located in the major population belt as delimited by census districts (Map 2). Few
places outside the main concentration had five thousand or
more inhabitants. Twelve of the thirteen cities of twenty-five
thousand or more inhabitants were located within the major
population belt and contained over 70 per cent of the total urban
population.

Singapore, at the tip of the peninsula, is by far the largest
city in Malaya (679,659 in 1947).[3] There were two cities
(Georgetown and Kuala Lumpur) of more than 150,000 but less
than 200,000 inhabitants. Over 50 per cent of the urban population and 17 per cent of the total population was in these
three cities. The cities function primarily as gathering and
processing centers of Malayan products and as centers of distribution of consumer goods, centers of maintenance and repair
of transportation facilities, and administrative centers. There
is virtually no secondary manufacturing function. In addition,
some of the cities are seats of learning and political centers.[4]
Most cities of western Malaya are centers of wholesale and
retail distribution and finance and gathering points for rubber
or tin. Transportation functions such as those of seaports, rail
points, or road centers are closely tied to the movement of
basic products and consumer's goods. The characteristics of
some of the mining towns and villages are discussed elsewhere.

The growth of urban population

The population of Malaya is not only becoming more urban,
it is becoming an urban population of large and medium-sized

---

3. In 1955 Singapore's population was estimated at well over
one million. At present rates of growth, it may double its 1947
population shortly after 1960.

4. E. Cooper, "Urbanization in Malaya," Population Studies,
November, 1951.

cities. The urban population of Malaya increased by 60.2 per cent between 1931 and 1947. This compares with an increase of 34.5 per cent for the total population in the same period. The large towns of the Federation and the city of Singapore increased at about the same rate (53 per cent). Only two of the twenty-three towns of more than ten thousand inhabitants increased less than 20 per cent in the period. They were Kampar, a tin-mining town, and Port Swettenham, a port. Two of the largest cities (Kuala Lumpur and Singapore) increased more than 50 per cent, while the third (Georgetown) increased by 25 per cent. Most of the larger towns increased from 30 to 100 per cent. The percentage increases in the population of the larger cities of Malaya between 1931 and 1947 are tabulated in Table 11. The principal characteristics of the cities is an unevenness of growth, some increasing greatly, others actually declining.

The increase in number of towns and cities in every size group has been considerable between 1911 and 1947. Probably the most noteworthy increase during the period 1931-1947 has been in the number of cities with populations between twenty-five thousand and fifty thousand. In 1931 there were two of these cities, and in 1947 there were eight.

Though no figures are available, it is generally believed that the urban population is considerably larger than the census shows because of ever-increasing suburbanization. The census-takers were aware that there was a substantial population clustered around some of the cities which was not enumerated as urban, though in fact the people were urbanites. To quote from the 1947 census:

> The foregoing figures represent, in every case, an increasing urbanisation of the population; but an examination of the populations in the areas immediately around the larger towns reveals that the proportion of urban population is, in fact, greater than these figures would suggest. There has, indeed, and for reasons which have been discussed elsewhere, been a considerable degree of what might be termed population-clotting around these towns, so that while the figures above indicate that one person out of every four in the Federation lives in a town or village, the proportion

89

would be nearer one in three if these dormitory
and food-supply areas were taken into account. [5]

It will be noted on Map 3 that the districts surrounding the
larger towns show high rural densities. It is likely that a proportion of these are not food-producing agriculturalists but
suburban dwellers. The pressures of population increases are
being felt in the larger cities to a great degree, and continued
expansion into suburban areas may be expected. [6] A sizable
government-planned suburb is being built and occupied adjacent
to Kuala Lumpur. [7]

Ethnic composition

Areal concentration of ethnic groups and further concentration of dialect groups within ethnic groups is a common feature
of Malayan cities. The localization of ethnic groups is based
on early and continued concentration on a particular site or in
a particular area and on nearness to places of employment in
occupational specialties.

In all but a few cities the Chinese form the bulk of the population, dominate finance, trade, and manufacturing, and provide most of the labor (Map 10). The Chinese shophouse as the
primary retail outlet is ubiquitous in Malayan cities. There is
no city or town of greater than village size, however, in which
representatives of each of the three major ethnic groups are
not found. The same is true to a remarkable extent of administrative divisions within the larger cities.

A study in Singapore has shown the marked localization of
ethnic groups within the city. [8] Singapore is essentially a Chinese city, and Chinese are found living throughout the city.
However, they are most heavily concentrated in the core of
the city, an area of many shophouses, under conditions of

5. Del Tufo, Malaya, pp. 43-44.

6. Ibid., p. 5.

7. T. A. L. Concannon, "A New Town in Malaya," The
Malayan Journal of Tropical Geography, March, 1955, pp. 39-
43. This development is surprisingly similar in appearance to
an American suburban "tract."

8. B. W. Hodder, "Racial Groupings in Singapore," The
Malayan Journal of Tropical Geography, October, 1953, pp.
25-36.

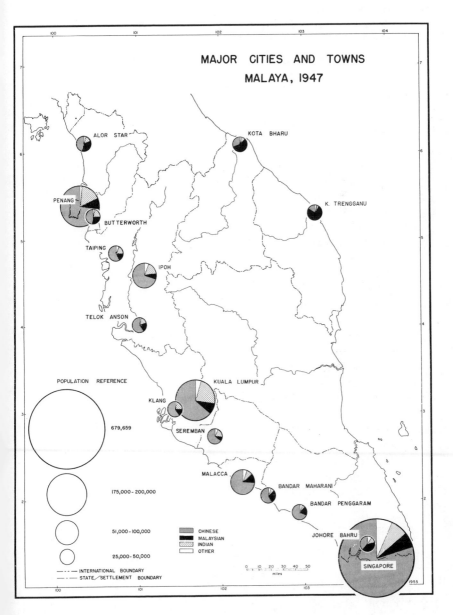

MAJOR CITIES AND TOWNS
MALAYA, 1947

ALOR STAR
KOTA BHARU
K. TRENGGANU
PENANG
BUTTERWORTH
TAIPING
IPOH
TELOK ANSON
KUALA LUMPUR
KLANG
SEREMBAN
MALACCA
BANDAR MAHARANI
BANDAR PENGGARAM
JOHORE BAHRU
SINGAPORE
1955

POPULATION REFERENCE

679,659

175,000 - 200,000

51,000 - 100,000

25,000 - 50,000

CHINESE
MALAYSIAN
INDIAN
OTHER

---·--- INTERNATIONAL BOUNDARY
---·-·--- STATE SETTLEMENT BOUNDARY

0   10 20 30 40 50
miles

Map 10

great congestion. In this area members of other groups are very few. Another concentration of Chinese occurs to the north of the centrally located government area in a former European sector. Not only do the Chinese concentrate as Chinese, but within the Chinese districts there are concentrations of Chinese of the same provincial origin and dialect group. Thus, the Hokkiens, early arrivals to Singapore and conspicuous in trade and business, are found in the older parts of the central-core "Chinatown." Tiechius are found close to the right bank of the Singapore river near the warehouses in which they work in great numbers. Other Chinese groups show similar localization.

Malaysians are found in greatest numbers in the outer districts of Singapore, especially in the western fringes and in the eastern swampy districts.[9] There are two small areal concentrations of Malaysians (one chiefly Indonesian) in the central core of the city. One is related to the early founding of a kampong on the site and the other is near the government offices where many Malaysians are employed.

Indians are most important south of the central core of the city near the docks and railway, where many of them work. Minor concentrations in the center of the city are related to early nuclei of settlement and occupational activities. Europeans and Eurasians are found mainly in the outer fringes of the city and in the suburbs.

Similar concentrations occur in Kuala Lumpur and in Georgetown. Malaysians, Chinese, and Indians live in all districts, though sometimes in small numbers. Europeans and others are found mainly in the outer fringes of the cities. The heaviest concentrations of Chinese are in the central districts. In Kuala Lumpur such districts were 75 to 90 per cent Chinese. In both cities Indians are found in greatest numbers in two or three concentrations. Two districts in Kuala Lumpur had one-third of all Indians in the city.

---

9. While only 6.4 per cent of the population of Singapore is Malaysian, the Malaysian inhabitants of Singapore constitute 12 per cent of all urban Malaysians. Singapore has the second largest urban Malaysian population in Malaya (19,513 in 1947), exceeded only by Kuala Trengganu, but nearly equaled by Kuala Lumpur (19,227).

Morphology and internal structure

Malayan cities consist of a nucleus of geometrically arranged streets lined with brick or concrete shops and godowns, surrounded by areas of irregularly spaced streets winding among sprawling dwellings of timber and thatch. The rectilinear pattern may sometimes be aligned along a waterfront or railroad. In peripheral neighborhoods government buildings and better residential districts are widely spaced along streets and roads which wind and twist in accordance with terrain. In many of the cities there are satellite districts of rectilinear street patterns usually not of the same orientation as the core.

The inner core consists of lines of two-storied shophouses. They almost invariably have a ground-floor business space and a second-floor or higher dwelling area. Government buildings are prominent just outside the central core, along with schools, churches, and the like. Surrounding the central commercial and administrative districts are the timber and thatch or timber and sheetmetal residential structures of Chinese, Indians, and Malays. The outer fringes of the cities are the sites of the houses of the Europeans and wealthier components of the other groups. These buildings are often modernized versions of the Malay house in appearance, although the structural materials are more varied. Newer government buildings are also found on the fringes of some of the cities. Industrial establishments are frequently found along the railroad or near the harbor areas. The railroad and its facilities are usually not part of the core of the city, although core areas may be immediately adjacent to harbor facilities in the seaports.

The land area of the cities of Malaya is relatively small, and average population densities are correspondingly high. Singapore, with a 1947 population near 700,000 in thirty-one square miles, had an average density of 21,800. This is a higher density in a smaller area than is commonly found in American cities of approximately the same population (Baltimore, Boston and Milwaukee). The same is true of Kuala Lumpur in comparison with Nashville or Grand Rapids, but the difference is not as great as in the case of Singapore. The commercial cores of Malayan cities are without exception the areas of greatest density, although this is not the case in many Western cities. In the center of Singapore densities range from 130,000 persons per square mile to 200,000 persons per square mile. Kuala Lumpur and Georgetown both have core densities of

100,000 or more. The other larger cities have less densely peopled core areas, but most are over 20,000.

Housing statistics for Malayan cities must be used with caution since in the census the term "house" means "dwelling unit." For example, the "line" house which is common enough in Malayan towns is a row of separate rooms under one roof. Each of these rooms is listed as a "house." Furthermore, each portion of a converted shophouse with a separate entrance is considered a separate "house." Most multifamily dwellings in the cities of Malaya are of this nature; there are relatively few structures of the multistoried apartment house type, although "high-rise" public housing is becoming important in Singapore.

The number of persons per occupied house increased somewhat in both the Federation and Singapore between 1931 and 1947 (4.8 to 5.2 in the Federation and 9.4 to 9.7 in Singapore), and in 1947 the figure was 5.6 for Malaya as a whole. Singapore has the greatest density of occupants per house. [10] In Singapore only one person in ten lives in a house having four to six occupants, while 50 per cent of the population lives in houses having seventeen or more occupants. Thirteen per cent of all houses in Singapore had twenty-one or more occupants. In eight of the eleven largest cities in the Federation, houses with twenty-one or more occupants equaled from four to nine per cent of all houses. These houses of twenty-one or more occupants are overwhelmingly confined to the cities. In the Federation outside of the eleven larger cities, 0.4 per cent of all houses contained twenty-one or more occupants. Outside Singapore city on Singapore island, 1.8 per cent of all houses had twenty-one or more occupants.

---

10. High urban densities in Singapore are reflected in an estimated 150,000 persons living under slum conditions. Public housing is the responsibility of the Singapore Improvement Trust, founded in 1927. Similar, though less extreme, conditions in the Federation resulted in the activation of the Federal Housing Trust in 1951. See V. Z. Newcombe, "Housing in the Federation of Malaya," Town Planning Review, April, 1956, pp. 4-20.

Mining Settlements

Tin mining in Malaya has given rise to a characteristic land-scape of mounds of detritus and water-filled pits over extensive areas (Map 11). It has also given rise to mining settlements, some transitory, some developing into cities and towns performing essential functions for the mining industry. The principal localities in which mining settlement is to be found are in Kinta valley in Perak and along the central mountain range in Selangor and Negri Sembilan.

The early settlements of the mining districts were little more than camps which could be abandoned readily as old tin areas became exhausted and new ones were opened to exploitation. A few of these camps took on a more permanent nature as transportation centers, commercial centers, and centers of dredging activities. Ipoh, Menglembu, and Batu Gajah arose from such beginnings. During the decade before World War II it became common for mine laborers to disperse in small shacks throughout the mining districts and cultivate small patches of land. These amorphously distributed shacks or single-roomed wooden huts and rows of shophouses along the roads became the principal features of settlement outside the villages and towns in mining districts. After the war this population became a problem in connection with terrorist activities. Some were gathered together in "New Villages" or regrouped on private mining properties. [11] A new pattern of settlement has evolved which is discussed further under "New Villages."

Estate Settlement

The estate, chiefly involving rubber estates, is the principal colonial-immigrant rural settlement form. In much of developed Malaya it is the chief rural settlement form. In 1947, 7 per cent of the total population lived on 1,104 estates of five hundred or more planted acres. Many of these people lived in estate housing, but some lived in villages just off the estate or as squatters around the boundaries of the estates. Perak, Negri Sembilan, Selangor, and Johore contained 816 estates with an

---

11. Ooi, Jin-bee, "Mining Landscapes of Kinta," <u>Malayan Journal of Tropical Geography</u>, January, 1955, pp. 52 ff.

SETTLEMENT IN A MINING DISTRICT

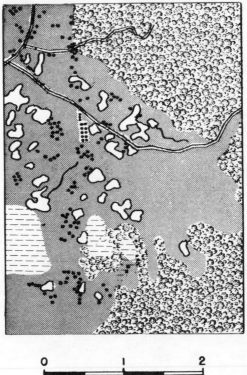

0   1   2

SCALE IN MILES

▦ MINING AREA	◠ PONDS		
• STRUCTURES	▤ SWAMP		
▦ BLOCK PATTERN	▨ FOREST		
═ ROAD	∼ RIVER		

TV   1955

Map 11

estate population of 310,087. No other state has as many as 100 estates, although the estate population in Kedah (50,209) exceeded that of Negri Sembilan, which had more estates.

Indians formed the largest single group dwelling on estates (Table 12). Over two-thirds of the rural Indians and 45 per

TABLE 12
ESTATE POPULATION BY ETHNIC GROUPS, 1947

Ethnic Group	Numbers
Malaysians	52,768
Chinese	114,422
Indians	241,369
Europeans	1,738
Eurasians	222
Others	1,811
Total	412,330

cent of all Indians in the Federation were estate dwellers. The Chinese were the next largest group of estate dwellers. Together the Chinese and Indians comprised 86 per cent of the entire estate population.

Estates early developed along roads and railroads and are still closely tied to transportation routes. In the older areas this transportation tie is less obvious, since estate settlement is continuous (Map 12A). In the parts of the country where estates are still being carved out of the forest the orientation to roads is pronounced (Map 12B).

The principal buildings of estates are houses for labor; small huts or shacks may be dispersed about the estate, or dwellings may be concentrated at a focal point on the estate as long, low, wooden structures divided into rooms. There are few other buildings. The residence of the manager and small smoking sheds and perhaps a plant for rolling rubber complete the list of structures. Nearby roads are frequently lined with shops which cater to the needs of the estate dwellers, such shop clusters generally having little functional unity.

Under the same measures which created the "New Villages," the estate population in many areas has been gathered in from the dispersed dwellings and regrouped in nucleated settlements.

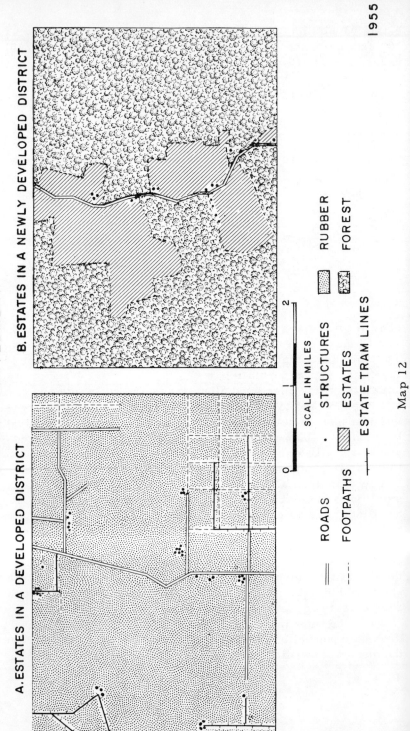

ESTATE SETTLEMENT

A. ESTATES IN A DEVELOPED DISTRICT

B. ESTATES IN A NEWLY DEVELOPED DISTRICT

ROADS
FOOTPATHS

STRUCTURES
ESTATES
ESTATE TRAM LINES

RUBBER
FOREST

SCALE IN MILES

0   2

Map 12

1955

TV

Subsequent to World War II, the activities of terrorist groups disrupting the administration and economic life of many parts of Malaya assumed alarming proportions. Squatter populations on the edges of towns and agriculturists dispersed in the forest and around estates became both the targets and the sources of support for rebels. The British administration decided to resettle this segment of the population into areas where they could be protected and supervised. Possibly a million persons in all were affected by the movement.

Between 1950 and 1953 some five hundred thousand persons were relocated in villages as part of the campaign to eliminate terrorist activities. [12] In addition, a possible two-thirds of a million people were brought together from dispersed quarters around estates and mining areas to nucleated sites. [13] The purpose of this movement was to bring dispersed agriculturists from the forests and estate laborers from the margins of estates together in defensible and more easily supervised agglomerations. Thus, an important source of food for the terrorists could be shut off, and their powers of intimidation reduced.

The program of moving the various peoples was carried out in two ways, "relocation" and "regrouping." "Relocation" meant that dispersed persons were brought together in villages. "Regrouping" meant that the dispersed estate and mining company labor population was brought together at some point of concentration on the property. The people affected were of three kinds, most of them squatters on land to which they had no legal right. One group consisted of estate laborers and miners, scattered about the mining areas and on the borders of estates. Another group consisted of Chinese squatters who had left the cities during the Japanese occupation and become agriculturalists. The third group consisted of urban dwellers

12. The Federation Annual Report, 1952, lists 509 villages and 461,822 persons. A more recent source states that 600,000 people are now settled in 550 "New Villages." Ronald Stead, "The 'New Villages' in Malaya," Geographical Magazine, April, 1955, p. 642.

13. E. H. G. Dobby, "Resettlement Transforms Malaya," Economic Development and Cultural Change, October, 1952, p. 167.

who moved to the peripheries of the cities, constructed shacks, and were engaged in work in town as well as in cultivating small plots. Regrouping on estates has generally formed agglomerations of Indians, and regrouping in mining areas has brought together Chinese populations on mining property. The population affected by relocation was almost entirely Chinese.[14] These people were gathered together in approximately 550 villages. "Thus great stretches of the Malayan countryside where once only isolated farmsteads existed have become converted into landscapes of entirely new towns and villages."[15] Since the purpose of the establishment of "New Villages" was primarily military, this fact has had much to do with the location and appearance of the villages. Accessibility and defensibility of sites were important considerations in locating the villages. They are located on or immediately adjacent to main roads and are surrounded by barbed-wire fences. Watch towers and flood lights are usually present. Some of the first villages were little more than shanty towns, but later ones were better planned and constructed. The villages are laid out in regular patterns. Construction materials are mainly wood and thatch, but concrete foundations and floorings and sheet-iron roofs are widespread. Shops, a meeting hall, a school, a post office, and other services and utilities are provided in each center. Some villages were built as extensions of existing villages or towns, but most are new aggregations in the countryside. Village sizes vary. Populations may range from a few hundred persons to six thousand or seven thousand. Four hundred houses has come to be considered an optimum size by administrators. Smaller villages are too costly and larger villages too difficult to administer.[16] In the Kinta valley the relocation of the dispersed population of miners and cultivators has accentuated the rows of villages and towns bordering both sides of the valley and coming together at Ipoh at the northern end of the valley. Thirty new villages have been added to fourteen towns and villages listed in the 1947 census. In 1952 the smallest of these villages had 140 inhabitants, and the

14. Indians and Malays have been resettled too to a lesser extent. See Katherine Sim, "Resettlement Camps in Malaya," Corona, July, 1952, p. 266.

15. Dobby, "Resettlement Transforms Malaya," p. 168.

16. Ooi, Jin-bee, "Mining Landscapes of Kinta," p. 53.

largest had 6,840. Most of the thirty villages had from 2,000 to 4,000 inhabitants, however. [17]

In Johore resettlement has brought a dispersed agricultural population into villages aligned along the roads. In 1947 there were nineteen villages and towns in Johore which had a population in excess of one thousand persons. Relocation created thirty-five villages of that size by 1952. In addition there were thirty smaller "New Villages." These villages are along the main road from Johore Bahru to Segamat and clustered within ten miles of Johore Bahru. [18]

Resettlement may have permanently altered the settlement pattern in parts of Malaya. The "New Villages" have increased Malaya's already high proportion of urbanization, although in many such villages the population is engaged primarily in agriculture. In the Kinta valley in 1947 one in two persons lived in a village or town of more than one thousand inhabitants. In 1952 five in every six people lived in towns and villages of that size. Formerly dispersed estate and mine workers have been brought together in nucleated villages on estates and mining property. However, since the movement of people was not in most cases for very great distances, district total populations have not been greatly affected, and overall population distributions remain about the same.

The political and economic effects of resettlement and regrouping already have begun to appear. Regrouping has generally been less unsettling than resettlement, but has worked some hardships on estate owners. Nucleation, for example, in some instances has increased the time necessary to reach the various parts of rubber estates and has affected the efficiency of tapping operations. The chief effects, however, have occurred as a result of relocation in "New Villages." In mining areas the villagers are primarily mine laborers, formerly highly mobile and able to follow the shifting mine operations. Now they are tied to a particular site. This means either

---

17. E. H. G. Dobby, "Recent Settlement Changes in the Kinta Valley," Malayan Journal of Tropical Geography, March, 1954, p. 62. See also Ooi, Jin-bee, "Mining Landscapes of Kinta," p. 53.

18. E. H. G. Dobby, "Recent Settlement Changes in South Malaya," Malayan Journal of Tropical Geography, October, 1953, pp. 6-7.

traveling long distances to work or possibly changing occupations. In "New Villages" adjacent to cities or towns the settlers have generally become urban workers. In rural areas a difficult problem has been to find work on estates for those who were deprived of their individual plots. In some villages, where relocation included the granting of a plot of farm land, many problems have arisen in making the village function as an integrated social unit and in agricultural pioneering in the Asiatic tropics.

Nevertheless, the "New Villages" have become a seemingly permanent part of the Malayan rural landscape and the urban fringe areas on the outskirts of the larger cities. In early 1957 it was reported that curfew restrictions were to be lifted after the granting of independence in August, 1957, and little shift in population is expected when restrictions in movement are removed.

5. Systems of Transportation

and Telecommunications

THE TRANSPORTATION system of Malaya is one of the most advanced in Southeast Asia. To a considerable extent, it consists of modern sea, air, road, and rail transport. On the other hand, slower, characteristically Asian forms of transport are also widespread. As with many other elements of Malayan life, recent Western technological systems and devices are found alongside older native forms. Both contribute to the over-all pattern of transportation, but the modern forms provide the principal and most effective means of movement within the peninsula and overseas.

Virtually all internal transportation focuses on Singapore; from Singapore external transportation reaches out to the world. The internal system is composed of land, water, and air connections of points within the Federation of Malaya and Singapore Island. The external system provides connections with the world outside Malaya, and includes some minor native shipping as well as modern sea and air transportation.

The Internal Transportation System

The best developed transportation network coincides with the areas of intensive settlement. Such a combination of intensive settlement and developed transportation includes virtually the entire west coast from north to south. In the west, the connection of inland points and the channeling of goods toward the sea for further shipment by water are provided by a system of improved roads and railroads. Air transport provides for regular and frequent movement of people between the larger towns. The transportation of products along the coasts is a function of both modern and native shipping, and cabotage is of considerable importance and proportions. The interior and the east coast of the peninsula have poorly developed transportation systems. Two long longitudinal land links (one rail and one road) connect the extreme northeast with the south. Only two modern roads run east and west to form direct links between the east-coast road and the west-coast road system (Map 13). Most movement in these undeveloped areas is by foot, cart, or small river or coastal craft.

The road system

The main road system provides for movement along the west side of the country from north to south, with many linkages and a few alternate routes. Roads penetrate all the developed districts and link the major focal points as well as most of the important villages and kampongs. However, dead ends are not unusual and some places of considerable size would be isolated by the cutting of a single road. The principal north-south route from Johore Bahru northward through Kuala Lumpur, Ipoh, and Alor Star to the Thai border is designated Route 1. This road follows the same general route and touches the same principal cities as does the main line of the Malayan railway. The east-coast road extends from near Johore Bahru northward along the east coast to Kota Bharu and Tumpat in the north, but only 195 miles out of 250 were surfaced at the end of 1955.[1] Virtually no tributary roads exist along its length. Indeed, the whole of the interior of Malaya is without improved roads except for the two east-west linking roads. The following, describing Trengganu, is true of much of Kelantan, Pahang, and eastern Johore as well: "Even today there are virtually no roads into the interior of the State and the British-made launch and various types of native water craft remain the most comfortable means of transport."[2]

One of the two east-west roads extends across the peninsula about forty miles north of Johore Bahru; the other and more important one crosses just south of center. This road (Route 2) originates at Port Swettenham, passes through Kuala Lum-

---

1. Federation of Malaya, Annual Report, 1955 (Kuala Lumpur: Government Press, 1956), p. 351.
2. Laura Andrews, "Welfare in Trengganu," Corona, September, 1954, p. 352.

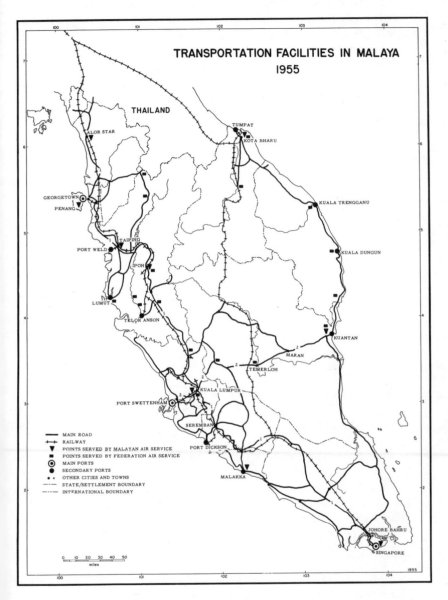

TRANSPORTATION FACILITIES IN MALAYA
1955

THAILAND

ALOR STAR

TUMPAT
KOTA BHARU

GEORGETOWN
PENANG

KUALA TRENGGANU

TAIPING

PORT WELD

KUALA DUNGUN

IPOH

LUMUT

TELOK ANSON

KUANTAN

MARAN

TEMERLOH

KUALA LUMPUR

PORT SWETTENHAM

SEREMBAN

PORT DICKSON

MALAKKA

JOHORE BAHRU
SINGAPORE

————— MAIN ROAD
+—+—+ RAILWAY
▼ POINTS SERVED BY MALAYAN AIR SERVICE
■ POINTS SERVED BY FEDERATION AIR SERVICE
◉ MAIN PORTS
● SECONDARY PORTS
• • OTHER CITIES AND TOWNS
– · – · – STATE/SETTLEMENT BOUNDARY
– – – – INTERNATIONAL BOUNDARY

0 10 20 30 40 50
miles

1955

Map 13

pur, and terminates at Kuantan on the east coast. The section
through Temerloh has been completed only recently. It reduces
the distance markedly over the Maran-Kuala Lumpur section.

Although the total mileage of the developed road system is
small (six thousand miles), a large part has paved surfaces
and adequate bridges and similar improvements. Two-thirds
of the six thousand miles of developed roads have paved surfaces (Table 13). Most of the trunk roads are asphalt-surfaced
and are at least eighteen feet wide. Gradients are usually not
over 1 in 30 and the width is adequate for the volume of traffic
carried.[3]

TABLE 13
ROAD SURFACES IN THE FEDERATION, 1952*

Class	Surface	Federal Highways[†] (miles)	State Highways (miles)
A1	Concrete	15.6	3.2
A2	Asphalt	1,744.0	2,254.5
B	Crushed stone watered and rolled	24.8	291.5
C	Hard surface oiled and rolled	40.0	192.0
D	Hard surface watered and rolled	162.0	643.5
E	Earth surface	158.0	532.3
	Total	2,143.4	2,917.0

*Federation of Malaya, Annual Report, 1952.
[†]Federal roads had increased to 2,270 miles in 1955
(Federation of Malaya, Annual Report, 1955).

The principal roads have steel or reinforced concrete
bridges. In the less developed areas ferries are still in use;
there are two ferries in Pahang and eight in Trengganu. Both
Federal and State governments administer and maintain the
road system. About two thousand miles of roads, the main
roads, are under the control of the Federal Public Works De-

3. K. E. Mackenzie, Malaya: Economic and Commercial
Conditions in the Federation of Malaya and Singapore (Great
Britain Board of Trade Overseas Economic Surveys [London:
H. M. Stationery Office, 1952]), p. 50.

partment. The other four thousand miles are under State and Settlement Public Works control. [4]

There is no secondary or strictly local system of improved roads in Malaya. Movement to and from the smaller kampongs and in the rural districts is over cart tracks and footpaths, and in some areas by boat on the streams. Apparently in the western districts movement by boat is of less importance than in eastern districts, where local movements are largely by small craft. Even in the west-coast areas the road system does not include improved local access roads. Estate roads, cart tracks, and footpaths make up the network.

The pattern of these routes varies with the nature of the locality they serve. In estate areas the roads, tracks, and paths form circuitous routes about the property (Map 14B). Their function is to permit the work of the enterprise to be carried on. Cart tracks and footpaths serving cultivators of small tracts are designed to provide access from the off-road settlements to the nearest road or in some places to a stream or railroad right of way.

Map 14C shows the paths in an area of paddy cultivation in Kedah. This is a drained and reclaimed area. The paths tend to be comparatively straight and often parallel drainage ditches. In those parts of the country having a rougher surface configuration and in thinly settled districts, paths and cart tracks are generally longer and follow winding, twisting courses.

Map 14A shows a locality in Pahang near the railroad and the Pahang river. Local paths focus on the railroad or the river as the next higher means of transportation. Many short roads have also been built to combat terrorist activities. Their purpose is to provide access to the radio stations established in remote kampongs and as part of terrorist control measures. [5] Some native means of local access have been superseded thereby, though such was not the intent.

Automobiles, buses, trucks, and foot-propelled vehicles

---

4. Mackenzie, Malaya, p. 51. In Singapore there are 131 miles of Public Works Department roads outside the city, including the Bukit Timah road linking the city with Johore Bahru.

5. Federation of Malaya, Annual Report, 1952, pp. 251-52; Annual Report, 1953, pp. 274-75.

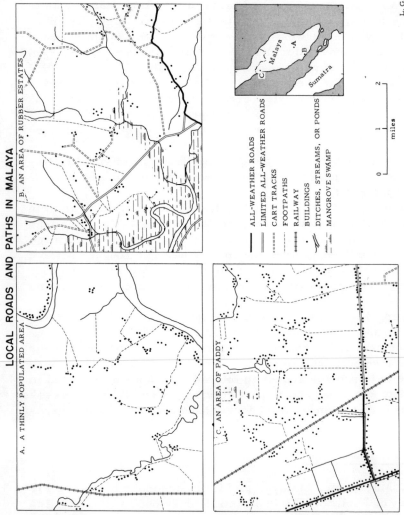

LOCAL ROADS AND PATHS IN MALAYA

A. A THINLY POPULATED AREA

B. AN AREA OF RUBBER ESTATES

C. AN AREA OF PADDY

ALL-WEATHER ROADS
LIMITED ALL-WEATHER ROADS
CART TRACKS
FOOTPATHS
RAILWAY
BUILDINGS
DITCHES, STREAMS, OR PONDS
MANGROVE SWAMP

Malaya
Sumatra
A
B
C

0   1   2
miles

L. G.

carry both passengers and goods in the cities. Trucks and buses carry most of the freight and passengers in both town and country. In rural areas and in the villages, bicycles, bullock carts, human porters, and small river and coastal sampans are used. It should be noted that in western Malaya river traffic has been largely superseded. Although measures of movement are lacking, it is possible to gain some impression of the magnitude of movement from a consideration of the kinds and numbers of vehicles.

Table 14 shows the number of vehicles in the Federation and in Singapore. It is clear that motor transport is increasing. In both the Federation and Singapore the number of private cars, motorcycles, and taxis has increased markedly. The number of trucks has increased also, but to a smaller extent. Not many people travel by private automobile. Although the number of private passenger automobiles nearly doubled between 1950 and 1953, there was still but one motor car for about ninety persons.

TABLE 14
NUMBER OF VEHICLES*

Federation	1947	1949	1951	1953	1955
Motorcars	13,714	20,837	30,750	44,552	51,337
Motorcycles	4,330	7,568	11,772	17,903	17,529
Buses	1,448	1,424	1,554	1,988	2,090
Taxis	1,234	1,352	2,078	3,258	3,172
Trucks	12,141	11,890	9,193	14,488	15,348
Other	488	851	5,153	9,754	11,101
Total	33,315	43,922	60,510	91,143	100,577

Singapore	1947	1949	1952	1954	
Motorcars	7,446	13,714	31,619	34,693	
Motorcycles	1,801	3,907	6,970	7,356	
Buses	290	356	796	970	
Taxis	1,867	1,081	1,610	1,610	
Trucks	5,377	6,578	9,390	9,525	
Trishas		7,927	4,559	4,064	
Tricycles		6,367	7,000	6,955	
Bicycles		94,347	163,072	178,708	
Others			2,259	2,113	
Total	16,781	134,277	227,275	244,994	

*Mackenzie, Malaya; Federation of Malaya, Annual Report, 1951, 1952, 1953, 1955; Colony of Singapore, Annual Report, 1954 (Singapore: Government Printing Office, 1955).

Some data on bus passenger movements do exist (Table 15). Travel by bus is becoming increasingly important. The number of passengers carried has more than doubled since 1947. The

TABLE 15
BUS TRAFFIC
IN THE FEDERATION

Year	Number of Passengers (millions)	Miles Traveled by Buses (millions)
1947	95	
1948	122	
1949	120	
1950	125	
1951	171	70
1952	193	77
1953	220	107
1955	228	108

number of miles traveled by buses also has increased greatly. The bus network in western Malaya is extensive. Buses operate over most of the six thousand miles of major and minor roads. Bus traffic will probably increase, since the road system serves many areas not reached by other modern means of transportation. In addition, passenger service has been eliminated on some railroad lines, and buses now furnish the only regularly scheduled land passenger transportation between some cities.

The role of sampans, carts, and pedaled vehicles must not be underestimated. While little information is available on the actual number of carts and river boats and the extent of human portering, such vehicles and activities are ever-present in city and countryside. The use of narrow two-wheeled, bullock-drawn carts is widespread. The use of the bicycle is common in Singapore and throughout the Federation. The great increase in bicycles in Singapore since 1949 is evident in Table 14. No similar figures are available for the Federation, but bicycles are numerous. The bicycle is used to haul commodities locally and is a means of travel for the individual. It can be used on rural cart tracks and footpaths as well as on improved roads.

The railways

The Malayan railway system furnishes arterial transportation between the major cities of Malaya and outlets to the principal ports (Map 13). The main route (north-south) connects Singapore with Penang (the rail head is on the mainland at Prai) via Kuala Lumpur. The ports of Port Weld, Telok Anson, Port Swettenham, and Port Dickson are connected to the main line by short east-west feeders. Other branches extend for short distances from the main line, especially near Kuala Lumpur. A long branch line extends northward from near Prai through Kedah and Perlis to the Thai border, connecting with the railway system of that country. Still another branch runs from Gemas at the Johore-Negri Sembilan border northeastward through the center of the country to Kota Bharu in Kelantan. This so-called east-coast line reaches to the port of Tumpat and beyond to the Thai border at Sungei Golok. Despite its name, this line does not parallel the coast but runs through the interior of the peninsula.

The expansion of the rail system was part of the extension of British control over all Malaya and accompanied the expansion of tin-mining. It also contributed to the extension of rubber planting, and the orientation of many rubber estates to the railroad is still evident today. The short feeder lines between the west-coast ports and their hinterlands were the earliest. They were constructed between 1885 and 1893 to afford outlets for the tin-mining industry. [6] The original operators of these lines were either private companies or the state governments. The extension and linkage of the east-west lines eventually led to the completion of the north-south line by 1920. The peculiar meandering of the main line is due in part to this process of integrating east-west lines into a north-south system. [7]

The physical plant of the government-owned Malayan railway is probably the best in Southeast Asia. Although operating speeds are not high, good roadbeds, rails, and signaling systems lead to efficient operation. The railway is meter-gauge throughout, with rails on the main line weighing eighty pounds to the yard. The main line is well ballasted, and has

---

6. C. A. Fisher, "The Railway Geography of British Malaya," Scottish Geographical Magazine, December, 1948, p. 125.

7. Ibid., p. 127.

adequate bridges, and a signal system. [8] Speeds are, however, limited to forty miles per hour for passenger trains and thirty miles per hour for freight trains. [9] Branch lines have lighter rails and in general do not equal the main line in other respects.

In 1955, 1,028 route miles were open to traffic (Table 16). The length of the system has declined somewhat from its maximum in 1931. Two branch lines went out of use prior to World War II, and the Port Weld and Port Dickson lines became freight lines only. [10] The Malakka branch, removed by the Japanese during the war, has not been restored. The in-

TABLE 16
MALAYAN RAILWAY OPERATIONS*

	Track Mileage	Passenger Journeys (thousands)	Passenger Train Mileage (thousands)	Tons of Paying Goods Traffic (thousands)	Goods Train Mileage (thousands)
1940	1,314	11,700	3,276	2,581	1,852
1947	1,011	4,409	1,056	1,389	1,426
1948	1,075	3,823	1,184	1,589	1,683
1949	1,091	4,442	1,353	1,761	1,784
1950	1,116	5,759	1,575	2,036	2,110
	Route Miles Open to Traffic				
1950	894	5,759	1,575	2,036	2,110
1951	912	6,735	1,194	2,038	2,268
1952	913	6,212	1,214	1,996	2,322
1953	984	6,632	1,385	2,043	2,257
1955	1,028	7,687	1,858	2,237	2,413

*Malayan Statistics, General Section, December, 1950 (Singapore: Government Printing Office, 1951); Federation of Malaya, Annual Report, 1951, 1953, 1955.

8. Henry Sampson (ed.), World Railways, 1954-1955 (London: Purnell and Sons, 1955), p. 281.

9. Ibid., p. 282.

10. Fisher, "The Railway Geography of British Malaya," p. 133.

creases in route mileage after the war were not new construction, but were due to the restoration of track removed by the Japanese, principally on the east-coast branch line. New railway construction is contemplated to bring the southeast coastal areas into more effective contact with the west. A new line will link Port Swettenham and Kuala Lumpur, through Raub, to Kuantan on the east coast; as a first step, reconstruction of the Kuala Lumpur - Port Swettenham line was reported underway early in 1957.

The western lines carry the heaviest traffic. The main line from Prai to Singapore carries the greatest passenger loads. Passenger trains between the larger intermediate cities are frequent, and two daily expresses run between Prai and Singapore. In 1954 the Bangkok-Singapore express resumed twice-weekly operations, thus re-establishing a prewar international service.

Table 16 shows the number of passenger journeys and passenger train mileage from 1947 to 1955, with 1940 shown as the last prewar year. The number of passenger journeys is markedly lower than before the war as a result of unrest and sabotage; freight tonnage also is lower than it was in 1940.

Freight movement still follows the general pattern of the early days before the completion of an integrated north-south system. Short sections of the main line and the east-west branches to the sea carry the heaviest freight loads. Freight traffic is concentrated on these lines as part of a funneling movement of export commodities to the seaports. There is some movement of foodstuffs over considerable longitudinal distances, but it amounts to only a small proportion of the total freight movement. In 1955 the Malayan railways moved over two million tons of paying goods and operated a freight train mileage in excess of 2.4 million miles.

Coastwise shipping

There are two salient characteristics of Malayan coastwise shipping: (1) shipping has an important, even vital, place in the internal transportation system of the peninsula, and (2) traffic focuses overwhelmingly on Singapore as a regional center. Coastwise shipping is an intermediate stage of the movement of goods into and out of Malaya. Small local craft and land transport vehicles concentrate outward-bound commodities at ports for transfer to large and small coastwise vessels. The coastwise vessels in turn deliver their cargoes to entrepôts

113

(principally Singapore, but also Penang). From Singapore or Penang, further shipment is world-wide. The pattern of distribution of import commodities is, of course, the reverse of the export pattern. Although coastwise shipping is considered as a part of the internal transportation system, the cargoes carried are part of the pattern of external trade.

Coastwise vessels consisting of small steamers, motor launches, and native craft call at the major and secondary ports and at many smaller places along both coasts. [11] A few of these smaller places have wharves and limited access for vessels of twelve or fifteen feet draft, but others are served by steamers standing offshore. In view of the generally poor communications along the east coast the importance of coastwise shipping by smaller craft and vessels is considerable, although the number of craft and the cargoes carried are much smaller than along the west coast. On both coasts, launches and native craft reach many coastal places not otherwise served and occasionally may reach up-river for short distances from the coast. Kangar in Perlis, for example, is thus served.

The ports with adequate harbors and facilities are served by larger modern vessels (Table 17). These ports are Singapore, Penang, Port Dickson, Port Swettenham, and Tumpat, and to a limited extent Malakka. Excluding Singapore, four of the remaining five ports are west-coast ports. The coast-wise trade in larger vessels is much more important along the west coast than the east, in part because of the lack of adequate harbor facilities and difficulties of navigation at certain times of the year along the east coast.

The major ports of the Federation are Penang and Port Swettenham. Both are on the west coast; Penang is an island near the northwestern extremity of the country, and Port Swettenham is roughly half-way between Penang and Singapore. The harbor of Penang is located between the northeastern part of the island of Penang and the mainland of Malaya. The distance between the shores is from one to three miles. Quays and piers line both shores for a distance of three miles. Port Swettenham is located near the mouth of the Klang twenty-seven miles from Kuala Lumpur. Deep-water wharf facilities

---

11. The secondary ports of Malaya are described in D. F. Allen, Report on the Minor Ports of Malaya (Kuala Lumpur: Government Press, 1953).

are limited, and about half of all cargo is handled by lighters.

Besides the major ports, Malakka, Port Dickson, and Tumpat (the last is the port for Kota Bharu in Kelantan) figure in both external and internal trade. Malakka, where ships must stand a mile offshore and use lighters for loading and unloading, and Port Dickson, which has a severely limited harbor and site, are minor west-coast ocean ports, as are Telok Anson and Port Weld. Tumpat has importance as the only east-coast outlet usable to some degree by larger vessels. [12]

TABLE 17
COASTWISE MOVEMENT OF VESSELS OVER 75 TONS
BETWEEN MALAYAN PORTS, 1950*

	Number		Vessel Tonnage	
	Arrived	Departed	Arrived	Departed
Singapore				
With cargo	467	463	118,157	114,626
In ballast	19	16	3,951	4,786
Penang				
With cargo	180	168	51,539	46,612
In ballast	4	17	425	6,125
Malakka and Port Dickson				
With cargo	357	356	108,074	107,625
Port Swettenham				
With cargo	320	323	83,238	83,730
Tumpat				
With cargo	99	99	33,149	33,149

*Malayan Statistics, General Section, December, 1950, p. 69.

Table 17 presents some measure of the coastwise trade in larger vessels for 1950, a representative year. It should be noted, however, that the table does not provide information concerning the actual tonnage of cargo carried. It does show

12. A specialized type of foreign traffic occurs between Dungun on the east coast and Japan. Iron ore, mined at Bukit Besi in Trengganu, is shipped by private rail line to the coast at Dungun and loaded on tramp steamers for shipment to Japan.

the number of arrivals and departures at particular ports as well as the vessel tonnage totals. Singapore stands out as the center of coastwise traffic. Other west-coast ports of greatest importance are Port Swettenham and Malakka-Port Dickson. The relatively minor status of the east-coast port of Tumpat is evident.

TABLE 18
COASTWISE SHIPPING IN
VESSELS OF 75 NET REGISTERED TONS
AND UNDER, AND
NATIVE CRAFT OF ALL TONNAGE, 1950*

	Tonnage	
	Arrived	Departed
Singapore		
With cargo	168,638	123,126
In ballast	63,060	111,053
Penang		
With cargo	130,711	35,314
In ballast	10,450	95,564
Malakka and Port Dickson		
With cargo	45,295	44,228
Port Swettenham		
With cargo	25,105	25,503
Tumpat		
With cargo	5,844[†]	5,844[†]

*Malayan Statistics, General Section, December, 1950, pp. 71-72.
[†]To and from Singapore only.

Movement of vessels under 75 net registered tons and native craft of all tonnages to and from the major ports is shown in Table 18. This table is approximate, but it permits some ranking of the major ports with respect to coastwise movement, although amounts and kinds of cargoes cannot be determined. Once again the pre-eminence of Singapore is apparent. The extraordinary tonnage of vessels departing in ballast from Penang suggests the dominant function of that port as a receiving rather than a distributing center for Malaya. Although exhibiting related characteristics, Singapore is clearly more significant as a distributing center than is Penang.

Internal air transportation

Major and secondary cities are linked by an air transportation system. Not unexpectedly, the most frequent service and the greatest numbers of passengers carried are between west-coast points. Six east-coast places do have service, however infrequent, and such service does tend to reduce the isolation of the east coast from the commercial and governmental centers of the country. Singapore is the great focal point of air movement, but the capital, Kuala Lumpur, is also a traffic center. This probably reflects the use and importance of air transportation in governmental affairs.

Internal Malayan air service is carried on by the privately owned Malayan Airways and the government-owned Federation Air Service. Actually, Federation Air Service is operated by Malayan Airways, which in turn is owned principally by the Blue Funnel Line and the Straits Steamship Company, Ltd., with BOAC holding a minority interest. Malayan Airways maintains its services between eight major cities in the Federation and the city of Singapore (Map 13). Federation Air Service connects some of these major points with other places throughout Malaya where payloads are few and small. Single-engine seven-passenger aircraft are used. Malayan Airways provides the main-line service; Federation Air Service functions partially as a feeder line, although administrative functions are basic. Daily or five-times-weekly service is maintained between Singapore and Malakka, Kuala Lumpur, Ipoh, Penang, and Taiping, which are the commercial, administrative, and production centers of Malaya. The number of flights varies, but the greatest frequency is maintained on the Singapore-Kuala Lumpur-Penang route. [13] The services of Federation Air Service are much less frequent. They vary from one flight a day between the better traffic-generating points to one a week at other places.

Table 19 shows the total number of arriving and departing passengers at Major Malayan airfields and airports. No sep-

---

13. Official Airline Guide (World-Wide Edition; Washington, D.C.: American Aviation Publications, Inc., August, 1955), C-565.

aration has been made between intra-Malaya arrivals and departures and international arrivals and departures, and so not all movement may be attributed to internal traffic. In general the number of passengers arriving and departing from Malayan points closely reflects the size and importance of the cities involved, although traffic at east-coast cities and Malakka may be disproportionately high. This large air traffic accords with their isolation in terms of other means of transportation. Singapore stands out as the dominant air center. Seventy-five per cent of all air passengers touching at the nine major airfields in 1953 for example, landed or departed at Singapore.

The Federation Air Service touches at smaller towns and moves considerably fewer passengers than does Malayan Airways. The routes flown have been subject to change. [14] Where the same places have been used both in 1953 and in 1952, increases over the 1952 passenger movement were usual. The better traffic-generating stations handle from one hundred to one thousand passengers per year, with sixteen hundred being the maximum handled, but this traffic represents only a small proportion of all Malayan traffic. Of all passengers handled at Federation airfields, less than 5 per cent were handled at the fifteen minor landing grounds of the Federation Air Service.

The External Transportation System

The external transportation of Malaya focuses on Singapore as the chief outlet and inlet of the country. In international shipping and air traffic other Malayan cities have some importance, but Singapore is outstanding in this respect. External land connections are limited by Malaya's peninsular position to routes northward into remote parts of Thailand. The only significant international land link is the railway connection with the Thai railway system which permits a through Bangkok-Singapore service. Sea transport has long been Malaya's principal form of external transportation. It is now supplemented by overseas air connections. Singapore, at an early date in modern times, became the chief port of the Malayan peninsula,

---

14. Compare Official Airline Guide, August, 1955, with Federation of Malaya, Annual Report, 1953.

TABLE 19

MAJOR AIRPORTS AND AIRFIELDS, AIRCRAFT MOVEMENTS, AND PASSENGERS CARRIED (ARRIVALS AND DEPARTURES)*

Airports and Airfields	Aircraft Movements 1955	Number of Passengers					
		1955	1953	1952	1951	1950	
Singapore	11,164	123,449†	123,956	130,783	135,605	87,277	
Kuala Lumpur	14,710	70,024	63,629	78,083	68,278	28,378	
Penang	4,786	45,120	45,113	50,999	46,339	32,001	
Ipoh	12,054	26,228	27,404	32,772	30,172	12,314	
Taiping	1,608	10,470	8,008	10,647	10,371	3,168	
Kota Bharu	1,270	15,049	19,093	20,249	16,452	11,143	
Kuantan	1,902	8,608	9,854	10,610	18,804	5,200	
Alor Star	648	7,501	4,373	5,278			
Malakka	21,206	17,994	10,282	3,099			

*Sources: For Singapore, Malayan Statistics, General Section, December, 1950; Colony of Singapore, Annual Reports, 1951-1954. For the Federation of Malaya, Annual Reports, 1950 to 1955.

†1954. About 4,500 movements concerned air services connecting Singapore with areas outside of Malaya and British Borneo. Thus, aircraft arrivals and departures at Singapore representing local services are substantially fewer than those at Kuala Lumpur, Ipoh, and Malakka.

but it is more than an outlet of Malaya. It is the regional trade and commercial center of Southeast Asia and a major cross-roads of world trade routes. Further, Singapore's strategic position at a constriction (the Strait of Malakka) in one of the great sea lanes of the world gives it an importance similar to that of such places as the Suez Canal or Gibraltar.

External shipping

Some of the great shipping companies of the world connect Singapore with Western Europe, Africa, the Americas, Australia, the Far East, and, regionally, with other points in Southeast Asia. Liner traffic, especially passenger traffic, is of greatest frequency on the main route westward to Europe and northeastward via Hongkong to Manila and Japan. Sailings between Singapore and points along these routes exceed twenty-five per week. Such frequencies are commonly exceeded only at Mediterranean and North Atlantic ports. Regional services from Singapore are also well developed. From Singapore many of the islands of Southeast Asia, as well as points on the mainland, may be reached by regular liner services. Service is most frequent to Jakarta in Indonesia; other regional connections are regular though much less frequent.

Singapore is also outstanding in number and tonnage of ships which call. In terms of net registered tonnage and total numbers, Singapore is a more important port than any other in Southeast Asia or the Far East with the exception of Hongkong. Functioning as an entrepôt, Singapore looms large in the movement of petroleum and petroleum products from Southeast Asia to points in the Far East.

Origins and destinations of imports and exports furnish further evaluation of the direction of movement to and from Singapore. In terms of value, the import trade is dominated by regional movements from Indonesia, Thailand, Indochina, British Borneo, and India. Imports from the United Kingdom rank high in total value of all imports, but imports from other European nations or from the United States are small. Export trade and traffic are oriented overwhelmingly to the United States and the United Kingdom. Regional exports to Indonesia, India, Thailand, and British Borneo are significant though much smaller. Singapore is the principal port for the export of Malayan products and the import of goods into Malaya. Federation trade with Singapore amounts to 40 per cent of its total foreign trade.[15] Singapore is also the most important port in Malaya in terms of movement of vessels between Malayan and foreign ports.

Table 20 shows the number of vessels calling at Malayan ports during a representative year, 1950, which had foreign origins or destinations. The pre-eminence of Singapore is clear; more ships called at Singapore than at all other Malayan ports combined. Ships in ballast do not call at such places as Port Swettenham or Malakka; the function of these ports as

TABLE 20
ARRIVALS AND DEPARTURES
BETWEEN MALAYAN AND FOREIGN PORTS
OF VESSELS OVER 75 NET REGISTERED TONS, 1950*

	Number		Tonnage	
	Arrived	Departed	Arrived	Departed
Singapore				
With cargo	5,129	4,770	13,536,088	12,817,744
In ballast	376	688	1,076,104	1,703,440
Penang				
With cargo	1,497	1,356	4,432,566	4,210,459
In ballast	163	269	651,928	783,736
Port Swettenham				
With cargo	191	914	3,494,413	3,465,987
Malakka				
With cargo	40	40	78,350	57,357
Tumpat				
With cargo	13	13	8,808	8,808

*Malayan Statistics, General Section, December, 1950.

provisioning, fueling, or focal points for shipping companies is small. Table 20 does not, of course, show the tonnages of cargo handled, but the ranking of the ports in this respect is similar to the ranking shown in the table. Nearly 75 per cent of the freight tonnage of cargo handled in Malaya in 1950 was handled at Singapore (Table 21). Penang and Port Swettenham accounted for most of the tonnage handled in the Federation. While much of the cargo handled at Singapore and Penang is

15. Federation of Malaya, Annual Report, 1955, pp. 126-7.

part of an entrepôt activity, most of the remainder is part of the movement of Malayan commodities to world markets and the movement of goods into Malaya for the Malayan market.

TABLE 21
CARGO TONNAGES HANDLED*
(freight tons of 40 cubic feet)

	Vessels over 75 tons		Vessels under 75 tons
	Discharged	Loaded	Discharged and Loaded
Singapore			
1950	3,881,704	2,331,649	626,450
1953	4,310,000	2,277,000	651,000
Federation			
1950	1,401,385	978,831	51,063

*Malayan Statistics, General Section, December, 1950; Singapore, Annual Report, 1953.

Regional trade is of two types: (1) cargo movement from points in Southeast Asia through the entrepôts of Singapore and Penang and (2) cargo movement between nearby countries and the peninsula. The second movement is chiefly between Malaya and Thailand and Indonesia. This trade is carried on by smaller vessels usually of less than 75 tons. The Indonesian trade, which originates largely in Sumatra, is confined chiefly to the west-coast ports, and the Thailand-Malaya trade is conducted principally through Penang.

The vast harbor and port facilities of Singapore consist of two parts: (1) the harbor proper with wharves, docks, and dry docks, and (2) the Roads, a fee-free protected anchorage used by both large and small vessels. [16]

Table 22 reveals that the major portion of cargo handled at Singapore passes over the Harbor Board wharves. However, the Roads traffic forms a significant proportion of all traffic in Singapore's port. Of a total of 7,288,000 freight tons of cargo handled in Singapore (excluding bulk oil at two points),

16. See D. F. Allen, Report on the Major Ports of Malaya (Kuala Lumpur: Government Press, 1951), pp. 5 ff.

nearly two-fifths were handled in the Roads. Much coastal and interisland traffic is carried on entirely from the Roads; little of this cargo passes over the main wharves.

TABLE 22
SINGAPORE HARBOR AND ROADS TRAFFIC*
(THOUSAND FREIGHT TONS)

Vessels	Roads		Harbor Board Wharves	
	Discharged	Loaded	Discharged	Loaded
Over 75 tons				
1950	1,691	645	2,190	1,686
1953	1,765	661	2,545	1.616
Under 75 tons and all native craft				
1953	391	206	1	
Rural landing places	Discharged		Loaded	
1953	33		10	

*Singapore, Annual Report, 1953; Malayan Statistics, General Section, December, 1950.

Not all the cargo passing in and out of Singapore, however, is handled in the Harbor Board area or the Roads. The Public Works Department maintains quays which are used by numerous small ships and native craft. Many privately owned jetties outside the municipal area are used by hundreds of small vessels. A considerable quantity of goods is handled in this manner (See Table 22, "Rural landing places.") The figures for "Rural landing places" are undoubtedly understated, since this traffic is poorly recorded.

External air transportation

Singapore, in keeping with the development of major air traffic centers throughout the world, has become an important focal point mainly because of its already established position as a commercial, trade, and traffic center. Nine international airlines maintain routes to or through Singapore. These include well-known European and North American airlines (BOAC, QANTAS, KLM, Pan American Airways). Regional connections with neighboring countries (Indonesia, Thailand, India), and the Far East are maintained by airlines of the various countries of the region including international routes of Malayan Airways. The chief centers of international air traffic are Penang, Kuala Lumpur, and, of course, Singapore. [17]

Singapore is on the main air route between Europe and Australia. It also lies on the secondary route between eastern Asia and Australia. However, it lies somewhat off the main Europe - East Asia route, which passes through Bangkok. Thus, Bangkok has become an air crossroads of an importance approximating that of Singapore as a maritime crossroads, and Singapore's significance is somewhat less in international air travel than Bangkok's. [18] The greater traffic-generating capacity of Singapore, however, and its role as a regional entrepôt for air as well as sea transport should continue to make it one of the major air centers of Asia.

Telecommunication Systems

The Malayan telecommunication system links neighborhoods, communities, towns, cities, and larger units of geographical organization. The two kinds of systems are wired carriers, such as telegraph, telephone, and cable; and wireless carriers, such as radio, radio-telegraph, and radio-telephone. Although telecommunication systems are essentially for interpersonal use, transmission of content intended for the mass media may make them indispensable to these media.

Interregional carriers

The telecommunication links between Malaya and the other regions of the world by overland lines, cable, radio-telegraph, and radio-telephone are shown on Map 15.

---

17. In 1955 the new airport at Paya Lebar was well on the way to completion. It is designed to accomodate the largest airplanes in service and will be among the best equipped fields in Asia.

18. In January, 1957, ninety-nine flights per week left Bangkok for foreign destinations; forty-six left Singapore (excluding Borneo services).

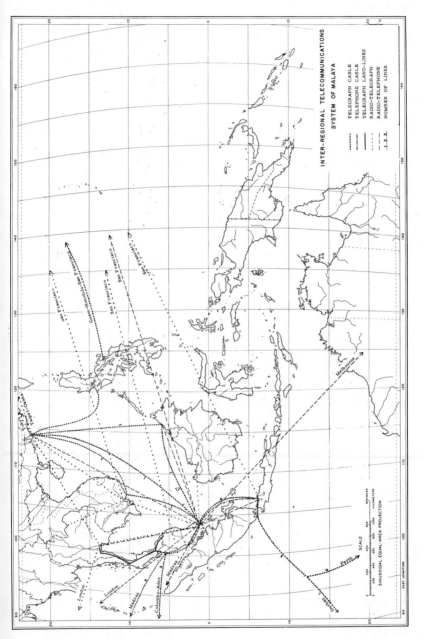

INTER-REGIONAL TELECOMMUNICATIONS
SYSTEM OF MALAYA

- - - - -   TELEGRAPH CABLE
          TELEPHONE CABLE
          TELEGRAPH LAND-LINES
. . . . .   RADIO-TELEGRAPH
- - - -   RADIO-TELEPHONE
1, 2, 3.   NUMBER OF LINES

SCALE
0 200 400 600 800 MILES
0 200 400 600 800 1000 KILOMETERS

SINUSOIDAL EQUAL-AREA PROJECTION

EAST LONGITUDE

Map 15

Overland lines. --The only land links are between Malaya and Thailand. Two telegraph lines cross the border: one on the west coast connecting Alor Star with the railway station at Kluang Ngae in Thailand, where it joins the Siamese State Railway communication system; the other on the east coast connecting Kota Bharu with Narathiwat. Both lines appear to connect ultimately with lines running to Bangkok.

Cables. --The international cable service for both telegraph and telephone service is maintained by Cable and Wireless, Limited, a British government-controlled company which operates a world-wide network connecting various parts of the British Empire.

Direct cable connections between Malaya and the outside world terminate in Singapore or Penang, which are connected with each other by a cable circuit. Four telegraph cables run westward from Penang: two to Madras and two to Colombo, Ceylon. The latter pair of cables connects at Colombo with cables to Europe and Great Britain through Aden, and to East Africa through Zanzibar. Singapore is a terminal for six telegraph cables: two to Jakarta; one to the Cocos Islands, where connections are made with a cable to Durban, South Africa, and with two cables to Perth, Australia; one to Jesselton, North Borneo; one direct to Hongkong; and one, apparently not in use at present, to Hongkong through Cap St. Jacques, south of Saigon. In addition, one telephone cable connects Singapore with Jakarta.

Radio. --Omnidirectional radio is used primarily by the major press services as a means of distributing news to a number of clients over a wide area simultaneously. Multiple transmission broadcasts are received in Malaya from London, San Francisco, Tokyo, and Manila. The United Press monitors its newscasts from all four of these points at Singapore, Penang, Ipoh, and Kuala Lumpur. The Associated Press monitors its newscasts from Tokyo and Manila at Singapore, and the same newscasts are monitored for the Associated Press by the postal and telegraph system receivers at Penang. Reuters maintains receivers at Singapore for reception of news from London. Although the Federation government has made its own transmitters available to the news services for news transmission from Singapore, it does not appear that they have been used to any great extent.

Radio-telegraph. --The three variations of radio-telegraph service, Morse-casts (code), Hell-casts (Hellschrieber print-

126

ing), and radio-teleprinter, are in use in Malaya. A fourth related system, radio-facsimile, is also used, primarily for the transmission of pictures and other graphic materials. Direct radio-telegraph circuits are maintained between Singapore and Bangkok, Medan, Kuching, and Saigon (Cap St. Jacques). The Singapore-Bangkok circuit connects at Bangkok with a circuit to London and another to Hongkong. The Singapore-Saigon circuit also connects with one to Hongkong, where, together with the circuit from Bangkok, it connects with circuits to Taipei and Tokyo. The Singapore-Medan circuit connects at Medan with a circuit to San Francisco. Because of the Singapore-Jakarta cable, telegraph connection can be maintained with San Francisco through the Jakarta-San Francisco radio-telegraph circuit.

For the most part, the radio-telegraph terminals in Malaya are equipped with teleprinters. Through combinations of circuit connections, direct teleprinter service is maintained with England, India, Australia, South Africa, Hongkong, the United States, the Philippines, Indonesia, and Borneo.

Apparently the only Morse-casts (outside of ship-to-shore and ship-to-ship communication) are those received by the Reuters station from London and by the Associated Press from San Francisco. Hell-casting is almost entirely confined to news service operations. Both Reuters and the Associated Press maintain Hell-cast receivers at their centers in Singapore. Radio-facsimile sending services are available between Singapore and Tokyo and between Singapore and Hongkong. In addition, facsimile material is received at Singapore from England, San Francisco, and Australia.

Radio-telephone. --Direct international radio-telephone services are maintained between Singapore and Jakarta, London, Melbourne, Jesselton, Hongkong, Bangkok, Madras, Colombo, and San Francisco. Through connections at these terminals with other circuits, service may be had with nearly any other part of the world.

Internal carriers

The paucity of available data concerning the telecommunication system in Malaya permits few generalizations. It is evident that the system is designed primarily to serve the west-coast population and commercial centers. The greatest density of connections appears in the former Federated States of Negri Sembilan, Selangor, and Perak. The east-coast centers appear as peripheral areas. In relation to community settlement, the system tends to favor the centers of Chinese, Indian, and European settlement. It also appears that the system tends, as is to be expected, to link the various high-literacy centers for all communities. It avoids to a great extent the areas of Malay predominance, particularly those along the east coast, and the interior regions are virtually without circuits. A rudimentary outline of the system from available sources has been plotted on Map 16. Both land-line and radio-telecommunication systems are in use.

Land-line systems. --The two predominant characteristics of the land-line systems are the tendency to be state- or settlement-based rather than nationally based, and the tendency toward nucleated structure. Most of the land lines are telegraphic, with only small telephone systems in Kelantan and Trengganu mentioned in available sources.

It appears that most of the present land-line systems were planned as essentially internal systems for each state or settlement. Thus, in such states as Johore and Negri Sembilan there appear to be well-integrated state systems only casually, if at all, connected to the systems of the other states. The most extensively developed land-line systems are along the west coast, apparently designed to serve the administrative and commercial requirements of those areas. Only one land-line circuit joins east- and west-coast states.

The land-line patterns within each state or settlement are usually nuclear, in that one or two major towns serve as the central focal point for a number of radiating lines. There appears to be little connection between the radial lines except through the focal center.

Radio-telecommunication circuits. --Although the available data do not make adequate distinction between radio-telegraph and radio-telephone circuits, the basic land-line system in Malaya is supplemented by a nation-wide pattern of radio-telecommunication circuits. In this pattern, Kuala Lumpur is the focal point, and Singapore, Penang, Kuala Lipis, and Kuala Trengganu are the primary termini. Here, too, the nuclear pattern is apparent.

Except for two small private systems run by the Central Electricity Board and the Marine Department, the telecommunication systems in the Federation are operated by the Telecommunications Department, which also operates the telegraph and telephone trunk circuits into Singapore. The

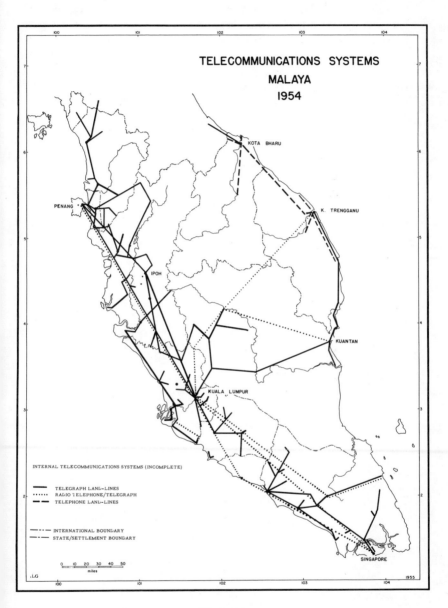

TELECOMMUNICATIONS SYSTEMS
MALAYA
1954

KOTA BHARU

K. TRENGGANU

PENANG

IPOH

KUANTAN

KUALA LUMPUR

SINGAPORE

INTERNAL TELECOMMUNICATIONS SYSTEMS (INCOMPLETE)

TELEGRAPH LAND-LINES
RADIO TELEPHONE/TELEGRAPH
TELEPHONE LAND-LINES

INTERNATIONAL BOUNDARY
STATE/SETTLEMENT BOUNDARY

0 10 20 30 40 50
miles

Map 16

Singapore island telephone system is operated by a public corporation known as the Singapore Telephone Board. This Board was instituted in 1955 following the expiration of the license of the Oriental Telephone and Electric Company, Limited, which had formerly operated the Singapore and Johore Bahru local services as well as the trunk connecting them. In 1955, Johore Bahru local service was taken over by the Federation Telecommunications Department.

6. Communication in a Plural Society

HUMAN COMMUNICATION presumes the understanding by a number of individuals of various conventional patterns of verbal and visual symbols. The individuals understanding a particular series of such symbols compose a general community. Within the general community, certain special communities may be defined by their common deviation or variation such as dialect differences or variations in syntactic structure. Furthermore, both the general and special communities characteristically contain certain specific communities composed of individuals living in close proximity to one another and maintaining close social relationships within specified geographical areas. The variety of communities in Malaya makes for exceptional difficulty in communication.

Malaya presents a picture of extreme linguistic heterogeneity. Four major communities are widespread on the peninsula and in Singapore: Chinese, Malay, Indian, and English (Map 17). The Chinese community is divided into a number of special linguistic communities, each distinguished by dialect variations. Other special communities are apparent among the Indian population from northern India, who use linguistic variations of Aryan origin. In addition, each of these general or special communities tends to be divided into specific communities centered in particular localities or regions, while within each particular locality or region different specific communities may be found living side by side or intermingled in the population complex of the area. It should also be noted that the many communities are not exclusive. Any individual may be a member of one or more such communities, and each major community tends to include individuals from different

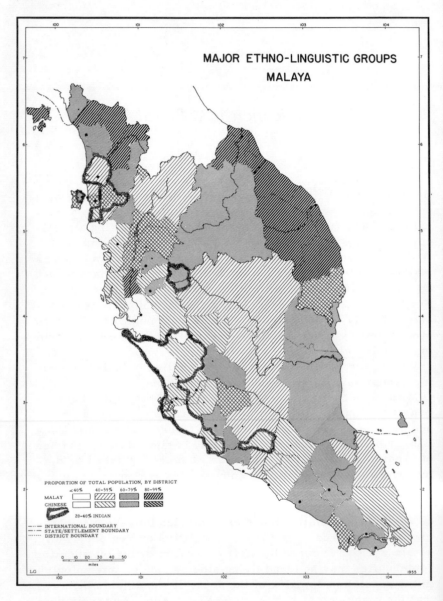

MAJOR ETHNO-LINGUISTIC GROUPS
MALAYA

PROPORTION OF TOTAL POPULATION, BY DISTRICT

	<40%	40-59%	60-79%	80-99%
MALAY				
CHINESE				

20-40% INDIAN

INTERNATIONAL BOUNDARY
STATE/SETTLEMENT BOUNDARY
DISTRICT BOUNDARY

0 10 20 30 40 50
miles

LG   1955

Map 17

ethnic or social groups. Finally, any individual may be affiliated with a community through an understanding of its speech
or its written symbols, or both. The first is affiliation through
linguistic ability; the second is affiliation through literacy.

The following survey of communication patterns in Malaya
attempts (1) to locate and define the various special and specific communities and outline their patterns of distribution and
associations, (2) to examine the media of communication related to each community through a description of the network
of communication flow and a study of sources and controls over
such media, and (3) to point out certain objectives in the control and utilization of the media through an analysis of overt
intentions in relation to content.

The Linguistic Communities

The Chinese communities

The Chinese settlers who migrated to Malaya and Singapore
originated, for the most part, in the south China coastal and
interior provinces south of Foochow (Map 18). [1] This region,
in Chinese history, was one of the last to be incorporated into
the Empire. Traditionally, it has retained certain distinctions
as compared with the older parts of China--culturally, politically, ethnically, and linguistically. Far removed from the
northern centers of Chinese culture, the area tended to develop
an amalgam of the indigenous local cultures with an overlay of
Chinese culture, usually in forms generations removed from
the contemporary forms of the northern centers. Imperial
control over the area varied in intensity, and a greater degree
of local autonomy was maintained than in other regions. Traditionally, revolutionary movements have tended to center in
the south, and secessionist movements have often been able to
maintain their independence for considerable periods of time.
To a considerable degree these distinctions are explained by
the ethnic heterogeneity of the people. Chinese expansion toward the south had tended gradually to push the native peoples
of the northern areas southward. As a consequence the indigenous peoples of the south were forced into the more isolated
and sequestered localities. Topographic features have tended
to create isolated riverine and coastal valleys, separated

---

1. Map after Purcell, Herrmann, et al.

133

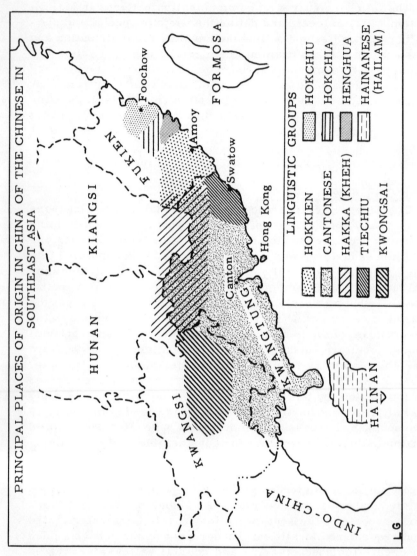

PRINCIPAL PLACES OF ORIGIN IN CHINA OF THE CHINESE IN SOUTHEAST ASIA

LINGUISTIC GROUPS

HOKKIEN
CANTONESE
HAKKA (KHEH)
TIECHIU
KWONGSAI

HOKCHIU
HOKCHIA
HENGHUA
HAINANESE (HAILAM)

Map 18

from one another by rugged uplands, thus allowing an unrestricted development of small homogeneous local populations distinct and separate from one another. As a result, the peoples of the region are divided into some ten or more related, but distinct, cultural groups.

These groups in turn utilize some seven different and usually not mutually intelligible dialects. These are (1) the Foochow dialect, spoken by the Hokchiu and Hokchia peoples around the city of Foochow and in the hinterlands, (2) the Hokkienese dialect, spoken north, south, and inland from Amoy and including a variation in the Henghua dialect, (3) the Tiechiu dialect, spoken around Swatow, (4) the Hakka dialect (Kheh), spoken over a wide area inland from Swatow and Canton, (5) the Cantonese dialect, spoken along the coastal areas north and south of Canton, (6) Hailam, a dialect used by the people of Hainan island, and (7) Southern Mandarin, spoken by the people of Kwangsi province inland from Canton and mutually intelligible with the Mandarin dialects of the north.

In Malaya the areal definition of these dialect groups does not exist as it does in China. Almost any section of Malaya will include representatives, in varying degrees, of each such special community.

However, certain dominant and significant nodal groupings of particular dialect groups in certain specific areas can be ascertained by (1) locating those areas where the Chinese form a majority of the total population of the area, (2) locating those areas in which the Chinese tend to be densely settled, and (3) determining the dialect groups predominant among the Chinese population of the above areas. Thus, Map 17 indicates roughly the proportional representation of the two major ethnic groups (which may tentatively be considered as coterminous with their associated specific linguistic communities) in each district in Malaya. The Chinese show a clear dominance in certain areas, particularly along the west coast. They are clearly minorities in the Malay-dominant areas along the east coast and the northern border region. Surrounding each major point of Chinese predominance, the proportion of Chinese in the total population tends to taper off to a point where they form only a small minority. In only a few districts is the ratio between Chinese and Malays relatively equal.

The fact that a certain ethnic group is predominant within a certain area, however, is not particularly significant in itself but must be considered in comparison with the relative

135

sizes of the districts and their total populations. Thus, ten thousand Chinese scattered over a thousand square miles are not as significant a community as one thousand Chinese grouped together within a single town. On Map 4 is shown the density of Chinese in each district of Malaya. Clearly indicated are the two extreme nodal areas of Chinese settlement, Penang-Province Wellesley and Singapore, and two other major centers, Ipoh-Kampar and Kuala Lumpur. Noticeably, Kuala Lumpur assumes a significance not indicated on Map 17, while Seremban, despite its dominant Chinese population, becomes less important because of its lower density. Malakka, too, assumes greater importance as a Chinese community center. Between the nodal points indicated, the densities tend to thin out, although it appears that the cities and towns outside the shaded areas of the map each contain a small, relatively close-knit Chinese community.

On Map 19 an attempt has been made to determine the dominant special communities of Chinese for each of the districts deemed significant on Maps 17 and 4. [2] Hokkienese-speaking Chinese predominate among the Chinese populations in four large areas along the west coast. Tiechiu peoples are also predominant in three coastal areas. Cantonese-speaking Chinese are found mainly in the long stretch of inland districts between Ipoh and Seremban. The large concentration of Cantonese in Singapore does not show up on Map 19. (See Table 47.) Hakkas are found associated with the Cantonese in the central valleys and elsewhere in Penang and in Malakka and Johore. Foochow-speaking people appear dominant only in the Dindings. The Hainanese (Hailam) and the Mandarin dialects, with one Hailam exception, do not appear on the map, indicating their broad distribution throughout the country with little central significance in any single district.

It is apparent that the various dialect groups are not equally intermixed in any particular district, except perhaps on Penang and Singapore islands. Each tends to predominate in some particular area to the near exclusion of others. In other districts an association of communities is found--Hokkienese with

2. Each special dialect community is represented to some extent in nearly every district. Only the more clearly defined and more comprehensive specific communities within each dialect group are shown.

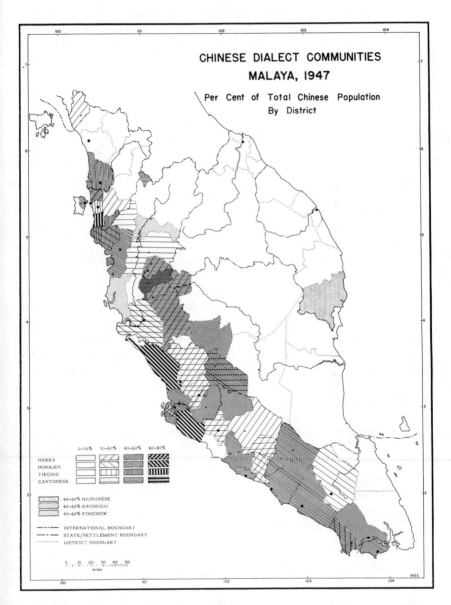

CHINESE DIALECT COMMUNITIES
MALAYA, 1947

Per Cent of Total Chinese Population
By District

	0-30%	30-40%	40-60%	60-80%
HAKKA				
HOKKIEN				
TIECHIU				
CANTONESE				

40-60% HAINANESE
40-60% KWONGSAI
40-60% FOOCHOW

–·–·–·– INTERNATIONAL BOUNDARY
–··–··– STATE/SETTLEMENT BOUNDARY
·············· DISTRICT BOUNDARY

0 10 20 30 40 50
miles

1955

Map 19

Tiechiu or Cantonese with Hakka. It appears that where such associations are noted, one of the community pairs will tend to be rural, the other urban. Otherwise, it appears that the intra-community cohesion is even greater than is indicated by the maps, since the largest segment of the Chinese population in each district appears to be urban rather than spread evenly throughout the district.

The Malay community

As the indigenous peoples of the country, Malays are found in numbers in every district. The special linguistic differences between different tribes and groups of Malays do not prevent mutual intelligibility, and divisions into special communities may be overlooked. [3] From Map 17 it can be seen that the districts of Malay dominance are along the east coast and interior regions and in the northwestern areas of Kedah. Two small areas of Malay dominance may also be noted in central Perak and in Malakka.

Malay density for each district is shown on Map 5. Five nodal areas are apparent, besides the high-density urban centers scattered throughout the country, but the vast interior regions, which appear predominantly Malay on Map 17, lose their importance because of low population densities. Only in the east-coast districts is there a relationship between high density and Malay predominance in the population. Along the west coast the Malays appear to predominate in those districts with relatively small total populations--i. e. , where other communities have not settled to any great extent--although their highest densities are found in Penang-Province Wellesley, Malakka, and Singapore, areas with such large total populations relative to area that the Malays are overshadowed by other communities. In the latter, however, as in the other urban centers, the Malays tend to be segregated into individual neighborhood communities.

---

3. One special community which might be noted, however, are the Indonesians residing in Malaya. Although the Indonesian dialects are generally intelligible to Malaya, their national origin makes them a significant, although minor, political community.

The Indian communities

The general Indian community is similar to the Chinese in being composed of a number of special dialect communities: Tamil, Telegu, and Malayalam from southern India; Punjabi, Maharatti, Bengali, Marwari, Pushtu, and Sindhi from northern India. However, the southern Indian dialects are predominant, accounting for almost 90 per cent of the total, and among these the Tamil is by far the most important, comprising nearly 80 per cent. Of the northern communities, only the Punjabi numbers more than five thousand. The other dialect communities are so small and spread so widely throughout the country as to lose any important individual identity.

Only in four areas do the Indian communities comprise more than 20 per cent of the total population (Map 17). These areas are (1) the area of Penang, Nibong Tebal, Kulim, and Kuala Muda, (2) the Cameron Highlands, (3) northern and western Selangor, and (4) Tampin.

Since the Indian community as a whole is much smaller than either the Chinese or Malay, the density factor was not considered suitable for comparative purposes. Instead, the Indian population of each district was computed as a percentage of the total Indian population for the Federation and Singapore. These percentage variations are shown on Map 20. Five areas of Indian concentration stand out: Singapore, the Klang-Kuala Lumpur area, Lower Perak, Ipoh, and Georgetown (on Penang). The urban character of Indian concentration is apparent. There is an urban nodality among the Indians, with increasing dispersion in the rural areas. However, the rural Indian population tends to be grouped in small communities on the various rubber plantations, maintaining a separate existence from the Malays and Chinese of the surrounding countryside.

The English community

Besides being the native tongue of the majority of the European population of Malaya, English forms a sort of lingua franca spoken with varying ability by some members of the Chinese, Malay, and Indian communities, and provides a means of mutual communication among them. It is probable that the distribution of English-speaking communities is centered around the major urban areas, with a rapid thinning-out in the rural districts.

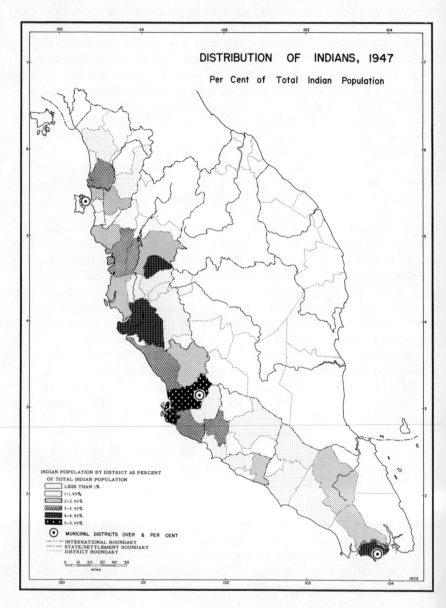

DISTRIBUTION OF INDIANS, 1947

Per Cent of Total Indian Population

INDIAN POPULATION BY DISTRICT AS PERCENT
OF TOTAL INDIAN POPULATION

LESS THAN 1%
1-1.99%
2-2.99%
3-3.99%
4-4.99%
5-5.99%

MUNICIPAL DISTRICTS OVER 6 PER CENT
INTERNATIONAL BOUNDARY
STATE/SETTLEMENT BOUNDARY
DISTRICT BOUNDARY

0   10 20 30 40 50
miles

1955

Map 20

The general pattern

Each of the various general and special linguistic communities in Malaya tends to concentrate in one, two, or more specific localities, distinct from one another on both the regional and local levels. With the exception of the Malay community along the northeast coast, all of the communities show their greatest concentrations along a ninety-mile-wide strip paralleling the west coast. Penang and Singapore are the only two areas showing concentrations of all three major groups. Concentrations of both Chinese and Indians are shown at Ipoh and Kuala Lumpur. Elsewhere, major concentrations of one community are correlated with low densities for the other groups. The English community, too, appears concentrated at Singapore and Penang and to a lesser extent at Kuala Lumpur and Ipoh. This tendency for the various communities to segregate themselves from one another--to cluster into fairly exclusive specific communities--is duplicated in the major urban centers and the smaller geographical units. Thus, the various cities and towns tend to have a Malay section, a Chinese section, an Indian section, and a European section. Within these sections there tend also to be clusters according to linguistic affiliation. The Hokkienese-speaking people tend to form a distinct neighborhood, as do the various other Chinese dialect groups, and the southern Indians tend to form a community distinct from that of the northern Indians. In the countryside a village will tend to be either Chinese, Malay, or Indian, but seldom will it be mixed to any great extent.

Tying these various disparate dialect communities together, however, are several "super-languages." Among the Chinese communities, Kuo-yü has been adopted as the means of inter-community communication. Malay, too, as the lingua franca of the region, assumes the character of a "super-language." Finally, English performs a dual role as a means of inter-community communication among certain elements of the various Indian communities and as a general language connecting elements of all the major groups--Chinese, Malay, Indian, and European.

The Literacy Communities

The data on literacy may be considered in relation to the population of an area as a whole, regardless of ethnic or linguistic variation; in relation to each ethnic group; or in relation to what has been defined as a literacy community composed of those persons understanding a particular linguistic symbol system regardless of their ethnic affiliation.

General literacy

The top set of figures in Table 23 indicates the literacy rates (number of literates per thousand population) for the Federation

TABLE 23
LITERACY
(rates per thousand)

	Males		Females	
	1931	1947	1931	1947
Federation	374	445	65	157
Singapore	416	519	139	199
Malaya	356	457	76	164
Ethnic Groups				
Malays				
Federation	260	379	43	118
Singapore	351	539	73	175
Malaya	263	387	44	120
Chinese				
Federation	431	495	94	193
Singapore	390	483	113	176
Malaya	421	492	99	188
Indians				
Federation	343	504	81	190
Singapore	503	680	211	319
Malaya	359	529	86	200

and Singapore for the two sexes in both 1931 and 1947. It is apparent that the general level of literacy is low. It also is apparent, however, that the general level increased significantly between the two census years, despite the turmoil of war and the Japanese occupation. The higher literacy rate indicated for Singapore in relation to the Federation reflects a general trend toward higher literacy in urban areas. This is, perhaps,

142

due as much to the attractive force of the large towns and cities upon literate persons as to the better opportunities for schooling provided by them.

The wide difference in the levels of literacy between males and females is particularly striking, although literacy among females shows a faster rate of increase than among males. Literacy rates are generally higher in the age groups under twenty-nine years. Literacy in such groups is about one-third again as high as those in the forty-and-over age groups. Increasing opportunities for schooling and settled conditions should accentuate the general improvement in literacy and the greater literacy in the lower age groups.

Literacy among ethnic groups

Of the three main ethnic groups the Malays are the least literate and the Indians the most literate, with the Chinese falling between the two. Europeans and Eurasians above the age of fifteen years are almost all literate.

The literacy rate among male Malays is 387, well below the 457 of the population as a whole. Malays have higher literacy rates than "Other Malaysians," a reflection of the better education of the indigenous population as compared with the immigrant.[4] There is undoubtedly a close relationship between low literacy and the predominant rurality of the Malaysians. City Malaysians have higher rates of literacy than rural Malaysians. Malaysian males between twenty-five and twenty-nine years of age, for example, have literacy rates of 87, 89, and 86 per cent in highly urbanized Singapore island, Penang, and Selangor, respectively. In the principal cities of each of these territories the percentages for such males are even higher: 89, 94, and 94, respectively.[5] Other areal differences exist; the literacy among Malaysians in the northeast, for example, is much lower than in the areas along the west coast.

Literacy among the Chinese is higher in the Federation than in the country as a whole, but it is lower in Singapore (Table 23). This is in contrast to the Malaysians and Indians, who have higher numbers of literate persons per thousand

---

4. T. E. Smith, Population Growth in Malaya: An Analysis of Recent Trends (London: Royal Institute of International Affairs, 1952), p. 26.

5. Ibid., p. 27.

in Singapore than in the country as a whole. The lower literacy among the Chinese in Singapore is probably related to the greater number of immigrants and to the large Chinese laborer population. In general, there are no wide regional differences in literacy rates among the Chinese or great differences among larger towns, smaller towns, and rural areas, in contrast with both the Malaysians and the Indians. [6]

The Indians have the highest literacy rates of the three major ethnic groups because the low number of females and children in the Indian population results in a high ratio of literate persons to the total Indian population. [7] It is essentially a reflection of the persisting immigrant character of the Indian population.

The extremely high literacy among the European and Eurasian population is in part related to their traditional engagement in public service activities which require the attainment of a minimum standard of literacy in English. [8]

The literacy communities

As with the linguistic communities, a literacy community is best defined and described in relation to the degree of contiguity pertaining among its members and the degree to which it forms a significant grouping within the total population of a particular area. The first may be measured in terms of areal density, the second in terms of the ratio of members to the total population. These two factors may be brought together to form an index of relative concentration of literacy between different areas. Such indexes of relative concentration have been calculated for the three major literacy communities and the English literacy community and are plotted on Maps 21, 22, 23, and 24. [9]

---

6. Ibid., p. 67.

7. M. V. Del Tufo, Malaya: A Report on the 1947 Census o Population (London: Crown Agents for the Colonies, 1949), p. 92.

8. Ibid., p. 96.

9. This index is adapted from that used by William Skinne in his work in Thailand. The full formula is: $\frac{X}{area} \times \frac{X}{total\ pop.}$ where X is any defined subgroup of the total population of given area (in this case that subgroup literate in a particula linguistic symbol system). In the following set of maps the in

Despite the diversity of dialects among the Chinese, the written language is standard and mutually intelligible to the literate members of any dialect group. The Chinese ideographs, however, are difficult to learn and tend to retard any widespread literacy among the Chinese. The concentration of literates in Chinese for each census district in Malaya is shown on Map 21. [10]

Literacy in Chinese is centered around four general areas: (1) Penang-Province Wellesley, (2) Ipoh-Batu Gajah-Kampar, (3) Kuala Lumpur, and (4) Singapore-Johore Bahru. The various urban districts of Malaya all show high concentration, even the Malay centers of Alor Star, Kota Bharu, and Kuala Trengganu. Between each of the major areas, concentration decreases rapidly (See also Map 25).

Malay is written either in rumi, the Romanized alphabet, or in jawi, a form of Arabic script. Literate Malays are usually familiar with both systems, and for purposes of de-

---

dex categories were formed to increase geometrically in such a manner that any single category indicates roughly twice the relative concentration of the next lower category and half the relative concentration of the next higher category. (See Appendix B.)

10. The 1947 census provides figures only for Chinese literate in "Any Language" and this map was based on these figures under the following two assumptions: (1) that few persons other than Chinese were literate in Chinese and that their exclusion from the figures would not be significant, and (2) that most Chinese literate in "Any Language" were literate in Chinese. The latter assumption was based on the reasoning that since of the total of those Chinese listed as literate in "Any Language," less than 15 per cent were recorded elsewhere as literate in any language other than Chinese, it would seem that at least 85 per cent of the literate Chinese were literate in the Chinese language. It seemed also reasonable to assume that of the remaining 15 per cent, the majority were literate in Chinese in addition to another language. Since the ratio of Chinese literate in languages other than Chinese appears fairly standard among the various districts, it was assumed that a concentration index based on the total figures would make possible a fairly accurate comparison of literacy concentration among districts.

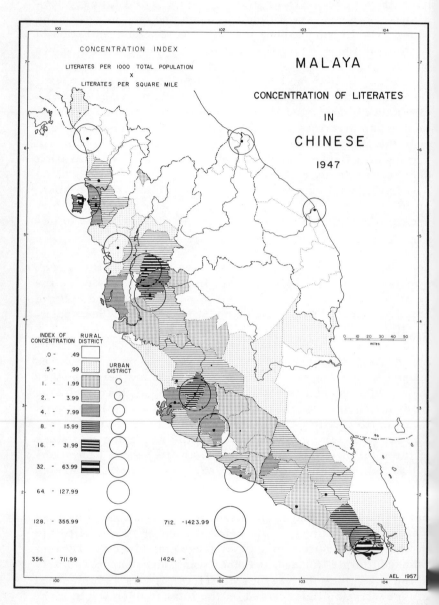

Map 21

fining community patterns the difference need not be taken into consideration. A relatively small number of non-Malays, twenty-five thousand, are shown as literate in Malay. Only three major centers of Malay literacy are noted: (1) Penang-Province Wellesley-Yen, (2) Parit, and (3) Malakka-Alor Gajah-Rembau (Map 22). As with the Chinese literacy community, there is a general concentration in all urban districts. In comparison with the relative density of Malay population in the northeast areas as shown on Map 5, the low concentration of literates in those areas is significant. In comparison with Map 21, showing the concentration of literates in Chinese, three factors are apparent: (1) there are very few points of coincidence between the two maps outside of the Penang-Province Wellesley area; those districts of high concentration for the Chinese literates show quite low concentrations of Malay literates and vice versa; (2) in the urban districts which show relatively high concentrations for both communities the Chinese literates show consistently higher concentrations, even where the urban districts are in such areas of Malay literate concentration as Malakka, Taiping, and Alor Star; and (3) the districts showing concentrations of Chinese literates are primarily those along the west coast south of Ipoh, while the largest number of districts showing a high concentration of Malay literates are north of Ipoh (compare also Maps 25 and 26).

The Indian peoples of Malaya use a number of different symbol and semantic systems, but as with their linguistic communities the Tamil predominates. The Malayan census makes no distinction among the various Indian communities insofar as literacy is concerned. There are some indications that the northern Indians tend toward a higher literacy rate than do those from the south, but the southern Indians so dominate the total as to nullify such a distinction. Of the southern Indians, the Tamil and Malayalam communities use different systems of writing, although they use similar dialects. The Punjabi are the only important northern Indian literacy community. Map 23 shows the concentration of persons literate in any of the Indian linguistic symbol systems. [11] Only three areas of signi-

---

11. As for the Chinese, the Malayan census provides data only on Indians literate in "Any Language"; the same assumptions were used in computing the literacy concentration indexes for the Indian as for the Chinese literates. (See note 10.)

147

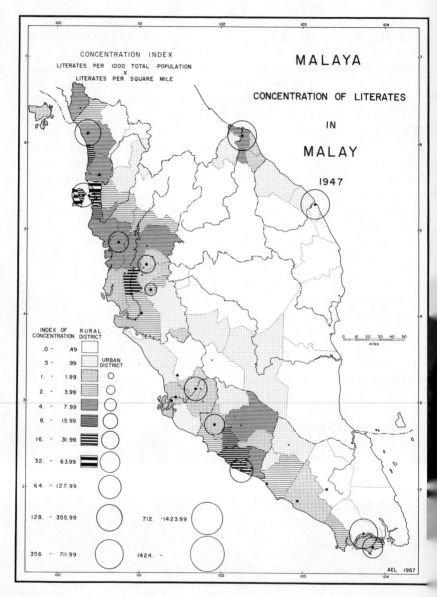

Map 22

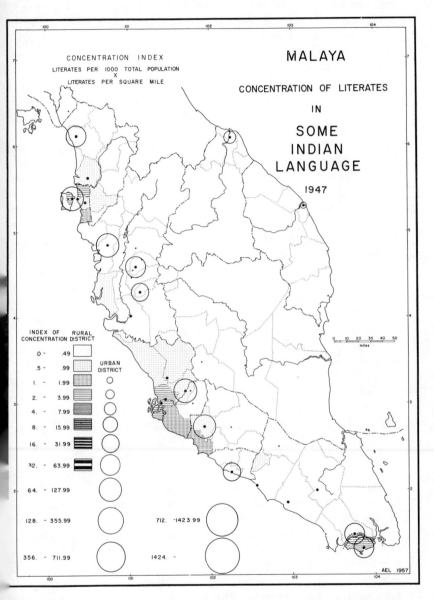

CONCENTRATION INDEX
LITERATES PER 1000 TOTAL POPULATION
X
LITERATES PER SQUARE MILE

MALAYA

CONCENTRATION OF LITERATES

IN

SOME
INDIAN
LANGUAGE

1947

INDEX OF RURAL
CONCENTRATION DISTRICT

.0 - .49
.5 - .99
1. - 1.99
2. - 3.99
4. - 7.99
8. - 15.99
16. - 31.99
32. - 63.99

64. - 127.99

128. - 355.99

356. - 711.99

URBAN
DISTRICT

712. -1423.99

1424. -

0 10 20 30 40 50
miles

AEL 1957

Map 23

ficance are apparent: (1) Penang-Province Wellesley, (2) Klang, and (3) Singapore. These show far less concentration than the centers for the Chinese or Malay literates because of the relatively small number of Indians. Surprisingly, the Indian literates show equal or greater concentrations in a number of the urban districts such as Kuala Lumpur, Seremban, Kampar, Ipoh, and Penang. The pattern of literacy in Indian dialects more closely approximates the pattern of Indian density as shown on Map 6 than do either the Chinese or Malay literacy concentrations in comparison with their respective density patterns.

English is a primary written language for the European and Eurasian residents in Malaya and a secondary language for a minor portion of the Malay, Chinese, and Indian communities. As with spoken English, written English is of great importance as the primary medium for official and commercial documents and, as will be noted later, for education, journalism, and radio presentation. It enables the various groups to communicate with the representatives of the colonial power and provides a means of written communication among members of the various other communities. This latter is of importance in view of the low literacy in languages other than their own among the major communities.

However, literacy in English is generally low. About 4.4 per cent of the total population of Malaya was literate in English in 1947, representing only a little more than 290,000 persons. Of the major ethnic groups, the Indians show the highest literacy in English, the Chinese the next highest and the Malays the lowest. Literacy in English among females of the major ethnic groups is extremely low. The centers of English literacy are shown on Map 24. Only two areas of any significance appear: (1) Penang-Province Wellesley and (2) Singapore, with a minor center at Kuala Lumpur-Klang. As is the case in the Indian community, English literates are more highly concentrated in a number of urban areas than are the more numerous Malay literates. The correlation between literacy in English and urbanization is apparent. It might be noted that the English and Indian literate communities are of about equal size, yet the former show a much greater concentration in the urban districts. While the Indian community shows some concentration in sixteen districts, the English community shows concentration in only six.

Those persons who are biliterate represent a special case.

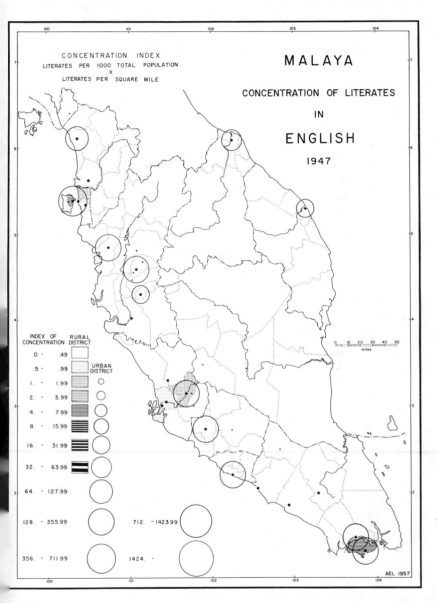

Map 24

Like the bilinguals they perform an important function as communication links between the other communities. Their role places them in positions of particular power in relation to others--they are the intermediaries and go-betweens of the multiliterate social, economic, and political whole. As has been noted, English is the principal secondary language of the biliterates. Malay is probably next in importance; the 1947 census lists some eighteen thousand Chinese and eleven thousand Indians as literate in Malay. It is doubtful that more than an insignificant number of non-Chinese are literate in Chinese or non-Indians literate in an Indian dialect.

The gross pattern of the literacy communities

For all the literacy communities--Chinese, Malay, Indian, and English--literacy tends to be concentrated in a few areas. Yet, with the exception of Penang-Province Wellesley, the centers of community concentration tend toward areal differentiation; literates in Chinese are concentrated in districts quite distinct from those in which Malay literates are concentrated (Maps 25 and 26). In eight of the twelve urban districts, some one of the major literacy communities (usually the Chinese) has a concentration predominance at least four times greater than that of any other community. These factors accentuate the community separateness noted previously in relation to the linguistic communities.

Secondly, it should be noted that literacy tends to develop among certain classes of people within each community, particularly the white-collar and commercial groups. Literacy is a prerequisite for government office employment and must be in either Malay or English. Chinese shopkeepers and traders tend toward increased literacy, and where their work brings them into contact with members of other communities, they are often literate in two languages. Also, literacy is predominant among the males; only European females show a rate of literacy equivalent to that of the males.

Finally, literacy within each community has taken slightly different trends dependent upon age and the introduction of mass education within the community. Thus, the older Chinese tend to be more literate than the young in Chinese, while the younger Chinese are becoming increasingly affiliated with the English community. In both the Malayan and Indian communities, literacy is higher among the younger members than it is among their elders.

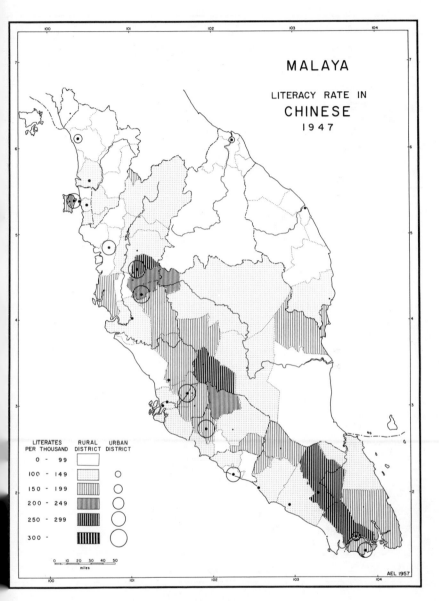

MALAYA

LITERACY RATE IN
CHINESE
1947

LITERATES PER THOUSAND	RURAL DISTRICT	URBAN DISTRICT
0 - 99		
100 - 149		○
150 - 199		○
200 - 249		○
250 - 299		○
300 -		○

0 10 20 30 40 50
miles

AEL 1957

Map 25

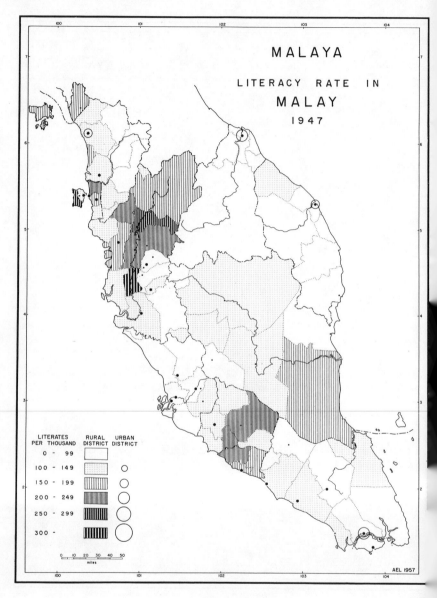

MALAYA

LITERACY RATE IN

MALAY

1947

LITERATES PER THOUSAND	RURAL DISTRICT	URBAN DISTRICT
0 - 99		
100 - 149		
150 - 199		
200 - 249		
250 - 299		
300 -		

miles

AEL 1957

Map 26

Education is a basic factor in communication behavior and community affiliation. The school is not only the place where various linguistic and literacy habits and abilities are developed, but also the source of many of the community values connected with language. There, too, ideas and impressions of the world and its peoples outside the community are formed. Information and propaganda from the outside can be effective only to the extent to which they fit into the complex pattern of attitudes and preconceptions developed in the individual by his community and group affiliations and by his teachers. Four elements of the educational process are of particular relevance: (1) the availability of educational opportunities and their future developmental trends, (2) the language of instruction and community relationships of the educational system, (3) the curriculum emphases, and (4) the nature of political, social, or economic controls placed on the schools.

The primary and secondary systems

The most general classification of schools in Malaya is according to the language of instruction. This reflects the variety of influences at work, from the early Moslem (Koranic) schools to the later government, missionary, Chinese, and Indian schools. There have been, therefore, four concurrent systems of education in terms of the language of instruction: Malay, English, Chinese, and Indian. Table 24 indicates the relative proportions of each type of school and the total enrollment in 1954.

The structure of education in the Federation has been characterized by a base of primary English and vernacular schools which lead to the English or Chinese secondary system and finally to either the University of Malaya or the Chinese Nanyang University. There are also technical, vocational, and adult education units within the system. The crossover of pupils from the vernacular primary systems to the secondary system, with the exception of the Chinese, has been insignificant. Few pupils go from the vernacular primary schools into the English secondary system, although special classes in English for advanced students in the Malay schools are designed to facilitate transfer of Malay students to the English secondary schools. In the Federation, only about one student in eleven goes on to secondary school. In Singapore, the figure is about one in seven or eight. In both cases, however, students from the English primary schools, whatever their ethnic origins, tend to go on to secondary schools.

TABLE 24
NUMBER OF SCHOOLS AND ENROLLMENTS
FOR EACH TYPE

	Singapore*		Federation†	
	Number of Schools	Enrollment	Number of Schools	Enrollment
Chinese	280	82,035	1,276	277,454
Malay	60	10,470	2,144	368,017
English	204	84,062	433	178,644
Indian	20	1,465	938	46,247

*Colony of Singapore, Annual Report, 1954 (Singapore: Government Printing Office, 1955), p. 95.
†Federation of Malaya, Annual Report, 1955 (Kuala Lumpur: Government Press, 1956), p. 208.

The historical development of the Federation has produced some areal variation in the availability of educational facilities. In the former Unfederated Malay States, where urbanization and other developments have lagged, there is a perceptible lag also in educational facilities and enrollments. Moreover, in these states the high proportion of Malays, with their informal education patterns, has deterred the development of formal educational facilities to the extent of the other Malayan states.

Malay schools developed out of the traditional Koranic schools. After the transfer of administration of the Straits Settlements from the East India Company to the Colonial Office in 1867, free education for young people of all races became a Colonial Office policy. The schools were gradually secularized, and religious instruction was restricted to the mosques and private instruction. The quality and quantity of the Malay schools improved with those of the English system, though always substantially behind.

English schools were established first by missionary societies as private schools. After the political transfer in 1867, the first government-aided schools were established, teaching in English, and English-language private schools were given financial support. Between the two world wars the English schools were influenced by the reforms in education then taking place in England, and there was a substantial increase in the number of secondary schools. In the same period, attention was given to more adequate preparation for higher education at Raffles College of Arts (established 1928) and King Edward VII College of Medicine (established 1905) in Singapore. After World War II the demand for English education received a new impetus, and enrollments in government and government-aided schools in the Federation rose from 44,000 in 1946 to 124,544 in 1955, when over 54,100 pupils were also enrolled in private English schools.

The Chinese schools were instituted and operated by private Chinese groups independently of government control up to 1920, when it was realized that they were fast becoming instruments of propaganda for Chinese nationalism and they were placed under the direction of a Department of Chinese Education. A system of governmental registration and inspection was instituted and a grant-in-aid program initiated to enable them to raise their standards and the quality of their personnel in order to bring them into line with the national educational policy. Because of the great interest of the Chinese community in education, the Chinese schools by 1937 were second in number (the Malay schools led), and Chinese pupils were the most numerous of the language communities enrolled in English schools. As a result of a study in 1951, the Chinese schools were given greater grants-in-aid to improve teacher training facilities, raise teachers' salaries, and revise textbooks to conform more closely to a Malayan, rather than Chinese, orientation.

The Indian vernacular schools sprang up during the 1870's with the influx of Indians to the new rubber estates. In 1912 rubber estate operators were required to provide schools with the aid of per capita grants from the government. In addition to the estate schools, other Indian schools have been supported by interested groups of Indians living in towns and by missionary societies. Schools and enrollments have increased sharply since the war despite the fact that the Indian population has decreased, indicating a backlog of pupils. The Indians also display a desire for an English language education, and they accounted for 22.2 per cent of the pupils in the Federation English schools in 1955. This percentage (39,624) represented an enrollment only slightly lower than that in the Indian schools (46,247).

Three recent developments will probably have a significant effect upon the future development of education in Malaya, particularly in the Federation. In 1952 the Federal Legislative Council established a national school plan in an effort to better meet the growing responsibilities for education. The aim of the system is to set up free, compulsory primary education for children of all races in the Federation, supported by government funds. The system is projected as bilingual, with English and Malay the languages of instruction, while Chinese and Indian vernaculars could be made alternative languages of instruction upon community demand. The central purpose of the system is, in addition to rationalizing the system in operation, to provide a Malayan orientation to the young people of the country, whatever their racial origin. Such an orientation is believed to be indispensable for the people of Malaya as they progress toward self-government. Recent modifications of the plan have placed a greater emphasis on English-language instruction and greater financial responsibility for the maintenance of the system upon the states and settlements. With the advent of independence in 1957 it is possible, however, that the government may be forced to accede to demands for greater Malayanization of the school system, although the great demand for English-language education indicates an increasing role for English as the dominant lingua franca.

A second development has been the rapid increase in the number of Malay schools, largely due to the inauguration of Ra'ayat or "People's" schools. These are a form of community development at the initiative of the people themselves. Usually a kampong or a group of kampongs will submit a request for government aid in setting up a local school. An officer of the Department of Education will inspect the plan and, if he approves, advise on the building site and courses of instruction. It is planned that those Ra'ayat schools which prove successful will be taken into the government school system.

A further significant increase in government-sponsored educational facilities has come with the institution of a number of new schools and classrooms in the "New Villages." Most of these are Chinese, but a number of Malay and Indian schools also have been built.

Mandarin has been adopted as the language of instruction in most of the Chinese schools. Most of the Indian schools use Tamil, although a few use other dialects such as Telegu or Punjabi. The Malay schools generally use local dialects, although a recent move has started toward the standardization of Malay throughout the country. Many of the Malay, Chinese, and Indian schools now offer courses in English, required for advancement into the secondary and higher schools. As a result there is a growing proportion of each of the communities developing bilingual and biliterate abilities. It is largely to these groups that the communities must look for future leadership.

The various vernacular school systems have tended generally to emphasize disparate and often opposing goals. Thus, the Chinese schools were designed primarily to perpetuate Chinese culture among their pupils, the Malay schools to instill a strong Moslem and Malay consciousness, and the Indian schools to provide a basically Indian background for the displaced Indian students. Even the mission schools, whether they taught in Malay, Chinese, or Tamil, tended to view their goal as the propagation of Christian virtues and Western cultural values. Few schools, if any, until recently viewed their goal as the creation of a unified Malayan society encompassing all the various ethnic, linguistic, and cultural groups. This diversity in education and indoctrination led the British after World War II to insist upon greater standardization and an increased Malayan orientation. The basic premises of the new national schools are stated thus:

(i) that education should aim at fostering and extending the capacity for self-government and the ideal of civic loyalty and responsibility;
(ii) that equal educational opportunity should be afforded to the children--both boys and girls-- of all races;
(iii) that upon a basis of free primary education there should be developed such secondary, vocational, and higher education as would best meet the needs of the country. [12]

The administration of educational services in the Federation is the combined responsibility of the federal Education Department and the corresponding department in each of the Malay states and settlements. The federal department is responsible

---

12. Colony of Singapore, Annual Report, 1953, p. 91.

to the Legislative Council and under the direction of the Member for Education. Policy and planning take place at the federal level, although no action may be initiated in the states or settlements without their agreement. The funds for education are essentially federal funds which have been allocated to the states and settlements in lump-sum grants. The allocation of state funds and the over-all direction of the education program in the states and settlements has been the responsibility of the state education departments. The various schools, besides being characterized by the language of instruction, may be distinguished by the degree of support each receives from the government. Thus, there have been schools receiving substantial grants-in-aid from the government, others receiving full support, and some receiving no funds.

The costs of the multilingual system of schools vary according to the type of school. A pupil-year in the Malay or Indian primary schools costs the government about M$100 (US$34), while the fees are only M$2.50 (US$.83) per month.[13] Aid to Chinese schools costs the government M$60 (US$20) per pupil-year. English secondary schools cost about M$400 (US$133) per pupil-year and charge fees of M$5 (US$1.67) per month. In 1953, 37 per cent of Federation education expenditures was for Malay schools, 15 per cent for Chinese schools, 4 per cent for Indian schools, and 6 per cent for the schools of the "New Villages." The amount spent on education for each ethnic group has been considered about proportional to the racial distribution of the population, although the Chinese claim that they are at a disadvantage on a per capita basis.

The administration of education in Singapore is the responsibility of the Director of Education, who is assisted by the Singapore Education Committee in matters of policy and the Education Finance Board in matters of finance. The Colony government, the City Council, and the Rural Board all share in the financing of education, which includes the salaries of teachers and the construction and maintenance of school buildings. School fees similar to those of the Federation add to the resources for education.

Education in Singapore particularly has been beset by problems resulting from increasing enrollments and the complex-

---

13. The average relationship of M$ to US$ is about three to one.

ities of a multi-lingual population. In 1947, 81,000 pupils were registered in primary schools, and in 1954 the enrollment reached 157,000. Secondary school registration increased in the same period from 5,900 to 21,200. Despite this tremendous increase, facilities have kept up with enrollment. Such progress has been made possible only by increasing the per capita cost of education from M$4 in 1947 to M$51 in 1954. Seventy-five per cent of the schools are government or aided schools. In late 1954 the Chinese schools were offered more complete government support, but many chose not to accept it for fear of greater government control over Chinese education. In government or aided schools the first six grades are free.

Specialized and higher education

The first government trade school was established in the Federation in 1926, and by 1941 there were four such schools teaching electrical installation, carpentry, motor engineering, bricklaying, and plumbing. Since that time the facilities have undergone considerable expansion, including the establishment of a combination school and factory at Kuala Lumpur and a modern technical secondary school, both of which have received financial aid from the Colombo Plan and loans of experts.

The Technical College at Kuala Lumpur was established in 1941 when a school for railway personnel, established in 1906, was reformed and broadened. The college, now completely financed by the federal government, offers three-year courses in civil, electrical, and mechanical engineering, telecommunications, surveying, and architecture. There also is provision for some holders of degrees from the Technical College to complete their education in overseas universities. In addition, a new technical college, Singapore Polytechnic, has been established in the Colony.

The College of Agriculture, like the Technical College, grew out of a departmental training school; it had been maintained for the training of Department of Agriculture employees. The college offers three-year courses in agriculture, including practical training on the college experimental station.

Nursing and teacher training schools complete the technical and vocational educational facilities of the country.

The University of Malaya was established in 1949 when the Raffles College of **Arts and the King Edward** VII College of

Medicine were consolidated. There are about nine hundred students enrolled in the university, and only the shortage of facilities has prevented much greater enrollment. Since the establishment of the university there has been an expansion of curriculum to include social sciences and extended engineering, agriculture, and medical training facilities. Special departments for Chinese, Malay, and Indian studies have been created. The University has been selected as the site of an educational testing center, supported by the ministries of education in both the Federation and Singapore, and operated under the guidance of personnel from the U.S. Educational Testing Service. Certain of the liberal arts and engineering faculties have been shifted to Kuala Lumpur, leaving the science and medical schools in Singapore.

The long-heralded Nan-yang University, aimed at increasing the opportunities for higher education for students advancing through the Chinese school system, was finally established in 1956 on Singapore island. The primary language of instruction is Chinese.

Adult education too has received considerable attention in recent years. This program has been expedited in order to raise the rate of literacy of the Federation in anticipation of self-government. The Adult Education Association of the Federation was organized in 1951 and has worked with experts of the United Nations on the problem of literacy. The association has received ample financial support from the government. Two courses of study which have assumed importance have been those in English and civics. In 1952 there were 11,000 students in 400 classes, and by 1953 the number had risen to 33,500 students in 1,180 classes. The Council for Adult Education in Singapore organizes classes for 10,500 students. For the most part, the classes are held in English, though there are also classes held in Tamil, Malay, and Chinese. Fees are charged for this program which, though small, are enough to cover the administration of the program. The Malayan Chinese Association has organized its own adult education program involving over 15,000 students. The Malayan Public Libraries Association also has been pursuing a successful program of adult education, especially in technical subjects in the "New Villages" and kampongs.

The distribution of the language and literacy communities, the availability of equipment, the reading habits and abilities of audiences, and transportation determine the structure and function of the mass media in Malaya. The press (newspapers, magazines, and books), radio, and motion picture distribution are affected by these factors.

The press

In 1954 there were published in the Federation and Singapore some 26 daily newspapers, 10 weekly papers, and more than 140 other general and special interest periodicals. These publications were printed in seven different symbol systems: English, Chinese, Malayalam, Tamil, Punjabi, Jawi, and Rumi.

The daily newspapers. --Table 25 shows the available total circulation figures for each language group of the daily press for the years 1947 and 1952. The increasing dominance of the

TABLE 25
DAILY CIRCULATION OF NEWSPAPERS,
1947 AND 1952

	1947*	1952†
English	110,500	124,500
Chinese	115,300	148,000
Malay	17,300	36,000
Tamil	25,400 ⎫	
Malayalam	5,000 ⎬ 30,900	21,500
Punjabi	500 ⎭	
Total	274,100	330,000

*UNESCO, Report of the Commission on Technical Needs in Press, Film, Radio, 1947 (Paris: UNESCO 1948), II, 158.

†UNESCO, Department of Mass Communication, The Daily Press, A Survey of the World Situation in 1952 (Reports and Papers on Mass Communication, No. 7 [Paris: UNESCO, 1953]), p. 26. The compilers appear to have mistakenly combined Malayalam with Malay. Therefore, the figures given above for the Malay and Indian vernacular press have been readjusted by comparison with the 1947 ratios.

English and Chinese papers is apparent. The Malay papers have more than doubled their circulation, but it remains small.

The Indian vernacular papers have apparently lost considerable circulation. In relation to the size of the various literacy communities the differences are even more striking, as indicated in Table 26.

TABLE 26
SIZE OF LITERACY COMMUNITIES
AND ASSOCIATED NEWSPAPER CIRCULATION

	Literacy Community*	Circulation[†]	Copies per 1000 Literates[‡]
English	294,406	124,500	0.423
Chinese	924,728	148,000	.159
Malay	674,297	36,000	.053
Indian	211,048	21,500	.102
Total	1,860,470	330,000	.178

*Del Tufo, Malaya, pp. 351-441. The figures for "Chinese" and "Indian" are for literacy in "any language" under the assumption that at least the major part of Chinese or Indians literate in any language are literate in Chinese or one of the Indian vernaculars, respectively.

[†] UNESCO, The Daily Press, 1952, p. 26. See note, Table 25, above.

[‡] Since the literacy figures are based on 1947 data and the circulation figures are for 1952, the "Copies per 1000 Literates" figures are not real for any particular time. However, it is believed that they do represent within a slight margin of error an adequate basis for comparison of newspaper coverage among the various communities.

It appears that the English-language press enjoys by far the greatest distribution in relation to its associated literacy community. Perhaps more important, only a relatively small number of Europeans and Eurasians are included in the English community. It seems reasonable to assume, therefore, that about three-fourths of the circulation of the English-language press is distributed to members of the Chinese, Malay, and Indian ethnic groups. The distribution of Malay papers among the Malay community, on the other hand, appears extremely low; this might indicate a large Malay readership for the English-language papers. Too, the distribution ratio for the Chinese papers appears low, considering the size of the Chinese literacy community and the fact that the Chinese enjoy the largest circulation of the four groups. The circulation ratio for the Indian vernacular papers is also small, although in consideration of its recent declining circulation it was probably much larger in 1947.

A third view of the press in Malaya is provided by figures showing the number of different papers published each year from 1947 to 1953 (Table 27).

TABLE 27
NUMBER OF DIFFERENT NEWSPAPERS, 1947-1953

	1947	1948	1949	1950	1951	1952	1953
English	13	11	10	8	7	7	7
Chinese	10	9	9	8	8	10	9
Malay	4	4	4	3	4	4	3
Tamil	7	7	5	4	4	4	4
Malayalam	1	1	2	2	2	2	2
Punjabi	1	1	1	1	1	1	1
Total	36	33	31	26	26	28	26

Both the English and Tamil papers show significant de-creases, but for apparently different reasons. Whereas the de-crease in the number of Tamil papers appears as a result of a proportionate decline in Tamil population and subsequent readership, the decrease in the number of English papers is accompanied by a considerable increase on total circulation. One result of the decline has been to increase the importance of Singapore as a newspaper publishing center for Malaya (Table 28).

Thus, although the number of papers publishing has declined

TABLE 28
PLACE OF PUBLICATION OF NEWSPAPERS, 1947-1953

	1947	1948	1949	1950	1951	1952	1953
Singapore	16	15	14	14	14	15	13
Federation (total)	20	19	17	12	12	13	13
Kuala Lumpur	8	7	7	5	5	6	6
Penang	9	9	8	6	6	6	6
Ipoh	3	3	2	1	1	1	1

in all four centers, the greatest decline has taken place in the Federation. This has been accompanied by an increase in the circulation of Singapore-published papers in the Federation. About half of the total English-language circulation in the Federation is published in Singapore; this represents about 40 per cent of the total number of copies published in Singapore. In 1950 Singapore-published papers accounted for 75,000 out of a total of 151,000 papers of all types distributed in the Federation, while circulation in Singapore alone accounted for an additional 112,000 copies. Of a total of 263,000 circulation in both Singapore and the Federation, Singapore-published papers accounted for some 188,000 or 71.5 per cent. Although valid data are not available, there is reason to believe that this ratio has been increasing steadily since 1950. There is apparently very little distribution of Federation papers in Singapore.

English-language papers are published at Singapore, Kuala Lumpur, and Penang. Of the seven published in 1953, four were published in Singapore, one in Kuala Lumpur, and two in Penang. Only three of the seven English-language papers are controlled by the British, although two of those three, the Straits Times of Singapore and the Malay Mail of Kuala Lumpur, are perhaps the most influential papers in the country. There is an apparent lack of competition among the various English-language papers. Two of the seven are essentially afternoon editions of their more important associated morning papers. The Straits Echo and Times and Penang Gazette combination in Penang and the Malay Mail at Kuala Lumpur enjoy near monopolies in their areas. The Indian Daily Mail's content tends to make it a specialized paper. The only true competition appears to be between the Straits Times and the Singapore Standard in the immediate Singapore-Johore Bahru area, but even there the editorial and managerial characteristics of the two papers probably appeal to widely different audiences--the Straits Times attracting a conservative, pro-British readership composed largely of Europeans, upper-class Malays, and perhaps a few Indians; the Standard attracting a largely Chinese audience.

Of the nine Chinese-language dailies published in 1953, four were published in Singapore, two each in Kuala Lumpur and Penang, and one in Ipoh. There is an apparent tendency among the Chinese-language newspapers to become organs in their circulation areas for particular dialect communities or special interest groups, thus mitigating their competitive nature. The

166

left-wing Chinese press is centered in Singapore and enjoys a predominant position in terms of circulation both there and in the Federation.

Three Malay newspapers are published--one each in Singapore, Kuala Lumpur, and Penang. All three Malay papers have very low circulations, as has been noted. However, the Malay habit of reading the paper aloud in the villages results in a far greater effective audience than is indicated by the mere facts of distribution. Majlis, in Kuala Lumpur, is considered the leading Malay paper, and it has become increasingly important, because of its location, as the organ of Malay officialdom and nationalism. There is little competition among the three papers for an audience.

Of the Indian vernacular press, the Tamil is the most extensive and the most important. Two Tamil papers are published in Singapore, and one each in Kuala Lumpur and Penang. The two Singapore papers possibly operate competitively, but distance separates the two Federation papers, and there is little probability of competition between them or with the Singapore papers. Two Malayalam evening papers are published in Singapore. About half of their combined circulation goes to the Federation, and it is probable that they are competitive papers. The sole Punjabi paper is published evenings at Kuala Lumpur. Its circulation is the smallest of any daily, around 750 copies.

Three factors have been stressed in this survey of the daily press in Malaya: (1) the intercommunity predominance of the English-language press, (2) the increasing importance of Singapore as the newspaper publishing center for both the Colony and the Federation, and (3) the relative lack of competition among the various papers.

The importance of the English-language papers lies in their function as intercommunity media. Whereas members of any particular community are unlikely to read the papers associated with any other community, it appears that a considerable segment of all of the three major communities tends to read English-language papers. It appears likely that these non-European readers of the English-language press are the bilingual and biliterate elite of their respective communities. It would seem, therefore, that whereas the various Chinese, Malay, and Indian papers tend to perpetuate community differences, the English-language press, at least on the upper lev-

167

els, leads toward a growing commonality of interest among a certain class of all the communities.

The importance of the growth of Singapore as the newspaper center for Malaya is associated with the division of the country between the Colony and the Federation. It appears that the greatest circulation increases for the Singapore papers have taken place in the Federation. In effect, at the present time nearly half the newspapers read in the Federation are published outside the Federation and thus outside the effective control of the government of the Federation. To some extent this situation appears detrimental to the growth of a national press in the Federation, although it tends to strengthen the commonness of interest between the Federation and Singapore.

The tendency for each newspaper to cater to a distinct group has led generally to a situation in which each newspaper becomes an organ of that group. In only a few cases is there any suggestion of competition between two newspapers for the attention of the same general audience. Editorial and content differences among the various papers appear to correspond to community differences, except, as noted above, in the case of the English-language papers, which divide along regional and political lines.

It must be concluded, however, that the daily press in Malaya appears adequate in relation to demand, even if not in relation to what is most desirable from some points of view. There is apparently little general demand for either prompt or general news coverage. The papers, in catering to particular groups, seem to express and satisfy the desires of the group, and little more is asked of them.

The weekly newspapers. --A number of the daily newspapers publish special Sunday editions, and there are also several weekly papers published in the Federation. [14] Unfortunately circulation figures on the weekly press are not available. As in the case of the daily press, Singapore, Kuala Lumpur, and Penang are the major publishing centers.

A considerable fluctuation in the weekly publishing field ap-

------

14. This discussion has omitted consideration of the "mosquito" press of Singapore. Since 1950 a considerable number of these four-page tabloid "scandal-sheets," all in Chinese, have appeared and disappeared from the Singapore publishing scene. Only a few have lasted for any appreciable length of time.

pears to have taken place between 1947 and 1953, as indicated in Table 29. In those years the number of English-language weeklies dropped considerably in the Federation, while the Tamil press moved completely to the Federation. The increase of the Malay weekly press by two papers is also significant.

TABLE 29
LANGUAGE AND PLACE OF PUBLICATION
OF WEEKLY NEWSPAPERS, 1947-1953

	English	Chinese	Malay	Tamil	Total
1947					
Singapore	2	4	1	1	8
Federation	6	1	0	0	7
Total	8	5	1	1	18
1953					
Singapore	2	3	2	0	7
Federation	2	1	1	2	6
Total	4	4	3	2	13

It seems likely that the weekly press in the Federation will become of increasing importance until such time as the demand for more up-to-the-minute news arises. Economically, the weekly is more feasible in a low-advertising area, while still fulfilling a needed communication function. In the Federation the importance of the government in the weekly field is noteworthy. Both government-sponsored weeklies enjoy large circulations, the first with fifty-eight thousand weekly copies in 1955, the second with twenty-five thousand.

The periodical press.--Periodicals published in Malaya, other than daily and weekly newspapers, range from tri-weeklies to quarterlies. They are published in English, Chinese, Jawi, and Tamil. The two main publishing centers are Singapore and Kuala Lumpur, with only a few published elsewhere. Only a few circulation figures are available for the periodical press, and those are concerned only with government-sponsored publications.

The kinds of periodicals and the language of publication for periodicals reported published in the Singapore Annual Report, 1952, are shown in Table 30. The predominance of Chinese-language periodicals in the Singapore periodical field has been apparent since 1946, although there was a temporary sharp

169

decline in 1948 when only three Chinese magazines were published. Also noticeable is an emphasis on triweekly, biweekly, and weekly publications, with nineteen of the twenty-six periodicals published in 1952 appearing weekly or oftener. Two other characteristics of the Singapore periodical press are the fairly rapid turnover in the field and the emphasis on commercial, entertainment, and consumer interests.

TABLE 30
SINGAPORE PERIODICALS: TYPE AND LANGUAGE, 1952

	Triweekly	Biweekly	Weekly	Bimonthly	Monthly	Total
English	-	-	2	1	-	3
Chinese	2	4	7	1	1	15
Malay	-	-	3	-	4	7
Tamil	-	-	1	-	-	1
Total	2	4	13	2	5	26

Of the total of fifty-two magazines listed as having been published in Singapore between 1946 and 1952, only twenty-six were still in publication in the latter year, and fifteen of these had been started only that year. Only three periodicals published continuously throughout the entire period. This instability appears due both to financial problems connected with insufficient capitalization and revenue and to audience limitations in relation to content.

Although the many Chinese names make thorough identification difficult, the prevalence of such titles as Radio Weekly, The Amusements, Rediffusion News, and Utusan Film, and Sports indicates the high preponderance of entertainment and consumer interest content among the Singapore periodicals.

In comparison with the Singapore publications, a number of significant differences appear in the Federation (Table 31). English and Malay are the predominant languages of publication, and there is greater emphasis on monthly and quarterly publication, with no periodicals published oftener than twice a month. The Federation periodical field had a later start than the one in Singapore, but its growth has been more even than the latter. Of the forty-two periodicals listed as published between 1947 and 1953, twenty-two were still in publication at the latter date, and each of these had been in publication for at least two years, and many longer. Also apparent is a greater emphasis on educational, indoctrinal, and informational periodicals, to the near exclusion of entertainment and consumer-interest magazines. One reason for these differences would appear to be the predominance of government-sponsored publications in the Federation. Of the twenty-two periodicals published in the Federation in 1953, thirteen were government-sponsored; among these were the only Chinese- and Tamil-language periodicals.

TABLE 31
FEDERATION PERIODICALS: TYPE AND LANGUAGE, 1953

	Bimonthly	Monthly	Quarterly	Total
English	1	4	4	9
Chinese	-	3	-	3
Malay	1	8	-	9
Tamil	-	1	-	1
Total	2	16	4	22

In the over-all picture of the periodical publishing field in Malaya, the most noticeable distinction is the contrast with the pattern of newspaper publishing. The Tamil periodical press is virtually nonexistent. The English-language periodical press is extremely weak in Singapore while comparatively substantial in the Federation. Chinese periodicals predominate in Singapore, with no independent publications in the Federation. The Malay periodical press is relatively strong in the Federation and in Singapore and is the only group with periodicals published in the Federation outside Kuala Lumpur (at Kota Bharu, Penang, Seremban, and Johore Bahru).

The periodical press, with the weekly newspaper press, appears in some ways to make up for the insufficiencies apparent in the daily newspaper field as far as the Malays are concerned. It is questionable, however, to what extent this would be true if it were not for the government-sponsored publications.

News sources. --There is no national or regional news-gathering agency servicing Malaya. Thus, news is either received from the various international agencies maintaining branches in the region or collected by the individual publications.

International agencies serving the papers of Singapore and

the Federation are Reuters, the United Press and the Associated Press of the United States, the Central News Agency of China, Persibiro Indonesia Aneta, Kantorberita Antara of Indonesia, Pan-Asia Newspaper Alliance, and the United Press of India. Reuters is the oldest and leading agency in both the Federation and Singapore, primarily providing foreign news for local distribution and in addition a small service in domestic news items. The United Press began operations after World War II. Their service includes general news, features, and photographs. The agency is generally stronger in the Federation than in Singapore, with the Chinese press as primary subscribers. The Associated Press was the third large agency to enter the area. Its primary business is in Singapore. Services include special commercial news releases (which compete with Reuters) and a large airmail feature service.

The Central News Agency of China is a Nationalist government-sponsored agency which distributes in Chinese to Chinese newspapers. Aneta is an independent Indonesian news agency with headquarters in Jakarta. Its operations are confined to Singapore. Antara is the national news agency of Indonesia and is the only agency providing a service in Malay. Pan-Asia, a regional agency operating out of Hongkong, specializes in news of Asian countries for Asian readers. Two of its subscribers to its services are located in Singapore. It is probably one of the few truly regional services in operation. The United Press of India maintains a correspondent at Kuala Lumpur who distributes UPI releases to the Indian press in the Federation.

Four of the latter services--CNAC, Aneta, Antara, and UPI--are engaged primarily in sending local news of China, Indonesia, and India to the Chinese, Malay, and Indian papers in the Federation and Singapore. It does not appear that they compete to any great extent with the larger international agencies on news of international affairs or events in other parts of the world. Local Indian news is also received by the Indian vernacular press through Reuters from the Press Trust of India.

The agencies also act to collect news of events in Malaya and Singapore for transmission to the outside world. The three large international agencies are fairly catholic in the news they select for transmission. The Chinese, Indonesian, and Indian agencies tend to gather and transmit news pertaining to the situation of the Chinese, Malay, and Indian ethnic groups. Singapore is a base for correspondents representing a number

172

of British and American newspapers and news-gathering agencies. Japan's Asahi Shimbun is also represented.

In addition to the regular news services, a number of official information offices of governments with representatives in Singapore or the Federation provide news bulletins for the press, while the governments of Singapore and the Federation maintain public relations organizations for the distribution of official information to the newspapers and news agencies. Some of the daily newspapers maintain arrangements with British and American newspapers and feature syndicates for the republication of features and articles.

For local news coverage each paper relies largely upon its own staff supplemented only slightly by material from the news services. Most of the larger papers maintain "stringers" throughout the country and permanent correspondents in the larger centers.

The relative importance and emphasis of the various news sources serving the press of the Federation and Singapore tend to condition the kinds and emphases of content. Three dominant characteristics might be noted: (1) large international press services offer a political, general, and economic service concerning world affairs in general; (2) smaller national press services from China, Indonesia, and India feed news of events concerning their areas to their nationals in Malaya; and (3) a small force, maintained largely by the English-language press, provides local news information.

Personnel. --The ethnic composition of personnel engaged in the publishing, advertising, and printing industry in Malaya in 1947 is shown in Table 32.

The Chinese predominate in almost all fields in the publishing industry. Most significant is their dominance as employers, managers, and foremen and as authors, journalists, and publishers. This predominance is of such a nature that they can be said almost to control the press in Malaya. Chinese dominance cannot be accounted for only by their employment on Chinese publications, and it must be assumed that they form an important element in the other language presses. Perhaps as surprising is the small number of Europeans employed in the publishing industry.

Summary. --The most significant factor concerning the press in Malaya is its diversity. The various publications appeal to different audiences, differ in content emphasis, and perform different functions.

The Chinese-language papers and magazines are primarily for the Chinese, the Malay-language publications for Malays, etc. Within these larger divisions, moreover, different publications appear as organs for different groups divided by community, location, and organizational affiliation. The English-language publications, on the other hand, appear to overstep community differences, being read by members of each of the other communities who are distinguished by their ability to read English and by a higher degree of education and status within the community.

TABLE 32

PUBLISHING INDUSTRY PERSONNEL, BY ETHNIC GROUP, 1947[*]

	Europeans	Chinese	Malays	Indians	Eurasians	Total
Industry						
Newspaper production	44	839	187	249	39	1,390
Government printing and bookbinding	21	2,719	633	797	30	4,266
Advertizing	9	251	21	8	8	302
Total	74	3,799	841	1,054	77	5,958
Occupation						
Employers, managers, and foremen	14	333	21	47	4	424
Hand compositors and typesetters	-	523	221	309	1	1,066
Linotype operators and stereotypers	-	120	25	56	2	211
Authors, journalists, publicists, etc.	48	254	43	57	23	445
Total	62	1,330	310	469	30	2,146

[*]Del Tufo, Malaya, pp. 448-549.

In catering to different groups the various newspapers emphasize content that appeals to the groups which they serve. Thus, Chinese newspapers emphasize news concerning the Chinese communities in Malaya and events concerning China and Chinese elsewhere. Indian newspapers are predominantly occupied with news of India, the Malay papers with events in the Malay and Moslem world, including Malaya. The English-language papers emphasize intercommunal and extralocal news demanded by their more highly educated and cosmopolitan audience. Different content emphases may also be noted between those periodicals published in Singapore and those in the Federation. The former emphasize entertainment and consumer interests; the latter, educational and informational content.

A relationship exists between the characteristics of the audience and the interval of publication. Among the Chinese publications, daily newspapers and weekly periodicals predominate; among the Malays, weekly papers and monthly periodicals. Most periodicals published in Singapore are weeklies; those published in the Federation are monthlies.

Largely because of the varying relationships between publications and their primary audiences, each tends to fulfill different but similar functions. Thus, the various Chinese, Malay, and Indian publications emphasize and enhance the group affiliation of their audiences, while at the same time perpetuating the differences between each group, while the English-language press attempts to create and perpetuate mutual interests among the biliterate elite sections of each community, fostering greater integration on the upper social and political levels.

Radio broadcasting

In Malaya there are two organizations concerned with the production and transmission of radio broadcasts, the British Far Eastern Broadcasting Service and Radio Malaya. In addition, a private company--Rediffusion (Malaya), Ltd., a subsidiary of British Relay Services, Ltd.--operates wired transmission services similar in content to radio broadcasting services in Singapore, Kuala Lumpur, and Penang.

The British Far Eastern Broadcasting Service. --This service was organized at Singapore in 1946 as the "Voice of Britain" for propaganda and military purposes in connection with British Army operations in the Far East. Under the policy control of the Foreign Office in London, its primary transmission area was the whole of Southeast Asia with the exception of Malaya. Originally conceived as a temporary operation, it was later decided that it should be made permanent. The British Broadcasting Corporation undertook the operation of the service in 1948, although policy remained under the direction of the Foreign Office. The service shares the studio and transmitter site at Jurong with Radio Malaya.

Because of the nature of the desired audience of the service, programs are divided on a linguistic basis, with an English-language section, a Siamese section, and an Indonesian section predominant. Broadcasts are also made in Burmese, French, Vietnamese, Dutch, Bahasa Indonesian, Kuo-yü, Cantonese, Japanese, and several Indian dialects. The programs are usually made up of relays from the BBC, mostly news bulletins and talks, and music from the service's record library.

Although the service is aimed primarily at audiences outside of the Federation, considerable areas of Malaya are probably within its reception range. It is likely that listeners within those areas tend to use it as an alternative station to Radio Malaya or other short-wave transmitters in the Southeast Asian region.

Radio Malaya. --The history of radio broadcasting in Malaya begins in 1922, when two amateur stations were placed in operation in Singapore. In 1936 the British Malayan Broadcasting Corporation, under the control of the Federated States government, began a regular broadcasting schedule. In 1940 the government of the Crown Colony organized the Malaya Broadcasting Corporation. Shortly after the end of World War II the two organizations were united under the Pan-Malayan Department of Broadcasting and operated under the name of Radio Malaya.

The Pan-Malayan Department of Broadcasting is responsible to both the Federation and Singapore governments. The main offices, studios, and transmitters are located at Singapore and Jurong, while stations and relay stations are maintained in the Federation at Malakka, Kuala Lumpur, Ipoh, and Penang, with Kuala Lumpur the central station. The entire organization is under the over-all control of a general director appointed jointly by both governments. Operationally, however, certain functions are divided between the independent Departments of Broadcasting of Singapore and the Federation, the former operating the Singapore installations, the latter the installations in the Federation, with the director and his staff as the coordinating agency. In 1952 the Federation Department of Broadcasting was combined with the Department of Information, the Malayan Film Unit, and the temporary Emergency Information Service under a Director General of Information Services responsible to the Member for Home Affairs, with headquarters at Kuala Lumpur. The operating budget for Radio Malaya is supported by contributions divided on a proportional basis between each government.

Radio Malaya operates three networks--Blue, Red, and

176

Green. The Blue Network broadcasts almost entirely in English; the Red Network in Malay, Tamil, several Chinese dialects, and a little English; and the Green Network entirely in Chinese dialects. With the inauguration of the multichannel VHF radio-telephone trunk system connecting Singapore, Kuala Lumpur, Malakka, Ipoh, and Penang, the older method of program relay from Singapore via short wave was eliminated. Now a single "general" program, made up of contributions from all four stations, is available over each network. Certain periods of each day are also allocated to purely local programs. The bulk of program material, however, still originates in Singapore.

The three networks' programs are broadcast from Singapore over medium-wave transmitter to the immediate Singapore-southern Johore area and over short-wave transmitters to those areas not within medium-wave range. At Kuala Lumpur significant sections from all three "general" programs are integrated for retransmission over both medium and short waves. In a similar manner, both the Penang and Malakka transmissions are made up of selections from the three "general" programs, interlaced with locally produced programs.

The specific objectives of Radio Malaya are:

> (i) providing a full and regular news service, (ii) focussing listener's loyalty and interest upon Malaya, (iii) encouraging responsible discussion on matters of public interest, (iv) stimulating interest in the work of Government, (v) raising cultural standards, (vi) broadcasting to schools, and (vii) providing entertainment. [15]

Programing on Radio Malaya has generally reflected these objectives. The networks stress three kinds of program: (1) general interest and news, (2) school broadcasts, and (3) community listening. Under "general" programs are included classical and popular music, variety, stories and drama, talks and features, religion, and sports broadcasts. The general category consumes the major share of total broadcasting time. Some of the music programs are produced locally by Radio Malaya's own orchestra, but a considerable number are tran-

---

15. Colony of Singapore, <u>Annual Report, 1954</u>, p. 187.

scribed or recorded. Music, drama, variety, and features in English are for the most part relayed or transcribed from BBC, Radio SEAC, Radio Australia, the National Broadcasting Company in San Francisco, All-India Radio, and other outside sources. Religion, lectures, and sports broadcasts and most of the vernacular programs are produced locally. The amount of time devoted to the different kinds of content varies among networks in view of the ethnic differences of the audiences. Increased local production has tended to emphasize "things Malayan." Audience participation and unrehearsed broadcasts on controversial subjects were introduced for the first time in 1952. Tape recordings made in villages, describing the lives and patterns of living of various peoples, are broadcast in an attempt to create a greater mutuality of understanding among all groups.

There appear to be considerable variations in the kinds of programs broadcast to different linguistic communities, as can be seen from Table 33.

TABLE 33

RADIO MALAYA: KIND OF PROGRAM IN RELATION TO AUDIENCE

(percentages of total broadcast time for 1948 and 1953)

	English		Malay		Chinese		Tamil	
	1948	1953	1948	1953	1948	1953	1948	1953
News	10	8	15	13	18	22	18	13
Talks	6	11	10	10	10	5	10	10
Entertainment	86	81	75	77	72	73	72	77

The growth of total broadcasting time is shown on Table 34.

TABLE 34

RADIO MALAYA

TOTAL HOURS OF NONSCHOOL BROADCASTING

PER WEEK FOR SELECTED YEARS

Year	Hours
1947	75
1948	86 1/4
1950	105
1952	184 1/2
1953	240
1954	230

The primary reason for the greater emphasis on news broadcasts for the Chinese shown on Table 33 and the considerable increase in total time between 1950 and 1952 shown on Table 34 is accounted for by the installation of the Green Network, which, in broadcasting to a number of different Chinese dialect communities, required a greater amount of total broadcast time. This factor is reflected in figures for proportions of total broadcasting time devoted to various linguistic communities, in Table 35.

Educational programs are produced and broadcast apart from the general broadcasts and are aimed directly at the

TABLE 35
RADIO MALAYA
PERCENTAGE OF TOTAL BROADCAST TIME
IN RELATION TO AUDIENCE

	1947	1948	1950	1952	1953
English	33.3	43.5	52.0	39.5	35.5
Chinese	28.3*	23.1*	18.0†	34.5‡	40.0‡
Malay	20.0	17.3	14.0	13.5	14.5
Tamil	18.3	15.6	17.0	12.5	14.0

*Includes Kuo-yü, Cantonese, Hokkienese, and Hakka.
†Includes Kuo-yü, Cantonese, Hokkienese, Hakka, and Tiechiu.
‡Includes Kuo-yü, Cantonese, Hokkienese, Hakka, Tiechiu, and Foochow.

classroom in the schools. The Schools Broadcasting Service operates as an independent subsection of Radio Malaya, with a permanent staff for each linguistic community under a general director. The permanent staff writes and produces almost all the school broadcasts, but from time to time the general broadcasting staff or outside artists and writers are called upon for special aid. The service is guided largely by a consultative committee composed of representatives of the Departments of Education of Singapore and the Federation who meet with representatives of the Broadcasting Department once each year or oftener to determine the policy and direction of the programs. During the year the Departments of Education remain in close cooperation with the schools broadcasting staff.

School programs are presented on weekday mornings during

179

the school year, with less time on Saturdays and Sundays. The number of hours devoted to school broadcasts has increased steadily since they were inaugurated in 1947, as shown in Table 36. Particularly noteworthy is the much greater proportional increase in English and Malay school broadcasts in comparison with Chinese school broadcasts over the period covered.

TABLE 36
NUMBER OF HOURS PER SCHOOL YEAR
DEVOTED TO SCHOOL BROADCASTS, BY AUDIENCE,
FOR SELECTED YEARS

	1947	1950	1953	Per Cent Increase 1947-1953
English	105	172	405	285
Chinese	108	172	207	92
Malay	76	80	162	113
Tamil	-	-	99	-
Total	290	424	873	201

A UNESCO report for 1950 notes the following subject emphases in the school broadcasts: ". . . Music, singing, literature, hygiene, civics, nature study, history, current affairs, etc., with, in addition, English courses for the Malay and Chinese schools." Particular attention appears to be paid to the teaching of English to Chinese. "In all the programmes for Chinese schools there was a judicious mixture of 'Malayanisation' material; e.g. a number of songs dealt with the Malayan scene, and a high proportion of the stories came from Malaya or India or England."[16]

The school broadcasts are intended for the age groups 8 to 19 years (for the English schools), 8 to 17 (for the Chinese schools), and 6 to 15 years (for the Malay and Indian schools). There are programs applicable to adult education, however, and some of the morning school programs are rebroadcast in the evening for adult consumption. In addition, some of the programs offered by Radio Malaya as general broadcasts have educational aims, such as weekly talks on health and hygiene, commentaries on progress in agriculture, medicine, and the

---

16. Colony of Singapore, Annual Report, 1949, p. 135.

social sciences (as they relate to life in Malaya), discussions of public institutions and democratic procedures, broadcasts on art and literature, and English-language courses.

In 1948 the governments of Singapore and the Federation began intensive efforts to provide broadcasting services to the large numbers of the population living in small villages and rural settlements throughout the country. In 1951, with the increase in the number of community listening receivers, a new division of the Department of Broadcasting was set up to provide special programs for this new audience. The Federation Annual Report for 1951 noted of this operation:

> Daily programmes for "community listening" broadcast in Malay (1 1/4 hours), Hakka (3/4 hour), Cantonese (3/4 hour), Kuoyu (1/2 hour) and Tamil (1/2 hour) include Malayan and a little world news, talks, dialogues and plays on health, farming, smallholding, the Rural and Industrial Development Authority, trade unions, elections, thrift and every aspect of the Emergency. . . .[17]

The aim of the community listening project in 1953 was "to bridge the gap between Government and people and to counter subversive propaganda."[18]

In conformity with the different kinds of programs, three primary audiences may be noted: (1) the general audience, (2) the school audience, and (3) the community audience. Each of these is, of course, divided by linguistic and dialect differences. The growth of the general listening audience may be seen in the figures on the number of receiver licenses taken out each year, shown in Table 37.

The only ethnic or linguistic breakdown on the general audience was made in the Federation Annual Report, 1947. At that time, of the total receiver licenses issued, "5,787 were held by Chinese, 1,912 by Europeans and 1,544 by Malays."[19] There is some reason to believe that a roughly similar ratio prevails at present, with the Chinese predominant. It also is probable that the saturation point among the European popula-

---

17. Federation of Malaya, Annual Report, 1951, p. 182.
18. Federation of Malaya, Annual Report, 1953, p. 315.
19. Federation of Malaya, Annual Report, 1947, p. 100.

tion has been reached and that further increases in receiver ownership will take place among the other ethnic groups. The figures in Table 37 include school listening sets, and those for the later years might include rediffusion receivers, although this is not clear from the data. Unfortunately, the distribution and location of receivers in the Federation cannot be determined from the available data, nor the proportions of sets equipped for short-wave reception, medium-wave reception, or both.

TABLE 37
RADIO RECEIVER LICENSES ISSUED, 1947-1953

Year	Federation	Singapore	Total
1947	11,043	11,818	22,861
1948	22,443	19,193	41,636
1949	34,711	24,547	59,258
1950	46,522	27,097	73,615
1951	60,000*	30,233	90,233*
1952	82,119	33,346	115,465
1953	121,660	42,470	163,130
1954	125,286	45,442	170,728
1955	135,347	-	-

*Approximate.

Data on the size and growth of the school audience are more plentiful than for the general audience. The governments generally equip government schools with receivers, while subsidized schools are allowed to devote a part of their subsidy for this purpose. About half the English schools fall into each category; nearly all the Malay and Indian schools are government-operated, while the majority of the Chinese schools are subsidized. Table 38 shows the number of schools for different linguistic communities having school receivers for selected years of the period 1947-1952. In the case of the school broadcasts to the Chinese, dialect differences do not appear to be a factor, since most, if not all, teaching is in Kuo-yü. The accelerated emphasis on school receivers in the Federation is apparent, as is the increasing tendency to favor the Malay schools.

The community listening audience is largely located in small rural villages, mining settlements, estates, etc. With

182

TABLE 38

NUMBER OF SCHOOL RECEIVERS, BY TYPE OF SCHOOL, 1947-52

	1947 Fed.	1947 Sing.	1947 Total	1950 Fed.	1950 Sing.	1950 Total	1952 Fed.	1952 Sing.	1952 Total
English	72	28	100	142	51	193	190	107	297
Chinese	26	29	55	319	61	380	379	74	453
Malay	20	7	27	221	13	234	403	20	423
Indian	-	-	-	-	-	-	184	8	192
Total	118	64	182	682	125	807	1156	209	1365*

*By the end of 1955, the number of receivers is estimated to have risen another 30 per cent.

the aid of grants from the Colonial Development and Welfare scheme the governments, especially that of the Federation, have been able to expand the community listening service throughout the country. By 1955, under the Colonial Development and Welfare grants, there were 1,050 community listening sets installed, mostly battery operated. [20] The allocation of these sets by state and settlement is shown in Table 39. The sets are allocated according to priorities based on Emergency needs and lack of the usual means of news dissemination. The scheme is administered on the basis of dual responsibility; the state and settlement governments are responsible for the

TABLE 39
FEDERATION: ALLOCATION OF COMMUNITY LISTENING SETS, 1955

State or Settlement	Battery Sets	Main-Connected Sets	Total
Perak	196	48	244
Pahang	149	9	158
Johore	96	11	107
Selangor	100	4	104
Negri Sembilan	84	11	95
Kelantan	87	2	89
Trengganu	71	8	79
Kedah	64	-	64
Malakka	53	2	55
Penang	32	7	39
Perlis	16	-	16
Total	948	102	1,050

20. Federation of Malaya, Annual Report, 1955, p. 395.

selection and changing of sites and the general supervision of the sets and their operators, and the federal Information Services are responsible for the administration of funds, documentation, and over-all supervision.

Radio Rediffusion. --In August, 1949, wired program distribution services were inaugurated in Singapore and in Kuala Lumpur by Rediffusion (Malaya), Ltd. A third service was opened by the company in Penang in 1954. All three systems operate under government charter.

In Singapore, programs are distributed from the company's studios to a number of substations over lines rented from the electric company. From these substations distribution is carried out over wire laid by the company to speakers installed for the use of the individual subscribers to the service.

Subscribers may choose either of two programs: the Gold Network or the Silver Network. The Gold Network is entirely in Chinese; the Silver Network uses English, Malay, and some of the less widely spoken Chinese dialects. The programs are about 60 per cent musical recordings, but in addition they include one newscast daily, edited by the company, a large number of live broadcasts from the company's studios, and broadcasts, program material, and newscasts relayed from Radio Malaya.[21]

Total transmission time per week in Singapore in 1954 was reported at 224 hours. Total subscribers in all of Malaya are about fifty thousand.

It is probable that the majority of this audience is Chinese, accounting for a preponderance of broadcast time in Chinese.

Summary. --Radio broadcasting in Malaya is under complete government control, with the two governments operating Radio Malaya on a partnership basis. It is the Singapore government, however, which appears as the dominant partner, and policy and direction are largely the function of the Singapore staff. In effect, the Federation system is largely dependent upon Singapore for programs, and Singapore determines the content of those programs.

Apparent in both policy and practice is the government's tendency to consider radio broadcasting primarily as a medium for indoctrination, information and education, with the entertainment function receiving the least priority. Content appears

---

21. Colony of Singapore, Annual Report, 1954, p. 192.

to be determined by the preferences of the government, rather than the preferences of the audiences. Emphasis is placed on broadcasts for the English-speaking audience, both general and in the schools, and a relatively large amount of time is devoted to news broadcasts to the Chinese communities.

The above factors assume increased significance in consideration of audience characteristics. The audience appears to be predominantly Chinese, despite the emphasis upon English-language broadcasts and the fact that most of the content is not particularly designed to appeal to the Chinese communities. It is, perhaps, this factor which has led to the success of the radio rediffusion companies in Singapore and Kuala Lumpur, whose content emphases are primarily entertainment and whose audience is predominantly Chinese.

Cinema

The per capita rate of film attendance in Malaya is probably the highest in the world. Although no total attendance figures are available, enormous numbers of the urban population are regular cinemagoers, and mobile cinema units reach a large audience in the rural areas. The latest available figures (1951) show a total of more than fifty-five permanent theaters, with a total seating capacity of over seventy thousand, and an even greater number of commercial mobile units operating throughout the countryside. In Singapore alone in 1953 there were thirty-seven permanent cinemas and forty-six open-air and mobile cinemas reported. Heavy attendance is indicated in Kuala Lumpur, with a weekly attendance of about one hundred thousand persons out of a population of 176,195 (1951).

Three types of films shown may be distinguished: (1) entertainment features and shorts, (2) newsreels, and (3) informational and educational films. Programs usually consist of a newsreel, one or two shorts, and a single feature. Most cinemas change their programs more than once a week, while the smaller ones often show up to five feature films per week.

The mobile cinemas usually make their showings at villages, estates, or mining settlements, remaining as long as business warrants, then moving on to the next spot. Rather than charging a single set of fees, as is the case with the permanent urban theaters, the mobile cinemas usually set a fixed expense-plus-profit price for each stop, which is then divided by the number of persons attending, the individual cost varying accordingly. Usually the admission price runs about a third of that at a permanent theater. The mobile cinemas usually use 16-mm. film, whereas the permanent theaters are equipped with 35-mm. projectors. The increase in the number of mobile cinemas is reflected in a gradually increasing number of 16-mm. entertainment films imported since 1950.

Most of the entertainment film used in Malaya is imported. Annual imports are between six hundred and seven hundred films. This includes almost the entire American and British production, a large part of the Chinese and Hongkong production (in both Mandarin and Cantonese), and a considerable part of the Indian production (in Hindi and Tamil). Films are also imported from Indonesia, the Philippines, Italy, Canada, Australia, France, Egypt, and the Soviet Union. Usually only one copy of each film is imported for distribution around the circuits.

Singapore is the center of film distribution for most of the Southeast Asian region, with more than ninety film distributors reported for 1950. Films are usually rented to exhibitors on a percentage basis. Block-booking, combined selling, and to a certain extent blind-booking are practiced, but booking more than six months in advance is prohibited.

A few entertainment films are produced in the country. In 1954 there were four local production companies producing films for distribution in Malaya, Thailand, and Indonesia. They produced a total of twenty-three films in that year. The primary producer is Shaw Brothers, Ltd., which usually runs its films in its own theaters first, then rents them for second runs to other houses. There are no available data on personnel, although the 1947 census suggests that a considerable share of the film industry, managerial and technical, is in the hands of Chinese.

The governments of the Federation and Singapore retain legal and financial controls on the industry. All films shown must be submitted to the Board of Film Censors, a body responsible to both the Colonial Secretary in Singapore and the Chief Secretary of the Federation. During the height of the Emergency, in 1949-51, a number of films were censored for excessive gunplay, violence, and sabotage, which it was feared might incite the audience.

American and British newsreels are imported regularly and usually are exhibited within two weeks of issue. The American newsreels in particular are exhibited in Chinese theaters, with dubbing-in of Mandarin and Cantonese. Newsreels are

imported occasionally from China. Local news stories are covered by the Malayan Film Unit cameramen and are often included in American or British newsreels, or are shown on programs in addition to the regular newsreels. Informational and educational films shown in Malaya include those made by the Malayan Film Unit in the Federation and those imported from other countries.

The Malayan Film Unit was established in 1946 for the production, distribution, and exhibition of informational and educational films concerning Malaya and Malayan problems and for bringing the various communities in the country into closer acquaintance with one another. More specifically, it was hoped that the unit could counter, to some extent, the disruptive tendencies following the war and aid in the creation of an informed and articulate public. The unit operates as a semi-independent organ of the Federation Information Services. Production by the unit in 1948 was limited largely to newsreels and an occasional short documentary film. The following year the operations were put on a commercial basis, with the unit contracting for special films as ordered and purchased by the various departments of the government. Films on cooperative marketing of rubber, mine defense, and army operations were made for the Cooperative Department, the Department of Mines, and the Defense Forces. As the Emergency continued into 1950, the emphasis on documentary films showing aspects of the fighting, defense methods, and political indoctrination were intensified.

The growth of the unit's documentary film production can be seen in the increase in the number of films delivered for distribution, from 19 in the period 1947-49 and 52 in 1950 to 111 in 1951. In 1952 the unit was reorganized and became part of the Films Division of the Information Services. The emphasis on production was changed from short-term Emergency topics to larger aspects of the policies of the government in education, youth organizations, agriculture, trade unionism, local government, rural and industrial development, and similar subjects. The unit's production is distributed primarily through the various departments which have ordered films or through the Information Services. However, the unit itself distributes copies of its newsreel stories to foreign newsreel companies. The unit also rents its documentary films to private exhibitors, in the Federation and Singapore and overseas.

Outside sources of informational and educational films are

governmental information services such as the Central Office of Information in London or the United States Information Service, or international agencies such as UNESCO or the World Health Organization. Films borrowed from such agencies are usually distributed through the Information Services film library.

Film is the most far-reaching and potentially the most effective of the mass media. This potential is, however, mitigated by content and the characteristics of the audience. The values, attitudes, and pictorial emphasis of the films vary widely in accordance with the numerous sources of origin. For example, Chinese films depict situations, problems, and values intimately related to the Chinese background and are therefore of limited meaning to individuals outside that cultural tradition; the same is true of films with other national origins. There is little general concurrence on specific standards for the various films and therefore little cohesive effect upon the audience.

The government of the Federation, through the Malayan Film Unit, has attempted to counter these factors and to achieve greater Malayan consciousness among the audience with films of Malayan backgrounds, while at the same time exercising a censorial right over the more disruptive aspects of films from outside sources. The government films, however, are largely of an informational and educational nature and lack the entertainment value of the imported films.

As is the case with other mass media, the Chinese are apparently predominant in both the production and the audience functions.

Other communications media

Government information services. --Both the Federation and Singapore, as has been mentioned, maintain information services charged with the dissemination of governmental information, maintenance of public relations and press liaison for the governments, and general administration of all indoctrinational and educational activities through the mass media.

The most recent activities of the information services have been of two kinds, the dissemination of general information and education through various forms of the mass media to the general public, and propaganda operations in support of the armed services during the Emergency. Perhaps the most important instrument for the first activity has been the mobile film and public address units located throughout the Federation. The allocation of such mobile units is shown in Table 40. It is estimated that these mobile units reach more than one million people each month. [22]

Emergency operations of the information services include the preparation of propaganda leaflets, posters, and booklets, radio material, and films designed either to weaken Communist sympathizers and subvert their resistance or to counter Communist propaganda among the general population. The chief direct medium for reaching the Communists is the leaflet. Second in importance is the use of "voice" aircraft, capable of delivering an audible message from a height of 2,500 feet. Less effective are direct radio operations.

TABLE 40
FEDERATION: ALLOCATION OF MOBILE UNITS, 1954

	Vans	Jeeps	Land Rover	River Units	Total
Perak	7	3	3	1	14
Johore	9	2	3	-	14
Pahang	5	-	3	3	11
Selangor	6	-	2	-	8
Kelantan	1	3	3	1	8
Kedah/Perlis	4	1	2	-	7
Negri Sembilan	4	1	2	-	7
Trengganu	1	3	1	2	7
Malakka	3	-	1	-	4
Penang	3	-	1	-	4
Headquarters (Kuala Lumpur)	-	3	3	-	6
Total	43	16	24	7	90

Rumor. --The Federation Annual Report for 1953 (p. 341) notes:

Quite as important as any direct channel to the Communist terrorists is the news which reaches them through their contacts with the rural population. . . . groups of defectors have been used

22. Federation of Malaya, Annual Report, 1955, p. 394.

189

to spread as widely as possible among the rural
people an understanding and rejection of communism, combined with the knowledge that Government welcomes and rehabilitates any genuine de-
fector from the Communist terrorist organization.

This is the only instance of the purposeful use of word-of-
mouth contact noted in any of the literature. It is apparent the
government feels it to be effective.

In a number of other countries in the less developed areas
of the world, word of mouth is perhaps the primary, if not the
only, means for the dissemination of information. Isolation
tends to make the trader a primary medium of communication,
linking one village with another and with the outside world. The
extent to which this is true in Malaya, however, is open to
doubt, since few areas of the country are truly isolated. The
bulk of the Malayan population lives in areas relatively well
serviced by the mass media of press, radio, and film. Furthermore, among this majority population linguistic differences tend to restrict free word-of-mouth circulation to particular communities and localities. Within such linguistic restrictions, however, there is undoubtedly considerable free
flow of rumor and word-of-mouth information. Among the Malays, the habit of reading the newspaper aloud to the inhabitants
of the kampong is a form of word-of-mouth communication.
News gained by the listener is passed along to other members
of the family and friends who were not present at the reading.
It is doubtful, however, that word-of-mouth plays much of a
role in intercommunity communication in Malaya.

7. The Malays in Malaya

MALAYA IS PART of the Malaysian realm of Southeast Asia. Immigration of Malaysian peoples, particularly from Indonesia, has taken place for centuries--sometimes as waves, such as those of the Bugis in the eighteenth century and the Javanese in more recent years, at other times as a mere trickle. Since all share common ultimate origins, the term "Malaysians" will be used here to identify all peoples who commonly speak a Malay language, are Moslems, and share a general culture. [1] This does not mean that there exists anything like perfect homogeneity among the peoples identified as Malaysians. Nevertheless, there is a fundamental cultural similarity among the Malaysian peoples in Malaya, based upon (1) a common origin in the so-called "Proto-Malay" or "Aboriginal Malay," (2) a common experience of first Hinduization then Islamization, (3) analogous ecological backgrounds which have helped produce a characteristic orientation toward the resources of the Malaysian world, (4) a basically common language, and (5) a common history of domination by a European power, whether Dutch or British.

In addition, there is a tendency on the part of all Malaysian peoples in Malaya to find a common political identity in the face of the threat of domination by the numerically equal Chinese population. There is a growing consciousness of the sep-

---

1. On this term there is some agreement among writers in the field. See Judith Djamour, "Adoption of Children among Singapore Malaysians," Journal of the Royal Anthropological Institute of Great Britain and Ireland, 1952, p. 159.

arate identity of the Malaysians with respect to the Chinese and Indians. This identity is reinforced by a growing sentiment for a pan-Malay unity and a concern with closer relationships with Indonesia. [2]

Historical Background

The ethnic origins of the modern, civilized Malay--the Deutero-Malay or Coastal Malay--are the subject of much controversy. It is said that he originated from the mainland of South Asia. How he came to the Malayan peninsula and what transformations he underwent en route are unknown. Suffice it to say that a southern Asiatic people did migrate from the mainland, probably around 2,000 B.C., [3] and populated the coastal regions of the peninsula.

From the basic physical stock provided by the migrations from mainland Asia, the modern Malay has been developed through accretions from other peoples. The importance of subsequent admixtures is stressed in the following statement about

---

2. The nature of the relationships which may develop between an independent Malaya and Indonesia are by no means clear, however. The importance of the Malays of Indonesian origin in Malaya's politics is unquestioned. At the same time, the economic and political record of the Republic of Indonesia has not been the most encouraging, and Abdul Rahman, the Federation prime minister, has indicated his disapproval of some of President Sukarno's policies. Malaya's ethnic diversity makes for problems which differ markedly from those of Indonesia. Immediate efforts at cooperation may be along cultural and linguistic lines, in standardizing a language usable in both countries. The Filipinos at the eastern extreme of the Malayan world maintain cordial, but far from intimate, relations with Indonesia, and the possibility of an integrated Pan-Malaysia seems both as near and as remote as a United States of western Europe. See Willard A. Hanna, "Indonesia and the New Malayan States," (American Universities Field Staff Report, WAH-5-'56), February 20, 1956.

3. R. O. Winstedt, The Malays, a Cultural History (rev. ed.; London: Routledge and Kegan Paul, Ltd., 1950), p. 11. Winstedt uses the estimates of Heine-Geldern and van Stein Callenfels.

192

the modern Malay by Winstedt: "This broad-headed individual with more or less Mongoloid features, olive skin, lank hair and thin beard is the Proto-Malay plus many foreign strains derived from intermarriage with Chinese from the Chou period onwards, with Indians from Bengal and the Deccan, with Arabs and Siamese."[4]

Of greater importance than the earlier immigrations and intermarriage, however, has been the more recent incursions of other Malaysian peoples from the adjacent Indonesian archipelago. Among the earliest immigrants were the Minangkabau from Sumatra, who in the fourteenth century were attracted by the wealth and commerce of Malakka and moved into what is now Negri Sembilan and Malakka. In the cultural field, the impact of their matriarchal background is felt to this day. In the early eighteenth century, Bugis from Celebes established themselves in what is now Selangor and somewhat later in the century became politically dominant in the Rhio-Johore empire. Cultural differences among these Indonesians and others, such as Balinese and Achinese, are said to be still visible, as are differences between the Malays of Kedah and Kelantan and the Malays in the southern part of the peninsula who have been more directly affected by the Indonesian invasions. Still other groups, such as the Patani Malays of northern Perak, were driven south from Thailand in the middle of the nineteenth century and retain aspects of the Thai culture.[5]

Immigration from Indonesia continues to diversify the Malaysian population in the peninsula. In 1947 Malaysians living in Malaya but born elsewhere comprised about 13 per cent (309,000 persons) of the Malay population.[6] The largest group of these were from Java (63,000). The existence of pan-Malaysian feeling makes the migrational link between the two Malaysian peoples more than a numerical matter. The numbers actually involved in this migrational stream to the Federation

---

4. Ibid., p. 15.

5. R. O. Noane, "Notes on the Kampongs, Compounds, and Houses of the Patani Malay Village of Banggul Arai, in the Mukim of Batu Karau, Northern Perak," Journal of the Malayan Branch of the Royal Asiatic Society, April, 1948, p. 125.

6. M. V. Del Tufo, Malaya: A Report on the 1947 Census of Population (London: Crown Agents for the Colonies, 1949), pp. 310, 316.

are cited in Table 41. Comparable data for the Colony of Singapore are not available. The number of immigrants to Singapore is believed to be very small, but the influence of Indonesian Malaysians in Singapore politics is known to be considerable.

TABLE 41
INWARD MIGRATIONAL SURPLUS OF INDONESIANS*

Year	1st Half January-June	2nd Half July-December
1949	-2,500	+2,905
1950	-2,023	-4,171
1951	-4,692	+2,305
1952	+4,085	+3,837
1953	-1,669	+9,748

Surplus 1949-1953: 7,734

*Federation of Malaya, Annual Report, 1953 (Kuala Lumpur: Government Press, 1954), p. 7.

Bases of Livelihood

Agriculture[7]

Table 42 shows the Malaysians to be pre-eminently an agricultural and rural people. Paddy cultivation and fishing together occupy about 75 per cent of those gainfully employed and may be subsumed under the category of a "peasant economy."[8] Common to the Malayan peasant economy, in both its agricultural and fishing sectors, is the use of rice as the primary food staple. The importance of this grain to the Malayan fisherfolk is illustrated by the use of the word nasi, or cooked rice, as a synonym for food. [9]

The demand for rice far exceeds the supply in Malaya, and

7. Malayan agriculture in general is discussed in Chapter 10.

8. For an elaboration of this concept of the peasant economy and its relevance to Malaya, see Raymond Firth, Malay Fishermen: Their Peasant Economy (London: Kegan Paul, Trench, Trubner and Co., 1946), pp. 22-23.

9. Rosemary Firth, Housekeeping among Malay Peasants (The London School of Economics and Political Science Mono-

TABLE 42

OCCUPATIONS OF MALAYSIANS, IN THE FEDERATION, 1947*

Occupation	Malays	Other Malaysians	Total Malaysians	Per Cent of Total Malaysians Gainfully Employed[†]
Fishermen	40,754	684	41,429	5.5
Agriculture (Paddy planters)	453,627	93,233	546,860 (386,570)	74.0 (51.1)
Food, drink, and tobacco mfr.	5,767	659	6,426	0.85
Wood and furniture mfr.	21,202[‡]	781	21,982	2.9
Transport and communication (excluding clerical staff)	24,221	1,616	25,837	3.4
Commercial and financial occupations	24,048	1,756	25,804	3.4
Public administration and defense	15,046	169	15,215	2.0
Professions	12,741	616	13,357	1.75
Personal service	8,476	1,084	9,560	1.4
Others	22,611	2,713	25,324	3.3
Total	628,493	103,311	731,804	97.0

*Less than 1 per cent of the Malaysian population lived in the Colony of Singapore in 1947.

[†]Total Malaysians gainfully employed: 751,310.

[‡]13,636 were women.

about one-half of the rice needed in the country must be imported. In the kampongs of Malaya, [10] rice is important not only for food but for certain ritual practices as well. [11] The Malaysian population, however, as distinguished from the other ethnic groups in the country, is estimated to be about 80 per cent self-sufficient in rice. The greater part of Malaya's

graphs on Social Anthropology, No. 7 [London: London School of Economics and Political Science, 1943]), p. 43.

10. The kampong is the basic rural settlement unit of the Malaysian population. It should be differentiated from Chinese settlements. See Chapter 4 for a discussion of Malay settlement patterns.

11. For ritual practices a form of glutinous rice is customarily used.

rice deficit is attributed to the urban and estate population. [12] While it has been noted that in Malaya, as elsewhere in Asia, World War II has decreased the dependence upon rice as a staple food, [13] the decrease has been difficult to evaluate. Wheat flour, introduced during the war in many Asian countries and increasingly favored among townsmen as a rice substitute, has been unacceptable as a substitute for rice among the Malaysians, [14] and rice has maintained its preferential status.

Malayan subsistence agriculture is, ideally, made up of self-sufficient kampongs. Paddy fields surround the house clusters. Within each cluster vegetable and tree gardens, including the coconut palms, durian, mango, and other fruit trees, clothe the settlement in green; and goats and chickens roam among the houses. To an essentially vegetarian diet may be added fish from the streams and drains around which the kampong is situated or from the sea if the kampong is near the coast. The need for money is theoretically small and may be met by occasional labor off the kampong during the rice off-season or by the cultivation of fruit, coconut, or rubber trees.

In fact, however, money and cash crops are immensely important. The fruit, coconut, or rubber cash crop not only assures the cultivator of a source of cash but tends to stabilize his agricultural economy by affording productive activities for the time when he is not working with rice. It is this economic balance which many observers have commented upon when the paddy-kampong complex is stressed. [15] Moreover the Malaysian paddy cultivator is becoming increasingly dependent on non-

12. P. T. Bauer, Report on a Visit to the Rubber-Growing Smallholdings of Malaya, July-September, 1946 (Great Britain, Colonial Office, Colonial Research Publication No. 1 [London: H. M. Stationery Office, 1948]), p. 20.

13. E. H. G. Dobby, Agricultural Questions of Malaya (Cambridge: Cambridge University Press, 1949), pp. 16-17.

14. David R. Rees-Williams, "The Malayan Situation in 1948," Three Reports on the Malayan Problem, Part I (New York: Institute of Pacific Relations, 1949), pp. 5-6.

15. See, for example E. H. G. Dobby, "Settlement and Land Utilization, Malacca," Geographical Journal, December, 1939, p. 471; or C. W. S. Hartley, "Establishment of New Rice Areas in Malacca," World Crops, May, 1951.

paddy sources of income such as rubber trees or labor in a nearby town, to the detriment of attempts to increase rice production.

Rice is, of course, the basic crop of the Malaysian peasant agriculturalist, as well as the most important commodity for which fish are sold by the Malay fisherfolk. In the traditionally typical kampong, such as those described by Dobby in Malakka, rice rarely leaves the kampong. The grain remaining after obligations are settled is stored as paddy and processed a few grains at a time as the need arises. [16] In the Kelantan villages studied by Rosemary Firth, from one-third to one-half of the food budget was spent for rice with cash earned by fishing. In the Kelantan case the attachment to rice was affirmed because, unlike the paddy planters, the fishermen have cash with which to purchase rice substitutes if they wish.

Most fruit and vegetables are grown in the kampong area for kampong consumption only. There seems to be no important vegetable cash-cropping such as that practiced by the Chinese, who have attained a high degree of specialization in truck gardening, especially around the larger cities. Similarly, there is no specialization in fruit, but each kampong has a few fruit trees supplying the local needs.

Livestock play only a restricted role in Malay agriculture, in part because there is little good natural pasture in the country, and where it does or can be made to exist it must compete with more productive land uses. Most of the larger beasts associated with kampong life are water buffalo, or kerabau; as in Indonesia, the Philippines, and some parts of mainland Southeast Asia and southern China they are used as draft animals. Some Siamese humped cattle are also employed as draft animals. Consumption of meat is low and is restricted for the most part to certain ceremonial occasions. This is explained by the basic importance of draft animals to the Malay cultivator and by taboos against pork among Moslems, which militate against the pig, ubiquitous in Chinese rural settlements. Every kampong, however, contains numerous fowl, chiefly chickens, and these provide an important source of animal protein in a typically low-protein diet.

Most of the paddy production is associated with a variegated

---

16. Dobby, "Settlement and Land Utilization, Malacca," p. 472.

kampong economy which inevitably is characterized by one or more nonrice cash crops; but rice also may be a cash crop, as it is in Burma and Thailand. The Malayan cash-grain areas are primarily in northern Kedah around Alor Star, northern Kelantan, and northern and central Trengganu, all areas of predominantly Malay settlement.

These primarily rice-producing areas have been settled relatively recently. Along the west coast, some, such as Krian, date only to the opening of the present century, while the others may be no more than twenty-five years old. Particularly significant has been the high proportion of Indonesian Malays associated with these areas. A possible explanation of this association is that the Malays of Malayan origin have been reluctant to move from their home kampongs because of the ritual and other associations which these places have for them and also because the newer, irrigated developments have not provided sizable enough kampong areas in relation to cultivable land to suit the Malays. In the absence of high native Malay interest in these developments, the Indonesian Malaysians have taken advantage of the opportunities afforded by them. [17]

The agricultural patterns in the "rice bowl" regions differ from those in other Malay areas in that the vertical monoculture of rice is practiced. In north Kedah, 95 per cent of the cultivated land below the fifty-foot contour is planted in rice, and only scant attention is given to the cultivation of other crops on the higher ground. [18] This region was developed at the same time as the areas now in rubber and tin, but the motive force for development was indigenous and traditional. The area has been reclaimed from mangrove forest and peaty swamps, and the rate of reclamation has been impressive. Population and paddy land have increased eightfold since 1850, when the region was first settled. Since that time 185,000

---

17. The Government in Malaya has, since the early 1930's, slowly extended the amount of land available for intensive wet-rice cultivation through the irrigation and drainage department of the Department of Agriculture. In addition, the rice farmers themselves have slowly reclaimed lands adjacent to their kampong bases from jungle, swamp, or beach.

18. Dobby, "The North Kedah Plain: A Study of the Environment of Pioneering for Rice Cultivation," Economic Geography, October, 1951, pp. 287-315.

acres of swamp have been converted to paddy land by the traditional technology and with no inducements for the pioneers beyond the immediate products of their labor. The reclamation was done communally by persons living contiguous to the swamp land in return for some share of the produce of the plots. The reclamation work was usually carried on during the slack season between February and April, and a crew of twenty to thirty men could develop seventy acres in about two months.

Such development demands substantial capital investment by farmers whose incomes are low and whose net surpluses are minute. In Table 43 is shown the capital investment for equipment by a Kedah paddy planter working ten relongs (one relong equals 0.75 acre) and having a buffalo of his own, in 1946.[19]

TABLE 43
COST OF RICE CULTIVATION EQUIPMENT, KEDAH

Buffalo	M$200.00
Cost of plow	25.00
Roller	25.00
Rake	30.00
Tajak	9.00
Changkol	4.00
Kuku kambing	4.00
Harvesting knives (3)	6.00
Wooden barrel for thrashing	15.00
Mats (10 pieces)	30.00
Nyiru jarang (sieve)	2.00
Bakol mengkuang	1.00
Sacks (6)	6.00
Total	M$357.00

19. The primary hand implements used in paddy cultivation are the following: kuku kambing, a pointed or double-pointed, frequently elaborately carved, stick for transplanting; pisau menuai, the small, curved knife used for harvesting rice; sabit, a sickle; kais, a hoe; tajak, an eighteen-inch cutting blade mounted on a three-foot handle; changkol, a hoe of Chinese origin; sikat, a rake; niru and lesong tangan, winnowing plates; bakol mengkuang, a fiber basket; intau, a rice sifter. Other implements of importance to the Malay agriculturalist

199

The relatively large amounts of capital required by the Malay paddy farmer provide one major barrier to the expansion of paddy agriculture, which must therefore be subsidized in some fashion. In addition, the Malay farmer is hampered by lack of credit, by insecurity of tenure, and by fragmentation of his holdings. Thus, the tendency of the sons of peasant cultivators to leave the farm for the towns and cities is partially explained by the difficulties facing the paddy farmer, which are only in part countered by the deep and near-mystic attachment of the Malay to his land, to rice, and to his kampong.

Fishing

Although fishing as a main activity occupied less than 6 per cent of the Malaysian population in 1947, there is a long historical if not actual commitment to it. Grist calls it a "trait" originating with the early Sumatran immigrants to Malaya. [20] Fishing the streams, drains, and sea is still an important subsidiary occupation for most of the Malaysians. In the Malakka and Kelantan-Trengganu regions the re-establishment of fishing as a main occupation among the Malays occurred between the years 1900 and 1930 when transportation facilities were increased in the eastern coastal region and the substitution of money for barter facilitated the division of labor which allowed for specialization in fishing. [21]

The degree of this specialization can be seen in the occupational distribution among the Kelantan-Trengganu fishermen, where, according to Firth, 75 per cent of the adult males had fishing as their main occupation, 10 per cent had some sort of middleman occupation, 10 per cent performed services asso-

---

are those associated with rubber tapping, such as knives, latex cups, spouts, buckets, coagulating pans, and sieves. See D. H. Grist, An Outline of Malayan Agriculture (London: Crown Agents for the Colonies, 1950).

20. Grist, An Outline of Malayan Agriculture, p. 10. Grist insists that the Malays were never "devoted" to agriculture.

21. Raymond Firth, Malay Fishermen, pp. 66-67. This section on fishing is based primarily on Professor Firth's work as well as that of his wife, Rosemary Firth. Because Firth studied a rather backward community some fifteen years ago, his work does not reflect the character of contemporary Malay fishing activity, particularly on the west coast.

ciated with fishing and the fishing community, and 3 per cent
had no particular occupation. The most important secondary
occupations of the fishermen were the cultivation of rice, which
occupied over 20 per cent of the men studied, and the building
and repairing of fish nets, which occupied another 20 per cent.
Subsidiary occupations assumed their greatest importance
during the northeastern monsoon from the end of November to
February, when strong onshore winds and high seas make
fishing difficult and dangerous.

The skills associated with fishing are simple, except for
those of the expert fishermen who direct the life-net fishing.
Here, five boats are used to manipulate the life-net which is
150 feet square. The expert fisherman not only is responsible
for the over-all direction but also must be skilled at "listening
for the fish" (locating the fish for placement of the nets),
drawing in the nets, and a variety of other activities. Most of
the expert fishermen come from families in which there is already at least one experienced fisherman.

The degree of specialization in fishing in the predominantly
fishing communities raises somewhat different problems of
household economics from those associated with the more balanced economies of the diversified agricultural kampongs.
Rice and other food items must be purchased from the pro-
ceeds of fishing. This results in a much greater familiarization
with the use of money in daily activities than is characteristic
in other Malayan communities, and it places the women, as the
household managers, in a somewhat more powerful position
within the family by virtue of their control over expenditures.

The main items of daily expenditure in the household budget
are rice, snacks, meat, eggs, vegetables, fruit, tobacco,
betel nuts, spices, sugar, and oil and matches for lamps. Together, rice and snacks comprise about two-thirds of the budget. Snacks are usually coffee plus a cigarette, a biscuit and
some sweetmeat, all of which may be had in a local Malay
coffee shop. They may also consist of lemonade and roasted
nuts sold on the beach by Indian vendors. Some foods are also
purchased in Chinese shops. Most of the items consumed
daily are grown in inland areas not far from the coast of Kelantan; others must be imported, such as salt from Thailand,
timber, turtle eggs, and some fruits from the Perhentian
Islands about twenty miles away from the Kelantan coast, and
betel leaf from Trengganu.

Rice cultivated in the areas near the coast is an important

source of food for the fishermen, although it does not usually meet the needs of the community. The usual system of land tenure is the pawoh system, whereby a man will lease a small plot of land and will commit half the crop to the landowner; the tenant must provide labor, seed, and tools. Vegetable cultivation along the Kelantan coast on any but a very small scale is difficult because of poor soils and a lack of acceptable fertilizers.

In addition to food, the coastal fishermen of Kelantan must purchase other supplies connected with fishing--bamboo for fish-curing trays, baskets, and net-drying structures, rattan for certain kinds of fish traps and lashing, pandanus leaves for covers, resin for caulking boats, and timber for boat building. From the west coast they procure mangrove bark for the dyeing of their nets. Before the war, ramie twine, nets, and cotton yarn came from China, through Singapore. Certain kinds of boats are purchased north of Kelantan in Thailand; others can be purchased in Trengganu. Fishhooks and other metal ware may come from Europe.

With the high degree of specialization and the dependence upon goods produced outside the fishing community, it is not surprising that there should be important middlemen operations. The Chinese have assumed many of these operations, although in the Kelantan-Trengganu area the degree of Chinese control is considerably less than in the western and southern parts of Malaya. The Chinese middleman, or towkay, advances money or goods such as rice and cloth to the fishermen against the security of future catches. He loans money for the purchase of boats or equipment or he may supply them at no cost in return for the option as first purchaser of the catch at a price which is usually below the free market price. This is called the daganang system. By this system the middleman assumes the risk of advancing capital and bears the burden of fluctuating market prices. On the other hand, he achieves a monopoly over much of the landed fish and reduces the Malay fisherman to the position of a debt-worker who cannot thenceforth take advantage of good market conditions to raise his own income.

Malay fishermen are for the most part coastal people who find in the sea a full-time occupation. During the heavy-catch season associated with life-net fishing some outsiders find their way to the Kelantan area, but for the most part crews are raised in the immediate locality of the coastal villages, and there tend to be bonds of physical neighborliness as well as common interests in fishing.

The crews of the Kelantan fishing boats change, since the fishermen will tend to seek out those boat captains who are having a good season. Another way in which a fisherman is likely to maximize his welfare is to associate himself with a boat captain who has adequate resources to tide his crew over the northeast monsoon season. This is an important consideration, since during the monsoon period most of the fishermen have no other source of income except small savings from the previous season.

Firth estimated the monthly income of the Kelantan fishermen to be around M$8 in 1939-40. This compared with an all-Malayan average for fishermen of about M$11 per month. The difference between east-coast incomes and that of the west and south generally and of the Chinese fishermen in particular is a function of proximity to larger markets and better organized systems of distribution. A much closer community life still exists on the east coast, however, and kinsmen of an impoverished fisherman are more inclined to come to his aid. The obligations of the boat captain to his crew during the monsoon season also act as a buffer to widespread deprivation.

The Malay fisherman must meet certain recurrent expenditures, such as a quit rent of about M$1 per year for the land on which his house stands and a license fee for his boat, which may be about M$5 for a large boat. In addition, he has the recurrent expenditures associated with being a member of the Moslem faith. If he lives in an area where he is able to grow more than four hundred gantangs of rice, [22] he must pay an annual tithe (zakat). Since east-coast fishermen do not cultivate rice to this extent, they are not liable for this due. The fitrah, however, is a household religious fee for everyone, which may be paid in rice or money. The fee varies with the price of rice for the year and in 1939-40 was M$0.20 per capita per annum. There are a host of other, smaller taxes to which most of the fishermen are subject, such as transfer fees for the sale of boats, market fees for small sellers in the local market, and fees for the killing of cattle and for the presentation of shadow plays or spirit performances. For wealthy men there are the additional burdens of charities which

---

22. Four hundred and twenty gantangs equal one ton.

they are expected to support, as well as the local Koranic school, praying places, and wells. The fees and taxes cited here for the fishermen effect the peasant agriculturist as well.

The determination of the value and ownership of capital in the fishing society is difficult. Much equipment is in co-ownership and much is secondhand. The per capita monetized value of the boats, boat gear, nets, traps, and line fishing gear for the Kelantan-Trengganu area was estimated by Firth to be from M$35 to M$40. One-third of the fishermen owned the boats they used; the remaining boats were owned by persons who did not go to sea or by fishermen who owned several. Three-fifths of the fishermen owned at least part of a net; the remainder either were too poor or were line fishermen, who use only a small hand net. In the Kelantan area the proportion of fishing capital owned by the Malays is considered high relative to that of southern Trengganu, Pahang, and other areas where Malay fishing is important and where Chinese control is much greater under the daganang system.

Important spatial relationships exist for the Malay fisherman in two directions: (1) along the coast with other fishing communities and (2) inland with agricultural and urban communities. In Kelantan, in addition to purchasing boats from one another, communities compete for the right to fish one another's waters when certain fish are running or when the approach of the northeast monsoon prevents intensive local life-net fishing. During the monsoon many Kelantan fishermen move to other communities where they have kin and where fishing is possible. Relationships between the fishing communities and the inland villages or towns are reflected in the exchange of fish for agricultural products, sometimes at large markets such as Kota Bharu, to which also come itinerant peddlers bringing manufactured goods, food products, and perhaps betel and tobacco.

Commercial and industrial activity

The Malaysian's agricultural and fishing occupations are generally considered subsistence, but they also have commercial attributes since members of the peasant economy are producing surpluses for trade. The term "subsistence," however, indicates a large measure of local self-sufficiency and suggests that the technology applied to wet-rice cultivation and fishing is low, and that net productivity is low. Incomes from these activities are barely enough to maintain the Malay capital stock; savings are small, and even when they exist there are few means of mobilizing and using them.

The principal commercial products of the Malaysians, rubber and coconuts, differ from the subsistence products in that they enter into a larger world economy. Their production frequently yields larger incomes capable of mobilization into further productive enterprise. Nevertheless, the differences between what are considered "subsistence" activities and commercial and industrial activities among Malaysians are small compared with those in the West.

Primary economic activities. [23]--The participation of Malaysians in estate agriculture, mining, and lumbering has been relatively small. However, the employment of Malaysians in these and other industries where Chinese and Indians had previously provided the bulk of the labor force has been increasing rapidly. Before 1945 Malaysians are said to have avoided work on estates or in mines, preferring certain forms of leisure instead. [24] Since that time there has been a significant influx of Malays into occupations traditionally held by Indians. Thus, in 1948, 22 per cent of the estate labor force in the country was Malaysian, in contrast to about 7 per cent in 1938. [25] A similar movement of Malaysians into mining, factories, and public works occupations is also taking place. The replacement of Indians in these occupations has been made necessary in part by the 1938 restrictions by the Indian government on Indian emigration to Malaya and in part by postwar Malayan legisla-

---

23. Other than the production of paddy or fishing for the market.

24. T. H. Silcock and Ungku Abdul Aziz, Nationalism in Malaya (Series Paper No. 8, Eleventh Conference of the Institute of Pacific Relations, Lucknow, October, 1950 [New York: Institute of Pacific Relations, 1950]), p. 2. The motives given by these authors need not be accepted without question since there has been no empirical examination of these matters. It is difficult at all times to know the functional importance of "leisure" to the working of credit and other aspects of economic activities.

25. A. G. Donnithorne, Economic Developments since 1937 in Eastern and Southeastern Asia and Their Effects on the United Kingdom (London: Royal Institute of International Affairs, 1950), p. 23.

tion which has tended to discourage Indian immigration. Moreover, the Indian Immigration Fund, created to aid in the immigration of Indians to Malaya early in the century, is now being used to bring Indonesian workers to the peninsula and to move indigenous Malays to labor deficit areas.

Mining, lumbering, and other primary productive occupations are of little actual consequence compared to rubber and, to a lesser extent, coconut production. The number of Malays employed in mining and lumbering in 1947 was only about ten thousand.

The coconut palm is found wherever there is a Malay settlement, and the crop forms an important part of the consumption pattern of almost all Malays. So ubiquitous and integral to the life of the Malay are these trees that he may date the birth of children by them as well as provide himself with drink (milk), food (nut), fuel (husk), and other materials for the maintenance of life. Of the 500,000 acres of coconut land, about 25 per cent is devoted to the estate form of cultivation, while the remaining acreage is in the hands of smallholders. In 1947 there were 23,669 Malaysians whose main occupation was associated with the production of coconut products.[26] The bulk of these were smallholders. The average holding was about ten acres.[27]

Coconut production beyond the consumption needs of the smallholder is usually in the form of copra. Coir and desiccated coconut do not appear to be important products of coconut cultivation. The preparation of the coconut for sale as high-quality copra necessitates the use of a kiln for drying, since solar drying cannot be relied upon because of rainfall variability. The cost of a kiln is frequently beyond the resources of the smallholder. The result is reliance on sun-drying and a low-quality product.

The income from the sale of copra is in cash if it is sold to a coconut dealer, or in cash or shop credit if the dealer is also a general shopkeeper. The income is highly variable since coconut, like rubber has a radically fluctuating price structure.

---

26. Del Tufo, Malaya, p. 477 (Table 88).
27. Ungku Abdul Aziz, Some Aspects of the Malayan Rural Economy Related to Measures for Mobilizing Rural Savings (New York: United Nations, 1951), p. 11.

Rubber is the Malaysian smallholder's most important source of cash. Bauer has said that this rubber is "easily the most valuable crop produced by any local population in the British Colonial Empire . . . and is a direct source of income of several hundred thousand people."[28] It is impossible to estimate the income of the smallholder from rubber because he does not keep records and the amount received cannot be recalled; the rubber is usually sold every three days and the money immediately spent. However, the effects of the cash income are evident in the enhanced level of living of the rubber smallholder compared to that of Malaysians who do not cultivate the crop. As security against a fall in the price of rubber an attempt is made to diversify sources of income. Rubber usually provides about 75 per cent of the cash income; coconut or durian trees, which yield an average of about M$200 per year, and other cash crops provide the balance. In addition, almost all smallholders resort to agricultural self-sufficiency in times of economic stress.

In 1947 about two hundred thousand Malaysians were engaged in the cultivation of rubber as a main occupation. However, the number of persons who derive income from rubber cultivation is much greater, since many persons chiefly occupied in subsistence activities also keep a few rubber trees.

Roughly half of the smallholdings in the country are in the hands of Malaysians. A substantial number of these are Javanese Malaysians. This fact is notable in terms not only of numbers but also of the superior skills as tappers and as entrepreneurs which the Javanese immigrants display. The peasant's rubber holding is usually three to five acres. In contrast to the holder of fifteen to one hundred acres, usually a Chinese or Indian, the Malaysian is more likely to receive the benefit of manuring from the draft animals used on the contiguous paddy fields. Occasional manuring of the trees almost compensates for the fact that the trees are old and carelessly tapped by women and children, resulting in a lower productivity than the larger stands which usually are tapped by the owner with the aid of professional tappers.

Most of the smallholders' rubber is marketed as "Chinese smoked-sheet No. 2-4," which generally brings a price which

28. Bauer, Visit to the Rubber-Growing Smallholdings, p. 5.

is from 3 to 5 per cent lower than the "Ribbed smoked sheet No. 1," the product of the best estates.

Bauer, in considering the cost factors in smallhold production, lists materials necessary in cultivating three acres (shown in Table 44). To this list must be added the cost of a coagulant, which has a variable cost depending on whether it is formic acid, which is preferred by the manufacturers of rubber goods and which is more expensive, or sulphuric acid, which is cheaper but results in a product less preferred and thus brings a lower price.[29] At the higher cost for the formic acid, the costs of equipping rubber land comes to about M$25 per acre. The total costs for opening the land, i.e., equipment plus clearing, are M$50 per acre.[30]

TABLE 44
COST OF RUBBER CULTIVATION EQUIPMENT FOR THREE ACRES

Item	Cost
400 Latex cups at $9 per 100	M$36.00
400 Spouts at $0.75 per 100	3.00
400 Cup hangers at $4.00 per 100	16.00
6 Coagulating pans at $0.70 each	4.20
1 Sieve	5.00
2 Buckets	4.00
1 Tapping knife	1.00
Total	M$69.20

Unable to meet the capital costs of reopening rubber land after the war, the Malay smallholder was compelled to turn to the Chinese rubber dealer for the capital. The latter would agree to clear the land, re-equip it, and give the Malay owner some cash sum, about M$50, for the right to tap the holding for six months or a year. The cash outlay by the Chinese would be M$250 for a five-acre stand, plus M$50 in cash to the owner, a total of M$300. The six-month yield from these five acres would be about M$1,500, one-half of which the Chinese dealer would have to pay for the costs of labor and coagulating

---

29. Ibid., pp, 71, 52-53.
30. Ibid., p. 72.

material. This left him with a net profit of M$450. Alternative sources of funds for the Malaysian smallholder are limited, and Bauer is of the opinion that, all things considered, this was a practicable means for the expansion of smallhold production. [31]

When the price of the commodity is high, Aziz suggests that Engels' Law operates; that is, as income increases, a smaller proportion of it is allocated to the purchase of essential consumption goods. The results are:

(a) Increased expenditure on consumption goods and the liquidation of some debt obligations.

(b) More consumer purchases of such items as clothes, shoes, hardware, and luxury foods; more leisure; expenditures at local coffee houses; some travel to visit relatives; more movies; and the purchase of jewelry, which is a form of saving for emergency but not for investment.

(c) Purchase of more durable goods such as sewing machines, radios, refrigerators, lawn mowers, and automobiles. There also may be some saving at the local credit society, bank, or even investment in some commercial activities.

(d) Pilgrimages to Mecca and the purchase of some land or buildings. [32]

Thus, it is only after a period of high income that the smallholder will bank his savings which then become potential investment capital.

Until recently, yields from all the smallholds were about the same as those for the estates--five hundred pounds per acre in 1950. The smallholder normally plants a greater number of trees per acre, but the yield from each is lower than on the estates. In 1952 it was estimated that about two-thirds of the smallholder's trees were over thirty years old and nine-tenths exceeded twenty years of age, a factor in the lower yields per

---

31. Ibid., pp. 72-73.
32. Aziz, Aspects of the Malayan Rural Economy, pp. 11-12.

tree. An additional factor, improper tapping, has already been mentioned. Also, the smallholder often fails to allow the bark rehabilitation cycle to run its optimum course of eight years tapping, eight years rest. This permits serious injuries to the bark and shortens the life of the tree. A comparatively large area of the tree is often tapped, a practice which exposes too much of the tree to injury. This also results in lower productivity per tree since the higher the tree is tapped, the less the yields are likely to be.

There are a growing number of Malaysians working on rubber estates as field laborers, and many are associated in other ways with the production of the crop. At the time of Bauer's study in 1946 there were several thousand casual laborers and share tappers on smallholdings. Share tapping is an arrangement whereby the owner of a small stand of trees shares his profit with the persons who help him tap. This practice is associated with marginal stands which are completely tapped only when prices are high.

There are no traditions impelling the Malaysian to produce rubber. Rather, there is a rational preference on his part to cultivate a crop which maximizes his income. Despite the exhortations of the government for more attention to the production of food crops and the subsidies offered for the production of food crops, the Malaysian apparently is determined to pursue rubber cultivation.

Secondary economic activities. --The number of Malaysians occupied chiefly in manufacturing or processing is small. In Table 42 it is shown that a substantial number of Malays and relatively few other Malaysians were in 1947 engaged in the manufacture of wood and furniture products. These are primarily rattan products, and the activity is organized in reasonably large, capital-intensive factory operations. This is the major manufacturing activity of the Malaysians and occupies about 3 per cent of the gainfully employed population.

In handicraft production the manufactures are of a traditional sort consumed by wealthy kampong people or a select few among the Malaysian aristocracy. Mats and baskets, on the other hand, are produced in the kampongs for the consumption of other kampong dwellers, and in some cases there is regional specialization. [33] Some of the important handicraft

---

33. Moyra Johnson, "Malayan Arts and Crafts," Far Eastern

goods are hand-woven and printed cloth, silver work, plaited baskets and mats, silver and gold embroidery, and lace edging. All of these articles may be purchased in Singapore, and nearly all bear the marks of the individual craftsmen who produce them.

The hand-woven cloth industry is the most aesthetically advanced of the handicraft and cottage industries of the country. The cotton and silk used has been imported from Japan, India, and China, and local dyestuff is used. The best of the cloth comes from Kelantan and Trengganu. The exceptional talent in these two predominantly Malay states can be traced to early Khmer influence. [34] In Trengganu the bulk of approximately fifteen hundred hand looms (kek) are located in the subdistrict of Chabang Tiga, including the town of Kuala Trengganu. In the Chabang Tiga area, looms employing about six hundred women and young girls are owned by one man and his sister. These entrepreneurs buy and process the material before distributing it to the weavers who work on a piecework rate. [35] Most of the cloth is of the sarong type. Cloth with silver or gold thread is made in small amounts because of a limited market and the technical skill necessary. This cloth is used primarily in the courts or by non-Malays in the towns for evening wear. [36] Some of the capital used in the production of the cloth is borrowed from the government, [37] and the marketing of the cloth is arranged centrally through a cooperative, the Trengganu Handicraft Committee, and with the help of the Department of Industry and Commerce.

The silverwork of Kelantan enjoys a reputation outside Malaya. Implements and methods have been passed on through

Economic Review, September 18, 1952, p. 369.

34. M.C.ff. Sheppard, "A Short History of Trengganu," Journal of the Malayan Branch of the Royal Asiatic Society, June, 1949, p. 3.

35. A. H. Hill, "The Weaving Industry of Trengganu," Journal of the Malayan Branch of the Royal Asiatic Society, June, 1949, p. 75-78.

36. Johnson, "Malayan Arts and Crafts," p. 369.

37. Federation of Malaya, Rural and Industrial Development Authority, Progress Report up to December 31, 1951 (Federation of Malaya Paper No. 24 of 1952 [Kuala Lumpur: Government Press, 1952]), p. 15.

successive generations, and each craftsman works at his own pace and with his own designs. The two main types of work are heavy repoussé work such as trays and bowls, and delicate filigree-patterned bracelets, brooches, and pendants. The appropriateness of Kelantan silver as a wedding gift has caused a change in the functional quality of some of the silver work, and more cigarette containers and toast racks have appeared recently. As in the case of the Trengganu cloth, the Kelantan silver work is cooperatively organized in the Kelantan (Malay) Arts and Crafts Society, which is able to borrow funds from the government as well as market the products. [38]

Plaited mats and baskets are made entirely by women from the leaves of the Pandanus palm. Two kinds of product may be distinguished: (1) mengkuang, a coarse fiber produced in most of the coastal villages, and (2) pandan, which is finer and is produced in Malakka, parts of Pahang, Province Wellesley, and Kelantan. Baskets and mats of either the mengkuang or pandan type are used for a variety of household tasks and for decorating homes.

Tertiary economic activities. --Among the Malaysians service and trade occupations are not important. However, Table 42 indicates that about 10 per cent of the gainfully employed find their main occupation in tertiary activities. If persons employed in public administration and defense are included, the figure is raised about 2 per cent. The latter specializations are a consequence of the British policy favoring the diversification and expression of economic opportunities for Malays. For the rest, personal and domestic service is an urban occupation almost entirely reserved for Malaysians, especially Javanese, because of employers' tastes and traditions in the matter. Most of the commercial and financial occupations are of the small-scale sort associated with the kampong economy.

In the Kelantan and Trengganu fishing economy studied by the Firths there were: (1) many middleman operations with a number and variety of traders, (2) a high development of exchange based on money, and (3) an active role by women in marketing activities. The first two result from the need of the fishing communities to realize cash for their fish in order to obtain the necessities of life, since the land contiguous to the coastal fishing villages is too poor to cultivate economically,

---

38. Johnson, "Malayan Arts and Crafts," p. 369.

and the Malay householder must turn to others for basic goods.

In the market of the village of Perupok[39] women played an active, even "dominating," role as both sellers and buyers. While the importance of women in some of these commercial activities has been noted for Malaya as a whole,[40] such a situation is more usual in the fishing areas, because fishing is restricted to the men, whereas in paddy areas women take part in cultivation.

The marketing activities at Perupok[41] were characterized by an irregular although fairly high number of sellers. The range observed was from eight to fifty-two, the average number of sellers at any time being about twenty. In Table 45 the numbers and kinds of shopkeepers are shown.

TABLE 45
OWNERSHIP OF SHOPS IN PERUPOK AREA
BY NATIONALITIES*

Type of Shop	Malay	Chinese	Indian	Total
Grocery	9	0	2	11
General store	2	4[†]	0	6
Coffee shop	1	2	5	8
Cloth shop	5	0	0	5
Goldsmith-dentist	0	1	0	1
Total	17	7	7	31

*Rosemary Firth, Housekeeping among Malay Peasants, p. 109.
†Includes the largest shop in the area.

To the Perupok market from the inland villages of Kelantan and Trengganu came the regular suppliers of betel leaf and the irregular sellers of snacks, vegetables, home-grown tobacco, palm sugar, and coconut oil. These Malaysians jour-

39. The following discussion is based upon Rosemary Firth, Housekeeping among Malay Peasants, pp. 90-105.
40. See Winstedt, The Malays, p. 131.
41. The region serviced by the Perupok market contained a population of 1,300 persons comprising 331 households.

neyed on foot to the fishing villages to sell their produce and buy fish for the inland kampongs. Other goods, usually fruits and vegetables not available from the inland villages, were carried by women from the towns of Kota Bharu and Jelawat by bus. Malay men sometimes were associated with this trade, as when a large amount of produce was purchased and resold in the Perupok market. This larger quantity was transported sometimes by bus and at other times by trucks of wealthier Malay merchants. The Perupok market also was supplied by sea from Thailand and the Perhentian Islands and from Trengganu. The commodities in this trade, often handled by Malays, were salt and rice from Thailand, fruit and turtle eggs from the Perhentian Islands, and fruit and betel leaf from Trengganu. In the immediate area of the Perupok market Malaysian women were engaged in producing snacks, a full-time activity usually handled by widows and divorcees.

Fish were sold on the beach as the boats arrived. Except for small sales to non-Malay middlemen for transport to other markets, most of the fish were purchased by women of the village. The fish were then piled on the beach for resale to retail purchasers both from the village and from other places nearby. The arrival of the fishing fleet signaled the opening of the village market, and the success of the day's fishing determined the vigor of the market in the same day.

The profits from the trade activities of the Malaysians are very small, in part a result of the very small inventories which the vendors, particularly the women, keep. In addition, profits are kept down by competition among the multitude of small traders. Numerous vendors visit each household with wares and produce in the hope of making a sale of a few cents' worth of their commodities. Because daily expenditures are dependent upon the daily income from fishing, which cannot be neglected, most of the Malay buyers cannot go directly to the market for many commodities which must therefore be purchased in small quantities and at a high price from vendors.

Nearly all Malaysians, whether fishermen or cultivators, have subsidiary sources of cash with which to make purchases in the local market. For inland Malaysians, as well as for fishermen, this income is in the main a daily one and the same general situation may be assumed to exist.

The degree of marketing activity by women tends to diminish with the general diminution of trade by Malaysians further south along the east coast of the country. Away from the northeast, trade becomes more specialized and more highly capitalized, and Chinese participation is much greater. There is substantially less Malaysian trade participation in the western part of the country, where the Chinese and Indians have long monopolized the middleman function.

Social and Political Organization

National and supranational organization

The Malaysians of Malaya, numbering about three million, are part of the Malaysian world which contains about one hundred million persons. In language, general culture, and increasingly in political identity, the Malaysian world--Malaya, Indonesia, and the Philippines--represents a symbol to which Malaysians in Malaya can, and increasingly do, attach strong value. The Moslem religion is an especially binding factor. The Shari'a, the canonical law of Islam, is noted by Firth as "a unifying force, extra-village and extra-national in character, linking even the most remote mountain farmer spiritually and emotionally with the farmer or townsman of the other Muslim communities in South-East Asia and far beyond."[42]

An important political value of the Malaysian world is a desire for pan-Malay unity. This desire cannot be dignified with the term "movement," much less "organization," but it does recognize the ethnic ties among the Malay peoples who comprise the bulk of the Malaysian world.[43] For the Malaysians of Malaya, Pan-Malaysia represents a potential loyalty, though its significance should not be overemphazied.

Of more immediate importance to the Malaysians of the peninsula is the system of Malay states. The system in its modern form has existed for over a hundred years. Within each state there exists a political structure which links the kampongs through subdistricts and districts with the sultan at the head of the state. The Malaysian in Malaya may move

---

42. Raymond Firth, "The Peasantry in South-East Asia," International Affairs, October, 1950, p. 511. On the other hand, it acts as a major repelling factor as far as the predominantly Christian Philippines are concerned.

43. Charles Robequain, Malaya, Indonesia, Borneo, and the Philippines, trans. E. D. Laborde (London: Longmans, Green and Co., 1954), p. 418.

with ease from one state to another to establish his home. The modes of life, the language, and the expectations of life for the Malaysian are nearly everywhere similar on the peninsula.

The exceptions to this homogeneity, however, are important and bear directly upon the Malaysian political and social organization. First, the large urban centers, particularly in the western part of the country, are not a part of the Malaysian world. These are the domain of the Chinese, the Indian, and the European. Second, in the state of Negri Sembilan and some of the adjoining territory the nature of Malaysian social organization is such as to preclude the easy adoption of new community members. With these exceptions, the peninsula is a common Malay domain. Although there is little internal migration of the Malaysians within the country, substantial homogeneity exists within the peninsula.

The key political relationship of the contemporary Malaysian is with the sultanate. This relationship takes two forms. First, a Malaysian is a citizen of the country by virtue of being a subject of the sultan, and all his prerogatives as a citizen originate from this relationship. This is more than a mere formality since there usually is a strong bond of loyalty between the Malaysian and his sultan which springs in part from an earlier feudal relationship. There is keen popular interest in the pomp and ceremony associated with the sultanate and in the general well-being of the ruler. The second form of the relationship is derived from the role of the sultan as the protector of the Moslem establishment in each state. As protector of the state religion the sultan is linked to the Malaysian people of his state through imams, the religious ritual officials in the mosques, and through the kadi, the local Moslem functionaries. This link is not personal, but it is nonetheless of basic importance.

Local organization

Like the peasantry throughout Southeast Asia, the Malaysians of Malaya are most meaningfully organized at the kampong level. In their world view prime importance is given to each man's house, his fields or stretch of beach, and his kin. Though he may acknowledge strong emotional and spiritual links with his sultan and with the Moslem-Malay world beyond, and may occasionally visit the other states of Malaya, the Malaysian peasant remains tied to his kampong.

The kampong provides the Malaysian with his essential primary group. The family households which comprise the kampong share a common physical environment in which they operate in a closely organized, communal manner. They also share a common religious belief which brings them together in prayer and celebration, and a common body of customary rules (adat) which govern most of their important social relationships.

Communal effort (kotong royong) is a conspicious and important part of kampong life. Typical activities affected by this are the establishment and improvement of certain items of "community capital," such as schools, roads, dams, and drainage channels.[44] The control of water is of special importance because of the reliance upon wet-rice cultivation. Every year, just before planting, dams and channels are worked on by all members of the community. The fields are cleared of off-season growth in the same way.[45] Communal labor is also of significance in the development of new rice lands, as on the north Kedah plain.

The face-to-face relationships in the kampong primary group are reinforced by common participation in important life-cycle ceremonies and in participation in the annual sacred days of the Moslem religion. There are holidays and observances in nine of the twelve months, which bring people of the kampong together in their mosques and in their homes.

The important life-cycle ceremonies attending birth, circumcision, marriage, and death are all occasions for interaction among kin and nonkin groups. At such times, people are congregated in a quasi-religious gathering to which all contribute some cash or goods in order to help defray the cost of the gathering. In most cases the cash or goods contributed are considered a debt which the recipient on some later and similar occasion must repay. There are, however, certain minimum payments which may be made (M$1. 00 in Kelantan) which are not considered as debt-binding but merely the expression of the desire on the part of a kinsman to participate, if only symbolically, in the obligation which he recognizes.[46]

---

44. Aziz, Aspects of the Malayan Rural Economy, p. 12.

45. Noane, "Notes on the Kampongs, Compounds, and Houses of the Malay Village of Banggul Arai," p. 127.

46. Rosemary Firth, Housekeeping among Malay Peasants, pp. 119-26.

A final aspect of the organizing function of the kampong in Malaysian society is the underlying body of customary rules. These are a counterpoise to the universal rules of the Moslem religion, the Shari'a, and serve to make each Malaysian community somewhat different from every other. The customary rules generally reflect aspects of the pre-Moslem Malaysian society and, along with the Moslem rules and the later statute law of the British, govern a wide variety of social relations. Some aspects of the adat have been made into statutory law, as in the case of land inheritance in Negri Sembilan and Malakka. Still other aspects are inextricably intermingled with the rules of the Moslem religion as these rules are made and enforced by the kadi in different parts of the country.

Corporate organization

Most of the rural Malaysians are organized in corporate units of greater or less cohesion. On the one extreme may be placed certain matrilineally organized groups in less-developed areas of Negri Sembilan, which exhibit considerable group solidarity and possess effective rules for socially binding persons to a common kinship-based group. At the other extreme are the bilaterally organized Malaysians living near some large towns of western Malaya where there is considerable involvement with certain aspects of urban life and thus marginal participation in the typical kampong life.

Kinship-based organization. --Despite the quantity of literature dealing with the matrilineal Malaysian groups in Malaya, the number of people actually involved in this form of social organization is small, about 10 per cent of the total Malaysian population.

Important immigration to the present state of Negri Sembilan began in the sixteenth century. [47] The influx of matrilineally organized Minangkabau people from Sumatra continued into the seventeenth century, and during the same period there occurred the settlement and the development of the "nine states," in Malay, "Negri Sembilan."

The Matrilineal society in Sungei Ujong, the most populous of the Negri Sembilan "states," is divided into clans (suku)

---

47. R. O. Winstedt, Malaya: The Straits Settlements and the Federated and Unfederated Malay States (London: Constable and Co., Ltd., 1923), p. 245.

having a traditional territorial base. [48] Clans are of two types:
(1) <u>waris</u>, those with political power stemming from the legendary marriage with and the gaining of political power from the
aboriginal Senoi inhabitants and (2) other clans without political
power. Every clan in Negri Sembilan has a territorial base,
but within any "state" only one or two clans will have the political power which makes them <u>waris</u>. Thus in Sungei Ujong
the <u>waris</u> are the clans <u>di-Ayer</u>, <u>di-Darat</u>, <u>Ulu Klawang</u>, and
<u>Rantau</u>; these are represented in other states but have <u>waris</u>
status only in Sungei Ujong.

Each clan is exogamous and is divided into subunits, <u>perut</u>,
which are extended family groups of a definite number com-
prising the <u>suku</u>. The chief of the <u>suku</u> is called the <u>lembaga</u>.
<u>Perut</u> are organized at the level of the kampong when there
are sufficient members in kampong residence; some clans are
organized only at the level of the <u>suku</u> when their numbers are
small. The head of the <u>perut</u> is called the <u>ibu buapa'</u>. [49] The
<u>perut</u>, because it is the local unit of social organization, is of
importance both for its social control and for functions of
economic cooperation.

At the head of the "nine states" of Negri Sembilan is the
ruler of Negri Sembilan, the <u>Yang di-pertuan</u>, who is also the
highest "state" official (<u>undang</u>) of the ninth state, Sri Menanti.
He and his family differ from the rest of the ruling groups in
the system in that they practice a system of patrilineal inheritance of political office. The ruler of Negri Sembilan is considered first among equals by the five <u>undang</u> representing the
matrilineal states, and he has the special functions of defending
the state of Negri Sembilan as a whole and acting as a court
of appeal for all of the states. Since the introduction and consolidation of British administration in Negri Sembilan, effective political power is no longer completely invested in the
Malay system. Control is restricted primarily to matters of
custom and the Moslem religion.

The political system of Sungei Ujong resembles that of the

---

48. Although Sungei Ujong is used as a model here, there
are deviations from its social patterns in the other districts of
Negri Sembilan.

49. G. A. de C. de Moubray, <u>Matriarchy in the Malay Peninsula and Neighboring Countries</u> (London: George Routledge and
Sons, 1931), p. 23.

other matrilineal states. All offices are filled by election on the condition that the next highest officer confirms the choice of the lower group. When there are more than two equal groups from which candidates for a single office may be taken it is customary to practice a rotational system (giliran). Women are active politically and even hold office on occasion. The participation of women in the political activities of the community constitutes one of the important differences between the adat perpateh (matrilineal system) and the adat temenggong (bilateral system) which characterizes most Malays in Malaya.

The principal offices of the political organization are as follows: The undang, or dato klana as he is called in Sungei Ujong, is the highest political officer. The dato klana represents Sungei Ujong in the council of rulers of Negri Sembilan, consisting of four other "state rulers" like himself who constitute the advisory body for the ruler of Negri Sembilan. The dato klana is elected from one of two dominant perut of the dominant waris, di-Darat, who rigidly rotate the office. [50] The dato klana confers and seeks the advice of the dato shah bandar, a sort of prime minister, and the council of lembaga tiang balai, leaders of all the waris in Sungei Ujong.

The dato shah bandar serves as the second executive officer of Sungei Ujong. The council of lembaga tiang balai consists of the clan chieftains (lembaga) of the four waris of Sungei Ujong, and it therefore has a territorial base. Each of the four councilors has administrative responsibility in matters of custom and the Moslem religion over a specific number of administrative subdistricts.

As Moslems, the men in the matrilineal groups could have as many as four wives. However, custom decrees that only the ruler of Negri Sembilan may take four wives, and the highest official of a "state" such as Sungei Ujong may have only three. A clan chief is limited to two, and common folk to one. The vast majority of Malays are monogamous, and the persistence of monogamous marriage has been explained largely in eco-

---

50. See P. E. de Josselin de Jong, Minangkabau and Negri Sembilan: Socio-Political Structure in Indonesia (The Hague: Martinius Nijhoff, 1952), pp. 178-79. It is Josselin de Jong's contention that this rotation of office is between dual-phratry divisions of the politically dominant matri-clans (waris) in the election of the undang.

nomic terms. In the case of the matrilineally organized Malaysians, monogamous marriage must be enforced in order to protect the integrity of the matrilineal structure as well as to afford special prestige roles to the important political officers.

Law in this matrilineal society is a matter of group responsibility. Criminal law and civil law are merged into a single system based on compensation to the group of the wronged by the group of the wrongdoer. [51]

Under adat perpateh justice is administered according to strict hierarchical principles. A case may be considered first by the immediate family members of a person. If it cannot be settled there, then the head of the extended family, the perut, considers it. If the case is still not resolved, it moves to the level of the clan, where the lembaga deals with it. Finally, the case may be brought before the undang. Some crimes are serious enough to be adjudicated only by the undang.

The system of inheritance in the matrilineally organized Malaysian society is complicated and controversial, not merely among students of the subject but also among the Malaysians themselves. [52] The three systems of inheritance operative in Malaya--matrilineal inheritance, bilateral inheritance, and traditional Islamic inheritance--differentiate between ancestral property and property acquired in marriage. In matrilineal inheritance there are distinctions between an ancestral property which belongs to the clan of the woman and one which belongs to the clan of the man. The suku and perut exercise a guardianship over this kind of property, and, in the case of

---

51. This becomes a complex matter, since a married man belongs to his wife's group for some matters and to his own matrilineal group for others. It is especially complicated when a man is a chief in his own matrilineal group and only a common member of his wife's group. The problem is made even more complex because of the residence pattern. A man lives in the house of his wife but leaves each day to work on the land of his own matrilineage (his sister's land). Thus the ties to his own clan remain strong.

52. The following works discuss this problem: de Moubray, Matriarchy in the Malay Peninsula, pp. 24-181; E. N. Taylor, "Inheritance in Negri Sembilan," Journal of the Malayan Branch of the Royal Asiatic Society, September, 1948, pp. 43-130; Josselin de Jong, Minangkabau and Negri Sembilan.

land, statute law helps these units in their guardianship by insisting on their pre-emption to any land which is to be sold. A consequence of the individual control of ancestral property is greater flexibility in its management and use. This flexibility is related to the changing views held on the matter of acquired property, which at one time was as restricted in terms of its dispositions as ancestral property.

Kampong-based groups. --For the 90 per cent of the Malaysians who are not organized matrilineally, the significant corporate groupings tend to be based upon kampong and neighborhood rather than kinship. [53] The kinship system of the large majority of the Malaysians is bilateral and is thus more in line with the general characteristics of preferred Moslem social organization.

The most inclusive bilateral kinship unit is the extended family. This usually includes three living generations who occupy a common residence, which may include more than one house, and who form a corporate unit in terms of important economic and religious activities. Within the extended family the descent of status and property may be through the male or the female line.

Distribution of the property of a deceased parent is deferred until the death of the other parent; thus is maintained the unit integrity of the lands for the extended family. [54] The extended family also acts cooperatively in the observance of the major Moslem festivals, on several of which they must join in common prayer and reading from the Koran and in the organization of an "open house" for kin and neighbors.

Beyond the extended family is the "circle of relatives" (kaum). The kaum operates in an apparently diffuse but generally supportive manner. An example of its action is the Malay

---

53. The social and kinship organization of the vast bulk of the Malaysians is only now undergoing anthropological examination. In 1948 Raymond Firth could remark that "the anthropology of the Malays is still in a very weak state; despite the great amount of attention devoted to subjects such as ritual, there is as yet no proper analysis of the fundamentals of Malay kinship and social structure. Report on Social Science Research in Malaya. (Unpublished MS; 1949), p. 17.

54. Winstedt, The Malays, pp. 48-49. This applies to the husband's parents because residence is patrilocal.

fishing industry where crews ordinarily consist of a nucleus of kinsmen or entirely of kinsmen if the captain of a vessel can raise no other crew.

The kampong and _mukim_ provide the community framework for the extended family. The kampong is the physical unit of settlement of the bilaterally organized Malaysians, and although it is without organized kinship base, it is not a fortuitously organized settlement. Each kampong has its own history and predominant ethnic origin (Bugis, Javanese, Malakka-Johore Malays, and so forth), and therefore its own body of custom and status differentiation.

The kampong is the basic unit for economic and religious cooperation and the minimal unit for administration. It is a center for the mobilization of local labor for the performance of local projects. Moreover, as a political unit it supports the local mosque and religious teacher. As an administrative unit it is linked to the system of state and national governments through the kampong headman, known variously as the _ketua kampong_, _sidang_, or _dato ampat_.

The _mukim_, or subdistrict, consists of several kampongs which are situated in an area of variable size depending upon the density of the population. Several _mukim_ (six to eight) comprise a district. At the level of the district the state and federal governments have direct control, for there the lowest level of the state or federal bureaucracy is found. The liaison between the state or.federal bureaucracy and the kampong headman is the _penghulu_, the traditional Malaysian official of the _mukim_. In the present century the increased demands of bureaucratic administration have required the kampong headman and _mukim_ officials to be away from their villages for considerable amounts of time, and to some extent the previous cohesiveness of the community-based social organization is being changed by the new and expanding responsibilities of the traditional leaders.

The family. --Like other aspects of the social organization, the family can be discussed only with reference to the prevailing systems of descent.

The marriage system among the matrilineally organized groups in Negri Sembilan is monogamy. Officials may take more than one wife in accordance with their status, but there are sanctions regarding the taking of more than one wife from any single clan. [55] The data on preferential marriage are not clear. Apparently cross-cousin marriage is a permitted, though perhaps not a preferred, form. The problem of whether the family or the clan is the ultimate exogamous unit in the marriage system is not at all clear. There is further confusion regarding the apparent existence of an asymmetrical connubium system. [56]

Among the bilateral peoples the rules of Shari'a provide injunctions regarding affinity of the prospective spouse. A bride price accompanies the marriage, but the recipient is the bride, not her parents. The bride price may be in the form of either a payment to her by the husband or a deferred payment which is realized only if the husband initiates divorce. Although polygamous marriages are recognized by the Koran, frequently the husband takes an oath at the time of the marriage that an automatic divorce is accorded his wife should he take a second wife or should he absent himself on land for six months or at sea a year. [57]

Child-rearing among the Malaysians is characteristically permissive in nature, with the child receiving considerable and constant attention and affection. The community sanctions which operate against parents who are brutal or negligent with their children are rather severe. [58]

The adoption of children is an important matter. Adoption may be of Malay children or Chinese children. [59] The apparent contradiction between the love and care accorded to Malaysian children and the high incidence of adoption is reconciled in the nature of the adoption. If the adopted child be Malaysian he is called anak angkat ("raised child") and is usually given over

55. Josselin de Jong, Minangkabau and Negri Sembilan, pp. 125-28.

56. Ibid., pp. 128-29. In an asymmetrical connubium system, one exogamous unit, Clan "A," is able to take brides from Clan "B" but not from Clan "C." It may give brides to Clan "C" but not to Clan "B." According to Josselin de Jong, this is a manifestation of the over-all dual-phratry division of the matrilineal society and one in which there is a subservience of the bridetakers to the bridegivers.

57. Winstedt, The Malays, pp. 47-48.

58. Djamour, "Adoption of Children," p. 159.

59. Ibid.; Rosemary Firth, Housekeeping among Malay Peasants, pp. 83-85.

to wealthier relatives who either have no children themselves or are better able to raise the child than the poorer relative with many other children. The parents may see the child in his foster home regularly. Other forms of Malaysian adoption are less lenient in this regard, but in all there is less of a separation of the parent and the child than in the case of the Chinese child.

The Chinese child adopted into a Malaysian foster home is called anak beli ("bought child"), and here the adoption of the child is complete; the child never sees the parents again. Chinese children are favored because of this unconditional adoption and because they are fairer in complexion and thus attractive according to the tastes of the Malaysians.

Social stratification

Malaysian society on the peninsula is characterized by both a traditional, essentially political, class structure and an emergent, essentially socio-economic, class structure corresponding to that of Western society. The traditional class differentiation exists between the Malay aristocracy and the commoners. Vestiges of the pre-British feudal relationship persist though the forms are disguised. As mentioned above, there remains a strong interest and feeling of loyalty among the commoners for the sultan of the state. Within the aristocracy there are certain marriage restrictions; women may not marry beneath their class. There is a similar convention for the sultan of a state in his first marriage. [60]

Of greater importance than this customary stratification is the class structure which is evolving from the gradual integration of greater numbers of Malaysians into the increasingly variegated national fabric of Malaya. Under the tutelage of the British, Malaysians have been drawn into a large variety of occupations and roles which set many of them apart from the rural Malaysian scene. These new occupations and roles, which have in great part been associated with the government service, imply changing relationships with not only other Malaysians but other ethnic groups in the country as well.

Taylor has used the term "kampong class" with reference to the majority of rural Malaysians. [61] The socio-economic

---

60. Winstedt, The Malays, pp. 50-52.
61. E. N. Taylor, "Malay Family Law," Journal of the

differentia generally used in the analysis of social stratification would justify the term. The residence patterns associated
with the kampong, the smallholdings economic operations, and
the social-community structure of rural Malaysian society all
tend to differentiate Malaysians in the kampongs from those in
more urbanized situations, on estates, or in road labor crews.

Within the kampong class itself there is increasing stratification as the leaders become involved in the administrative
functions of mukim and district government. The feeling is
that the real issues of the kampongs are being neglected in the
interest of personal advancement on the part of these officers.[62]

In the towns the stratification of society would appear to be
occurring at a more rapid rate than in the rural areas. This
is not unexpected since the number and variety of opportunities
is much greater in the towns. In the social survey of Singapore in 1947 there was evidence of substantial stratification
and role differentiation particularly related to economic activities.[63]

Legal institutions

Three systems of law can be differentiated: statute law, the
most consistent and general;[64] customary or indigenous law;
and Moslem law, also with an autonomous development historically. The relationship between the latter two systems is
ambiguous.

The complex law of Islam is a complete body of rules which
was developed in the Arabic countries, but indigenous Malaysian law has occasioned variation and accommodation in Moslem law. Another variable in modifying the introduction of
Moslem law was the societal differentiation of Malaysian society into matrilineal and bilateral groups.

Malayan Branch of the Royal Asiatic Society, May, 1937, p. 5.

62. Charles Gamba, "Rural Development in Malaya," Eastern World, May, 1952, pp. 20-21.

63. Colony of Singapore, Department of Social Welfare, A
Social Survey of Singapore: A Preliminary Study of Some As-
pects of Social Conditions in the Municipal Area of Singapore,
December, 1947 (Singapore: G. H. Kiat and Co., n.d.), p. 52.

64. Statute law was initiated by the British, and the penal
code is that which was developed by the British in India.

At present, two factors appear to be fundamentally responsible for the continued confusion surrounding customary law and Moslem law. First, the <u>kadi</u>, those responsible for the administration of Moslem law, are themselves so steeped in the indigenous law of their region that they are unable to differentiate it from Moslem law for purposes of settling disputes. Thus, it frequently happens that a decision will be rendered in the name of the Shari'a when in fact it is in contradiction with Moslem, though consistent with the indigenous, law. More often still, the two systems of law will be compounded into a single pronouncement in the name of either one or the other. [65]

The second factor in the persistence of confusion between the two bodies of law is the ignorance of many of the civil servants responsible for the adjudication of disputes. Most of these officers are inadequately prepared in the intricacies of either system to perform their functions well. The problem is especially difficult in the case of officers transferred from the matrilineal areas, particularly in the northern part of Malaya where Moslem law dominates over indigenous law, to bilateral areas. In such cases, Moslem law is likely to be administered with little or no account taken of the important matrilineal character of the indigenous law. [66]

The sources of the Malaysian legal system are digests, dating from the sixteenth century and consisting of early unwritten law, and translations of the basic Moslem works from the Shari'a, dealing with marriage, divorce, and the legitimacy of children, which the Malaysians in Malaya have adopted almost unchanged. [67]

Religion

Landon states that the Moslems of Indonesia "are Moslemminded and have sanctified all their practices with Moslem sayings and prayers. The names of Allah and Mohammed are

---

65. Taylor, "Malay Family Law," p. 9.

66. Winstedt, <u>The Malays</u>, p. 99.

67. <u>Ibid.</u>, pp. 91-92. The sources are summarized in great detail by Winstedt. See also R. O. Winstedt and P. E. de Josselin de Jong, "A Digest of Customary Law from Sungei Ujong," <u>Journal of the Malayan Branch of the Royal Asiatic Society</u>, July, 1954, pp. 25-37.

on their lips daily. They stubbornly resist all attempts to convert them to any other religion."[68] The same is equally true of the Malaysians. There remain, however, deep commitments to pre-Moslem ritual and spiritual values.

Ritual and belief

The belief system of the Malaysians of Malaya, particularly of the rural population, incorporates a body of superstitions and ritualistic practices which are not derived from Islam. In many areas these beliefs and practices have established a recognized place in the Islamic religion of the Malaysians. Thus, at the outset, the statement that the Malaysians are unquestionably Moslems must be qualified by the statement that Islam as practiced in Malaya would not, in many of its aspects, be recognized by Moslems of the Near East. Far from detracting from the faithfulness of the Malaysian Moslems, this merely accentuates the fact that Islam is a living religion in Malaya.

Some specific beliefs, such as that in the unpropitious qualities of certain numbers and the consequent avoidance of an even number of steps on the ladders leading into the elevated Malay house, are universal in the country.[69] Of greater importance, however, in terms of the time allocated to their performance and the intensity with which they are held, are the folk rituals associated with agriculture and fishing.[70]

The best known of the ritualistic practices, even after almost six hundred years of Moslem influence, is the propitiatory ceremony preceding the planting of paddy at the onset of the rainy season. At this time goats and buffalo are slaughtered as part of the festivities marking the planting season. Trans-

---

68. Kenneth P. Landon, Southeast Asia, Crossroad of Religion (Haskell Lectures in Comparative Religion [Chicago: University of Chicago Press, 1948]), p. 163; H. Fauconnier, Malaisie, trans. Eric Sutton (New York: Macmillan and Co., 1939), p. 236.

69. Noane, "Notes on the Kampongs, Compounds, and Houses of the Malay village of Benggul Arai," p. 136.

70. By "folk ritual" is meant the body of practices which existed before the introduction of the universal religion of Islam and which continue to have a place within the cultural tradition of Moslem Malaya.

planting of the young seedlings occasions another period of ritual behavior when the shaman (pawang) ritually makes the initial planting; thereafter the transplanting is carried out by women in silence and under the prohibition of not planting an accidentally dropped seedling. Harvesting of the rice in the dry period of December and January is also accompanied by a ceremony which lasts from two to three days after the first reaping by the shaman. Harvesting is characteristically done with a special knife, the blade of which is hidden in the belief that the grain, if frightened by the sight of the blade, would lose its taste. There are other minor practices accompanying the cultivation of rice which antedate Islam in Malaya. [71]

Among the fishermen, propitiatory offerings over the boats and nets is an essential part of the routine of fishing. Considerable resources are expended as offerings, and payments are made to the shaman (bomoh) whose prayers are considered essential to the success of the venture. Just as in rice cultivation, there are definite prescribed rituals for the various stages and seasons of fishing. [72]

Important magic and mystical cults constitute a discrete system within Islam although predating it in Malaya. These cults satisfy the immediate and local needs of the Malaysian peasant in terms of his economic activities and the aspects of his health and general welfare. The peasant's world is populated with spirits (hantu), some of which are bad, others good. There are sea spirits and land spirits; all have names and "personal" characteristics. The "good" spirits must be propitiated in order to assure their constant solicitude. The "evil" spirits must be controlled by prayer and exorcised by rite through the intervention of a medium.

An important element in the cults is the recognition that a man's lot cannot be improved simply by supplication of the good spirits. Thus, the fishermen state that by propitiating the spirits they improve their chances for the full execution of their skill, but spirits cannot make a good fisherman out of a mediocre or poor one.

In addition to these manifest functions of the cult system,

71. Lim, Joo-jock, "Tradition and Peasant Agriculture in Malaya," Malayan Journal of Tropical Agriculture, October, 1954, pp. 44-45.

72. Raymond Firth, Malay Fishermen, pp. 122-24.

there are important latent aspects. The cults give Malaysians an outlet for fantasy needs and even reward particularly imaginative individuals with roles like the spirit medium which provide status as well as income. Moreover, the cult provides explanations about phenomena of the world.

Orthodox Islam provides ritual requirements and facilities for salvation, an elaborate cosmology, and a feeling of community with other Moslems in the country as well as in the whole of the Moslem world. In the acceptance of the two systems the Malaysian is aware of no contradictions. The Malay fisherman conceives of both systems as aspects of Allah and as contributing to greater prosperity. The hantu are invoked in the name of Allah, and Moslem terms sprinkle the rites and prayers to the spirits. The Arabic word kun, meaning "to come into being," is used to call the spirits. Many of the shamans of the cults are haji, that is, Moslems who have made the pilgrimage to Mecca, and frequently the shamans are called in to tend sick members of the Moslem hierarchy.

There is, of course, some resistance on the part of the pious and informed Moslems who deride the cults as ineffective and unnecessary for good Moslems and decry the recognition of the efficacy of the spirits as against the tenets of Islam. These people claim that the cults cannot really reach the spirits in any case. This confusion of religious systems corresponds to the conflict of custom and Moslem rules in the legal system, mentioned above. The two sets of rules are so intermingled at so many levels that, in effect, it is more like a single system with a division of function between the two principal elements. [73]

Organized religion

For the bulk of the Malaysians, organized Islam is represented by the local mosque with its officers--the imam or leader of prayer, the kadi, and the religious teacher or guru. The links with the Moslem world at large, through the sultan

---

73. This point was made by Raymond Firth in a series of lectures entitled "Religion and Human Organization" delivered at the University of Chicago, April-May, 1955. The discussion here is based primarily upon the lecture entitled "Orthodox Religions and Local Cults," delivered April 26, 1955.

and the hierarchy of the state religion, are more remote from the experience of the peasant.

In terms of immediate experience, the Malaysian's association with organized Islam is restricted in large part to participation in the weekly services and in major holidays, support of the religious organization through payments of religious dues, and the process of socialization and indoctrination which young people undergo as part of their religious education.

The peasants attach considerable importance to the weekly attendance of religious service in the local mosque. In part, the importance of this practice is attested to in the refusal of the Malay fishermen to stay at sea for periods longer than a week and to risk being absent from these services on Friday, the Moslem sabbath. The weekly participation in the proceedings at the mosque is more than a personal religious experience; as in the case of Western religious practice, there are important ancillary functions performed in the mosque associated with vital life-cycle events. Thus, there are important religious procedures which must be completed at the birth of children, at the time of circumcision, at the completion of Koranic studies, at the time of betrothal and marriage, and at the time of death, and even after death at the various memorial services. These important personal and social activities make the mosque and the services of its officers essential.

Certain major annual holy days are also celebrated. Most of these celebrations are carried out in the mosque; others are carried out by all the people in their homes or at other specific places. The Hari Raya are the most important of the holy days. These consist of two festivals, the Hari Raya Haji (pilgrimage festival) and the Hari Raya Puasa (fast-ending festival), the latter occurring in the tenth Moslem month and marking the end of the ninth month of fasting (ramadan), and the former celebrated in the twelfth Moslem month at the same time as the great sacrifice and pilgrimage at Mecca. In these holy days, which the Malaysians share with the rest of the Moslem world, the Malaysians pay greater attention to the fast-ending festival than to the pilgrimage festival; in the Arabic countries or in Pakistan, the two festivals are accorded equal weight. [74]

---

74. Al-Abidin bin Ahmad Zain, "Malay Festivals and Some

On the Hari Raya it is customary for the Malaysians to visit their parents and their religious teachers early in the morning, after which they dress in their best attire and attend services at the mosque. It is also customary at this time to keep open house for friends and neighbors.

The importance attached to minor holy days varies according to the region and reflects some of the differences among Malaysians in Malaya. Another important aspect of these holy days is the degree to which some of the traditional Moslem practices have been modified to conform with certain pre-Islamic usages and in general with local preference.

The Moslem New Year tends to be a day of celebration for urban more than for kampong Malaysians except in the northern part of the country. Later in the first month, the tenth day, 'Ashura day, is celebrated, especially among the Penang Malaysians; in Penang there are large numbers of a particular Moslem sect, the Shi'ites, for whom this is an important day. On the last Wednesday of the second Moslem month the Mandi Safar is celebrated. This holiday marks the end of the month of Safar (the month of the Prophet's illness) and in the past was a time for the solemn cleansing of sin at a river or the sea. Now, especially in Malakka, the Mandi Safar is celebrated with much joy and in the spirit of a picnic at the sea or river site. The traditional dance form which was performed for this holiday, the ronggeng, has given way to a modern and popular dance (joget moderen), and the solemnity of the occasion is somewhat lessened by the fact that this is a favorite time for the making of marriage matches and thus a time for courting, flirtation, and display. [75]

From the first to the twelfth day of the third month of the Moslem calendar the Prophet's birthday is celebrated. In the kampongs it is customary to read from the Koran and conduct panegyric chants, all in Arabic, which few if any understand, in a large open meeting which is accompanied by refreshments and a good deal of noise. After a lull during the fourth, fifth, and sixth months when there are no religious holidays, the important Mi'raj festival takes place. In the seventh month

Aspects of Malay Religious Life," Journal of the Malayan Branch of the Royal Asiatic Society, March, 1949, p. 94.

75. Katherine Sim, "Mandi Safar in Malakka," Corona, June, 1954, p. 225.

on the twenty-seventh day, the accession of the Prophet to heaven is celebrated. During this very colorful festival the kampongs and their approaches are lighted with torches, and the Koranic story of the journey to heaven is read. The final minor festival, Nisfu night, held during the eighth month, commemorates the dead and prepares for the dead to revisit the kampongs on this night. On all of these days part of all of the services associated with the festivals take place in the mosque.

An important adjunct to the religious system of the Malaysians is the period of Koranic study which each young boy theoretically undergoes. Not only is this a method for the indoctrination of the Islamic religion, it also serves as an important period of general orientation to the Malaysian society. The experience which the young man has with his teacher (guru) is expected to provide an essential part of his socialization. The general socializing influence which Koranic instruction imparts helps explain its continuation despite the difficulties involved in it for young people. "Learning to chant the Koran from cover to cover is a grinding task for Malay children and retards secular education, but it is still a universal practice, a martyrdom establishing them in their faith."[76]

Education[77]

Of the three dominant ethnic groups in Malaya, the Malaysians alone have both an informal and a formal system of education. Aspects of the informal system have been discussed above in the context of religion. For the Malaysians, as for the Chinese and Indians, formal education includes the vernacular schools and the government English schools.

Vernacular education
There have been Malay vernacular schools in the country for about a century and a half providing a primary education for

76. R. O. Winstedt, "Malaysia," in Islam Today, ed. A. J. Arberry and Rom Landau (London: Faber and Faber, 1943), p. 218.

77. Education in general in Malaya is discussed in Chapter 6.

children of any ethnic group from the age of six to twelve. The number of Malay children in these schools has almost trebled since 1941, to 336, 311 in 1953. [78] This increase has not been paralleled by a corresponding increase in facilities and poses one of the most difficult problems for the Federation.

The Federation has attempted to maintain adequate facilities for the constantly increasing number of Malaysian children seeking education. The major portion of the expenditures in new buildings and facilities has gone to the government English schools, where 26, 215 Malaysians, or 25. 5 per cent of the total enrollment, received training in 1953.

Of much greater importance has been the creation of new facilities by the Malaysians themselves. A kampong or group of kampongs acting as a community may request funds for the construction of a school from the federal Department of Education. The request is channeled through the penghulu and the district officer. If on inspection of the demand for the school, the desirability of the site, and the availability of teachers, the education officer feels that the venture would succeed, the grant is made. It is the intention of the government that when these Ra'ayat schools appear to be permanent, they will be integrated into the government school system. The community aspect of the schools is sustained in most cases through a committee of local interested persons who help in the sponsorship of sport days, concerts, and exhibitions of student handicraft art. These committees also aid in the maintenance of the school buildings, teachers' quarters, and the grounds.

In addition to maintaining adequate facilities in the Federation, there is the problem of providing enough adequately trained teachers for the schools. To some extent this demand is being met from outside the country, as in the case of the recruitment of thirty-one graduates from Indian and Pakistani universities for work in the English schools in 1953. There are also two teacher-training colleges, a federal one for men at Tanjong Malim, Perak, with a capacity of 418, and a college for women at Malakka with a capacity of 196. Because the pressure upon the existing resources for training teachers has been so great, there were 2, 777 part-time teacher trainees instructed on weekends and during intensive school holiday periods in 1953. There also were some 3, 500 additional young

---

78. Federation of Malaya, Annual Report, 1953, p. 174.

people being instructed once a week in preparation for intensive training at one of the institutions at a later time. A similar acceleration of the teacher-training program for teachers in the English language schools has taken place, including the construction of a teachers' college at Kota Bharu and the establishment of a training college in Kirkby, England.

In Singapore there were only ten thousand pupils in Malay-language schools, [79] and, as in the Federation, these were almost all Malaysians. The problems faced in Singapore are similar to those noted for the Federation.

Less than 10 per cent of the total enrollment at the University of Malaya consists of Malaysians: 90 out of 954 in 1953. Moreover, over half of these are enrolled as arts majors as distinguished from the Chinese, for example, of whom over half were in the medical school.

The future program of the educational system as it concerns the Malaysians is not clear. In 1952 an education ordinance was enacted creating a national school system which was bilingual. English and Malay were to be taught in all schools, regardless of whether the basic language medium of the school was English or Malay. The national school establishment, affording as it did free and compulsory education to all children from the ages of six to twelve, immediately ran into the problem of financing. As costs were estimated, it became clear that the program could not be administered without curtailing expenditure on other necessary social services. Matters have been substantially at this point since 1954 with the apparently emergent trend being a national system wherein a priority is to be given to the establishment of English-language schools. This policy has inspired the animosity of the Chinese, Malaysian, and Indian politicians, all of whom have claimed that this English-language priority program is being operated at the expense of the vernacular school systems. However, evidence seems to indicate that most of the influential Malaysians are aware of the necessity of learning a language capable of communicating modern ideas and feel that English, as opposed to Chinese as an alternative modern language, would be far better for Malaysians.

---

79. Colony of Singapore, Annual Report, 1953 (Singapore: Government Printing Office, 1954), p. 90.

Internal affiliations

The two most important affiliational factors operating within the kampongs seem to be (1) the corporateness based upon a common economy, common labor, common belief and value system, and common residence, or upon kinship (matrilineal) principles and (2) the bureaucratization of the traditional offices of authority. The corporateness of the kampongs and the development of a special, qualified group of Malaysians from within the kampongs are not opposed. Indeed, the concurrent existence of unit solidarity and specialized links with the outside world are important features of the changing function of the Malayan kampong.

The kampong has been undergoing important changes for the past forty years. Two aspects of the change may be identified. With the introduction of rubber as an important cash crop has come the monetization of the kampong economy and greater involvement in the national economy. The second stage has been the recent focusing of attention upon the kampong as the fundamental political unit of the Malaysian population. This political attention has been stimulated by the need of the federal government to win the loyalty of the kampong people in the fight against the Communists and by the recognition on the part of the Malaysian politicians that their greatest strength lies in the kampong.

Malayan affiliations

The effective mobilization of political and social pressure by the Malays in 1946 in opposition to the Malayan Union proposal of the British Colonial Office showed a degree of cohesive national sentiment among the Malaysians which came as a surprise to many. Since that time more serious attention has been given to the understanding of Malay "nationalism," and some of the salient characteristics of it have become apparent. It differs from nationalism elsewhere in Asia in three ways: (1) it is a recent development; (2) it is not dominated by a middle class; and (3) it is characterized, as in Thailand, as much by an anti-Asian as an anti-Western orientation. The nationalist ideology seems not to have developed until the 1920's when, following the successful revolution in Turkey and later the articulation of the pan-Islam doctrine, many young Malaysians engaged in a mild sort of anti-British, anti-Christian agitation primarily through the circulation and reading of illegal magazines from Cairo and India. Somewhat later, Malay intellectuals brought out their own magazines, but these stressed not the broad aims of the pan-Islamic movement for uniting Moslem countries of the world, but the modernization of Islamic life in Malaya. [80]

Devotion to Islam and dedication to modernization as parts of the nationalist ideology were consistent with the then developing policy of the Colonial Office. To the British the principal threat to their maintenance of power and political stability came not from the Malaysians, who were becoming a smaller portion of the total population in the face of Chinese immigration, but the Chinese, who had been stimulated politically by the Chinese revolution and the rise of Kuomintang. The policy of the British was therefore to concentrate as much political power within the Malay state as was consistent with over-all administration. This was accomplished through the Malay sultanates tied together tenuously at the formal level but in fact centrally controlled through a system of British advisors and residents. In this way the indigenous aristocracy came to be favored in the political system. This favored position continues and in effect divides the Malays into two political groups, the aristocracy and the middle-class-oriented United Malayan Nationalist Organization (UMNO).

Perhaps the unique aspect of Malay nationalism is its orientation against the Chinese. This sentiment is based on the fear that Chinese economic power and potential political power could together make Malaya a Chinese country. This fear in turn rests on the assumption that Malaya is the land of the Malaysians and that the Chinese, Indians, other Asians, and Europeans are exploitative and temporary residents of the country. On the other hand, modern Malaya lacks a single dominant national character. Illustrative of the impression of the country on a stranger is the following statement by a French rubber planter: "Learning that the Malays were Mohammedans I had set sail for a sort of Algeria, but landed in a Chinese City [Singapore or Penang]. Since my arrival I have lived in India [among the Tamil estate workers]. And suddenly

---

80. Ratman, S. Raja, "The Changing Malay People," Asia, August, 1942, p. 453.

[on coming to know the Malays] I find myself in Polynesia. "[81]
According to Silcock:

> The Malays make much of the fact that Malaya is
> their country. The claim may be conceded in a
> limited sense, . . . [but] apart from the river
> valleys the Malay peninsula was almost wholly
> unoccupied at the time of the first British settle-
> ment and vast areas have never at any time been
> occupied by Malays. It is hysterical nonsense to
> claim that the Malays ever owned Malaya [in the
> sense of political ownership of the unoccupied land]
> in the same sense as the modern European state
> owns the territory it administers. [82]

Modern Malaya is, in point of fact, not a Malaysian nation,
not even a plural national society in the sense in which it exists
in other countries where the Chinese or Indians form an important but numerically small portion of the population. In Malaya there is the beginning of a "national" character only now
emerging, and this character is as distinctively Chinese as it
is Malaysian. The claim on the part of the Malaysians that the
country is theirs is therefore important only as one theme in
the political development of the country.

Two kinds of influence militate against real Malaysian
political unity. These are (1) a class division between the aristocracy sultanate group of Malays and the middle-class, essentially government-employed and professional Malaysians
and (2) state particularism. The latter is important though
little stressed in national politics. It has been observed that
any one state might be disinclined to defend another state vigorously in the defense of the country as a whole. [83] At the
present time the propensity toward a state localism is being
reinforced by the increasing number of Chinese in the Federation legislature. The economic advancement of the Malaysians,

81. H. Fauconnier, Malaisie (New York: Macmillan and Co.,
1939), pp. 83-84.
82. T. H. Silcock, Dilemma in Malaya (London: Fabian Publications, Ltd., 1949), pp. 11-12.
83. Theodore Adams, "The Malay in Malaya," Asiatic Review, January, 1944, p. 98.

238

for example, requires far more than the mere reservation of rice lands for Malaysians. The needs are such that the Malaysians must depend on governmental support, [84] and there is a tendency to seek support in the state organs rather than submit to the power of the Chinese in the federal structure.

In recent years the problem of state particularism has been approached through mass education. The Federation government has conducted "Civic Days" which are meant to inform the people, primarily the Malaysians, of the problems which the Federation government faces regarding economic, political, and social aspects of life in Malaya. "Civic Days" are organized by the local district officers; they last a week and are attended primarily by the important kampong officers (headman, prayer leader, teachers) but also by Malaysians in the lower ranks of the bureaucracy. [85]

External affiliations

The two important external links of the Malaysians in Malaya are the ancient ties with Indonesia and the more recent ties to the United Kingdom. Affiliations with other Moslem countries were never important, and there has been a partial disavowal of the uniting tendencies of Pan-Islam, although there are signs of increasing concern with the Arab world. Affiliations with neighboring countries have been unimportant in recent years except for the relations between the Patani Malays of peninsular Thailand, and the Malays of Kelantan and Kedah.

As for the Patani Malays, an irredentist movement originating in Kedah has had a significant following including rather highly placed persons. The movement was led by Tengku Mahmood Mahyddeen, a former official in the Federation government and a man of high prestige in Kelantan, where the irredentist movement enjoys its greatest support. [86] Its aim apparently was to reintegrate the Patani Malays into the Malayan body politic, but diplomatic progress on the subject between the British and Thai governments has been slight.

84. Silcock and Aziz, Nationalism in Malaya, p. 46.
85. Sim, "Malayan Notebook," Corona, April, 1953, pp. 142-44.
86. Virginia Thompson and Richard Adloff, Minority Problems in Southeast Asia (Stanford: Stanford University Press, 1955), p. 160.

The ties between Britain and Malaya have been important for a variety of reasons. Probably most important has been the mutual recognition that a close relationship was indispensable to maintaining political stability and Malay political hegemony. At the time of the union proposals in 1946 and in the present period of transition to greater self-government, the close relationship between the Malay political leaders and British civil servants has been apparent on both institutional and personal levels. Young Malaysians traditionally have obtained their higher education in British Commonwealth countries, and the British have supported free education for the Malays throughout their history in the country. The policy of favoring Malaysians for the middle and higher bureaucratic positions has also produced the situation, indeed the need, for the exchange of ideas, values, and aims, and has enhanced mutual understanding. All of this interaction has, of course, been intensified through personal relationships nurtured through generations.

The ties to the various parts of what is now the Republic of Indonesia have long been important. The link between the matrilineal people of Negri Sembilan and the Sumatran Minangkabau has been especially strong because lineal descent of the former is traced to some of the clans of the latter. In the selection of a candidate for one of the high offices in this society, one consideration which can be of considerable advantage to the candidate is his relationship to the Minangkabau (Sumatran) nobility and high office holders. In fact, amidst the political uncertainty in Malaya there has been at times a strong feeling on the part of many of the Negri Sembilan leaders that closer formal connection should be established between the Minangkabau and themselves. [87]

The ties between Java and the Javanese immigrants to Malaya have in recent years become increasingly important. There is much unpublicized intercourse between the two places by businessmen, by young Javanese immigrants seeking wives, and by Javanese workers returning for a time to their former

---

87. During the Japanese wartime control of Southeast Asia, Malaya and Sumatra were administered from Singapore as one unit, reflecting the strong economic, cultural, and geographic relationships which connect the shores of the Strait of Malakka.

homes with the earnings from commercial and labor activities in Malaya.

Unarticulated affiliational antagonisms

The Malays have been characterized by two forms of insecurity and antagonism. The first is the diffuse and only fragmentally articulated resentment against their alleged relegation to an economic rural backwater.

> Since he began producing rubber, the Malay grower has been prevented by policies--from his viewpoint--economically unsound, to achieve a higher standard of living. For instance, officially or covertly he has found it most difficult to obtain permission to plant new areas of land with rubber. Or, the terms of trade have been against him when he has attempted to market rice and other crops. Finally he has been exploited by other groups and made to pay the price of ill-conceived one sided schemes--as in the case of the share certificates of 1939-40. [88]

A consequence of the feeling of economic deprivation has been the focus of Malaysian hostility upon the economically powerful Chinese.

The second unarticulated affiliational antagonism is that which exists between the British and Malaysians over the catastrophic withdrawal of the British in 1942. The subsequent loss of prestige was evident after the reoccupation of Malaya in 1945.

> The general emotional background [of the reoccupation] was one of shame for the debacle of 1942, accentuated by the fact that many of the senior civil servants returning from prison camps had seen nothing of the subsequent war. The feeling

---

88. Gamba, "Rural Development in Malaya," p. 20. According- ing to the share-certificate plan, the Malaysian smallholders were granted a grossly inadequate and disproportionate share of the restricted rubber quota for Malaya. See Bauer, Report on a Visit to the Rubber-Growing Smallholdings, p. 31.

was aggravated by a sense of disappointment that events had robbed the British Army of the chance to wipe out the score by a victorious campaign in Malaya. [89]

The loss of prestige in this wartime experience has apparently never been rectified, and the persistence of British explanations of their 1942 position as late as 1953, in reports on the "Civic Days" courses, indicates the importance placed by the British upon the loss.

---

89. Silcock and Aziz, Nationalism in Malaya, p. 32.

242

8. The Chinese in Malaya

OF THE APPROXIMATELY twelve million overseas Chinese, [1] about five-sixths reside in the countries of Southeast Asia. Of this number, three million live in Malaya. [2] Not only does this segment represent the principal concentration of Chinese people outside of China proper, but it also constitutes the largest Chinese proportion of the total population of any of the Nan-yang nations. [3] Significant as these numerical figures may seem, there are other factors which further reflect the posi-

1. American Consulate-General, Hongkong, "Current Background," No. 301 (Hongkong, November 1, 1954), p. 1. (Mimeographed.) The official Chinese Communist census placed the total population of China at 601,938,035 as of June 30, 1953. The number of overseas Chinese was tabulated at 11,743,320. The former figure includes the population of Formosa.

2. Federation of Malaya, Annual Report, 1953 (Kuala Lumpur: Government Press, 1954), p. 3; Colony of Singapore, Annual Report, 1953 (Singapore: Government Printing Office, 1954), p. 9. Estimates placed the total at 3,013,415; the Federation had 2,152,906 and Singapore had 860,509.

3. Victor Purcell, The Chinese in Southeast Asia (London: Oxford University Press, 1951), p. 2. The author graphically illustrates the position of the Chinese in each of the countries of Southeast Asia, clearly demonstrating that those in Malaya are the largest concentration for any country in the region and represent about one-half of the total population. The term Nan-yang has come to have reference to the countries of Southeast Asia, although its literal meaning is "South Seas."

tion of the Chinese in contemporary Malaya--their economic strength, their social organization, and a recent but rapidly developing political consciousness.

The Chinese own and operate most of the non-British commercial enterprises throughout Malaya and are second in terms of volume of capital investment. [4] They are the chief middlemen and shopkeepers and generally dominate the service industries. Although their historical importance in tin mining has been lessened under European competition, they still account for over 40 per cent of the annual tin production. Similarly, the Chinese dominate the pineapple industry and own many of the small and medium rubber holdings which account for a large proportion of the annual output. The Chinese also are the principal vegetable gardeners, supplying the urban centers with fresh produce.

The traditional forms of Chinese social organization are intimately related to their economic activities and provide the basis for small centers of Chinese culture amidst an indigenous people that equal them in number. When the Chinese went to Malaya they took their religious concepts, clan and dialect associations, and guilds and secret societies. Although the latter were made illegal in the latter part of the nineteenth century, they again have assumed importance especially since the end of World War II. The other associations form a series of interlaced social groupings which embrace every facet of Chinese existence. The social cohesiveness resulting from the activities and functions of these various social groupings has led Purcell to characterize the Chinese in Malaya as being "more ethnographically exact than in any other country of Southeast Asia because since large-scale immigration from China began over half a century ago there has been no miscegenation of any importance. Before then it was comparatively small."[5]

---

4. B. K. Madan (ed.), Economic Problems of Underdeveloped Countries in Asia (New Delhi: Indian Council of World Affairs, 1953), p. 151. The author sums up the role assumed by the Chinese in the Malayan economy, stressing the difficulty involved in accurately determining the actual proportion of total investments held by the Chinese.

5. Purcell, The Chinese in Southeast Asia, pp. 2, 3. See also Victor Purcell, The Chinese in Malaya (London: Oxford

The embryonic political consciousness of the Chinese is largely a recent and externally induced phenomenon. It also is the most conspicuous and potentially significant development in postwar Malaya. Governed traditionally as an alien group, the Chinese were never encouraged to participate in government. Indeed, it was the stated policy of the British authorities to protect the indigenous Malays from the encroachments of the ambitious and aggressive Chinese. Supporting this policy, moreover, was the highly transitory nature of Chinese settlement, their allegiance to another country, and their apparently indifferent attitude to the vagaries of government and administration.

Postwar events in the Far East and Southeast Asia have modified the traditional framework which molded the Chinese role in Malayan political life. A large percentage of Chinese (over 62 per cent) now claim Malaya as their birthplace. Most of these have come to regard Malaya as their permanent residence, thereby developing increasing interest in its political future. The emergence of China as a world power has also brought into sharper focus the necessity for declaring political allegiances; and British intentions to relinquish national control have crystallized the apparent need for more active participation in government life. The Chinese fear the possibility of the Malays' depriving them of their economic supremacy through political machinations. It is in part the need for protecting these vital interests that impels the Chinese to assume a more active and even leading role in the political arena.

The general identification of the Chinese with the small but tenacious Communist movement has stimulated Malay fears of the motives which might lie behind Chinese efforts to acquire political power. Nevertheless, the Chinese are beginning to enlarge rapidly their political role in Malaya. The protection of well-established economic interests, the heritage of a national regime, and the conflicts induced by the rise of Communist China are the main factors in this development.

University Press, 1948), pp. 293-95. The author includes an appendix on the Straits Chinese who are descendants of mixed marriages between Chinese men and Malay women. These are unique, however, and represent a very small proportion of the total Chinese population. Their language, "Baba Malay," is based on the Hokkien dialect but is spoken with a Malay accent.

Earliest Chinese literary evidence pertaining to the Malay Peninsula dates from the sixth century A. D. [6] Little more is known about Chinese interest or settlement in the area until the early fifteenth century. From 1405 to 1433 the famous Chinese Admiral Cheng, Ho carried out a series of sea-borne expeditions that brought him into contact with Malaya and other countries of the area. [7] They were the first large-scale organized Chinese efforts to explore Southeast Asia and beyond by means of the sea. A form of tributary relationship was established and continued for the next hundred years or so but then declined, contact being made only by occasional Chinese traders and pirates. Evidence indicates that Chinese trading activities and settlement were largely confined to the present-day settlement of Malakka.

From this early period to the establishment of Singapore in 1819, the number of Chinese in Malaya was never great and fluctuated as economic conditions under the Portuguese and Dutch improved or waned. [8] Penang island was leased from a local sultan by the British East India Company in 1786, and shortly afterward Chinese settlers arrived in comparatively large numbers. It appears that British policy was admirably suited to Chinese interests. This correlation is most evident in the founding and expansion of British interests on Singapore island. By controlling the Strait of Malakka from Singapore, Sir Stamford Raffles and his complement of administrators were able to construct the basis for a great entrepôt trade within a few years after the establishment of Singapore as a

---

6. W. P. Groeneveldt, "Notes on the Malay Archipelago and Malakka," Verhandelingen van het Bataviaasch Genootschap van Kunsten en Wetenschappen, 1880, pp. 111-44. The author has translated and commented upon every reference to the various parts of Southeast Asia contained in Chinese documents. After two other references from the seventh century, no more evidence on Malaya appears in Chinese literature until the fifteenth century.

7. J. J. L. Duyvendak, "The True Dates of the Chinese Maritime Expeditions of the Early Fifteenth Century," T'oung Pao, 1939, pp. 341-412.

8. Purcell, The Chinese in Malaya, pp. ix, x.

port city in 1819. In general, the Chinese went to the Nan-yang in expectation of making a livelihood far and above that available at home. Whereas the British were interested primarily in establishing political control and orienting the economic development of Malaya toward the needs of Europe, the Chinese capitalized on the advantages offered them in trading, shopkeeping, and spice cultivation. From the start the Chinese were considered so important to the visionary Raffles that special areas of settlement were designated for them in the new colony which still constitute the principal and most heavily populated Chinese sectors of the colony. [9]

Even though the influx of Chinese increased to the point where Singapore early became a largely Chinese settlement, it was not until the late nineteenth and early twentieth centuries, when the rubber and tin industries developed in response to world-wide demand, that their numbers were augmented appreciably throughout Malaya. This period in Chinese immigration reflected the need for laborers to clear the jungles, construct roads, expand mines, and establish plantations.

Immigration and labor recruitment

The system of labor recruitment involved the agents of tin mines and agricultural estates, who, retaining ties with their former hsien (small administrative district in China) or villages and speaking the dialects characteristic of those areas, were able to induce peasants from their own "home" districts in China to seek jobs with their respective employers. Once these men were delivered to the ports for shipment, the agents' responsibility for the sinkeh ("new recruit") ended. Normally, before the laborer embarked for Malaya, he would agree to work for the particular employer for a stipulated period of time in return for payment of passage, subsistence, and clothing. Often he was "Shanghaied" to Penang, Malakka, or Singapore where he was subjected to the scrutiny of hiring agents and then shuttled off to the rapidly expanding tin mines and agricultural estates. [10] It was this indentured class that bore the

9. B. W. Hodder, "Racial Groupings in Singapore," Malayan Journal of Tropical Geography, October, 1953, pp. 25-26.

10. Chen, Ta, "Chinese Migrations with Special Reference to Labor Conditions" (Bulletin of the United States Bureau of

brunt of the evils characterizing the system of recruitment. After the "Chinese Protectorate" was established by the British in 1877, a contract system became the rule for employing new recruits, but the indenture system continued until 1914 when the British finally prohibited it.

One of the principal reasons for this unfortunate situation was that the Chinese imperial government denied any protection to its nationals when they emigrated. Government decrees during the Ch'ing dynasty ordered emigrants to be punished severely if they returned. Therefore, once they did leave, they had no recourse from the nefarious practices associated with recruitment. For the most part, the British remained aloof from Chinese labor problems until the latter part of the nineteenth century. [11]

It was only when internecine struggles among the Chinese occurred, threatening the peace and the continuation of normal economic activities, that the British administration took an active part in pacifying the Chinese, introducing a less harsh recruitment system, and improving the labor conditions of the sinkeh.

From the late nineteenth century up to the early 1930's the Chinese population increased spectacularly, except for a short period at the beginning of World War I. Up to 1929 immigration was completely free, but from this date on it came under the control of the British administration. Monthly quota restrictions in accordance with economic need were instituted and applied to all groups, but because of their predominant numbers the Chinese were the first to be affected. The policy of restriction continued until World War II when all surplus labor was utilized to meet the increased needs engendered by the growing world tension. After the war, the quantitative control

---

Labor Statistics, No. 340 [Washington: Government Printing Office, 1923]), pp. 111-237. The author discussed this subject in illuminating detail.

11. They did, however, manifest some interest in the conditions associated with Indian recruitment, but this was at the insistence of the government in India. It should be recognized that all the early British civil servants in Malaya were seconded from the India Civil Service and for that reason may have been more inclined to protect the newly arrived Indian laborer.

system established earlier was superseded by a policy of continued restriction of immigration on a selective basis in which both economic and political considerations have played a significant role. This general policy was formulated as late as 1948 and further defined in 1953. [12]

Regional origins

Archeological and linguistic evidence serve as guides to the origin of the Chinese immigrants to Malaya. Most have come from China's southeastern provinces of Kwangtung, Fukien, and Kwangsi, and from the island of Hainan directly south of Kwangtung (Map 18, Chapter 6, above). Various reasons have been proposed to account for this restricted place of origin, ranging from geographical propinquity to the superior enterprise of the natives of this area. [13] None has been wholly satisfactory, although the poverty of coastal Fukien and eastern Kwangtung is notorious. Before the Chinese began to take an interest in their position, and before the number of immigrants admitted to Malaya was reduced, individual Chinese migrated with the idea of returning to their homeland after having made their fortunes. Naturally, most did not realize this ideal and instead remained, sending money home to support their families in China. Their relative success provoked visions of wealth and opportunity for those in their native villages, and thus emigration from certain areas continued. [14]

There are nine major linguistic groups among the Chinese in Malaya, plus a scattering of others, each from different areas. The Hokkiens (natives of Amoy and its hinterland) are predominant, whereas the Cantonese are the second largest group. The Hakka (Kheh), who originate from northwestern Kwangtung and southwestern Fukien, form the third largest group; the Tiechiu from around Swatow and the Hainanese

---

12. Federation of Malaya, Annual Report, 1953, pp. 9 ff. See also Chapter 3 of this study, "Demographic Patterns."

13. Chen, Ta, "Chinese Migrations," Chapter 1.

14. See Chen, Ta, Emigrant Communities in South China (New York: Institute of Pacific Relations, 1940), pp. 161-66. The author examines the effects that emigration has had on specific communities in China, which are actually referred to as "overseas Chinese communities," with their main source of income based on remittances from the overseas members.

(Hailam) from Hainan island constitute the fourth and fifth principal segments of the Chinese population. The Kwongsai come from central and western Kwangsi province, the Hokchiu from the coastal town of Foochow and its hinterland in Fukien, the Hokchia from a small area directly below Foochow, and the Henghua from a section of Fukien north of Chuanchow. [15] As is apparent from Table 46, the first five linguistic groups constitute the bulk of the Chinese population, amounting to 92.9 per cent in 1947, 92.7 per cent in 1931, and 96.2 per cent in 1921.

TABLE 46
CHINESE IN MALAYA*

	1921	1931	1947
Hokkien	379,028	538,852	827,411
Cantonese	331,757	417,516	641,945
Hakka	217,697	317,506	437,407
Tiechiu	130,026	208,681	364,232
Hainanese	68,200	97,568	157,649
Kwongsai	998	46,095	71,850
Hokchiu	13,821	31,908	48,094
Hokchia	4,058	15,301	12,754
Henghwa	1,659	31,025	17,065
Others	24,496		36,260
Total	1,171,740	1,704,452	2,614,667

*M.V.Del Túfo, Malaya: A Report on the 1947 Census of Population (London: Crown Agents for the Colonies, 1949), p. 75.

The Singapore Annual Report for 1953 places the Chinese population at 860,509, or 76.6 per cent of the total. This sum is divided into six major linguistic groups--Hokkien, Tiechiu, Cantonese and Kwongsai, Hainanese, Hakka, and "Others." The remaining population is composed of Malaysians (12.2 per cent), Indians and Pakistani (7.5 per cent), Europeans (1.4 per cent), Eurasians (0.98 per cent), and others (0.93 per cent). As can be observed from Table 47, the various dialect

15. See Map 18 for the geographical distribution of these groups in China.

groups in Singapore resemble those in Malaya as a whole, except for the Hakka, who are relatively insignificant and who tend to be identified with rural occupations.

TABLE 47
CHINESE IN SINGAPORE
(1953 ESTIMATE)*

	Number	Per Cent
Hokkien	341,000	39.6
Tiechiu	185,300	21.7
Cantonese and Kwongsai	186,000	21.7
Hainanese	62,400	7.2
Hakka	47,200	5.4
Others	38,600	4.4
Total	860,500	100.0

*Colony of Singapore, Annual Report, 1953, p. 11.

During the 1930's there was a considerable movement of Chinese back to the China mainland, some at British expense, and a monthly immigration quota was imposed on adult males. During the period from 1934 to 1938 female immigration was unrestricted for those planning to join their husbands already in Malaya.[16] There was evidence, however, that many women were going to Malaya precisely because restrictions were placed upon men; the women began to assume the same position of support to the family left at home that men had done previously. It has been estimated that about two hundred thousand women emigrated to Malaya during this period. Because of the large numbers involved, the authorities were forced to impose restrictions upon women also shortly before the start of World War II. The resulting more balanced sex ratio was extremely important in alleviating some of the earlier social problems of the Malayan Chinese.

The Chinese first settled in Malakka, later on the island of Penang and in Province Wellesley, and then in Singapore. These three areas, and especially the last, continue to be the

16. W. L. Blythe, "Historical Sketch of Chinese Labour in Malaya," Journal of the Malayan Branch of the Royal Asiatic Society, 1947, pp. 64-114.

foci of major Chinese settlement. The principal region of settlement lies along the west coast of Malaya extending from Singapore to Penang, with localizations in urban areas. In 1947 the four principal Chinese linguistic groups--Hokkien, Cantonese, Tiechiu, and Hakka--formed nearly 87 per cent of the total Chinese population in Malaya. Although significant concentrations of these four groups are to be found wherever the Chinese are present in numbers, there are few sharply defined divisions of the country based on these dialect groups (see Map 19 and the discussion of linguistic communities in Chapter 6). In only twenty-six of the eighty-nine census districts into which Malaya was divided in 1947 did one of these groups form more than 50 per cent of the total Chinese population, and many of these twenty-six contained only a very small Chinese merchant community serving a predominantly Malay population.

As for the distribution of these Chinese dialect groups, the Hokkiens are more of an urban people than any other; the Hakkas form a predominantly rural community associated largely with mining areas; and the numerically smaller groups tend to bunch in small geographical areas. [17] One example of this singular concentration is in the Dindings, a district of Perak. The total population in 1947 was a little over seventy thousand, and the Chinese represented more than half of this figure. The linguistic groups settled there are the Hakchiu, the Hakchia (both from the general area of Foochow), and the Hokkiens. The first two groups constitute 34 per cent of the total Hokchiu and Hakchia population in Malaya, whereas the Hokkiens in the Dindings represent only 0.12 per cent of the total number of Hokkiens living in Malaya.

The strip of land forty to seventy miles in width along the west coast of Malaya is the most highly developed, and about 80 per cent of the Chinese are settled there. This correlation is a natural result of the use of Chinese labor to clear the jungles and to expand and develop the tin mines and rubber estates during the latter part of the nineteenth century and the first decades of the twentieth.

---

17. T. E. Smith, Population Growth in Malaya, an Analysis of Recent Trends (London: Royal Institute of International Affairs, 1952), pp. 64 ff.

Urban-rural settlement

The Chinese historically have been the predominant element in the urban population of Malaya.[18] In 1947, the Chinese represented nearly two-thirds of the total urban population in the Federation and over three-fourths in the Colony of Singapore.[19] Whereas both the Chinese and Malaysians represent increasing percentages of the total urban population, the Indian proportion in this category has actually decreased since 1931. However, the ratio of urban Chinese to the total Chinese population increased from 1931 to 1947 at a slower rate than those of the Indians and the Malaysians. Whereas the Malaysian ratio increased by 25 per cent and the Indian ratio by 22 per cent, the Chinese increase was only 9 per cent. These figures would seem to indicate that even though a greater proportion of the total Chinese population in 1947 was classified as urban (53.7 per cent), as compared with the Malaysians (14.1 per cent) and Indians (39.0 per cent), a more stable urban-rural balance of settlement has been established for them.

Nativity and sex ratio

Of particular interest in light of proposals to foster Malayan national loyalties is the enormous increase in the proportion of Malaya-born Chinese, who numbered over 60 per cent of the total Chinese population in 1947. This is a direct result of immigration policies and other developments following the world depression in the early 1930's, for in 1931 less than one-third of the nearly one and three-quarter million Chinese living in Malaya were born in Malaya. After the Aliens Ordinance Act was passed in 1933 and subsequent legislation was instituted further defining the categories of individuals permitted to immigrate, this low proportion gradually changed. The advent of World War II, the following political instability, and the loss

---

18. S. M. Middlebrook, "Yap Ah Hoy," Journal of the Malayan Branch of the Royal Asiatic Society, 1951, pp. 3-127. This is an historical study of a Chinese merchant who was largely responsible for the growth of Kuala Lumpur. In many areas of Southeast Asia the growth of towns has been associated largely with Chinese settlement and enterprise.

19. M. V. Del Tufo, Malaya: A Report on the 1947 Census of Population (London: Crown Agents for the Colonies, 1949), pp. 46, 47, and tables.

of contact with members of families still in China were other contributing factors.

A related development is the relatively high ratio of males to females in Malaya, as shown in Table 48. Originally only the male members of families emigrated with the intention

TABLE 48
CHINESE FEMALES PER 1,000 MALES*

	1911	1921	1931	1947
Federation of Malaya	215	371	486	815
Colony of Singapore	356	469	602	882
Malaya	247	384	513	833

*Del Tufo, Malaya, p. 45.

of sending for their wives when they could afford it, but in many instances the new settler would establish another family in Malaya and return to his homeland only occasionally when a death or other emergency occurred. [20]

Bases of Livelihood

The economic hierarchy of the Malayan Chinese ranges from a leading rubber baron in the former Straits Settlements to an egg collector in a suburb of Singapore city, and from the gigantic Tiger Balm industry to a single pawnshop. Chinese are engaged in all occupations but are associated primarily with service industries of every conceivable kind and vegetable gardening, and act as middlemen in daily village and town transactions. Initially active in the tin industry and the cultivation of agricultural export crops, they soon became aware that service and related industries would better satisfy their immediate desires to make money and return to China. The creation of Malay reservations and nonalienation of paddy land in the early

20. The present ratio augurs well for a more stable social group. The decreased incidence of prostitution and interracial marriages are external manifestations of these more balanced sex ratios.

twentieth century reinforced this development. The pattern was not changed substantially in the postwar years except for a temporary period of relatively widespread subsistence agriculture occasioned by "squatter" settlement.

Dialect-group occupation pattern

Occupational structure among the Chinese tends to vary with the dialect groups. According to Purcell:

> First of all, and particularly to-day, Chinese of all tribes engage in agricultural pursuits--the Hakkas and Cantonese probably to the greatest relative extent and the Hainanese and Hokchias the least. For the rest: (a) the Hokkiens are of an'urban habit and have a genius for trade and shopkeeping. That, and their old association with it, accounts for their predominance in Singapore, Penang, and Malacca (over a quarter of a million live in the three municipalities alone); but they are also found in great numbers in Johore, Selangor, and Perak where they are widely engaged in agriculture. (b) The Cantonese are rather more versatile. They are strongly represented in agriculture and are also numerous in the towns, but their predilection, if they have one, is for mining in which large numbers of them are employed--for instance in the Kinta Valley of Perak. (c) The Hakkas, or Khehs, are probably the most rurally inclined of all the tribes and with the Cantonese provide the bulk of the tin-mining population (about 80 per cent of the Chinese population of the Kinta Valley for instance). They are also widely engaged in agricultural pursuits and are found in considerable numbers in non-mining rural districts. (d) The Teochius [Tiechiu] like the Cantonese, are catholic in their tastes but, apart from the peculiar case of Kedah, seem on the whole slightly to prefer urban occupations. In Kedah an accident of early association makes them (as they have been since 1921) the most numerous tribe. (e) The Hainanese (Hailams) in the towns and villages (for which they show a preference) are chiefly employed in shopkeeping and domestic service, but they are also

widely distributed in the rural and in particular
the rubber-growing districts.[21]

This general diversity of occupation is highlighted by the
pattern exhibited in Singapore.[22] The Hokkiens account for
35.9 per cent of the total population on the island and dominate
local mercantile activities, export trade, and big business.
The Cantonese, the second largest Chinese group, are predominantly artisans. The Tiechius, the third largest group,
are engaged in lighter transfer of goods from tongkangs (small
boats) to warehouses and in interisland trade with British
Borneo and Thailand, where there are Tiechiu trading communities. Whereas the Hainanese are employed principally as
domestics and service employees, the Hakka do not appear to
have any occupational specialization.

A recent specialized study of Chinese physicians in Singapore[23] reveals that all the major dialect groups possess
medical practitioners. Of the 424 recognized Chinese physicians, who almost equaled the number of Western-trained doctors in the colony, 152 were Hokkien and 143 Cantonese. The
remainder were divided into three groups: Hakka (59), Tiechiu
(53), and others (7). Cantonese-speaking physicians are reportedly sought only by Hakkas and Cantonese. Furthermore,
since the Tiechiu and Hokkien dialects are similar, speakers
of each go to doctors of either group. This may explain in
part the apparent lack of correlation between dialect groups in
the general Chinese community and Chinese physicians belonging to those groups.

Data concerning the Chinese communities become more
valuable when compared with similar material for the other
racial groups. For example, the 1947 census indicates that
56 per cent of the Chinese males were gainfully occupied (that
is, in "the occupation at which the person spends most of his
time and from which he received the greater part of his income"), as compared to 53.4 per cent for the Malays and 71.3

------

21. Purcell, The Chinese in Southeast Asia, pp. 271-72.
22. Hodder, "Racial Groupings in Singapore," pp. 25-36.
23. Choo, Oh Siew, The Chinese Physician in Singapore: A
Study of His Popularity among the Chinese and People of Other
Races (Singapore: University of Malaya, May, 1955), pp. 41,
67.

per cent for the Indians. A further breakdown reveals that over one-half of the male Chinese working population is engaged in mining, manufacture, transport, and commerce, although of the remainder, one-third is occupied in agricultural pursuits. In comparison, almost three-fourths of the total male Malay working population and over two-fifths of the Indian population are engaged in agriculture.

Rubber holdings

The Chinese play an exceptionally important role in the rubber industry as estate owners, smallholders, processors, and middlemen. Although the Chinese own about one-half of the total number of rubber estates, their proportion of the total planted acreage is less than one-quarter (Table 49). This is principally because the Europeans own over 80 per cent of the estates one thousand acres or larger in size. On the other hand, the Chinese owned over 65 per cent of the smaller estates in mid-1953. This table further reveals that the smaller units were least productive for both Europeans and Chinese, and that the smaller Chinese estates were only about one-half as productive as the smaller European units.

From 1951 and 1952 the total number of estates owned by the Chinese had increased 13 per cent by mid-1953, whereas the number of estates owned by the Europeans had decreased by 6 per cent; the total high-yielding acreage owned by the Europeans during this three-year period increased from 522,000 to 583,000 acres, or about 11 per cent, and the Chinese acreage of high-yielding material increased from 82,000 to 113,000 acres, or about 27 per cent. Larger estates are better managed and conduct systematic replanting practices enabling consistent production over a protracted period of time. When rubber prices are depressed, as in 1953, some of the smaller estates especially European-owned smaller estates, often cease production. However, since the smaller units often represent the only source of cash income for the Chinese family, rubber trees owned by the Chinese continue to be tapped regardless of price fluctuations. Therefore, the management of the smaller holdings is usually characterized by continuous and extensive over-tapping without regard to replanting.

To a degree the same problem applies to the true small-holdings, those under one hundred acres in size, which occupy about 1.7 million acres. It is estimated that about half this acreage, chiefly those holdings under fifteen acres, is operated by Malaysians. The remainder is held by both Chinese and Indians, although the available data do not distinguish among the three ethnic groups. The Chinese, however, may well be the most important of the three, indirectly if not directly, since many of the Malaysian-operated smallholdings are actually owned by Chinese. In any event, it is customary on the smallholdings to tap constantly and often indiscriminately, and it is uncommon to find systematic replanting of higher-yielding clones taking place, since this is a costly matter.

TABLE 49
RUBBER ESTATES*

Acres	Number of Estates	Total Planted Acreage	Total High-yielding Acres	Per Cent High-yielding of Total Planted Acreage
Europeans				
100-499	85	24,974	8,054	32.2
500-999	143	108,022	44,267	41.0
1,000-1,999	253	366,593	143,519	39.1
2,000-4,999	184	569,146	234,707	41.2
Over 5,000	48	343,703	152,752	44.4
Total	713	1,412,438	583,299	41.3
Chinese				
100-499	1,033	206,541	34,216	16.6
500-999	134	94,110	23,086	24.5
1,000-1,999	55	77,579	24,713	31.9
2,000-4,999	19	53,366	17,671	33.1
Over 5,000	4	30,510	13,430	44.0
Total	1,245	462,106	113,116	24.5
All Nationalities				
100-499	1,598	322,486	52,942	16.4
500-999	312	227,366	72,237	31.8
1,000-1,999	319	460,416	171,684	37.3
2,000-4,999	206	630,865	255,564	40.5
Over 5,000	54	388,573	175,328	45.1
Total	2,489	2,029,706	727,755	35.9

*Federation of Malaya, Annual Report, 1953, p. 115.

The problem of replanting has long been recognized by the government, and in 1953 the Rubber Industry (Replanting) Fund Ordinance, designed to pay the planter M$400 (later M$500) for each acre replanted (about one-half the actual cost of plant-

258

ing), succeeded in getting almost as much rubber replanted in one year by smallholders as had been done in the six previous years. However, since gross smallholder production amounts only to about two-thirds that of the estates, aid to the smallholders (apportioned on a production basis) has been smaller than that given the estates, which need it less.[24]

Estate population

The Chinese population resident on estates over five hundred acres ("Class A") represented over 27 per cent of the total Class A estate population in 1947. This represented an increase of 19 per cent over the 1921, and 20 per cent over the 1931, figures.

The distribution of the Chinese estate population does not, however, conform closely to the distribution of the total estate population. For example, whereas Johore, Selangor, Perak, Kedah, and Negri Sembilan have the largest proportion of the total estate population in the order given (about 87 per cent), the largest concentrations of estate Chinese are located in Johore, Negri Sembilan, Selangor, and Perak.

The role of the Chinese in the estate economy is reflected in Table 50, which attempts to translate gross numbers from the census into percentage ratios for the various occupation categories. The table shows, first, that the Chinese are foremost in the service sector as witnessed by their roles as truck gardeners, poultry and livestock rearers, and foresters and woodcutters. Secondly, when the Malaysian and Indian elements are considered together, the Chinese appear relatively unimportant in the other forms of agricultural cultivation except for rubber, in which they show a structure comparable with the Malaysians, except in the category of owners and managers. Although the Chinese are represented in all agricultural occupations, there appears to be a greater percentage in rubber and the least in coconut production. Whereas the Malaysians predominate in coconut cultivation, the Indians have the largest interest in oil-palm cultivation. A very high proportion

---

24. Federation of Malaya, Taxation and Replanting in the Rubber Industry. Statement of the Federal Government on the Report of the Mudie Mission and on Certain Proposals Made by the Rubber Producers' Council (Kuala Lumpur: Government Press, 1955), pp. 1-41.

of paddy planters are Malaysians; only 8 per cent are Chinese. It must be borne in mind, however, in evaluating these statistics that only 12 per cent of the total Chinese population is classified as agricultural, whereas 26 per cent and 33 per cent of the Malaysians and Indians, respectively, are in this category.

TABLE 50
PERCENTAGE ANALYSIS OF AGRICULTURAL OCCUPATIONS*

	Percentage			
	Chinese	Malaysians	Indians	Others
Rubber cultivation				
Owners, managers, etc.	32	57	6	5
Tappers	38	40	21	1
Factory workers	18	16	63	3
Other agricultural occupations	22	13	63	2
Coconut cultivation				
Owners, managers, etc.	8	89	1	2
Factory workers	16	50	34	-
Other agricultural occupations	9	36	54	1
Oil palm cultivation				
Owners	27	9	36	28
Factory workers	15	23	60	2
Other agricultural occupations	28	10	61	1
Other agricultural industries				
Paddy planters	8	88	0.2	3.8
Fruit, vegetable growers	79	17	3	1
Poultry, livestock raisers	62	9	25	4
Foresters and occupations	65	33	Negligible	
Other agricultural occupations	43	39	16	2

*Del Tufo, Malaya, p. 477, Table 88.

Chinese occupation pattern in Singapore

The Chinese, who account for over 75 per cent of Singapore's population, are dominant in every one of the chief occupation categories outlined in the census except public administration, in which the Malays are chiefly represented (as police officers). The Malays also form a large proportion of the fishermen in Singapore, but even in this normally indigenous occupation the Chinese are predominant both as fishermen and fish brokers.

Commercial occupations dominate among the Chinese. About one-half of those represented in this category are peddlers, hawkers, and vendors, whereas the other large segment of this category are salesmen, commercial travelers, and the like. The next largest category is transport and communication. In this they are largely represented as ship owners, managers, agents, stevedores, boatmen, and ship's crew, and also as pedicab pullers and drivers. [25] The next two largest occupation categories consist of domestic service and office employees in which Chinese form over 90 per cent of the former and over 75 per cent of the latter. Similar distribution exists for each of the other occupations. For instance, the Chinese constitute over 70 per cent of all the occupations of professional status and over 90 per cent of such occupations as cabinet-making.

Of the 7,223 persons employed in public administration and public defense in 1947, however, only 684 were Chinese. Although both the Indians and Malays have larger absolute numbers employed in this general category, the Chinese have more central government officials than either. This situation is true also of the municipal officials, police officers, and inspectors. As pointed out previously, the bulk of the police ranks are made up of Malays. Thus, it would appear that Chinese supervise a predominantly Malay police force. However, over one-half of the police administration is European. The existence of a predominantly Malay constabulary in an almost wholly Chinese population is in itself suspect and has been recognized by the British authorities as such. Reasonably successful efforts have been made to recruit more Chinese, although their representation was less than 20 per cent as late as 1952. This is reflected in the national distribution of the Singapore Regular Police Force for 1952. [26] Of the 3,675 persons employed, only 468 were Chinese, and of this number 288 were C.I.D. (Criminal Investigation Department) men, meaning that over 60 per cent of the Chinese, as members of the police force, did not come into face-to-face contact with the native population. On the other hand, of the 2,523 Malays represented on

_____

25. The pedicab is a three-wheeled, foot-propelled vehicle introduced to Southeast Asia by the Japanese.

26. Colony of Singapore, Annual Report, 1952, p. 201.

the force, 2,433 were in the uniform branch and only 70 were C. I. D. men.

In some respects this situation is a result of the Emergency conditions existing in Singapore, as throughout all of Malaya. The Communist movement is largely Chinese, and therefore it is relatively common to associate all Chinese with terroristic activities. Thus, the British understandably have been reluctant to recruit Chinese on a large scale because of altercations that might occur between them and the Malays in pursuance of their duties. From the standpoint of a young Chinese, this form of occupation is not especially favored as it conflicts with a cultural ethos traditional to Chinese society. The soldier or anyone connected with law enforcement tends to have little prestige and ranks low on the scale of Chinese social stratification. Furthermore, there is a discreet feeling that people should be able to govern their own affairs as much as possible without the policing activities of a specially constituted force. Such intracommunity maintenance of law and order is manifested in the form of clan and dialect groupings, whose activities and responsibilities traditionally have embraced many features of social life that today are a function of law enforcement agencies. Besides, the exclusiveness of the Chinese and their ability to govern their own affairs was originally recognized by the British through the appointment of Kapitans China as the spokesmen of their particular communities. Although the exclusiveness and traditional method of governing their affairs has undergone some change, the principle remains the same. [27]

Chinese occupation pattern in the Federation

The Chinese bases of livelihood in the Federation resemble those in Singapore in that Chinese predominate in the professions, mining, personal services, and commercial services. Of the two occupation categories in which they are not pre-eminent, agricultural and public administration, the Chinese represent about one-fifth of the former and only one-

---

27. The employment of some Chinese as high officials in government does not conflict with these cultural values. The greatest social prestige is attached to any government position; even members of the Imperial Chinese "Censorate" (an essentially investigatory body) were held in high esteem.

twentieth of the latter. Two occupations are of particular significance to the Chinese, tin-mining and pineapple cultivation.

Tin-mining. --Tin-mining has been one of the principal sources of livelihood for the Chinese since earliest times. Today this continued interest is reflected in the fact that nearly 40 per cent of the tin produced comes from mines owned by Chinese who employ more than one-half of the tin-mining labor force.[28] Although 600 of the 740 tin mines are Chinese operated, the more extensive holdings of the European-owned mines, together with the methods of extraction used in them, account for their greater productivity. Labor in the tin mines up to the nineteenth century was principally Malay, but when the rich deposits in Larut were discovered in the 1850's, Chinese laborers flocked to the fields. Until the early 1930's, when European capital began to flow into the tin industry, Chinese owners produced about two-thirds of the total. Since that time Chinese production has declined to between 35 and 40 per cent of all production.

Chinese traditional social organization is reflected in the organization of the Chinese sector of the tin industry. "Kongsi," or partnerships, form the financial basis of most of the Chinese mines, although more recently an increasing number have been owned by companies with the same shareholders as the former kongsi.[29] Normally, the individuals working in each mine are from the same linguistic group and often originally came from the same general community in China. It appears that the Hakka, Cantonese, and Hokkien dominate both as owners and employees, with the Hokkien a poor third. Whereas previously the latter group had been primarily the shopkeepers and provision-store dealers on mines supplying the needs of the laborers, they seem now to be taking a more direct interest in actual mining operations.[30] Thus, certain

---

28. Malayan Tin Bureau, There Is Plenty of Tin (Washington: Malayan Tin Bureau, 1952), p. 6.

29. Federation of Malaya, Annual Report, 1953, p. 160. Cf. J. B. Perry Robinson, Transformation in Malaya (London: Secker & Warburg, 1956), p. 74. He defines a "Kongsi" as being any functional assembly of members of the same clan, guild, or craft.

30. Siew, Nim Chee, Labor and Tin Mining in Malaya (Data Paper No. 7, Southeast Asia Program, Department of Far

organizational traditions have been established which, together with the heavy capital investments made, assure continued Chinese participation in industry.

The proportion of immigrant as compared with locally born laborers is increasing. Until the early thirties, all the laborers were poorly educated immigrants from the rural districts of China. Even after the passage of the Aliens Ordinance Act in 1933 and other legislation restricting the number of Chinese entering the peninsula, those who did enter were shuttled off to the tin mines. During the war and directly afterward as a result of the Emergency, immigration of laborers was at a virtual standstill, thereby causing an influx of locally born Chinese into the mines when the need for labor arose. Yet, as late as 1950 it was estimated that two-thirds were born in China; in prewar times the proportion was closer to four-fifths. The number of Malaya-born would have been greater had not many laborers abandoned their jobs during the war and failed to return. [31]

Pineapple industry. --It has been said that the economic development of Malaya is a result of two chief factors--British political control and Chinese enterprise. [32] The growth of the pineapple industry in Malaya reflects a merging of the two. It had developed during the forty years preceding World War II "from a small 'cottage' industry to become one of the largest fruit-canning industries in the world and it ranked third amongst Malaya's export industries."[33] Particularly suitable to Malaya because it is the only known crop of economic importance which can be grown satisfactorily on peaty soil, pineapple-growing is confined largely to the state of Johore, with subsidiary concentrations in Selangor and Perak. Until the occupation of Malaya by Japan, seventeen processing factories had been established by the British to service the produce of

----

Eastern Studies [Ithaca: Cornell University, February, 1953]), p. 24.

31. Ibid.

32. H. G. Callis, Foreign Capital in Southeast Asia (New York: Institute of Pacific Relations, 1942), pp. 48-58.

33. Great Britain, Colonial Office, Economic Survey of the Colonial Territories, 1951, Vol. VII, The Products of the Colonial Territories (London: H. M. Stationery Office, 1952), p. 30.

the more than sixty thousand acres of pineapple, most of which were in smallholdings worked by Chinese. In 1937, Malaya provided the United Kingdom with 90 per cent of its imports of canned pineapple.

At the end of the war the industry had practically disappeared. Only one of the factories remained, and only three thousand acres were producing. Within a relatively short time exports increased from 13 tons in 1946 to 17,368 tons in 1953, representing a change in value from about M$11,000 to approximately M$12,000,000. In proportion, the area under cultivation increased to about twenty-seven thousand acres, with about fifteen thousand acres in smallholdings ranging between twelve and eighteen acres each. Production has been affected by the resettlement program operated under the Emergency and involving five to six hundred thousand persons, since much of the postwar production came from the "squatter" population being resettled. The Pineapple Industry Ordinance of 1951 was designed for the specific purpose of building up a fund for the improvement of the industry, including, at least in principle, the provision of some financial assistance to the smallholders' overage plantations. The provincial agriculture department and the Ministry of Supply have been active in fostering the continued expansion of the industry. Model projects have been started with emphasis on proper drainage, selected seedlings, and the use of more adequate fertilizers. Meanwhile, the Ministry of Supply has controlled pineapple prices until recently in an effort to check inflationary tendencies.

Political and Social Organization

Clan relationships, dialect similarities, and occupation identifications form the common basis of all Chinese groupings whether they be benevolent and secret societies or guilds and labor unions. There is even more indication that individual Malayan Communist Party units are organized along such patterns. [34] Those groups which have gained the interest of the outside world have been widely publicized and consequently there is a considerable body of literature about them. This is

---

34. "The Emergency in Malaya," The World Today, November, 1954, pp. 476-87.

true particularly of the Communist party of Malaya and the Malayan Chinese Association.

The general political order

In Malaya today there is at least one political organization that claims the support of the entire Chinese population. This is the Malayan Chinese Association (MCA), which was formed in February, 1949, by Sir Tan, Cheng-lock for the apparent purpose of organizing Chinese public opinion on the 1948 Federation Agreement. [35] Until this date there had never been any such organization, political or otherwise, that pretended to represent the interests of all the Chinese. Its continued existence through the Emergency and its relative success in elections indicates its support by a large segment of the Chinese community. In 1952 it merged with the United Malay National Organization (UMNO).

Prior to the postwar MCA, organized political activity was externally oriented. The emergence of the Chinese republic in 1912 and the revolutionary movements associated with it received considerable financial and sympathetic support from overseas Chinese in general and from the Chinese in Malaya in particular. Sun, Yat-sen and his supporters were active in soliciting financial assistance and in organizing branches of the Kuomintang, or of predecessors of that political organization, as early as 1906 in Malaya. Although the active supporters were few in number, there had always been deep feelings among Malayan Chinese for the establishment of a strong China.

These sympathies have become the source of the ambivalent position in which many Chinese in Malaya now find themselves. On the one hand, support of the Communist regime in China evokes a fear on the part of the Malayan Chinese that their economic power would be curtailed should the Chinese Communists win in Malaya. On the other hand, nonsupport effectively severs their ties with the homeland. Furthermore, because the creation of Malayan loyalties has become a tenet of

---

35. Tan, Cheng-lock, rubber baron from Malakka, is the elder statesman of the Malayan Chinese. He has been active in public affairs and government circles since the early 1930's and more recently has been identified with the growing political consciousness of the Chinese.

colonial and Malay policy, the Chinese are considered disloyal if they reveal any overt sympathy toward China. These conflicting pressures appear to have been resolved superficially on the basis of the MCA's success in both the Singapore and Federation of Malaya elections in 1955.

There are few data on the numerical or the qualitative strength of the Nationalist cause. Some information, however, indicates that because the Chinese Communists are attempting to intimidate wealthy overseas Chinese into paying ransom for imprisoned relatives and are employing other similar tactics, some of the funds previously remitted to the mainland are now finding their way to Taiwan. Because of the nature of the movement, the activities of the Kuomintang in Malaya always have been oriented toward the mainland and had little concern with the political development of Malaya proper. Proof of a continued China-oriented interest held in common by most Chinese became apparent when the self-exiled leaders of the Kuomintang returned from Sumatra shortly after the end of the war and were able to make deep inroads into the progress achieved by the Malayan Communist Party. Purcell claims that whenever the Communist party advocated policies detrimental to China, it would inevitably lose followers, to the benefit of the Kuomintang membership. [36]

The Communist party did not become active until 1934 when it was responsible for work stoppages, boycotts, and other manifestations of labor dissension. During the war, this organization fought against the Japanese, [37] and afterward it determined to establish a Malayan republic. It apparently has never received widespread active support from the Malayan Chinese, but it does constitute the most serious source of trouble to the British administration at the present time.

One of the major deterrents to the formation of an effective total Chinese political organization has been a general apathy toward political activity. Traditionally, organized political

---

36. Purcell, The Chinese in Malaya, p. 276. He cites the instance of a Penang Chinese newspaper with a strong Communist bias that lost most of its subscribers when it defended the action of Russia in remaining in Manchuria at the end of World War II.

37. It was the only organized anti-Japanese group in Malaya for two years following the fall of Singapore.

expression took the form of secret societies in China. As they normally formed the basis of revolutionary movements, the concept of a legal political party was foreign to Chinese political ideology until the formation of Nationalist China; an interesting parallel can be seen in the rise of the Communist Party in China. Because of the growing insecurity among the Chinese in Malaya as a result of rumors that the British, who have been protecting their interests against the encroachments of the Malays, [38] are seriously considering vacating the area, they have begun to take a more active interest in their own future political status.

Malayan Chinese Association. -- The only qualification for membership in the Malayan Chinese Association is the intent to live permanently in Malaya. There are no limitations with regard to race since it is one of the cardinal objectives of the association to "promote and maintain inter-racial good will and harmony in Malaya."[39] The central headquarters is located in Kuala Lumpur, with branch associations in each state and settlement in the Federation and with a Singapore branch. Each branch association is made up of a number of district associations, which in turn consist of area associations.

The MCA has assumed a heavy responsibility with regard to the resettled "squatters," providing financial aid for the building and maintenance of schools, constructions of homes, and other necessities, until they are able to provide for themselves. This money has been administered through welfare funds of the association and was, until mid-1953, acquired through national lotteries that were sponsored from time to time. Up to that date, when the Templer administration prohibited the operation of lotteries by political associations, the association had disbursed two and one-half million Malayan dollars for welfare work to the "New Villages."[40] Although

_____

38. This is the "other side of the coin." The colonial authorities have officially protected the Malays and their landholdings against foreigners, including the Chinese and the Europeans. In the process, however, Chinese autonomy and freedom also were insured.

39. Quoted from a government publication of the MCA's charter.

40. Victor Purcell, Malaya: Communist or Free? (London:

268

expressly stating that one of the objects of the association was "to foster and safeguard the social, political, cultural and economic welfare of the Malayan Chinese by legal or constitutional means," it had relegated "politics" to the bottom of the list for the duration of the Emergency. But by labeling the MCA as political, the government prevented it from conducting its welfare activities and as a result incurred considerable resentment. The association believes that the government directed legislation specifically at it by referring to it as "political," and the government has publicly reproached the MCA because it has stopped its welfare work, thereby placing a heavier financial burden on the already hard-pressed government.

With the proscription of some political parties after the declaration of the Emergency and the fading out of others, the UMNO and the MCA, after February, 1949, were the only two organizations in the Federation with any sizable representation. In September, 1951, however, the IMP (Independence of Malaya Party) was founded by Dato Onn bin Jafaar, the founder of UMNO and Member for Home Affairs in the Federation government. Largely because of the "official" atmosphere in which it was conceived and the policy of racial equality it advocated, the IMP failed to win the support of either the Malays or the Chinese. The political composite was further crystallized in February, 1952, when the UMNO and the MCA united to defeat the IMP candidates in the Kuala Lumpur municipal elections. The UMNO-MCA alliance won a total of twenty-six out of thirty-seven seats in the general municipal elections of early 1953, in Johore gaining all nine vacancies, in Muar seven out of nine, in Kuala Lumpur three out of four, and in Malakka two out of three.

To counteract the intention of the government to wean popular support away from the alliance by having the mentris besar (head ministers) of seven of the nine states convene in April, 1953, for the purpose of determining how a "free, united, and independent Malayan nation" could be constructed, the UMNO-MCA merger held its own conference in August of that year. Taking as a keynote the statement of the Colonial Secretary that Malaya would be given independence as soon as its various races were united, the UMNO-MCA stressed the

---

Victor Gollancz, Ltd., 1954), p. 83, n. 1.

importance of showing the British and all others concerned that unity between the two main racial groups was possible. It passed a resolution to work for a sovereign and independent state within the British Commonwealth and urged that elections for the Federal Legislature be held in 1954. The government decided, as a result of these resolutions, that general elections would be held in mid-1955, at which time the alliance was markedly successful in capturing the majority of elected seats.

The Malayan Communist Party. --The MCP cannot be appropriately designated as an ethnic political organization, but because of its almost exclusive Chinese membership a discussion of it at this point is included. The historical development of the Communist party in Malaya is associated largely with the vicissitudes of its counterpart in China. As a result of the cleavage between the Communist and Kuomintang parties in 1927 and singular instances of party defection in Malaya, the MCP maintained a precarious existence until the early thirties. Even after this, because of government policies, it never really became a potential threat to the internal peace of Malaya until the summer of 1948 when it inaugurated a policy of open terrorism for the ultimate purpose of establishing a Malayan republic by August of that year. [41]

It was the advent of World War II that crystallized the formation and organizational effectiveness of the Malayan Communist Party. During the last few months before the invasion of Malaya by the Japanese, British commando units were active in the recruitment and training of guerrilla groups. MCP members were trained by the British along with others, because it was well known that the Chinese, and especially the Chinese Communists, were the implacable enemies of the Japanese, and all those who showed any inclination to oppose the common enemy were welcomed regardless of political affiliation. [42] Because of the rudimentary nature of the organizations thus formed, most were ineffective in constituting any real opposi-

---

41. G. Z. Hanrahan, "The Communist Struggle in Malaya," (New York: Institute of Pacific Relations, 1954). (Mimeographed.)

42. F. Spencer Chapman, The Jungle Is Neutral (New York: W. W. Norton, 1949). This author describes the efforts of the British to organize an effective force to combat the rapidly advancing Japanese.

tion to the Japanese and accordingly were forced to go underground shortly after the fall of Singapore in February, 1942. Those who escaped the rounding-up tactics of the Japanese retreated into the jungles and there formed closely knit guerrilla units that constantly harassed the occupying power, necessitating the diversion of special constabulary forces to keep them under control.

Official British contacts were made with these guerrilla units in 1943, and the British managed to obtain an agreement from them promising cooperation with the Southeast Asia Command in return for supplies and other forms of material support. Shortly after their retreat to the jungles the guerrillas called themselves the Malayan People's Anti-Japanese Army (MPAJA), and it was this organization with which the British officers negotiated in making the above agreement. At the end of the war, but before the British military administration was able to assume administrative control over all the internal communities, the MPAJA emerged from the jungles and assumed political supremacy in certain areas.

After an uneasy period during which the British showed definite intentions of resuming their former status, the MPAJA reluctantly relinquished its nominal control over these areas in December, 1945, by surrendering its arms in return for a small gratuity to compensate for its efforts during the war. But there were many individuals, the hard core of the MCP, who refused to succumb to the returned colonial power. This initial refusal and later attempts at labor strikes through control of the General Labor Union (GLU) represented the first efforts of the MCP to initiate and continue an essentially anti-British policy. When it became evident that their program was not successful in influencing the Malayan population, the MCP declared an all-out struggle against the British for the control of Malaya in June of 1948. This policy of open terrorism was replaced in late 1951 by one of subversion and infiltration into the ranks of labor unions, election to public offices, and the acquisition of influence in various political and social organizations. Present MCP policy is characterized by sporadic and isolated attacks on police stations, tin mines, and rubber estates, coupled with its program of subversion

One of the chief problems connected with combating the activities of the MCP is the existence of a "fifth column," nominally known as the <u>Min Yuen,</u> the "masses work force," which is estimated to number about twenty thousand members. Composed of young people, it collects food and money, distributes propaganda, and works as a contact between guerrilla groups and the population. Because of the military policies pursued by the British, the MCP was forced to organize its jungle forces into special mobile units made up of members of the <u>Min Yuen</u> and the terrorists. Resettlement of squatters, psychological warfare among the villagers, and other measures have undermined the activities of this fertile group, but their strength is still latent and unpredictable. Effective control of young teenage groups, especially in high schools, constitutes a prevalent problem; its abatement may come only with the decline of Communist power.

The British administrators and the Federal and state governments continue to adopt new measures to cope with the persistent Emergency situation. Some are temporary in nature, such as the special "Ferrent Forces" composed of volunteers and including Iban trackers from British Borneo, language specialists, and specially assigned technicians. Other measures are more permanent, such as the Home Guard units and a working cooperation between police, army, and government employees, perhaps the most hopeful recourse. Such measures as the tight control over food-supply movements or a surprise raid on a suspected village, are apparently beginning to succeed, but in spite of the cost involved (about one-third the annual budget) they have not reduced substantially the number of terrorists (between 3,000 and 6,500 at any one time). A hard core has allegedly established headquarters across the border in Thailand and still hopes to establish a Communist republic through ruthless means.

Another government approach to the problem was made in the September 15, 1952, amendment to the 1948 citizenship laws, providing more political rights for Chinese.[43] All Malaya-born Chinese, estimated at about 70 per cent of the adult Chinese population, were made eligible for citizenship and, after fulfilling certain residence requirements, were enabled to vote. Although the granting of such rights does not automatically weaken the power and influence of the MCP among the politically uncommitted, it does deprive that organization

43. Purcell, Malaya: Communist or Free?, pp. 218 ff. See this work for details of the law and criticisms directed to it by prominent members of the Chinese community.

of a potent political weapon. Another favorite propaganda point of the Communists, the absence of Malayan independence, has also been effectively negated through the announced plans for independence in August, 1957. As the terroristic features of the MCP program come under control and the "British Protectors" simultaneously project such fundamental schemes to meet the growing aspirations of the Malayan peoples, the MCP may be undermined as a potent political force.

Local organization

Village or neighborhood social and political organizations are normally based on dialect or place-of-origin similarities. Homogeneous groupings of Chinese who speak a particular dialect are common throughout Malaya, especially in Singapore where specific settlement sites were designated by Raffles shortly after that city was founded.[44] Mutual unintelligibility among the dialects compels an individual to settle in an area where his special language is spoken. The custom of immigrants to take up only temporary residence was additional reason for them to seek out the area where it was easiest to communicate with their neighbors. Recent changes in this traditional pattern of settlement, together with the emphasis placed upon learning kuo-yü (the national language which will probably become the lingua franca) in the Chinese school system, operates to break down some of the traditional social and occupational cleavages.[45] Areal agglomeration of dialect groups, however, will continue as long as high population densities continue in the urban centers dominated by the Chinese. Furthermore, the grouping and settling of large numbers of individual Chinese households into "New Villages" serves to intensify these elementary bonds of social life.

Evidence from Sarawak and North Borneo also indicates

---

44. Hodder, "Racial Groupings in Singapore," pp. 25-36.

45. J. A. T. Horsley, "Resettlement of a Community" (Singapore: University of Malaya, April, 1955), pp. 71-82. "Kampong Henderson," three miles northwest of Singapore, originated from the settlement of one Chinese family. It now has three main families from the same Fukien district in China and is mainly Hokkien, with a few Cantonese and Hakkas. It is described as "typical of the many Chinese 'Kampongs' in Singapore and also in Malaya."

that in many instances local recreational clubs or youth groups and sometimes entire towns are commonly named after the region or city in China from which most of the inhabitants emigrated.

Corporate organization

As of December 31, 1954, there were more than 4,500 societies in the Federation of Malaya.[46] Of this number more than 2,300 were Chinese in membership, representing over half of the total Chinese population of the Federation. The number of such societies in Singapore has been estimated at 900.[47] In terms of actually performing some useful social function, these numbers would be drastically reduced, but they do indicate the extent to which Chinese are "organization" conscious. Another factor is the requirement that all groups with a membership of over ten be registered with the government under a Societies Ordinance enactment established in 1934 and revived in 1947.

As a result, these organizations include everything from a labor union to a religious group. Furthermore, a person is normally a member of more than one group; formal membership, therefore, does not accurately reflect the numbers who participate in and benefit from the numerous activities sponsored by these groups.

Kinship-based groups. --Clan relationships have traditionally assumed an important role among the Chinese of southeastern China. Emigration served to accentuate this importance since it was common practice for members of the same clan to provide the means and even employment for their "brothers" to go to the Nan-yang region. Making a livelihood was a precarious enterprise, and therefore all the assistance that

---

46. Federation of Malaya, Attorney-General's Chambers, "Return of Societies in the Federation of Malaya, as at 31st December, 1954," Appendices I, II, III. (Kuala Lumpur, 1955). (Mimeographed.)

47. Directory of Chinese Schools and Associations in Singapore(1948), No. 109, quoted in T'ien, Ju-kang, The Chinese in Sarawak (The London School of Economics and Political Science Monographs on Social Anthropology, No. 12 [London: London School of Economics and Political Science, 1953]), p. 10.

similarity of surname promised was eagerly sought. An example of the importance that clan relationships obtain throughout the Nan-yang is taken from the personal experience of a Western-trained Chinese scholar:

> Shortly after my arrival in Sarawak I had occasion to visit a certain Mr. T'ien who lived at some distance from Kuching. I took with me a young student friend named Yang. On our arrival we were treated with all the ordinary marks of hospitality, but there was perhaps a hint of constrained politeness in the air until our host, on enquiring, was told that my friend's surname was also T'ien. Immediately all constraint was dropped, and we were both treated as members of the family. . . . Later, I myself experienced the advantages of the intricate network of this kind of surname relationship. I could always find hospitality with other T'iens anywhere in the Colony, and in each district I would be told of T'iens whom I would meet at my next stopping place. [48]

If this kind of experience occurred to one who could not claim recent emigration from China, it is certain that clan ties among those who can is indeed strong.

The clan, or as it is commonly rendered in Chinese, tsu (族), "includes all persons of a single surname who can trace their descent from a common ancestor."[49] There is no distinction made on an occupation basis, as members of a particular tsu can range from the most successful entrepreneur to the most menial of laborers. The only qualification is that the individual involved has the same Chinese character for his surname. This similarity of surname is associated with the assumption that all those who share it must be patrilineally related. Every person is proud to claim a particular genealogy, and some wealthy Chinese have traced their ancestry back to the early dynasties of Chinese history.

---

48. T'ien, The Chinese in Sarawak, pp. 23 ff.

49. Marion J. Levy, Jr., The Family Revolution in Modern China (Cambridge, Massachusetts: Harvard University Press, 1949), p. 49.

Theoretically clans remain single corporate structures, but in practice areal segmentation takes place, and there are cases where one clan is divided among several villages. Such cases occur primarily in the Yangtze valley and in the southeast provinces of Fukien and Kwangtung, from which most of the overseas Chinese originate.[50] These segments are referred to as subclans or fang (房), and they can usually trace a common descent and thus can be termed a lineage. Broadly, then, kinship structure consists of the widest clan, comprising a very large number of dispersed localized subclans whose members may, although not always, be able to trace a mutual kinship. These in turn are subdivided on a lineage basis into nuclear units of family organization called the chia (家).

It is the tsu which holds property, exercises extralegal functions, makes proper arrangements for ancestor worship, and performs various other functions as an organized unit.[51] The segmentation of clans has also brought about a segmentation of functions, and therefore the subclan assumes the roles, at the village or regional level, which would be performed by the larger group in an unsegmented clan. One of the principal activities of these subclans is to maintain and disburse welfare and educational funds that are collected periodically from the various members. Traditionally the eldest men of the eldest generation are the nominal heads of the clan responsible for setting ancestor worship dates, settling disputes within the clan, and supervising other activities associated with it. Recently clan leadership has been based not only on age but also on social prominence and education of the individual.[52] The actual leaders of the clans, however, are the managers, treasurers, and committee members, who come from the more wealthy families and who tend to constitute self-perpetuating factions in many cases. Generally most of the control is in the hands of the business and professional members of the clan, and the majority of membership, represented by the poorer groups, has little power.

Clan relationships cut across other forms of social groupings. Because clans are exogamous, members of the same

---

50. Olga Lang, Chinese Family and Society (New Haven, Connecticut: Yale University Press, 1946), p. 174.
51. Ibid., p. 175.
52. T'ien, The Chinese in Sarawak, pp. 23 ff.

clan can be members of different dialect groups. Thus, one of the larger clan associations in Singapore, the Shen association, has members from six different Chinese provinces (Kansu, Chekiang, Anwhei, Kwangtung, Kwangsi, Fukien) and has branch organizations in several countries in Southeast Asia. [53] It publishes a newsletter relating pertinent details about famous members of the clan and providing information on the movements of others.

Increased urbanization and wartime dislocations have had some detrimental effect upon the strength of clan ties. [54] Lang claims that at least in China urbanization has tended to break down clan relationships, particularly among the lower income classes. The proliferation of social services normally associated with urban areas tends to supplant some of the mutual-help and benevolent characteristics of the clan groupings. Changes wrought by the Japanese in Malaya also affected Chinese clan groupings. Families were separated, established ways of settling intracommunal problems were disrupted, and leaders of the community were forced to go into hiding. In addition, the resettlement of more then five hundred thousand Chinese, or about one-sixth of the total Chinese population, into "New Villages" cannot help but have repercussions on all facets of Chinese social organization.

Nonkinship-based groups. --Most of the Chinese corporate organizations in Malaya are nonkinship-based groups. The official register for the Federation of Malaya has classified them according to ten different categories. They are (1) religious, (2) kongsi, (3) houy (hui) kuan, (4) social, (5) sports, (6) benevolent, (7) guild, (8) cultural, (9) political, (10) general. [55] There is evidence of some overlapping of these with the strictly kinship-based (or clan) groups and the general ethnic or political organizations. Nevertheless, over 1,500 of the 1,612 non-kinship-based groups are listed as independent

---

53. Ibid., p. 24, n. 4.

54. Lang, Chinese Family and Society, p. 180; Willard H. Elsebree, Japan's Role in Southeast Asian Nationalist Movements, 1940-1945 (Cambridge, Massachusetts: Harvard University Press, 1953), pp. 146 ff.

55. Federation of Malaya, Attorney-General's Chambers, "Return of Societies in the Federation of Malaya."

of clan or political societies. Similar proportions probably hold for Singapore.

Dialect associations exist for every major linguistic group among the Chinese. They appear to be the largest in membership and the most inclusive of the nonkinship-based groups outside of the general ethnic political organization already discussed. They are organized on the basis of clan relationships, occupation similarities, and place of origin. Although all members of dialect associations speak the same dialect, which is the basis upon which the organization is founded, these three factors are the reasons for its group status. All three are interrelated and serve to unite the members through a series of complex and overlapping loyalties. T'ien states that the "intricate system of clanship should be considered as the fundamental basis on which the social relations of the overseas Chinese are regulated, and by which the sense of mutual solidarity is made very real. This is especially true of the rural districts."[56] This kind of basis for social relations is most clearly demonstrated in the dominant groups of these dialect associations, which normally consist of one large clan. The institutional structure of the association and the relations maintained among the various members are controlled and manipulated by this leading clan. This dominance is associated with their economic status in relation to the other members.

The economic ties among the various members are maintained through an elaborate credit-debit structure that affects all members. In most instances the leading clan controls the "purse strings," insuring its financial position by charging high interest rates on short-term loans. Once such a relationship is established, it will continue, since it is standard practice for debtors to pay back only a certain percentage of their loans for the specific purpose of obtaining an additional loan. The creditor, who is probably a clansman and most certainly a member of the same dialect association, is compelled to increase the loan even though he knows that the original capital will not be repaid. Therefore, the interest charges are designed to compensate for this and also for the possibility that a debtor will abscond with the loan and settle elsewhere. The legal system enables creditors to press charges through the courts, but because of the loyalties engendered by clan and

---

56. T'ien, The Chinese in Sarawak, p. 17.

dialect affinity, most prefer to settle such problems without recourse to law.

In some instances the most tangible identification of an association is through the place of origin claimed by most of its members. It is the factor that initially brings overseas Chinese together and provides the basis for social cohesion and unity. As a result, many of the organizations are named after the hsien, province or region, in China from which the majority originated.

The chief function of these associations is in connection with their economic and benevolent assistance. [57] Such assistance ranges from advancement of education and the promotion of religion to the relief of poverty and the provision of employment services. Every Chinese community, whether organized or not, provides some funds for the education of its children. The Hokkien association in Singapore has been notable among the organized groups for its work in education affairs. It manages four schools in Singapore, each of which has over one thousand students. The Hokkien children, who constitute only 10 per cent of the enrollment, attend free of charge, and members of other dialect groups pay a small sum. Additional money is obtained from public contributions and temples. In addition, the Hokkien association has been intimately connected with the initial steps in erecting the Nan-yang university in Singapore. It not only donated large sums of money but also provided the land on which the university was begun. [58]

Promotion of religion normally consists of building temples, maintaining cemeteries, sponsoring certain religious festivals, and providing burial services through an insurance fund. [59] Most of these activities are engaged in by the individual associations, but temples appear to have been erected by specific groups for the worship of certain overseas Chinese heroes. [60]

---

57. Kwok, Swee Soo, An Account of the Sources of Benevolent Assistance Which Are Asian in Origin and Organization (Singapore: University of Malaya, April, 1954), p. 80. (Microfilm.)

58. Richard Butwell, "A Chinese University for Malaya," Pacific Affairs, December, 1953, p. 345.

59. Kwok, An Account of the Sources of Benevolent Assistance, p. 72.

60. S. M. Middlebrook, "Ceremonial Opening of a New

Because of the unusual powers associated with the gods worshipped, many of the temples have come to be attended and supported by all dialect communities. Indeed, Confucian, Taoist, and Buddhist religious symbols all may be found in the same temple. One of the dialect organizations revealed that its monthly budget was divided into three sections: (1) 70 per cent for the burial fund, (2) 20 per cent for the general fund, and (3) 10 per cent for the charitable fund. It is claimed that burial fees and other affairs connected with death demand a comparable proportion of the budgets of most associations.

Labor unions. --The first of two principal factors influencing the growth of trade unions among the Chinese in Malaya is the early identification of the Chinese Communist movement with labor organization and activity. Although a few Chinese employees' associations existed before 1922, it was only after this date, when the first National Labor Conference was held in Canton, China, that the modern labor movement in Malaya developed.[62] During the 1923-1927 period when the Nationalists and Communists in China were working together, Chinese revolutionaries, under the direction of the Far Eastern Bureau of the Comintern located in Shanghai, were active in disseminating propaganda, organizing cadres, and infiltrating labor unions in Malaya.[63] Their activities involved the supplying of leadership and revolutionary overtones to some of the labor strikes occurring in the twenties.

By 1924 Communist influence in the labor movement was formalized in the Nan-yang Federation of Labor. It was centrally located in Singapore but had jurisdiction over many of the other countries of Southeast Asia. Government policy permitted such organizations to exist until the Nationalist-Communist split in 1927 when general precautionary measures were taken.

Chinese Temple at Kadan, Malakka, in December, 1938," Journal of the Malayan Branch of the Royal Asiatic Society, 1939, pp. 98-106; Marjorie Topley, "Chinese Rites for the Repose of the Souls, with Special Reference to Cantonese Custom," Journal of the Malayan Branch of the Royal Asiatic Society, pp. 149-60.

61. Kwok, An Account of the Sources of Benevolent Assistance, p. 77.

62. Purcell, The Chinese in Malaya, p. 208.

63. Hanrahan, "The Communist Struggle in Malaya," p. 7.

After a small shoemakers' strike for higher wages in early 1928 was turned into a violent demonstration against "British imperialism" by the Nan-yang Federation, the government declared the federation illegal. Labor agitation by Chinese Communists was further blocked by the deportation of several leading members of the party following the confession of a Comintern agent in 1930. For several years the Malayan Communists assumed an inconspicuous role in the labor movement, but by 1934 they again emerged as the leading members of the Malayan General Labor Union, successor to the defunct Malayan Federation of Labor. [64] The following years, up until the advent of World War II, were marked by sporadic strikes, some of which involved many thousands of laborers.

Although the government was able to bring labor dissension under control through the banishment ordinance of the late thirties and other legislation designed to introduce trade unionism in 1940, Communist organizers had been successful in creating a core of trade union leaders and a multitude of supporters. It was this legacy which formed the basic elements of the newly organized trade unions following the war. Through the general labor union organized in Singapore the Chinese Communists were able to control virtually every Chinese labor organization ranging from longshoremen to tin miners and from pedicab drivers to construction laborers. The postwar implementation of the 1940 ordinances brought experienced British trade unionists to Malaya who worked with various government departments in an effort to introduce responsible trade unions based on the collective bargaining principle. Continued demonstrations of strength by the Communist-dominated unions and the later eruption of terrorist activities in 1948 led to the purging and deportation of undesirable leaders. Since that date Chinese have been reluctant to join labor unions for fear of being identified with the Communist uprising. At present less than 15 per cent of the total trade union membership (185, 000 in the Federation and 64, 000 in Singapore) is Chinese; Indians represent about 60 per cent of the membership. [65] Increasing the Chinese membership to a point comparable to their repre-

---

64. Ibid., p. 21.

65. J. Norman Parmer, "Trade Unions and Politics in Malaya," Far Eastern Survey, March, 1955, pp. 33-39.

sentation in the general labor force constitutes the principal problem faced by trade unionists in Malaya.

Another primary factor affecting the growth of trade unions among the Chinese involves the essentially social rather than industrial basis of their organization. Chinese labor associations grew out of former guilds, secret societies, and mutual-benefit associations. 66 Guilds were and continue to be governed by committees composed of employers and employees who decide rates of wages, hours of work, holidays, and terms of apprenticeship. In addition they normally provide many welfare and beneficial activities that are now associated with the modern labor union. Because these traditional social groupings provide, in many instances, the same benefits as labor unions, the Chinese have not felt compelled to join the unions to the same degree as the Indians.

It can readily be seen that these two factors tend to perpetuate the present complex of trade union movement in Malaya. Continued tension as a result of the Communist uprising makes the average laborer reluctant to join a labor union and he is thus obliged to depend upon other forms of social groupings. The traditional guild system, therefore, has been reinforced by the somewhat new duties placed upon it. Chinese representation in trade union membership will probably change in direct proportion to the degree to which terrorist activities are gradually neutralized.

Secret societies[67]

Another form of nonkinship-based group which has existed in China for centuries is the secret society. Originally religious or benevolent self-help associations, they assumed a political and antidynastic character especially at the time of the Manchu conquest of China, and they later degenerated into criminal organizations.

In Malaya it is customary to trace the origin of Chinese secret societies to the Triad Society, otherwise known as the Hung League (洪家), or Heaven and Earth Society (天地會), which according to Chinese annals dates from the seventeenth century A. D.; the history of secret societies as such goes back

---

66. Purcell, The Chinese in Malaya, p. 207.

67. Except for minor editorial changes, the section on the secret societies is the work of Mr. Leonard Comber.

much further than the seventeenth century and probably dates from the primitive initiatory rites of remote antiquity. The origin of the first name is in the symbol of a triangle used by the society in its esoteric ritual, which signifies the trinity of Heaven, Earth and Man.

The secret rites of Chinese secret societies nearly always represent symbolically three distinct stages in the evolution of mankind: (1) the end of man's alloted span in this world, (2) a period of initiation and purification to prepare him for the other world which lies beyond, and (3) rebirth into this world whence he came. The symbols used in Chinese secret society ritual are, generally speaking, those connected with fertility rites, reproduction, and astrological lore.

Although fundamentally all secret societies are an offshoot of the primitive initiatory rites of prehistoric man trying to solve the riddle of the universe, Chinese secret societies do present certain problems peculiar to themselves. This is due to the complexity and difficulty of the Chinese language, both written and spoken, which readily lends itself to the use of homophones and rebuses. For example, the name of some quite irrelevant object may perhaps be used to suggest another word of the same sound with an entirely different meaning, or a word or phrase may be represented by a picture of objects whose names resemble those words. Another inherent characteristic of Chinese secret societies is their reliance on Buddhism and Taoism to provide a reservoir of quasi-religious, mystic symbols, about which, even to this day, very little is known.

The Triad Society, which is the common ancestor of nearly all the Chinese secret societies in Malaya, was originally a quasi-religious cult, with the virtuous aim to "obey Heaven and act righteously" (順天行道). Early in the eighteenth century it came into prominence in China as a revolutionary political organization with the avowed intention of supporting the cause of the native Chinese Ming dynasty, which had been overthrown by the non-Chinese Manchu, or Ch'ing, dynasty in 1644. It then adopted as its slogan, "Overthrow the Ch'ing, and restore the Ming" (反清復明) and on account of its subversive activities was soon proscribed by the Manchu government.

In China proper the part played by secret societies in making history has never really been evaluated completely by Western scholars, and it would be fascinating to rewrite Chinese history from the point of view of secret societies and their influence on the course of events. There are numerous occasions when secret societies shaped Chinese history in a momentous way--in the Taiping Rebellion of 1850, the Franco-Chinese war of 1883, the Sino-Japanese war of 1894, the Boxer Rebellion of 1900, and even the revolution of 1911 which resulted in the overthrow of the Ch'ing.

The Triad Society was first brought to Malaya from South China by Chinese immigrants during the nineteenth century. There is little or no information concerning its early years in Malaya. This is due to four reasons: (1) The Chinese community governed itself largely through the society up to 1870; (2) the secrecy of the society forbade members, on pain of death, to disclose information regarding its activities; (3) there was no European official in Malaya who understood the Chinese or their language and customs; and (4) upon the suppression of the society in 1890 all records were destroyed.

It seems likely that the earliest Triad headquarters were in Thailand, and later in Malakka and Penang, and that the Malayan headquarters of the society moved to Singapore in about 1850. Chinese traders had come to Singapore from the year of the city's foundation by Sir Stamford Raffles in 1819, but they had settled in Malakka and Penang even earlier. Nevertheless, it was only in the middle of the nineteenth century, with the growth in importance of Singapore and the development of tin-mining in the Malay Peninsula, that the rate of Chinese immigration into Malay increased considerably and with it the influence of the Triad Society. It seems likely that it started as a mutual aid and protection society, but despite its seemingly unobjectionable aims and the apparently high moral tone of its ritual, it gradually degenerated into a criminal organization prepared to use any means to impose its own form of "government" upon the Chinese community.

An examination of the rules of the Triad Society reveals that they contain three main provisions, secrecy, mutual help in trouble, and respect for one another's womenfolk. At first sight these regulations seem harmless enough, but they have been interpreted traditionally in practice to prevent brethern from informing about the criminal activities of brother members to the police, to assist brother members to escape from police custody, to ignore the law of the country, and to acknowledge allegiance only to the society's own rules and regulations. The society also assumed the power of life and death over its members and any others who ran afoul of them. Thus it constituted virtually a rival government, an "imperium in imperio," obviously intolerable to constituted authority.

In those days, the British government of the Straits Settlements impinged little upon Chinese life. As there were no officers who spoke their language, the Chinese were left largely to their own devices. They soon organized themselves into their own political, economic, and social groupings, with their own headmen in charge. In doing this they were helped by the fact that traditional Chinese society encourages such groupings by division into family groups bearing the same surnames, by parochial loyalty felt for particular districts and provinces, and by their division according to vocation into various trade guilds. This system gives every individual a recognizable label and a definite rallying point.

In the system which sprang up in Malaya the headmen acted as buffers between the Chinese community and the British officials. It was not until long afterward that the British officials realized with something of a shock that the very headmen on whom they had been relying were secret society leaders. The power of the secret societies grew apace with the phenomenal development of Singapore and became a serious menace to the peace of the settlement. It became more and more difficult to recognize the old and benevolent aims of the Triad Society in its degeneration. Secret society activity was encouraged by an ignorant and terrified population which paid one side or the other protection money to be protected from the extortions of their rivals. The money levies went into the pockets of the headmen and of the "strong-arm" section of the secret societies, paid for legal fees, and provided periodic funeral feasts and elaborate religious ceremonies and celebrations to encourage tradition and ritual among the members.

In 1824, 1846, 1851, and 1854 in Singapore, and in 1867 in Penang, there were serious secret society clashes. Of these, the last was probably the most serious and warrants special attention.

In 1868 the Penang riot commission, appointed to inquire into the origin and causes of the 1867 Penang riots, which covered Penang island and a wide area of Province Wellesley and involved some thirty thousand Chinese and four thousand Malays and Indians, reported:

> That the late riots and their origin in a trifling
> quarrel between two rival Muhammadan societies

[were] fostered by two other rival societies of Chinese, with one of which each of the former had joined in alliance. That all these societies joined in the riots by the direction and under the instigation of their respective headmen or office-bearers, who directed their principal movements and who, from the funds of their societies, supplied them with provisions and arms, with rewards for the heads of their enemies, and with gratuities and pensions for the wounded and for the relations of those who were killed when fighting. That the organization and discipline of the Societies appear to be as complete as that of any disciplined force of the Government. That it is therefore evident that these secret societies are extremely dangerous to the peace and welfare of the community.

The Penang riots were in fact an extension of the struggle between rival factions of the Triad Society and allied Malay groups for possession of rich tin workings in Perak, which had already been the cause of the first Larut War of 1862. The Penang riots came to an end when both sides had wearied of the fighting, which was, however, destined to break out again a few years later in the second and third Larut Wars (1872-74). This is the period in Malayan history when secret societies played a vital part in shaping the course of events leading to British intervention in the interior of Malaya. In 1873 the situation in the western Malay states had deteriorated as a result of a dispute over the succession to a sultanate and quarrels, in which Chinese secret societies took a prominent part, over the ownership of land rich in tin. Civil war spread throughout the interior of the country. The three main reasons for rivalry between opposing Chinese and Malay secret societies, often allied, were possession of tin mines in the Larut district of Perak, possession of the monopoly of opium supply to the miners, and the possession of the monopoly of revenue, liquor, and other "rackets," obtainable from the Malay rajahs.

The result was less tin mined, and there was a danger that the secret society war would spread to Singapore, Penang, and Malakka, where the society headquarters were situated. The leading Chinese merchants in Malaya petitioned the British

Government to intervene in what they described as the "half-civilised States of the Malayan Peninsula."

In the light of these factors, the British government decided to change its policy of noninterference in the Malay States, and in 1873, when a new governor of the Straits Settlements, Sir Andrew Clarke, was appointed, he came out to Malaya armed with instructions from the home government which he interpreted as authority to intervene in the affairs of the Malay states, restore law and order, and establish a system of British residents. After a series of desultory skirmishes, the warring factions agreed to cease fighting and submit their differences to arbitration. For the first time, the British government used the services of a British official (William Pickering) with a knowledge of the Chinese language and Chinese customs to establish direct contact with the rival Chinese secret society factions and to persuade them to agree to negotiation. This important chapter in Malayan history was finally brought to a close by the signing of the Treaty of Pangkor (1874).

By this time the British government had been thoroughly alarmed at the power wielded by Chinese secret societies and their continual threat to peaceful government, and it decided upon a policy of suppression. In 1869 the Suppression of Dangerous Societies Ordinance was promulgated. The practical result of this ordinance was not suppression or dissolution, but formal registration. Its name is therefore misleading. It inaugurated in fact a period of unrestricted registration from 1870 to 1882, during a decade when the immigrant Chinese population of Malaya was increasing by hundreds of thousands, following the development and expansion of the tin-mining industry. The decision for final suppression was sponsored by Sir Cecil Clementi Smith, the first governor of the Straits Settlements who possessed an intimate personal knowledge of the Chinese, and in 1890 the societies ordinance became law. It made all Chinese secret societies unlawful but provided them with a loophole for survival by designating societies formed for "Recreation, Charity, Religion, and Literature" as exempt from the provisions of the new ordinance. In the years to come many of these seemingly harmless clubs and societies became cover organizations for secret society intrigue. This ordinance, with its multitude of amendments, remains in force in Malaya today.

In China proper, secret societies had been suppressed since

the promulgation of a sacred edict by the Manchu Emperor, K'ang Hsi, in 1662, and similar action had been taken by the British authorities in Hongkong in 1845. It was perhaps due to the fact that the Straits Settlements were, until 1867, governed from India by officers appointed from India, who did not understand the Chinese, that the power of the Chinese secret societies was allowed to grow to such proportions before a policy of suppression was decided upon.

Mention has already been made of William Pickering and the part he played in contacting the rival Chinese secret societies taking part in the Larut Wars. Pickering was the first official Chinese interpreter and "Protector of Chinese" to be appointed by the Straits Settlements' government (1871). He had been born in Manchester of Scottish parents in 1841 and had had a chequered career as third mate on a tea clipper in the China trade and as an officer of the Imperial Chinese Maritime Customs, before coming to Malaya. On his return to Singapore from his mission to Perak he set about organizing a government department staffed by Chinese-speaking British officers, which was the forerunner of the present-day Chinese Affairs Department. Pickering's first office was a room in a Chinese shophouse in Canal Road, Singapore, but he later moved to Macao Street, subsequently renamed Pickering Street in his honor. His role in the suppression of secret societies inevitably made him many powerful enemies within their ranks. That Sir Cecil Clementi Smith, governor of the Straits Settlements, was highly pleased with Pickering's work is evident from the following quotation from a despatch which he wrote on the twentieth of June, 1888, to the Secretary of State for the Colonies:

> The Government is not now weak in regard to Chinese affairs, as it was when in 1869 the first Ordinance dealing with these secret societies was passed. I believe that I am right in saying that at that time there was not a single Officer of the Government who had any knowledge of the Chinese language, or of their habits or customs. Since 1871, it had the very marked advantage of the services of Mr. Pickering, who possesses extraordinary qualifications for the post of Protector of Chinese and of adviser to the Government on all

matters connected with the Chinese community. His department has grown by degrees until it is second to none in importance, and there are now other offices which are presided over by gentlemen who have passed in the Chinese language and have been trained in the public services. This strengthening of the Government Departments in the direction referred to will continue, and the Government can and will give to the Chinese inhabitants a real and honest protection in lieu of that protection which they believe they obtain by joining a secret society.

The secret societies' disapproval of Pickering's diligence was, unfortunately, in direct ratio to the governor's approval, and in July, 1887, an attempt was made on his life by a Chinese secret society member. Pickering never fully recovered from this murderous attack and retired the next year.

The official suppression in 1890 of secret societies had the effect of driving them underground and doubtless loosened society discipline. Paradoxically, society discipline was very strict when the societies were themselves an integral part of the governing of the Chinese through the headmen system and again during the period of unrestricted registration (1870-1882), when they were officially recognized. After 1890 they degenerated into dangerous gangs, and although their overt activities were restricted to a large extent by the strenuous afforts of the Chinese Protectorate and the police, they were responsible for much of the crime throughout Malaya.

Just before the outbreak of World War I, it was confidently claimed by the government that the hard core of the secret societies had been broken, but it seems in the light of present-day knowledge that this claim was not based on fact. Nevertheless, it is true to say there was a period of outward calm, during which a radical internal reorganization was taking place. The gangster epidemic was an evil growth which the common sense of the Chinese people was glad to see suppressed. It was definitely a matter for local government. But the same Chinese did not understand why the British government in Malaya should expect them to be as enthusiastic over a ban on the local development of political societies whose roots were in China, even if such societies were unfortunate enough to cause local disturbances. From the Triad Society to the Kuomintang was less than a step. To some it was merely a change in name. When in due course of time the inevitable split, latent in all Chinese secret societies, occurred within the ranks of the Kuomintang and a separate left-wing party emerged as the Chinese Communist Party, the two resultant factions were the cause of prolonged disputes and disturbances in Malaya. Rival members of the Triad family of secret societies were quick to align themselves with the opposing political parties of the Kuomintang and the Chinese Communist Party, then clandestinely establishing themselves in Malaya.

After World War II, both the Kuomintang and the Malayan Communist Party were refused official recognition and registration under the societies ordinance in Malaya and automatically became illegal societies, with their activities necessarily shrouded in secrecy. Both were conflicting political parties which from their inception carried on "underground" war against each other.

It should be remembered that the Kuomintang had always had close connections with the Triad Society because of the support given by the latter to Dr. Sun, Yat-sen's anti-Manchu revolutionary movement. In particular, two branches of the Triad family in Malaya have always staunchly supported the Kuomintang and bitterly opposed the MCP. They are the Hua Chi Society (華記會) and the Hung Min Society (洪民會).

As far as is known, the Hua Chi Society was originally formed some forty or fifty years ago by Chinese tin miners in the Sungei Besi district of Selangor. In the beginning, when its object was the unobjectionable one of providing mutual help and benefits to its members, it was known as the Hua Ch'iao Society (華僑會), or Society of Overseas Chinese; but as its activities assumed a more political flavor, its name was changed to its present form. Branches were established in the states of Selangor, Negri Sembilan, Johore, Pahang, and Perak, although its main strength was concentrated in Kuala Lumpur, where in 1949 five ostensibly innocuous Chinese clubs used as "cover" organizations accounted for two thousand of its members. As it is so bitterly opposed to communism it is not surprising that it numbers among its ranks many Chinese members of the police and Home Guard.

Since the outbreak of the Communist insurrection in Malaya in June, 1948, there has been a close connection between the

Hua Chi and Hung Min societies, brought together as allies against a common foe. The Hung Min Society came into existence in Penang during September, 1945, immediately following the Japanese surrender at the end of World War II. Its title was previously unknown in the history of Triad Societies in Malaya and should not be confused with the Hung Men Society (洪門會), which is another generic name for the Hung League mentioned at the beginning of this section. In other words, the Hung Min Society is a new progeny of the mother Hung Men Society. The Hung Min Society soon proved itself to be a lusty, troublesome child addicted to murder, armed gang robbery, kidnapping, and other crimes of violence. It did not take long for the new society to create a reign of terror on Penang island and parts of the adjoining mainland by its reliance on brute force to achieve its ends. For the first time since the enforcement of the societies ordinance in 1890 a Chinese secret society was stronger than the government.

At the height of the Hung Min Society's power many influential Chinese merchants in Penang, who were also known to be Kuomintang members, emerged as office-bearers. If further proof was needed of its Kuomintang affiliation, the Kuomintang Chinese Consul-General for the Malayan Union attended its inauguration ceremony. With the police helpless in face of an increasingly deteriorating situation, many of the Chinese merchants in Penang decided to approach the Hung Min Society for protection. One large importers' and exporters' association, for instance, paid as much as M$18,000 per month for the provision of a guard for its cargoes in the Harbour Board area. Other rich Chinese merchants were only too eager to pay equally large sums of money for "protection." The revenue of the society was also augmented by smaller "voluntary" contributions from hawkers and shopkeepers. At the beginning of 1946 the estimated monthly income of the society from all sources was reliably reported to be M$100,000. It was only in May, 1946, after vigorous counteraction by the police, supported by the army, that the situation was brought under control. By then it was too late. There were then estimated to be one hundred thousand members in Penang and Province Wellesley alone, and many thousands of other members were scattered throughout the Federation of Malaya and Singapore.

In May, 1948, a joint meeting of representatives of the Hua Chi Society and Hung Min Society was held secretly in Kuala

Lumpur, at which it was decided to cooperate fully with each other and to settle any differences that might arise by peaceful negotiation rather than by force. This, then, obviated any police interference. It was unanimously agreed that their common enemy was communism. In passing this resolution they were only confirming what in fact had been their policy for some time. In the previous year, when some of the ringleaders of the Penang Hung Min Society had been arrested, they had stated quite bluntly that if the government suppressed their activities, then the field would be left wide open for communism.

Among the Chinese secret societies in Malaya the branch of the parent Triad Society in support of the MCP and opposed to the Hua Chi and Hung Min societies was known as the Chi Kang Party (致公堂). The Chi Kang Party in China originally had given considerable monetary and material support to the revolutionary party organized by Dr. Sun, Yat-sen to overthrow the Manchu dynasty, but in 1925 had swung to the "left" in support of the left-wing Kuomintang and had become involved in an unsuccessful uprising against the right-wing elements. Consequently, many of its members were forced to flee for their lives and came to Malaya, where there was already an overseas branch in existence. The society remained dormant for many years, but at the end of World War II its activities were resuscitated in Hongkong by General Li, Chi-shen, the chairman of the Kuomintang revolutionary committee, who was later elected vice-chairman of the Central Peoples' Government of the Peoples' Republic of China. In 1946 General Li sent his personal representatives to establish contact with the overseas branches of the Chi Kang Party in Southeast Asia and to encourage them to resume activities in support of the indigenous Communist movements in their countries. At the end of 1946, following a visit by General Li's emissary, the Kuala Lumpur branch of the Chi Kang Party was reorganized and started functioning again. It shared office space in the Wai Chow Building with the Kuala Lumpur MCP headquarters, and in view of its left-wing affiliations it is not surprising that its inauguration ceremony was attended by many prominent MCP representatives, including the secretary of the Selangor State Committee, MCP, and the representative of the MCP in the Federation of Malaya.

In October, 1952, the Chi Kang Party is known to have been in secret contact with the MCP concerning its intention to form a "Peoples' Righteousness and Justice Unit" (人民正義团) to combat the activities of "secret societies whose activities are harmful to the livelihood of the people." There is little doubt that the secret societies referred to were the Hua Chi and Hung Min societies.

During the present Communist revolt in Malaya the Chi Kang Party has been delegated to carry out outrages for the MCP; in a similar fashion, the Hua Chi and Hung Min societies have struck for the Kuomintang against the MCP. There also have been gang fights between these two opposing factions. All secret societies of the Triad family are singularly well equipped to carry out armed forays of this kind, for they always have had "killer sections" as an integral part of their organization. These sections consist of an "Executioner" or "Military Affairs Officer" known in Chinese as a "Red Rod" (紅棍), a number of armed guards, used for initiation ceremonies and gang fights, known as "Vanguards" (先鋒), and five "Tiger Generals" (虎將) in each headquarters unit who are in charge of the "killer sections."

After the establishment of the Peoples' Republic of China in 1949 and the consequent wane of Kuomintang influence, there was a noticeable swing in all the Triad group of secret societies in Malaya toward the "left." Triad societies always have supported Chinese racialism and nationalism, and it was reasoned that as the Communists were in control of China and were therefore the national government of China, Triad and communism should present a combined front for self-preservation against the anti-Triad and anti-Communist British Malayan government. Much play was made of the fact that in the past secret society men had been "persecuted" by being arrested, imprisoned, and sometimes banished to China. Now was the time to retaliate, it was urged, while the British government was fully extended in dealing with the threat of militant communism, because if the MCP should fail in its present armed uprising, then the government would be free to concentrate again on suppressing Chinese secret societies. The short term aims of both organizations were seen to coincide in the support of Chinese nationalism and the defeat of the British in Malaya.

Consequently the Hua Chi and Hung Min societies became fundamentally less antagonistic toward the MCP than they had been hitherto. But with the constantly changing pattern of the Communist revolt in Malaya, with its emphasis one moment

293

on the "shooting war" and the next on "underground" subversion, it is becoming increasingly difficult, at such close range, to determine actually what part the secret societies are playing and whether or not their over-all policy has undergone a radical change.

In Singapore, where the Communist uprising has never assumed such a violent appearance as in the Federation, the Triad Society from the early days of the MCP revolt has not taken a great interest in subversive political activities, although it has certainly been responsible for much of the ordinary crime in the Colony. In this, it obviously has sought to take advantage of a situation where nearly all the available resources of the police have been deployed against militant communism. Of course, it can be said that by carrying out criminal activities in this way, it has helped create a diversion for the MCP, but on the surface it appears that the objectives of the society have been entirely criminal--the efficient running of well-organized rackets covering hawkers, shopkeepers, hotel keepers, laborers, prostitutes, opium smugglers, and gambling dens. In June, 1955, an official police spokesman is reported in the Singapore Standard to have said that the existing powers of the Singapore police were "inadequate to smash the rising menace of secret society gangsters." According to this report, "secret society activities--rival gang clashes, stabbings, extortion, and murder-- have risen sharply during the last three months." Three murders were committed by secret society gangs during the same period, and "gangs battle it out frequently in the Chinatown area for the right to control and extort protection money from covering hawkers, shopkeepers, trisha riders and gambling dens." The police spokesman continued, "A great deal could be done by parents and social welfare workers, especially among the Chinese community, to prevent youths from joining these gangs. They are responsible for much of the petty crime as well as crimes of violence in Singapore today." The secret society subbranch of the Singapore police was said to be maintaining constant pressure on secret society members, but "the effect of this preventive action with the existing laws of the Colony is not great."

According to statistics published for 1954 by the Singapore Commissioner of Police, there were 360 secret societies in Singapore, with a membership of 11,000. Of these, 130 societies, with 8,500 members, were known to be active. During the same year 2,281 secret society members were arrested, and six revolvers, one sawed-off rifle, grenades, twenty-six shells, and ten detonaters were recovered by the secret societies subbranch of the police.

Unfortunately, no comparable figures are available for the Federation of Malaya, and it is unlikely, since armed communism has tended to mask secret society activities and there is a lack of police officers trained and experienced in secret society work, that the authorities there are so well informed. There is little doubt, however, that the number of secret society members is large and their activities extensive.

Family
The family structure is the most important element in the social organization of the Chinese. Although modified in certain respects during the last one hundred years, and more especially within the last thirty years, it has retained its principal pattern for over two thousand years. The family, chia, is understood to be a unit consisting of members related to one another by blood, marriage, or adoption, and having a common budget and common property. [68]

This economic group includes the temporarily absent members and also those who are staying together in the home village. "The relatives outside the family belong to one's kin and clan. 'Family, kin and clan' are three concentric circles. The relations within the family are the most intimate, in the clan the most external." [69] There are generally three types of families, the conjugal, the stem, and two forms of joint family. The conjugal family consists of the husband, wife (or wives), and children. The stem family consists of the parents, their unmarried children, and one married son with his wife and children. The joint family consists of the parents, their unmarried children, their married sons and sons' wives and children, and sometimes a fourth or fifth generation. One type of joint family prevails when the head of the family is the father staying with his married sons, and the other type exists when the eldest brother (most commonly) presides over his other married and unmarried brothers and their wives and children and occasionally other relatives.

68. Lang, Chinese Family and Society, p. 13.
69. Ibid., p. 13.

The joint family, as here described, was the principal form of family organization throughout Chinese history. Such a family was considered as a unit of production, that is, the members usually worked together, all contributing to the harvest of crops or employed in the business owned and managed by the father or grandfather or other male member of the family recognized as the head of the family. Ideally, the relationship established among the various members of the family--for example, father to son, elder brother to younger brother--was the prototype of the relationship existing between the individual and the state. One who was filial to his father would make a good and responsible citizen, since it was this kind of relationship that made for stability and security. Therefore, the essence of good government had its roots in the family structure itself. The role of the family in traditional Chinese social organization also persists among the Chinese in Malaya.

Children, especially males, play important roles in the Chinese family. The value placed upon having a progenitor to carry on the family name is so important that it has been the basic reason for a man to acquire a second wife. In those families where male children are absent and where a secondary wife (concubine) has not been taken, one of two alternatives is available for continuing the family name. Either the son-in-law (assuming that the family has female children) acquires the name of his wife, or the family adopts a boy. Because of the high value placed upon male children, however, those offered for adoption are almost exclusively female. Sale of children for adoption accurs within a few weeks after birth, and because Chinese parents sever all connections with the child upon selling, Chinese children are preferred for adoption among all Malayans to those of other ethnic groups.[70]

Although kinsmen are divided into paternal and maternal relatives, the Chinese clan is an exogamous group of the same surname whose members are held to be related to one another by descent from a common ancestor. Clan members worship the ancestors of the whole group. The actual clan usually comprises only those whose origin can be traced to the same vil-

---

70. Judith Djamour, "Adoption of Children among Singapore Malaysians," Journal of the Royal Anthropological Institute of Great Britain and Ireland, 1952, pp. 159-68.

lage. Particularly important are the responsibilities each member of the joint family assumes for the economic welfare of the group and the relationships existing among the various members of the household.

When a member emigrated from China, it was understood that he would periodically remit funds to those members of his family remaining in the village. They would be used for purposes ranging from contribution to a dowry for his daughter's marriage to the establishment of hygienic facilities for his entire village. Normally the emigrant was a young unmarried man who had not yet become the head of a family but who was still expected to send part of his savings (the largest part) to his parents.[71]

The proportion of China-born Chinese in Malaya is considerably less than it was twenty years ago. Immigration quotas and wartime prohibitions on travel are chiefly responsible for the trend outlined in Table 51. The number of Chinese born in

TABLE 51
CHINESE NATIVITY AND IMMIGRATION*

	Number of Chinese Born in Malaya			Per Cent of Total Chinese Population		
	1921	1931	1947	1921	1931	1947
Federation	178,503	383,172	1,196,089	20.9	29.9	63.5
Singapore	79,686	150,033	437,243	25.1	35.6	59.9
Malaya	258,189	533,205	1,633,332	22.0	31.2	62.5

*Del Tufo, Malaya, p. 84.

Malaya increased by about 50 per cent during the first inter-census period and by over 100 per cent during the second inter-census period. Because political unrest and instability has con-

71. Chen, Ta, Emigrant Communities in South China. The author, who made his field study in 1934-35, estimated that two-thirds to three-fourths of those emigrating to the Nan-yang were not heads of households, though many of them may have been married.

tinued since 1947, it is reasonable to assume that the proportion of China-born has continued to decrease. New generations
of Malaya-born Chinese do not have the same strong personal
ties with the mainland as their parents. Familial bonds are
tending to be concentrated in Malaya or in Southeast Asia. This
localization of family interest and separation from the traditional ties that bind the average Chinese to China eventually
will have the effect of creating new loyalties for the country of
their adoption. The process, however, will not be without
strains. As older members of the community observe the di-
vergence of interests between themselves and the younger
generation, there will be conflicts, and as the former control
the "purse strings" of present-day Malaya, the tensions will
be manifested in those activities where contributions from this
group are requested.

The most noticeable example of this tension is in the school
system. In Singapore the younger groups want to manipulate
the school curricula for their own purposes, and the older
members are powerless to intervene except at the cost of closing the entire school. However, the majority of Chinese are
said to remain apathetic or at least ambivalent toward these
conflicts. A second major conflict arises from Communist
China's strength as a strain on the loyalties of a large number
of Chinese in Malaya who now consider Malaya their home.

Social stratification

Economic strength, family ties, and education, in this order,
are the indices of social stratification among the Chinese.
From the period of the earliest British political control of Malaya, leaders of the community were appointed on the basis
of their acknowledged influence and social prestige arising
from economic dominance.[72] The "life members," for example, of the societies in Singapore are the big businessmen who

---

72. Goh, Soon Phing, A Research Paper on Some Aspects of
Woman's Life in a Singapore Chinese Fishing Village (Singapore: University of Malaya, mimeographed, 1955). Appendix A:
"Headman and His Assistant," p. 104. In this specialized study,
the author discusses the role of those nominal leaders who settle
minor problems, family quarrels, discontent of employees,
and also are responsible "for anything that goes wrong in the
village." The headman claims with pride that "he is recognized

"solve" any financial problems faced by the group.[73] They normally are not active in the affairs of the society but are the actual "backers" and operators behind the scenes who determine the success of failure of its activities.

Status in the community deriving from family ties is also implicitly based on the economic wealth possessed or formerly possessed by that family. A successful newcomer may easily assume greater importance if accompanied by a decline or even static position of the former leaders of the community. The significance of education is reflected in the creation of an almost completely independent school system for Chinese extending from nursery schools to the Nan-yang university.

Among the dialect groups, the highest levels of the social pyramid are shared by the Hokkien and Tiechiu. Both are long residents of Malaya and are pre-eminent in commercial and financial occupations. Their recognized status in the Chinese community is expressed in the Chinese chambers of commerce which are almost exclusively staffed and headed by members of either of these two groups.

Legal institutions

Until the latter part of the nineteenth century when legal statutes were codified defining the relationship between Chinese customary law and colonial law, the Chinese community was governed almost wholly according to the tenets of Chinese custom. Kapitans China, community leaders appointed by the British, administered the law until progressive restriction on the operation of it gradually brought the Chinese under the growing body of case law based on the English system. Deference to Chinese custom is retained in some instances. This is true particularly of the rights of a secondary wife to share intestate property.[74] But generally English common law applies to the Chinese and is modified only where necessary by Chinese custom.

Extreme forms of punishment under customary law for in-

---

by the Govt." (see also p. 6). It is evident that this early tradition persists, especially in rural areas.

73. Kwok, An Account of the Sources of Benevolent Assistance, p. 66.

74. Purcell, The Chinese in Southeast Asia, p. 327.

fractions of secret society codes and rituals in early years was one of the criteria for making such organizations illegal. Today only minor intracommunal disputes are settled by the community itself. The importance of "saving face" is valued highly, and therefore any arrangement through intermediaries equitable to the injured parties is preferred to recourse to the courts.

Religion

The patterns of Chinese religious behavior in Malaya are generally the same as in China, although there are modifications because of long contact with foreigners and unique circumstances surrounding their early residence in Malaya. One of the recognized authorities on Chinese history has characterized the Chinese religion as being "eclectic, tolerant, optimistic, confident in the moral trustworthiness of the universe, ethical, ritualistic, superstitious, concerned with an attitude of this-worldliness, and not separated from the State. "[75]

Confucianism, Taoism, and Buddhism, the three principal religions of China, hold some of these conceptions in common. At times, as during the Ch'ing dynasty, the Chinese state has officially sponsored Confucianism at the expense but not necessarily by the castigation of the other two. Such tolerance is reflected in the capacity of an individual Chinese to profess belief in all of the above religions and to practice those rituals which he thinks will best serve him for particular purposes. It is an expression of his conviction that all contain some good and are to be judicially observed when the occasion demands.

Confucianism

Confucianism has been concerned largely with the organization of the state, society, and social relationships. For this reason it has been criticized as being "nonreligious," but because of the religious rites connected with ancestor-worship as encouraged by Confucius and officially countenanced by the government for centuries afterward, it is considered to be

---

75. Kenneth S. Latourette, The Chinese: Their History and Culture (New York: The Macmillan Company, 1951), Vol. II, Chapter 16.

one of the world's great religions. Under Confucianism the emperor was thought to be the religious as well as the secular head of the state. He had certain functions to perform at periodic ceremonies and conferred titles on divinities in connection with his position as the religious leader of the realm. These official religious responsibilities were administered through a special branch of the government called the board of rites, with local officials undertaking functions at that level.

Confucianism also stresses the proper code of ethics to be practiced with regard to social relations between the various members of the family. Children customarily have been taught to memorize the basic four books expounding the principles of Confucianism, which until recently represented the core of Chinese school curricula in the countries of Southeast Asia. The older generations and the Chinese in rural areas especially cling to these traditional cultural and educational forms.

Confucianism has been particularly important in contributing the rites and ceremonies connected with death, mourning, and burial. These practices observed with regard to the departed form one of the principal fabrics upon which the Chinese family is structured and have a profound influence on molding Chinese life and thought.

Buddhism

Buddhism reached its peak in popularity and appeal in China during the T'ang dynasty and has been on the decline ever since, but it still has considerable strength and is therefore considered one of the three main religions of China. "One source of Buddhism's power is the belief that through the friendly offices of Buddhist divinities present evils are to be avoided and desirable goods of this life to be obtained." Another source of its hold "is the determining influence which can be entered through Buddhism upon the soul's lot after death."[76] Through its conception of reincarnation and karma, individuals are motivated to do good in this life so as to acquire merit for a future existence. The devoted practitioners of Buddhist doctrines are confined largely to monks and nuns who enter the monastery or nunnery after a series of trials

---

76. Ibid., p. 641.

including oaths of celibacy, vegetarianism, and the keeping of other vows.

Hinayana (or Theravada) and Mahayana constitute the two main divisions of Buddhism. The latter predominates in China and among the overseas Chinese. Probably the most generally worshipped bodhisattva is Kuan-yin, the "Goddess of Mercy," who is very popular among the Chinese in Malaya. In addition, there is a whole pantheon of divinities to which the Buddhists play host and which are found not only in temples and shrines but also in the average home. Buddhism has a vast literature which is propagated through temples, shrines, and monasteries and also reaches the masses through folklore, stories, and legendary accounts.

Taoism

Having its roots in ancient China, as does Confucianism, Taoism seems to gain its popularity and strength from its emphasis on superstition. It has, on the other hand, borrowed from Buddhism its priesthood, its canon, and its acceptance of the idea of transmigration and of karma. The role of the Taoist practitioner in the community is one of saying services for the dead, writing charms, exorcizing evil spirits, and communicating with the dead through automatic writing. Like Buddhism, immortality can only be obtained through the practice of exacting rituals, meditation, and cultivation of attitudes like inaction and placidity. Voluminous literature and numerous gods exist in this religion, providing the means for the attainment of its ideals. There is also a strong ethical element inherent in Taoism that tends to complement the teachings of Buddhism and Confucianism.

Special Malayan religious characteristics

The above outline of the three main beliefs upon which Chinese religious behavior is based attempts to spell out the characteristics of Chinese religious belief. Superimposed upon this structure are the influence wrought by Christianity and Islam. In addition, animism has also played an important role in Chinese life and by some is claimed to be the one common belief held by all Chinese. The "eclecticism" ascribed to Chinese religion, then, is made more lucid by these converging influences which all serve to reveal a very complex and intricate pattern defying accurate analysis.

Early Chinese residence in Malaya compounds this complexity through the deification of local heroes. Whereas in most of China the Shen and the Fu represent spirits of Buddhism and Taoism, in Malaya (Penang and Malakka especially) the eunuch admiral Cheng Ho is worshipped as the Shen and is known as Sam Po Tai Shan.[77] Accounts of his legendary efforts to save his countrymen in these unknown lands found their way into the folklore and beliefs of the Malayan communities. Toh Peh Kong (Ta Pai Kung), representing the Fu, is the most popular hero in Malaya. He is propitiated by businessmen who ask for inter- cession in their affairs. Purcell believes that this god is merely the personification of the pioneer spirit generally (of those who suffered hardships in early days) and is not the dei- fication of any special person, as Sam Po Tai Shan is of Cheng Ho.

The same author enumerates the overseas patron saints to whom the Malayan Chinese pay their respects depending upon their individual occupations:

> Overseas patron saints include Wu Ku Lao Yeh for farmers, Chiao Sheng Lao Yeh (whose festival is on the 7th of the 5th moon) for carpenters, Shui Hsin Lao Yeh for incense-stick makers, Kwan Ti, the God of War, for tradesmen (in his capacity of God of Wealth), and T'ien Hou Sheng Mu, the Taoist Queen of Heaven, for fishermen and sailors.[78]

It appears that a number of religious festivals, which formerly entailed much preparation and expense, have now been dis- continued although they are resurrected occasionally in com- memoration of some particular event.

There is no information available on the numbers of Chinese who claim allegiance to a particular religion, other than super- ficial data contained in the 1931 census. The census specified the number per thousand Chinese who were Christians and Mo- hammedans with the former claiming eighteen, and the latter two, per thousand. With this and other related information the editor of the 1947 census estimated that of the 2,614,667 Chi- nese living in Malaya in that year, about 2,560,000 professed

---

77. Purcell, The Chinese in Malaya, Chapter 6.
78. Ibid., p. 124.

adherence to the Chinese "national religion," which he described as Confucianism or ancestor worship.

Purcell sums up the effects of Chinese beliefs on the other peoples of Malaya in the following statement:

> There is little evidence to show how far this exists. I am inclined to think to a very small degree. The tolerant nature of the Chinese and their ability to adhere to two or three sets of beliefs, even contradictory ones, at the same time, deprives their religion of proselytizing force. It has no threats of hell for the disbeliever or promises of heaven for the believer--whatever the Buddhist canon may say. And of the other peoples, the Mohammedans and the Christians are constantly threatened with dire punishment if they dabble in superstitions unauthorized by their creed, while the caste Hindus are in danger of losing their caste. [79]

In conclusion, some mention should be made of the numerous festivals held throughout the year, some of which are religious in nature, others merely traditional. For example, it is traditional that all debts be paid up on New Year's Eve, and 106 days after the winter solstice the Cheng Beng feast is celebrated, during which honor is paid to the dead. Recent political events and the encroachments of the West have tended to change to some degree the observance of festivals. Celebration of the start of the Chinese Revolution in 1911, the death of Sun, Yatsen, the Marco Polo Bridge incident, and dates associated with the war in Malaya all have found a place in the calendar of observances for the Chinese.

Chinese Education

Learning and education occupy a high place, perhaps the highest place, in traditional China's hierarchy of values. The Hua-ch'iao, overseas Chinese, have implemented this tradition almost wherever they have settled. In all of the Southeast Asian countries, except where official government policy has made it impossible for periods of time, the Chinese have maintained

---

79. Ibid., pp. 129-30.

and financed their own system of education in which Chinese, in recent years kuo-yü, the national language, has been used as the medium of instruction. Curricula have been oriented toward matters of Chinese cultural interest, and in recent years political orientations too have been toward China. To the various Southeast Asian countries the Chinese schools have appeared to be a threat to national integrity, and various means have been employed to limit their growth and influence.

In Malaya the Chinese schools have been a focus for the Chinese community and a center for the growth of Chinese nationalism, although not all Chinese children attend Chinese-language schools by any means. Since World War II, they also have been centers, at least in the middle schools of Singapore, for Communist propaganda and political unrest. In short they have been barriers to the Malayanization of the Chinese.

The tremendous increase in the number of Chinese students seeking education since World War II is also gravely overtaxing existing Malayan educational facilities and presents other problems that only recently have been faced realistically. With the Emergency and the rise of China as a world power, the government has seen the necessity for bringing the Chinese educational system more and more under its control. Various schemes have been legislated to realize this end. The most recent involves changing all the vernacular schools into national schools, thus in effect eventually diminishing the differences that now exist among the various racial schools.

Another factor of importance is the increasing concentration of the more complete educational facilities in the urban areas. Because the Chinese constitute the major urban group in Malaya, a greater proportion of students receiving secondary and higher education are Chinese. Efforts to modify this imbalance are reflected in the desire to construct high schools in the rural areas so that more Malays can obtain a secondary education.

Government policy appears to be directed at establishing English and Malay as the national languages. Because English is the language of the commercial and business world, Chinese students are already interested in learning it. Malays would like to gain some proficiency in the language in order to raise their economic position. Therefore, English appears to be the future lingua franca of Malaya. Although the kinds of problems are similar in Singapore and the Federation, those in Singapore are more intense because of the dense concentration of Chinese.

305

As in the Federation, Singapore has four kinds of primary schools based on the languages of instruction (English, Chinese, Malay, and Indian), and English and Chinese secondary schools. All of the registered schools,[81] including the Chinese, come under the jurisdiction of the director of education of the Singapore government. There is an assistant director of education (Chinese), however, who is in direct charge of the Chinese schools. The Chinese schools fall into two categories: government-aided and nonaided. The former are required to measure up to certain conditions and standards and receive aid on the basis of capitation grants and salaries for English teachers. Government aid to the 111 Chinese schools has been relatively small, about S$3.5 million in 1954 as compared with about S$6 million to the 44 English-language schools. Nonaided schools are supported by dialect associations, school fees, and the general Chinese community through annual fund-raising drives.

Government educational policy is based upon the premise of incorporating all the existing schools into a general educational system subject to government supervision and control. This policy was recently reinforced through the issuance of proposals requiring that all Chinese schools in Singapore "provide an education centred on Singapore and Malaya and designed to turn out good citizens of the Colony with a sound working knowledge of Chinese and English."[82] Those schools already receiving aid would have their grants increased and others would receive new grants, provided they adhered to these conditions. By assuming the responsibility for publishing new textbooks, standardizing teaching techniques, and establishing certain norms for qualified teachers, the government hopes to achieve better management. The reaction of the Chinese to these proposals is mixed or hostile. In late 1954, when full grants-in-aid to the Chinese schools were authorized, over

80. See A. D. Barnett, "Notes on Growing Forces among Singapore Chinese: Political Parties, Students, and Workers" (Report ADB-9'55, [New York: American Universities Field Staff, 1955]).

81. Fewer than two thousand students are in nonregistered schools.

82. Colony of Singapore, Annual Report, 1953, p. 92.

three-quarters of them refused the grants on the grounds that they would result in government control over Chinese education.

The following table indicates the numbers of Chinese schools, pupils, and teachers in the total Singapore educational system.

TABLE 52
SINGAPORE: CHINESE EDUCATION, 1953*

	Schools	Pupils	Teachers
Government-aided	111	58,586	1,740
Nonaided	162	20,686	536
Total Chinese schools	273	79,272	2,276
Total registered schools	508	160,897[†]	5,412

*Colony of Singapore, Annual Report, 1953, p. 90.
†Increased to 178,000 in 1955.

Included in the "Total Registered Schools" are the English schools attended by Chinese. The government operated eighty such schools and provided aid to forty-four others in 1954. In addition there were fifty-three nonaided English schools which also were attended by Chinese students. Most of the educational institutions in Singapore are probably attended by Chinese students.

Only a small percentage of Chinese students enter secondary school, and fewer acquire a university aducation. It is estimated that only one out of every six primary school graduates enters the higher grades. The total number of higher-school students including all races was only 5,900 in 1947, whereas by 1954 there were 21,900. Because of the predominance of the Chinese in the Singapore population, it can be assumed that most of these were Chinese. Although there are only about 10,500 pupils in the Chinese-language middle schools, they are the foci of discontent and unrest among the youth of Singapore, assuming active roles in political agitation and revolt against both the Chinese and colonial societies within which they were bred.

The main center for higher education in both the Federation and Singapore is the University of Malaya in Singapore. Al-

307

though the number of Chinese students enrolled in the University in 1953 was only about six hundred, these represented two-thirds of the total enrollment. University education in Malaya, then, is Chinese-dominated, although the language of instruction and the teaching methods employed both are English. Only recently, in 1955, have studies in Chinese civilization been instituted at the University of Malaya.

Many Chinese youths still leave for the Chinese mainland, although they are not permitted to return thereafter. One estimate is given as eight to nine hundred per year. A small number seek a higher education at the universities of Taiwan, chiefly the National Taiwan University in Taipeh. The demand for a "Chinese" education also led to the founding of the Nan-yang university in Singapore, opened officially in 1956, after a vicious two-year struggle which resulted in the ousting of anti-Communist educators, led by Lin, Yu-tang, the chancellor. Its future role remains uncertain, and it may simply degenerate into a continuing haven for agitators who grow too old for the Singapore middle schools. [83]

The establishment of Chinese schools by independently organized groups has been the source of many current problems. These were accentuated as a result of the war when education practically ceased. Textbooks printed in China and teachers with little training were used in the early postwar years. Some success has been made in revising the textbooks and setting up normal schools for improving the caliber of teachers. All schools are overcrowded. In addition, because of the wartime absence of education, nearly two-thirds of the students attending the middle schools are overage. Some are "professional students" who carry on agitation and undermine discipline.

Little governmental control over Chinese schools has per-

---

83. The Nan-yang university was established in order to provide higher educational opportunities for Chinese students who did not have sufficient command of the English language to qualify for the University of Malaya. It also was designed for the use of all Southeast Asian (Nan-yang) Chinese. At first a united Chinese effort, it appears that Communist-China oriented elements, even among the wealthy in the Singapore Chinese community, may have come to exert considerable influence on university policies. See Butwell, "A Chinese University for Malaya," pp. 344-48.

mitted tensions between younger and older members of the Chinese community to develop into open conflict. Whereas those financially supporting the schools are reluctant to espouse actively policies akin to anticolonialism or in sympathy with Communist agitation, the younger leaders have been interested in orienting school curricula and teaching toward China. The alternative to complete closing of the schools has been to acquiesce in receiving more government aid, thus coming more and more under the "protection" of the government.

<u>Federation</u>

All of the registered Chinese primary and secondary schools come under the jurisdiction of the Federation department of education and the immediate supervision of the state, and these schools either receive government aid or are fully supported by the particular communities which initially established them. Aid has been changed from a per capita basis to a grant-in-aid scheme which contributes toward the salaries of teachers on a fixed incremental salary scale. All schools are free to accept or reject this plan, but if it is accepted, the school must measure up to certain conditions designed to improve the standards and tone of the school. By the end of 1953, 453 schools accounting for 73 per cent of the students had applied and were admitted to this relatively new scheme.

As of 1953, there were 1,210 Chinese primary schools, most of which offered courses up to and through the first six grades. It was estimated in 1951 that only one-fifth of all those who entered primary school actually finished. Because of the general increase of the number of students, this proportion may have risen slightly. Only about one student in every forty enters the first year of the middle school, and of this number a similar proportion finish the entire six years of secondary education. Lack of adequate facilities, insufficient funds, and old-fashioned curricula constitute the basic reasons for this low ratio of students attending the higher schools.

In addition to the Chinese vernacular primary schools, there are both primary and secondary English schools which accept all racial groups. English is the medium of instruction, and they are government-operated, receive government aid, or are privately managed. Those receiving government aid are operated by large missionary bodies, teaching orders, and other private organizations. The essential difference between the vernacular and English school rests in the cultural orientation inherent in both. The proportion of Chinese attending English as opposed to vernacular schools is about one to four and presumably will become more balanced as more of the latter are incorporated into the national school system. [84] Because of the emphasis placed upon learning English, many students in the Chinese middle schools transfer to the English schools for more intensive study.

According to the education ordinance of 1952, all vernacular schools are to be converted eventually into national schools, with Malay and English as the major languages of instruction. Chinese and Tamil are to be offered as subjects in any grade which has fifteen or more students desiring them. There has been considerable opposition to this policy by the Chinese community on the grounds that it sacrifices Chinese language and culture to Malay nationalism. Aware of this problem, the government has settled for a policy of gradually introducing the national schools.

Teacher training

Of considerable importance to the stabilization of the Chinese school teaching profession was the establishment of the first government-operated Chinese normal school in Green Lan, Penang, in 1952. It offers a two-year course of full-time instruction to Chinese students who have passed the government examination and completed their first three years of secondary school. In addition, a large number of Chinese school teachers have been affected by the recent plan to send selected English school teachers to Britain for specialized study in the Malayan Teachers' Training College at Kirkby.

One of the chronic problems associated with teaching in Chinese schools has been the highly temporary status of tenure of office. Insufficient wages, inadequate training, low prestige, and other sources of higher remuneration have been responsible for the annual migration of teachers from one school to another. Government aid to augment teacher salaries, positive steps to raise the qualifications of teachers through advanced training, and efforts to standardize teaching technique

---

84. Victor Purcell, "The Crisis in Malayan Education," Pacific Affairs, March, 1953, pp. 70-76. The ratio is slightly lower in Singapore.

and curricula all serve to correct and stabilize this perennial problem.

Political and Social Aspirations

The largely apathetic attitude of the Chinese toward involvement in the political affairs of Malaya derives from two chief factors. First, there is no historical background or experience upon which they can rely for expressing their wishes in such affairs. Their only precedent is the secret society. Secondly, political control has been guarded jealously by the British and Malays under a system tacitly recognized by the Chinese. Indeed, their own leaders had their positions of authority enhanced by being appointed Kapitans China of their individual communities. Although prevented from acquiring land in many areas by the nonalienation enactments of the early twentieth century, they were reasonably content with being permitted to govern their own affairs with a minimum of interference and to exercise freedom in economic matters. Thus, political and social aspirations among the Chinese were more a function of maintaining contact with the homeland and of social cohesiveness than an espousal of a particular ideology or governmental system in their adopted country. These passive attitudes have been subjected to diverse and disintegrating influences.

Within the past fifty years or more three political forces have affected the political and social aspirations of the Chinese in Malaya. The first, nationalism, is the earliest and the most persistent. It is interrelated with the second, communism, and strongly influences the direction taken by the third, Malayan loyalties. Communism is a more recent phenomenon in Southeast Asia, but is particularly important because of the precipitous rise to power of China. Apart from its ideological appeal, it has harnessed the attraction of nationalism and therefore increased its dubious popularity among the peoples of Southeast Asia. The effort to create Malayan loyalties is more recent than either of the others. It is also the most disputable. On the other hand, it may prove to be the only logical alternative that the Chinese can choose to extricate themselves from their present ambivalent position. Recent elections in Singapore and the Federation indicate that the Chinese have been able to exert political strength when the desire has been strong enough. Out of twenty-five seats on the Singapore legislative assembly up for election in the spring of 1955, sixteen were captured by Chinese representing various political parties.

Of chief concern to the leaders of the Chinese community in recent years has been the acquiring of political privileges commensurate with their economic position. At the same time, the Malays want to maintain their political control and acquire economic status too. Colonial policy has supported the Malay sentiments. The securing of limited political franchise by the Chinese,[85] however, has already indicated how effective they are in realizing, at least in an initial way, their objectives. It is to be stressed, moreover, that Chinese political prestige and success, particularly in the Federation, appears to be associated with the alliance of the Malayan Chinese Association with the United Malay National Organization. The merging of these two communal parties is without precedent in the history of Malaya. It appears that basic differences in aspiration have been buried by the victories achieved in the present. Well-informed observers are unable to analyze accurately the reasons for the coalition, much less explain its ability to remain intact. For the present, however, and perhaps for the immediate future, it represents a successful effort to combine the resources of each group for the purpose of solving a mutual problem.

One of the major factors involved in defining the political aspirations of the Chinese in Malaya, as throughout Southeast Asia, concerns their relationship to China. Besides the periodic remittance of funds to families in China, Malayan Chinese have financially supported political and other causes in their homeland. This was true particularly during the rise to power of the Kuomintang and the eventual overthrow of the Ch'ing dynasty in 1911. After the Japanese invasion of China in 1937 huge amounts of money were sent to the Kuomintang treasury. It has been estimated that immediately after World War II and up to February, 1946, funds from Southeast Asian Chinese amounted to US$5 million monthly. [86] Even after the Communist regime was installed at Peking, substantial sums continued to flow to the "Motherland."[87]

---

85. Lack of such rights was a propaganda point of the MCP.
86. Virginia Thompson and Richard Adloff, Minority Problems in Southeast Asia (Stanford: Stanford University Press, 1955), p. 13.
87. Ibid. Radio Peking announced in late 1949 that these

The active support given by Malayan Chinese to Communist China presents issues that differ fundamentally from their former support of the Nationalist regime. The motivation is the same, [88] but the consequences that such support has for the economic security of the Chinese middle class, in the event of Communist expansion and control throughout the area (as in northern Indochina), has raised conflicting feelings. The announced aims of the British to prepare the Malayan peoples for independence reinforces the necessity for thinking in terms that go beyond remitting funds and the desire for a strong China. Thus the issue of establishing loyalties to Malaya as opposed to supporting a regime that may mean curtailment of economic power imposes conflicting influences on the action of the individual Chinese. Remittances, though restricted in amount since 1950, [89] are still sent to China, while concurrently the Chinese economic position in Malaya is being protected by increased activity in the political sphere.

Communist China has not been backward in cultivating sympathies for China. For example, Malayan overseas Chinese were represented by the largest number of delegates (five) to the First National Peoples Congress held in 1954. [90] It has established special banking facilities and investment opportunities for overseas Chinese either returning to China or remitting funds to their families. Opportunities to further their education is offered young overseas Chinese students by assuring them that a certain percentage admitted to Chinese universities will be from abroad and that their passage will be paid by the gov-

---

remittances provided the Communist regime with its second largest source of foreign exchange.

88. It can be defined loosely as supporting policies that raise the power position of China. Both regimes espoused it; the Communists were notably effective.

89. About M$45 a month per person, estimated at M$15-21 million each year.

90. American Consulate-General, Hongkong, "Current Background," No. 290 (Hongkong, September 5, 1954), p. 5. The complete breakdown is included: Thailand (4); Indonesia (4); Vietnam, Laos, Cambodia (2); North Borneo and Sarawak (1); Burma (1); Philippines (1); Korea and Mongolia (1); Japan (1); India and Pakistan (1); Europe (1); Americas (2); Africa (1); Oceania (1); Reserved (4).

ernment in China.[91] Since 1950 special broadcasts have been beamed to the Nan-yang in Tiechiu, Hakka, Cantonese, and Hokkien from China, and bureaus for overseas Chinese have been organized at Peking, Hainan, and in some of the China provinces, which function as servicing and protection agencies for individuals returning to China. In addition, contact is maintained with home villages through various newspapers and other periodicals published in Singapore and catering to specific dialect groups.[92] Not all the methods used by Communist China, however, have resulted in closer harmony with that country. Efforts to increase amounts of remittances have involved the intimidation of wealthy overseas Chinese by imprisoning their relatives in China on trumped-up charges. Although at first successful, when the rates became too high these methods had the effect of alienating the prosperous middle class.[93] It has been recently reported that some returnees are put on collective farms, their property confiscated by the government.[94]

Government policy in Malaya, of course, has not encouraged the development of closer relations with China. It has deported all undesirables, limited the amount of money that can be remitted, restricted immigration to specifically defined categories, and prevented individuals from returning to Malaya once they have left except for special occasions. These and other regulations impose severe handicaps on the retention of family ties and firsthand knowledge on what is occurring in China. The effect has been to widen the breach between the countries, stimulate the growth of Malayan loyalties on the part of some, neutralize the feelings of most, and crystallize the antagonisms felt by many against the restrictions emanating from both the Peking and the Malay governments.

Some of these problems have been most clearly isolated in connection with the policy pursued against the Communist

---

91. Thompson and Adloff, Minority Problems in Southeast Asia, p. 12.

92. T'ien, The Chinese in Sarawak, pp. 81 f.

93. Thompson and Adloff, Minority Problems in Southeast Asia, p. 13. See A. Doak Barnett, "A Contest of Loyalties: Overseas Chinese in Thailand" (New York: American Universities Field Staff, December, 1954), p. 23.

94. American Consulate-General, Hongkong, "Review of Hongkong Chinese Press," No. 213 (Hongkong, January, 1955).

"bandits" in Malaya. There appears to be no direct material assistance provided by Peking, but "individual agents are believed to have been helping them with strategy and indoctrination."[95] Because the Malayan Communist Party initiated its revolutionary activity before the Communist regime came to power in China, it has been difficult to accuse Peking of initiating the terror. On the other hand, as almost all persons identified with this activity have proved to be China-born Chinese, and since the Communist regime is now in power, the authorities in Malaya feel that Peking could effectively end this "bandit" activity if it wished.[96] Overtures of peaceful intentions expressed at Bandung in April, 1955, were realized concretely in the form of China's abandoning her support of a dual nationality status for Chinese residents in Indonesia.[97] Further overtures, if they materialize, may constitute a guide for solving the vexing problems that characterize the complex relationship between Communist China and the Malayan Chinese.

95. Thompson and Adloff, Minority Problems in Southeast Asia, p. 18.

96. C. P. Fitzgerald, "East Asia after Bandung," Far Eastern Survey, August, 1955, pp. 115 ff.

97. "The Sino-Indonesian Treaty on Dual Nationality," Far Eastern Survey, May, 1955, pp. 75-76.

9. The Indians in Malaya

THERE HAVE BEEN Indians and Indian influences in Malaya since the beginning of the Christian era. In the earliest period, during the first Christian millennium, a great Indian civilization sent forth its commercial and cultural ambassadors to seek trade and establish colonies. Between the fifteenth century and the mid-nineteenth century a second form of Indian immigration became dominant, based upon increased trade and commercial opportunities, especially after the British establishment of Penang and Singapore. Until the final phase of immigration began in the nineteenth century, the number of Indians never exceeded twenty thousand. Since the late nineteenth century most of the Indians in Malaya have been plantation laborers who would work on estates for a few years and then return to India. Today, the Indian population is undergoing a further transition based upon its integration into an emerging national polity in Malaya.

During the early period of Indian influence, which came to a close in the late fifteenth century when the peninsula was Islamized, trade contacts were established in Kedah, and by the fifth century there also were Indian settlements in Kedah. There seems to have been established several Hindu states whose culture closely resembled that of the contemporary states of south India. In the eighth century the Buddhist Sri Vijaya empire controlled several of the states on the Malay Peninsula and neighboring Sumatra and Java.[1] Tin produc-

---

1. For an excellent discussion of this early period in Malayan history see D. G. E. Hall, A History of South-East Asia (New

tion, for export to Bagdad by Arab traders, was an important economic activity in this early period.

The conversion to Islam of the state of Malakka in the late fifteenth century and the expansion of Islam over the rest of Malaya ended one thousand years of Hindu cultural influence. Hindu temples and relics were destroyed, and Hindu practices anathematized. However, elements of Hindu culture appear in several aspects of modern Malayan culture. Winstedt draws attention to the similarity between traditional Hindu purificatory rites as practiced in India and certain of the ritual incidents of the Malay's life-cycle ceremonies of birth--puberty rites, early education, and marriage.[2] Evidence of Indian exorcism exists in Perak and Kelantan where the Malay shamans invoke the god Siva as well as gods of Sufi (Islamic) mysticism. Two aspects of modern Malay culture in which Indian influences persist most vigorously, however, are in the enthronement of Malay sultans and the preludes to traditional Malay shadow plays, wherein Indian sacrificial and invocational ceremonies take place, and in the plays themselves, which re-enact stories from Hindu epic, the Ramayana. Sanskrit words referring to religious and ritual experience, such as those meaning religion, fasting, teacher, heaven, and hell, also are incorporated into the Malay language.

The period between the coming of Islam to Malaya in the fifteenth century and the era of modern Indian immigration left little of significance. Many of the Indian families in Penang and Singapore claim to trace their origins to this period, and some of the older Indian mercantile houses were founded shortly after the British arrival there. Also, there is on Penang a people known as Jawi Pekan who trace their ancestry through original Indian-Malay unions. (Beyond indications that the Jawi Pekan are an industrious folk closely associated with Penang's thriving trade, little has been written of them.)

Immigration and Demography

Most of the nearly eight hundred thousand Indians who live in

---

York: St. Martin's Press, 1955), Chapter 3.

2. R. O. Winstedt, The Malays, a Cultural History (rev. ed.; London: Routledge and Kegan Paul, Ltd., 1950), pp. 14-33.

Malaya are associated with the commercial plantation agriculture and mercantile activities which developed in the nineteenth century. Indians have provided most of the labor force for the estate sector of the modern economy. The Indian population may be divided into "indigenous" and "immigrant" groups. An "indigenous" person is one who was born in Malaya, and an "immigrant" person is one who was born elsewhere and has migrated to Malaya. [3] Half the Indians in Malaya were "immigrants" in 1947.

Modern Indian immigration began in the early years of the nineteenth century when sugar estates were being developed on Penang and in Province Wellesley and coffee plantations in Perak were appearing. At the same time, and until 1873, the Straits Settlements served the government of India as a convict station, so that Indians were introduced into the peninsula from this quarter. However, Indian immigration arose primarily from the demand for laborers for the expanding coffee estates, and increasingly after 1900 for the rubber estates. From 1880 to 1900 the average annual number of Indian immigrants was about 20,000; between 1901 and 1910 the number rose to 48,000; in the next decade it rose to 90,000; and for the period 1925 to 1929 it increased to 119,790. Between 1931 and 1940 it was 76,000. [4]

Between 1901 and 1929 the number of Indian immigrants grew rapidly. [5] After this date, migrational deficits became regular, that is, there was a net outflow of Indians from Malaya. Between 1938 and 1949 the deficit amounted to about 20,000 per

---

3. This distinction, while rather simplified, is useful: as a consequence of the prevailing conjugal imbalances within the Indian population, a person born in Malaya of Indian parents may be considered to come from that portion of the population which is more stable. Correlated with favorable conjugal circumstance has been a more stable economic and social foundation which has permitted the maintenance of the Indian family in Malaya.

4. N. V. Sovani, Economic Relations of India with Southeast Asia and the Far East (Madras: Indian Council of World Affairs, 1949), p. 49.

5. G. St. John Orde-Browne, Labour Conditions in Ceylon, Mauritius and Malaya (Command Paper No. 6423 [London: H. M. Stationery Office, 1943]), p. 113.

year.[6] In 1951 the flow reversed, and migrational surpluses of Indians began, reflecting the expansion of rubber production as a response to the boom market created by the Korean War. The Indian surplus in 1952 was 18,000 and in 1953, 22,000.[7] Whether this recent surplus migration is a trend which reflects world prices alone, and might therefore be temporary, is difficult to judge. However, since 1953 showed a surplus even higher than that of 1952, at a time when the world rubber market was sharply contracting after the boom of 1951-52, this surplus could well be caused by other factors. One cause might be the replacement of Chinese who have been forced out of their traditional occupations on estates or in mines as part of the re-settlement program taken on under Emergency legislation. Another seems to be the policy of allowing alien wives and children to join their male family members, in line with the intent and practice of the immigration ordinance of 1952.

Immigration to Malaya has been a south Indian phenomenon, the south Indian states having provided about 93 per cent of the total Indian population in Malaya in 1931[8] and 90 per cent in 1947.[9] Of the south Indian population, the Tamil-speaking Indians have supplied the largest group. The Tamils were about 90 per cent of the south Indians in 1947, though the Malayalam-speaking people, who more often work in towns as laborers than on estates, have shown a relative increase in recent years. Another aspect of the composition of the immigrating Indian population has been the high representation of the lower strata of Indian society; more than one-third of the immigrants were of the lower Indian castes.

The relatively small number of northern Indians who have migrated to Malaya has been primarily from one region--the

6. T. E. Smith, Population Growth in Malaya: An Analysis of Recent Trends (London: Royal Institute of International Affairs, 1952), p. 81.

7. Federation of Malaya, Annual Report, 1953 (Kuala Lumpur: Government Press, 1954), pp. 53-57. But in 1955, it had declined to 3,125 in the Federation. All figures refer to both Indian and Pakistani nationals.

8. C. A. Vlieland, British Malaya: A Report of the 1931 Census (London: Malayan Information Agency, 1932).

9. M. V. Del Tufo, Malaya: A Report on the 1947 Census of Population (London: Crown Agents for the Colonies, 1949).

Punjab. The Punjabis (and Sikhs) are not associated as exclusively with the estate economy as are the south Indians, though they frequently serve in the capacity of estate watchmen and policemen, occupations which they have held since their early immigration period in the nineteenth century. More generally, the north Indians are engaged in commercial and financial occupations in the towns.

The Indian emigrating from south India was compelled to do so by the increasingly adverse conditions of life in India due to higher taxes, famines, debt, and the decline of handicraft industries with increasing competition from machine-made goods. Employment on the estates of Malaya, either as indentured labor (under contract), recruited labor, or free labor, was made relatively easy after 1890. At that time the Straits Settlements government in cooperation with the government of India set up an immigrant depot at Negapatam near Madras, where laborers could be housed and fed while awaiting transportation to Malaya. In the early years the length of contract was usually three years, and this period has been the average length of service by Indian immigrants since that time. Figure 3 gives a diagrammatic summary of the immigrant flow between the years 1928 and 1940.

Indian immigration has been regulated almost from the beginning, in contrast to the immigration of Chinese labor. In addition to the regulation in 1890 already mentioned, the Indian Immigration Committee was established by the Malay government in 1907, and an immigration fund was created, derived from compulsory contributions by the employers of Indian labor, to cover the costs of feeding, shipping, and housing the migrant workers en route to Malaya, as well as to defray the costs of repatriation of ill or unemployed Indian laborers.

In 1910 the recruitment of indentured labor was prohibited, and the kangany system of recruitment took its place. This system was designed to increase control over the immigration process. The kanganies usually were Indian foremen on estates in Malaya who were licensed to recruit labor in their own villages in India. Licenses were issued under the direction of both Indian and Malayan officials, and the number of recruits was limited in every case. An engaged laborer could leave his Indian village only with the consent of his village headman. This system had the advantage of assuring better care of the laborers, though at best conditions were poor, and it also had the effect of channeling labor to the labor-deficit areas in Ma-

MIGRATION OF INDIAN ESTATE LABORERS
BETWEEN MALAYA AND INDIA

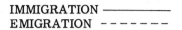

IMMIGRATION ——————
EMIGRATION – – – – – –

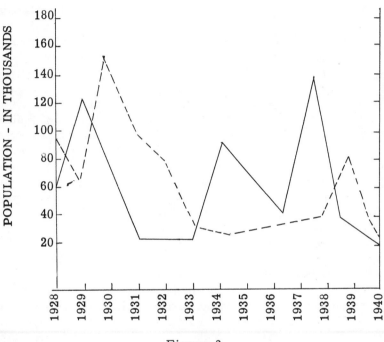

Figure 3

laya. There was further regulation in the Indian emigration
rules of 1922 which provided for a lower limit in the numbers
to be recruited by the <u>kanganies</u> and more supervision over the
entire process in India. Under the same legislation a standard
wage was established, hospital and maternity benefits were as-
sured, provisions were made for compulsory education on the
estates, and penal sanctions for breach of labor contract were
abolished.

During the 1930's free, unassisted, unrecruited immigration

became increasingly important for unskilled laborers, whereas it had previously been restricted primarily to merchant and professional occupations. Unassisted immigration increased from 12 per cent of total immigration in 1920 to 38 per cent in 1934, and to a prewar high of 89 per cent in 1937. 10 Ultimately, unrecruited labor became prevalent, having grown from 12 per cent in 1920 to 91 per cent in 1938. 11 Thus, by the middle of the 1930's the kangany system, after successive modifications, had become an insignificant part of the migrational system.

The functions of assisting and recruiting laborers for Malaya had by the 1930's come under the supervision of governmental agencies which, in the case of India, sought to provide maximum protection for the workers and which, in the case of Malaya, sought the most stable possible labor force. In 1938 the kangany system was ended in India. In the same year, the government of India banned all emigration to Malaya.

The ostensible reason for the ban was the glut of Indian labor in Malaya, which operated against the Indian laborers there. The actual reason for the ban seems to have been to place pressure upon the Malayan employers, who in 1937 had refused to consider an increase in the minimum wage for Indian workers as advised by an agent of the Indian government, Srinavasa Sastri, following a survey of estate conditions in 1936. The ban reflected a growing consciousness of the conditions under which Indians had to work in Malaya and their implications upon the sensibilities of an increasingly influential Indian "nationalism."

In the post-World War II period the same political and social forces became apparent on the Malayan side, as evidenced in the regulations governing the immigration of Indians. From the time of the reoccupation of Malaya after the defeat of Japan until 1952 the government of Malaya controlled immigration through passport regulation and through the passenger restrictions ordinance which made the possession of the means of livelihood a condition of entrance into Malaya. In August, 1953, an immigration ordinance set up a selective mechanism

10. Bruno Lasker, Asia on the Move (New York: Henry Holt and Co. , 1946). p. 60.

11. Virginia Thompson, Labor Problems in Southeast Asia (New Haven: Yale University Press, 1947), p. 67.

for immigration and employed a system of entry permits, which was directed at restricting the immigration of hawkers, shopkeepers, and others "not necessary to the economy of Malaya."[12]

Change in the Indian population has been influenced as much by economic and political factors as by internal demographic matters (age-sex structure, fertility, and so forth). As an illustration, between 1931 and 1947 the Indian population decreased from about 622,000 to 600,000. The brunt of the decrease fell upon south Indians whose population decline of 6.3 per cent was not offset by the normal 38.6 per cent increase of the much smaller north Indian population.[13] This decrease in south Indians reflects the long-term decline in the rubber industry which struck the states of Perak, Selangor, and Negri Sembilan. Between 1938 and 1951 there was a migrational deficit of 20,000 per annum, largely south Indians.[14]

The noneconomic variables in the population process, however, are moving toward normalcy, as evidenced by the changing ratio of women to men in the Indian population. In 1947 there were 11.1 per cent more men than women in the age range of fifteen to nineteen, as compared with 15.9 per cent in 1931.[15] Male and female imbalance had been considered as evidence of the impermanent nature of Indian settlement in Malaya. Now, as the imbalance slowly corrects itself, an increasingly permanent population of Indians can be postulated, supported by other political and social evidence. For example, under the most recent immigration ordinance (1952) the largest category, 50 per cent of all persons granted entry to Malaya, were alien wives of residents, alien children under twelve years of age belonging to residents, and alien females "on compassionate grounds."[16]

Characteristics of Settlement

Thirty-nine per cent of the Indian population lives in towns

---

12. Federation of Malaya, Annual Report, 1953, p. 9.
13. Del Tufo, Malaya, p. 79.
14. T. E. Smith, Population Growth in Malaya, p. 84.
15. Ibid., p. 86.
16. Federation of Malaya, Annual Report, 1953, p. 9.

and villages. [17] The implications of this in terms of style of
life for these "urban" Indians are difficult to elucidate because
there is no adequate discussion of the characteristics of Malayan urban settlement. Still, the crude fact that one out of
every three Indians is not directly a part of the estate "culture" is important. It should also be noted that there is a considerable difference between what might be considered "rural
living" among Malaysians and the style of life of the Indian
workers on the estates. On the estates the Indians have formed
an entirely different ecumene than the rural Malays, since they
have been specialized agricultural wage workers; they have
lived under conditions which have been controlled and regulated
by the Malayan government in cooperation with the government
of India; and they have been culturally homogeneous and isolated from the Malay rural scene. For these reasons, a simple
rural-urban dichotomy fails to describe clearly the Indian population.

There is, however, a clearly defined urban population of
Indians in the commercial cities of Georgetown and Singapore.
The Indian population of the municipalities is 63 per cent and
79 per cent, respectively, of the entire Indian population within
the administrative units of Penang and Singapore. The numbers
involved are, however, small: 49,000 in Singapore and 26,000
in Georgetown. In addition to these clearly defined urban dwellers, 110,000 Indians lived in towns over ten thousand, of
which there are twenty-three in Malaya. The remaining 42,000
Indians listed by the 1947 census as urban dwellers lived in
towns of one thousand to ten thousand.

Because there has been no detailed study of urbanization
in Malaya, it is impossible to characterize the distinctive
elements of the Indian urban population. It may, however, be
significant that in districts of the Federation with the highest
percentage of Indians, i.e., parts of Perak, Selangor, and
Negri Sembilan, there is a correspondingly high percentage of
urbanization of Indians. This would seem to suggest a functional dependence of the Indian estate dweller upon the services
of the Indian town dweller based upon set tastes and preferences in food and clothing.

Most of the remaining 60 per cent of the Indian population
in Malaya is settled in rural settlements ranging from large,

_____

17. Del Tufo, Malaya, p. 47.

highly efficient and highly capitalized rubber estates to subsistence smallholdings. About 51 per cent of the gainfully employed Indians are engaged in some sort of commercial agricultural activity. Of this number most are engaged in the production of rubber; the remainder are in coconut and oil-palm production, and stock-raising. Only eight thousand Indians were counted as being engaged in subsistence occupations in 1947.

The spatial distribution of most of the Indians has followed the environmental demands for the cultivation of rubber (Map 6). The bulk of the rubber cultivation occurs on the west coastal plain in a band which begins in northern Perak and ends at the tip of Johore and which does not usually extend over fifty miles from the western coast.

The Indian estate population appears to be isolated from the Malay rural scene by reason of different economic activities, different cultural activities, and the self-sufficient nature of the estate existence. Thus, though Malay kampongs may, and frequently do, border on the estate lands, propinquity does not assure social intercourse between the two peoples. The same situation holds for similar reasons with regard to the Chinese population, there being many Chinese laborers on estates or in the tin-rich Kinta valley. The isolation of the three ethnic groups from one another in the population belt of Malaya constitutes one of the central sociopolitical problems.

The traditional residence facilities for the Indian estate laborer have been "coolie lines" consisting of long houses divided into partitions for workers with families or left undivided in dormitory fashion for single men. During the past twenty years, under the pressure of the Indian agent in Malaya and the Malayan health and welfare officers, these establishments have gradually been replaced by individual dwelling units of a cottage type, which house the primary family, or at least by long houses which are not set back-to-back, thus assuring maximum ventilation and cooking space.

Another aspect of the changing internal settlement patterns relates to social organization. The traditional "coolie line" consisted both of buildings and of laborers who worked under a foreman (kangany). The laborers were responsible to the foreman in matters relating to life in the lines. The "coolie lines" on any estate were responsible to the oldest foreman, who served as liaison between the planter or his agents and the laborers on the estate. Since early legislation on immigration provided that the foreman recruit laborers from the village of his origin in India it must be supposed that there was a significant relationship between the social organization of the home village and the transplanted society on the Malayan estate. Most of the Tamil laborers were recruited from the most depressed castes, which meant that in addition to originating from the same village the social organization transplanted was probably consistent with caste organization in India.

Since the recruitment of Indians through the foremen has been prohibited for the last twenty years and the average length of stay in Malaya for the Indian laborer has been estimated at from three to eight years, an almost complete replacement of the population recruited through the old system has probably taken place. Therefore, the close relationship between settlement on estates and the native Indian social organization postulated above probably no longer holds. The regulation and improvement of labor conditions has undoubtedly reduced dependence upon the autocratic powers of the foreman. Moreover, other developments probably have acted to impersonalize the labor community on these estates, such as trade unionism and the growth of literacy and political consciousness. Finally, with unassisted and relatively free immigration during the late 1920's and early 1930's the significance of the Indian village group in any given "line" has been reduced, though the immigrant laborer still comes from the south Indian states. All of these factors have probably weakened the earlier group solidarity of Indians on estates.

Internal migration

Table 53 and Table 54 indicate that the internal migration of indigenous Indians is not nearly as significant to the total Indian population as is external migration. The overall percentage of indigenous Indians by state reveals that less than 20 per cent of the Indians born in Malaya have residence in states other than those in which they were born. This does not cover the internal migrational tendencies of immigrant Indians at all. It does indicate a propensity on the part of the indigenous Indians to remain settled in their states of birth. This is related to the probability that a large proportion of the indigenous Indians are engaged in stable economic activities which provide enough employment opportunities.

Low internal migration has been explained by one observer as: "common unwillingness of the labourer to sever . . . ties and uproot himself from particular areas and estates. "[18]

Though the immobility may not be general or widespread--

TABLE 53
INTERNAL MIGRATION OF INDIANS, 1947*

State or Settlement	Total Indian Population	Born in Malaya	Per Cent Malaya-born of Total Indian Population	Born in State Enumerated	Per Cent of Malaya-born Indians Born in State Enumerated
Penang	57,157	33,041	58	29,339	89
Malakka	19,718	9,970	51	8,287	83
Perak	140,176	77,615	55	69,464	88.5
Selangor	145,184	77,208	53	70,195	91
Negri Sembilan	38,082	18,076	47	13,583	72
Pahang	14,744	6,396	43	4,595	72
Johore	55,044	22,195	40	16,691	75
Kedah	51,347	25,954	51	20,599	76
Kelantan	4,940	1,788	36	1,570	88
Trengganu	1,761	436	25	no data	no data
Perlis	1,684	815	48	no data	no data
Federation average	-	-	-	-	81.5
Colony of Singapore	68,978	25,018	57	21,002	84
Malaya average	-	-	-	-	82

*Del Tufo, Malaya, p. 329, Table 45.

there is some mobility--the reluctance on the part of many estate workers to move to better opportunities is important. It
has been quite common also for estate workers to take a wage
reduction with equanimity rather than seek other employment
when the rubber market is weak, since, if unsuccessful, they
would risk the possibility of being found indigent and repatri-
ated to India. Certainly the immigrant Indian worker is not as
migratory as might be supposed.

Health and sanitation

In matters of health, sanitation, and availability of public
welfare services, the Indian estate population is favored.
During the early 1920's considerable pressure was exerted
upon the planters to provide adequate medical and hospital
facilities for the estate workers, as well as latrines and pure
water supplies. The Malayan government also pursued a program of establishing centrally located government hospitals
and ample well water. In comparison with the facilities avail-

18. C. Kondapi, Indians Overseas, 1832-1949 (New Delhi:
Indian Council of World Affairs, 1951), pp. 97-98.

able to the Malay rural dweller, the facilities upon estates are very good. Moreover, the government has recently been concentrating upon rural health measures, and this undoubtedly will work to the advantage of the estate workers.

TABLE 54

DISTRIBUTION OF IMMIGRANT INDIANS, 1947*

State or Settlement	Per Cent Immigrant of Total Indian Populatio..	Tamil Population (Born in Madras)	Indian Population Born in Other Indian Areas†	Indian Population Born in Other Areas
Penang	42	20,943	2,737	436
Malakka	49	8,423	1,185	140
Perak	45	51,004	10,337	1,220
Selangor	47	58,116	8,655	1,205
Negri Sembilan	53	17,433	150	377
Pahang	57	6,843	1,277	243
Johore	60	26,293	5,847	709
Kedah	49	22,098	2,853	442
Kelantan	64	2,194	885	83
Trengganu	75	873	389	63
Perlis	52	623	180	66
Federation average	54	-	-	-
Colony of Singapore	44	32,119	11,017	824
Malaya average	50	-	-	-

*Del Tufo, Malaya, p. 329, Table 45.

†Including Indians born in Ceylon, in the British Commonwealth outside of India, elsewhere, or not stated.

Several factors militate, however, against the fullest use of the health and sanitation facilities on the estates. Health regulations for estates demand that there be a dispensary and hospital space available to estate workers. These have been reported as being inadequately staffed, usually by persons who have had some instruction in emergency dressing but who are incapable of handling serious injuries, much less disease. To ameliorate this problem the government has attempted to establish hospitals, within reach of the estate population, which could care for illnesses and injuries beyond the competence of the estate dispensaries, particularly childbirth and maternity cases. However, persons suffering from malaria, the most common of the debilitating diseases, and those needing maternity care have been reluctant to leave the estates for the hospitals, which frequently are as far as fifty miles away. In part this results from a suspicion of hospitals and their methods; in part it is a reluctance to leave family and friends on the estate. Similar factors impede the raising of sanitation levels on the estates themselves, and, as one observer has reported, the latrine is likely to be the cleanest and most odor-free building on an estate because it is hardly ever used. [19] In short, the facilities available to the Indians working on estates probably have been adequate, or nearly so, in terms of the actual demand for them.

Bases of Livelihood

The livelihood base of the Indians in Malaya is closely associated with economic activities of national or international rather than local character, and involves specialized labor, clerical and mercantile skills which are usually wage-remunerative as opposed to subsistence agricultural occupations. Value commitments are associated with economic activities which are by their nature less highly localized and more flexible than those of the Malay population. This association tempers all aspects of Indian life. It partly explains the relatively impermanent status of the Indian in Malaya and ties his economic well-being not merely to the local but also to the international economy, the markets of which absorb his industrial raw materials or use his skill as a businessman.

In Table 55 the Indian population is analyzed in terms of the most important industries and industrial groups wherein they find gainful employment. In the Federation 85 per cent of the Indians engaged in agricultural occupations work at rubber, coconut, and oil-palm cultivation or stock-rearing, activities which are part of the export economy of the country. In both Singapore and the Federation public employment also is important. Personal service occupations, although not occupying an important proportion of the gainfully employed, are aggregated with the "commercial" occupations, not by reason of their intrinsic character (cooking, gardening, valet services, etc.) but because they are most readily associated with urbanism.

---

19. H. Fauconnier, Malaisie (New York: Macmillan and Co., 1939), p. 236.

TABLE 55
INDUSTRIAL AFFILIATIONS
OF GAINFULLY EMPLOYED INDIANS, 1947*

Industrial Group	Federation		Singapore	
	Total Recorded	Per Cent of Total Recorded	Total Recorded	Per Cent of Total Recorded
Fishing	586	0.2	10	-
Agriculture	182,546	60	561	1
Transportation and communication	14,348	5	5,943	14
Commerce and finance	25,930	9	8,827	21
Public administration	35,245	11	16,745	40
Personal service	19,509	6	3,931	9
All other	22,737	8.8	6,685	15
Total	300,901	100.0	42,702	100.0

*Del Tufo, Malaya, pp. 442,473, Tables 78, 87. These figures cover only 91 per cent of the gainfully employed Indians of the Federation and 85 per cent of those in Singapore in 1947.

Basic needs and subsistence occupations

The absence of subsistence occupations among the Indians is notable because these are of such importance in the home communities in India. Despite substantial remittances from Indians in Malaya there seems never to have developed in south India the sort of emigrant community which characterizes much of south China, considerably dependent upon funds remitted by members of the family overseas. In great part, the funds which have been remitted to India from Malaya have come from small wage workers on the estates or clerks in small shops whose remittances, though in the aggregate considerable, merely help support numerous substandard households in India.

Food, clothing, and other necessities are purchased by the Indians out of their wage earnings. The estate Indians usually have had special subsidies available to them. In the case of rice, for example, in 1941 estate workers could buy at about 13 per cent below the prevailing market price, and this price was maintained at a stable level despite the considerable fluctuations in the open market price. Clothing has presented a special problem. The Tamils traditionally have preferred Indian-made cloth to that made in Malaya or elsewhere. During World War II this created an intense problem for the Indian workers in Malaya because of the impossibility of obtaining

330

south Indian fabrics. The tastes of the Indians were so inflexible on this point that they wore the tattered remnants of their prewar wardrobes until trade relations became normal after the defeat of Japan. [20]

The provision of basic needs for the Indians in Malaya has been complicated further by cost of living increases since the war. Table 56 makes this immediately apparent. Increased wages have not matched the rising costs of living, and the Indian householder has had to stint on some of his expenditures in order to balance his budget. It has been observed that the Indian, much more than the Malay and Chinese, is likely to "economize at the expense of his stomach."[21]

TABLE 56
COMPARATIVE COSTS
OF SELECTED COMMODITIES FOR INDIANS

Commodity	Cost per Unit (Straits Dollars)	
	1941	1945
Rice	0.05	0.90
Salt	0.03	0.80
Sugar	0.08	3.50
Fish	0.43	3.50
Ragi	0.03	0.53
Soap	0.10	1.50
Cloth	0.30	6.00
Firewood	0.25	2.90
Dried chillies	0.16	4.20

This tendency has undermined the health of the estate population. Indians more and more revert to the traditional Tamil diet of rice plus a fish relish, a diet extremely low in protein. This tendency is re-enforced by the character of the stores at which the Tamil must shop for his food. These are small establishments with modest inventories. Because of inadequate storage facilities they seldom carry fresh foods. Milk, dairy products, and eggs are absent from the diet because of their

---

20. P. Kodanda Rao, "Indians Overseas: The Position in Malaya," India Quarterly, April-June, 1946, p. 154.

21. Orde-Browne, Labour Conditions, p. 102.

prohibitively high cost and because they are foods not commonly eaten in India. When these products are produced by estate workers in their supplemental agricultural activities, they are usually sold rather than consumed. The incidence of beriberi (vitamin B_1 deficiency), xerophthalmia (vitamin A deficiency) and malaria, which is frequently endemic in the estate regions, results in high morbidity within the estate population.[22]

There is some evidence that Indians would take up subsistence agriculture if permitted to do so. At no time in the modern period has there been substantial land suitable for subsistence cultivation available for Indians. Such land has rather been reserved for rubber or some other commercial crop or for Malay subsistence farming. Several small agricultural settlement schemes were developed for Indians. These were in Bagan-Serai, Perak, and in Chua, Negri Sembilan. The former was established by the Roman Catholic mission in the 1870's. The latter involved 243 acres of thickly wooded jungle and 500 acres of dry land unsuitable for rubber.[23] One private land settlement plan was concerned with land contiguous to a large rubber estate at Sungei Ujong.

Indians do own some land. In 1935 they owned 36,535 acres in the Straits Settlements and 272,447 acres elsewhere. However, about 70 per cent of this land was in the hands of middle-class Indians whose use of it was commercial. On many plantations Indians are encouraged to cultivate subsistence crops on small garden plots but there is extremely little individually owned land devoted to subsistence-type agriculture.

These conditions have rankled the politically conscious Indians. They do not object to the land reservations for the indigenous Malays, but they do object to the preferential treatment accorded the Malays of Indonesia, who are entitled to land for subsistence agriculture though they are nationals of another country, and to the discrimination in the use of the highlands of the peninsula, about five thousand square miles, which have been available easily to Europeans, Malays, and Chinese, but only with difficulty to Indians.[24]

---

22. Erich H. Jacoby, Agrarian Unrest in Southeast Asia (New York: Columbia University Press, 1949), p. 129.
23. Kondapi, Indians Overseas, p. 120.
24. Ibid., pp. 130, 310.

Commercial and industrial activities

Primary occupations. --Over half of the gainfully employed Indians are owners of plantations or, much more frequently, wage earners on estates. It is in the cultivation and processing of rubber that the largest group of Indians gain their livelihood. On the European-owned and -operated estates, where the Indians have comprised about 80 per cent of the labor force,[25] working conditions are most regularized and the information most reliable and ample.[26]

The estate force can be divided into three large groups: the field force, the factory force, and the clerical force. In the field occupations are the following classes: managerial, tapper, and other field labor. In the managerial class the labor foremen, kanganies or mandors, are a combination of labor boss and patriarch depending on personality factors and on the strength of the trade-union organization. The foreman is the liaison between the planter and the laborer in the organization of daily tasks; he also is in charge of the "lines," and of maintaining a modicum of order and sanitation. In these latter functions the labor foreman is aided by the estate policeman, usually a Sikh, and subordinate field foremen. Since the abolition of the recruitment system the foremen have risen more frequently through the ranks of the ordinary field workers, their performance as skilled tappers and their industriousness, not their capacity for recruitment, being the decisive factors. It is common for foremen to use their savings to purchase smallholdings and in time to leave the estate and develop their own holdings.

The tappers are the most skilled of the rubber workers and the most highly paid. Each tapper is allotted a group of trees which may cover a wide area. The skill of the tapper in making his cut in the bark is important in the life and productivity of the tree. Of the sixty-nine thousand tappers listed

---

25. Thompson, Labor Problems in Southeast Asia, p. 72.

26. It is from the European estates that most of the census information was gathered, and the discussion below is based primarily upon employment conditions on these holdings. However, conditions elsewhere are likely to vary greatly from those on the European-managed estates and, for that matter, among the European estates themselves.

in 1947, about thirty-nine thousand (57 per cent) were men. [27]

The tapper's day begins at dawn, for the latex flows best in the early hours. Every tree in his charge is visited, a slanting cut taken in the bark, a strip of which is then removed and a small cup attached to the bottom of the cut along which the latex runs. After all the trees are so attended, the tapper retraces his route collecting the latex accumulated during the interval of about four hours. This is taken to the factory, weighed by a clerk, and credited to the worker. The Indian, however, unlike the Chinese, is paid by the day and not by the weight of the latex. The tapper's day is usually finished by noon or shortly thereafter; it consists of six to seven working hours. [28]

Rubber factory workers numbered something over seven thousand in 1947. The occupations are for the most part skilled, and the rate of remuneration is usually as high as that of the tappers. In the estate factories, the tapped latex is converted into sheet rubber for transport to further processing or export. Factory work is usually for nine hours a day, and the conditions have been described as fair according to industrial practices in Asia--the rooms being fairly well ventilated, the machinery frequently provided with safeguards, and most of the odors adequately drawn off.

Of the remainder of the field operations performed by the Indians, weeding is most important. For the first six years of the life of the rubber tree, before it is tapped, weeding is important. It is generally done by old people, both men and women, and by children, as well as by tappers when they are required to work a full nine-hour day.

The few Indian clerical workers on the estates form a somewhat different labor group from the field workers. The clerks

---

27. Del Tufo, Malaya, p. 477 (Table 88).

28. The length of the tapper's day is subject to controversy since the work day for Indian estate workers was fixed at a maximum of nine hours by Indian Immigration Committee despite the practice of stopping tapping by noon. Thus, on some estates, tappers have complained that after completing their tapping function they were compelled to perform other field jobs to fill in the nine-hour day. It is conceded, however, that most tappers work a six-hour day. See Kondapi, Indians Overseas, pp. 95-96; Orde-Browne, Labour Conditions, pp. 96-97.

are literate, are in close contact with the administrative staff, are usually indigenous, and accompanied by their families. Though the clerical workers enjoy free housing and services, as do the field or factory workers, their salaries are low because of the many candidates for white-collar positions. Not until recently have they received the same sort of welfare and holiday privileges as the field workers.

Wages beyond a standard minimum in the rubber industry have been determined by the price of rubber and the accessibility of the estates to labor.

The world price for rubber fluctuates considerably. The result for the Indian worker has been a highly fluctuating wage rate which has been tolerable only because of the free services to which he is entitled. One of the consequences of the fluctuating wage situation is that less nutritive foods often are consumed, the Indians are more susceptible to illness, and they frequently are compared unfavorably with the Chinese as being less energetic workers.

The second factor in the wage situation of the Indians has been the delineation of so-called "key" and "nonkey" areas of rubber cultivation based upon the availability of the estates to labor. Estates in regions well served by roads and rail connections may offer their workers from 15 to 20 per cent less than regions not so favored. The argument that the price differential will induce a worker in the former areas to move to the latter areas is unsound when applied to the Indians because of their reluctance to leave an estate which has come to be home. The "key" and "nonkey" wage differential has, therefore, probably not produced a more economically responsive Indian labor force, but has merely discriminated against the Indians in the more highly developed rubber cultivation areas.

During slump periods the Indian laborer's income may fall by almost 25 per cent, not so much from his own decreased employment, since labor laws guarantee the worker a minimum of work days, but from the decreased employment of the women and children of his family, whose incomes contribute about 25 per cent of the household income. It should of course be remembered that the Indian rubber worker receives free housing, fuel, water, hospital and medical services, entertainment, and a subsidy for rice, his major food staple. Also, in the event of unemployment or decreased employment he does not have to depend on savings to tide him over to pay his passage back to India. If the Indian must be released by an estate, relief funds

335

are available from the Indian Immigrant Fund, and there are depots in various parts of the country which house and feed unemployed Indians and find employment for them on public works projects. The same funds are used to provide transportation for unemployed Indians to areas which have a labor deficit or back to India in the event that the unemployment situation is of more than short duration. [29]

In other commercial agricultural occupations the Indians are far less numerous. In 1947 there were 9,500 Indians in coconut cultivation, 190 of whom were owners or managers; in oil palm cultivation there were 6,200 Indians, of whom 56 were owners or managers; Indian truck farmers totalled about 3,400, livestock raisers 2,600, and forestry workers 133. The Indians in the other primary productive occupations such as fishing, mining, and forestry, numbered only 8,040.

Wages for Indian agricultural laborers outside the rubber industry have been tied to the minimum legal wage for the estate workers. It has been argued by Indians that the free services available to the estate worker tends to discriminate against nonestate labor and serves to keep estate labor from seeking other employment. In 1938 the Indian agent in Malaya, with the support of the government of India, had the uncontrolled aspects of unassisted immigration of Malaya brought under closer regulation in order to minimize the effects on wages of an oversupply of nonestate Indian labor in Malaya. As a result the wage level of the nonestate Indian was somewhat improved as the supply more nearly matched the demand for immigrant Indian labor.

Secondary occupations. --About 5 per cent of the gainfully employed Indians in 1947 were involved in secondary productive pursuits, exclusive of factory workers on estates. Indians were employed almost exclusively as semiskilled and unskilled workers (Table 57). A significantly smaller proportion of Indians are owners or managers than is true among the Chinese in the same fields of employment. This is evident especially in the category of occupations associated with metal-working, where the largest group of industrially employed Indians is to be found. Also, there are significantly few Indians in handi-

---

29. P. P. Pillai (ed.), Labour in South East Asia: A Symposium (New Delhi: Indian Council of World Affairs, 1947), p. 146.

craft industries. This is noteworthy in the cases of textile and fiber production and is correlated with the dependence upon imported fabrics from south India.

TABLE 57
SECONDARY EMPLOYMENT OF INDIANS, 1947*

	Federation	Singapore
Bricks, pottery, glass	179	171
Chemical processes, paints, etc.	39	6
Metalworkers (nonelectroplate or precious metals)	3,502	2,125
Electroplate and precious metals	755	140
Watches, clocks, scientific instruments	21	16
Skin, leather, and leather substitutes (not footwear)	6	3
Textiles (not processing or clothes makers)	19	7
Textile goods and clothes	1,381	747
Food, drink, tobacco	2,716	404
Wood and furniture	1,249	541
Paper, cardboard, bookbinders	101	36
Other metals	2,101	90
Total	12,069	4,215

*Del Tufo, Malaya, pp. 480, 522, Tables 88, 97.

Tertiary occupations. --Table 55 indicates that about one-third of the employed Indians in the Federation are engaged in tertiary productive occupations. Table 58 shows the distribution of Indians in trade and service employment.

In general, the service and trade occupations are filled by Indians from the north of India. Many of the medium and small tradespeople in the Indian population are Moslems of the Marakkayar community (from Madras) and Chettiars, whereas the Sikhs and Pathans provide most of the policemen and watchmen and perform many of the other public service functions.

Of the non-labouring classes, the most thriving are the Nattukottai Chettiars. They generally do their usual business--money lending and banking-- and in the course of that business have acquired rubber estates, house properties, etc. They have their own chambers of commerce in different centres of Malaya. Next to them come the merchants, both North Indians and South Indians. They are engaged in all sorts of trade from petty hawking and street vending to the big import and export trade. They have also got their associations in different

337

TABLE 58
TERTIARY OCCUPATIONS OF INDIANS, 1947*

	Federation		Singapore	
Trades				
Builders, bricklayers, etc.		666		775
Painters		319		303
Clerical		5,879		3,002
Stationary engineers and dynamo technicians		1,192		610
Warehousemen		424		600
Total		8,480		5,290
Public service				
Transportation, communication		17,024		7,070
Public administration, defense		2,418		1,054
(police)	(1,500)		(830)	
Professional		5,324		902
(medical technicians)	(2,500)		(400)	
(teachers)	(1,500)		(106)	
Entertainment, sports		459		131
Total		25,225		9,157
Personal service		17,471		3,493
(Domestic)	(7,000)		(1,400)	
Commerce and finance		22,459		6,922
(Retail establishments, proprietors, managers)	(7,324)		(1,885)	
(Vendors, hawkers, salesmen)	(14,022)		(4,941)	
Other		33,616		11,498
(Unspecified labor)	(26,000)		(7,734)	
(Watchmen)	(5,000)		(2,500)	
Total		107,251		36,360

*Del Tufo, Malaya, pp. 480, ·522, Tables 88, 97.

centres. There are also a few advocates and soli-
citors and also a number of medical men working
in Government and as private practitioneers. There
is a small number of Indians holding responsible
positions in the Government service, such as the
police, railways, posts and telegraphs, etc. A
number of Punjabis are employed in the ranks of
the military. The rest, forming the bulk of the
non-labouring classes, are to be found in the clerical ranks of the various Government departments,
mercantile firms and banks, rubber estates and
oil-palm plantations and other places of employment. [30]

30. Sovani, Economic Relations of India, p. 50.

Recruitment for service and trade occupations is in the first instance from the children of those already established in these fields. The transfer of values from the parents to the children, the status accorded "white collar" and "trades" occupations, and the greater availability of means for an adequate education are factors involved. The deficit is made up from immigrants and by recruitment from second-generation estate children. In March, 1946, the Indians in Malaya appealed to the Indian government to persuade the Malayan government to relax the postwar restrictions on Indian immigration of shop assistants, clerks, and artisans. [31] Before 1941 there was a trend toward increased proportions of such workers. In 1940, for example, of the 15, 320 Indian deck passengers to enter Malaya, only 1, 314 were estate workers; the rest were tradesmen, shop-keepers, and clerical workers. [32]

Indian commercial influences upon the Malayan economy may be measured by the magnitude of Indian investment in Malaya. In an official Indian publication it was estimated in 1950 that this investment was between 170 and 250 million rupees. The lower figure, which is probably an underestimate, represents over US$36 million, or M$108. 5 million. This is equal to about 2 per cent of the gross national product of Malaya in 1950, es-timated at M$5, 418. 9 million, or about 25 per cent of the total private investment fund in Malaya. [33] Most of the Indian invest-ment is by the small Chettiar group, whose principal activities have been in business, trade, and banking. To an increasing extent, until 1941, money was also being invested in land.

Tertiary occupations are associated with the towns and cities of Malaya, especially Singapore. There has been a single south Indian group, the Malayali, who follow somewhat different occupational patterns from those of the other south Indians. The Malayali population characteristically has been associated with semiskilled and unskilled labor in the towns, just as the Tamils have been associated with the estates. Another sort of differentiation has been that between the immigrant and native-born Indians in the towns, particularly Singapore. In 1947

---

31. Kondapi, Indians Overseas, p. 189.

32. P. S. Narasimhan, "The Immigrant Communities of South East Asia, " India Quarterly, January-March, 1947, pp. 36-37.

33. While these figures are estimates of estimates and are therefore suspect, they do indicate something of the magnitude

occupational distribution in Singapore varied according to the immigrant-native born dichotomy in the following manner: 35 per cent of the native-born Indian wage earners were in clerical occupations; 33 per cent were semiskilled workers; 11 per cent were unskilled workers; whereas among the immigrant Indian wage-earners 15 per cent were shopkeepers or assistants, 30 per cent semiskilled, and 32 per cent unskilled.[34]

A 1938 survey of Indian shop workers in Singapore, reported in the Straits Times, disclosed marked differences between the northern and southern Indians in Singapore. The northern group consisted mainly of Indians whose places of origin were in Sindh, Gujerat, and the United Provinces; the southern group exclusively of Tamils and south Indian Moslems. The former group operated most of the fashionable establishments, though the majority of shops were operated by the southerners.

> The Northern Indians recruited their labor from India on the basis of an agreement whereby assistants were required to work in Singapore for two or three years, and their passage, board and lodging were paid for by the employer. But the quarters provided by the employers--ones which the employee was bound to accept--were usually located on the floor above the shop and consisted of a small, ill-ventilated room situated under the watchful eye of the employer. Working hours were generally from 8 A.M. to 9 P.M. with a half holiday on Sundays and only one full holiday at Deepa-

---

of the investment. See Indians in the Malayan Economy (New Delhi: Manager of Publications, 1950), cited in S. Nanjundan, "Economic Development of Malaya," India Quarterly, 1952; the Indian investment estimate given is in crores of rupees. This estimate is corroborated by Kondapi, Indians Overseas, p. 301. The gross national produce estimate is from Frederic Benham, The National Income of Malaya, 1947-49 (Singapore: Government Printing Office, 1951), p. 172.

34. Colony of Singapore, Department of Social Welfare, A Social Survey of Singapore: A Preliminary Study of Some Aspects of Social Conditions in the Municipal Area of Singapore, December, 1947 (Singapore: G. H. Keat and Co., Ltd., n. d.), p. 52 (Table 16).

vali. Two hours were allotted for lunch and tea but dinner could be eaten only after the shop was closed. Wages were scheduled on a rupee basis. Sindhi merchants paid a minimum of 30 rupees monthly, with annual increments ranging from 5 to 10 rupees, and also supplied food and lodging. But half the salary was sent to the employee's family in India and the remaining credited to the employee's account. No actual money was paid to the employee, in addition to the advance given him before leaving India, unless a specific agreement to that effect had been made in the contract. Stringent as were such working conditions they were generally far better than those prevailing for Southern Indians. The latter not uncommonly had to work from 6 A.M. to 11 P.M., with only three half-hour breaks for food. Most of the Muslim and Tamil employers recruited their Indian assistants locally; nevertheless, they, too, forwarded half the salary earned to the employee's family in India. Employers uniformally claimed that they and their assistants were one, big happy family, mutually concerned with each other's morale and physical welfare. They blandly asserted that their assistants loved long hours, disliked holidays, and did not know what to do with the leisure time they had. Their assistants, however, told the investigating reporters another tale. They complained of the crowded living accommodations, which also served as dining rooms, of poor food, of a 15-hour working day, of inadequate wages ranging from Straits $7 to $35 irregularly paid and of punishment meted out to them on the slightest pretext. Their employers took charge of computing salaries and refused to render them any accounting; having no means of redress the employees had to accept all the fines and items marked "personal expenditures" which were chalked up against them. Their chief grievance, however, was the lack of privacy and of leisure time. [35]

35. Ibid.

The publicity from the _Times_ investigation forced the south Indian Chamber of Commerce to recommend a reduction of hours
and increased leisure time, but these minimal reforms were
resisted by a significant section of the Indian mercantile community. [36]

The postwar debtor ordinances. --The conditions under which
the Indian merchant has plied his trade in Malaya have been
reasonably secure and stable, since Indians have enjoyed the
privileges of British subjects. There are cases, however, of
disabilities to which the Indian merchants are susceptible because they are a minority in a restive multiracial community.
The postwar ordinances dealing with titles to land and debtor-
creditor relations during the period of occupation under Japan
stipulated that all transactions in land during the war were to
be recognized as valid, except when these transactions were
consummated under conditions and principles not in accordance
with prewar practices or when the transactions were made
under duress. The debtor ordinance provided for the validation
of all monetary transactions made during the occupation period,
except those involving the interests of persons who had fled
the country with the coming of the Japanese, i. e. , primarily
the Europeans.

The Indians in Malaya prior to the war had been important
creditors and held considerable land in the form of mortgages.
These Indians, of whom the most important were the Chettiars,
had advanced loans to Malays before the war in British currency, and while many of the Chettiars fled at the time of the
Japanese invasion, most had delegated agents to carry on their
business. These agents were compelled to accept highly in-
flated Japanese currency as repayment and to release the titles
and mortgages they held as collateral. Because the Indians had
agents in Malaya during the war period, their businesses were
considered to be in operation by the postwar authorities and
therefore not eligible for the special consideration given to
European creditors who had fled. Moreover, the ordinances
discriminated against Indians in that they granted more ample
repayment of prewar obligations to banking institutions than
to private creditors, which most Indians were.

The ordinances were passed in 1947 but were held in abey-

---

36. Summary of the _Times_ investigation cited in Thompson,
Labor Problems in Southeast Asia, pp. 89-90.

ance until 1949 at the request of the government of India, which was protecting the Indian interests in Malaya. The pressure of the Indian government was of no avail, and an additional ordinance was passed in 1948 for Singapore, setting up a revaluation schedule for certain loans repaid during the war, which in the opinion of Indians was too low. The position of the Indians throughout the negotiations on these ordinances was that they did not expect to realize the full value of their prewar loans since the exigencies of war had operated against all in Malaya. In fact considerable land was acquired by Indians during the period of occupation, indicating that while there was some loss, there was also some gain to the community as a whole. The Indians argued, however, that during the occupation period duress was general and all cases should be reviewed in this light; they complained that in the final settlement European creditors were favored over the Chinese and Indians because the latter were not in general organized as banking institutions and were not able to leave the country when it was invaded by the Japanese. [37]

Social and Political Organization

The estate-dwelling Indians form a fairly insular subsystem within the total Malayan social system. To a lesser extent, the same is true of the Indians who dwell in the towns of Malaya. While the Indian urban dweller is not isolated physically from other communities in the way that the estate Indian is, he nevertheless tends to create his own social and business associations from among his own kind. His colleagues are almost certain to be Indians, whether he lays track for the railroad or is a clerk in a Singapore shop, and he will try to raise his children to speak the Indian mother tongue.

It has been noted that personal connections and relationships are important to Indians in the emigrating communities of India. Personal assurances of a tolerable experience in Malaya, when added to the impoverishment of most Indian emigrating communities, help the prospective immigrant break the ties to his home village and venture forth into a new world. Moreover, the immigrant knows that it will be possible to return in a rather short time, three years, and that the world in-

---

37. Kondapi, Indians Overseas, pp. 301-4.

343

to which he is venturing is not a strikingly new one. He goes to an estate where people more or less of his own caste, locale, or economic status live. At the end of three years, if he has not brought his wife and family, he returns home; if he has brought his family, his stay is likely to be longer and more pleasant, but he will return to India eventually. As for the non-estate immigrant Indian population, similar conditions have operated among certain sections of the laboring groups and petty mercantile groups.

> The Malayan Indian having been born and bred in the country [Malaya] has come to love the country of his adoption. He knows little of India, as it is only through newspapers and magazines that he sees it. He is modern and as much Anglicized and Americanized as any other Malayan. He meets all on the same level and has an affectionate approach. Being thoroughly cosmopolitan in his ideas, he has inter-married with the many nationalities that reside in the country. Many Indians can be seen with Chinese, Malay, Eurasian, Siamese and occasionally European wives. Sometimes inter-marriage has occurred for two or three successive generations, consequently the latest offspring have neither much knowledge of, nor need to return to, India. In some cases contact with relations in India has been lost. [38]

There are on the other hand the native-born or "Malayan" Indians whose home and the home of their parents and grandparents is Malaya. There undoubtedly are Indians born in Ma-

---

38. H. I. S. Kinwar, "India's Link to Malaya," United Asia, June, 1950, p. 424. The quoted paragraph will prove startling in the light of some of the material which follows regarding the native-born "Malayan" Indian. By way of explanation, it is impossible to know what the writer may have meant by "Anglicized and Americanized" except to convey that there are many such Indians who are urbanized, who speak English and perhaps no Indian language, and who are associated with modern business or professional occupations.

laya who have lived there all of their lives but still harbor the desire to return "home" to an Indian village. More important, it would be desirable to distinguish within the native-born Indian population second-generation from first-generation Malayans, but such information is scarce.

The "Malayan" Indian probably is much more like the Indians in East and South Africa than those in that important center of Indian migration, Ceylon, where ancient Indian invasions left an important land-based population which now comprises about 20 per cent of the population. These so-called "Ceylon Tamils" are distinguished from the dominant Sinhalese population and an almost equal number of so-called "Indian Tamils" who work upon the tea and rubber estates. Ceylon Tamils are comparable to the Malayan Indians in that they are distinguished from the more transient estate population by having been born in Ceylon and by having a full family pattern. However, in contrast to the Malayan Indians, the Ceylon Tamils have an independent culture both because they have existed as a detached subculture for six to eight centuries and because the culture, like that in India, is based upon agricultural village settlements.

The Malayan Indians, like the Indians in Africa, are not associated with a strong Indian culture and must be studied as an element of urban and commercial society.

Religion

Religion as an aspect of Indian social organization in Malaya apparently is not of as great significance as its role in India might suggest. There are over four hundred Indians whose occupations are entered as priests and monks, though their precise functions are difficult to determine. It cannot be expected that the religious values and activities of India should appear unchanged in Malaya since in India religion is vitally bound up with the cultivation of the land, the welfare of family or lineage, and the deification of the place of family or lineage residence. These vital elements are absent in Malaya, though there has been some attempt to continue the forms in the new setting:

> Each estate possesses different gods; but the coolies [Indian estate workers], if moved to another, do not seem to object to transferring their worship--even possibly from a benevolent Vishnu to a terrifying Kali, God of Vengeance. Often one saw

a ruined temple near the coolie lines, deserted because the gods had been unpropitious and the disappointed worshippers had decided to start all over again with a change of gods in a new temple.[39]

Education

The education of young Indians in Malaya is confined to formal teaching and instruction. Divorced from the social structure of which it is a part, the informal, ethnic education by which the roles and attitudes of the Indian in India are imparted has no significant function. In Malaya the attitudes necessary in the socialization of the young are better imparted through formal classroom techniques dealing essentially with Malayan matters. Moreover, on the estates where most culturally unadulterated Indians are found, the relative brevity of their stay in Malaya has undoubtedly militated against the development of informal educational techniques. Indian informal education suffers also from the fact that the wage-earning estate population does not have as much free time as in India.

TABLE 59
INDIAN VERNACULAR SCHOOLS AND ENROLLMENTS*

	Enrollment	Teachers	Number of Schools
Singapore	1,271	49	21
Federation	46,247	1,648	898

*Colony of Singapore, Annual Report, 1953, p. 90;
Federation of Malaya, Annual Report, 1955, p. 241.

Indian schools in Malaya are of three types: government, government-aided, and private. In the Federation, around 10 per cent of the 42,043 Indian pupils enrolled in the Indian vernacular schools in 1953 (4,813) were enrolled in government schools; about 62 per cent (25,226) were in the government-aided estate schools; while 28 per cent (11,518) were in government-aided schools operated by committees of Indian citizens or by religious, primarily Roman Catholic, organizations.

---

39. Katherine Sim, Malayan Landscape (London: Michael Joseph, Ltd., 1946), p. 110. The choice of the god Kali may be significant since in India it is the god historically associated with rural unrest.

About 1 per cent more were enrolled in private schools.[40] In the main, the government or private Indian vernacular schools are found in the towns, and the government-aided schools, which are primarily estate schools, are in the countryside. In addition, Indian pupils (40,000) account for 22.2 per cent (1955) of all enrollments in the English schools in the Federation and a substantial percentage in Singapore. Thus, the Indians show a more marked preference for an English education than any other Asian group.

The supply of trained teachers in the Indian vernacular schools is rising. Of the 1,648 teachers listed in 1955, 922 were trained, whereas 726 were not trained. However, there is no provision for the full-time training of teachers for the Indian schools as yet.[41]

Education on the estates has not received the same attention from either the government or the planters as have medical services or housing, probably because the last-named services bear more immediately on the productivity of the workers. Although the controller of labor in the Federation has had the power to force planters to establish schools for children between seven and fourteen years if there are over ten children on an estate, the facilities provided have been few in number and poor in quality. In 1947 there were 64,565 male and female children between the ages of five and fourteen years living on estates; in 1953, when this population had increased by at least 2 per cent, there were only 25,266 in estate schools. Indifference on the part of the planters and the government has not been the sole reason for these conditions. Schools which have been set up and have been carefully, even enthusiastically, maintained by the estate managers, have faced the problem of procuring adequately trained teachers. In the 1936 survey by Srinavasa Sastri it was noted that on many of the estates the teachers frequently were field foremen, estate clerks, or accountants whose competence was rudimentary at best.[42]

For the nonestate Indians the demand for schools teaching in the vernacular has been small. Living in cities and towns and composed to a greater degree of native-born Indians, the nonestate Indians make use of the English schools to a much great-

40. Federation of Malaya, Annual Report, 1953, p. 181.
41. Federation of Malaya, Annual Report, 1955, p. 241.
42. Cited in Kondapi, Indians Overseas, p. 150.

er degree. In fact, the availability of better educational facilities to the Indians in the towns tends to re-enforce the Malayanization of the more permanent, urban-dwelling Indian. In addition to learning English and having the advantage of better instruction, the town-dwelling Indians also are indoctrinated with the values meant to be conveyed in the national school system of Malaya.

Affiliations in the Indian community

Since the end of the war the government of Malaya has attempted to stabilize the Indian immigrant family through its immigration policy. As the family becomes more "normal" and the accommodations for family life are enhanced, the function of the Indian in the Malayan economy will become even more important. The Indians increasingly are regarded by the Malayan authorities as a part of the national core of Malaya with its multiracial population. The orientation of both the Indians and the government during the Emergency strongly supports this assumption.

The trade unions. --Trade union activity on a significant scale has been a post-World War II development in Malaya as a whole. Trade union activity is of major potential significance for the Indians for two reasons: (1) approximately 75 per cent of the Indian working population is associated with the commercialized sector of the Malayan economy as skilled and semiskilled workers who believe that trade unions represent a logical development of a maturing labor force within a democratic society; (2) the Indian workers are aware that organized labor plays an increasingly important political role in modern democratic societies.

Organization of the Indians on the estates has lagged considerably behind the Chinese and other elements of the Malayan labor force. One of the reasons was the delay in resuscitating estate industry after the Japanese occupation. It was not until 1946 that the estates were, for the most part, in a condition to resume normal operations. More important perhaps was the fact that most of the Indians who could be expected to lead in the organization of the estate workers were jailed, deported, or otherwise harassed by the British military administration for their participation in the Azad Hind movement under Bose, which was supported by the Japanese.

During the immediate postoccupation period other factors also worked against the development of Indian trade unions.

348

One of these was the tension existing between the Chinese and the Indian laborers. This tension had its roots in the discrimination against Indians in that the Chinese traditionally have been paid by the pound of latex tapped and their money wages have been substantially higher than those of the Indians who have worked by the day. Moreover, the Chinese had usually assumed control of the estate labor organizations despite the numerical superiority of the Indians, who accounted for perhaps three-fourths of the memberships.

A final handicap to the organization of trade unions by the estate Indians had been the split in the ranks of the Indians themselves. Immediately after the defeat of Japan and the reoccupation of Malaya by the British, a fissure was observed among the organizationally conscious Indians, which divided the former Azad Hind supporters, now organized as the Indian Independence Association (IIA), and the Indians who were organizing within the framework of the Communist-influenced General Labor Union (GLU). Ultimately open violence between the two factions broke out. Although this fissure was narrowed after India achieved independence, there are still substantive issues which provide a basis for conflict.

The lag in organizing of the Indian labor force has undoubtedly served as a counterpoise to the gradually increasing costs of using Indian labor on the estates. These increasing costs are a result of the constant improvements in work conditions, health, education, and relief which have had to be provided. If, in addition, there had been an effective organization of Indian laborers demanding wage increases and greater benefits from the planters of Malaya, Indian estate labor probably would have lost its important role in the economy. However, the planters have long known of the reluctance of the Indians to organize, and according to one Indian writer they have used this knowledge to their own ends:

> The European planter feared the Chinese labour and their Kapalas [the Chinese labor contractor and labor leader on a particular enterprise]. The Chairman of the Planter's Association stated that there were grounds for fearing that in any dealing with the Chinese [the planters] would encounter organized opposition of a kind not so easy to break through. In the disorganization of Indian labour lay the clue of the cheapness of Indian labour and its

frequent wage reductions in spite of the indispensability of over six lakhs [600,000] of Indian labourers to the Malayan estates. [43]

Nevertheless, some trade union organization has been carried on since the war. The postwar organizational program was given impetus by the 1946 visit to Malaya of Pandit Nehru, who addressed the Penang GLU and described the working conditions in Malaya as "shocking." During that year and 1947 the activities of the Indian trade unionists, working on rubber estates primarily, became intense. The eruption of the Communist terror in 1948 and the subsequent establishment of the Emergency curtailed these activities.

Indian participation in the estate unions, however, has been increasing. The head of the National Union of Plantation Workers is an Indian, and in 1955 he was elected president of the Malayan Trade Union Council. Moreover, Indians have been extremely active in labor movements off the estates. Since the leadership in many of the trade unions of necessity must be English-speaking and somewhat "Western" oriented, and since such a high proportion of the Indians are educated in the English schools, the Indians tend to play a major role in certain unions, particularly those representing "white-collar" workers. It has been easy for many of these union leaders to move into politics, particularly in Singapore.

Chambers of commerce. --Another category of social groupings within the Indian community includes the middle-class societies usually referred to as "chambers of commerce." [44] In addition to pursuing merely economic objectives, these organizations aim at consolidating the Indian trading community politically and socially to act as a pressure group for Indian interests.

To some extent these middle-class Indian organizations reflect the divisions created by different origins within the Indian population. Thus, there are expressly "south Indian" organizations which are concerned with problems more or less

---

43. Ibid., p. 108.

44. There are also noncommercial associations of Indians in Malaya, such as the Federation of Indian Organizations (Kuala Lumpur), the Indian Association (Singapore), and various Sikh associations, but information about them is lacking.

350

separate from the more general Indian associations. They are similar to the Chinese societies which represent the various Chinese dialect groups. The northern Indians, however, form an important proportion of the total membership among most of the Indian pressure groups and may, therefore, exert a political influence greater than their proportion in the total Indian population.

The lower middle-class Indians have suffered considerable deprivation since the war. They were hard hit during the period of Japanese occupation when the shortage of retail goods and the fall of purchasing power produced a crisis for the small entrepreneur. Many of them were recruited into the Azad Hind movement and into the Indian National Army. As a consequence, when the British returned to Malaya, they came under suspicion as collaborators in Japanese-sponsored anti-British movements, and they have had a difficult time finding employment, especially in the public service occupations. In problems of this kind the associations are likely to be called upon for action and support in their quasi-political capacities. [45]

Such affiliations contribute to the stabilization of the Indian community. The normal family is, at the present time, the agency most conducive to stabilization. As Malaya becomes increasingly a home and Indian children are drawn into the organs of Malayan socialization such as the national school system, Indian labor becomes more reliable and stable. The trade union movement, at the moment somewhat disorganized, holds the potential of offering to the Indian laborer an alternative to the dependence which he has had upon the government of India for his protection in Malaya, with a consequent weakening of the link with his native land. More of the laborers' problems will be resolved in Malaya by dealing directly with the employer groups and the Malayan authorities. In all likelihood the political functions of the trade unions, which until now have proved a handicap, will continue, at least until the political status of the Indians has been established in a manner satisfactory to them and political parties have been organized within which the Indian laborer has a voice.

The predominantly middle-class, commercial Indian associations have served to protect the interests of the Indian commercial minority. While these organizations are much older

---

45. Rao, "Indians Overseas," pp. 154-55.

and more stable than the trade unions, there is no indication that they can serve as rallying points for the entire Indian population because they are concerned with problems somewhat alien from those of the unskilled or semiskilled majority. Most of the middle-class Indians are what have been described as "Malayan" Indians, whereas most of the laborers are "immigrants." Even this divisive aspect of the Indian population, however, is being modified since under existing immigration regulations most Indians will be "native-born" in a generation or two.

Malayan affiliations

From another major standpoint--that of Indians in relation to all other communities within Malaya--the prominent motif is the separateness of the Indians. The Malay term for the dominant Indian group in Malaya, the Tamils, is "Kling." This apparently is derived from Malay orang Keling, which probably has reference to the medieval Hindu kingdom of Kalinga, a source of early Indian migrants. Similarly, the Malays are prone to call all northern Indians by the term "Bengali." These blanket terms reflect Malay indifference toward the Indian minority and have become offensive to the Indians over the years. Offense must have deepened since the independence of India, from which the Malayan Indians, regardless of their intention to remain in Malaya, derive considerable pride.

In the typical Chinese urban and Malay rural community the Indian, particularly the Tamil, is considered the fair object of all sorts of humor, especially of the wit of the Malays in their customary dramatic recreations. The caricature of the Indian is frequently that of an extremely agitated man with an offensively high-pitched voice which is contrasted to the calm reserve of the "typical" Malay.

Political participation. --The Indians have not been successful in achieving as much political representation for themselves in the postwar period as the other major communities because of their rather protected and regulated life in the past and because, where political interest has been expressed by the Indians, it has been almost always in terms of India.

In the prewar period the Indians were not represented at all within the legislative councils of the Federation or in the state councils and were not represented in the Straits Settlements government until after 1924, and then only on a minimal level. Even their present political role in the Federation remains relatively small. The two principal reasons are, first, the effect of having to share a relatively small number of political offices with the Ceylon Tamils. [46] In 1951, when the unofficial majority, which had fifty of the seventy-five seats in the Federation legislative council, insisted upon placing unofficial members in the position of ministers over some of the departments of government, no Indians were appointed, but one Ceylonese Tamil was. [47] Moreover, the Ceylonese population in the Federation--2. 5 per cent of the Indian population--had one unofficial member in the legislative council, as did the Indians. However, Indians found their way into the council as members representing labor and the Indian chambers of commerce, thus raising their number to five as compared to the one Ceylonese member in 1950. [48] In 1951 the Indians also were fewer in the unofficial representation than the Europeans, who had seven members, though their population was only 5 per cent of that of the Indians. In Singapore this situation did not exist because the Indians were more prone to act in the elective process for the Colony legislative council. [49] Also, there was greater opportunity for the Indians to find representation in such capacities as members for commerce and labor, as well as ethnic representatives.

The second reason for the modest Indian role in political life is the complexity of the matter of citizenship, a problem shared also by the Chinese. However, in September, 1952. Malayan nationality was opened to the Indians by changes in the Federation laws. According to these changes, the Federation government estimated that over 222, 000 of the estimated 665, 000 Indians in the Federation in 1953 would fulfill the requirements for citizenship automatically; another 186, 000 fulfill the birth qualifications toward this eligibility. Thus about 62 per cent of the Indians are moving rapidly toward full eligibility for citizenship. [50]

It is still too early to tell whether the Indians now eligible under the new liberal ordinances will take advantage of their

---

46. Kondapi, Indians Overseas, pp. 415-16.

47. S. W. Jones, Public Administration in Malaya (London: Royal Institute of International Affairs, 1953), pp. 184-85.

48. Kinwar, "India's Link to Malaya," p. 426.

49. Jones, Public Administration in Malaya, pp. 180-83.

50. Federation of Malaya, Annual Report, 1953, pp. 16-19.

opportunities for citizenship. In any event ignorance and illiteracy will work against the number who might acquire and exercise the right of citizenship. It has been estimated that about 50 per cent of the potential Singapore electorate in 1951 would have to be discounted as too illiterate to participate in the elections.[51] This probably would be no less true elsewhere in Malaya. On the isolated estates and rubber smallholdings the Indian's lack of information and interest about suffrage is likely to be re-enforced by attitudes associated with his traditionally neutral political role. Subject to a paternalistic wardship, only the more emancipated Indians have moved into the sphere of political action in recent years.

As for the real opportunities to exercise suffrage, the present structure of state and local government ordinances are such as to exclude significant portions of an Indian electorate. In general, the municipalities of the states seem to have the most restrictive electoral laws, that of Kuala Lumpur being perhaps the most extreme and municipalities of Johore being perhaps the most liberal. The restricted municipal laws are, of course, significant for the Indians because of their degree of urbanization. In the former Unfederated Malay States with their predominantly Malay population the restrictions against the non-Malay minorities are less severe than in the states of Selangor, Perak, Negri Sembilan, and, to a lesser extent, Johore, where the non-Malay population is large and important.[52]

Political organization. --Organized Indian opinion has been articulated by two major organizations: the Central Indian Association of Malaya (CIAM), prior to 1942, and the postwar Malayan Indian Congress (MIC). The MIC is exclusively Indian, as opposed to Pakistani. Both organizations have been rather more spasmodic than continuing, and it seems that only on specific issues and in certain situations have they made their positions known. At those times the CIAM and the MIC tended to speak as though they were stating the positions of the Indian community as a whole.

Of the two organizations, the CIAM was less political and more oriented toward the improvement of the conditions of labor. Since there was no organized trade union movement with

51. Jones, Public Administration in Malaya, p. 181.
52. Ibid., p. 188.

a method of collective bargaining, such improvement had to be pursued by propaganda and indirect political pressure. This meant that only the most spectacular of the labor problems were used by the CIAM to mobilize public opinion in Malaya and India on behalf of the Indian laborers. For example, in 1941 in Klang (Selangor) the authorities used the police as well as the army to quell a strike in that area. Several persons were killed or injured; about two hundred Indians were prosecuted as rioters; and almost four hundred others were detained on various charges. The CIAM was able to generate enough public (Indian) resentment over the issue, particularly against the use of Indian troops against the strikers, that the government of India took a strong position in the matter and paid the legal costs of the defense of the arrested Indians in the case. [53]

Prior to the Klang strikes, which were the high point of CIAM prewar activity, there had been a sharp infusion of political purpose into the CIAM. In 1937 Pandit Nehru visited Malaya as an emissary of the Indian government following up the Sastri report of the preceding year, which dealt with labor conditions of Indians in Malaya. Following the Nehru visit there was a visible increase in the political activities of the CIAM, which culminated in the Klang incident. [54]

The Malayan Indian Congress emerged immediately after the war as an overtly political organization whose aim was to further the political security of the Indian in Malaya through alliance with moderate political organizations of the other ethnic groups. It has presented itself frankly as the voice of the politically sensitive portion of the Indian community. It was different from the CIAM in that it was not concerned primarily with Indian labor, though it took a deep interest in it. With its broader political aims the MIC has been able to draw upon the strength of the powerful Indian commercial class. This has given a more moderate tinge to the political configuration of the organization than that of the labor-oriented CIAM, but the leadership is probably still considered, if not radical, at least politically challenging to the British because of the presence

---

53. Kondapi, Indians Overseas, p. 112.

54. T. H. Silcock and Ungku Abdul Aziz, Nationalism in Malaya (Series Paper No. 8, Eleventh Conference of the Institute of Pacific Relations, Lucknow, October, 1950 [New York: Institute of Pacific Relations, 1950]), p. 15.

of such men as J. A. Thivy, who was a high official in the anti-British Azad Hind movement.

One of the earliest acts of the MIC was its leadership of the widely publicized campaign for the abolition of the toddy drink shops on or near the estates. Toddy is a juice obtained from the coconut palm and, if consumed immediately, is a healthful beverage, but if it is allowed to ferment for a day or two, it becomes an unhealthful intoxicant. It is perhaps a testament of the inadequate recreational activities on the estates that the consumption of toddy has been a major form of leisure activity. It has been considered a smirch upon the Indian estate workers by politically oriented Indians sensitive to the criticism of non-Indians. Indians have been incensed that the tax revenues from toddy sales have caused the authorities to resist its prohibition, despite the sympathy which they have expressed publicly for prohibition. The Indians also have resented the fact that the revenues derived from the toddy shops on or near the estates have not been used to the benefit of labor. The toddy issue was used skillfully by the Indians to mobilize public opinion in favor of the Indian estate workers, and at the same time the issue served to bring to the attention of the government a serious health and morale problem of the Indians upon the estates.

Another important issue, of considerably greater substantive importance, was the campaign of the MIC in Singapore prior to the 1948 legislative council elections. The MIC took the position with the Chinese in the city that the composition of the council, with only six members elected by secret ballot, and those British subjects, was undemocratic, and they boycotted the elections that year.

In the period of increased self-government which begins in 1957, the stage will be set for the amalgamation of the Indian political forces in Malaya. For the next several years the elections undoubtedly will be conducted along community lines, reflecting the problem which is central to an emergent "Malayan" nation--multiracialism. In this process the development of the MIC should be important.

A final aspect of the relations of the Indian community with other communities within Malaya is that of the Indians and the Emergency. In general, the Emergency has proved to be a depressant upon the development of key institutions which may ultimately aid in the integration of the Indian community into the emergent Malayan polity--trade unions and political organizations. However, one of the decisive results of the Emergency has been to place the Indian community substantially in the camp of the government. This has in turn given the Indians considerable status as supporters of the dominant interests in the country and has created the feeling that the Indians, along with most of the Malays and a smaller proportion of the Chinese, constitute the population out of which the new Malaya will grow.

Pronouncements of both the Communist forces in Malaya and the constituted British authority have given evidence of the role of the Indians in the Emergency. Captured Communist documents have complained that the Indians do not understand the struggle being waged by the Communists and are inclined to be unsympathetic toward the forms of Communist terror, such as the destruction of rubber trees, the burning of rubber factories, and the disruption of other means of livelihood which for the Indians mean unemployment and homelessness.[55] On the other hand, the British authorities have repeatedly expressed confidence in the role of the Indians in the struggle against the Communist terror. No influential Indian has become associated with the Communist movement, nor has there been a position of noninvolvement taken by the Indian community. On the contrary, the Indians have expressed condemnation of the terroristic methods of the Communists, especially where the terror has touched their communities.

Since 1951, when the Communists modified their campaign of full terror to one which was reserved for those construed as traitors, such as police and informers, there have been several murderous incidents which have provoked the hostility of the Indians.[56] Being the object of Communist terrorism has probably moved more Indians closer to a position of sympathy with the government and antipathy toward the Communists than any amount of governmental persuasion and propaganda.

External affiliations: India

The economic link of the Indians with India has been heavy and strong. So long as Malaya had a need for Indian estate labor, this economic relationship was bound to be primary. Moreover, the importance of skills, labor, and capital from

---

55. Kondapi, Indians Overseas, p. 113.
56. Han, Su-yin, "Malaya: The 'Emergency' in Its Seventh Year," The Reporter, December 16, 1954, p. 24.

India was an important element in the economic development of the country. In addition to the flow of labor for the estates in Malaya there has also been a steady and increasing flow of clerical and general business personnel between India and Malaya. Another important link though of smaller magnitude, is that formed by the practice of rotating the staffs of Indian concerns in Malaya which have their home offices in India. This is a practice current among the medium-sized concerns rather than the largest ones, since the latter are in the hands of native-born Indians who have resided in Malaya for twenty years or more. This flow of urbanized Indians between the two countries may have a significance far exceeding their number.

There also have been secondary economic connections, such as the substantial remittances from men in Malaya to their families in India. It is difficult to know the magnitude of the cash remittances transferred because the individual amounts have been small and fairly widely distributed in India. In 1947 the amount remitted by the Indians undoubtedly was less than that remitted by the Chinese, though more than that of the immigrant Malaysians. [57] There seemed to be an inverse relationship between the time of residence in Malaya and the frequency of remittances. [58]

The sentimental links, those connecting the immigrant Indian with the Indian village and the Indian family, have become of less consequence with the stabilization of the Indian population in Malaya and their subsequent change in economic function. In prewar days Indians in Malaya attempted to visit India once every three or four years. The disruption of shipping services and the long period of the war changed this pattern so that now the frequency is considerably less. Another deterrent has been the doubling of the fare between Malaya and India since the war. [59]

Despite the decreased traffic for brief visits, it has been estimated that in relation to their respective numbers the proportion of Malaya-born Indians visiting India has been almost twice the corresponding proportion of local-born Chinese

---

57. Colony of Singapore, Department of Social Welfare, A Social Survey of Singapore, p. 112.

58. Ibid. , p. 123. These findings are subject to possible error because of the small Indian sample.

59. Rao, "Indians Overseas, " pp. 155-56.

visiting China, and that the proportion of Indians who had lived in the country for over twenty years revisiting India was greater than the corresponding proportion of Chinese.[60] In addition, this group of Indians visited India more times than the corresponding group of Chinese visited China.

The sentimental link is likely to be affected also by the adjustment of Indian citizenship in Malaya. In the draft constitution of India it was specifically provided that no Indian could enjoy Indian citizenship while being a citizen of another country, and that Indian citizenship depended upon residence and domicile in India.[61]

The Indians nevertheless retain a strong political orientation toward the motherland. The latent political orientation of the Indians in Malaya to India in the prewar period was brought into the open with the establishment of the Indian National Army (INA) in Malaya. During the early days of the occupation of Malaya the Japanese carried on a vigorous propaganda campaign, the substance of which was to remind the Indians in the country of their patriotic duty toward India and the Indian nationalists who opposed the continuation of the war with Japan. The response was very favorable among the Indians, and when the Japanese brought Subhas Chandra Bose into the country, the Indian National Army was born.

Support of the INA was widespread among the Indians, particularly among the urban lower middle and middle classes. For the estate workers the appeal was probably not as attractive because of the large drafts of labor the Japanese took to complete the work on the Burma-Siam railroad and the general remoteness of the estate Indians from the sources of Japanese propaganda. The response of the urban Indians is indicated by the following statements:

> Indians in Malaya realized that freedom was a thing worth fighting for, and gave their all to achieve the national [India] cause. They enlisted freely in the INA. The whole situation caused a complete change of outlook in their lives. For the first time Indians in Malaya came closer to their mother-

60. Colony of Singapore, Department of Social Welfare, A Social Survey of Singapore, p. 112.

61. Cited in Kondapi, Indians Overseas, p. 419.

land and proved that they could be of service even if it came to sacrificing their lives. Many of them fought against the British in Burma and around Kohima (Assam) and gave their lives in the cause of India's freedom. [62]

The Indian National Army and its achievements fired the imagination of the Indians in East Asia and wrought a tremendous psychological revolution in their minds. In addition to strengthening the freedom movement in India, the courageous stand of the Indian National Army helped in securing respectable treatment to Indians at the hands of the Japanese. [63]

The moral support of the Indians in Malaya did not go unmarked by India in the years just preceding and following the achievement of independence. In late 1945, as soon as it was feasible, the British Indian government re-established official contact with the Indians in Malaya through a representative and liaison officer stationed at Singapore whose main function was to protect the mass of Indians who were detained by the British military administration for their part in the INA or its political counterpart, the Indian Independence League.

In December, 1945, the British Indian government dispatched a mission of inquiry into the condition of the Indians in Malaya. This mission in its report stressed the economic deprivation of the Indian estate workers and the political persecution of the followers of the Indian National Army and the Indian Independence League. [64] In addition, the mission of Nehru to Malaya in 1946 and the subsequent aid tendered the Indians in Malaya by India (in the form of relief grants and the services of two medical missions) went far in modifying the attitudes of the British toward the Indians in Malaya who had collaborated with the Japanese. Finally, with the establishment of Indian independence, the new government appointed as its agent in Malaya J. A. Thivy, who was an Indian, born in Malaya, and who had held a high office in the INA as well as the presidency of the Malayan Indian Congress. Thus, in every way the Indian gov-

---

62. Kinwar, "India's Link to Malaya," p. 425.
63. Kondapi, Indians Overseas, p. 178.
64. Rao, "Indians Overseas."

ernment went to considerable lengths to aid in the rehabilitation of the Malayan Indian population in a direct and official manner. The intervention of the Indian government in these matters was all the more remarkable since it preceded the granting of independence to India by Great Britain.

Beginning with the war and the INA, the Indians in Malaya have been drawn increasingly into a sphere of active interest in the affairs of the new India. This interest reflects both pride in the achievement of the motherland and an expectation of benefits to be gained from this achievement by the Indians in Malaya. The expectations of aid are not without foundation. Independent India has shown abilities for leadership in Asia and has been accorded commensurate respect and consideration by Great Britain as the leading Asian member of the Commonwealth. In this regard it is important to note that all of the projects for the advancement of self-government in Malaya have proceeded with the consultation of the government of India. [65] Moreover, while India's position regarding self-government in Malaya has been moderate, it has nevertheless stressed the need for the improvement of the conditions of labor among the Indian workers in Malaya. [66]

This increasingly important focus upon India may have important ramifications regarding the position of Indians in Malaya. It is a counterpoise to the integrative tendencies of recent political movements of the Indians. A reliance upon the prestige of India to help in the solution of some of their problems might align the Indians in Malaya against the establishment of a strong political interest in Malaya and the definition of their future political role there. There is some evidence of this possibility in the desire on the part of many Indians in Malaya for dual citizenship in Malaya and India in an effort to enjoy the benefits of both, an idea vigorously condemned by Nehru. [67]

---

65. Werner Levi, Free India in Asia (Minneapolis: University of Minnesota Press, 1952), pp. 117-18.

66. Vidya Prakash Dutt, India's Foreign Policy, with Special Reference to Asia and the Pacific (Indian Paper No. 1, Eleventh Conference of the Institute of Pacific Relations, Lucknow, October, 1950. New Delhi: Indian Council of World Affairs, 1950), p. 14.

67. Cited in "Indian Periodicals," The Modern Review: A

Another consequence of the focus upon India may be friction between the Indian Moslems and Hindus as a result of the creation of an independent Pakistan. Although there has been no reported friction, an increased intimacy between Indians in Malaya and the Indian government may lead to overt expression of Indian-Pakistani hostility.

Monthly Review and Miscellany, May, 1953, p. 412.

10. The Economic System

THE ECONOMY OF MALAYA is the product of two often autonomous economic systems interacting over time. [1] One of these may be described as the indigenous system. It is Malay, agrarian, subsistence, noncommercial, wet-rice oriented, and village organized. It tends to be located in those sections of Malaya where there is a Malay or Malaysian majority and where urban populations are small.

The second system of economic activity is predominantly foreign and commercial. It in turn may be divided into two segments. The first of these is Asian, chiefly Chinese and partly Indian. It characteristically has been dual in its orientations. On the one hand it has been directed toward the primary production of rubber or tin, the two major products of Malaya, with both labor and entrepreneurial elements active in the whole. On the other hand it has been partly urban, commercial, and trade-oriented. The second foreign segment has been European, chiefly British, but with other non-Asian nationalities represented. It has been almost entirely commercial and has developed through the primary exploitation of natural resources (rubber estate lands and tin-bearing formations) and the organization of commerce on a national and regional scale.

On the basis of this ethnic specialization of economic activity, Malaya is often said to possess not only a plural society

---

1. The economic problems of Malaya are discussed at length in the report of the International Bank for Reconstruction and Development, The Economic Development of Malaya (Baltimore: Johns Hopkins Press, 1955).

but also a plural economy. Unlike the situation in some other colonial or former colonial territories, however, the indigenous Malays are not the haulers of water and hewers of wood, providing labor for the commercial economy. This labor has been provided by Chinese and Indians. To a substantial degree the Malay sector of the economy has been even more isolated from the foreign sectors than is the case in southern Indochina, for example, where the peasant cultivator has been engaged in rice cultivation on a primarily commercial basis and therefore has acted as the foundation for a rice-export-oriented economy. The Malay has tended to pursue a subsistence type of activity, raising paddy primarily for his own use, together with fruits and vegetables in his kampong gardens.

Though this has been so traditionally, and legislation forbidding non-Malay ownership of land in large areas of Malaya has tended to maintain a division between Malay and non-Malay economic activity, the lines of demarcation have long been blurred. One of the major economic and social problems in Malaya has resulted from the widening of the zone of interaction between the Malay and non-Malay sectors of the economy and resultant changes in the traditional Malay way of life. Such interaction is not new. The Chinese, for example, long have acted as middlemen in Malaya between the Malays and the rest of the country, and the two ethnic groups have been characterized by a symbiotic relationship of value to both. Chinese merchants and traders have dominated whatever commerce has taken place in rural areas, and the rice mills of Malaya also have been under their control. Their role has been discussed briefly in Chapter 7 in connection with the Malay fishing villages of the east coast.

As Malay peasant colonization, with governmental assistance in recent times, has taken place in new rice lands in the northwest and northeast, more paddy has been raised as a cash crop than ever before, and an increasing number of Malays have moved toward a money economy from a barter and exchange economy. This tendency has been accelerated greatly in the last few decades by the transformation of Malay paddy farmers into rubber smallholders. It is estimated that over two hundred thousand Malays are occupied primarily in the care of rubber estates, and more are becoming wage laborers every year. Many Malays also have been incorporated into the administrative labor force, particularly as a result of the increased policing and military activity associated with the Emergency.

In all of these ways the villager has come to be supplied with important amounts of cash income, and this in turn has made him reluctant to concentrate on the production of foodstuffs, even for his own consumption. Cash incomes also have made the Malay more important in the national economy as a consumer as well as a producer.

In the recent past, the Malay produced nearly enough food to feed himself, with little or no surplus for the other ethnic groups in Malaya. Thus, Malaya has not fed itself, and the trend is in the direction of less rather than greater self-sufficiency in foodstuffs as the Malay himself becomes oriented toward activities other than food-producing.

The line separating the two commercial segments of the economy, the Asian and the European, also has been far from clear. Indians form the chief portion of the rubber estate labor force, together with Chinese, and most of the estates are European-owned. However, many sizable estates are Chinese-owned, and most of the smallhold rubber production is channeled through Chinese hands. The Chinese have also played an extremely important role in the tin industry, the second primary industry of Malaya. Finally, they have developed both national and international trading organizations, in many instances familial or clan-based, which compete with the European trading houses.

The total level of economic achievement in Malaya has been exceptionally high for Asia. The per capita product for the country is estimated at about US$298. [2] Although this figure is only about one-ninth that in the United States and about one-sixth that in Great Britain, it is somewhat higher than the per capita product in Japan and is several times greater than those for most other Asian countries.

The explanation for this economic development lies in a complex of factors. A favorable population-resource ratio, an environment suitable for the cultivation of rubber trees, large

---

2. See the appendices in B. F. Hoselitz, et al., The Role of Foreign Aid in the Development of Other Countries, a Report prepared for the U.S. Senate Special Committee to Study the Foreign Aid Program of the U.S. (Chicago: The University of Chicago Research Center in Economic Development, 1956). Published also as Report #3 (Washington: Government Printing Office, March, 1957).

deposits of tin-bearing ores, and the accessibility of a great entrepôt, Singapore, have provided the framework for the system. Foreign capital and enterprise, attracted by the commercial activities and the financial and service facilities associated with the entrepôt trade have played a significant role. Foreign labor also has been important. In short, the Malayan economy as a dynamic organism has been created out of the energies and ingenuity of foreigners--Europeans, Chinese, and Indians--who have maximized the opportunities offered within a favorable physical setting by a laissez-faire system of economic values associated with British rule. Malaya thus possesses a complex of economic facilities of exceptional potency --an established transport and communications system, a stable currency, an expanding educational system, widespread banking facilities, and a relatively skilled labor force which has grown within a framework in which entrepreneurial abilities have loomed large.

TABLE 60
GROSS NATIONAL PRODUCT BY ORIGIN*

	1949 Value (million M$)	%	1951 Value (million M$)	%	1953 Value (million M$)	%
Rubber	420	11.8	2,025	26.9	715	12.4
Mining	250	7.0	480	6.4	325	5.6
Other agriculture and forestry	840	23.7	1,380	18.4	1,430	24.7
All other activities	1,825	51.4	3,260	43.4	2,925	50.6
Gross national income	3,335	93.9	7,145	95.0	5,395	93.3
Indirect taxes	215	6.1	375	4.9	385	6.7
Gross national product (at market prices)	3,550	100.0	7,520	100.0	5,870	100.0

*International Bank for Reconstruction and Development, The Economic Development of Malaya, p. 21.

The bases for the economy have been fourfold: rubber, tin, the entrepôt trade, and the indigenous agricultural system. The first three of these have made rapid economic growth in Malay possible, and rubber and tin together contribute about 20 per cent of the gross national product (Table 60). That portion of the national product not associated with the production and processing of these two commodities or directly with the entrepôt trade is derived from the production of other agricultural products and from economic activities, largely of a service nature, associated either with the entrepôt trade or with the processing and distribution of domestically consumed goods.

Superficially, Malaya is characterized by relatively high levels of living, which suggest economic stability and the absence of many of the economic problems identified with the densely populated states such as India and China. In fact, however, the economic problems of Malay are great. The extreme dependence of the economy upon a limited number of exports for which world demand cannot be controlled is significant. The entrepôt trade, too, depends upon the good will of neighboring countries, and the dependence upon foreign areas for nearly half the food supply of the country presents similar potential difficulties. A major fall in the price of rubber and tin is felt throughout Malaya, even in those sectors of the economy not directly dependent upon them.

Thus, Malaya is faced with the need for diversification of its economic structure and for minimizing its dependence on the outside world for markets and foodstuffs. The direction of expansion is already twofold, first, in the direction of the development of secondary processing and manufactural industries, and second, in the development of primary products other than rubber and tin, such as palm oil and cacao. These activities will tend to broaden the economic base somewhat and lessen Malaya's vulnerability to fluctuations in world prices.

Occupational Structure of the Population

The character of the economy is reflected in the occupational structure of the population. In 1947 there were 1, 773, 182 gainfully employed males and 488, 494 females. This was about two-fifths of the total population. Eighty per cent of the males and 90 per cent of the females were employed in the Federation; the balance was employed in Singapore.

In Malaya as a whole the largest proportion of gainfully employed persons was in agriculture. Over one-fifth of the total population and 53 per cent of the gainfully employed were engaged in agriculture. The next largest industrial category, commerce and finance, accounted for slightly more than 4 per cent of the total population and about 11 per cent of the employed persons (Table 61).

Other classes of activities in which considerable numbers were employed include manufacturing (9.8 per cent), public administration (7.4 per cent), personal services (6 per cent) and transport and communications (5 per cent). Mining, of major importance in the economy, employed only about 49,000 persons (2.1 per cent).

TABLE 61
TOTAL POPULATION BY INDUSTRIAL GROUP, 1947

Industrial Group	Numbers	Per Cent of Total Gain- fully Employed	Per Cent of Total Population
Fishing	65,169	2.9	1.12
Agriculture	1,198,822	53.0	20.60
Mining and quarrying	48,937	2.1	0.84
Manufacturing	221,270	9.8	3.80
Transport and communications	112,212	5.0	1.93
Commerce and finance	256,169	11.3	4.40
Public administration and defense	167,717	7.4	2.88
Professional service	26,325	1.2	0.45
Entertainment and sport	11,716	0.5	0.20
Personal service	135,060	6.0	2.32
Other	18,279	0.8	0.32
Total gainfully employed	2,261,676	100.0	38.86
Not gainfully employed	3,557,586	-	61.14
Total population	5,819,262	-	100.00

Not unexpectedly, there are major differences between the Federation and Singapore. Well over half of the gainfully employed males in the Federation were employed in agriculture, but only very small numbers were so employed in Singapore. In the Federation rubber and paddy cultivation each accounted for about 25 per cent of the persons engaged in agricultural activities. Market gardening and stock-raising occupied 6 per cent of the agriculturally gainfully employed. In Singapore the largest industry group was commerce and finance (19.2 per cent of the Singapore gainfully employed) followed closely by manufacturing (19 per cent). Public administration and transport and communications are relatively more important in Singapore, though smaller numbers are actually employed than in the Federation.

Out of the 441,443 gainfully employed females in the Federation, 79 per cent were in agricultural industry. Other industries accounted for only small proportions of the female work-ers. In Singapore the women were employed mainly in personal service (40 per cent of the employed females), transport and communications (16 per cent), and commerce and finance (14 per cent).

There are varying degrees of areal concentrations of the industry groups. As is usual, commerce, administration, transport, and manufacturing occupations are localized prin-cipally in the cities. Singapore, the largest of the cities, has the greatest number of workers in these industries. Many workers in manufacturing in Singapore are engaged in ship-yards and industries directly servicing transport. About one-fourth of all the gainfully employed in Singapore, therefore, are concerned with transportation. Thus, transport, commerce and finance, and manufacturing tend to identify the dominant functions of Singapore.

Other localizations of industry exist. For example, 86 per cent of the 49,000 workers in the mining industry were located in Perak and Selangor. Most of the gainfully employed in mar-ket gardening, rubber, and coconut cultivation are in west-coast states. Rice cultivators occur in greatest numbers in Kedah, Perak, and one of the east-coast states, Kelantan.

Chinese and Malaysians in the Federation and in Singapore have 34 to 40 per cent of their total numbers gainfully em-ployed. In each of these latter instances the high proportions are closely related to the fewer females in the total population of the ethnic group. In the Federation, the Chinese and Malays account for nearly four-fifths of all those gainfully occupied, with the Indians accounting for about 16 per cent. In Singapore the Chinese form the bulk of the gainfully occupied.

The three major ethnic groups are found in some industries in greater proportions than in others. The Malays are found in greatest numbers in agricultural or related pursuits. With the "Other Malaysians" they constituted nearly 55 per cent of the 1,174,673 employed persons in agriculture in the Federation. Although total numbers involved are much lower, two-thirds of the persons in the fishing industry were Malays. Malays also were conspicuous in public administration (nearly half of the people in this industry were Malays). In Singapore Malays do not constitute very large proportions of any of the industrial groupings, but are most numerous in public administration, reflecting their importance in the police forces.

Chinese are found in greatest proportions in agriculture

(half in rubber growing), in manufacturing, and in commerce. The proportions of the gainfully employed Chinese males in the Federation in 1947 were 42 per cent employed in agriculture, 15 per cent in manufacturing, and 16 per cent in commerce. Singapore Chinese are found in large numbers in manufacturing, transport, and commerce. Manufacturing in both the Federation and Singapore is dominated by the Chinese; 77 per cent of those employed in manufacturing in the Federation and 84 per cent in Singapore in 1947 were Chinese. In Singapore the Chinese dominate virtually all the industrial groups including the small number (24, 000) of agriculturalists (mostly market gardeners). They are nearly matched in numbers by Indians in public administration.

Indians are found chiefly in rubber growing (36 per cent of all Indian females gainfully employed). They also appear in considerable numbers in commerce. In Singapore, Indians are found in relatively high proportions in manufacturing, transport, and commerce. Indians have for years been associated with the Malayan Railway, their numbers comprising a high proportion of the total number of railway employees.

Trade Unions [3]

The trade union movement is underdeveloped and beset with important problems. In the period before World War II, trade union organization was carried on largely by Communists and thus was repressed by the government. During this period labor conditions in the country were, as they are now, fairly good for Asia, though there were still enough labor difficulties and unrest for legitimate organizational activity.

Between 1945 and 1948 trade union activity became increasingly vigorous because of wartime declines in levels of living and the atmosphere of freedom created by the British. This led to the creation of several large labor federations which only loosely bound their constituent bodies but which had pronounced left-wing political commitments. At the time of the eruption of the Communist terror in 1948 these unions were repressed by the authorities as centers of subversion.

---

3. See Chapters 8 and 9 for details on labor organization. Most of the history of the trade union activity in the country has been along communal lines.

Since 1948 trade union activities in the country have been revived slowly under the tutelage of an advisory group of British trade unionists. The Trade Union Advisory Department of the Federation, staffed by British unionists, has attempted to develop "democratic and responsible unions." In Singapore the same function has been served by the Labour Department. In both places the offices undoubtedly will become a part of the permanent staff of the agencies responsible for labor.

In the Federation in 1955 there were 281 trade unions with a membership of 150,480. This compares with 425 unions and a membership of 290,000 in the 1945-1948 period. The most important trade unions represent about 25 per cent of the 300,000 rubber estate workers. These unions are weak and besieged with financial problems. They were unable to prevent wage reductions after the Korean war boom and have been powerless to prevent still further reductions since that time. Under these conditions the members are restive, and morale is low. In 1954 the National Union of Plantation Workers was organized to consolidate the larger of the dozen unions representing rubber workers.

The second most important group of unions in the Federation represents government employees. These are among the oldest and most experienced unions and have a good record of successful bargaining. Among the more notable of this group are the unions of civilian employees of the British armed forces in the country.

In Singapore in 1954 there were 136 unions representing 76,452 workers, or 8 per cent of the working population. Most of the unions in Singapore represent a small number of workers, about one-third of them having a membership of less than 200 persons. [4]

There are two principal national trade union organizations: (1) the Malayan Trade Union Council in the Federation and (2) the Singapore Trade Union Congress. Both have been beset with financial problems and factional conflicts around dominating personalities. Both are members of the International Confederation of Free Trade Unions.

Three important characteristics have marked the development of trade unions: (1) unbalanced racial composition and

---

4. For example, there are four unions representing 825 members of the tailoring trades.

participation, (2) the tendency toward multiple unions in the same industries, and (3) the tendency toward restriction to larger enterprises.

The racial aspects of the trade union movement have been particularly significant. Indians have been important beyond their number and now constitute about 75 per cent of the organized workers in the Federation. Almost all of the rubber unions consist wholly of Indians. The greater importance of the Indians as compared with the Chinese has been caused by (1) the propensity of Indians to participate in trade union activities as members through custom and principle and (2) the fact that the Indians have been less affected by the restrictions of Emergency legislation. The Chinese, on the other hand, were the core of the organizational movement in the period 1945-1948. Now many Chinese are out of unions. The reasons are several: (1) the fear that to belong to a trade union would make a non-English-speaking Chinese suspect of Communist sympathies; (2) the fear that membership in a non-Communist union would bring reprisals from the Communists; and (3) a repugnance against the governmental and Indian domination of the trade unions.

The multiplicity of unions in a single industry or occupational category has two important causes: (1) at the present state of organizational activity independent unions restricted to the particular enterprise--company unions--are the rule, and about 50 per cent of the unions are of this sort; (2) unions are frequently restricted to persons of the same racial origin, thus creating the situation of separate Chinese, Malay, and Indian unions for the same industry; in Singapore this tendency is manifest in the case of eight teachers' unions and nine seamen's unions.

The tendency of unions to be restricted to large enterprises is a consequence of the fact that these enterprises, frequently European-operated, have accepted the principle and usefulness of trade unions and accept such organizations. On the other hand, the middle- and small-sized enterprises fear the power of unions and may resort to violent means to prevent their establishment.

One of the defects from which the trade union movement suffers most is the lack of capable leadership. Most union leaders are young, idealistic, and, because they speak English and have some education, somewhat detached from the workers whom they represent. This has been a central problem in the post-1948 developments and is manifest in a bureaucratic crust which does not inspire the confidence either of the members or of the employers.

In conclusion, there seem to be several factors which stand in the way of successful trade union organization. Cultural and linguistic differences which result from the multiracial population lead to a lack of understanding and unity; the geographical isolation of important segments of the labor force, such as the estate laborers, has made communication and organization difficult; the paternalistic values of the government and of many employers have led to formidable resistance to unionism and to considerable violence; illiteracy and the retention of important traditional values, such as the failure of the Chinese to distinguish between a trade union and their traditional guild, prevent the acceptance of many of the ideas of the trade union movement.

Land Utilization

The gross pattern of land use

The pattern of land use reflects the extraordinary localization of different kinds of economic activities, especially those of a primary sort. As indicated on Map 27, most of Malaya is unoccupied and to a large degree unused. Most of the central and eastern parts of the country remain under forest. The forested area is around thirty-eight thousand square miles, nearly 75 per cent of the total area of the country (Table 62). Patches of land in rubber, paddy fields, or other crops have been carved out of the forest, but these kinds of land use are localized to a marked degree in a relatively narrow band of highly developed territory along the western portion of the peninsula and in two major areas in the northeast.

About one-third of the forested area is set aside as reserves for various purposes. The remainder consists primarily of Crown and State Land. Most of the reserves lie below the one-thousand-foot contour, covering forested areas of greater importance than those at higher levels. It is the more valuable lower forests, however, which are being cut into most vigorously, either in the course of lumbering or in the expansion of agricultural and mining land. The need for greater control over forest exploitation has been growing, therefore, and one of the recommendations of the World Bank report on Malaya was for the development of plans by which the higher-level

373

forests above the one-thousand-foot contour can be brought under a system of forest management in which cutting would be on a sustained-yield basis. In addition, some of the forested areas consist of both mangrove and freshwater swamps, the economic value of which is surprisingly high, since wood from these areas is used as fuelwood and construction material. These also represent opportunities in some areas for the expansion of agricultural land, particularly where peat formations underlie the swamp forest growth, although the difficulties of bringing peat lands into economic production have yet to be resolved adequately.

The developed portions account for less than 21 per cent of the total area of the country. As stated, their chief concentration is in the western littoral, generally less than 50 miles wide and extending down the entire coast from the Siamese border to Singapore. Here are found the greater part of the population of the country, almost all of the estates, almost all of the tin mines, and a very large proportion of the paddy lands. Within this area are located most of the facilities for commercial activities as well, and it is identified by the densest populations, the largest proportion of transportation and communications facilities, most of the controlled irrigation facilities, power installations, and the largest proportion by far of the processing installations for Malaya's primary production.

TABLE 62
LAND USE, 1949*

	Area (sq. mi.)		Per Cent of Total Land Area	
Area alienated[t]	10,535		20.7	
Forested area	38,133		74.9	
Reserve		14,456		28.4
Crown and state land		23,677		46.5
Crown and state land not under forest	2,243		4.4	
Total	50,911		100.0	

*R. G. Heath, Malayan Agricultural Statistics, 1949 (Kuala Lumpur: Caxton Press, 1951), Table 1.
[t]Includes buildings, agricultural land, and built-up areas. Cultivated area equals 84.6 per cent of the area alienated.

374

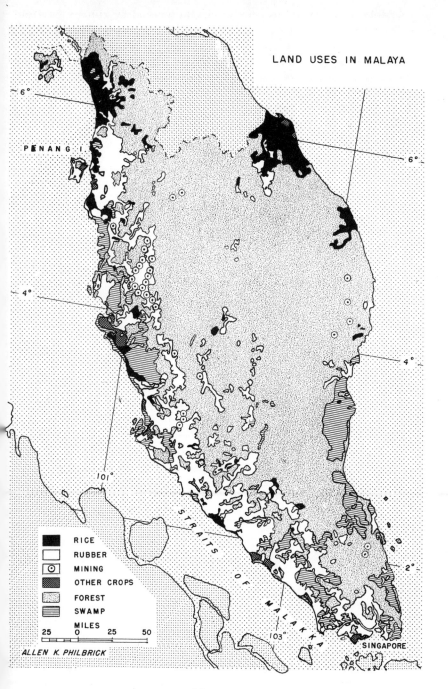

LAND USES IN MALAYA

6°

PENANG I.

6°

4°

4°

101°

STRAITS OF MALAKKA

RICE
RUBBER
MINING
OTHER CROPS
FOREST
SWAMP

MILES
25 0 25 50

ALLEN K. PHILBRICK

103°

2°

SINGAPORE

Map 27

Most of the western area is characterized by rubber estates. These extend in a discontinuous band from northern Kedah southward to Singapore itself. The rubber belt tends to be most broken in Perak, where swamp and peat areas extend over considerable acreages and where tin-mining tends to be highly localized. Almost all of the rubber estates lie below one thousand feet in altitude, and although many have been located near sea level, the greater number are sited upon somewhat higher ground characterized by better drainage.

The total area under cultivation is about 16 per cent of the country. This is not dissimilar to the percentage in Japan, for example, but the similarity of agricultural occupance between the two countries ends there. In Japan, agriculture is oriented primarily toward the production of foodstuffs for domestic consumption, and the areas in nonfood crops are conspicuously small. In Malaya, the situation is almost reversed. As shown on Table 62, less than one-fourth of all the area in agricultural land uses in Malaya is concerned with the production of food. Even if it is assumed that the areas in strictly subsistence market and tree gardens associated with the kampongs are understated, which they probably are, the dominance of commercial agricultural land uses is striking. In no other country in Southeast Asia is this imbalance between food and nonfood crop acreages so remarkable.

Actually, of course, food is produced almost everywhere in Malaya where there are people, with the exception of the cores of the larger cities, but plots are too small and scattered in many cases to be shown at the scale of Map 27. Each city and town tends to be ringed with small areas of vegetable plots in which an extremely intensive form of horticulture is practiced, chiefly by Chinese.

The conspicuous elements of the food-producing sectors of the economy appear on Map 27 in black, indicating the predominantly paddy regions. These are concentrated in two major regions and several minor ones. The most important in terms of acreages are in the northwest, in Kedah, Province Wellesley, and Perlis, and in the northeast in the deltaic and coastal lowlands of Kelantan and Trengganu. Smaller areas of rice concentration are found along the coast of Perak, around Malakka, and in a number of still smaller areas of predominantly Malay kampongs widely scattered throughout the western belt of development.

Land tenure

Most of the land in the Malay states is the property of the ruler. "Most alienated land is held in perpetuity, subject to the payment of a fixed annual rent and, in the case of agricultural land, to certain express or implied cultivation conditions."[5] The trend in recent years, however, has been to alienate land on a leasehold basis. In the case of paddy land particularly, ownership depends upon actual productive use of the land. If after a certain period of time, two or three years in many cases, a plot of land has not been continuously cultivated, title reverts to the ruler. In most of Malaya, the Torrens system of registration of land is in force. In the Settlements it is not. In general, the implementation of land registration legislation in Malaya has been slow and inefficient, and many problems arise which reflect the lag in the official registration and measurement of landholdings.

A conspicuous feature of land tenure is the so-called Malay Reservation. Beginning in 1913, and continuing until just before the war, the various states enacted legislation setting aside large areas of land primarily for Malay occupation. These were designed to protect the Malay landowner and farmer against the loss of his land by forbidding transfer of title to non-Malays within these areas. Since the reservations account for about one-fourth of the total area of the country,[6] their influence upon settlement patterns and land utilization are of exceptional importance. Special cases exist in Trengganu and Malakka where special rights of state nationals are associated with land tenure. In the former case the effect is one equivalent to that of the reservation enactments.

The argument for the Malay Reservation has been particularly strong in those areas of predominantly Malay settlement where increasing fragmentation of holdings and the inroads of the other ethnic groupings, chiefly Chinese smallholders and European estate operators, have disenfranchised the economically vulnerable Malay peasant farmer. The argument for the continuance of the reservations is less strong, however, in areas of relatively sparse settlement which must remain unused until and unless Malay pioneers decide to move into them.

---

5. International Bank for Reconstruction and Development, The Economic Development of Malaya, p. 307.

6. See Map 7, "Malay Reservations," in ibid., facing p. 312.

Since these areas contain large forest resources (some of them forest reserve lands) and might contain substantial deposits of tin ores, their continued reservation militates against the expansion of the Malayan economy as a whole.

The entire matter is, of course, a major political issue. To the Malays, the reservations represent a means by which they can maintain themselves against economically more vigorous groups within the country, especially the Chinese. To the Chinese, the reservations are the symbol of a second-class citizenship to which they heartily object and which they are inclined to cite as reasons for their reluctance to submit to increasing Malayanization. To the European and Chinese tin industry, the inability to prospect adequately in the reservations may mean a rapid deterioration of the industry as tin reserves decline.

The fact that land in the reservations cannot be alienated to non-Malays has also worked hardship upon the Malay farmer himself. Since he is unable to pledge his land as security for loans, his sources of credit have tended to be fewer than before, especially since adequate substitutes for Indian and Chinese money-lenders have not yet been created. In fact, lending is still practiced, and non-Malays have acquired de facto though not de jure control over considerable areas of paddy land.

Before the reservation legislation was passed, many non-Malays purchased land both in and out of the reservations, and they have retained their property, but in general it was very difficult in the States, as compared with the Settlements, for Chinese to obtain land suitable for paddy cultivation. Since relatively few Chinese had been interested in moving into paddy agriculture, however, so long as other employment opportunities existed in the cities and mines and on the estates, it is not clear how much of a hardship this worked on the Chinese. Nevertheless, the fact that discrimination was practiced scarred Malayan Chinese pride and resulted in Chinese resentment which has had political repercussions.

Food-Producing Agriculture

Although it is customary to divide agricultural activities in many Asian countries into subsistence and commercial categories, it may be more meaningful in Malaya to discuss them in terms of the products they produce, whether foodstuffs or other agricultural products. Almost all of the foodstuffs produced in Malaya are consumed internally. Only a small amount of specialized food products are exported, whereas foodstuffs are a major retained import. Almost all the nonfoodstuffs produced, on the other hand, are exported, although some, like coconut oil, are also consumed within the country. The division is not, however, a simple one between subsistence and commercial agriculture, since a large quantity of Malay-produced paddy, for example, has come to be produced partially as a cash crop, although most of it is consumed in the kampongs.

Rice

Rice is the basic foodstuff in Malaya, yet it accounts for only 16 per cent of the total cultivated area in the country. Its production is entirely in the hands of smallholders. The large-scale commercialized paddy farming practiced in the Irrawaddy delta and in southern Thailand and Indochina is not characteristic of Malayan paddy cultivation. Paddy culture is important in every state of the Federation, but is of greatest significance in the so-called rice bowls of Kedah, Perlis, Province Wellesley, Perak, Kelantan, and Trengganu, where over two-thirds of Malaya's rice is produced.

The distribution of rice acreages is shown on Map 27 and described on Table 62. The greatest concentrations are in the northwest and northeast. The three most important rice-producing provinces are Kedah, Kelantan, and Perak, which together account for 64 per cent of the country's rice acreage. When Perlis, Province Wellesley, and Trengganu are added to these, the total percentage of rice acreages located in the north is just under 80 per cent. For the most part these are the provinces with the highest percentages of Malaysian population (except for Kedah).

Rice plays a more significant role among the Malays than any economic description can suggest. Rice production has been called a way of life rather than an economic activity. Recent studies completed by the Department of Geography at the University of Malaya have noted the continuing importance of paddy-farming among the predominantly Malaysian communities in northwestern Malaya. [7] Equally important, however, were the findings which indicate changes in the traditional way of life associated with paddy production. In each of the areas

7. E. H. G. Dobby et al., "Padi Landscapes of Malaya," Malayan Journal of Tropical Geography, October, 1955.

TABLE 63

AGRICULTURAL LAND USES, 1949*

State or Settlement	Total Acreage	Rubber	Per Cent of Malayan Rubber Acreage	Paddy†	Per Cent of Malayan Paddy Acreage	Coconut Palm	Per Cent of Malayan Coconut Acreage	Oil Palm	Pineapple	Minor Crops‡	Total Cultivated Acreage
Perlis	198,400	5,370	0.1	43,430	5.1	3,218	0.6	-			
Kedah	2,342,400	35,405	10.4	273,200	32.7	31,538	6.2	-			
Kelantan	3,677,440	115,814	3.4	141,550	16.9	41,152	8.1	550			
Trengganu	3,232,000	42,111	1.2	44,110	5.3	20,486	4.0	-			(16.1% of the
Penang, Province Wellesley	256,000	66,730	2.0	39,400	4.7	42,397	8.3	503			total area is
Perak	5,107,200	555,164	16.4	119,370	14.3	112,304	22.1	22,120			cultivated)
Selangor	2,026,880	511,479	15.1	40,850	4.8	101,104	19.9	17,585			
Pahang	8,878,720	194,979	5.7	46,740	5.6	13,513	2.6	5,830			
Negri Sembilan	1,632,000	388,213	11.5	34,290	4.1	4,768	0.9	2,841			
Malakka	405,120	215,179	6.4	31,810	3.8	11,165	2.2	-			
Johore	4,685,440	920,016	27.2	20,710	2.5	117,965	23.2	41,078	16,000§		
Singapore	142,080	20,764	0.6	-	-	7,900	1.5	-	535		
Total	32,583,680	3,385,224	100.0	835,460	99.8	507,510	99.6	90,507	34,850‖	392,536	5,246,087
Per Cent of all cultivated acreage		64.6		16.0		9.7		1.7	0.6	7.4	100.0

*From Heath, Malayan Agricultural Statistics, 1949. †Area planted.

‡Chiefly fruits, starchy tubers, and vegetables, but including tea and other commercial crops §1954.

‖1955, chiefly in Johore, Selangor, and Perak.

studied, the trend is toward greater commercialization, not only of the rice industry but also of kampong life.

> "The interaction between . . . [the commercial and self-sufficient phases of paddy cultivation] is complicated not only because the original self-feeding community [the Malays] is learning other ways of earning a living and being drawn into the towns, but also because a newer commercial-farming community (from South China) is moving into the padi-lands and diffusing other ways of dealing with the land and other modes of getting a living from it."[8]

These changes in paddy production and in the attitudes of the Malay toward paddy farming are part of the general cultural transformation which all ethnic groups have been undergoing in Malaya, although it is the Malay for whom changes are most radical. One reflection of these changes is the continued dependence of Malaya upon foreign areas for 50 to 60 per cent of its rice needs. This is a crucial factor in the national economy and creates a major balance-of-payments problem. Thus, much developmental planning has been in the direction of increasing domestic paddy production. The fact that subsidies and other aids to food-producing agriculture also help gain the good will of the Malay community should not be overlooked, nor is the relative unreliability of rice supplies in the troubled Asian world to be ignored.

The rice deficit is associated less with the Malaysian community than with the other ethnic groups, and less with the kampong rural areas than with the estates and the towns and cities. The Malaysian community is estimated to be about three-quarters self-sufficient in rice, or even more in many parts of the country. On the other hand, the other ethnic groups are unimportant as paddy producers and are almost totally dependent upon rice imports, chiefly from Thailand and Burma, for their basic food staple. The long-standing rice deficit has been accompanied particularly since the war by a rise in the consumption of rice substitutes. Wheat and wheat flour have become increasingly important net import items and Malaya

---

8. Ibid., p. 8.

(chiefly Singapore) imports about 130,000 metric tons of wheat flour annually. The effect of these imports is restricted primarily to Singapore and the other cities where the European or Western-educated population is greatest; it does not suggest a major change in the dietary tastes of the Malaysian.

The rice deficit is a reflection in part of the separation among the various sectors of the economy. As Chinese and Indian labor moved into the country, they were so isolated economically from the Malay's predominantly subsistence agriculture that the Malaysian paddy farmer responded only slowly to the increased domestic demand for his product. 9 Rice imports were contracted for by the large estates. In Singapore, it was no more difficult, and sometimes cheaper, to import Siamese or Burmese rice instead of rice from northern Malaya.

In addition, neither neutral nor cultural conditions of Malay rice cultivation have been conducive toward rapid increases in total paddy production or in yields. Extensive cloudiness, poor drainage, periods of drought, sometimes poor soils, and the difficulties of reclaiming peat swamps or jungle for cultivation all have militated against increased acreages and yields. The former have risen from about 662,000 acres in the period 1926-30 to some 835,000 acres in 1953-4, but the increase has been erratic and has barely kept pace with population increases. Yields have risen in general, especially as the result of government-sponsored irrigation projects which now cover about a quarter of the total planted acreage. Gross production has about doubled in 30 years, but so has population. In general, too, Malay paddy farming is rather extensive as compared with that in East Asia, and yields are between one-third and one half those of Japan, though they are relatively high for much of southern Asia.

Finally, the Malay cultivator has been diverted to other means of livelihood. Rubber smallholding has perhaps been the most important of these, but there has also been a flight of young Malays into the towns, often after service in the police forces. An increasing number of wage laborers also has been

---

9. Nevertheless, up to two-thirds of the Malaya-grown paddy is likely to find its way into the market. See D. W. Fryer, "Food Production in Malaya," The Australian Geographer, May, 1954, p. 36.

Malay in recent years. In addition, skilled technical personnel in government agricultural services has been short, and the disruptions associated with the Emergency also have taken their toll of rural Malays.

Rice cultivation. --Rice technology in Malaya may be divided into "wet" cultivation, in which the crop grows in a partially controlled water environment at least part of the time, and "dry" or "upland" cultivation. Wet-rice cultivation is the most important of the two systems and is associated with permanent kampong settlement. [10]

Though cultivation techniques vary in different parts of the country, the following account is fairly representative. [11] Most of the wet rice in the country is grown during the wetter season, that is, from September to January. Plantings may be made a few months earlier in the case of some of the longer growing varieties. From February to April little is done in rice cultivation, and the time is used for the cultivation of other crops and the reclamation of land. Transplanting of the seedlings from nurseries is common, and in Krian, Perak, as many as three transplantings may occur. Prior to transplanting, the seeds are soaked for several days in order to encourage germination. The fields are cleared of their fallow vegetation with a shortbladed scythe and then plowed. The bunds around the fields are then repaired, and the land is reduced to a soft mud in order to receive the transplanted plants. The transplanting is done by women. Water, where there is controlled irrigation, is allowed to flood the field, the level of flooding corresponding with the development of the plants, until the flowering begins. At this stage, the water level is reduced until, at the time of harvest, the soil is just moist. In Malaya, the usual term of maturation of the rice plant is from five to nine months depending on the variety of seed. Only one crop a year is usual, and double cropping is rare.

Another cultivation system is the tenggala, a variation of

---

10. In the postwar years of 1946-49, for example, the average planted acreage of wet paddy per annum was 782,600, as compared to 76,431 of dry paddy. See Heath, Malayan Agricultural Statistics, 1949, Table 30.

11. This discussion is based on D. H. Grist, An Outline of Malayan Agriculture (London: Crown Agents for the Colonies, 1950), pp. 122-27.

shifting cultivation which is becoming less important than it was a century ago. The term tenggala means plow. Under the system, a small plot is cleared and plowed three times in different directions. Varieties of paddy are planted, which will do about as well under drought conditions as in inundated areas. After about four croppings, the field will be abandoned to grass or secondary jungle for several years, and adjacent plots will be cleared and cultivated in the same way. Yields are relatively low, being about 40 per cent less than those under more standard practices.

Relatively little fertilizer, either farm-originated or commercial, is used in Malayan paddy cultivation. Cattle grazing over rice stubble during periods of fallow fertilize the fields with their manure. Some guano is used in Kedah and Perlis where the manure is obtained from local limestone caves. Night soil is not used. Recent experiments in subsidizing the use of fertilizers in Kelantan have resulted in expanded yields and suggest one course for development that may or should be followed.

Once the grain is harvested, usually ear by ear by means of a small hand knife, the tuai, and thrashed by hand, it is stored as paddy until required for household use. Then it is husked by means of wooden mortars and pestles or by small hand grindstones, passed through a small hammering apparatus, indik, where it is milled, and finally winnowed in a platelike wicker basket, tampi. If rice dough is desired for Malayan noodles, the rice is soaked until soft, then pounded into a smooth paste. 12

Increasing quantities of paddy are milled in rice mills rather than at home. These mills tend to be of two kinds: (1) cooperative mills which generally operate throughout the year and mill rice for the local consumption of the peasant farmers; and (2) Chinese-owned mills of larger size (though still small compared with those in Siam and Burma) which purchase local rice through agents over wider areas and mill it for cash sale. There also are some government-operated mills. Most of the larger mills are located in the rice bowl areas of the north. Government-established minimum prices prevail at the mills,

---

12. Dobby, "Settlement and Land Utilization, Malacca," Geographical Journal, December, 1939, p. 472.

M$14 per picul at the end of 1955. [13] Price controls at the consumer level, however, were removed in 1954.

Problems in Malayan rice cultivation. --There are a number of disabilities which operate upon the cultivator of rice, whether it be in the intensive rice areas of northeast or northwest Malaya or further south where crops other than paddy are important. Fragmentation of holdings, indebtedness, and insecure tenure are three important and related problems.

It is difficult to evaluate the extent of fragmentation throughout the country because there have been no surveys on ownership, tenancy, or land utilization at the requisite scale. However, it is known that fragmentation has taken place, and the assumption is that under the Moslem inheritance laws the extent of excessive fragmentation is considerable. Under the laws of Moslem inheritance there are precise rules for the distribution of the property of the deceased persons, and there is no distinction made between real and personal property. The application of these laws leads to a multiplicity of persons with rights in the same plot of land, and in order to realize these rights the land may be subdivided into extremely small, uneconomical holdings under the so-called "open-field" system. [14] The results of this excessive subdivision are well known--concealed unemployment, increased indebtedness, and the abandonment of holdings too small to be worked, which tend to become breeding places for rodents and other plant pests.

Also, as the number of paddy plots increase, there is a corresponding demand for kampong area for the completion of the paddy cultivator's balanced holding. This demand upon the limited kampong area in turn results in ever greater subdivision of the area devoted to other than paddy crops and a subsequent fall in income from cash crops as well as less balanced diets. One observer has pointed out that under this pressure the kampong area available to each paddy cultivator falls well below the optimum area of about six or seven acres, which the

---

13. The picul varies from one area to another, but its average weight is about 140 pounds.

14. Individual "lots" tend to range between two and seven acres, but portions of each lot may be used for kampong or other purposes, and a lot may be divided into two or more fields depending on drainage and surface considerations. A single farmer may cultivate several widely scattered fields.

cultivator can use profitably for vegetables, cash crops, and stock-keeping. [15]

Like fragmentation, indebtedness is judged to be considerable especially in those areas where tenancy is common and other forms of insecure tenure exist. Debts arise from the relationships which exist between the cultivator and the processors and purchasers of the grain. The problems of debt are most manifest in the rice-surplus areas, where rice is a cash crop processed in mechanized and centrally located mills owned by Chinese and, to a lesser extent, by Indians. The Chinese and Indians serve also as the source of loan capital, which might not be used for productive purposes but rather for consumption needs such as weddings, funerals, feasts, and so forth. The debt obligation ties the cultivator to the miller from whom he borrows, and the rice must be sold to that creditor in order to liquidate the debt. Since the cultivator has only one purchaser, the pricing is largely to the disadvantage of the seller, and the debt, if it is reduced at all, declines slowly.

Two forms of debt exist: (1) that contracted with Indian Chettiars and others for which the collateral is land and loss of the land the sanction for nonpayment, and (2) that contracted with Chinese shopkeepers where the borrower pledges some part of his production. Of the two, the latter is most widespread largely because of the Malay reservations enactments which prevent a non-Malay from owning certain lands. [16] It may be supposed that indebtedness is appreciably less severe in areas which are not so monocultural or so involved in the cash nexus as is, for example, Krian in Perak. In 1954 in part of Krian about 80 per cent of the residents of the area owned no land, and only 29 per cent of the lots in the area were owner-worked. [17]

The peasant debt may be minimized in two ways: first,

---

15. C. W. S. Hartley, "Establishment of New Rice Areas in Malaya," World Crops, May, 1951, p. 173. Hartley points out that kampong holdings under two acres become much too small whereas the largest kampong holding a family can utilize is around ten acres.

16. Alan Pim, Colonial Agricultural Production, the Contribution made by the Native Peasants and Foreign Enterprise (London: Oxford University Press, 1946), p. 57.

17. Dobby, "Padi Landscapes of Malaya," p. 78.

diversification of income-producing activity tends to reduce dependence upon the merchant in a predominantly rice-producing community and thus reduces the possibility of debt accumulation; second, in communities where social interdependence has not been so severely impaired as in the monocultural, highly monetized areas, wealth is distributed among the less fortunate members of the community through the kinship system and through certain ceremonial practices such as feasts.

Insecure tenure is, like fragmentation and indebtedness, a major problem primarily in the rice-surplus regions of the country, particularly north Kedah, Province Wellesley, and Krian in Perak. The rate of tenancy in these areas, like indebtedness, is very high, and though tenancy in itself is neither bad nor good, insecure tenure and unfavorable rental arrangements raise considerable problems for the cultivators. An increase in tenancy has accompanied that of fragmentation. As plots become smaller through subdivision, the cultivator finds that his smallholding does not afford him enough income on which to live, and he seeks still more land. That a plot which will be leased to a tenant already has a number of co-owners does not seem to prevent the further encumbrance by a tenant, though it does explain why the tenant's return on labor might be small.

The postwar developments have increased the burdens of tenancy. First, the prewar practice of granting renewal of tenancy has changed since the war, and owners now tend to increase the obligation of the tenant as a precondition for renewal. This development is in part a consequence of the increased pressure upon the land resources of the country and in part a breakdown of some of the traditional values associated with land. A second postwar development regarding the conditions of tenancy is that regarding rental arrangements. Prior to the war, it was the accepted practice for the tenant to pay his rent after the harvest either as a fixed amount or a proportion of the crop. In recent years landowners have come to demand cash rent in advance. Thus, the cultivator must contract a cash debt from a credit cooperative, if he is fortunate enough to belong to one, or more likely from a money-lender or local shopkeeper. In the latter case, there is a Malay term describing the debt arrangement, padi kuncha, whereby the cultivator must repay cash or credit advances with a predetermined quantity of paddy.

Other problems of paddy cultivation center about physical

rather than cultural difficulties. The possibility of expanding paddy acreages is limited by the fact that the best paddy lands are already under cultivation and by the high costs of bringing into cultivation areas under swamp or jungle. Government assistance in these directions has been given, and large areas in Perak have been earmarked for development.

The use of fertilizers also means considerable outlays of cash by the peasant farmer, who may be unsympathetic toward their use in any case. Again, government assistance appears necessary. In addition, however, relatively little is known about the fertilizer requirements of tropical soils. Similarly, mechanization in paddy agriculture is in an experimental stage. Although techniques have been developed for the use of machinery in preparing the fields for planting, relatively little progress has been made in adapting machines for use in cultivation after planting and in harvesting.

One of the biggest problems is that of water. Despite the high rainfall in Malaya, some areas, particularly in the northern districts, experience considerable periods of near-drought. The so-called "wet" cultivated areas under native technologies are dependent in the main upon direct rainfall retained in the fields or on the fluctuations of river levels over which the cultivator has little control. Controlled irrigation is limited to less than one-fourth of all paddy acreages. Expansion of irrigation facilities has accelerated since the establishment in 1932 of the Federation Department of Irrigation and Drainage, and further expansion is anticipated. Between 1950 and 1955, three hundred thousand acres of paddy land were improved and one hundred thousand acres of new land were added. [18]

Nevertheless, double-cycle harvesting of paddy is little practiced, although the year-round growing season would permit it. The chief limiting factor is water; a second is soil infertility and a lack of fertilizers; a third is a lack of incentive on the part of the cultivators to modify their annual pattern to a double cycle of cultivation. Under the Japanese considerable progress was made in encouraging double harvesting through the use of early-maturing paddy varieties developed in Thailand, but only small areas now employ them.

---

18. International Bank for Reconstruction and Development, The Economic Development of Malaya, p. 295.

Other food production

The value of other food production in Malaya is nearly double that of paddy production, but relatively little is known about its economics. The acreage of food crops other than rice is about 7 per cent of the total cultivated area of the country, as compared with 16 per cent in paddy, but the value of output is about 12 per cent of all agricultural production as compared with 8 per cent for rice.

Fruits and vegetables. --The kampong is virtually self-sufficient in its fruit and vegetable production, as well as in rice. The importance of kampong mixed-garden produce is described by Terra for Java, but the significance of his generalizations applies also to Malaya. [19] It may be that the mixed gardens supply a substantial portion of the caloric intake among the villagers as well as the greater proportion of the protein and protective elements in their diet. Among the important fruit trees are the durian, custard apple, soursop, papaya, rambutan, guava, mangosteen, and various citrus fruits--oranges, limes, and pomelos.

Bananas are ubiquitous and form an important addition to the Malayan diet for all ethnic groups. Every kampong contains banana "trees." In addition, considerable areas of slope have been put into bananas for the urban markets, with resultant problems of soil erosion.

Within the kampong starchy tubers and supplementary grain foods and pulses are raised in the mixed gardens. Yams, sweet potatoes, corn, soybeans, peas and beans, and peanuts are among the chief crops. Market gardening of leafy vegetables, however, is a Chinese specialty, and Chinese market gardens are found around all the major cities. A typical minute Chinese one-acre market garden farm has been studied in detail by Blaut, who describes an intensive system of multiple cropping, completely controlled irrigation, heavy fertilization, and round-the-clock cultivation that is probably unparalleled in the non-Sinitic agricultural world. [20] European vegetables

---

19. G. J. A. Terra, "Mixed Garden Horticulture in Java," Malayan Journal of Tropical Geography, October, 1954, pp. 33-43.

20. James Blaut, "The Economic Geography of a One-Acre Farm on Singapore Island," Malayan Journal of Tropical Geography, October, 1953, pp. 37-48.

are raised in higher gardens around the Cameron Highlands and Fraser's Hill.

Tapioca (or cassava or manioc) is raised over a considerable acreage, especially in Johore and particularly by Chinese who use it chiefly as pig food.

Pineapples. --Pineapples are grown widely but account for less than 1 per cent of the total cultivated acreage in the country. Much of the crop is raised as a cash crop, with Johore the center of production. Before the war much of the area under pineapples was cultivated under a system of modified shifting agriculture by Chinese croppers, and Malaya became the second largest pineapple exporter in the world, next to Hawaii. Postwar production declined markedly but is beginning to rise once more to prewar levels. In 1955 some thirty-five thousand acres were under cultivation. Since pineapples do well on peaty soils, the possibilities for expanding the industry are considerable. Nearly half of the existing acreage is estate acreage, in contrast to the prewar period when smallholdings were most important.

Tea, coffee, pepper. --Tea is of modest importance as a cash crop grown primarily on estates for both local consumption and export. Production is over five million pounds of tea annually from both highland and lowland estates, of which nearly three million pounds are exported. Coffee, formerly of considerable importance, is primarily a smallholder's crop, grown without shade and often as a catch crop. Almost all of the product of about ten thousand acres of coffee trees is sold locally. Pepper is a secondary crop of less importance than ever before, grown primarily in Johore by Chinese cultivators. Coconuts, described below as a nonfood crop, are an important addition to Malaya's food supplies. Grown almost everywhere, either on estates or in the kampongs, the coconut supplies cooking oil and most of the fats in the Malay and Indian diets, and a smaller percentage in the diets of the Chinese.

Major Nonfood Crops

Rubber

Rubber is one of the three externally oriented bases of the Malayan economy. Rubber alone accounts for up to 60 per cent of domestic exports by value, and during periods of high prices, nearly 30 per cent of Malaya's gross national product. The indirect contributions of this industry are immense. There are, for example, the host of service and secondary industrial activities which, while not associated directly with the production of tin or rubber or the merchandise trade at Singapore and Penang, exist only because of them. Thus, the income-yielding opportunities in the sale of food, drink, and clothing to estate and urban workers are derived from the existence of the directly productive and ancillary service activities associated with tin and rubber. Further, the earnings from the export of rubber and tin and from the trade at the entrepôt, help to defray the costs of necessary imports. In fact, it is by virtue of the accessibility of a wide assortment of imported goods that the margin in economic standards between Malaya and the rest of Asia is maintained. Finally, the impetus given to the modern Malayan economy by the introduction of foreign capital and enterprise has been dependent upon the continuing development of the three basic industries. The distribution of the wealth from this development, it is true, has not been even, the Chinese and Europeans having received the greater portion, but all people in the country have profited from it, and the plant for maintaining a relatively high level of living is well established.

The Para rubber tree (hevea brasiliensis) was introduced into Malaya in the 1870's, and the plantation cultivation of the crop began on a wide scale after 1905. From 1905 to the early 1920's the expansion of the industry was rapid, and by 1924 Malaya was the chief producer of rubber in the world. During this period of expansion, the bulk of the capital was European, primarily British, and the management of most of the estates was in British hands. Labor for the estates was provided by southern India.

During the 1920's and 1930's the industry was forced by the condition of the world market to restrict production, and there was a period of general retrenchment. One of the important effects of this retrenchment was the diminution of the smallholders' production, as compared with the estates. The rubber smallholders, owners of less than one hundred acres, were generally accorded an inequitable share of the total rubber production under the various restriction schemes. In the same period, between the 1924 Stevenson restriction plan and the outbreak of World War II, the smallholders of the Netherlands East Indies were permitted to expand their acreages to such a degree that Malaya was displaced by the new Republic of Indonesia in the production of rubber.

Rubber is not only the most valuable agricultural product in Malaya; it is also the largest user of cultivated land. As Table 62 shows, rubber accounted for about 65 per cent of the cultivated land in the country in 1949. A gradual increase in planted acreages, particularly among smallholders, indicates an acreage of about 3. 8 million acres in 1955, or about two-thirds of the total cultivated acreage. About 54 per cent of the acreage is in estates, with the remainder in smallholdings. Production is divided into about the same proportions, although in recent years the smallholders have continued to make gains at the relative expense of the estates in part through the expansion of illegally planted holdings, in part through excessive and destructive tapping practices.

Rubber is produced in all of Malay's major political units, but the major areas of production are in the so-called "rubber belt" along the western littoral zone of the country. In 1949 Johore contained 27. 1 per cent of the rubber acreage, Perak 16. 3 per cent, Selangor 15. 1 per cent, Negri Sembilan 11. 4 per cent, and Kedah 10. 3 per cent, these states accounting for 80 per cent of the total acreage. New plantations, however, are appearing in the previously less developed states, such as Pahang, Kelantan, Trengganu, and Perlis, as well as in Perak and Kedah.

Rubber is the product of two different forms of economic organization: the estate, i. e. , areas exceeding one hundred acres, and smallholdings.

The acreage criterion for the demarcation of the estate, one hundred acres, disguises more than it reveals. Estates are owned by Europeans, Chinese, and Indians, and they vary widely according to ownership. Most European estates are between 1,000 and 5,000 acres, the average being about 1,800 acres, while most of the Chinese and Indian estates are less than 500 acres. While the average size of the Chinese and Indian estates is about 340 acres, most of them are between 100 and 200 acres.

The same wide variation is seen in nature of ownership. Of the 832 European estates in 1950, 600 were owned by public liability companies and the remainder by private liability or simply private companies. Only 15 of the 981 Chinese and none of the Indian estates were owned by public liability companies in the same year. Moreover, there has been a tendency for the Indian Chettiar owners to have several rather small estates or smallholdings, while the Chinese owners tend to hold fewer, somewhat larger units.

Smallholdings comprise 46 per cent of the rubber acreage in Malaya and produce 44 per cent of the rubber. Within the "smallholdings" are a great variety of production units. There are significant differences between a three- or four-acre, Malay-owned holding tapped by a resident owner, a Chinese holding of sixty to eighty acres tapped by contract labor, or a number of holdings each of three to twenty acres owned by an individual Chettiar. Holdings under fifteen acres may be called "peasant" holdings since these usually are tapped by the peasant family without additional labor. Most Malay holdings fall into this category, though there also are some Indian and Chinese peasant holdings.

Rubber production has been characterized by wide fluctuations in price due primarily to the highly variable demand for the product. Part of the present critical situation of the rubber industry in Malaya is caused by unstable demand due to strategic stockpiling and competition from synthetic rubber. There has been a corresponding low elasticity of supply because of the rather inflexible cost structure of the industry. A diminution in the tapping of rubber, for example, on the estates, does not substantially reduce costs of production because of the relatively fixed overhead costs of labor, maintenance, processing, and transportation.

As Table 64 shows, Malaya competes with two major kinds of rubber production. The first is Indonesian, and Indonesian rubber continues to account for a major proportion of all natural rubber production. The second kind of competition is that between natural rubber and the synthetic product. In 1954 synthetic rubber, although cut back from previous highs, nevertheless accounted for 28.5 per cent of the total world rubber production, and it was 33 per cent in the previous year. Even the United Kingdom is now a producer of synthetic rubber, which is superior to the natural product for certain uses.

The problem of the Malayan rubber industry, therefore, has been to increase the efficiency of its production so as to compete with production elsewhere. The heart of the problem has been the large percentage of average and low-yielding trees in the industry. In 1954 about two-thirds of all the estate acreage and most of the smallholding acreage were in low-yielding trees. The replacement of these plantings has been regarded as a high-priority matter, and the government has adopted a

policy of assistance to the industry. Subsidies to rubber planters therefore have been established of M$400 per acre to es-
tates and M$500 per acre to smallholders, financed by a local
tax imposed upon rubber production and an export tax. In 1954
and 1955 about one hundred thousand acres of estate rubber
trees were replanted with high-yielding clones. Previously, the
estates had launched sizable replanting schemes even under the
handicaps of the Emergency. Smallholder replanting has been
much less, only fifty-three thousand acres in 1954 and 1955,
partly because relatively high rubber prices have discouraged
replanting, and partly because no detailed scheme of smallholder assistance had been worked out. New planting has not
been a major part of the government's efforts at increasing
production and efficiency, but the evidence points to increasing
expansions of acreages, especially in newly developed areas,
so long as rubber prices continue favorable. The problem is
complicated by considerable rubber plantings on peat soils
which are relatively poorly drained and in which the trees find
it difficult to root and maintain themselves in high winds.
Another difficulty is lalang (Imperata cylindrica), a noxious
grass which spreads rapidly and deprives young rubber plants
of moisture, nutrients, and space.

TABLE 64
PRODUCTION OF NATURAL AND SYNTHETIC RUBBER (thousand long tons)*

Annual average for 3-year period:	Malaya	Indonesia	Other Countries	World Natural	World Synthetic	Total World
1923-25	182	167	102	451	-	451
1935-37	414	350	210	974	-	974
1947-49	672	381	372	1,425	510	1,935
1952-54	573	704	457	1,734	840	2,574
1954[†]	584	730	479	1,803	716	2,519
Per Cent of Natural World Production						
1923-25	40.0	37.0	23.0	100	-	-
1954[†]	32.5	41.0	26.5	100	-	-
Per Cent of Total World Production						
1954[†]	23.2	29.3	19.0	71.5	28.5	100

*Report of Mission of Enquiry into the Rubber Industry of Malaya (Kuala Lumpur,
1954), p. 6. (Mimeographed.)
†One year only. United Nations, Statistical Office, Statistical Yearbook, 1955
(New York: United Nations, 1956).

Coconuts

The second most important nonfood agricultural product, the coconut, accounts for less than 3 per cent of the total estimated gross national product of Malaya, but it occupies nearly 10 per cent of the total cultivated area. In the kampongs it is an essential ingredient for daily living and an important source of cash in the form of copra. About one-fourth of the estimated half-million acres in coconut palm are on estates. Johore, Selangor, and Perak are the chief producers. Yields of copra per acre vary enormously, from fifteen hundred to two thousand pounds per acre on some of the estates to less than five hundred pounds in the smallholdings. The latter production in particular is hampered by plantings on poorly drained sites, although lack of knowledge concerning cultivation practices and overage trees are common.

Oil palm

The oil palm is a relatively recent element in the Malayan agricultural landscape. Most production is on estates, and the acreage in 1954 was estimated at 109,000 acres. Palm oil production in 1955 was fifty-six thousand tons; that of palm kernels, fifteen thousand tons; and both acreages and output have increased markedly since the war.

Livestock in the Economy

Livestock are raised primarily as draft animals rather than for food. In general, natural pastures are rare in Malaya, as in much of the tropics, and the agricultural systems, both indigenous and foreign, have not been conducive to the practice of animal husbandry on a large scale. The value of livestock in

TABLE 65
LIVESTOCK, 1955

Water buffalo	242,600
Cattle	279,000
Goats	268,100
Sheep	26,700
Pigs	403,600
Horses	610

the Federation is estimated at about M\$200 millions, [21] and in relation to the native agricultural sector in which they are most important, this represents a sizable proportion of all capital investment other than land.

Ownership of the various types of animals tends to reflect Malaya's ethnic diversity. Most buffalo are owned by Malays, who use them in paddy cultivation. Most of the cattle, except for a small number of milch cows, are also Malay-owned. Goats are owned chiefly by Malays and Indians, the mutton-eating portion of the population. Pigs are an almost exclusively Chinese possession and form an important export from the Federation to Singapore. The crop-livestock associations commonly associated with middle-latitude agriculture are not found in Malaya. Pig-rearing is associated in part with tapioca cultivation, but most of the swine population depends on scavenging, as in China itself.

Meat imports are relatively small. Some chilled and frozen beef is imported from Australia primarily for the European segment of the population. Sizable quantities of Australian mutton are imported, however, for consumption primarily by the Indian estate population.

Poultry is ubiquitous, even in some urbanized areas. Singapore is a surplus producer of poultry and eggs, and engages in a lively export trade with the Federation.

It is estimated that about five and one-half pounds of beef are consumed per capita annually by beef eaters (chiefly Muslims); three pounds of goat and sheep mutton by the mutton eaters (Indians and Malays); and about twenty-five pounds per capita by the pork eaters (chiefly Chinese). Poultry consumption is at a rate of some five pounds per capita annually; egg consumption is about thirty per capita. [22] In general, animal protein is low in all diets, least so in the Chinese diet. In all cases, average meat consumption is high for Asia.

Fishery Products

Fish produced within Malay is said to contribute some 15 per cent of all domestic foodstuffs by value and about 10 per

_____

21. Federation of Malaya, Annual Report, 1955 (Kuala Lumpur: Government Press, 1956), p. 189.

22. Ibid., p. 190.

cent of all food consumed. [23] It also accounts for about 3.5 per cent of the gross national product. Fish is the chief source of animal protein in the Federation, and fifty-three pounds per capita are consumed. In Singapore per capita consumption is lower.

The shallow waters off the coast for a distance of about thirty-five or forty miles are the principal fishing grounds of the country. The west-coast grounds, however, normally supply two-thirds of the total catch. Traditional Malay methods of fishing prevail but are characterized by much local variation. Chinese fishermen in considerable numbers on the west coast and out of Singapore use Chinese methods primarily (73 per cent of the Singapore fishermen and about 30 per cent of all fishermen in Malaya are Chinese). Picturesque Malay craft of various sizes and styles, still largely wind-propelled but becoming increasingly mechanized, are most numerous. [24] Much fishing is carried on from the beaches and in estuaries, using beach seines and stake traps. Other equipment includes offshore seines, long lines, troll lines, and drift nets. Brackish water ponds in former mangrove areas also are used as tidal fisheries for prawns and crabs.

In general, surface species of fish are taken in greatest numbers, with pelagic species being almost untouched. Off the east coast almost the entire catch is of surface species. On the west coast fishermen out of Penang use long lines to catch deep-water fish along the edge of the continental shelf at depths of sixty fathoms.

The production of fish for human consumption in Malaya is around 140,000 tons annually, of which about 4,500 tons are taken by Singapore fishermen. [25] About 25,000 tons are freshwater fish. In addition, some sea products are used for animal consumption, and about 15,000 tons are used for ferti-

---

23. International Bank for Reconstruction and Development, The Economic Development of Malaya, p. 325.

24. One of the principal innovations in the Malayan fishing industry has been the motorization of many fishing vessels. Outboard motors have been most common and find ready acceptance among the fishermen. In 1954, nearly one-fourth of fishing vessels were motor-driven.

25. International Bank for Reconstruction and Development, The Economic Development of Malaya, p. 326.

lizer. Salting and drying are the main methods of preservation. Some sea products, such as shrimp, are made into paste-type foods which are fermented and keep well. [26] Icing is a common practice, and iced fish come to the market in good condition, considering the climate. In general, preservation is not a major problem of the fishing industry as presently constituted. Distribution problems arise, however, when there is a local surplus due to an exceptional catch or when government stimulus through improved methods increases the catch without improving distribution facilities. On occasion, while a ready market has waited in one area, a surplus of fish in another has gone to waste because of inadequate transportation. [27]

The industry is based principally on private operators financed with borrowed capital. The individual fisherman so financed sells his fish to his creditor. A few cooperative marketing groups exist, and fish dealer associations are widespread.

It is evident from the fishing methods used and from the present lack of knowledge concerning the habits, seasonal movement, and usual foods of the marine life in Malayan waters that the fish catch could be improved greatly. However, efforts to introduce temperate-water fishing methods have not been particularly successful, nor have the methods of other areas been adaptable to Malayan waters or, sometimes, acceptable to the Malayans. Output should increase, however, with greater numbers of powered vessels, although knowledge of fish species and their movements needs intensive emphasis. In 1955, the Regional Marine Fisheries Station at Singapore was completed, and the Fish Culture Research and Training Institute at Malakka was under construction. Problems of improved credit and marketing facilities have yet to be solved.

Forest Products

Although most of Malaya is under forest, it is not self-sufficient in forest products. Exports are sizable (M$28.6 million

---

26. Fish pastes and condiments are an essential addition to bowls of rice in Southeast Asia and southern coastal China.

27. Low-grade dried and salted fish chiefly from the east coast are a traditional export to Indonesia, but in recent years these have been hampered by Indonesian trade controls.

in 1955, chiefly of graded sawn timber), but imports are equally sizable, although some of the imported wood may be processed for re-export. Paper, however, accounts for a sizable item in the country's import trade, and economical processes for manufacturing paper products from tropical hardwoods have yet to be developed.

The total value of timber products in Malaya ranges between M$100 and 150 million. The sawmill industry, composed of some 373 sawmills in 1955, employs about twenty thousand persons, chiefly Chinese. Most of the mills are small; almost all are Chinese-owned.

The forest is a source of lumber, fuelwood, and household materials (mattings), and of resins, gums, and other gathered products. Timber is cut for local use and for urban uses and export. The concern here is with the use of the forests for timber, since other uses are relatively minor.

Lowland forest is the chief source of timber, including both rain forest and freshwater swamp forest. Mangrove is also exploited for charcoal, firewood, and poles. The preferred species in the lowland forest are tropical hardwoods. Timber production in 1955 was seventy-four million cubic feet in log form. About fifty-five million cubic feet were for lumber; the remainder was for charcoal and firewood.[28] It is estimated that fifty-five million cubic feet were consumed in the Federation, while twenty million were exported to Singapore or overseas.

About 45 per cent of the total output of timber comes from the easily accessible reserved forests, which include 12,500 square miles (one-fourth the land area) of the approximately 37,500 square miles (three-fourths the land area) of Malaya that is forest-covered. Only 8,000 square miles of the reserved forest are classed as productive.

Forest management practices vary. Reserved areas generally are opened for lumbering, with some, although wholly inadequate, provisions for regeneration. Regeneration is carried on by the government as part of the silviculture program, with the avowed aim of making Malaya self-supporting in timber through forest culture. Plans for regulated exploitation were completed for all states in 1955 except Kelantan and Trengganu. The larger mangrove forests in all states are utilized under controls.

---

28. Federation of Malaya, Annual Report, 1955, p. 171.

The forestry department of the government works toward the expansion and more effective utilization of forest resources through (1) maintenance, protection, and replanting in the present forests, (2) road construction, making the forests accessible, and (3) expansion of uses for tropical woods through research and through sales promotion.

The potentials of the forests are limited by several factors: low average quality of timber; inaccessibility; competition in world markets from areas of cheaper production; mixed character of forests; and lack of knowledge of proper seasoning and preservative treatment of tropical woods. It should be noted that none of these difficulties is insurmountable. The first condition is perhaps open to question even on the basis of present knowledge. Assessment of these forests as tropical forests in a position to supply tropical markets, rather than in terms of comparison with temperate forests, may lead to different views concerning their usability.

Tin and Other Minerals

Tin is a second pillar of the Malayan economy. Other minerals are of minor significance. The extraction and export of tin long antedated the development of the rubber industry of the country, and it was an important Chinese industry as much as five hundred years ago. The production of tin has remained fairly constant since 1900, whereas rubber was just beginning its era of expansion at that time. Tin exports constitute about 20 per cent of the total Federation exports and, through the duties levied on tin exports, provided about 11 per cent of the Federation's custom revenue in 1955. [29]

Cassiterite (SnO_2) is the only important tin-bearing mineral in Malaya. The methods used in the extraction of the mineral are dredging and gravel-pumping, both of which are made possible by the predominantly surface alluvial ores. [30] The ability

---

29. Although the customs revenues on tin exports were virtually the same in 1954 and 1955, the percentage of revenue derived from tin was twice as high in 1954 as in 1955 because of higher rubber prices and duties in 1955. Federation of Malaya, Annual Report, 1955, p. 103.

30. For a discussion of the various methods of tin-mining, as well as an historical treatment of the industry in Kinta, see

to use surface mining techniques, as opposed to the underground mining necessary in Bolivia, has given Malayan tin a price advantage.

As between the methods of gravel-pumping and dredging, the latter is the more important in terms of production. The prominence of the dredging method corresponds with the increasing pace of mechanization of the industry since the early years of the century. Thus, while output has remained the same since that time, the number of workers in the industry has fallen by 80 per cent; now forty thousand workers produce the same product as two hundred thousand workers did in 1914. The mechanization of the industry (horsepower applied to production increased sixfold between 1913 and 1950) has been a function of the increased participation by Europeans and European capital. At the present time, 50 per cent of the total output of tin is provided by European dredging companies, 40 per cent by Chinese gravel-pumping companies, and 10 per cent by hydraulic, open-cast, and underground facilities, which are primarily European in ownership. All Malayan ore is smelted at domestic refineries in Singapore (Palau Brani), Penang, and Butterworth.

The tin industry is the largest single industrial consumer of electrical power on the peninsula, requiring 72 per cent of the Federation power in 1953. According to some analysts of the Malayan economy, the increasing competition for the power in the Federation has caused a shortage for tin producers and has prevented, it is implied, the fullest development of the industry. To some extent, this shortage of power was ameliorated by the construction of the Connaught Bridge power station at Klang, Selangor, in 1952. [31]

Ooi, Jin-bee, "Mining Landscapes of Kinta," Malayan Journal of Tropical Geography, January, 1955, pp. 1-57.

31. The power facilities of the Federation are organized under the Central Electricity Board (CEB), created in 1949. The CEB is an autonomous corporation which operates some stations, including Connaught Bridge, and grants licenses and oversees the operation of other power facilities. The principal licensee is the Perak River Hydroelectric Power Company, which is the chief supplier for the tin industry. The present installed capacity in the Federation is 445,000 kilowatts, of which steam and oil generation provide 90 per cent (159,000

There are two problems which seriously threaten the tin industry and therefore the Malayan economy. One is the unfavorable market prospects for tin in world trade. Between 1949 and 1953 the average annual production of tin for the world was 163,000 tons, of which the contribution by Malaya was about one-third. During the same period, the annual world consumption was about 134,000 tons. The surplus of tin production over consumption was stockpiled on a year-to-year basis by the United States for strategic purposes. In 1953, when world production rose to 169,000 tons, consumption fell to 129,000 tons, leaving a surplus of 40,000 tons. In the same year the United States considered its stockpile sufficient, but it continued its purchasing policy through 1955, when 43,454 tons were purchased from Malaya.

Combined with the price implications of increasing over-production of tin is the high taxation of the Malayan product. At present the Malayan tin industry is subject to an export duty and a federal income tax. Another charge, although small, is an assessment which goes to support the Tin Research Institute. The effect of this encumbered cost structure for the industry has been to discourage the development of marginally productive tin areas and to deter new investment in the industry.

The second major problem of the tin industry has been the near exhaustion of the present tin deposits and the need to survey and develop new areas. In 1933 a careful survey of the tin industry estimated that the reserves on the then leased tin lands would not last beyond twenty years. Since that time the extraction has been fairly heavy, and there has been no concomitant exploration for new ore bodies. Further exploration has not taken place for a number of reasons. In the first place, geological surveying is expensive. For the most part the present tin-mining regions in Malaya have been known for many decades and were exploited by Chinese miners long before the British intercession in Malaya. Second, the need for exploration and development did not become clear until shortly before World War II. Thereafter, the Japanese occupation halted ex-

---

and 248,000 kilowatts, respectively) and hydroelectric generation 10 per cent of the total capacity. The states of Perak, Selangor, Negri Sembilan, Malakka, and Johore have 82 per cent of the installed capacity of the Federation.

ploration, and the postwar Emergency made exploration difficult and dangerous, since aerial methods of exploration have not been well developed for tin-bearing ores. Finally, and perhaps most important, the acquisition of mining lands presents many uncertainties to the developer. Prospecting licenses do not automatically bring with them the rights to exploitation from the individual states. On the grounds that tin-mining conflicts with other more important land uses, particularly agricultural land uses, prospecting permits especially in the Malay reservations are difficult to acquire. In addition, existing legislation in the Mining Enactments places a heavy burden on the developer by making him responsible for costly rehabilitation measures in the tin-mining areas where surface mining leaves ponds, tailings, and exposed areas of infertile subsoils. One partial solution might be a greatly accelerated program of mineralogical surveying under government control to ascertain the best areas for exploitation, together with a comprehensive survey of land uses and needs for land devoted to alternative uses.

Other mineral production is of distinctly less importance. Among the metallic minerals, iron is perhaps the most significant. Production of ore in 1955 was nearly one and one-half million tons, almost all of which was shipped directly to Japan. Bauxite production, chiefly in Johore, has been rising and reached 222,000 tons in 1955, primarily for export to Taiwan, Japan, and Australia. Except for gold, other metallic mineral production is minute. Coal remains an important resource, although production has been falling because of the relative availability of fuel oil from the Southeast Asian region. In 1955, 206,000 tons of coal were produced. In the prewar period a peak production of 781,000 tons was reached in 1940. Low calorific values, high costs of production even from open-cast mines, the increased use of oil for space heating, and the proposed shift from coal to oil for the Malayan Railway, all point to declining or at least stagnating coal outputs.

Trade

The per capita value of trade for Malaya is higher than that of any country in Asia, including Japan. Although the value of trade fluctuates markedly from year to year, on the average it amounts to about M$1,300 for each resident of the country. Malaya, therefore, is a trading country among the Asian nations, but it differs markedly in the character of its trade not only from some other Asian countries but more significantly from the countries of the West.

There are two trades rather than one. The first is the merchandise trade based upon domestic production and consumption. The second is the entrepôt trade which consists of goods and services originating in and destined for areas outside of Malaya. The two are so intimately intertwined that it is virtually impossible to separate them, but with the use of some tables and assumptions, it is possible to describe and relate them below.

The domestic merchandise trade

The domestic merchandise trade may be assumed to be primarily that of the Federation. This is true particularly of the export trade, to which Singapore contributes relatively little in the way of domestically originated merchandise. It is true, of course, that the growth of secondary industries in Singapore results in significant values added to imported raw materials which may then be exported in a transformed state. For the most part such exports are subsumed under the heading of re-exports, though this may be controversial. In the import trade, Singapore is a major consumer of imported materials in its own right, and the portion of its imports which are concerned with retained items for Singapore itself surely should be considered domestic trade, but the value of these items may not exceed 10-15 per cent of the total trade of Singapore (see below).

The trade of the Federation. --Tables 66 and 67 show the trade of the Federation in 1954 and 1955 by commodity values and by direction. The contrasts between the commodity trades in these two years is striking, especially in exports. These contrasts reflect the basic instability in the Malayan external economy, which is dependent upon world prices for raw materials over which Malaya has no control. In each year, the dominance of rubber and tin over all other commodities is conspicuous. In 1954 and 1955 these two materials accounted for 80.3 per cent and 85 per cent of the export trade, respectively. Exports in 1951 were of much greater value than in 1955, reflecting the high price and demand for rubber because of the Korean crisis. Even if allowances were to be made for retained imports in Singapore and for Singapore-originated exports, the share of rubber and tin in the export trade would be overwhelming.

404

The import trade is considerably more diversified. Foodstuffs are conspicuously important, followed by petroleum products, "hard" manufactures, and "soft" manufactures. This is
a pattern characteristic of most underdeveloped regions. Although Malaya's economy in some ways fits the "underdeveloped" criteria less well than many others, in terms of domestic merchandise trade, it qualifies as an arch-type of the
underdeveloped or "colonial" economy.

TABLE 66
FEDERATION: TRADE, BY COMMODITY*

| | 1954 | | 1955 | |
	Value (million M$)	%	Value (million M$)	%
Exports				
Food, beverage, and tobacco	91.6	5.6	93.9	3.9
Copra and coconut oil	63.5	3.9	52.3	2.2
Palm oil and kernels	36.8	2.3	40.8	1.7
Rubber	902.6	55.5	1,583.3	67.1
Wood, lumber, and coal	20.7	1.2	28.6	1.2
Tin concentrates	183.0 ⎫		191.4 ⎫	
Tin blocks, ingots, etc.	220.8 ⎭ 24.8		231.4 ⎭ 17.9	
Iron ore	21.8	1.3	32.6	1.4
All others	86.1	5.2	104.7	4.4
Total	1,626.9	99.8	2,360.0	99.8
Imports				
Rice	93.5	7.1	125.6	8.1
Others	312.5	23.7	352.1	22.8
Beverages and tobacco	76.0	5.7	79.7	5.2
Tin concentrates	47.5	3.6	64.0	4.1
Rubber	44.0	3.3	59.4	3.8
Copra	14.5	1.0	11.4	0.7
Mineral fuels	115.2	8.7	125.8	8.1
Chemicals	72.9	5.5	88.0	5.7
Textile products and footwear	114.8	8.7	134.1	8.7
Base metals	44.4	3.4	52.7	3.4
Machinery	99.3	7.5	99.1	6.4
Transport equipment	49.2	3.7	74.3	4.8
Others	235.3	17.9	276.8	17.9
Total	1,319.1	99.7	1,543.0	99.7

*Based on Federation of Malaya, Annual Report, 1955.

The most significant trading partner of Malaya is Singapore.
This is to be expected, since in large measure Singapore functions less as an independent entity than as a port for Malaya as
a whole. In short, Singapore accounts for around 40 per cent
of all the trade of the Federation. It tends to be rather more
important as a distributing center for non-Malayan imports

405

consumed in the Federation than as an outlet for Malayan produce, although this distinction becomes blurred in times of very high rubber and tin prices. The United Kingdom, North America, and western Europe tend to be the most significant markets for Malayan exports. The other Southeast Asian countries tend to be much less significant in the Federation export trade, thus reflecting the similarities in production patterns that characterize the Southeast Asian world.

TABLE 67
FEDERATION: DIRECTION OF TRADE*

	1954 Value (million M$)	%	1955 Value (million M$)	%
Exports				
Singapore	693.8	42.6	985.4	41.8
United Kingdom	181.9	11.2	323.4	13.7
Canada	25.8	1.6	33.7	1.4
India	44.9	2.8	45.1	1.9
Other Commonwealth countries	36.5	2.2	50.1	2.1
U. S. A.	200.7	12.3	326.7	13.8
Indonesia	6.3	0.4	11.2	0.5
France	74.2	4.6	101.6	4.3
Germany	69.2	4.3	125.3	5.3
Italy	52.0	3.2	79.3	3.4
Netherlands	30.5	1.9	31.5	1.3
Japan	64.9	4.0	89.7	3.8
Thailand	25.0	1.5	30.7	1.3
All others	119.7	7.4	124.6	5.3
Ships and aircraft stores	1.5	0.1	1.7	0.1
Total	1,626.9	100.0	2,360.0	100.0
Imports				
Singapore	509.1	38.6	586.9	38.0
United Kingdom	260.4	19.7	295.3	19.1
Australia	48.3	3.7	52.1	3.4
India	24.6	1.9	28.3	1.8
Other Commonwealth countries	49.6	3.8	58.6	3.8
U. S. A.	16.1	1.2	17.9	1.2
Indonesia	133.9	10.2	133.3	8.6
Burma	21.6	1.6	41.0	2.7
China	19.2	1.5	24.7	1.6
Thailand	121.5	9.2	160.2	10.4
All others	114.8	8.7	144.7	9.4
Total	1,319.1	100.1	1,543.0	100.0

*Based on Federation of Malaya, Annual Report, 1955.

An increasingly significant potential market for Malayan exports, especially rubber, appears to be China. A marked decline in the rubber stock-piling policies of the United States after 1955 has encouraged negotiations with China, and it is expected that some of the trade slack resulting from changes in American policy will be countered by the China trade. Agreements with China indicate a triangular trade whereby some Chinese imports of rubber will be paid for with Burmese rice previously contracted for by the Chinese. Trade with Japan also may be expected to rise, as Japanese trading companies intensify their activities in Singapore and the Federation.

Apart from Singapore, the United Kingdom is the major source of the Federation's imports. The United States is insignificant, in part reflecting currency controls within the Federation. The Southeast Asian countries, however, are particularly important, Indonesia and Thailand alone accounting for about 20 per cent of the Federation's imports. This apparent anomaly, when contrasted with their minor role in the export trade, is explained in part by imports of rice from Thailand, and primarily by the import of rubber from Sumatra and of tin from peninsular Thailand for processing and re-export through Penang.

Penang is a free port and entrepôt. It handles about one-third, by value, of all the trade of the Federation, chiefly exports of domestically produced rubber and tin. However, from 15-20 per cent of Penang's trade is with Indonesia, Thailand, and Burma. Most of this involves rubber, tin concentrates, and petroleum products. Of these three, the first two, rubber and tin, are primarily imports and re-exports and represent a segment of the Federation merchandise trade which is not truly domestic. If most of this trade, valued at about M$210 million in 1955, were deducted from the other trade of the Federation, the result would be a more accurate picture of the true domestic trade balance of the Federation. Also, if that were done, the significance of Singapore (as well as that of the non-Southeast Asian countries) would tend to rise, and Singapore might be described as handling about 50 per cent of the Federation's domestic trade rather than 40 per cent.

The trade of Singapore. --The trade of Singapore cannot be described so simply. Its outlines are shown in Tables 68 and 69. Table 68 shows Singapore's trade with areas other than the Federation in 1954. Singapore's imports are extremely diverse, nearly 50 per cent of them falling under the heading "Other commodities." This reflects the role of the city as a distributing and marketing center for the Federation and much of insular Southeast Asia. Rubber and petroleum products account for about a third of its imports by value. Tin is insignificant since virtually all of Singapore's tin imports come from the Federation. Formerly, significant quantities of tin came to Singapore from Indonesia, but these imports have dwindled to nearly nothing. Rice is important, as are regional products such as spices and manufactured goods.

Exports from Singapore are also rather diverse and tend to be similar in nature to imports. Thus, rubber and petroleum products are of prime importance, and "Other commodities" remain significant. Tin is exceptionally important and represents the results of the processing of imports from the Federation which do not appear on the table.

TABLE 68
SINGAPORE: TRADE, BY COMMODITY, 1954*

Commodity	Imports		Exports	
	Value (million M$)	%	Value (million M$)	%
Rubber	328.7	14.1	785.1	38.2
Tin	-	-	196.0	9.6
Petroleum products	469.2	20.2	295.3	14.4
Rice	94.6	4.0	23.1	1.1
Textiles	117.0	5.0	35.6	1.7
Spices	71.1	3.1	73.2	3.6
Iron and steel manufactures	98.9	4.2	33.5	1.1
Other commodities	1,150.6	49.4	622.5	30.3
Total	2,330.1	100.0	2,054.3	100.0

*Exclusive of trade with the Federation of Malaya. Based on Colony of Singapore, Annual Report, 1954.

On Table 69, which shows the directions of Singapore's trade, the values of exports and imports to and from the Federation have been included. The Federation is the dominant trading partner, in 1954 taking nearly 20 per cent and sending nearly 23 per cent. In terms of imports alone, Indonesia is most important with 26.3 per cent, although its role varies with rubber prices and with the commercial policies of the Indonesian government. The United Kingdom and the rest of Europe are of major importance, with the remainder of the import trade highly diversified. Imports from British Borneo, chiefly petroleum from Sarawak, account for most of the imports from "Other British territories. "

TABLE 69
SINGAPORE: DIRECTION OF TRADE, 1954*

Country	Imports Value (million M$)	%	Exports Value (million M$)	%
Federation of Malaya	693.8	22.9	509.1	19.9
Indonesia	795.2	26.3	135.6	5.3
United Kingdom	340.7	11.3	270.2	10.5
Europe	222.1	7.3	391.3	15.3
Other British territories	189.9	6.3	315.0	12.3
U. S. A.	132.6	4.4	259.9	10.1
Japan	120.1	4.0	100.4	3.9
Thailand	136.5	4.5	56.2	2.2
Australia	84.9	2.8	137.1	5.3
India and Pakistan	48.2	1.6	84.3	3.3
Hongkong	78.4	2.6	45.5	1.8
China	68.0	2.2	13.9	0.5
Other countries	113.5	3.8	244.9	9.6
Total	3,023.9	99.9	2,563.4	100.0

*Based on Federation of Malaya, Annual Report, 1955, and Colony of Singapore, Annual Report, 1954.

Export schedules are different in several ways. The Federation is most important, but Indonesia is relatively unimportant. Trade with the United Kingdom and "Other British territories, " Europe, and North America are extremely important, and Australia becomes more prominent. Trade with "Other countries" likewise is more important than in the import trade.

The trade with the Federation is markedly understated, however. Since Singapore acts as a port for Malaya and since most of its imports from the Federation are rubber and tin which are processed and then re-exported, Singapore acts as an entrepôt for the Federation. Thus, allowing for retained imports from the Federation in Singapore, we may estimate that about 80 per cent of Singapore's Federation imports are re-exported (with allowances for value added, M$600 million). Assuming this to be the case, the significance of the export column becomes quite different. Not only does Singapore send about 20 per cent of its exports to the Federation, but about 30 per cent of its other exports originated in Malaya. Thus, of the total export of Singapore, about 50 per cent by value in 1954 originated in or was destined for the Federation. A similar situation may be assumed, on a somewhat smaller scale, with regard to imports. Thus, we can argue that about 40 per cent of all of Singapore's trade concerns the Federation. If this is so, then trade with or on behalf of the Federation is the single most important function of Singapore.

The entrepôt trade

Any discussion of the entrepôt trade of Malaya should take into account the relations between the Federation and Singapore. Most discussions do not. Available sources define the entrepôt trade of Malaya, quite properly in their context, as referring only to the traffic in goods which originate out of and are destined for points foreign to Malaya as a whole. The following discussion of the entrepôt trade therefore refers only to this more limited use of the term. Figures include values added in Malaya (by processing and semimanufacture) to imported goods. Data are drawn from Benham's study[32] and from the International Bank report on Malaya.

On Table 70, the entrepôt trade of Malaya as a whole, which moves through Singapore and Penang, is estimated at between 40 to 50 per cent of its total trade. This estimate is probably high, since it seems not to have taken sufficient account of the special trade relations between Singapore and the Federation discussed above and the very large market function of Singapore itself. If it is assumed that some 90 per cent of Malaya's entrepôt trade passes through Singapore, there is considerable doubt that the entrepôt percentage estimate allows for a sufficient amount of retained imports in Singapore. Nevertheless, it marks the significance of the entrepôt trade to the total economy.

In general, the total volume of the entrepôt trade tends to be understated. For one thing, there is a considerable carriage of goods in native vessels through Singapore, which, as is necessarily the case in even a well-regulated free port, may not be recorded. Secondly, many smaller vessels, particularly coasters and native craft, use Singapore as a calling station for supplies, water, and passengers en route from one place to another, although they may not unload or load cargoes. The

---

32. Frederic Benham, The National Income of Malaya (Singapore: Government Printing Office, 1951).

TABLE 70
MERCHANDISE TRADE*

EXPORTS

	1949		1951		1953	
	Value (million M$)	%	Value (million M$)	%	Value (million M$)	%
Domestic produce						
Rubber	558	32.4	2,279	37.5	898	29.7
Tin	241	14.0	506	8.3	351	11.6
Coconut products	49	2.8	85	1.4	58	1.9
Palm oil and kernels	42	2.4	45	0.7	37	1.2
All others	53	3.1	136	2.2	142	4.7
Subtotal	943	54.8	3,051	50.2	1,486	49.2
Re-exports	779	45.2	3,025	49.8	1,534	50.8
Total exports	1,722	100.0	6,076	100.0	3,020	100.0

IMPORTS

	1949		1951		1953	
Domestically consumed						
Rice	200	10.8	222	4.7	277	8.6
Other foodstuffs	315	17.0	538	11.3	516	15.9
Drink and tobacco	63	3.4	106	2.2	101	3.1
Petroleum products	78	4.2	120	2.5	170	5.3
Textiles	169	9.1	355	7.5	135	4.2
Machines	181	9.8	432	9.1	337	10.4
All others	185	10.0	539	11.3	328	10.1
Subtotal	1,191	64.3	2,312	48.6	1,864	57.6
Import for re-export	660	35.7	2,443	51.4	1,374	42.4
Total imports	1,851	100.0	4,755	100.0	3,238	100.0
Total trade	3,573		10,831		6,258	
Entrepôt trade, total and as per cent of all merchandise trade	1,439	40.3	5,468	50.5	2,908	46.5

*Based on International Bank of Reconstruction and Development, The Economic Development of Malaya, p. 23

cargoes they carry, however, might well be considered part of the entrepôt trade, since if it were not for Singapore's facilities, the vessels would not stop there. This is characteristic of all ports, of course, but is particularly significant at Singapore.

The importance of Singapore and Penang long antedates the rise of the modern rubber and tin industries. The favorable location of Singapore with regard to archipelagic Southeast Asia was significant from the first. Its facilities as a free port were unmatched by any other port (with the exception, in part, of Penang) in the region. Political stability and sound currencies under the pax Britannica encouraged trade, and an increasing population and rising production made the Straits Settlements an attractive calling place for vessels of all sorts. In the case of Penang as well as Singapore, strong regional ties exist with northern Sumatra (which significantly enough was administered from Singapore under part of the Japanese Occupation). In any event, major British trading houses based many of their commercial and developmental operations in Singapore, and Chinese merchants have long used Singapore as their base of operations for trade with Southeast Asia and with China.

The composition of the entrepôt trade has varied in recent years, though its main character has remained stable. In 1949, for example, about 65 per cent of the value of the trade consisted of the handling and processing of tin and rubber products, petroleum products, and manufactured goods, the most important of which were cotton piece goods, other textiles, and vehicles and other mechanical equipment. In 1953 these commodities comprised about 75 per cent of the entrepôt trade. As a percentage of the total entrepôt trade[33] in the respective years, tin and rubber products rose from 20 to 22 per cent, petroleum products rose from 19 to 29 per cent, and manufactured products fell from 26 to 23 per cent. (See Table 71.)

The fluctuations in the composition of the trade, as indicated above, are significant not only because of their magnitude but also because they reveal the sorts of influences which operate upon the entrepôt trade. The case of rubber is an excellent example. In 1950-51 the price of rubber rose steeply in response to the Korean war. This price increase led to greater production (especially smallholder production) in Indonesia and other neighboring areas, most of which found its way to Singapore. High prices produced a corresponding increase in income which could be used to purchase goods handled in the Singapore trade. Thus, both the volume and value of the trade increased

---

33. This total includes the value, import and export, of the goods plus the value added in trade and processing.

TABLE 71
ENTREPÔT TRADE, 1949-53*
(million M$)

	1949	1950	1951	1952	1953
Values of entrepôt trade					
1. Rubber and tin (import value)					
Rubber	123	612	1,249	497	308
Tin concentrates	31	60	68	47	38
Subtotal	154	672	1,317	544	346
2. Other Malayan products (import value)					
Copra	55	60	65	37	40
Pepper	20	33	37	38	50
Arecanuts	12	7	10	13	10
Sago and tapioca	5	4	8	7	6
Others	25	35	33	30	31
Subtotal	117	147	153	125	137
3. Other food, drink, tobacco (export value)	89	143	260	252	168
4. Petroleum products (export value)	146	197	275	414	446
5. Other manufactures, including textiles and machinery (export value)	203	383	561	473	356
6. Total import-export value	709	1,542	2,566	1,808	1,453
Estimated values added	119	421	582	248	160
Total costs of imports for re-export (item 6 minus value added to foodstuffs, petroleum products, and other manufactures	660	1,466	2,443	1,698	1,374
Total values of re-exports (item 6 plus values added to rubber, tin, and other "Malayan" commodities)	779	1,887	3,025	1,946	1,534

*From International Bank for Reconstruction and Development, The Economic Development of Malaya, pp. 129-30. Fuller explanations of the calculations are to be found therein.

in this period. As the price of rubber began to fall in 1952 and with it the supply of rubber and incomes, the entrepôt trade suffered severely. Moreover, some of the Southeast Asian countries, notably Indonesia, initiated severe import restrictions on goods handled through Singapore in an attempt to overcome balance-of-payments difficulties. [34] All of this has meant unstable conditions for the Singapore entrepôt trade even though the trade situation had once again improved by mid-1955.

The case of rubber also illustrates another recent trend in the entrepôt trade. The natural products of Southeast Asia,

413

which before the war provided the bulk of the value of the trade, are no longer finding their way to Singapore for grading, processing, and shipment to Europe. Tin, copra, jelutong, sawlogs, sago, rice, and fish products, as well as rubber, have not really recovered from the interruption of the war in terms of contributing to the entrepôt trade. One important reason has been the creation of facilities for processing and shipping in the producing countries, although official trade restrictions remain more significant.

There has been, however, an increase in the volume of trade in manufactured goods from Europe and North America, and an even greater increase in the volume of petroleum products which now enters the entrepôt trade. This postwar trend more than compensates for the small decline in the regional products trade and represents a qualitative change in the character of the total trade. Of the manufactured items, cotton piece goods and other consumption items such as food, cigarettes, and canned milk have been less important than durable goods, in which trade has increased rapidly. The postwar development of the petroleum industry in and around Singapore has occurred primarily because of Singapore's function as a center for petroleum blending and transshipment, its proximity to the rapidly developing fields in British Borneo, and its expanded consumption of petroleum as bunker fuel.

To an important extent, the gradual stabilization of the entrepôt trade following World War II and the Korean war has been due to the changing nature of the trade as evidenced in the importance of "Western" manufactured goods and petroleum products. Singapore is assuming the character more of a distributor to, rather than a gatherer from, Southeast Asia. The future of the entrepôt trade in Malaya is, despite the trials since the end of the war, fairly secure. Notwithstanding the postwar emergence of nationalism and associated exclusionist

---

34. These and other restrictions are not new to Singapore. Even before the war, some of the countries within the area served by the entrepôt trade of Singapore, notably the Dutch holdings, attempted to restrict the trade. It was the severity of the restrictions in 1952 which was notable. In 1955, many restrictions on regional trade were lifted, but the trades with Indonesia and, to a degree, Thailand, still remained somewhat depressed.

policies in some of the countries in the region, there continues to be a need for the special services and skills which Singapore is able to provide. In fact, it has been suggested that the development of greater economic autonomy in some of these countries--a development which would appear to threaten Singapore's importance--would actually work to the advantage of the more advanced center since one result of economic development should be an increase in the volume of trade in the region as a whole.

Economic Development

Malaya has, like other Southeast Asian states since the end of the war, entered upon a program of planned economic development with the aim of achieving a higher and more stable level of living for its people. Malaya is also a member of the Colombo Plan, which encourages the maximum utilization of the domestic resources of the country through the exchange of technical and economic assistance between participating countries.[35]

It is possible to identify two major aspects of the developmental program. The first is the broadening and the diversification of the commercial sector of the economy. The second is the intensification of the program of rural development. This is

---

35. The Colombo Plan for Co-operative Economic Development in South and Southeast Asia was formed in 1950 under the auspices of the British Commonwealth Consultative Committee on South and Southeast Asia. The consultative committee represented the following states: Australia, Canada, Ceylon, India, New Zealand, Pakistan, and the United Kingdom. In addition to these participating states, the following regional states were participants as of 1955: Federation of Malaya, Singapore, British Borneo (North Borneo, Sarawak, Brunei), Burma, Cambodia, Thailand, Vietnam, Japan, and the Philippine Republic. There is no over-all master plan for the participating nations, since each develops its own program. The organization as such exists only insofar as the participating nations share the maintenance costs of the administration of the plan and the Technical Assistance Scheme and meet together annually to report on progress and discuss common problems.

not a unique pattern of development. Other Asian states with a similar dual quality in their economies have followed a similar pattern. In this process Malaya has great advantages because of the advanced character of the established economic system.

The commercial sector

The broadening and diversification of the commercial sector of the economy is proceeding along two somewhat autonomous lines. There has been a sharp infusion of governmental investment into the economy. This investment has been closely associated with Malaya's participation in the Colombo Plan, and the resources of other members of the Plan--notably Australia, New Zealand, and the United Kingdom--have been drawn upon. As of 1955, twenty-five experts and seventy-nine trainee positions have been provided by these to the Federation and three experts and forty-five trainee positions provided for Singapore. About £25,000 worth of equipment has been provided to the two areas, and about £65,000,000 in grants and loans have been provided to Malaya and Borneo, with most going to Malaya.

Under the program of governmental investment in the Federation, new agricultural lands are being developed through the drainage and irrigation of land not previously cultivated. Notable successes have been achieved in the Tanjong Karang and Trans-Perak areas; in the latter region, 180,000 acres of swampland will be brought into cultivation. The Rural and Industrial Development Authority, which will be discussed below, has continued to employ greater funds and personnel. Electrical power capacity has been extended through the construction of the Connaught Bridge power station, and future capacities will be enlarged by the proposed hydroelectric station in the Cameron Highlands. The east-coast railway, destroyed during the war, has been reopened, and plans for a £21,000,000 east-west line from Port Swettenham, Selangor, via Kuala Lumpur to Kuantan, Pahang (two hundred miles) have been announced. Additional deep-water berths at Port Swettenham are being constructed; the airport facilities at Penang and Kuala Lumpur are being increased; and telecommunications connecting Kuala Lumpur with Singapore, Ipoh, Penang, and Malakka are being improved.

In Singapore investment and development by the government have followed different lines. Housing, water supply, and education have been the chief targets for developmental activities.

The second line of development of the economy is related to the greater increase in income-producing capacity of Malaya's secondary and tertiary industries as compared with the previously dominant primary industries. There has been an appreciable increase in manufacturing, commercial, and professional services in recent years. Data on labor in industrial employment, figures on electrical consumption, and information on installed industrial horsepower all indicate this secondary and tertiary growth. Most of the new establishments are of the small-scale variety which have typified much of the commercial and industrial activity in the country.

The rural sector

The program of rural economic development, the second broad aspect of economic development in Malaya, is implemented through the general agricultural assistance programs of the state and federal governments and through the Rural and Industrial Development Authority (RIDA). The former are concerned with the improvement of crops, the extension of acreages, and the provision of basic educational and welfare needs for the rural population of the country. RIDA is concerned primarily with the utilization of the capital and labor resources of rural Malaya based upon a partnership of the villagers and the government. In both the general agricultural and RIDA programs, the principle of self-help is important, and in both there is an effort to involve and integrate the traditionally somewhat isolated villagers into the total Malayan economy.

The improvement of rice production, which has occupied the government agriculture departments for about twenty-five years, forms a major part of the assistance program. Irrigation and drainage facilities have been developed throughout the country, but most extensively in the "rice bowl" areas in the northern part of the country, by the Drainage and Irrigation Department of the Department of Agriculture. In these areas the same department provides subsidies for the new cultivators and part-time employment opportunities as a source of additional income. The Federation government has provided the rice cultivators with a guaranteed price for their product delivered at government rice mills, as well as pure-strain seed at little or no cost. Loans have been granted to cultivators for the purchase of draft animals and fertilizers. Extensive experimentation has been carried out with a view to introducing mechanical techniques.

417

Other food crops--maize, ragi, fruits, and groundnuts--
similarly have been supported by subsidies and pure-strain
seed, and there has been research upon food preservation.
Rubber smallholders have received attention from the government through the smallholder division of the Rubber Research Institute. This agency, supported by an assessment
upon each pound of rubber exported, has instructors in the
field who deal with the problems of the smallholders. Through
the Rubber Research Institute the smallholders have been provided with high-yielding seeds and assisted in the acquisition
of coagulants and other necessary materials.

The government of Malaya has for some years had a policy
of rubber replanting which applies to smallholders as well as
to estates. The replanting policy received a new stimulus
with the development of the bud graft and clonal seedlings,
which produce trees of substantially higher yields than those
which have been used in the past, therefore effecting much
greater yields for the same inputs of labor and materials. However, the peasant smallholders, those with under fifteen acres,
rarely replant their existing stands, and few smallholders with
under fifty acres replant to any extent. The reasons for this lie
in some of the deepest problems of the Malaysian smallholders. First there has been the economic consideration. A smallholder with from three to five acres cannot afford to take perhaps a fourth of his trees out of tapping for the period necessary for the growth of new trees (about six years). Government
efforts to remedy this situation by offering a subsidy for the
period of maturation of new trees have so far failed because
of inadequate compensation. Moreover, when the Malaysian
smallholder allows a part of the stand to go out of production,
he deprives himself of the income from his cheapest resource--
his labor--which now, because of the smallness of the holding,
is not realizing its maximum return.

A second chain of problems concerns the replanting of rubber
trees amidst mature trees. Root competition between the im-
mature and the mature trees results in inadequate nutrition for
the new trees and the failure or distortion of many of the new
plantings. Moreover, there is a constant struggle between wild
vegetation and cultivated crops, which demands the expenditure
of considerable effort on the part of the cultivator. Further,
replanting new trees upon old land always raised the problem
of soil fertility and viability of the new trees. As a conse-

quence, fertilization becomes almost necessary, leading to increased costs both in money and labor.

Finally, there is the problem of inadequate motivation. It has been argued that the peasant smallholder cannot be expected to replant his present holdings and deprive himself of needed income when lying nearby are vast amounts of land, suitable to the cultivation of rubber, which the government will not alienate for the production of rubber. The costs of planting these unused lands would be lower than replanting costs, even after clearing, because of the natural (though temporary) fertility of the land.

In addition to replanting problems, difficulties arise regarding the processing of smallholder rubber. In centralized processing the latex must be carried from the smallholding to the plant. Most of the weight of the latex at this point is water, and the costs of transporting this water content are high. Centralized processing of smallholder rubber has been attempted by private companies and has usually failed because the cost of transportation proved too high.

Research and education have been supported by the governments in such matters as the rural economy and mobilization of rural savings, fruit cultivation, and pest control for tree crops. Important research has also taken place concerning specific smallholder crops such as cocoa and pineapple. Poultry and goat strains have been imported in an effort to improve the existing stock and attention has been given to the local strains of pigs and cattle.

A final aspect of the governmental assistance to smallholders has been the administration of rural relief assistance, the organization of weekly fairs and periodic competitions for the best of certain types of cultivation, and annual exhibits of crops and implements.

Assistance to the smallholders by the governments has been neither uniformly successful nor consistently practiced, although since 1950, with the establishment of RIDA and the post-Korean-war trade slump in 1952-53, there has been a more consistant policy of support for smallholders. In part this consistency has been a function of the nature of RIDA, since in contrast to the more general forms of governmental assistance RIDA has depended heavily upon the efforts of the smallholders and not merely the capital and experts of the governments. Much of the work of RIDA has been the planning and execution of schemes for rural economic development which stress the processing and marketing of the producer's own product. In this respect RIDA has affected the handicraft industries of the country as much as the producers of foods.

RIDA, like rural development efforts in other Asian countries, has been slow to develop the sort of organization and spirit of receptiveness among the rural population necessary for the full success of the aims it has set. In matters like the construction of dams, bridges, and roads there has been success, since here there is one large effort on the part of the village people, and the task is finished at one time except for minor upkeep. The establishment of rice mills in the major rice-producing areas and the provision of motorized transport for collection also have met with success, for the need was great. However, in other cases, such as that of cooperative rubber smokehouses, small rubber growers have been reluctant to allow their shares of a venture to be reinvested in the extension of such cooperative activities. They choose rather to realize their gains in immediately disposable income.

Despite these efforts to diversify and broaden the Malayan economy and introduce developmental stimuli into rural Malaya, the economy remains primarily dependent upon the export of rubber and tin and the entrepôt trade. A change, however, has begun and may lead to the ultimate transformation of the Malayan economy.

11. Political Organization and Development

Administrative Development

PERHAPS THE MOST notable aspect of administrative development in Malaya has been its multiplicity of forms and structures. Various experiments in administration in the Straits Settlements were entered into by the East India Company and later by the Colonial Office. The pattern of administration in the early Malakka and Rhio-Johore sultanates was discussed in Chapter 2. [1] During the early 1800's each of the states maintained different kinds of administrative structures, which were changed notably with the introduction of the resident system. Union of the Federated Malay States in 1895 brought further changes for some of the states. The cyclical pattern of centralization-decentralization was continued in the Union proposals of 1946 and the establishment of the Federation. Local government has assumed many and varied forms--municipalities, town boards, rural boards, town councils, and local councils. The synthesis of Western ideas of democracy with remnants of indigenous political forms can be seen in every state.

---

1. In addition C. A. Fisher admirably reviews the political geography of Malaya in his chapters "The Problem of Malayan Unity in Its Geographical Setting," Part I: "Historical Geography," and Part II: "Recent and Contemporary Political Geography," in R. W. Steel and C. A. Fisher (eds.), Geographical Essays on British Tropical Lands (London: George Philip & Son, 1956).

The Straits Settlements under the East India Co. (1786-1858)

Penang was administered as a residency under the government of Bengal from 1786 to 1805. Province Wellesley, acquired in 1800, was administered as a part of Penang. Francis Light, founder of the settlement of Penang, was appointed its first superintendent. Light, unfortunately, was not an administrator, nor was the East India Company much interested in the settlement, except as a safe harbor for its ships and a factory for trade. Adequate pay was not forthcoming for even the few officials under Light's charge. Consequently most of them entered into private trade to supplement their incomes, eventually becoming more concerned with their own businesses than with administering the settlement. A formal legal system was not instituted until 1807; land alienation was common; no system of registration was enforced; and administrative revenues were virtually nonexistent. Despite a rapidly growing population few, if any, social services were offered by the government. Although trade grew rapidly, the settlement suffered.

In 1805 the company, possibly anticipating an increase in its operations in the area with the capture of Malakka and the Dutch East Indies, suddenly reversed its previous policy, elevated Penang to the status of a presidency of India and dispatched to it a governor, three resident councillors, a colonel, a chaplain, and fifty or more other officials. Instead of recovering from its former lack of administrative attention, Penang suffered even more from an overdose of officialdom. Trade prospered, but the presidency could never manage to cut down on its staff, and the annual deficit grew to £ 80, 000 per year, with little evident improvement in the quality of government. In 1826 Malakka and Singapore were brought into the presidency in an effort to make better use of the large staff.

In Malakka, following its conquest from the Dutch in 1795, the uncertainty of the times and the indecision of the East India Company held up effective administration. Fearful that the Dutch would return and enter again into competition with Penang, the company was on the verge of destroying the port, but owing largely to Thomas Raffles the plan was not carried through. After being returned to the Dutch in 1818 for a short period, Malakka was ceded permanently to the company by the treaty of Holland in 1824. Between that time and its incorporation into the Penang presidency in 1826, Malakka was administered as a dependency of the Governor-General of India.

Singapore was established in 1819 under the twin hazards of Dutch resistance and Penang jealousy. The Dutch objected vigorously to the establishment of a British factory so close to their commercial sphere, while Penang, too, feared the competition that the new settlement might give to its trade. From 1819 to 1823 Singapore was governed as a part of an East India Company factory at Bencoolen on Sumatra and in the latter year was transferred to the direction of the Governor-General of India. Under Bencoolen, Singapore was governed by a resident in consultation with the sultan of Johore and the Chief of Police. The consent of all three was required for the imposition of customs and duties and the establishment of farms, and in addition they handled all grievances, listened to petitions and issued proclamations. Unfortunately, the natural attraction of the situation for migration and trade produced strains on the settlement. The rapidly increasing population was soon out of control, and lawlessness was rife. The legal system was chaotic and unmanageable, and revenue was low in comparison to the demands for increased services. In 1823 Raffles, then Lieutenant Governor of Bencoolen, persuaded the sultan and the chief of police to put the whole of Singapore in British hands, a move which was formalized the following year. Two years later, in 1826, Singapore was incorporated into the Penang presidency along with Malakka.

By 1826, largely because of its free trade policy, Singapore had far outstripped the other two settlements as a center for trade. Upon incorporation of the three settlements in the presidency, the free trade policy which had proved so successful in Singapore was applied to Penang. But instead of reducing Penang's administrative deficit, the move increased it. Faced with an increasingly adverse financial situation which threatened the viability of all three settlements, the East India Company in an economy move in 1830 reduced the status of the settlements to that of a residency under Bengal. Two years later the capital was moved from Penang to Singapore. With this move, the administrative structure was readjusted, leaving a governor and two assistants in Singapore, a resident councillor and two assistants in Penang, and a resident councillor with one assistant at Malakka. Each of these officials divided among themselves a number of functions. In Singapore, for example, the governor and his assistants functioned as superintendent of lands, chief of police, superintendent of convicts, magistrate and commissioner of the court of requests, and superintendent of public works. The governor and the resident councillors also acted as judges. In time, as the demands for better services increased and the burden on the existing officials grew too great for efficiency, the various staffs were enlarged.

In 1851 the Governor-General of India took over the control of the settlements from Bengal. The East India Company was dissolved in 1858, and the settlements passed under the control of the British India Office. The connection with India was severed only in 1867 when the settlements were transferred to the Colonial Office as a Crown Colony.

Throughout the period of company rule, the administration of the settlements suffered from three major problems: 1) the inability of the company to adopt a permanent attitude and policy toward the settlements; 2) the tendency to consider the settlements as appendages of the Indian government; 3) the lack of a civil service capable of coping with the special problems arising in Malaya.

The company had entered Penang only under force of circumstances--the temporary need for a base on the eastern shores of the Bay of Bengal. Similarly, the company's interest in Malakka was transitory; it desired to keep the colony out of Dutch hands, without necessarily wishing to assume responsibility for its administration. The company was governed essentially by profit motives, rather than by any particular concern over the welfare of the settlements themselves; thus at every point liabilities were weighed against gain, and that policy adopted which appeared to yield the greatest revenue with the least expenditure on a short-term basis. For decades, therefore, the settlements suffered from changing policies.

Perhaps a more basic problem was the company's concern primarily with its operations and role in India; the settlements were never considered as more than mere extensions of the Indian administration and outposts for the Indian trade. The uncertainty of the company concerning the function of the settlements appears to have resulted from its inability to make the settlements fit into the Indian administrative scheme. Distance, too, prevented adequate control by the Indian authorities and contributed to the reluctance of ambitious officials to accept appointments so far from the center of authority and promotion. Under the presidency an attempt was made to create a Straits Settlements civil service, recruited from the Bengal civil service. Few such recruits, however, had any training in or any knowledge of Malay language, customs, or law, and most tended to consider their appointments as temporary and therefore made little attempt to acquaint themselves with Malayan problems. Fortunately, one small group of men who had been trained at Penang and in Bencoolen managed to retain some power in the settlements, and from them eventually developed an efficient and knowledgeable civil service, when the connection with India had been severed.

The Straits Settlements under the Colonial Office (1867-1941)

Following the transfer of the Straits Settlements to the control of the Colonial Office a conscious effort was made to eradicate the problems which had plagued the East India Company administration. A fairly consistent policy of administration was developed which survived for some seventy-four years with little change. A Malayan civil service was instituted to provide personnel trained in the problems unique to the settlements. The administrative and judicial functions were divided; no longer would the administrators act like judges, as they had under the company. Even more important, however, was the introduction of the idea of local responsibility and participation in government.

The chief officer of the Crown Colony of the Straits Settlements was a governor, appointed by the secretary of state for the colonies. The governor was usually brought to the settlements from service in other colonies, thus introducing new ideas and preventing the formation of a self-perpetuating bureaucracy. There were, in exceptional cases, variations from this rule, as in the cases of Sir Frank Swettenham and Sir Hugh Clifford, both of whom rose through the Malayan civil service.

The day-to-day administration of the Straits Settlements was carried on under the direction of the colonial secretary, an official usually chosen from the local civil service. He was head of the civil service, general administrator, and the channel for all communications from and to the governor. Under the colonial secretary were the resident councillors of Penang and Malakka, who were in charge of the particular affairs of those settlements. Similar functions for Singapore were fulfilled by the colonial secretary, in addition to his other tasks.

An executive council functioned as an advisory body to the governor. This council consisted of the general officer commanding the troops, the colonial secretary, the two resident councillors, the attorney-general, the treasurer, two other nominated official members, and three unofficial members, one of whom was Chinese. It served as a cabinet and a board of experts on particular problems. The unofficial members were chosen for their knowledge of special problems, the Chinese member representing the Chinese population and serving as a liaison agent between the government and the Chinese community. The council met only at the summons of the governor, and the governor was left free to reject the council's advice. The governor possessed both an ordinary and a casting vote in all decisions of the council, and these, in addition to his hold over the official members, usually impelled council agreement on government plans. The power of the governor was held in check, however, by the ability of the British Colonial Office to review any of his actions. Thus, the minutes of each council meeting were submitted periodically to the secretary of state for the colonies. In any case where the governor chose to disregard the advice of the council, he was obliged to make a full report to the Colonial Office.

Legislative power in the colony was vested in a legislative council, subject to the dissent of the secretary of state for the colonies. The competence of the legislative council was sufficient for independent legislation on most matters, but in some special points the consent of the British government was required. The primary problem of the legislative council was concerned with membership, which changed frequently, chiefly along the lines of increasing and diversifying the unofficial membership. Although the considerable majority of officials was greatly reduced, government superiority was maintained. Prior to 1924 all the unofficial members were appointed by the governor. In that year the number of unofficial members was increased to thirteen, or equal to the number of official members, excluding the governor. Two of the unofficial members were elected by each of the Chambers of Commerce of Singapore and Penang. The others were selected from the three settlements and from the several racial communities in an attempt to secure representation from the various elements in the population. Of the thirteen unofficial members, seven were Europeans, three Chinese, one Malay, one British Indian, and one Eurasian. Of the thirteen official members, eight were the official members of the executive council, three were the heads of the departments of education, medical and health, and Chinese affairs. The judiciary also was represented in the earlier days but was later dropped. The vote of the official members was at the command of the governor, and it was usually a foregone conclusion that bills receiving the support of the governor were passed. Essentially, the council functioned in order that the unofficial representatives might make known the desires of their constituencies, without being allowed any voice in the final decisions.

There was little move in the colony toward the introduction of self-government above the purely local level, nor was there much demand for it. The essential character of the settlements was that of the marketplace. Few of their inhabitants considered them permanent places of residence. What was desired was some form of government which could regulate and control lawlessness and provide the services necessary for the maintenance of equitable living conditions with the minimum of interference in commercial activities. Of those who could claim the settlements as home, few had had any experience of representative government, and even fewer had the requisite degree of political education for the formation of an intelligent constituency.

In general, the colonial government was good, clean, and efficient. To some extent it was faced with financial problems similar to those which plagued the East India Company. The British government expected the settlements to be financially self-sufficient, and the ability of the administrators to overcome this handicap and maintain independently a high level of political and social development for the colony attests to their general competence. Little change occurred in the form and direction of colonial government in the Straits Settlements from its institution up to 1941, when the Japanese invasion suddenly put an end to the situation in which that government had been maintained.

The residency system in the Malay States

The events which led to the acceptance of British residents by the Malay states of Perak, Selangor, Negri Sembilan, and Pahang have been discussed in Chapter 2. The suggestion concerning the placement of residents in some of the states had been sent by the Colonial Office to the governor of the settlements, worded thus: "I should wish you specially to consider whether it would be advisable to appoint a British Officer to reside in any of the States. Such an appointment could, of course, only be made with the full consent of the Native Government. . . ." The governor gave a broad interpretation to this suggestion and through pressure concluded the Treaty of Pangkor with the chiefs of Perak in 1874, by which the new sultan agreed to "receive and provide a suitable residence for a British Officer to be called Resident, who shall be accredited to his court, and whose advice must be asked and acted upon on all questions other than those touching Malay religion and custom." Within a year the Sultan of Selangor also requested the services of a British resident.

The collection and control of all revenues and the general administration of the country were to be regulated with the advice of the resident. The cost of this officer, his assistants, and their establishments were to be a first charge upon the revenue.

The first resident in Perak entered upon his duties with zeal, lending a broad interpretation to his function. Intent upon reforming the state and the character of its people along liberal Christian lines, he immediately encountered the opposition of the Perak chiefs who felt, not unjustly, that he was impinging upon their prerogatives and interfering in native custom. The newly appointed governor of the Malay States, investigating the problem, was informed that the Pangkor Treaty was unworkable, since the chiefs would pay little heed to advice. The governor decided that henceforth the residents were to be "Queen's Commissioners" with powers to carry on the administration in the name of the sultan. Thus, what had originally been merely a move toward greater liaison with a Malay government had ended with the British taking over that government. The radical interpretations of the original suggestion were to have repercussions both in Perak and England. The zealous approach of the Perak resident led in 1874 to a rebellion of the Perak chiefs in which the resident was assassinated. Immediate retaliation was instituted by the British, and within a short time the rebellion was quelled. The incident had immediate consequences in the Colonial Office. The governor advised annexation as the solution to Malay problems, but this suggestion was immediately quashed by the secretary of state, who at the same time defined the Colonial Office's conception of the duties of the resident:

> The residents are not to interfere more frequent-
> ly or to greater extent than is necessary with the

minor details of government; but their special objects should be, the maintenance of peace and law, the initiation of a sound system of taxation, with the consequent development of the resources of the country, and the supervision of the collection of the revenue. . . .

Two years later the Colonial Office again admonished the residents that they were to act as advisers and not as rulers, and that if they chose to disregard that principle they would be held responsible for any trouble springing from their neglect of it. In practice most residents did choose to disregard the injunction. The Malays had realized their inability to combat the British successfully and easily acceded to their demands, while the British on their part tempered their administration with greater consideration of Malay custom and feelings. Gradually complete control over the state governments was taken by the residents.

Under the residents, rudimentary systems of taxation and land registration were instituted, British law was introduced, educational facilities were built, and public works projects initiated. The finances and trades of the states increased rapidly, and population grew apace, bringing new demands upon the governments for public services and facilities. Nearly all of the early residents were imbued with dreams of even greater prosperity, and surplus funds were quickly put to work in transportation and communication systems, governmental buildings, city planning, and other forms of Western development.

Perhaps the most significant administrative development under the residency system was the creation of state councils. Their membership comprised the rulers, the principal chiefs, several of the leading Chinese, and the resident for each state. Their functions were mainly legislative, but the annual financial estimates and other important matters were also presented for consideration. The councils served as sounding boards for new ideas. Each resident was able to assess the feelings of the other groups involved in relation to a particular issue, while membership in the council gave back to the sultan and the chiefs some of the prestige they had lost by the institution of the resident system.

The size of the administrative areas involved and the greater number of functions taken on by the residents led eventually to the establishment of a civil service in each state, under the control of the resident. The higher officers of the service were English wherever possible; the lower levels were staffed with Malays, Chinese, Eurasians, and Indians. Each of the states was divided into administrative districts under the charge of a Malay official, the penghulu, who was entrusted with powers which gave him a part in keeping the peace and assisting in the processes of orderly government.

As the four states continued to develop politically and economically, the resident system began to perpetuate an anomaly. While economically the states were developing as an interrelated and integrated unit, the resident system tended to maintain and intensify inherent localism. Each resident tended to consider his state a separate domain whose development need not take into consideration the other states of Malaya as a whole. Meanwhile, commercial, agricultural, and mining interests came to demand integrated transportation and communication facilities. It was lack of these facilities, too, which allowed the residents to maintain their independence from the centralized control of the colonial government at Singapore, and the latter was beginning to realize the economic and political dangers inherent in this separatism. On July 1, 1895, the four states were federated under one administration.

The Federated Malay States

The Federated States were administered by a structure identical in form to those of the separate states. At the head was a resident-general, functioning over the larger unit as the residents had over their individual states. Residents remained in charge of the state governments, and each department of the state governments had its head answerable to the resident. But for every important department there was also a federal head responsible to the resident-general. In theory the resident-general worked under the direction and control of the colonial governor (as high commissioner) and the secretary of state for colonies, but in reality he was allowed a broad area of freedom with only slight interference. The capital of the Federated States was established at Kuala Lumpur, and in a short time a considerable secretariat and bureaucracy had been created.

Under the new arrangement the functions of the state councils diminished. Legislative matters required the assent of

the resident-general and passage by each state council in nearly identical form. The law was to be drafted by a legal adviser.
In this situation discussion of legislation was of little avail,
and the councils became in effect mere ratification bodies for
legislation promulgated by the federal government.

The new centralization meant considerable reorganization.
The judicial and police departments were integrated and enlarged. A federal civil service was formed. The public works
department was centralized and reinforced. The bits and pieces
of individual transportation and communication lines which had
been established in the various states were connected to form
a rudimentary federal system. The financial system was reorganized and standardized and a unified land registration
system adopted.

Throughout all this the fiction of the independence and sovereignty of the states and the sultans was maintained. The
British rulers insisted that their administration was on behalf of the sultans. Largely in order to satisfy the demands of
the sultans and the states for some share in their own administration, a conference of Malay rulers was established, including members of state councils and chiefs all under the
presidency of the high commissioner. Although this body had
no legislative jurisdiction, it did furnish an arena for the airing
of grievances and the discussion of common problems.

By 1909 practically all aspects of administration rested in
the hands of the federal government. The powers of the sultans,
the residents, and the state councils were restricted largely
to matters of immediate and local importance and to carrying
out the mandates of the resident-general. In 1909 a reorganization move attempted to bring the sultans, residents, and
state councils back into the governmental organization through
the creation of a federal council. The president of the council
was the high commissioner; next in order of importance was
the resident-general, then the four sultans, followed by the
four residents. In addition there were four unofficial members
nominated by the high commissioner, three British and one
Chinese. Thus, of the fourteen members, six were members
of the British administration, four, as appointees of the high
commissioner, were associated with the administration; only
the four sultans were not associated with the British rule.
Since the deliberations of the council were in English, which
none of the sultans then understood or spoke, their influence

on council decisions was negligible. The practical effect of the council was to further reduce the powers of the sultans and the state councils, although the introduction of the residents to the council did enable the resident-general to gain a slightly more accurate outlook regarding local affairs and the effects of federal enactments.

Also in 1909 the status of the resident-general was reduced by altering his title to chief secretary to government, equal in rank to the colonial secretary. There was no apparent diminution of the powers of the office, however. This move, which was viewed as an attempt to place the Federated States directly under the control of the colonial government at Singapore, encountered considerable resistance from the more vocal elements of the European, Chinese, and Malay communities, who were later placated by a provision giving the council full control over the finances of the Federated States.

Although the reorganization of 1909 quieted criticism for some time, particularly during World War I, the issues of centralization - decentralization and state sovereignty reappeared after 1920. Rupert Emerson cites the three primary factors leading to the renewed demands for reorganization:

> These were: (1) the finances of the F. M. S., which had taken a decided turn for the worse in the post-war slump; (2) the growing sense in the Federation that the Malays, both rulers and ruled, had been unwisely and unjustly pushed too far into the background by the ponderous machine of European finance, industry and administration; and (3) the complexities and absurdities of the general constitutional structure of Malaya. [2]

The target for attack became the office of chief secretary. The attempt of the high commissioner to abolish the position was strongly opposed, however, by the British and Chinese commercial interests who disliked either the extension of colonial control over the states or any re-emergence of state autonomy which might tend to hinder the free movement of

---

2. Rupert Emerson, Malaysia (New York: Macmillan and Co., 1937), p. 155.

trade across interstate boundaries. The move toward greater state autonomy appears to have been sparked by the sultans, exercising their first major bit of political initiative since the institution of the resident system. An important factor in the colonial government's move in support of decentralization was a desire to bring the Unfederated States into the Federation. To do this it seemed necessary to give the sultans some assurance that their prerogatives and sovereignty would not disappear. This could only be done by returning the lost sovereignty of the sultans of the Federated States. It was, in turn, the relatively greater independence of the Unfederated States which led the sultans of the Federated States to seek a return to greater state autonomy.

The primary outcome of the demand for reorganization, however, was a shake-up in the federal council. In 1920 the size of the council was increased by the addition of a legal adviser and a financial adviser as official members, and two more Europeans, one Chinese, and a Malay as unofficial members, still leaving the official members with a clear majority. In 1927, the new reorganization move recognized the impotence of the sultans in the council and provided for their removal. The places of the rulers in the council were taken by the heads of the four major departments--medical, labor, public works, and education. In addition, one more official member and three Malay unofficial members were added. This then gave the council a membership of thirteen official and eleven unofficial members. The rulers were reduced to meeting in an annual durbar, with the residents, the high commissioner, and the chief secretary, to discuss the affairs of the country. However, the agenda of each council meeting was usually discussed beforehand by the sultans with their residents.

The 1927 arrangement quieted opposition for a while, but a renewed demand for decentralization was to arise in 1930-31 from the Colonial Office which argued that regardless of the efficiency of the centralized federal government, it was not consistent with British policy in the area, which was based on the theory of Malay sovereignty under the advice and direction of the British. Despite vigorous protests, the office of the chief secretary was reduced to that of federal secretary, with a status one rank lower than that of resident. Former department heads of the federal government became advisers on departmental affairs, while the control of state departments was transferred to the states. The state councils were rehabilitated, although the federal council maintained its position as the supreme authority under the high commissioner. Under the new proposals the federal government retained control of finance and the promulgation of general enactments, but it was the state councils which worked out the budget proposals for federal disposition, and legislated on local matters. One further move was the appointment of unofficial federal councillors to be members of the state councils.

One proposal which was not accepted at this time was the establishment of a Malayan Union, including all the Malay states and the Straits Settlements. Immediate protests were raised by the sultans of the Unfederated States, who foresaw the impairment of their sovereignty; by the Singapore merchants, who thought their free trade might be impaired; by the sultans of the west-coast Federated States, who feared their revenues might be spent to support the much poorer eastern states; and by commercial interests in the states who saw it as a move toward even greater centralization under the control of Singapore.

In general, the reorganizations of the early 1930's remained in effect until 1941, despite some controversy both in Malaya and in Great Britain. It is apparent that during the periods of the residency system and the Federated Malay States, the British government was plagued with indecision and conflict between policy and implementation similar to that in the Settlements under East India Company rule. The Colonial Office repeatedly stated that British intentions were not to deprive the sultans and the individual states of their rights and prerogatives, yet the administrators found it impossible to develop adequate governmental institutions without disregarding both the Colonial Office and the sultans.

The prime controversy from 1875 to 1941 revolved around this problem. Various suggested compromises proved either unworkable or unacceptable. At nearly every point uncompromising opposition was encountered resulting from the mutual antipathies, fears, and dissatisfactions of the various special-interest groups. Political and commercial elements feared greater centralization and control from Singapore. The Malays resented the growing dominance of the Chinese population and their control of the economic life of the country; the Chinese feared the potential consequences of any growth in Malay political power. Unable to institute needed political and administrative reforms and equally unable to withdraw, the British administration was forced to vacillate between sometimes contradictory policies in an attempt to placate its more extreme critics while maintaining a modicum of consistent development. The one move which might have alleviated a number of the problems, the institution of representative government, never appears to have been seriously considered above the local levels.

The Unfederated Malay States

Because of attention to developments in the Federated States, political developments in Johore and the former Siamese states of Kedah, Perlis, Kelantan, and Trengganu were overlooked to some extent. The Federated States had come into being before the Unfederated States were brought under British control, and, having witnessed the effects of the resident system and federation upon the sovereignty of their colleagues in the Federated States, the sultans of the Unfederated States were at considerable pains to maintain their independence. Because of this independence, the development of administrative and political institutions must be considered separately for each of the states.

Johore--Johore was the first state to come under British influence and the last to enter into formal political control. To a considerable extent the temenggong rulers of Johore had maintained their authority over the state owing to British support, and in return they acted as mediaries between the British and the other Malay sultans. A relationship of trust and understanding developed which was unlike the coercive relationship between the British and the other sultans. In 1866 the temenggong Abu Bakar assumed the title of Maharajah of Johore with British consent. In 1885 a treaty elevated the Maharajah to Sultan and brought Johore under British protection, without mitigating the sovereignty of the sultan except in regard to international relations. This relationship was cited by the Colonial Office as one "of alliance and not of suzerainty or dependency."[3]

British control was not extended over Johore as it had been in the Federated States in part because it was not necessary. The Johore sultans maintained a steady hand on their administration and early developed the practice of employing private

---

3. Cited in ibid., p. 22.

British and European consultants on special problems. In 1895 a written constitution drafted by an English law firm was promulgated, which remained in force until 1946. Under this constitution the sultan was head of the state and chief administrator. He was to be aided by a council of ministers and a council of state, the members of the former being ex officio members of the latter. The council of State contained, in addition to the ministers, other members appointed by the ruler with the advice or concurrence of the council of ministers. By an amendment of 1912 a third body was added, the executive council, the members of which were appointed by the sultan.

In 1914, by arrangement with the British, the sultan admitted that rapid increases in population and commercial development demanded some reorganization of his government and agreed to the services of a general adviser, whose advice was to be heeded on all matters excepting Malay religion and custom and under whose cognizance revenue and customs were to fall. However, the theory was never relinquished that the administration was to be carried out by the mentri besar (chief minister) and the state secretariat and that it was essentially a Malay rather than a British administration. Under the new arrangement, some of the departments were headed by British; others remained in charge of Malays. Some British were allowed membership in the councils. The council of ministers became somewhat anachronistic, devoting itself primarily to affairs concerning Malay religion and customary law. A sort of dual civil service was developed with each British officer having his Malay counterpart. Legally Johore was not a part of that structure headed by the high commissioner which included the other Malay states, but rather it maintained relations directly with the governor and the colonial staff at Singapore. Symbolically, too, the British flag did not fly over the general adviser's house, as it did over those of the residents and advisers in the other states.

In many ways the most independent of the sultans, the rulers of Johore became the leading spokesmen for the Malays in the controversies over centralization and the Malayan Union. As perhaps the most progressive and forward-looking rulers on the peninsula, they were virtually the only ones to encourage Chinese immigration and foreign investment. The result was rapidly increasing economic development and prosperity at the expense of maintaining Malay hegemony in population and land holdings. To a greater extent than in most of the other states

436

the Johore civil service is staffed at various levels by Chinese and Indians. This has been perhaps the predominant reason for the insistence of the sultan that the upper levels of government remain in Malay hands and under Malay control.

Kedah. --Through a treaty in 1909 the British government acquired "all rights of suzerainty, protection, administration and control . . . over the states of Kelantan, Trengganu, Kedah, Perlis, and adjacent islands" which had formerly been held by Thailand. However, the exact nature of Siamese rights in these areas had been defined imperfectly. During most of the nineteenth century a relationship of only token vassalage existed between several of the states and Thailand, and even this had tended to disappear by 1900. In Kedah Thailand enjoyed only the precise and provisional right of financial supervision in return for a large loan which had been advanced some years earlier. De jure British protection and control for that reason was not instituted until the conclusion in 1923 of a treaty with the sultan of Kedah, although de facto British intervention into the internal affairs of the state was under way by 1910.

Under the treaty of 1923 the sultan accepted a British adviser on the usual terms, with the proviso that no appointments would be made without his being informed beforehand. The treaty also stipulated that the British would not attempt to merge Kedah or her territories with any other state or colony without the consent of the sultan in council. Malay was to be the official language. A state council was also provided to assist the sultan in governing the state. The council was composed of the sultan as president, three other Malays selected by the sultan with the consent of the high commissioner, and the British adviser. Additional members were to be added only with the consent of both the sultan and the high commissioner.

Developments in Kedah were based primarily on the principle that Malay hegemony must be maintained in the face of British political infiltration and Chinese economic expansion. The Kedah sultans have clung jealously to the prerequisites and power of their office. Although the formulation and direction of administration rested largely in British hands, the latter gave careful attention to the advice and criticism of their Malay colleagues, whose intervention and resistance could be expected at any time they felt that the independence and separate identity of Kedah were threatened. Many of the offices filled by British in the other states were filled by Malays in Kedah. Particularly was this true on the level of the district and land offices, all of which were staffed by Malays. An administrative structure parallel to that in Johore was maintained. The administrative heads of government were the Malay secretary of government and the assistant adviser, the first responsible to the sultan, the second to the British adviser.

The potential economic power of the Chinese was recognized early as a threat to the maintenance of Malay rule in Kedah. The economic policy of the government aimed at making Kedah a land of prosperous Malay smallholders engaged in rice agriculture and cattle-breeding, with rubber cultivation as a source of cash income. Foreign intrusions outside the area of south Kedah already devoted to large-scale rubber planting were discouraged. Chinese were found only rarely in government office, outside the strictly local councils. It was largely an antipathy toward the Chinese which was at the root of continued reluctance in Kedah to enter into any form of Malayan union which might open the country to further Chinese immigration.

The Kedah state council acted both as an advisory body and as a legislature. It was the smallest body of its type in the states. Rarely were decisions made in meeting, agreement upon policy and legislation usually having been arranged beforehand. The council was never just a rubber stamp for orders handed down to it by the sultan or the British adviser. Discussion and debate were usually handled in informal caucuses, and some bills were given extensive revision before acceptance.

Perlis. --Prior to the British-Siamese treaty of 1909, Thai control in Perlis, as in Kedah, was exercised only over the finances of the state. This control was to continue only until a previous Thai loan had been paid off. Under the treaty of 1909 a British financial adviser replaced the Thai adviser. During the following decade the financial adviser gradually assumed a more direct hand in administration in all departments. Good administration placed the British in an embarrassing position in 1929 when Perlis paid off the final installment of its loan, and the British found themselves with no further legal standing in the country. However, the rajah was willing to admit that he and his people were not prepared to run the country without outside assistance, and upon that basis a new agreement was negotiated in 1930 legitimatizing the position of the British adviser.

Supreme authority in Perlis was vested in the rajah in council. The council met once a week under the presidency of the ruler to enact legislation and consider important administrative matters. It included the British adviser, a Malay vice-president, and other Malay members, usually the heads of government departments. For practical purposes the administration was in the hands of the British adviser. The civil service was almost wholly Malay; the number of British officials was kept at a minimum.

Kelantan. --Kelantan prior to 1903 was perhaps the most isolated and backward of the Malay states. Anarchy was rife; the sultan exerted little control over his officials or his people; the financial position was weak. Thai suzerainty was acknowledged, but actual Thai control was minimal. This state of affairs led in 1902 to an agreement between Britain and Siam defining Thai rights over Kelantan and providing for the appointment of a Thai adviser. The adviser appointed was, however, a British civil servant, and other officials were borrowed by Thailand from the Federated Malay States service. Thus in 1909, at the time of the treaty of cession, the Thai exercised full administrative rights over Kelantan, but their established civil service was staffed largely by British officers. It was this anomalous administration which the British took over intact.

The sultan in council possessed the formal sovereignty of the state, but actual administration was under the control of the British adviser and his staff. The British staff was held to a minimum, acting only as heads of key departments, while all other positions were filled by Malays. The council consisted of fourteen appointed members, almost exclusively Malay, and the British adviser, under the presidency of the sultan. Its primary function was the ratification of decisions arrived at elsewhere. There was little open discussion or deliberation.

Trengganu. --Siamese rights in Trengganu prior to 1909 were minimal and largely symbolic. The sultan had left the rule of his country to his relatives to devote himself to religious seclusion. In general the governmental situation in Trengganu was even worse than in Kelantan.

By agreement in 1910 Trengganu accepted British protection and control of its foreign affairs. For the following nine years the only British official was the British agent, whose powers were little more than those of a consular official. During this period, however, a state council was instituted, and regularization of the legal and financial systems along British lines was begun.

A treaty in 1919 provided for the acceptance of a British adviser with the usual powers over all matters of Malay custom and religion. As in Kelantan, British officials were kept to a minimum necessary to ensure control, with all other posts in Malay hands. The sultan was the legal head of the state, with the administration under the mentri besar and the British adviser. The state council consisted of fifteen appointed members under the presidency of the mentri besar. The British adviser was not a member of the council, although he usually attended all meetings and his advice was inevitably sought before any resolution was passed.

In contrast with British rule in the Federated States, the actions and policies of the advisers in the Unfederated Malay States appear to have conformed more fully with the views of the Colonial Office. In effect, the nature of the administration tended to remain Malay, although its guiding force was British. The various advisers tended, much as did the early residents in the Federated States, to identify themselves with the interests of the Malay subjects and to adopt their attitudes concerning the maintenance of Malay hegemony in political and economic affairs, the continuation of a policy of independence and separatism from the other states, and the tendency to view economic developments as an internal and local matter. In comparison with the residents, the actual powers of the advisers was limited, although their legal powers were similar. The difference appears to have arisen largely as a result of the ability of the Malay rulers and the British advisers of the Unfederated States to compromise their differences and integrate their aims for the benefit of each state. Only rarely are any overt clashes recorded. Too, the advisers were forced to a much greater extent than in the Federated States to rely upon Malays in the lower levels of administration.

Perhaps the most striking similarity of interest among all the Unfederated States has been their insistence on independence from any type of inter-Malayan association and their emphasis upon internal self-development. Their isolationism has resulted largely in an economic developmental continuity quite distinct from that of the Federated States. The economic base of the latter was predicated largely on commercial agriculture and tin production and was characterized by large-scale investment and development by foreign interests, while the economies of the Unfederated States, with the possible exception of Johore, were based on the Malay smallholder largely engaged in subsistence production of rice. Opportunities in the Federated States attracted large numbers of foreign immigrants, mostly Chinese and Indians, while the policies of the Unfederated States, again with the exception of Johore, tended to block such immigration. The fact that Johore is an exception in the two cases merely points to the greater community of attitudes among the four former Thai vassal states.

The Japanese occupation

The Japanese wrought very little change in the administrative structure of either the Settlements or the States in Malaya. Essentially government remained as before, with the exception that the Settlements came under even more direct control as Japanese territory than they had as British colonies. In the States Japanese advisers replaced the British residents and advisers. Japanese plans even continued the former British policies, in that an eventual federation of the states was envisioned under Japanese protection, with control centered in a governor-general in Singapore. Independence was not included in the plans for Malaya as it was in the plans for other states of Southeast Asia.

Perhaps the most significant development under Japanese rule came in 1943 when the decision was made to grant the Malays a more direct participation in government. Local councils were established in each district, composed of from ten to thirty Malay members, of whom one-half were appointed by the Japanese and the other half elected by the village headmen. The primary function of these councils was advisory rather than legislative. They were to answer questions from the governor and furnish opinions reflecting local attitudes on matters pertaining to the district. Although local councils of various sorts had existed in Malaya for some time prior to the Japanese invasion, these new councils apparently were the first attempt to bring any elective representative body into the state or national administrative scheme.

A second development of importance was the attempt just after the invasion to combine Malaya and Sumatra under a single administration centered in Singapore. Thus, for the first time since 1824 the old lands of the Rhio-Johore empire were reunited. The Japanese made considerable propaganda capital out of the fact. Ethnic and linguistic ties between the peoples of the two areas were stressed. It was claimed that the economies of the two areas were complementary and that the new political arrangement would work to the best interests of both, especially by taking Sumatra from the control of Java. It appears doubtful that the new structure succeeded in its aim of bringing about any greater community of interest between the two peoples, although there was a slight increase in communication between the two areas, particularly on religious and governmental levels. By 1944 the plan was discarded, and Sumatra was made a separate administrative area. There was some sign, however, of an increasing Malay interest in Indonesian independence and a tendency to identify with their Malay-Moslem neighbors. This tendency appears to have been encouraged by the Japanese, and it is probable that the real growth of a pan-Malay movement should be dated from this period.

A third development was the increasing enmity between the Malay and the Chinese populations of Malaya. Japanese actions against the Chinese in Malaya assumed the character of ruthless persecution, and in return it was the Chinese who led and largely manned the resistance movement. The Malays, on the other hand, tended to cooperate with their new overlords, much as they had with the British, and were rewarded with preferential treatment. This disparity in treatment and attitude aroused bitterness on both sides, with the Malays calling the Chinese troublemakers and charging that they were attempting to take over the country, while the Chinese accused the Malays of sympathizing with and aiding the enemy in an attempt to liquidate the Chinese. Charges and countercharges were to lead to armed clashes and terrorism, continuing far past the end of the Japanese reign and forming an important factor in the postwar Emergency.

The Malayan Union proposals

During the war considerable attention was paid by the British government and the Colonial Office to problems of postwar reorganization and rehabilitation in the colonial territories and dependencies. In October, 1945, the government announced its plans for the future of Malaya. Specifically these called for (1) the creation of a Malayan Union for all the separate governments of Malaya with the exception of Singapore, (2) the establishment of a common Malayan citizenship, embracing alike all Malays, Chinese, Indians, and others who were qualified by birth in the country or residence for a suitable period of time, and (3) the replacement of the sovereignty and prerogatives of the sultans with complete British jurisdiction in all matters. Through the Union proposals the historic distinctions between the various states (between Federated and Unfederated states and between the Malay states and the British settlements of Malakka and Penang) were to be eliminated.

A common Malayan citizenship admitting Chinese and Indians on a basis of equality with the native Malays clearly would have ended the preferential political status of the Malays and extended potential political power to an essentially alien group, whose loyalty to an independent Malaya was doubtful. As one critic charged, the move would in effect have made Malaya another Chinese province. The citizenship criteria were so lenient as to be almost all-inclusive. Included were all persons born in the territory of the Union or of the Colony of Singapore before the date on which the order came into force and persons who had been ordinarily resident in those territories for ten years during the fifteen years preceding February 15, 1942. In addition, certificates of naturalization were to be granted to persons who had resided in those territories for one year before making application and for a further period of four years during the previous eight years.

Under the plan the sultans were no longer to preside over their states councils or even attend them; their assent was no longer required for the passage of bills, this becoming the prerogative of the governor; and perhaps most important, they were no longer to have powers concerning Malay religion and custom. Instead they were to become members of two advisory bodies:(1) the council of sultans, presided over by the governor and attended also by the chief secretary, attorney-general, and financial secretary, which would meet to consider legislation relating solely to matters of the Islamic religion and to advise the governor on any question which he might present to it; and (2) the Malay advisory councils in each state, over which they were to preside and which were to offer advice on matters concerning religion.

The reaction among the Malays to these proposals was almost immediate as they burst from their previous dormancy into a torrent of political activity. Demonstrations and public meetings spread throughout the country. Political groups and parties were formed overnight. Adding fuel to the reaction against the proposals was the manner in which they were forced

443

upon the country. The sultans were virtually forced to sign the agreements, without consultation with their state councils, or face forcible removal and replacement by someone more amenable to the dictates of the British government.

The two most important effects of the British proposals were (1) the awakening of political consciousness among the formerly dormant Malay population and (2) the intensification of Malay-Chinese enmity due to the determination of the Malays to maintain their preferential status. The Malays were not alone in their protests. Former governors, civil servants, and commercial interests joined their voices in opposition to the scheme, and even the Chinese, who had the most to gain, refrained from open support of the proposals. Though the weight of logic and need rested with the Colonial Office, it was counterbalanced by the traditional relationship between the Malays and the British and the prior policy of the Colonial Office itself, the outcry of public opinion both in Malaya and in Great Britain, and the lack of strong support from any quarter. Although refusing to retreat from its position in favor of the establishment of a strong central government and the creation of a common citizenship for all who regarded Malaya as their homeland, the British government agreed to drop the Union proposals and to consult with Malay, Chinese, and Indian leaders before taking any new steps. Through such consultation the Federation of Malaya Agreement was brought into force in 1948.

The Federation of Malaya

The Federation agreement was essentially a compromise between the demands of the Malays and the needs for centralization. Under the agreement the British retained complete control of the defense and external affairs of the Federation, and the sultans retained the prerogatives, powers, and jurisdiction enjoyed prior to 1941.

The Federation was to consist of the nine Malay states and the settlements of Malakka and Penang. A federal government was established consisting of a high commissioner, a federal executive council to aid and advise him, and a federal legislative council.

The federal executive council consisted of the high commissioner as president and three ex officio members, not less than four official members, and not less than five or more than seven unofficial members, of whom not less than two of the official members and three of the unofficial were to be Malays.

The federal legislative council consisted of the high commissioner as president, three ex officio members, eleven official members, the nine presidents of the state councils in the Malay states, and one representative from each of the two settlements' councils, who would count as an unofficial member. Fifty other unofficial members were allocated to labor (6), planting (6), mining (4), commerce (6), agriculture and husbandry (8), professional, education, and cultural groups (4), settlements (2), states (9), Eurasians (1), Ceylonese (1), Indian (1), and Chinese (2). The official languages were English and Malay.

In addition, a council of rulers (Majlis Raja Raja Negri Melayu) was provided for, which would meet whenever necessary under the chairmanship of a ruler chosen by the conference and would meet with the high commissioner at least three times a year. The approval of the council was to be given to every draft salary change, and its advice was to be asked on questions regarding the immigration policy of the Federation.

A careful delineation of the rights, duties, and functions of the Federation and the individual states was made in the agreement. The authority of the state governments was extended to all matters not specifically reserved to the Federation. In each state constitutional machinery similar to that of the Federation was instituted. A state executive council and a council of state functioned as an advisory board and a legislative body respectively, although the latter was restricted to the making of laws which did not infringe upon the legislative powers of the federal legislative council. The state executive councils consisted of at least five ex officio members, including the mentri besar, the British adviser, the state secretary, the legal adviser, and the state financial officer. Other members could be added as prescribed by the state constitution. The executive councils met under the presidency of the ruler. The councils of state were presided over by the mentri besar and included at least the other four ex officio members listed above.

The powers of the governments of the two settlements also were extended to all matters not specifically reserved to the federal government. Both were under direct British rule, with a settlement council acting as advisory body to the resident commissioner. The major portion of the revenues of the states and settlements was obtained through block grants voted by the federal legislative council upon presentation of a yearly estimate. There were, however, other minor sources of revenue reserved for the use of the states and settlements.

The citizenship requirements under the agreement were considerably stiffened. Automatic citizenship was to be granted only to those born in the territories covered by the new Federation or to anyone whose fathers were Federation citizens at the time of the birth of the children. Federal citizenship was to be acquired by application and by fulfilling the requirements of adequate residence--fifteen years residence out of the preceding twenty years immediately preceding application, knowledge of English or Malay, declaration of intention of permanent settlement, and willingness to take a citizenship oath. Malayan citizenship, at first, did not necessarily mean a definite change in nationality. Thus, British, Chinese, or Indian nationality was not impaired by acceptance of Malay citizenship, except through the action of the parent nation. In 1951, amendments to the Federation agreement further liberalized the citizenship regulations regarding birth and residence and at the same time extended the criteria for determining the "Subjects of the Ruler" in the various states, thus opening their legislative councils to non-Malays. The new amendments, however, required a much greater identification with the Federation and the state on the part of citizens; they conferred the status of nationals and demanded allegiance from the citizenry.

The Federation agreement, in a sense, can be considered more than a mere compromise. Under the agreement the sultans and the states not only regained the powers which were threatened by the Union, but even strengthened their position, particularly in the former Federated States. Noticeable aspects of this change were the virtual elimination of the powers of the residents and their replacement by the mentris besar, the increased authority of the state councils, and the improved position of the unofficial members in both the Federation and state councils.

The unofficial members were quick to realize their powers under the new administrative system. It was they who introduced the member system into the Federal government, whereby unofficial members were appointed as spokesmen for certain departments in the legislative council in place of the official departmental heads. The plan was placed in effect in 1951 with the appointment of six members. Each was responsible to the high commissioner for the operations of his department as its political head and as its spokesman in the legislative council.

A civil servant continued to serve as the administrative head of each department, and another civil servant acted as secretary and personal assistant to each unofficial member. Most of the new members also assumed seats on the executive council. The departments thus transferred to unofficial leadership included home affairs, health, education, agriculture and forestry, and lands, mines, and communications. The unofficial members appointed included three Malays, one Ceylonese, one Chinese, and one European. Thus two important results of the move were to weaken further the authority of the chief secretary over the administration and to eliminate the federal secretariat. The chief secretary under the new provision became primarily a coordinator of the new departments and a deputy to the high commissioner. With responsibility divided among the new members the monolithic nature of the federal secretariat was fractured, and its remnants were to be found only in the personal staffs of the high commissioner and the chief secretary.

One further step toward loosening the strong centralization of the federal system came in 1953 when the high commissioner relinquished his presidency of the legislative council, and the council installed its own speaker, an unofficial member.

With the gradual loosening of control over the federal government and the institution of the new citizenship provisions, the next step in administrative development was the institution of a representative form of government, and an electoral working committee of the legislative council met early in 1954 to recommend the appropriate constitutional changes. Two reports were issued by the committee, a majority report which recommended the inclusion of thirty-four elected members in a ninety-eight-member legislature, and a minority report which favored sixty elected members. The minority is reported to have expressed the views of the powerful UMNO-MCA Alliance of Malays and politically active Chinese. The latter group favored an extremely rapid move to independence, and under the leadership of Tengku Abdul Rahman, later Chief Minister, fought vigorously to have its report adopted by the British authorities, the legislative council, and the council of rulers. Both reports were in agreement, however, in favoring the retention of the official members of the council and the mentris besar. "There would be six members for commerce, four for mining, two for agriculture, and two for the trade unions, all nominated by the organizations concerned. For the first time there would be seats . . . specially reserved for representatives of the minorities--the Eurasians, the Ceylonese and even the aborigines"[4] (Figure 4).

There was considerable disagreement concerning the dates of the elections, the minority report demanding elections before the end of 1954 and the majority recommending a later date. In April, 1954, an agreement was reached whereby the elections were to be held as soon as possible in 1955, and the number of elected members of the legislative assembly, as the new law-making body was to be called, was set at fifty-two. The official languages were to remain English and Malay. In this way the Federation passed directly from a form of government in which the legislature was wholly appointed to one in which a clear majority was elected. [5]

The Crown Colony of Singapore

Under the union proposals and the Federation agreement, Singapore was to remain a British colony, while Malakka and Penang were joined with the Malay states. This break-up of the former Straits Settlements called for reconsideration and reorganization of the Colonial government structure.

By the Singapore Colony Orders in Council of March, 1946, a new administrative structure was instituted. The governorship was retained with its previous status. An executive council was to consist of the governor as president, four ex officio members, two other official members, and four unofficial members, all appointed by the governor. A legislative council was instituted, with the governor as president, and the four ex officio members of the executive council, five nominated official members, four nominated unofficial members, one unofficial member elected by each of the three chambers of commerce (European, Chinese, and Indian), and six other elected mem-

---

4. Vernon Bartlett, Report from Malaya (London: Derek Verschoyle, 1954), p. 94.

5. For a detailed description of the decisions reached in amending the constitutional structure of government see the Federation of Malaya, Report of the Committee to Examine the Question of Elections to the Legislative Council; Introduction of Elections to the Federal Legislative Council; and Report of the Proceedings of the Federal Legislative Council, June 23-4, 1954 (Kuala Lumpur: Government Press, 1954).

THE NEW FEDERAL LEGISLATIVE ASSEMBLY

Elected

52

State and settlement
representatives--9
mentri bezars (prime
ministers) of states,
and 2 representatives
of Penang and Malakka
11

Nominated represen-
tatives of "scheduled"
interests--chambers
of commerce, trade
unions, etc.

22

Nominated represen-
tatives of racial mi-
norities--aborigines,
Ceylonese, etc.
3

Nominated reserve--
at the governor's dis-
cretion for underrep-
resented minorities

7

Ex officio, British
officials

3

LG

Figure 4

bers. Of the latter, two were to be elected from each of the two municipal electoral districts and one from each of the two rural electoral areas. Thus, a clear unofficial majority obtained in the legislative council, with nine of the thirteen unofficial members representing distinct constituencies.

More recent amendments to the orders in council have raised the membership of the executive council to twelve (with the addition of two unofficial members elected by the members of the legislative council) and the membership of the legislative council (by two more unofficial elected members). In 1951 the legislative council also elected a vice-president to act in the place of the governor when the latter was absent. Elections to the legislative council are held every three years.

In the first election, in 1948, the franchise was confined to British subjects, and the registration was extremely low-- 22,440, primarily Indians and Europeans. Two parties, the "Progressives" and the "Independents," presented candidates, but the political differences between the two were small. Of the registered electorate 63 per cent went to the polls. Of the six councillors elected, three were Indians, one was Chinese, one European, and one Malay.

The colony's second legislative council elections were held in 1951, with nine seats at stake. The franchise had been extended to Singapore residents born in the Federation, Sarawak, North Borneo, and Brunei, and the total registered vote was more than doubled, with slightly more than half going to the polls. Two organized political parties took to the field, the "Progressives" and the "Labour" party. Of the nine councillors elected, six were Progressive, two were Labour, and one was Independent. Of these, three were Indians, three were Chinese, one was Eurasian, one was Ceylonese, and one was European.

The question arose at the time of the 1951 elections concerning the representativeness of the electorate. It was obvious that less than 2 per cent of the total population was participating in the elections, with the Indians, a minority group, dominating the electorate. A short study revealed that of the colony's near-million population, less than three hundred thousand were eligible to vote; the rest were underage or alien.

In 1953 a commission under the chairmanship of Sir George Rendel was appointed to review the constitution with special reference to the question of increasing the number of elected members, to the state of the electoral register, and to the relations between the colonial and municipal governments. The commission's report recommended a legislative assembly with twenty-five out of thirty-two members elected and a council of ministers composed of three British senior officials and six appointed Asian members drawn from the membership of the assembly, in place of the executive and legislative councils. Elected terms were to run for four years. The three chambers of commerce were to be excluded from special representation in the assembly. The report also proposed an automatic registration of eligible voters, recognizing the failure of voluntary registration.

On April 2, 1955, the new plan was put into effect, and elections were held for the twenty-five assembly posts. Automatic registration had created an electorate of 300,309 registered voters divided among the twenty-five electoral districts. Of these, 158,134 voted. Candidates from five parties with a small scattering of Independents contested for the twenty-five seats. The Labour Front scored an unexpected victory, capturing ten seats. The Progressives took four seats, the Peoples Action Party and the Alliance three seats each, and the Democrats two seats, with three seats going to Independents. Surprising, also, was the increased interest in the elections among the Chinese. Although there was little indication of voting along strictly communal lines, fifteen of the new members were Chinese, giving them a clear majority. Three Malays, three Europeans, two Eurasians, and two Indians also gained seats. Through the formation of a coalition the Labour Front party was able to assemble enough votes to entitle it to form the government, with the party leader chosen as chief minister to the colony.

The post of chief minister assumes most of the functions formerly exercised by the colonial secretary. A greater direction of government by the chief minister was ensured in the first legislature when the governor sought and accepted the advice of the new chief minister in naming members to the appointive seats. This tends to assure the party or coalition in power of a clear majority.

Local self-government

The passage of the Local Authorities Elections Ordinance in 1950 instituted a period of considerable change in the function and structure of local government in Malaya, although the consequence of this change has yet to be evaluated. A short review of local government as it operated prior to 1950 might, however, provide insight into the significance of the changes being made.

Municipalities. --Municipal committees had been formed at a fairly early date by the citizens of Penang, Singapore, and Malakka, functioning primarily as pressure groups attempting to ensure governmental response to the needs of the three cities. In Singapore a municipal commission having authority over certain public service functions was created in 1856. Similar commissions were instituted in Penang in 1888, somewhat later in Malakka, and in 1948 at Kuala Lumpur. Several other of the larger towns in the Federation are slated for municipal government in the near future.

Up to 1951 the municipal commissioners of Penang, Singapore, and Malakka were appointed by the governor. At least five were to be selected; the majority were rate-payers and nonofficials in the government. The president of the commission, however, was always an official. The president also, by virtue of his position, was the chief administrative officer of the municipality and thus the most powerful individual in the local administration. His activities, however, were held in check by the control of the commission over finances and by the weight of public opinion; he was answerable both to the commission and to the high commissioner or governor.

The general functions of the municipal government included the provision of public services such as sanitation and welfare, recreational facilities, construction and maintenance of roads, town planning and zoning, street lighting, fire protection services, licensing, water supply, and, in Penang, electricity and public transport. Noticeably, the municipalities do not maintain their own police services, handle education on the primary and secondary levels, or maintain public libraries, museums, or art galleries. These are handled by the central government.

The work of the commissions is handled in committee. The regular meetings of the commissions are rarely deliberative, the principal business being to pass on the decisions already approved in committees.

Under the control of the commissions and directly under the authority of the president of the commission are the various departments, each headed by a chief and usually a deputy chief, the first functioning primarily as a planning officer, the latter as the operations officer.

The municipalities are expected to be self-sufficient financially, although their budgets are subject to the scrutiny of the

452

central government. Largely because of this self-financing feature the municipalities have been able to claim and gain a major degree of autonomy. Seldom does the central government interfere in municipal affairs. The municipalities recruit their own departmental staffs individually and set their own taxation rates.

The primary changes which have appeared under the local authorities regulation are not so much in the functions and operations of the municipalities as in the composition of the municipal councils, successors to the commissions. In Penang in 1948 the commission was composed of two official and ten unofficial members, all appointed. Under the regulations six of fifteen members are appointed and nine elected. In Singapore eighteen of the twenty-seven members are elected. In Malakka nine of thirteen members are elected, and in Kuala Lumpur twelve of eighteen are elected. In Kuala Lumpur, it should be noted, the appointees are responsible to the Sultan of Selangor rather than to the high commissioner. In all four municipalities the president of the council continues to be an official.

Rural boards. --Those areas in the former Straits Settlements and the Crown Colony not under the authority of the municipalities of Penang, Malakka, or Singapore are administered by rural boards. In 1955, there was one board each on Penang Island, in Province Wellesley, in Malakka, and on Singapore island. The rural boards are the creation of the governor or high commissioner in council and are recognized as corporate bodies and distinct legal entities. All members are appointed. The chairman of each board is an official who exercises the executive powers of the board. Although the rural boards are empowered to collect revenues, their finances are under the control of the central government, which takes all surpluses and reimburses any deficits. The various departments under the rural boards are staffed from the central government.

In early 1954 the Singapore Constitutional Commission recommended that the two local authorities, the city council and the rural board of Singapore, should be reconstituted as a single island-wide local authority; in 1955 they were combined into a City and Island Council. A similar move has been made in the Federation regarding the relationships between the rural boards and the municipalities. The Municipal Amendment Ordinance of 1954 provides for the establishment of "a complete system of local government within the rural areas, which, while providing for local administration on a democratic basis, would remain within the general scope of the Municipal Ordinance and would be fully integrated with the existing rural Boards. . . ."[6] There appear to be no present or contemplated changes for the rural board structures under the local authorities regulations.

Town boards and councils. --Town boards exist only in the states and are organs of the state governments specially created to deal with local affairs. Members are appointed by the rulers in council and all activities are undertaken in the name of the state governments. Membership is composed of both officials and nonofficials, the former often in the majority. The usual effect is to place the nonofficials in the role of advisers and organs of public opinion rather than of participating members in government. To an even greater extent than in the municipalities and the rural boards, the chairman of the town board dominates the local government. As an organ of the state government the town board is dependent upon it for revenues and personnel. In general the functions of the town boards are similar to those of the municipalities.

Perhaps the unique factor in the town boards is their ability to reach out from the towns in which they are based and assume jurisdiction over villages elsewhere in the state, over road strips, and over such features as lakes, dams, airports, and so forth. The result has been that most town boards have extended their jurisdiction over large sections of the districts in which they are located, and a list of the town boards is virtually coterminous with a list of districts. Large scattered areas of each district, however, may not be under the jurisdiction of the town board but left rather to the jurisdiction of the district officer and the penghulus, although surrounded by town board areas.

In a move to establish democratic self-government, Johore in 1952 superseded the town boards of Johore Bahru, Muar, and Batu Pahat with town councils, each with a majority of elected members. This early move has been followed in most other states, and by the end of 1954 the number of elected town councils had increased to twenty-two. At the same time

---

6. Federation of Malaya, Annual Report, 1954 (Kuala Lumpur: Government Press, 1955), p. 449.

there has been a strong move to increase the financial autonomy of the town boards and town councils. An amendment to the Town Boards Ordinance in 1954 gave powers to the state governments to confer such autonomy.

Local councils. --The Local Councils Ordinance of 1952 provided for the establishment of local councils in the more advanced rural areas and the "New Villages." At the end of 1954, 210 local councils had been established and 92 more were scheduled for establishment in 1955. All of the "New Villages" have local councils. The membership of the local councils is predominantly elective.

Other forms of local self-government. --In addition to the above, there exist a number of special boards with jurisdiction over special areas or functions. Such boards are the Harbour Board of Singapore, drainage boards on the coastal areas, special licensing boards, and the Singapore Improvement Trust. Membership on these boards is usually appointive, although nominations may sometimes be made by public groups concerned with the functions of the particular board.

Political Parties and Elections

Active political partisanship and representative government are relatively new, primarily postwar phenomena in Malaya, although their development has been in part gradual. The present emphasis on democratic development stems from a number of factors: (1) the early stimulus of Western political theories carried to the country by missionaries and students returning from other lands; (2) the impetus provided by the Japanese during their occupation of Malaya in the formation of elective and representative local bodies; (3) the examples of independence and anticolonial nationalism by such neighboring states as Burma, India, and Indonesia, and finally, (4) the pronounced reaction of the Malay people to the union proposals and the growing realization by the British that the status quo ante bellum in Malaya was never to return.

The development of political parties and organizations

Active political organization among the peoples of Malaya developed in three stages: (1) the formation of a number of small, weak, "intellectual" political groups before 1941; (2) the creation of large pro- and anti-Japanese organizations supported by substantial numbers of the Malay, Indian, and

Chinese communities during the period from 1941 to 1945; and (3) the organization of representative parties after 1945 espousing special platforms and appealing to various segments of the population for support of their political ambitions.

The early period. --Two contradictory tendencies came to dominate and divide the early political groups in Malaya, as they did elsewhere in Southeast Asia: (1) the policy of rejecting the West by a resolute reversion to pre-Western values and practices; and (2) the attempt to compete with the West through the adoption and incorporation of Western standards and techniques into the indigenous culture.

Particularly was this division apparent among the Malays, who developed two distinct political groups: the conservatives (Kaum Tua), and the modernists (Kaum Muda). Early partisanship of a quasipolitical character was expressed primarily in pan-Islamic movements. These arose in the Islamic world, under the leadership of Egypt and Turkey, largely as a reaction to Western dominance. Before 1922 the pan-Islamic movement in Malaya was under the control of the orthodox and conservative groups centered in the religious seminaries of Perak and Kelantan. Moslem clubs sprang up, a strenuous attempt was made to eradicate English words from the Malay vocabulary through the introduction of Egyptian and Arabic synonyms, while even the traditional role of the sultans was subverted for allegiance to an anticipated universal Islamic Federation. To a considerable extent the pan-Islamic movement was supported by the British as less dangerous to them than nationalism or Pan-Malayism. Pan-Islam received a serious blow, however, in 1922 as a consequence of the revolution and modernization program in Turkey. The abolition of the caliphate removed the political bias from the movement, while British support gradually won over the orthodox Moslems.

A further consequence of the new situation in Turkey was the rapid rise of modernism, largely in imitation of Turkey, chiefly among the younger, English-educated men in the towns. The Kaum Muda, a party of about one hundred young Malays from the growing middle class, advocated progress along Western lines through democracy and the seizure of new economic and cultural opportunities. Increasing liberalism among the Malays also was expressed through the Anjaman-i-Islam and the Ahmadiya movements under the leadership of Sir Syed Amier Ali and Mira Ghulam Ahmed and supported largely by the Western-educated and urban Moslems. Nationalism does not seem

456

to have appeared much before 1920, but during the decade of the twenties a number of Malay associations were formed, among them the Malay Association for the Advancement of Learning, the aims of which were largely educational but which possessed a nationalistic bias, and the Malay Union movement, centered on Singapore, which aimed at organizing all Malays for the preservation of their rights and their political economic advancement. By 1941 the influence of the modernist movements in Malay political thought was marked, although the conservative elements remained active and enjoyed the support of the Malay masses and their tradition-bound leaders who felt threatened by the modernist movements.

Political organization in the early period among the Chinese also reveals both traditionalist and modernist tendencies, although in markedly different ways than those among the Malays. Traditionalist organizations were of two types: (1) the secret societies, characterized by political terrorism largely within the Chinese community, and (2) the community associations, such as the Hokkienese Association, and certain special-interest groups of Chinese, such as the Chinese chambers of commerce, traditional Chinese craft guilds, and so forth. The secret societies had been active politically in several of the states, particularly in Perak and Selangor, before British intervention. Their particularly ruthless activities were viewed as a threat to political stability by the British who have persistently attempted to quash them, but with only limited success. The community associations and special-interest groups generally have restrained their political activities, although purposefully applying pressure upon the governments in pursuit of their interests. It was owing largely to their activities that the Chinese were given special representation in the Colony and Federated States legislative bodies.

The modernist trend is seen in the growth of two revolutionary movements among the Malayan Chinese: the Kuomintang and the Communist Party of Malaya. Malaya was an early center of outside support for the Nationalist revolution in China. Under the urgings of Sun, Yat-sen a strong branch of the Kuomintang was established, particularly among the Cantonese on Penang. The primary aim of the Malayan Kuomintang was to maintain among the Chinese an intense interest in the revolutionary movement in China, focus their primary allegiance on the southern Chinese movement, and support Chinese independence and nationalism with funds and personnel. To a considerable extent the Kuomintang in Malaya, as in China, was closely associated with some of the antidynastic secret societies. Both the British and the Malays tended to view with distrust growing Chinese nationalism within Malaya, which threatened to orient the allegiance of the majority Chinese population toward a political entity other than Malaya. The Kuomintang was declared illegal by the government until 1930, when it was allowed to function only under strict governmental supervision and control.

The chief rival of the Kuomintang became the Malayan Communist Party (MCP). Communism in Malaya received a relatively late start in comparison with other Asian countries, primarily because of three factors: (1) the relative absence of social and economic conditions which made communism seem attractive; (2) the failure of the British Communist Party, which had been charged with the responsibility of organizing the British colonial areas, to extend their activities to Malaya; and (3) the tendency of the Comintern to emphasize activity in the more industrialized countries of Europe. The first organizational work in Malaya appears to have been attempted in 1924. The following year a special representative from the Chinese Communist Party was sent to Malaya to effect a liaison with resident Chinese and Indonesian revolutionaries. At the same time, because of the Nationalist-Communist accord reached in China, a number of Communist agents were able to infiltrate the Kuomintang organization in Malaya. Communist power within the Kuomintang grew considerably in the years before 1927, when the break between the radical elements of the Kuomintang in China and the conservative faction led by Chiang, Kai-shek led to a similar break in the Malayan organization. The Communist-infiltrated Malayan revolutionary committee broke away from the overseas branch headquarters of the Kuomintang, thus instituting a bitter rivalry between the two groups. Communist activities centered particularly within two of the Chinese communities: the Hailams from the island of Hainan, who were looked down upon by the other Chinese communities, and the Hakkas, who also were viewed as a group apart from the other Chinese. Local Communist leadership has continually drawn heavily upon these two communities.

The break with the Kuomintang temporarily weakened the strength of the Communists in Malaya, and in 1928 the Comintern dispatched several agents to Singapore to organize the region-wide Nan-yang Communist Party, uniting Chinese Communist elements in Malaya, Burma, Indochina, and Thailand. Several special organizations also were formed by the Communists as adjuncts to the central party, such as a Communist youth league in 1926 and a Nan-yang Federation of Labor in the same year.

In 1930 the Nan-yang Communist Party was dissolved, to be replaced in Malaya by the Malayan Communist Party. The move appears to have been based largely upon Comintern distrust of the overemphasis on organization among the Chinese (at this time the Soviet Union had withdrawn virtually all support from the remnants of the Communist movement in China) and the lack of organization among the other ethnic groups. At the same time the Nan-yang Federation of Labor was renamed the Malayan Federation of Labor, with a new emphasis on the organization of Malay workers. Shortly thereafter, however, the entire Communist organization in Malaya was badly shaken by a series of wholesale arrests and deportations of Communists by the British authorities in Malaya and by a similar series of blows in other Southeast Asian countries.

The party was not completely killed, however, and during the 1930's a series of events served to revive and actually encourage its growth in Malaya. These were: (1) the effects of the worldwide economic depression which led many of the unemployed and destitute to lend support to any organization which could promise them relief and hope for the future; (2) the change in Communist policy from militant revolution to popular front tactics in which attention was focused on such issues as anti-imperialism, which could attract groups otherwise hostile or indifferent to Communist aspirations; (3) the Japanese attacks on China and the reinstitution of cooperation between the Communists and Nationalists in China, which led many Malayan Chinese to adopt a friendlier attitude toward the Communists in view of danger from a common enemy; and (4) the growing preoccupation of the British with the danger from Germany in Europe. Communist activity during the 30's was characterized by a series of riotous labor strikes, anti-Japanese movements, and, between 1939 and 1941, by an anti-British campaign which was suddenly reversed after the German attack on Russia. The Communists had succeeded once more in infiltrating the Kuomintang in Malaya and weakening it from within, so that with the launching of the Japanese invasion in 1941, the Communist Party was virtually the only well-organized resistance group in the country.

Before 1936 the Malayan Indians had no strong political organizations similar to those of the Chinese. In that year the Central Indian Association of Malaya was formed under the leadership of N. Raghavan and C. S. Goho. The association became the champion of better labor conditions, education, and political privileges for Malayan Indians. Although for a time it succeeded in awakening an interest in politics among the Indians, its involvement with congress politics in India and with the Malayan Communist Party in labor strikes served to divide the local-born from the immigrant Indians and to antag- onize the employers of Indians. The association also aroused the opposition of the government, and it did not survive the Jap- anese invasion.

The Japanese period. --The Japanese occupation of Malaya affected political organization among the three major ethnic groups in markedly different ways. The Japanese encouraged pan-Malay nationalism among the Malays and anti-British and Indian independence movements among the Malayan Indians; the Chinese communities became more actively united in op- position to the Japanese.

Political activity among the Malays was dormant throughout the period of the Japanese occupation except for the formation of a few anti-Japanese guerilla groups, such as the Malay wataniah in Penang. In general, the Malays tended to be co- operative with, or at least obedient toward, Japanese rule. Nor do the Japanese appear to have made any effort to form polit- ical organizations among the Malays. Malaya, in Japanese pol- icy, was not slated to become one of the "free" Asian nations. Rather, British policies were adopted, and Malaya was given the role of a Japanese protectorate. A temporary attempt to arouse an active pan-Malay attitude among the people by bring- ing Malaya and Sumatra under a unified administration was not successful. Japanese propaganda in the schools tended to emphasize the "Asia for the Asians" line in an attempt to a- rouse Malay support for Japanese activities, but there ap- pears to have been no overt attempt to create a pro-Japanese supporting organization.

The situation was quite different among the Malayan Indians. India was still in British hands, and the Japanese felt the nec- essity for the creation of a fifth column in Southeast Asia, which could aid in the eventual overthrow of the British in south Asia. Immediately after the fall of Singapore in 1942 the Japanese began to organize a movement among the Southeast

Asian Indians aimed at eventual Indian independence. Raghavan and Goho, the leaders of the defunct Central Indian Association of Malaya were chosen to organize and lead the new Indian Independence Leagues in Malaya (IIL). Various difficulties hindered the growth of the movement, however, until the arrival in July, 1943, of S. Chandra Bose. Bose was named commander of the Indian National Army and head of the provisional government of Azad Hind, which, though an autonomous government in nationalist Indian eyes, was largely the creation of the Japanese. By June, 1945, there were nine IIL branches in Malaya, with headquarters at Singapore. Recruits for the Indian National Army came primarily from the ranks of unemployed estate workers, but support for the movement stemmed from all classes of Indians, partly from national loyalties, partly from fear of retaliation if support were not forthcoming. Others like the Sikhs, employed almost entirely as policemen by the British, found it much to their personal advantage to shift their allegiance to the Japanese. Support for the Japanese was not wholehearted, however, as evidenced by the recognition of such IIL leaders as Goho and K. P. K. Menon that Japanese support for Indian independence was not wholly altruistic. A few Indians joined anti-Japanese guerrilla forces in Malaya, while others were imprisoned in camps as recalcitrants. During the final stages of the war, as Japanese reverses were compounded, relations between the Indians and the Japanese became progressively strained. Following the return of the British in 1945 a relatively mild policy was taken toward the Indian adherents of the Azad Hind. A few of the leaders were tried and later released. The consequences of the movement were to live on, however, in a new political consciousness among the Indians, even though it tended to be oriented toward India rather than Malaya.

Following the German attack on Russia, the Malayan Communist Party changed its policy to one of cooperation with the British, who were then allies of the Soviet Union. With the Japanese attack on Malaya in 1941, the party immediately sided with the Malayan government, and cooperation with government forces was offered. London, after some deliberation, accepted the offers of both the Communists and the Kuomintang. A Chinese mobilization committee was formed to recruit a militia. The Communists proceeded to organize their own guerrilla forces in anticipation of the British defeat. A training school for guerrilla activities was instituted with some British aid.

461

With the fall of Singapore in February, 1942, the Communist organization went underground. Four classes were graduated from the guerrilla training school before Singapore's fall and sent into operation in the field. In March, 1942, these forces were officially designated as the Malayan People's Anti-Japanese Army, while the civilian supporters of the MPAJA were organized as the Malayan People's Anti-Japanese Union. Both were almost entirely Chinese and under the control of the Malayan Communist Party. The Japanese invasion, in effect, united the Chinese (and some minor segments of the Malay and Indian communities) in common opposition to the Japanese under the leadership of the Malayan Communist Party and provided the MCP with the opportunity to organize a broad base of popular support for its activities and to recruit, train, and indoctrinate an armed force for use not only against the Japanese, but after the end of the war, against the British.

Japanese policy toward the Chinese in Malaya was somewhat confused. Ruthless attempts to suppress Chinese support of the MPAJA by intimidation, mass evacuation, and imprisonment were made, but their success was slight. At times the Japanese also attempted to woo the Chinese by appealing to their dislike of the Malays and the Indians as well as the British, again with little success.

As a consequence the MPAJA became the most powerful political-military agency in Malaya, especially during the final part of the war. Whereas the Japanese controlled the routes of communications and the major urban areas, the MPAJA controlled all the rural areas at night and many of them during the day as well. The parallel to the situation in China during the war, especially in North China, is conspicuous. There, too, the network of Japanese control overlay a countryside only occasionally under Japanese domination.

The postwar period.--Political organization in Malaya was dominated by two tendencies in the postwar period: (1) the formation of essentially communal parties, and (2) the growth of alliances among the parties due to the inability of any one of the communal parties to gain political power by itself. Characteristic differences also appear between political organizational activity before mid-1948 and the outlawing of the Malayan Communist Party and its affiliated organizations, and activity after that date, with the institution of representative and elective government.

The Malayan Communist Party emerged from World War II

as the dominant political organization in the country. Intent upon preserving the organization which it had created during the war, the Communist leadership immediately began the conversion of the Malayan People's Anti-Japanese Union into a People's Democratic Movement, and members of the disbanded Malayan People's Anti-Japanese Army were organized as the MPAJA Ex-Service Comrades Association, which functioned under close Communist supervision. Among the Chinese the MCP and the New Democratic Youth Corps replaced the formerly strong Kuomintang and the San Min Chu I Youth Corps. Affiliated with the MCP was a small Indian Communist Party formed in 1945 in Singapore. This latter organization, strangely, appears to have maintained closer ties with the Chinese Communist Party, through the MCP, than with the Communist Party of India, thus further indicating the central role of the Chinese in Communist affairs in the country. MCP tactics before 1948, in line with the Communist world strategy, stressed cooperation with and infiltration of other organizations. Particular emphasis was placed on union organization. In late 1945 the General Labor Union was organized, and by February of the following year it had come to dominate the entire trade union movement in Malaya. Governmental resistance to a general strike in February, 1946, and the reinstitution of the Trade Union Enactment of 1940, requiring that all union officers have a previous record of actual work in the trade represented by their union, resulted in the reorganization of the GLU into the Pan-Malayan Federation of Trade Unions (PMFTU). This organization claimed to represent some 463,000 workers and was affiliated with the Communist-led World Federation of Trade Unions. By mid-1948 the PMFTU controlled some 214 out of a total of 277 registered unions in Malaya, including the key tin, rubber, and longshoreman's unions.

Close contact was also maintained by the MCP with the many other political parties and organizations which were founded before 1948. One of the first of these appears to have been the Malay Nationalist Party, founded by a Dr. Barhanuddin at Ipoh in late 1945. Though nominally Malay, the MNP appears to have been primarily dominated by resident Indonesians intent upon gaining Malay support for some sort of pan-Malayan independence movement. Although it remained active for some time, the conservative Malays failed to rally to it. Its platform was noticeably similar to the eight-point program of the Communists at the time: (1) establishment of a government representative of all nationalities, the improvement of living conditions, and the development of industry, agriculture and commerce; (2) granting of free speech, association, and so forth; (3) increased wages and abolishment of high taxation and interest rates; (4) establishment of a national defense army; (5) establishment of free education in several major languages; (6) restoration of property confiscated by the Japanese; (7) acquisition of tariff autonomy; and (8) aid in freeing the oppressed people of the East. This program appears designed particularly to integrate the Communist movement with the nationalist movements of the day.

In December, 1945, the Malayan Democratic Union movement was formed by two Eurasian lawyers, Philip Hoalim and John Eber, with the support of Chinese of the professional class. Its principal aim was the uniting of the non-Malay communities in a program for racial equality and self-government for Malaya within the British Commonwealth. Significantly, several members of the MCP participated in its inauguration, although its platform certainly had little to attract Communist sympathy. The primary attraction for the Communist appears rather to have been the antigovernment bias of the movement.

Several communal Indian parties were formed shortly after the war, among which were the Malayan Indian Association, the Ceylon Tamil Association, and the Pan-Malayan Muslim Indian League. The latter was primarily a self-protection organization oriented toward Pakistan and formed in the wake of Indian-Pakistan disturbances. The most important of the Indian groups, however, was organized in August, 1946, by John Thivy. As the Malayan Indian Congress, it self-consciously patterned itself after the Congress Party of India, and most of its membership was drawn from the ranks of the former Indian Independence Leagues.

The Malayan Union proposals sparked the formation of a number of small parties among the Malays, such as the Perak League, most of which united in March, 1946, in the United Malay National Organization under the leadership of Dato Onn bin Jaafar, founder of the Malay Peninsula Movement in Johore. The aims of the UMNO were the defeat of the union proposals and the political, social, and economic progress of the Malays toward self-government. Support for UMNO came primarily from the Malay aristocracy and bureaucratic and intellectual circles. By November, 1946, the clamor aroused by the UMNO had caused the British to withdraw certain of the union proposals, particularly those regarding citizenship and the rights of the Malay rulers. This apparent victory of the UMNO aroused the fears of large segments of the non-Malay population who viewed the UMNO platform as a move to disenfranchise them and place all power in Malay hands.

Under the leadership of the Malayan Democratic Union, headed by Hoalim and Eber, a federation of all parties and organizations opposed to the UMNO was organized. Named the All-Malayan Council of Joint Action, it included the MDU, the Malay Nationalist Party, the Malayan Indian Congress, the Pan-Malayan Federation of Trade Unions, the MPAJA Ex-Service Comrades Association, the Malayan New Democratic Youth Corps, Angkatan Wanita Sedara (Women's Party), Angkatan Permuda Insaf (Youth Party), the Ceylon Tamil Association, and the Malay Students' Union, among others. This unwieldly coalition of groups with widely disparate objectives was based only on common opposition to the UMNO. A compromise platform was finally agreed upon which aimed at ensuring the political status of the non-Malays while appeasing the Malays. It included (1) the unification of Singapore and the Federation; (2) a fully elected and representative legislature; (3) equal political rights for all who regarded Malaya as their home; (4) assumption by the Malay sultans of the position of fully sovereign and constitutional rulers; (5) Malay control of matters concerning Malay custom and Moslem affairs; and (6) encouragement of the advancement of the Malay community. The last three points were to be the price for Malay concurrence on the first three.

The divergent views of the various groups comprising the AMCJA, however, soon led to its partial fragmentation. The Malay Nationalist Party bolted the coalition with Angkatan Permuda Insaf to form the Malay Council of Joint Action. One Malay objection to the AMCJA was its predominant Chinese membership through both the MDU and the Communist-affiliated groups. Later the other Malay groups affiliated with the AMCJA joined the Malay Council of Joint Action, which was renamed Pusat Tenaga Ra'ayat (People's United Front), popularly called PUTERA. To the six points of the AMCJA platform, PUTERA added a demand that Malay become the official language of the country and that the British relinquish at least part of the conduct of foreign affairs. AMCJA and PUTERA continued to cooperate, especially after the announcement that the union proposals had been scrapped. AMCJA represented essentially the Chinese view, while the PUTERA represented the anti-UMNO Malay view. The bulk of the AMCJA's popular support came from the Indian and Chinese trade unions, which were largely Communist-affiliated, while PUTERA apparently stayed clear of any Communist associations. Between May and August of 1947 AMCJA and PUTERA cooperated in drawing up a draft constitution for the Federation, of which Purcell notes, " . . . [It] will prove to have had a great influence, for most parties since have drawn heavily upon it. "[7]

For the Malayan Indian Congress, participation in the AMCJA had rather severe consequences in that a considerable part of its following was alienated, both because of the affiliation with Communist organizations and because of the feeling of many Indians that Indian interests were being subverted by Chinese dominance in the AMCJA.

Non-Malay dissatisfaction with the terms of the new federal constitution, particularly the citizenship and immigration provisions, brought the AMCJA back into the field in 1947, without the PUTERA faction, at the head of a joint Chinese-Indian effort to protest the new constitution through a boycott of the impending Singapore elections and nonparticipation in the new federal legislative council. In Singapore the AMCJA was abetted by a largely Chinese group headed by Tan, Cheng-lock, and called the Pan-Malayan Council for Joint Action. The Chinese share in the boycott was relatively successful, with the result that only some twenty thousand of the one hundred thousand to two hundred thousand eligible voters went to the polls, and only one Chinese was elected. The Indians were much less successful. In the end nearly half the votes cast in the Singapore election were Indian, and three Indians were elected.

In early 1948 Communist policy in Malaya made an abrupt change, possibly as a direct result of the failure of the AMCJA to prevent inauguration of the new federal scheme and also reflecting increasing disaffection among the Chinese supporters of the party, particularly among the unions. More generally, however, the change appears concomitant with an over-all change in world Communist strategy. The first signs of the change were an increase in terrorism. Counter-measures by

7. Victor Purcell, Malaya: Communist or Free? (London: Victor Gollancz, Ltd., 1954, p. 60.

the government led in June, 1948, to full-scale guerrilla warfare--the Emergency had begun.

Immediately, the MCP went underground. Communist influence in the labor unions collapsed, and the Communist leadership absconded with union funds. The number of unions shrank from 399 to 162. The Communist supporting organization, the People's Democratic Movement, was reorganized as the Min Yuen and was assigned the task of furnishing the guerrilla units with supplies, intelligence, and recruits, carrying on propaganda activities and general liaison with the "masses," and generally assisting the guerrilla forces through sabotage, strikes, agitation, and espionage.

The outbreak of the Emergency played havoc with the remnants of the AMCJA. The PUTERA faction carefully avoided any further connection with it. Such Communist-affiliated organizations as the MPAJA Ex-Service Comrades Association, the New Democratic Youth League, and the Pan-Malayan Federation of Trade Unions were declared illegal and went underground. The Malayan Democratic Union decided to dissolve itself "in the present political situation and curtailment of civil rights," and one of its leaders, Eber, was imprisoned and later exiled to Great Britain. The Malayan Indian Congress, sole surviving member of the AMCJA, announced a voluntary suspension of all political activity until the end of the Emergency, although it was to return to the political arena in the following year.

The collapse of the AMCJA coalition hit the Chinese community particularly hard, leaving it without any effective political leadership or organization. Between June, 1948, and February, 1949, the only active political organization in the Federation was the UMNO, although a few smaller local Malay parties continued to exist. This collapse of the political leadership of the non-Malay communities left an unfortunate vacuum. There was no longer any organized structure for negotiation or arbitration among the various communities. Even UMNO became almost impotent in its inability to deal directly with some counterpart organization among the other communities in the furtherance of common objectives. To counter this vacuum the Communities Liaison Committee was formed, headed by Dato Onn, E. E. C. Thursisingham, and Dato Syed Kadir. As an informal body the committee attempted to define areas of common agreement among the various communities and to achieve action on its objectives through appeal to pub-

467

lic opinion. The primary success of the committee, perhaps, lay in its clarification of a number of points of tension which formerly had divided the various communities. Its work was important in the formation of the intercommunity cooperation leading to the later successes of the UMNO-MCA Alliance and of the "Merdeka" mission to London.

Before the Singapore elections of March, 1948, there were no political parties in Malaya in the modern sense of the term. The organizations which have been noted were principally lobbying groups using pressure and propaganda in efforts to influence government policy. Since they had no official representation in government, their platforms were statements of a group desire, rather than actual outlines for administrative policy. Since there were no elections, they could sponsor no candidates, nor were they able to place effective control over any of their members who might be appointed to office, since the organizations had little influence on the mechanics of the legislature.

Coincidentally, the introduction of the elective processes in Malaya occurred just at the demise of most of the early postwar organizations, thus paving the way for the creation of political organizations capable of operating under the new system and functioning as true parties. Before this time it was not necessary to distinguish between organizations in the Federation and in Singapore, since all such organizations had an all-Malay basis. But with the establishment of separate electoral systems within which the parties must operate, political development in each of the political units took sharply divergent turns.

Singapore. --Two political groups appeared on the ballots in the 1948 Singapore election for seats on the legislative council, neither of which could be called a party. Candidates offered themselves for election under the labels "Independent" and "Progressive." Neither group appears to have been well organized, and the political differences between them were minimal. Both campaigned for an elected majority on the legislative council, more government and municipal appointments for local aplicants, more social services, and union with the Federation.

The success of the Progressives in the 1949 election apparently encouraged the creation of a more formal organization. By the time of the Singapore municipal election in December, 1949, the Progressive party was beginning to appear as a well-functioning machine. Adopting a policy of conservative moderation and gradual progress toward independent self-

government, it captured the majority of seats in the municipal council.

The Independent candidates in both the legislative council
and the municipal elections apparently never found sufficient
common ground for the formation of a party. Thus the Progressives were unopposed by any other political organization
until the legislative council elections in April, 1951, when a
Labor party was formed. The Labor party was patterned
largely after the Labor party of Great Britain, basing its platform on social and economic welfare reforms, immediate
self-rule and union with the Federation. In the 1951 elections
the Progressives won six of the nine contested seats, the Labor
party two, and the Independents one.

The slight participation of the electorate in the 1951 elections led to a review of the entire system of representative
government in the Colony and the recommendation of a primarily elected legislature (twenty-five out of thirty-two seats).
The election was set for April, 1955. It was apparent that under
the new scheme one or another of the political parties could,
by gaining a majority representation in the legislature, take
over the government. This realization splintered the Labor
party and brought forth four new parties. An internal struggle
for power among the leadership of the Labor party caused its
disruption. One splinter group joined with the newly formed
Singapore Socialist Party in August, 1954, to form the Labor
Front, which was more a coalition than a party. The platform
of the Labor Front aimed at immediate independence, the creation of a socialist state and repeal of the Emergency regulations.

Even further to the left was the People's Action party (PAP),
formed in November, 1954, largely through the initiative of
Lee, Kuan Yew, a Chinese lawyer. Most of the support of the
PAP came from the Chinese trade unions and, according to its
detractors, from the Malayan Communist Party.

The parties of the right in the 1955 elections included the old
Progressive party, under the leadership of C. C. Tan, which
pursued its usual conservative course of moderation and gradual development. According to pre-election estimates the Progressive party was scheduled to win easily. The issue of multilingualism brought the second right-wing party into existence,
the Democrats. Made up of wealthy bankers and merchants of
the Chinese chamber of commerce, the sole objective of the
party was to gain admission of Chinese as one of the official

languages in the legislature. A third rightist party developed with the entrance of the UMNO-MCA Alliance into Singapore politics. [8] The small Singapore Malay Union was brought into the Alliance after it had sought support from both the Progressives and the Labor Front. The primary objectives of the Alliance were a fully elected legislature, multilingualism, and amendment of the Emergency regulations and the Trade Union Ordinance.

In the elections the Labor Front scored a surprising victory, winning ten of the twenty-five contested seats. The Progressives took only four seats, the PAP and the Alliance three each, and the Democrats two seats, with three seats going to Independents. According to Carnell, the unexpected results of the election were due to two factors: (1) the alluring and extravagant promises made by the parties of the left (in the expectation that they would probably lose and would not have to be responsible for their fulfillment); and (2) the splitting of the right-wing vote between the Democrats and the Progressives.[9]

David Marshall, a Singapore lawyer, emerged as the leader of the Labor Front and Chief Minister of the Singapore government. In order to form a government, however, Marshall was forced to seek a coalition with one of the other parties. [10]

Marshall rejected a coalition with the more extremist PAP and turned to the Alliance, a move which immediately brought the PAP out as the leading opposition. This situation has also led to a quandary among the other right-wing parties, who hesitated to join the PAP as a general opposition, yet were opposed to the policies of the government. As a result the legislature was divided into three sections: (1) the govern-

---

8. For an explanation of the MCA (Malayan Chinese Association), see below.

9. Francis G. Carnell, "Political Ferment in Singapore," Far Eastern Survey, July, 1955, p. 99.

10. Control of eighteen of the thirty-two seats is necessary to form a government. Marshall could count on his own party's ten seats, plus the votes of the three senior British officials, who must vote with the government. If the governor allowed Marshall to name two of the other appointive members, then with personal control of only fifteen votes, he still would need at least threee more.

ment coalition, supported by one of the three Independents; (2) the right-wing opposition of the Progressives and one of the Democrats; and (3) the left-wing opposition of the PAP supported by the other Democrat. The remaining two Independents were uncommitted. At the same time the Labor Front was sundered by internal disagreement concerning the speed of governmental reorganization. One faction insisted that the government live up to its campaign promises immediately. The other, led by Marshall, took the more realistic view that reorganization must follow careful planning. The position of the Labor Front was complicated further by the continued hold of the Progressive party on the Singapore municipal council. Partisan differences were expressed in several severe clashes between the two bodies over jurisdictional matters.

The relatively weak showing made by both right-wing parties in the election led, in February, 1956, to the formation of the Liberal Socialist party composed primarily of members of the former Progressive and Democratic parties. The new party controls eight seats in the Legislature, placing it second behind the Labor Front. The platform of the new party is primarily a synthesis of the nearly identical platforms of the old parties and no new emphasis is apparent.

Another significant series of party developments has been the tendency for Federation parties to expand to the Colony and vice versa. Most significant is the avowed drive of the MCA to expand its Singapore membership to four hundred thousand by 1958. It is interesting that no mention is made of strengthening the Alliance, but only the Chinese section of the Alliance. This suggests an intentional attempt of the MCA to build up its strength in Singapore as a counter to the overwhelming hegemony of the UMNO in the Federation. The Pan-Malayan Labor Party, too, seems to be looking toward the Colony as a fresh source of support. In the other direction, the PAP has become increasingly active among the labor unions in Johore, possibly presaging an expansion of its political activities into the Federation. All three of these moves, along with the earlier entrance of the Alliance into Singapore politics, seem to point to an increasing awareness of the eventual union of the Colony and the Federation and the present need for their development of concurrent and cooperative policies.

Perhaps the most noteworthy characteristic of Singapore politics is its comparative lack of communal bias. Only the old Democratic party was overtly communal in nature, although the growth of the MCA and its possible split from the Alliance in Singapore may lead to a new communal political alignment. The other parties, although dominated by Chinese, express no communal sympathies and hold their memberships open to individuals from all races.

The Federation. --The demise of the All-Malayan Council for Joint Action left the UMNO in sole command of the political field in the Federation, while leaving the Chinese community without any organized political representation. The Malayan Indian Congress lay temporarily dormant.

The first move to fill the void among the Chinese was taken in September, 1948, by Tan, Cheng-lock, who contemplated the formation of a Malayan Chinese League. Out of this plan came the Malayan Chinese Association (MCA) in February, 1949. The original aims of the MCA were both political and eleemosynary, seeking political equality for the Chinese, while carrying on welfare activities for displaced persons. A basic part of MCA policy under Tan was the growth of political cooperation with the Malays.

Recognizing the need for intercommunal unity if the common objectives of independence and self-rule were to be obtained, Dato Onn in September, 1951, resigned as head of UMNO and founded the Independence of Malaya Party. The new party appeared at the outset to have strong backing from a number of other groups for its aim of uniting the various communities for a common cause. A promise of support was secured from Tan, Cheng-lock and from P. P. Narayanan, president of the Malayan Trade Union Council, while Onn himself insisted that while the UMNO must remain a communal party, it must also cooperate with the other communities in winning independence, with the IMP as the common rallying ground. Onn's platform for the IMP included a united Malaya, with the powers of the sultans drastically reduced, a common citizenship, and the admission of Chinese and Indians into the administrative service.

Onn had not counted upon the resistance of the conservative leadership of the UMNO, which, under his successor as head of the organization, Tengku Abdul Rahman, denounced the IMP as a destructive move. The failure of the UMNO to support Onn appears to have led also to the disaffection of Tan, Cheng-lock who, realizing that the Malays were failing to support IMP, turned instead to the conservative leadership of the UMNO for an alliance.

Dissension threatened all three groups temporarily. A minority pro-IMP faction of the UMNO threatened to bolt the party. Misgivings among the Chinese over the new alliance impaired its power for a short while. Dato Onn and the IMP, weakened by the lack of adequate Malay and Chinese support, came to lean more and more upon the revived Malayan Indian Congress and the Indian trade unions for support.

The first contest of strength among the new groups came with the municipal election in Kuala Lumpur in February, 1952. Through an astute scheme of gerrymandering, the UMNO-MCA Alliance made certain that both Chinese and Malays would be elected from their respectively strong electoral districts and that competitive candidates would not be entered by both parties in any one district. Therefore, the IMP in each district faced either an UMNO or a MCA candidate, but not both, while UMNO-controlled votes in a strongly Chinese district were thrown behind the MCA candidate, and vice versa. Of the twelve seats contested, the MCA and UMNO candidates won nine, the IMP two, while one went to an Independent.

This proof of the workability of an intercommunal alliance almost immediately set in motion the creation of a more formal and permanent arrangement between the UMNO and the MCA which was to emerge as the UMNO-MCA Alliance party. The Alliance demonstrated its power at the municipal elections in Johore Bahru, Muar, Malakka, and Kuala Lumpur at the beginning of 1953 by winning a large majority of the contested seats in each case.

The failure of the IMP led to a series of new political arrangements and the creation of two more parties. In June, 1952, delegates from Singapore, Selangor, Penang, and Perak decided to form a Pan-Malayan Labor Party, since it was apparent that the IMP could no longer support labor's political objectives. The platform adopted called for national independence, social justice, and the equitable distribution of the fruits of labor through cooperative ownership and democratic control. The moving spirit of the new party was Inche Mohamed Sopiee. The PMLP continued for a short while to support the IMP, and later supported the Alliance for a time, but generally followed its own course of supporting those who supported its platform, regardless of their other affiliations. The Alliance victories tended to heal the breaches within the UMNO so that by early 1953 the pro-IMP faction had returned to the fold, and party strength had greatly increased. Finally, the Malayan Indian

Congress, as in the past, found itself backing the wrong horse and belatedly attached itself to the Alliance bandwagon, with a promise of proportional representation in future Alliance successes.

In April, 1953, in anticipation of the forthcoming federal elections, the mentris besar of Perak, Kelantan, Kedah, Negri Sembilan, Johore, Trengganu, and Selangor called upon delegates from all political parties to attend a national conference at Kuala Lumpur. The conference was announced as a move to consider how best to achieve the common ideal of a united, free, and independent Malayan nation. The UMNO and the MCA, perceiving the hand of Dato Onn behind the scenes, boycotted the conference and called its own conference for August of that year. The keynote of the UMNO-MCA conference revolved around unification of the various communities in Malaya, establishment of a sovereign and independent state within the British Commonwealth, and the holding of federal legislative elections in 1954. The mentri besar conference met the following day and recommended federal elections not later than 1956 and an enlarged, but still largely nominated, federal council. Patently the mentri besar conference reflected the desire to delay the development of representative government as long as possible, in order that their prerogatives might be retained.

Having set the stage through the mentri besar conference, Dato Onn returned to the political scene early in 1954 with a new Party Negara. The Party Negara, in line with its antecedents in the mentri besar conference, developed as a moderate conservative Malay party. Its communal nature was apparent despite its avowedly intercommunal objectives. [11] Its true nature was revealed also in its stand on maintenance of the existing citizenship laws, under which citizenship is first and foremost the province of the individual states rather than the Federation, and its insistence that Malay become the only

---

11. The argument of the Party Negara supporters concerning its noncommunal character is related to its internal party structure. Thus, they point out that the members of the party vote on party policy on an individual basis rather than by communal blocs, as in the Alliance. This does not, however, mitigate the fact that it represents the desires and aspirations of a group drawn almost solely from one community, the Malays.

national language, that immigration be curbed, and that the civil service be Malayanized.

The first test of the relative strength of the Alliance and the Party Negara came in February, 1955, in the state election in Trengganu, a normally conservative state in which the Party Negara was expected to carry considerable strength among the peasantry. The Alliance won handily. This was, however, only a prelude to the federal elections in July, 1955, for a new legislative assembly, the results of which are shown on Map 28. Here the Alliance faced both the Party Negara and several other smaller nationalist parties--the Pan-Malayan Islamic Association and the regional National Association of Perak, [12] and the Pan-Malayan Labor party. Again the gerrymandering techniques of the Alliance were successful; every seat except one was taken by it. The single seat not taken by the Alliance, in Krian district, was won by the Pan-Malayan Islamic Association.

By the end of 1955 the Alliance appeared to be in complete control of the politics of the Federation, and with the mandate of the electorate behind him Abdul Rahman proceeded to enforce his policies. Within one year, however, the invincibility of the Alliance came into question, and its leadership was successfully challenged by the previously impotent Pan-Malayan Labor party. The most resounding defeat for the Alliance in the municipal and town elections held on December 1, 1956, came from Penang, where it lost all eight seats contested. Five of the seats were taken by the labor party; the other three went to independents. The labor and independent members together were thus placed in a position to overthrow the previous Alliance administration. In Seremban, too, the Alliance lost the one contested seat to the labor party. In Malakka the Alliance lost one seat to the local Malayan party. In Kuala Lumpur, Ipoh, and Butterworth, however, the Alliance retained all the seats contested.

Although the defeats were relatively minor and the Alliance's power in the Federal government remained unchanged, both Abdul Rahman and the opposition leaders recognized their sig-

---

12. The National Association of Perak was, to all purposes, identical in policy and objective with the Party Negara. It apparently remained separate because of the antipathy of its leaders toward Dato Onn.

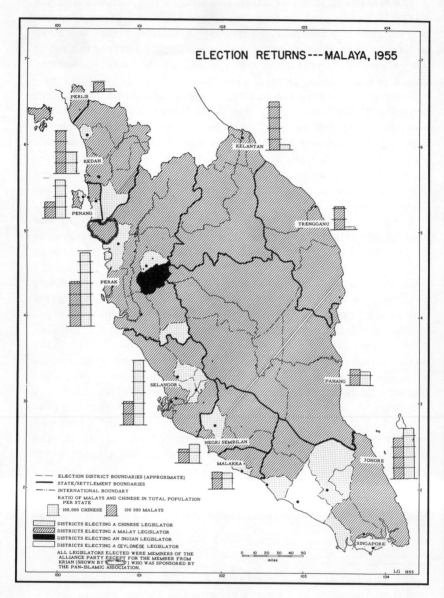

ELECTION RETURNS --- MALAYA, 1955

PERLIS
KEDAH
PENANG
PERAK
SELANGOR
NEGRI SEMBILAN
MALAKKA
KELANTAN
TRENGGANU
PAHANG
JOHORE
SINGAPORE

ELECTION DISTRICT BOUNDARIES (APPROXIMATE)
STATE/SETTLEMENT BOUNDARIES
INTERNATIONAL BOUNDARY
RATIO OF MALAYS AND CHINESE IN TOTAL POPULATION
PER STATE
100,000 CHINESE   100 000 MALAYS
DISTRICTS ELECTING A CHINESE LEGISLATOR
DISTRICTS ELECTING A MALAY LEGISLATOR
DISTRICTS ELECTING AN INDIAN LEGISLATOR
DISTRICTS ELECTING A CEYLONESE LEGISLATOR
ALL LEGISLATORS ELECTED WERE MEMBERS OF THE
ALLIANCE PARTY EXCEPT FOR THE MEMBER FROM
KRIAN (SHOWN BY   ) WHO WAS SPONSORED BY
THE PAN-ISLAMIC ASSOCIATION.

0 10 20 30 40 50
miles

LG 1955

Map 28

nificance as symptomatic of an underlying malaise within the Alliance. Rahman, commenting on the defeat in Penang, attributed it to three factors: (1) his government's actions in closing the Chung Ling Chinese Middle School in Penang, (2) disagreement in the ranks of the Alliance in Penang, and (3) fear among the Chinese that the UMNO would dominate Penang politics. Opposition leaders also charged that the defeats were a reaction to the rising taxes under the Alliance government.

The defeats may also have been a result of the growth and development of the labor party into a functioning political organization after its long years of indecisiveness. The labor party during 1956 increased the number of its branches in the Federation in seeking a broad base of popular support, and was reported to have held "cooperation" talks with the left-wing Malay Nationalist People's party (Partai Ra'ayat). If communal tensions within the Alliance continue to develop the labor party may well serve as the rallying place for the dissident Chinese and Indians. In such a situation it might then become the primary source of opposition to the UMNO.

Merdeka

Both the Alliance in the Federation and the Labor Front in Singapore achieved their success in the 1955 elections largely because of promises of independence and complete self-government within the near future. "Merdeka!" (freedom) was to become the rallying cry and basic principle of the new governments. Concerned with merdeka, however, were a number of factors, both internal and external, which had to be taken into consideration in determining the exact manner by which it was to be achieved, the degree of freedom and independence which was to be allowed, and the nature of the body politic after merdeka. The differences between the Federation and Singapore have led to different courses of development toward merdeka in each.

The Federation

As of October, 1955, the primary opposition to the Alliance government in the Federation was the outlawed Malayan Communist Party. A part of the platform on which the Alliance came to power was the granting of a general amnesty to all Communist guerrillas. The amnesty was designed to (1) divide the hard-core Communists from their wavering followers who might be ready to call off their losing fight, (2) more strongly unify the Federation behind the anti-Communist fight should the offer be rejected, and (3) bring a rapid end to the Emergency should the appeal succeed. A meeting was arranged in December, 1955, between the chief ministers of the Federation and Singapore, and Chin, Peng, Malaya's Communist leader. The chief ministers demanded that the Communists surrender their arms, submit to a short period of detention for investigation, and agree to the dissolution of the Malayan Communist Party. The Communist leadership balked particularly at the third proviso, despite the reported assurances of Abdul Rahman that former terrorists would be permitted to enter politics within the framework of present political organizations or new non-Communist parties after a period of rehabilitation. The meeting ended in deadlock. The offer of amnesty was withdrawn the following February.

The Communists took cognizance of the changed situation in the Federation, however, in January with a major reorganization and reorientation of the policies of the party. Placed as second and third in command of the party, following Chin, Peng, were a Malay and an Indian, in an effort to give the Chinese-dominated party more of a "united front" and noncommunal character. The revised party manifesto admittedly was aimed at identifying the aims of the party with the general goals of the country and its people. It was announced that the party was willing and ready to join in cooperation with all other segments of the population for the attainment of those ends. This reorganization also marked a change in Communist tactics from terrorism to political maneuvering and subversion. During the Federation's "Merdeka mission" to London, the MCP was quite active in the villages attempting to undermine confidence in the mission through a rumor campaign. In September, 1956, at the Eighth National Chinese Communist Party Congress in Peking, a formal request was read from the MCP suggesting that the Chinese Communists attempt to mediate an acceptable peace in Malaya. This idea was rejected immediately by Rahman, who pointed out that complete surrender now was the only acceptable course for the Communists. With their numbers drastically reduced, the Communist guerrillas appeared to be in a hopeless position, yet they remain a substantial source of threat and irritation to the new government which will have to face merdeka with the Communist problem still hanging over it. [13]

The Federation's "Merdeka mission" left for London in January, 1956, under the leadership of Abdul Rahman. The Colonial Office had already agreed in principle to Malayan independence. The issues before the conference concerned procedure, timing, and the new relationship which would pertain between the Federation and the Commonwealth. The Alliance platform had called for complete independence within two years. The date set by the Conference was September 1, 1957. Independence was to be achieved in two stages: (1) immediate authority over the internal affairs by the Federation government, and (2) relinquishment of control over external defense and foreign affairs by the British on Independence Day. Agreement was reached on changes in regard to external defense, internal security, finance, economic development, and the future Malayanization of the public services. It was agreed that a commission would be set up to review and draft suggestions for a new federal constitution. The Federation announced that it intended to remain within the Commonwealth and the sterling bloc. The conference and agreement produced by it were self-consciously designed "to reconcile the factors of continuity and efficiency, on the one hand, with recognition of the evolving political facts of the situation, on the other." [14]

The constitutional commission established at the London conference was headed by Lord Reid of Britain as chairman and included a member each from India, Pakistan, Australia, and Great Britain. The commission began its work in spring, 1956. Its specific task was to "make recommendations for a federal form of constitution for the whole country as a single, independent self-governing unit within the Commonwealth, based on parliamentary democracy and a bicameral legislature." [15] The commission was also instructed that its recommendations must (1) safeguard the position and prestige of the Malay rul-

---

13. One of the first acts of the Paramount Ruler of Malaya after independence was acquired on August 31, 1957, was to make a final offer of amnesty to the Communist guerillas, good until December 31, 1957, on terms similar to those of December, 1955.
14. Cited in the Christian Science Monitor, April 2, 1956.
15. Cited in the Times of Indonesia, September 6, 1956.

ers, and (2) safeguard the special position of Malays and the legitimate interests of the other communities.

The commission's report was made public in February, 1957, after nearly a year of study and deliberation. As expected, the primary problem which the commission faced concerned citizenship criteria and the rights of the non-Malay communities in the new nation. Jus soli was established as the basis for citizenship. The commissioners recommended that a person should be considered a citizen of the Federation if he was a citizen of either the Federation or one of its states prior to Merdeka day, or is born in the Federation on or after that day. Persons born in the Federation before independence and who are not citizens, should, on application, become citizens if they are over seventeen, have lived for five of the preceding seven years in the Federation and intend to stay there permanently, and have an elementary knowledge of Malay. Persons living in the Federation on Merdeka day but not born there, should be entitled to become citizens if they have lived there for eight of the previous twelve years and intend to stay, and have an elementary knowledge of Malay. Future naturalization would require a ten-year residence period. The commission did not recommend that new citizens be required to renounce their former citizenship, but only to swear that they would not "exercise any rights or privileges they may have under the nationality laws of any foreign country." The commission also felt that under the new unitary state, all citizenship must be primarily in relation to the Federation, rather than to the individual states and their rulers.

Regarding the special rights of the Malaysian community, the commission found it difficult to reconcile the granting of such special privileges to one community only and not equally to all citizens of the state, although it recognized the need for safeguarding the right of the Malaysians. It recommended that present preferences for the Malaysians, such as land reservation and quotas for public services and for business licenses, should remain for the present, but should gradually disappear. They also agreed that Malay should be the national language, but that English should continue to be an official language for at least ten years.

The commission recommended a return to greater centralization of government, although agreeing that the states should enjoy a measure of autonomy. It recommended that the head of state of the Federation should be elected for five years by

the Malay rulers from among themselves on the basis of sen-
iority in office. He must be a constitutional ruler bound to
accept the advice of a prime minister. In the states, too, the
rulers would be bound to accept the advice of their mentris
besar, while the mentri besar of each state should be responsible to the state legislative assembly.

The Federal legislative assembly would have the right to
restore constitutional government in any state, or to introduce
the new constitution in any states which have refused to do so
by January 1, 1959. In return for these restrictions on the
states, the commission recommended that they be given greater control over their own financial matters. The Federation
government, however, would have greater power over the
planning and execution of nationwide development and land reform programs, even where these impinged on what have been
rights reserved to the states.

Other significant changes suggested by the commission were:
(1) that the former Straits Settlements be completely severed
from their connection with the British crown and become states
equal in rank to the other states in the Federation, with a governor and chief minister equivalent to the sultans and mentris
besar; (2) that the new parliament for the Federation consist
of a house of representatives of one hundred members elected
from single constituencies for five years, and a senate of thir-
ty-three members, one-third nominated, chosen for six-year
terms; (3) that the number of the constituency districts be
doubled to 104; and (4) that the present Emergency regulations
should be continued only one more year.

The constitution suggested by the commission was a compromise and synthesis of demands from various groups. It
was not designed to please any one group entirely. In fact, the
problems of the commission in framing an equitable and acceptable proposal on citizenship became increasingly complicated
in the last months of 1956 by a marked rise in communal tension, apparently prompted in some cases by fears of the consequences of independence. The heightened tension found expression in the "letters to the editor" newspaper columns, in
the formation of numerous new communal organizations, in
conflicts between interracial athletic teams, and in the pronouncements of the major communal political groups. The vice-
chairman of the UMNO was prompted to predict that civil war
would quickly follow independence unless the racial differences

481

were settled before independence. The Communists took every opportunity to intensify the intercommunal conflict.

One political observer has noted that the future of the new nation must lie in a solution to the communal problem and that the question of how the various communities are going to get along together when administrative responsibility rests in their hands has been side-stepped at every juncture in the progress toward self-government. It is clear that the Malays are unwilling to relinquish their special position and status; it is equally clear that the non-Malay population will not be content with less than equality in the new nation.

Nonetheless, in May, 1957, representatives of the Federation and of the Colonial Office were reported to have reached "agreement on all the outstanding issues" concerning the new constitution based on the Reid Commission report, and it was announced that the constitution would go into effect on August 31. These issues centered about the status of those Malayans now British citizens, chiefly Chinese living in Penang and Malakka, under the new constitution. It was agreed that these might be given Commonwealth citizenship, as well as Malayan, but according to the Economist of May 25, 1957, they "would owe undivided loyalty to Malaya." The Commonwealth citizenship grants them only free entry into and residence in the United Kingdom. It was also agreed that Islam was to be recognized as the state religion.

In mid-August, the agreement between Britain and Malaya was signed under which Malaya became an elective monarchy on August 31. Tengku Sir Abdul Rahman, the Yang di-Pertuan Besar of Negri Sembilan, was elected Yang di-Pertuan Agong, or Paramount Ruler of Malaya. Tengku Abdul Rahman (no direct relation), the former Federation chief minister, was to continue as Prime Minister of the new state.

Singapore
The situation which led the British to look favorably on independence and self-government for the Federation did not exist for Singapore. The requirements of Commonwealth security and strategy demanded Singapore's retention under British control. Its ambiguous situation as, in effect, a Chinese outpost in Malayan waters seemed to make it a handy weapon of Communist activity. Too, the Singapore government under the leadership of David Marshall had neither the solid backing of an electorate nor the internal stability that was apparent in

the Alliance in the Federation. The relevance of these factors was exposed repeatedly in a number of major crises faced by the Singapore government during its first year in office.

Hardly had the new government taken over when the colony was virtually paralyzed by a series of strikes and riots that reached their peak on May 12, 1955, when three persons, including an American newspaperman, were killed. The main dispute was between the management and workers of a Chinese-owned bus company over the firing of some workers. The strike of the bus workers was followed by a rash of sympathy strikes in other industries, many undoubtedly Communist inspired. The Singapore Middle School Students' Union next joined, and became a major agitating force. For four days transportation and business in the colony were at a standstill. The bus company dispute was finally settled on May 14, but the repercussions of the strikes and riots remained to plague the government's claims that it could maintain its own peaceful self-development and control its own internal security. The chief secretary, at a meeting of the legislative assembly, laid the blame for the disorders on the People's Action Party and its leader, Lee, Kuan-yew, together with Communist agitators. [16]

The second major crisis arose in the latter part of July with the governor's refusal to appoint two additional vice-ministers as requested by the chief minister. Marshall appealed to a special assembly session and announced he would resign if the governor did not modify his stand. The assembly framed a resolution demanding an end to colonial rule, a liberal interpretation of the present constitution for the interim period before full self-government, and a new constitution providing self-government. The real point of issue was whether the governor was bound to accept and act upon the advice of the legislative assembly and the council of ministers, or whether, in effect, he had a veto power over the acts of the assembly through his refusal to accept them. On August 2, 1955, the assembly voted to suspend its sessions until an acceptable answer was received from the secretary of state for the colonies, who was traveling in the area at the time. After three days of consultation between the secretary and the chief minister it was announced that the governor had agreed to act in

---

16. Reuters release, May 16, 1955.

the future on the advice of the chief minister in all matters, reserving his power to dissolve the legislative assembly and suspend the constitution. In addition, the chief minister was invited to form a delegation to meet with the Colonial Office in London the following spring to discuss the grant of self-government in the light of a year's experience. It was readily noted that the settlement, although solving the immediate problem of the relations between the governor and the assembly, made few other concessions and implied that the colony's right to self-government was conditional upon its ability to prove that it deserved such a privilege before the spring meetings.

A third crisis threatened at the end of October when a minor opposition within the Labor Front attempted to seize control of the party and remove Marshall from power. Reconsideration of the vote, however, revealed that many of those voting against Marshall were not party members, and the election was declared null and void. In retaliation the leaders of the party opposition and their supporters walked out of the party conference. Ten days later the two assembly members who had led the opposition within the party left the government side of the assembly and took their seats with the opposition. By the move the thirty-two-seat house was split into equal halves, and the government majority was erased. It was able to continue only because of a constitutional technicality whereby two of the nominated members seated with the opposition were required to vote with the government. With this unstable control the government was supposed to prove, during the following six months, its ability to maintain a stable government.

Against this background the chief minister set out in early December for London to make preliminary arrangements for the spring meeting. The chief minister hoped during the preliminary talks to have the civil service removed from control of the chief secretary and attached to the office of the chief minister, to have Singapore's military trainees (national service) removed from the authority of the governor and placed under the council of ministers, to have debate permitted in the assembly in languages other than English, and to urge support of a move to grant citizenship to those Singapore residents who were not then British subjects.

In general Marshall's talks with the secretary of state for the colonies were successful. Six points were agreed upon for the spring meeting: (1) a definition of internal self-government; (2) establishment of a date for the introduction of internal self-government; (3) the future structure of the legislative assembly (Marshall requested that the elected seats be doubled); (4) the future of the public services; (5) external relations and external defense problems; and (6) any other business. The opening of the conference was set for April 23, 1956. In addition, Marshall gained agreement that the council of ministers should control the national service men and that the number of ministers should be increased to allow for a minister of commerce and industry. The question of language for use in the assembly was left for constitutional amendment if desired. It was decided to postpone decision on the citizenship problem until the April meeting. It finally was decided that the civil service would be kept divorced from politics and maintained under the chief secretary, but that the staff associations should have the right to approach the chief minister on general conditions of service and public policy relating to the public service. Marshall returned to Singapore with supreme confidence that the political aspirations of his government and the people of Singapore would be amply fulfilled at the April meetings.

In the few months before April a series of relatively minor events, strikes, small riots, and intercommunal strife began to lead to reconsideration of the government's ability to maintain internal peace and stability. The various racial minorities--Malay, Indian, Eurasian, and European--began to consider their own possible futures in an independent, but Chinese-dominated, state. Increasingly they voiced fears of immediate and future violence. Although Marshall had admitted the necessity and desirability of a major degree of British control over the external defense of the island, his previous statements on independence had been largely based on the government's own control of all internal defense. In the face of rising doubts, Marshall was forced to revise his previous stand, and in late March he announced an arrangement whereby "the Prime Minister of Singapore would recognize a duty to consult with the Governor-General and to act on his advice, if and when, in the opinion of a committee composed of the services affected, the locally recruited defense forces are inadequate to maintain public order."[17] This would place the ultimate police and security power in the hands of the "com-

_____

17. Quoted in London Times, March 27, 1956.

mittee, " and it was to be over the definition of the composition of such a committee that the London talks were to break down.

The Singapore delegation, composed of leading members of the various parties (including the PAP), left for London in early April. Marshall previously had promulgated the doctrine that the entire question of Singapore's independence and self-rule must be settled at the meeting--that partial solutions to the problem would be unacceptable--and that Singapore must not be placed in a position of having to beg for more at some later date. For slightly more than three weeks the talks continued, until on May 15 the Colonial Office announced that "the Singapore constitutional conference ended today without agreement." The basic cause of the breakdown is pointed up in the announcement:

> "In their first proposals the Singapore delegation demanded sovereign independence within the Commonwealth by April next year. They proposed that in the independence Act conferring this upon them there should be provision to allow Her Majesty's Government to maintain bases on the island and to have a concurrent interest in external affairs, though the effect of the provisions they proposed was that the Singapore Government would at all times have a veto on the proposed arrangements.
>
> The Secretary of State in reply explained why Her Majesty's Government could not accept these proposals at the present time. There had been no appreciable period of stable democratic government in Singapore. No political party at present held a commanding majority. The subversive forces of communism were strongly at work in Singapore, as the Chief Minister himself had recognized, and it was impossible to foresee what the future might hold in internal political development. Her Majesty's Government did not therefore think they would be honourably discharging their responsibilities if they now took the irrevocable step of abrogating all rights and powers of any sort in connection with Singapore for all time." [18]

18. Quoted in London Times, May 16, 1956.

The Singapore delegation then modified its original demands, while the Colonial Office offered an eight-point proposal which would: (1) change Singapore's status from a colony to a "state"; (2) supplant the governor with a high commissioner; (3) double the elected seats in the assembly and withdraw completely the nominated members; (4) provide for a separate Singapore citizenship within the Commonwealth on the same basis as that enjoyed by the fully self-governing members of the Commonwealth; (5) provide for full internal self-government, including responsibility for internal security, subject only to the reservations in (8) below; (6) leave the United Kingdom in control of external defense and external affairs with the exception of commercial and trade relations; (7) establish a defense and security council composed of three representatives from the Singapore government, three from the United Kingdom government, and with the high commissioner as chairman. The council would not only discuss matters of external defense, but would also receive reports on the internal security situation and consider what action, if any, was called for; and (8) provide that Her Majesty's Government would retain authority to make orders in council for Singapore, restricted to those circumstances where it was clear, in the light of advice from the defense and security council, that it would be unable otherwise to carry out their responsibilities for external defense and external affairs. [19]

Although the provisions represented a significant advance, the Singapore delegation recognized that the fifth and eighth provisions placed ultimate authority in the hands of the defense and security council which, at any time, under the plea of defense or security, could ask for intervention into Singapore's internal affairs. By the end of the negotiations the Singapore delegation had announced itself ready to acquiesce in the retention of limited powers by the United Kingdom government, but only on the two conditions that the use of these powers would depend on the recommendation of the defense and security council, and that United Kingdom representatives would not be in a majority on the council. It was suggested that a chairman for the council be appointed by a neutral body such as the United Nations, or even by the government of the Federation. Such an alternative was unacceptable to the Colonial Office,

---

19. Ibid.

however, and with the final statement that "to accept this position . . . without any certain power to take any action other than to suspend the constitution and to take over the entire government of the territory [in case of an emergency] would place them in a quite unacceptable situation," Her Majesty's Government terminated the talks.

The Singapore delegation returned home. Lee, Kuan-yew, of the PAP, the first to arrive, announced at the Singapore airport the intention of his party to seek new elections and, if successful, to make certain through a program of passive resistance that the Colonial constitution did not work. The members of the newly formed Liberal Socialist Party moved in the assembly that "the offer of Her Majesty's Government should have been accepted by the delegation at the constitutional conference in London as an interim measure"; but the motion was voted down. David Marshall returned to resign his post as chief minister.

With his resignation, Marshall recommended as his successor a fellow member of the labor front and former minister for social welfare and labor in his cabinet, Lim, Yew-hock. This recommendation was accepted by the governor, and Lim was asked to organize a new government. Although it was not expected that the new government would change drastically the policies of its predecessor, the quiet, purposive assurance of Mr. Lim was a significant change from the flamboyant dramatics of the previous chief minister. By the end of September a unanimous vote of confidence had consolidated the new chief minister's position, and he had launched a large-scale roundup of subversives and agitators, dissolved the Communist-dominated Middle School Students' Union, and negotiated plans for a second series of talks on independence with the Colonial Office in London the following spring. Attempted opposition to these moves by students, unions, and opposition members was successfully quelled. The anti-Communist Singapore Trade Unions Congress came out in full support of the government, and the attempt of the PAP to push a vote of censure through the assembly was roundly defeated and turned into a second vote of confidence. By the end of the year Lim had obtained assembly approval of his moves to reform the public services by placing local personnel in all key positions as they were available. He could look forward to bringing to a second London conference an impressive record of achievement during his relatively short time in office.

The second London conference convened in mid-March, 1957, and continued until mid-April. Basic agreement was reached on most controversial issues. The internal security council (referred to above as the defense and security council) was to be composed of three British members, with the high commissioner as chairman, three Singapore ministers, and one Federation member who would hold the deciding vote. Singapore citizenship would be independent, British trade interests would be protected, and the Head of State would be a Malayan. The conference broke down over the British insistence that "no person involved in seditious activities may stand in the first elections for the new legislature of the State of Singapore."[20] This demand threatened to become a major issue after the return of the Singapore delegation to Singapore, and most of the major political leaders of the delegation's stand. The controversy did not, however, prevent the drawing up of new Singapore citizenship legislation as agreed upon at the London conference, and the bill had passed its first reading by the end of September with little opposition. By early October the seeming barrier to a Britain-Singapore agreement had apparently been forgotten in the press of other events. The PAP, leading vocal opponents to the British proposal, became torn by internal strife, with the more extreme leftist elements seizing control from Lee, Kuan-yew and the more moderate group. This move was shortly followed by a wholesale roundup by Singapore police of the leaders of the leftist PAP faction and of several of their supporting labor union leaders. In late September a second series of raids led to the arrest of a number of Chinese Middle School students charged with subversive activities, and issuance of a deportation order on the principal of the leading Chinese Middle School in the Colony. It began to appear that Chief Minister Lim was intent upon proving to the British that the Colony could quite adequately handle its subversive problem by itself, and that the British fears of the previous April had little relationship to the realities of the situation in October. If, by the time of the elections, expected in the latter half of 1958, the subversive elements were either imprisoned or deported, then there was little basis for further disagreement.

---

20. As repeated in the Economist, April 13, 1957.

Malayan union

One of the most important factors that will have a significant impact upon the future development and status of both Singapore and the Federation concerns their mutual relationship. A former colonial secretary of the states, Sir Patrick McKerron, commenting on the breakdown of the Singapore talks, noted as a primary cause of the trouble the fact that "the Federation and Singapore have been allowed, or have allowed themselves, to develop constitutionally on different sets of rails when they ought both to have been on the same track."

The statement reflects the feelings of many in both the Federation and Singapore that integration must come eventually, and that moves perpetuating the separateness of the two units will only postpone that step to the detriment of both. Several times Marshall made tentative moves toward discussion of the subject, but there was little interest expressed by the Federation government. There, the primary fear is, of course, of the numerical superiority which would accrue to the Chinese population through the integration with Singapore.

In a statement rejecting the possibility of integration in the near future, Abdul Rahman pointed out that (1) Malay is the national language of the Federation, while the majority of the people of Singapore speak Chinese; (2) the Chinese of Singapore would be unlikely to accept a Malay ruler; and (3) they would be unlikely to accept Islam as the official religion. The chief minister's statement, coming just before the second series of London talks, cast a considerable shadow over the Singapore leaders, since a primary point in Chief Minister Lim's program for the island's self-governing future was based on a union.

Shortly after Rahman's statement, the Singapore branch of the UMNO announced that it would withdraw from the Singapore Merdeka mission unless seven points were included in the memorandum to be taken to the talks. These were that (1) five-eighths of all government posts in Singapore should be reserved for Malays; (2) those who intend to become Singapore citizens should be able to speak Malay fluently; (3) only a Malay should be appointed as a governor-general; (4) only citizens of the Federation and Singapore should be entitled to political rights; (5) Islam should be made the official religion; (6) Malay should be made the official language within ten years; and (7) Malays should be recognized as the indigenous people of the island and as such should be helped in improving their lot.

Although the UMNO later withdrew the first two demands and modified the second two, it was apparent that the price of Malay support, either from the Federation or within Singapore, would be recognition of predominant Malay rights on the island.

The general reaction in Singapore to Rahman's statement was expressed by the Straits Times:

> Singapore cannot be quarantined, thrust behind a cordon sanitaire on the causeway.
>
> The belief it can is not only unrealistic but dangerous. The two countries [Singapore and Malaya] are the nearest approach to Siamese twins that geography and economics have produced. They must live together, not to be cut asunder. The question is how they shall live together. [21]

21. Cited in the Christian Science Monitor, "Singapore-Malaya: Merger Hopes Fade," January 22, 1957.

12. A Recapitulation

THE FUTURE COURSE OF DEVELOPMENT in Malaya, with an independent Federation and a self-governing Colony, will be dependent largely upon factors derived from its own past and its present character. The diverse contending ethnic, social, economic, and political factions pose an immediate problem for the new governments, which somehow must forge a workable unity and common purpose if they are to survive. Opposing these divisive trends are a number of developments which may lead toward greater cohesiveness and integration. The nature and relationships of these various centrifugal and centripetal forces at work in Malaya can be summarized in terms of a number of factors and developments acting through both space and time.

Geographic situation has given Malaya a unique strategic and economic importance in Southeast Asia and in the world at large. Malaya lies at the juncture of the primary transportation and communication lines running through the region and connecting western Europe with eastern Asia; it is located centrally in relation to the other population centers of Southeast Asia; and as the end of the attenuated Malay Peninsula, it is the southernmost part of the Asian mainland and the natural point of connection between the mainland and the Indonesian archipelago. These situational relationships have served to make the control of Malaya a key to the extension of control over the entire region. The Sri Vijaya and Malakka empires, the Portuguese, the Dutch, the English, and the Japanese all have recognized and based their struggles in the area upon these facts.

Location has also made Malaya a focal point for commerce

in the region, as attested by the growth of the great trading centers at Malakka, Penang, and especially Singapore, the entrepôt for archipelagic Southeast Asia. In addition, location has exposed Malaya to numerous cultural contacts and ethnic infiltrations over both land and sea. In prehistoric time successive waves of migrations down the peninsula from continental Asia appear to have contributed to a diversity of basic ethnic and cultural patterns.

Desire for commerce brought early Indian cultural influences, and intermarriage between Indians and indigenes contributed to the evolution of the deutero-Malay. Other early Indian influences arrived indirectly through Fu-nan, Java, and Sumatra. Early Chinese influences were important primarily in commercial and political terms, but they also contributed to the ethnic fusions out of which have developed the modern Malay. Later Arab and Indian trade brought Islam to the region and transformed the culture of the Malaysian world from an introverted provincialism to an extroverted universalism characterized by proselytizing zeal. Portuguese and Dutch rule had both political and commercial consequences. The British introduced Western social, economic, and political ideologies and structures. The Japanese contributed largely to the growth of political consciousness and nationalism among the indigenous peoples. The Chinese immigrants of the past one hundred years were responsible for introducing an economic and political dualism in the country which has been characterized by interracial tensions. Nationalism and communism are two of the responses to these cultural intrusions.

Present-day Malayan society is, in effect, three or perhaps four societies--Malaysian, Chinese, Indian, and European--all welded under British rule into a highly interdependent social, economic, and political complex. It may be described as a plural society according to both general meanings of the term: it is a society consisting of two or more major ethnic groups, and it is a society composed of an indigenous cultural and economic component overlaid by an essentially foreign, colonial, and Western element.

As early as 1500 the confluence of diverse cultural and economic influences had led to a synthesis which was identifiably Malay, in contrast to the ethnic and cultural patterns of the surrounding areas. Further outside influences have contributed increasingly to the formation of distinctly Malay patterns of social, economic, and political development. The common Malay patterns are characterized by a social organization based on the kampong, or in the case of the Minangkabau people of Negri Sembilan, on the matrilineal family; a general adherence to Islam; a common language; and a traditional economic system based primarily on subsistence agricultural production, handicraft industry, and fishing. The primary centers of this Malay culture and settlement are in the north and along the east coast.

A number of factors since the end of World War II have contributed to the internal integration of the Malay community, and to its integration with other communities. The prospect of self-government has produced an awareness among all Malaysians of the need for organizing internally in order to achieve common objectives, and of cooperating with other communities in achieving political stability. Increasing participation in local, state, and national governments at the bureaucratic level has given the Malays experience in administration and in understanding the problems of other Malays throughout the country, and has created a group of trained leaders no longer bound to localistic and parochial perspectives. The Malay community has come to participate in the national economic life of the country through greater cultivation of cash crops and participation in such urban occupations as mercantile activities and public service. A common fear of Chinese economic dominance has served as an impetus to internal integration. In part as a counterpoise to the threat of Chinese dominance and in part as a manifestation of the self-awareness of the national community of Malaysians in Malaya, there has developed a focus upon other Malaysian peoples in Asia, particularly those of Indonesia. Pan-Malay unity has become an important part of the world view of the Malaysians in Malaya and has made itself felt in the political pronouncements of the Malaysian leaders.

Opposed to these centripetal factors and in part an outgrowth of them, are the centrifugal factors which hinder intra-Malaysian and Malaya-wide integration. Class differentiation has developed among the Malaysians in both the urban and rural areas. In the urban areas it has come as a consequence of socioeconomic differences; in the rural areas it has come with the increasing involvement of some of the kampong leaders in the bureaucratic functions of the state and national governments. The development of political organizations has led to factionalism among the Malaysians, as illustrated by the plethora of Malaysian parties which have come into being and contend with each other in pursuit of divergent objectives, such as the UMNO, the Party Negara, the Pan-Malayan Islamic Association, the National Association of Perak, and the Malay Nationalist People's Party. The Malaysians, for the most part, have been and probably will continue to be basically subjects of different states within the Federation, and their loyalties have been directed toward the various state rulers, rather than toward a nebulous and abstract concept of a unified Malaya.

Many of those factors which tend toward greater cohesion within the Malaysian community tend also toward the greater differentiation of the Malaysian community from the other communities in Malaya; while those factors working against Malaysian cohesion, often tend toward greater cooperation of certain Malaysian elements with elements of the other communities in pursuit of common objectives. Thus, political factionalism among the Malaysians has resulted in the UMNO-MCA Alliance, while the better-educated Malaysians increasingly appear to find more in common with members of other communities on their own social and economic level than with other members of their ethnic groups.

About half of the total population of Malaya is Chinese and the ratio appears to be rising each year because of the high reproduction rates of the Chinese. They form the largest concentration of ethnic Chinese outside China. In Malaya they form a distinctive community characterized by their different social organization, settlement patterns, economic and occupational characteristics, and political affiliations.

The Chinese in Malaya are almost all either immigrants, or descendants of immigrants, from the southern provinces of China. As such they have tended to perpetuate the linguistic and provincial differences which characterize their homeland. The Hokkien, Cantonese, Tiechiu, and Hakka predominate, with lesser numbers from the Hainanese, Foochow, Hokchiu, Hokchia, and Henghua communities. Although no strict lines of differentiation can be drawn, various Chinese communities tend toward distinctive settlement and occupation patterns. The Hokkien tend to be urban-centered and are engaged largely in commerce; Cantonese and Hakkas tend toward rural settlement and agricultural pursuits and mining; the Tiechiu and Hainanese seem to prefer living in towns and cities, the latter being known especially as shopkeepers and domestic servants. The predominant settlement of the Foochow community is in the Dindings.

The Chinese immigrants brought with them a distinctive social organization characterized by a close-knit system of clan
and family relationships and an involved pattern of organizational affiliation based on locality of origin, occupation, and
economic relationships. Both of these systems are interrelated
and serve as a form of extralegal control within the Chinese
community, while at the same time ensuring the welfare and
security of its membership. A result of this interlocking set
of social systems has been a strong inner cohesiveness among
the Chinese, which has tended to resist penetration from the
outside and efforts toward enforced assimilation of the Chinese
with the other communities in Malaya.

Chinese dominate a large and significant sector of the Malayan economy. The original impetus for Chinese immigration was tin mining and trade, and these two activities, in
addition to commercial agriculture, form the basis for livelihood of the majority of Chinese. Of the two primary bases
of the economy, tin and rubber, the Chinese-operated mines
produce about 40 per cent of the total tin production, and Chinese smallholders account for a considerable proportion of the
total rubber production. Chinese completely dominate the pineapple industry, the third largest export item in the Malayan
economy.

An equally important role of the Chinese in the Malayan
economy is their function in relation to the Malaysian subsistence agriculturalist and smallholder. They are a primary
source of risk capital, supplies, and equipment, and the primary trade outlet for the production of the Malaysian farmer.
Although this relationship keeps a large proportion of the Malaysian population under their obligation, it in turn provides
the Malaysian with his only readily available supply of capital
and equipment, which he must have if he is to exist at all.

The political orientation of most of the Chinese is marked by
a dualism which is directed on the one hand toward China,
their land of origin, and on the other hand toward Malaya, their
land of residence. Political affiliations in one sphere tend to
affect affiliations in the other. Most of the Chinese immigrants
came to Malaya with the intention of eventually returning to
China. Although Malaya is now their home and the expectations
to return have diminished, most of the Chinese maintain strong
ties and sympathies with their homeland and its internal politics. At present they find themselves faced with the necessity
of choosing between the Communist government in Peking and

the Nationalist government on Taiwan as a focus for their loyalties. They face a similar choice in Malaya, between cooperation with the other communities in the maintenance and development of an independent nation, or, in resistance to the political dominance of the Malaysians, support of the largely Chinese Communist movement.

In both cases the consequences of affiliation and support in either direction are not yet clear, and the Chinese generally have expressed a reluctance to make any decisive choice until the issues are further clarified. This has resulted in a general nullification of their potential political pressure in either China or Malaya.

The third largest ethnic group in Malaya is the Indians. Predominantly from south India, they, like the Malaysians and Chinese, are characterized by distinct social, economic, and political patterns.

Unlike the Chinese, who came primarily as entrepreneurs, the Indians were brought to Malaya primarily under contract, to fill a need for agricultural workers. Before World War II most of the Indian laborers stayed in Malaya for only a few years before returning to India. More recently the Indian population has stabilized, and increasing numbers of Indians have taken up permanent residence in Malaya. The greatest number of Indians continue to live in the rubber-producing areas of the west coast, while most of the remainder are urban dwellers. Among the rural population, settlement is largely based on the estates, with a tendency for persons of a common village origin in India to congregate.

Rubber production remains the basis for livelihood among the rural Indians, either as estate workers or as independent smallholders. The urban Indians are engaged primarily in public service activities or professions.

An especially articulate minority, the Indians have assumed a role out of proportion to their total numbers in such activities as union organization and politics. In the Federation, Indians play an especially strong role in union activity; they form the core of the Pan-Malayan Labour party. In addition, the Malayan Indian Congress is a participant in the UMNO-MCA Alliance. In Singapore also their contribution to the labor movement has been significant, and their role in Colony politics has been even greater than in the Federation. It appears that the Indians are becoming increasingly Malayanized, and it seems likely that as they tend to identify their interests with the future of

497

Malaya they will assume an even greater role in its political and economic development.

The European population of Malaya is insignificant numer-ically, but it is important primarily for its past control over Malayan political and administrative development and its con-tinued control over the commercial sectors of the economy. It is predominantly British.

Although the civil service and administrative functions for-merly performed by the British are rapidly being transferred to Malayans, the concepts and structure created by the British are virtually unchanged. Both the Federation and Singapore will remain tied to the British Commonwealth after the political changes in 1957, and it is probable that the two units will con-tinue to rely for some time upon British advice and assistance in their internal development.

Foreign, mainly British, interests continue to control the major share of tin and rubber production in Malaya, largely as a result of superior capital resources and improved tech-nological processes. Malaya's economy relies on its export trade, and this too is largely controlled by Europeans.

Malaya's physical setting is unique, but it bears a strong resemblance to that of the rest of archipelagic Southeast Asia. This setting consists of a peninsula and its nearly surrounding seas, a backbone of forest-clad hills and mountains set in swampy or marshy plains, and mantling soils, easily eroded when cleared of forest. Frequent torrential downpours, cloudy skies, humid air, and uniform temperatures characterize the climate. The resource base of Malaya consists of its land, its forests, the bordering seas, and the mineral deposits under-ground.

Some of the plains have been cleared and put under cultiva-tion; others remain forest and swampland. Future expansion of settlement and cultivation will involve either clearing the lowlands and lower hill areas of forest or draining and filling the lowland marshes. Like most tropical soils, those of Ma-laya are generally deficient in plant nutrients or quickly lose nutrients under cultivation, and they may erode easily under the heavy Malayan rainfall. Heavy precipitation and the vary-ing directions and loads of the Malayan streams also contribute the hazards of occasional flooding.

The forests of Malaya, while extensive, form more of a potential than a present resource. They await techniques of efficient extraction and preservation for tropical woods and, more importantly, increased demand. Accessibility is also a problem, but will tend to diminish under increasing settlement and development.

The waters surrounding Malaya, although fished for centuries by Malays, still constitute an underutilized resource by modern standards. Though little is known of the habits of the fish of these waters, and the introduction of improved techniques is thus hampered, it is certain that catches can be increased by fairly simple measures. One of these is mechanization of the fishing boats. Increased utilization is also dependent upon concurrent solution of present marketing problems.

Mineral resources of present importance in Malaya are tin, iron, bauxite, and coal. Tin is the only mineral presently extracted in quantity. While the outlook for the industry does not indicate immediate exhaustion, it still is one of short-run reserves. Present reserves of high-grade ore are definitely limited, and lower grade ores cannot yet be profitably processed. Iron-ore deposits in the east coast areas can apparently be further developed. They are at present a major source of supply for the steel mills of southern Japan, and known reserves are substantial. Bauxite deposits are substantial, but at present only one or two mines are in operation. Increased exploitation is dependent on outside factors, chiefly those of international supply and demand, and improved processing techniques. Coal is of poor quality and limited in quantity. Very little is presently mined.

To effectively utilize and manage its resources, modern Malaya has developed transportation and communication systems binding together the various parts of the country-production areas, processing facilities, administrative centers, markets, shipping points, and overseas terminals. The transportation complex consists of modern means of movement-- motorized road vehicles, trains, airplanes, and ships, and the associated roads, railroads, airfields, and harbors--and older, native means of movement-- human porters, bullock carts, and river and seagoing native boats. The best developed land transportation network is in western Malaya, where the connection of inland points and the channeling of goods toward the sea for further shipment by water is provided by a system of improved roads and railroads. The communication systems consist of well-developed postal and telecommunication networks, especially serving the commercial and more populous centers of the western zone, and word-of-mouth transmission, which is of course limited by linguistic differentiation.

The Malayan economy is based on rubber production, tin-mining, the entrepôt trade, and the indigenous agricultural system. It is characterized by a relationship between certain occupations and ethnic affiliations, by areal differentiation of basic commodities, by a heavy reliance upon foreign trade and markets, and by a relatively high per capita gross product.

Two relatively distinct economic systems can be distinguished: an indigenous Malay system based on noncommercial, subsistence agriculture and organized on a village basis, and a foreign, commercial production system based on resource exploitation for overseas export and the organization of commerce on a national or regional scale. The latter element also is composed of two parts. The first is Asian, based on the entrepreneurial and labor activities of Chinese and Indians. The second is based on European capital, technologies, and management.

The centers of foreign Asian and European economic activity in Malaya are found along the west-coast areas and in the southern extremities of the peninsula. The indigenous agricultural areas are mainly in the north and along the east coast. The first areas are well serviced with modern industrial and commercial service facilities and with an experienced and skilled labor and entrepreneurial force. The latter areas are relatively underdeveloped.

The major sources of instability in the Malayan economy arise from its reliance on foreign markets for the disposal of its limited number of export commodities, and on the continued goodwill of other nations in the area for the maintenance of its entrepôt trade.

Despite its relatively high per capita product, the Malayan economy is faced with a number of problems. Among these are the need for diversification of production and minimization of dependence on the outside world for markets and foodstuffs, and the need for development of a more equitable economic balance among the various areas of the country and among the different ethnic groups. Recent trends toward solution of these problems are the development of primary products other than tin and rubber and the development of secondary processing and manufactured industries. The Rural and Industrial Development Authority is seeking to raise levels of living and productivity in rural areas, particularly those settled by Malaysians, and to integrate the native economy with that of the commercialized areas along the west coast.

The modern economic development of Malaya has tended to bring the various political divisions together as an economic unit. Technical developments in transportation and communication also have brought the various states into closer physical relation with one another. Increasing economic interdependence, especially after independence, may be expected to bring the various ethnic groups together in a closer functional relationship.

Administrative structure and practice in Malaya have developed as a synthesis of two distinct systems: a traditional pattern of government derived from Hindu concepts of royalty, Islamic law, and customary precedents established during the Malakka empire; and British concepts of administration derived from Western liberal and laissez-faire ideals. Largely as a result of this dualism, an indeterminate cyclic pattern of centralism-decentralism has marked the course of administrative development in Malaya. The Federation agreement and the constitution proposed by the Reid commission are both attempts to arrive at some mediation of administrative structure which would permit maximum unitary development on a national level, while maintaining the independence demanded by the various states. In effect, local government in the rural areas maintains its traditional bases, running upward through the penghulu to the mentri besar and sultan at the state level, while the British-evolved system begins at the district level and in the cities and towns, and works upward through the state bureaucracies to the federal level. It is at the district and state levels that the two systems are forced to coexist and where they tend to meet in conflicts of interest.

Political organization in Malaya has tended to develop as an outgrowth of older forms of social groupings, ethnic, religious, class, or economic. This diverse base has impelled the formation of political coalitions for the attainment of common objectives. At the same time these coalitions lead to instability, since not all their member parties retain common objectives in all matters. Signs of such differences have appeared among the governing coalitions in both the Federation and Singapore, with the MCA, in the first instance, finding it increasingly difficult to align Chinese support behind an alliance that is overtly working for Malaysian hegemony, while in the latter case it is the UMNO which has threatened to pull out of its coalition with the labor front because of fears of impending Chinese control in the Colony.

Increasingly, Malaya has become an important factor in world affairs, and events elsewhere are assuming ever greater consequences for Malaya's internal political and economic development. Its strategic value is recognized by both the Communist and non-Communist nations. Malayan natural resources, particularly tin and rubber, continue to play an important role in the economic power relationships of the world order. In connection with the effort to contain communism in Southeast Asia, political events in Malaya are of increasing importance in the world balance of power. Malaya represents in microcosm the world-wide struggle against subversion and stands as an example of the policy of containment to which the Western powers are committed.

It appears probable that the future in Malaya will be influenced by world conditions nearly as much as by internal developments. Economic stability within Malaya is predicated largely on the world price for tin and rubber. The degree to which the large Chinese community will become integrate with the Malays is likely to be determined by factors and conditions in China leading to greater or less identification of Malayan Chinese interests with those of Chinese cultural and political imperialism. The future role of the Western nations or the Communist nations in Malayan affairs will probably be a function of the relations between the two groups on a world basis.

In view of all the above factors, the course of future development is neither clear nor certain. The following problems appear paramount at the moment: the Federation agreement was essentially a compromise between the extremes of centralization and decentralization; its continuation in the new constitution does not appear to be a final solution to the problem of Malayan unity. The primary problem still remains.

Efforts to create democratic and representative political forms are still in the experimental phase, with the primary problem that of creating a Malayan-oriented constituency out of several diverse and antipathetic ethnic groups, speaking several languages and possessed of little sense of national identification.

The dependence of the Malayan economy on the price of rubber and tin makes it vulnerable to extreme fluctuations in world markets. Competition from other sources, both regional and technological, has removed Malaya from its dominant position as a source of these two commodities, and there is increasing uncertainty as to the future stability of an economy largely dependent upon their production and export.

Problems arising from the pluralistic nature of Malayan society have not been resolved, although some activity in that direction has taken place. Basic differences and interests continue to separate the Chinese, the Indians, and the Malays, the urban populations from their rural brethren, and the ruling elites from the masses.

As for Singapore, perhaps the most pressing problem of the future will be the definition of its relationship to the Federation in view of the announced refusal of the Federation leaders to consider unification.

Some moves have been taken in partial resolution of the above problems, but their effectiveness is as yet uncertain.

The immigrational streams from India and China have been virtually closed, and the percentage of Malayan-born Chinese and Indians is increasing rapidly.

The self-sufficiency of the Chinese as an ethnic and economic group is gradually diminishing, thus helping to integrate them more fully into the general Malayan political economy. The Chinese also are beginning to participate in the internal political affairs of the country, although to a lesser degree than the Malays and Indians.

There is a growing emphasis on peasant self-sufficient agriculture, both in rubber and subsistence production on the one hand and in diversified light industries on the other.

The shift from British administration to local self-government appears to be taking place without serious disruption or internal disturbance, thus permitting a continuity in administrative control.

Growing Malay identification with other Malaysian and Moslem peoples looks toward the creation of either a greater pan-Malay or a pan-Islam federation, although the Chinese would strongly oppose the submergence of their interests to either of these alien conceptions. Identification by the Malayan Malays with the rest of the Malay world, and their conception of Malaya's centrality in that world, are suggested by a proposed name for the independent Federation: "Malaysia." At the same time, the economic and political difficulties in which Indonesia finds itself act as powerful deterrents to a pan-Malaysia for Malays accustomed to the relative stability of British institutions, judicial, commercial, and political.

Appendix: Note on Concentration Index Maps

THE CONCEPT "concentration" usually embodies two related factors: (1) compactness, and (2) purity. The corresponding factors in demography are density and homogeneity of a population. The concentration index (CI) is an expression of the relationship between these two factors. It is formed from three variables: (1) the size of the area concerned (A), (2) the total population of that area (TP), and (3) the size of the referent subclass (SC), which is determined in relation to any generalized characteristic. The index formula is then expressed as $CI = \frac{SC}{A} \times \frac{SC}{TP}$, or simply, the areal density of the subclass (D) times its ratio in the total population (R).

The nature of the index can, perhaps, be illustrated by the following examples:

	A	TP	SC	D	R	CI
A	100	20,000	20,000	200	1.0	200
B	100	20,000	10,000	100	0.5	50
C	50	20,000	10,000	200	0.5	100
D	50	40,000	10,000	200	0.25	50
E	50	40,000	20,000	400	0.5	200

It is apparent from example A that where the referent group is identical with the total population, then the concentration index is identical with the population density. In example B only the size of the subclass has been changed--reduced by half-- yet significantly the concentration index is reduced by three-fourths, since the halving of the subclass reduces both its density and its ratio in the total population. In example C, both the area and the size of the subclass have been halved, and since the change is proportional the density remains the same. The ratio is halved, however, resulting in a halving of the concentration index. The other two examples show similar variations in the index dependent upon changed relationships among the three variable factors.

It has been noted that in a situation where the subclass is identical with the total population, as in example A, the concentration index is identical with the density of the total population. If there were no members of the subclass in the total population the index would be zero. The index, therefore, always defines a relationship between the subclass and the total population somewhere along a continuum whose terminals are a theoretical zero and a figure equal to the density of the total population. This relationship can be expressed as a fraction with CI as the numerator and the total density as the denominator. Thus, with a total population density of 100 and a CI of 25, the fraction 25/100 indicates that the degree of concentration of the particular subclass is equal to one-fourth the maximum possible degree of concentration (where the subclass would be identical with the total population).

When the concentration index of some subclass is mapped (as in Map 22 for example) and compared with a map of total population density (Map 2), the degree of homogeneity in the area mapped becomes apparent. The greater the variation between the two map patterns, the less the homogeneity within the population.

If, on a graph, two series of numbers representing the areal density of the subclass and its ratio in the total population are assigned to the X and Y axes, the concentration index for any particular combination of the two factors can be indicated by position on the graph. If a large number of indexes were so plotted on a single graph, it would be found that all concentration indexes of a particular value lie on a parabolic arc focused on that point of the graph farthest away from 0. If coordinates were drawn on the graph for a number of indexes of equal value, it would be seen that the areas of the graph enclosed within the coordinates for each index are identical, regardless of the numerical value of either factor, density or ratio. Thus, each CI of 50, for example, indicates an identical degree of concentration of a subclass, regardless of the size of the areas concerned, the size of the subclass, or the size of the total population of which it is a part. It is this quality which makes the

506

index particularly useful for comparative purposes among geographical units, such as census districts, of various areas and
populations.

The primary problem which use of the index solves can be
shown in relation to Maps 4 and 17, concerned with density of
Chinese population and proportions among the total population
of the major ethnolinguistic groups. On the first map the districts of Balik Palau on Penang, and Butterworth and Bukit in
Province Wellesley are all in the same category, while Nibong Tebal, the third district in Province Wellesley, is in
a lower category. Since these four districts all appear to have
about the same area it might seem logical to suppose that the
Chinese are of about equal significance in the populations of
the first three districts, and of less significance in the fourth.
If the same districts are observed on the second map, just the
opposite impression is given--that the Chinese are most significant in Nibong Tebal, of less significance in Balik Palau
and Bukit, and of relatively little significance in Butterworth.
In order to gain any realistic impression of the significance of
the Chinese in the four districts it would be necessary to compare the two maps with each other and with Map 2, "Density
of Population," and probably with the density maps for the
other ethnic groups.

Thus, neither of the two measures, density (Map 4), or
proportion (Map 17), can be considered an adequate index of
population significance by itself; a subclass with a density of
fifty persons per square mile in a city of small area and a total
population one hundred times that of the subclass cannot be
considered equal in significance to a subclass with a density
of fifty in an area where the subclass is nearly equivalent to
the total population. In the case of a subclass of Chinese one
would have to say that the second area is "more Chinese" than
the first. Similarly a subclass with a . 50 ratio in an area of
high general density must be considered more significant than
a subclass with the same ratio in a low-density area. The concentration index is intended to bring these variable relationships together in a single common system which will allow
comparative estimates of subclass significance among areas
and populations of wide variability.

In the maps in this book showing the concentration indexes
for the various literacy communities, the indexes for each census district have been grouped and categorized for ease of
comparison. The categories used are common to all four maps.

The wide range of indexes did not allow the use of equal-interval categories; nearly one hundred categories would have had to be indicated. Instead, the categories used are based on a geometric progression in which each category indicates about twice the degree of concentration as the next lower category. Thus, on Map 21, "Concentration of Literates in Chinese," Penang Northeast and Singapore Island may be interpreted as containing within their populations roughly twice the concentration of literates in Chinese as Ipoh district, while Ipoh may be interpreted as having roughly twice the concentration of such districts as Balik Palau, Bukit, or Kuala Lumpur. Similar interpretations can be made in comparisons between districts on all four maps.

Bibliography

Adams, Sir T. "The Malay in Malaya," Asiatic Review, XL (January, 1944), 98-100.

Allen, D. F. Report on the Major Ports of Malaya. Kuala Lumpur: Government Press, 1951.

-------. Report on the Minor Ports of Malaya. Kuala Lumpur: Government Press, 1953.

Allen, G. C., and A. G. Donnithorne. Western Enterprise in Indonesia and Malaya. London: George Allen and Unwin, Ltd., 1957.

American Consulate-General, Hongkong. "Current Background," No. 290. Hongkong, September 5, 1954. (Mimeographed.)

-------. "Current Background," No. 301. Hongkong, November 1, 1954. (Mimeographed.)

-------. "Review of Hongkong Chinese Press," No. 213. Hongkong, January, 1955.

Andrews, Laura. "Welfare in Trengganu," Corona, VI (September, 1954), 352-55.

Awberry, S. S., and G. W. Dalley. Labour and Trade Union Organization in the Federation of Malaya and Singapore. (Colonial Office Publication No. 234.) London: H. M. Stationery Office, 1948.

Aziz, Ungku A. Some Aspects of the Malayan Rural Economy Related to Measures for Mobilizing Rural Savings. New York: United Nations, 1951.

Barnett, A. Doak. "A Contest of Loyalties: Overseas Chinese in Thailand." Circular letter of the American Universities Field Staff, ADB-15-54, New York, December 15, 1954.

-------. "Notes on Growing Forces among Singapore Chinese:

Political Parties, Students, and Workers." Circular letter of the American Universities Field Staff, ADB-9-55, New York, July 11, 1955.

-------. "Self-Rule and Unrest: Overseas Chinese in Singapore." Circular letter of the American Universities Field Staff, ADB-8-55, New York, July 7, 1955.

Bartlett, Vernon. Report from Malaya. London: Derek Verschoyle, 1954.

Bauer, P. T. Report on a Visit to the Rubber-Growing Smallholdings of Malaya, July-September, 1946. (Great Britain Colonial Office, Colonial Research Publication No. 1.) London: H. M. Stationery Office, 1948.

-------. The Rubber Industry: A Study in Competition and Monopoly. Cambridge: Harvard University Press, 1948.

Benham, Frederic. The National Income of Malaya, 1947-49 (with a note on 1950). Singapore: Government Printing Office, 1951.

Blaut, James. "The Economic Geography of a One-Acre Farm on Singapore Island," Malayan Journal of Tropical Geography, I (October, 1953), 37-48.

Blythe, W. L. "Historical Sketch of Chinese Labour in Malaya," Journal of the Malayan Branch of the Royal Asiatic Society, XX (1947), 64-114.

Burdon, T. W. Fishing Industry of Singapore. (Background to Malaya series, No. 5.) Singapore: Donald Moore, 1955.

Burge, William. Commentaries on Colonial and Foreign Laws, Vols. I, IV. London: Sweet and Maxwell, Ltd., 1907, 1928.

Burkill, I. H. Dictionary of Economic Products of the Malay Peninsula. London: Government of the Straits Settlements and the Federated Malay States, 1935. 2 vols.

Burnett, F. Report on Agriculture in Malaya for the Year 1946. Kuala Lumpur: Government Press, 1947.

-------. Report on Agriculture in Malaya for the Year 1947. Kuala Lumpur: Government Press, 1949.

Butwell, Richard. "A Chinese University for Malaya," Pacific Affairs, XXVI (December, 1953), 344-48.

Callis, H. G. Foreign Capital in Southeast Asia. New York: Institute of Pacific Relations, 1942.

Carnell, F. G. "Communalism and Communism in Malaya," Pacific Affairs, XXVI (June, 1953), 99-117.

-------. "Malayan Citizenship Legislation," The International and Comparative Law Quarterly, Ser. 4, Vol. I, Part IV (October, 1952), pp. 504-18.

--------. "Political Ferment in Singapore," Far Eastern Survey, XXIV (July, 1955), 97-102.

Carter, G. F., and R. L. Pendleton. "The Humid Soil: Process and Time," Geographical Review, XLVI (October, 1956), 488-507.

Chapman, F. Spencer. The Jungle Is Neutral. New York: W. W. Norton, 1949.

Chen, Ta. "Chinese Migrations with Special Reference to Labor Conditions," Bulletin of the United States Bureau of Labor Statistics, No. 340. Washington, D. C.: U. S. Government Printing Office, 1923.

--------. Emigrant Communities in South China. New York: Institute of Pacific Relations, 1940.

Cherry, W. T. Geography of British Malaya. Singapore: Malaya Publishing House, Ltd., 1928.

Chin, Kee-onn. Ma-rai-ee. London: George C. Harrap & Co., 1952.

Chinese Schools and the Education of Chinese Malayans: The Report of a Mission Invited by the Federation Government to Study the Problem of the Education of Chinese in Malaya. Kuala Lumpur: Government Press, 1951.

Choo, Oh Siew. The Chinese Physician in Singapore: A Study of His Popularity among the Chinese and People of Other Races. (Unpublished research paper for the Diploma of Social Studies.) Singapore: University of Malaya, May, 1955. (Available on microfilm.)

Colony of Singapore Annual Report. Singapore: Government Printing Office.

Colony of Singapore Department of Social Welfare. A Social Survey of Singapore: A Preliminary Study of Some Aspects of Social Conditions in the Municipal Area of Singapore, December, 1947. Singapore: G. H. Keat and Co., Ltd., n. d.

Colony of Singapore Government Printing Office. Catalogue of Government Publications, January, 1953. Singapore: Government Printing Office, 1953.

Colony of Singapore Marine Surveys Department. Report of the Government Marine Surveys Department 1949, by A. Graham. Singapore: Government Printing Office, 1950.

Comber, Leonard. Chinese Magic and Superstitions in Malaya. Singapore: Donald Moore, 1955.

Commonwealth Consultative Committee on South and South-East Asia. The Colombo Plan for Co-operative Economic Development in South and South-East Asia. (Cmd. 8080.) London: H. M. Stationery Office, 1950.

Concannon, T. A. L. "A New Town in Malaya," Malayan Journal of Tropical Geography, V (March, 1955), 39-43.

The Conflict in Asia of Capitalism, Communism and Indigenous Culture. A Report to the Twelfth Conference of the Institute of Public Relations, Kyoto, September and October, 1954. (New Zealand Paper No. 3.) Wellington: New Zealand Institute of International Affairs, 1954.

Cooper, Eunice. "Urbanization in Malaya," Population Studies, V (November, 1951), 117-31.

Corry, W. C. S. A General Survey of the New Villages. Kuala Lumpur: Government Press, 1954. (Restricted.)

Del Tufo, M. V. Malaya: A Report on the 1947 Census of Population. London: Crown Agents for the Colonies, 1949.

"Development of Mineral Resources, Federation of Malaya," Colonial Geology and Mineral Resources, IV (1954), 185-88.

Djamour, Judith. "Adoption of Children among Singapore Malaysians," Journal of the Royal Anthropological Institute of Great Britain and Ireland, LXXXII (1952), 159-68.

Dobby, E. H. G. Agricultural Questions of Malaya. Cambridge: Cambridge University Press, 1949.

-------. Malaya and the Malayans. (The Golden Hind Geographies First Series, Book Three [A].) London: University of London Press, 1947.

-------. "Malayan Prospect," Pacific Affairs, XXIII (December, 1950), 392-401.

-------. "Malaya's Rice Problem," Pacific Affairs, XXVII (March, 1954), 58-60.

-------. "The North Kedah Plain: A Study in the Environment of Pioneering for Rice Cultivation," Economic Geography, XXVIII (October, 1951), 287-315.

-------. "Recent Settlement Changes in the Kinta Valley," Malayan Journal of Tropical Geography, II (March, 1954), 62.

-------. "Recent Settlement Changes in South Malaya," Malayan Journal of Tropical Geography, I (October, 1953), 1-8.

-------. "Resettlement Transforms Malaya," Economic Development and Cultural Change, Vol. I (October, 1952).

-------. "Settlement and Land Utilization, Malacca," Geographical Journal, XCIV (December, 1939), 466-78.

-------. "Settlement Patterns in Malaya," Geographical Review, XXXII (April, 1942), 211-32.

-------. Southeast Asia. London: University of London Press, 1950.

--------, et al. "Padi Landscapes of Malaya," Malayan Journal of Tropical Geography, Vol. VI (October, 1955).

Donnithorne, A. G. Economic Developments since 1937 in Eastern and Southeastern Asia and Their Effects on the United Kingdom. London: Royal Institute of International Affairs, 1950.

Draft Development Plan of the Federation of Malaya. Kuala Lumpur: Government Press, 1950.

Dutt, Vidya Prakash. India's Foreign Policy, with Special Reference to Asia and the Pacific. (Eleventh Conference of the Institute of Pacific Relations, Lucknow, October, 1950, Indian Paper No. 1.) New Delhi: Indian Council of World Affairs, 1950.

Duyvendak, J. J. L. "The True Dates of the Chinese Maritime Expeditions of the Early Fifteenth Century, T'oung Pao, XXXIV (1939), 341-412.

Elsbree, Willard H. Japan's Role in Southeast Asian Nationalist Movements, 1940-1945. Cambridge: Harvard University Press, 1953.

"The Emergency in Malaya," The World Today, X (November, 1954), 477-87.

Emerson, Rupert. Malaysia. New York: Macmillan, 1937.

--------. Representative Government in Southeast Asia. Cambridge: Harvard University Press, 1955.

Fauconnier, H. Malaisie. Trans. Eric Sutton. New York: Macmillan, 1939.

Federated Malay States. Laws, Statutes, etc., 1920-1938. Kuala Lumpur: Government Press, 1940.

Federation of Malaya. Annual Report on Education. Kuala Lumpur: Government Press.

Federation of Malaya. Taxation and Replanting in the Rubber Industry. Statement of the Federal Government on the Report of the Mudie Mission and on Certain Proposals Made by the Rubber Producers' Council. Kuala Lumpur: Government Press, 1955.

Federation of Malaya Annual Report. Kuala Lumpur: Government Press.

Federation of Malaya, Attorney-General's Chambers. "Return of Societies in the Federation of Malaya, as at 31st December, 1954." Appendixes I, II, III. Kuala Lumpur, 1955. (Mimeographed.)

Federation of Malaya, Rural and Industrial Development Authority. Progress Report up to December 31, 1951. (Federation of Malaya Paper No. 24.) Kuala Lumpur: Government Press, 1952.

Ferguson, D. S. "Sungei Manik Irrigation Scheme, " Malayan Journal of Tropical Geography, II (March, 1954), 9-16.

Firth, Raymond. Malay Fishermen: Their Peasant Economy. London: Kegan Paul, Trench, Trubner, 1946.

-------. "The Peasantry in South-East Asia, " International Affairs, XXVI (October, 1950), 503-14.

-------. Report on Social Science Research in Malaya. 1949. (Unpublished MS.)

Firth, Rosemary. Housekeeping among Malay Peasants. (The London School of Economics and Political Science Monographs on Social Anthropology, No. 7.) London: London School of Economics and Political Science, 1943.

Fisher, C. A. "The Problem of Malayan Unity in Its Geographical Setting, " Part I: "Historical Geography"; Part II: "Recent and Contemporary Political Geography, " in Geographical Essays on British Tropical Lands, eds. R. W. Steel and C. A. Fisher. London: George Philip and Son, Ltd., 1956.

-------. "The Railway Geography of British Malaya, " Scottish Geographical Magazine, LXIV (1949), 123-35.

Fitzgerald, C. P. "East Asia after Bandung, " Far Eastern Survey, XXIV (August, 1955), 113-19.

Freedman, M. "Colonial Law and Chinese Society, " Journal of the Royal Anthropological Institute, LXXX, Parts I, II (1950), 97-125.

Fryer, D. W. "Food Production in Malaya, " The Australian Geographer, VI (May, 1954), 35-38.

Gamba, Charles. Labour Law in Malaya. (Background to Malaya series, No. 8.) Singapore: Donald Moore, 1955.

-------. "Malaya and Self Government, " Eastern World, VI (September, 1952), 16-17.

-------. "Rural Development in Malaya, " Eastern World, VI (May, 1952), 20-21.

-------. Synthetic Rubber and Malaya. (Background to Malaya series, No. 11.) Singapore: Donald Moore, 1956.

General Index of Ordinances, Enactments, Proclamations etc. in Force on the 31st of December, 1954. Kuala Lumpur: Government Press, 1954.

Ginsburg, Norton S. "The Great City in Southeast Asia, " The American Journal of Sociology, LX (March, 1955), 455-62.

-------- (ed.). The Pattern of Asia. New York: Prentice Hall, 1958.

Goh, Soon Phing. A Research Paper on Some Aspects of Woman's Life in a Singapore Chinese Fishing Village. (Unpublished research paper for Diploma of Social Studies.) Singapore: University of Malaya, 1955. (Available in microfilm.)

Great Britain Colonial Office. Economic Survey of the Colonial Territories, 1951. Vol. VII, The Products of the Colonial Territories. London: H. M. Stationery Office, 1952.

Great Britain, Secretary of State for Colonial Affairs. Report of Advisory Commission on Constitutional Development. Rome: Food and Agriculture Organization, 1957.

Grist, D. H. An Outline of Malayan Agriculture. (Malayan Planting Manual No. 2.) London: Crown Agents for the Colonies, 1950.

Groeneveldt, W. P. "Notes on the Malay Archipelago and Malacca," Verhandelingen van het Bataviaasch Genootschap van Kunsten en Wetenschappen, XXXIX (1880), 111-44.

Gullick, J. M. "Sungei Ujong," Journal of the Malayan Branch of the Royal Asiatic Society, XXII (May, 1949), 1-69.

Hall, D. G. E. A History of Southeast Asia. New York: St. Martin's Press, 1955.

Han, Su-yin. And the Rain My Drink. Boston: Atlantic Monthly-Little, Brown and Co., 1956.

-------. "Malaya: The 'Emergency' in Its Seventh Year," The Reporter, XI (December 16, 1954), 23-27.

Hanna, W. A. "Japan's Current Interests in Singapore and Malaya." Circular letter of the American Universities Field Staff, WAH-6-56, New York, March 5, 1956.

-------. "Indonesia and the New Malayan States." Circular letter of the American Universities Field Staff, WAH-5-56, New York, February 20, 1956.

Hanrahan, Gene Z. The Communist Struggle in Malaya, New York: Institute of Pacific Relations, 1954. (Mimeographed.)

Hartley, C. W. S. "Establishment of New Rice Areas in Malaya," World Crops, III (May, 1951), 171-74.

Hawkins, Gerald. "Marking Time in Malaya," International Affairs, XXIV (1948), 76-88.

Heath, R. G. Malayan Agricultural Statistics, 1949. (Federation of Malaya Department of Agriculture, Economic Series, No. 15.) Kuala Lumpur: Caxton Press, Ltd., 1951.

Hill, A. H. "Wayang Kulit Stories from Trengganu," Journal of the Malayan Branch of the Royal Asiatic Society, XXII (June, 1949), 85-105.

-------. "The Weaving Industry of Trengganu," Journal of the

Malayan Branch of the Royal Asiatic Society, XXII (June, 1949), 75-84.

Hill, L. C. Report on the Reform of Local Government. Singapore: Government Printing Office, 1952.

Hodder, B. W. "Racial Groupings in Singapore," Malayan Journal of Tropical Geography, I (October, 1953), 25-36.

Horseley, J. A. T. Resettlement of a Community. (Unpublished research paper for the Diploma of Social Studies.) Singapore: University of Malaya, April, 1955. (Available on microfilm.)

Hoselitz, B. F., et al. The Role of Foreign Aid in the Development of Other Countries, a Report Prepared for the U. S. Senate Special Committee to Study the Foreign Aid Program of the U. S. Chicago: The University of Chicago Research Center in Economic Development and Cultural Change, 1956. Published also as Report #3. Washington, D. C.: Government Printing Office, March, 1957.

India, Ministry of Labour, Labour Bureau. The Indian Labour Yearbook: 1947-48. Delhi: Manager of Publications, Civil Lines, 1949.

Indian Emigration. London: Oxford University Press, 1924.

"Indian Labour in Ceylon, Fiji, and British Malaya," International Labour Review, XLII (July, 1940), 57-76.

"Indian Periodicals," a review of an article by H. I. S. Kinwar, The Modern Review: A Monthly Review and Miscellany, XCIII (May, 1953), 412.

International Bank for Reconstruction and Development. The Economic Development of Malaya. Baltimore: Johns Hopkins Press, 1955.

International Tin Study Group. Review of the World Tin Position 1947-1948. The Hague: International Tin Study Group, 1948.

-------. Tin 1950-1951. The Hague: International Tin Study Group, 1951.

Jacoby, E. H. Agrarian Unrest in Southeast Asia. New York: Columbia University Press, 1949.

John, I. G. Malayan Meteorological Service, Summary of Observations, 1953. Singapore: Government Printing Office, 1954.

Johnson, Moyra. "Malayan Arts and Crafts," Far Eastern Economic Review, XIII (September 18, 1952), 369-70.

Jones, S. W. Public Administration in Malaya. London: Royal Institute of International Affairs, 1953.

Josey, Alex. Trade Unionism in Malaya. (Background to Malaya series, No. 4.) Singapore: Donald Moore, 1954.

Josselin de Jong, P. E. de. Minangkabau and Negri Sembilan: Socio-Political Structure in Indonesia. The Hague: Martinus Nijhoff, 1952.

King, F. H. H. Money in British East Asia. (Colonial Research Publication No. 19.) London: H. M. Stationery Office, 1957.

Kinwar, H. I. S. "Indians in Malaya," Eastern World, VI (December, 1952), 14-15; VII (January, 1953), 19.

———. "India's Link to Malaya," United Asia, II (June, 1950), 423-26.

———. "Malaya's Cultural Contacts with India," Asia, III, No. 12 (March, 1954), 536-44.

Kleinsorge, P. L. "Employers' Associations in Malaya," Far Eastern Survey, XXVI (August, 1957), 124-27.

Knorr, I. E. Tin under Control. Palo Alto, Calif.: Stanford University Food Research Institute, 1945.

Kondapi, C. "Indians Overseas: A Survey of Developments in 1947," India Quarterly, IV (January-March, 1948), 60-77.

———. Indians Overseas: 1838-1949. New Delhi: Indian Council of World Affairs, 1951.

Kwok, Swee Soo. An Account of the Sources of Benevolent Assistance Which Are Asian in Origin and Organization. Unpublished research paper for the Diploma of Social Studies, University of Malaya, 1954. (Microfilm.)

Ladejinsky, W. I. "Agriculture in British Malaya." Foreign Agriculture, V (March, 1941), 103-25.

Landon, K. P. Southeast Asia, Crossroads of Religion. (Haskell Lectures in Comparative Religion.) Chicago: University of Chicago Press, 1948.

Lang, Olga. Chinese Family and Society. New Haven: Yale University Press, 1946.

Lasker, Bruno. Asia on the Move. New York: Henry Holt, 1946.

———. "Mineral Resources of Southeast Asia," Journal of Geography, XLII (October, 1943), 241-48.

Latourette, Kenneth S. The Chinese: Their History and Culture, Vol. II. New York: Macmillan, 1951.

Levi, Werner. Free India in Asia. Minneapolis: University of Minnesota Press, 1952.

Levy, Marion J., Jr. The Family Revolution in Modern China. Cambridge: Harvard University Press, 1949.

Li, Dun J. British Malaya: An Economic Analysis. New York: The American Press, 1955.

Lim, Joo-jock. "Tradition and Peasant Agriculture in Malaya," Malayan Journal of Tropical Agriculture, III (October, 1954), 44-47.

Lim, Tay Boh. Problems of the Malayan Economy. (Background to Malaya series, No. 10.) Singapore: Donald Moore, 1956.

Mackenzie, K. E. Malaya: Economic and Commercial Conditions in the Federation of Malaya and Singapore. (Great Britain Board of Trade Overseas Economic Surveys.) London: H. M. Stationery Office, 1952.

Madan, B. K. (ed.). Economic Problems of Underdeveloped Countries in Asia. New Delhi: Indian Council of World Affairs, 1953.

Malayan Statistics, General Section, December, 1950. Singapore: Government Printing Office, 1951.

Malayan Tin Bureau. There Is Plenty of Tin. Washington: Malayan Tin Bureau, 1952.

Markandan, Paul. The Problem of the New Villages of Malaya. Singapore: Donald Moore, 1954.

Mason, Frederic. Schools of Malaya. (Background to Malaya series, No. 3.) Singapore: Donald Moore, 1957.

Means, Gordon. New Villages in Malaya. Unpublished manuscript, University of Washington, 1957.

Meek, Charles K. Land Law and Custom in the Colonies. London: Oxford University Press, 1949.

Meek, J. P. Malaya: A Study of Governmental Response to the Korean Boom. (Cornell University Department of Far Eastern Studies, Southeast Asia Program, Data Paper No. 17.) Ithaca: Cornell University, April, 1955. (Mimeographed.)

Middlebrook, S. M. "Ceremonial Opening of a New Chinese Temple at Kadan, Malacca, in December, 1938," Journal of the Malayan Branch of the Royal Asiatic Society, XVII (1939), 98-106.

------- . "Yap Ah Hoy," Journal of the Malayan Branch of the Royal Asiatic Society, Vol. XXIV (July, 1951).

------- , and A. W. Pinnick. How Malaya Is Governed. 2nd ed. New York: Longmans, Green, 1949.

Miller, Eugene H. Strategy at Singapore. New York: Macmillan, 1942.

Mills, Lennox A. British Rule in Eastern Asia. London: Oxford University Press, 1942.

Mitchell, Kate L. Industrialization of the Western Pacific.

(Institute of Pacific Relations Inquiry series.) New York: Institute of Pacific Relations, 1942.

Morrison, Ian. "Aspects of the Racial Problem in Malaya," Pacific Affairs, XXII (September, 1949), 239-53.

--------. "The Malay: Lover of Colour and Ceremony," Geographical Magazine, XXIII (1950-51), 239-53.

Moubray, G. A. de C. de. Matriarchy in the Malay Peninsula and Neighboring Countries. London: George Routledge and Sons, 1931.

Nanjundan, S. "Economic Development in Malaya," India Quarterly, VIII (1952), 289-311.

Narasimhan, P. S. "The Immigrant Communities of South East Asia," India Quarterly, III (January-March, 1947), 32-41.

Nathan, J. E. The Census of British Malaya, 1921. London: Waterlow & Sons, Ltd., 1922.

Newcombe, V. Z. "Housing in the Federation of Malaya," The Town Planning Review, XXVII (April, 1956), 4-20.

Noane, R. O. "Notes on the Kampongs, Compounds, and Houses of the Patani Malay Village of Banggul Arai, in the Mukim of Batu Karau, Northern Perak," Journal of the Malayan Branch of the Royal Asiatic Society, XXX (April, 1948), 124-47.

Official Airline Guide. World-Wide Edition. Washington, D. C.: American Aviation Publications, Inc., August, 1955.

Onraet, Rene. Singapore: A Police Background. London: Dorothy Crisp, n. d.

Ooi, Jin-bee. "Mining Landscapes of Kinta," The Malayan Journal of Tropical Geography, Vol. IV (January, 1955).

Orde-Browne, G. St. John. Labour Conditions in Ceylon, Mauritius and Malaya. (Command Paper No. 6423.) London: H. M. Stationery Office, 1943.

Owen, G. "A Provisional Classification of Malayan Soils," The Journal of Soil Science, II (January, 1951), 20-41.

Parkinson, C. N. Britain in the Far East. (Background to Malaya series, No. 7.) Singapore: Donald Moore, 1955.

--------. A Short History of Malaya. (Background to Malaya series No. 1.) Singapore: Donald Moore, 1956.

Parmer, J. Norman. "Trade Unions and Politics in Malaya," Far Eastern Survey, XXIV (1955), 33-39.

--------. Colonial Labor Policy and Administration: A History of Labor in the Rubber Plantation Industry in Malaya, 1910-1941. Unpublished Ph. D. dissertation, Cornell University, February, 1957.

519

Parry, M. L. "The Fishing Methods of Malaya and Trengganu," Journal of the Malayan Branch of the Royal Asiatic Society, XXVII (1954), 77-144.

Pelzer, Karl. Population and Land Utilization. New York: Institute of Pacific Relations, 1941.

Pillai, P. P. (ed.). Labour in Southeast Asia: A Symposium. New Delhi: Indian Council of World Affairs, 1947.

Pim, Sir A. Colonial Agriculture Production, the Contribution Made by the Native Peasants and Foreign Enterprise. London: Oxford University Press, 1946.

Purcell, Victor. The Chinese in Malaya. London: Oxford University Press, 1948.

------. The Chinese in Modern Malaya. (Background to Malaya series, No. 9.) Singapore: Donald Moore, 1956.

------. The Chinese in Southeast Asia. London: Oxford University Press, 1951.

------. "The Crisis in Malayan Education," Pacific Affairs, XXVI (March, 1953), 70-75.

------. Malaya: Communist or Free. London: Victor Gollancz, Ltd., 1954.

Pye, Lucian W. Guerrilla Communism in Malaya. Princeton: Princeton University Press, 1957.

Raghavan, Nedyam. India and Malaya: A Study. (India and Her Neighbors series of the Indian Council of World Affairs.) Bombay: Orient Longmans, Ltd., 1954.

------. Indians in the Malayan Economy. New Delhi: Government of India Press, 1950.

Rao, P. Kodanda. "Indians Overseas: The Position in Malaya," India Quarterly, II (April-June, 1946), 150-62.

Ratnam, S. Raja. "The Changing Malay People," Asia, XLII (August, 1942), 449-53.

Rees-Williams, D. R. "The Malayan Situation in 1948," Three Reports on the Malayan Problem, Part I. New York: Institute of Pacific Relations, 1949.

Robinson, J. B. Parry. Transformation in Malaya. London: Secker & Warburg, 1956.

Robequain, Charles. Malaya, Indonesia, Borneo and the Philippines. Trans. E. D. Laborde. London: Longmans, Green, 1954.

Sampson, Henry (ed.). World Railways, 1954-1955. London: Purnell and Sons, 1955.

Service, H., and I. L. Patterson. "Mineral Resources for Non-Ferrous Metals in the Federation of Malaya," in United

Nations Department of Economic Affairs, Development of Mineral Resources in Asia and the Far East. Bangkok, 1953.

Sheppard, M. C. ff. "A Short History of Trengganu," Journal of the Malayan Branch of the Royal Asiatic Society, XXII (June, 1949), 1-74.

Siew, Nim Chee. Labor and Tin Mining in Malaya. (Data Paper No. 7.) Ithaca: Cornell University Press, 1953.

Silcock, T. H. Dilemma in Malaya. (Fabian Colonial Bureau Pamphlet, Research Series No. 135.) London: Fabian Publications, Ltd., 1949.

-------. The Economy of Malaya. (Background to Malaya series, No. 2.) Singapore: Donald Moore, 1956.

-------, and Ungku Abdul Aziz. Nationalism in Malaya. (Eleventh Conference of the Institute of Pacific Relations, Lucknow, October, 1950, Series Paper No. 8.) New York: Institute of Pacific Relations, 1950.

Sim, Katherine. Malayan Landscape. London: Michael Joseph, Ltd., 1946.

-------. "Malayan Notebook," Corona, V (April, 1953), 142-44.

-------. "Mandi Safar in Malacca," Corona, VI (June, 1954), 224-25.

-------. "Resettlement Camps in Malaya," Corona, IV (July, 1952), 264-66.

"The Sino-Indonesian Treaty on Dual Nationality," Far Eastern Survey, XXIV (May, 1955), 75-76.

Smith, T. E. Population Growth in Malaya, an Analysis of Recent Trends. London: Royal Institute of International Affairs, 1952.

Sovani, N. V. Economic Relations of India with South-East Asia and the Far East. Madras: Indian Council of World Affairs, 1949.

Stead, Ronald. "The New Villages in Malaya," Geographical Magazine, XXVII (April, 1955), 642-52.

Tan, T. H. "Chinese in Malaya," The Nation, December 25, 1954, pp. 549-50.

Taylor, E. N. "Inheritance in Negri Sembilan," Journal of the Malayan Branch of the Royal Asiatic Society, XXI (September, 1948), 41-129.

-------. "Malay Family Law," Journal of the Malayan Branch of the Royal Asiatic Society, Vol. XV (May, 1937).

Taylor, W. C. Local Government in Malaya. Kedah: Government Press, 1949.

Ter Haar, Barend (trans.). Adat Law in Indonesia. New York: Institute of Pacific Relations, 1948.

Terra, G. J. A. "Mixed Garden Horticulture in Java," Malayan Journal of Tropical Geography, III (October, 1954), 33-43.

Thompson, Virginia. Labor Problems in Southeast Asia. New Haven: Yale University Press, 1947.

------, and Richard Adloff. The Left Wing in Southeast Asia. New York: William Sloane, 1950.

-------. Minority Problems in Southeast Asia. Stanford, Calif.: Stanford University Press, 1955.

T'ien, Ju-kang. The Chinese in Sarawak. (The London School of Economics and Political Science Monograph on Social Anthropology, No. 12.) London: London School of Economics and Political Science, 1953.

Tinker, Irene. "Malayan Election: Electoral Pattern for Plural Societies," Western Political Quarterly, IX (June, 1956), 258-82.

Topley, Marjorie. "Chinese Rites for the Repose of the Souls, with Special Reference to Cantonese Custom," Journal of the Malayan Branch of the Royal Asiatic Society, XXV (1952), 149-60.

Tweedie, M. W. F. Prehistoric Malaya. (Background to Malaya series, No. 6.) Singapore: Donald Moore, 1955.

UNESCO. "Report of the Commission on Technical Needs," in Press, Film, Radio, 1947. Vol. II. Paris: UNESCO, 1948; Second Supplement. Paris: UNESCO, 1950; Vol. V. Paris: UNESCO, 1951.

------, Department of Mass Communication. The Daily Press: A Survey of the World Situation in 1952. (Reports and Papers on Mass Communication, No. 7.) Paris: UNESCO, 1953.

United Nations, Department of Economic Affairs. Development of Mineral Resources in Asia and the Far East. Bangkok: United Nations, 1953.

-------. Economic Survey of Asia and the Far East, 1953. Bangkok: United Nations, 1954.

United Nations Economic Commission for Asia and the Far East. Coal and Iron Resources of Asia and the Far East. Bangkok: UNECAFE, 1952.

United States Board on Geographic Names. Decisions on Names in the Federation of Malaya and Singapore. Washington, D.C.: Department of the Interior, January, 1952.

United States Department of State, Division of Publications. Malaya: Trouble Spot in Southeast Asia; Background. (Department of State Publication 5061, Far Eastern Series, No. 57.) Washington, D. C.: U. S. Government Printing Office, 1953.

Vlieland, C. A. British Malaya: A Report of the 1931 Census. London: Malayan Information Agency, 1932.

Wales, H. G. Quaritch. "Archeological Researches on Ancient Indian Colonization in Malaya," Journal of the Malayan Branch of the Royal Asiatic Society, Vol. XVIII, Part I (February, 1940).

Watts, I. E. M. "Line-Squalls of Malaya," The Malayan Journal of Tropical Geography, III (October, 1954), 1-14.

Wickizer, V. D., and M. K. Bennett. The Rice Economy of Monsoon Asia. Palo Alto, Calif.: Stanford University Food Research Institute, 1941.

Williams-Hunt, P. D. R. An Introduction to the Malayan Aborigines. Kuala Lumpur: Government Press, 1952.

Winstedt, Sir R. O. Britain and Malaya. London: Longmans, Green, 1944.

-------. "A History of Malay Literature," Journal of the Malayan Branch of the Royal Asiatic Society, XVIII, Part I (January, 1940), 1-141.

-------. A History of Malaya. Singapore: Malayan Branch of the Royal Asiatic Society, 1935.

-------. Malaya: The Straits Settlements and the Federated and Unfederated Malay States. London: Constable, 1923.

-------. The Malays, a Cultural History. Rev. ed. London: Routledge and Kegan Paul, Ltd., 1950.

-------. "Malaysia," in Islam Today, ed. A. J. Arberry and Rom Landau. London: Faber and Faber, 1943.

-------, and P. E. de Josselin de Jong. "A Digest of Customary Law from Sungei Ujong," Journal of the Malayan Branch of the Royal Asiatic Society, XXVII (July, 1954), 1-71.

Zain, Al-Abidin bin Ahmad. "Malay Festivals and Some Aspects of Malay Religious Life," Journal of the Malayan Branch of the Royal Asiatic Society, XXII (March, 1949), 94-106.

-------. "Malay Journalism in Malaya," Journal of the Malayan Branch of the Royal Asiatic Society, Vol. XIX, Part II (October, 1941).

-------. "Modern Developments in Malay Literature," Journal of the Malayan Branch of the Royal Asiatic Society, XVIII, Part II (1940), 142-62.

Index

528

Municipal Amendment Ordinance, 453-54

Rubber industry, 44, 45, 46, 111, 196, 198, 318, 357, 363-70 passim, 372, 373, 376, 382, 390-94, 418-20, 438; and estate patterns, 95, 97, 333-36; implements used in, 199-200n; and Malays, 205, 207-10, 241, 258; and Chinese, 244, 252, 257-59; and Europeans, 257; and Indians, 258, 325, 329; and trade, 404, 406-7, 408, 412-13, 414

Rubber Industry (Replanting) Fund Ordinance, 258-59

Rubber Research Institute, 418

Rumor, as communication, 189-90

Rural and Industrial Development Authority, 416, 417, 419-20, 500

Sakai, 17

Sanitation problems: and Indians, 327-28

San Min Chu I Youth Corps, 463

Sastri, Srinavasa, 322, 347

Schools: English, 155, 156-57, 159, 160, 306-11 passim; Malay, 155, 156, 158, 159, 160; Indian, 155, 157, 158, 159, 160; Chinese, 155, 157, 158, 159, 160, 306-11 passim; and advanced education, 161-62; radio programs for, 179-82

Schools Broadcasting Service, 179

Secret societies: Chinese, 282-95

Selangor: natural environment of, 9; mineral resources of, 15; history of, 25, 30, 31, 32, 33, 35-41 passim, 43; population of, 55, 61, 63, 64, 67, 68, 69, 73, 139, 259, 324; mining in, 95; transportation in, 127, 416; literacy in, 143; immigration into, 193; occupations in, 255, 264, 323, 369, 392; political participation in, 290, 354, 355, 457, 473, 474; power resources of, 401, 402n; and residency system, 427-30

Selangor, Sultan of, 39, 41, 428, 453

Semang, 17

Senoi, 17

Sequeira, Diego de, 27

Seremban, 136, 150, 171, 475

Settlement patterns: of Malays, 80-86, 92, 93, 195n, 225-26; of Chinese, 90, 92, 93, 97, 195n, 246-47, 259-60, 273-74; of Indians, 92, 93, 97, 323-26

Setul, 39

Shaw Brothers, Ltd., 186

Silcock, T. H., 238

Singapore: natural environment of, 7, 9; history of, 20, 23, 35, 36, 38, 42, 246, 247, 316, 317, 422, 425, 426; population of, 50, 51, 54, 56, 57, 61, 64, 65, 66, 67, 68, 69, 73, 76, 88, 89, 93, 94, 136, 138, 139, 141, 324; ethnic groups in, 90-91; transportation in, 103, 107, 109, 110, 111, 113, 114, 116, 117, 118, 124; as leading port, 120-23; communications in, 126, 127, 128, 172, 188, 416; literacy in, 142-45 passim, 150; education in, 155, 160-61, 162, 235, 305, 306-9; publications of, 163, 166, 167, 168, 169, 173; radio broadcasting in, 175, 176, 177, 179, 181, 184; cinema in, 185, 186, 187; immigration into, 194, 251; occupations in, 202, 255, 256, 260-62, 329, 339, 340, 367, 368, 369, 374, 376, 382, 391, 396, 397, 398, 399; social organization in, 226, 240n, 277, 278, 279, 298; settlement patterns in, 252; political participation in, 267n, 268, 271, 273, 274, 280, 281, 291, 294, 311, 350, 353, 354, 356, 360, 370, 371, 372, 432, 436, 441, 442, 443, 452, 453, 457-66 passim, 473, 497, 501; secret societies in, 284, 285, 286, 288; trade of, 366, 404, 405, 407-10, 411-15 passim, 493; mineral resources of, 401; establishment of, 423; political parties in, 450-51, 468-72; and merdeka, 482-91; relationship with Federation, 490-91, 503; mentioned, v, 1, 284, 343

Singapore, Crown Colony of, 47, 448-51

Singapore Colony Orders in Council, 448

Singapore Constitutional Commission, 453

Singapore Improvement Trust, 455

Singapore Malay Union, 470

Singapore Middle School Students' Union, 483, 488, 489

Singapore Polytechnic, 161

Singapore Socialist Party, 469

Singapore Standard, 166

Singapore Telephone Board, 130

Singapore Trade Union Congress, 371, 488

Skinner, William, 144-45n

Smith, Sir Cecil Clementi, 287, 288

Smith, T. E., 72

Social affiliations: of Malays, 236-42; of Chinese, 311-15

Social organization: of Malays, 215-27; of Chinese, 244, 263-64, 265, 273-99; of Indians, 343-45

Social stratification: of Malays, 225-26; of Chinese, 298-99

Societies. See Associations

Societies Ordinance, 274

Society of Overseas Chinese. See Hua Ch'iao Society

Soils, 10-12

Sopiee, Inche Mohamed, 473

Law and Status among the Kiowa Indians. Jane Richardson. (Monograph I) 1940. 142 pages, bibliography. Out of print

Rank and Warfare among the Plains Indians. Bernard Mishkin. (Monograph III) 1940. 73 pages, bibliography. $1.50

Disease, Religion and Society in the Fiji Islands. Dorothy M. Spencer. (Monograph II) 1941. 92 pages, chart. Out of print

An Analysis of Inca Militarism. Joseph Bram. (Monograph IV) 1941. 93 pages, bibliography. $1.50

A Primitive Mexican Economy. George M. Foster. (Monograph V) 1942. 123 pages, plates, maps, bibliography. Out of print

The Effects of White Contact upon Blackfoot Culture, with Special Reference to the Role of the Fur Trade. Oscar Lewis. (Monograph VI) 1942. 79 pages, maps, bibliography. $1.50

Arapesh. R. F. Fortune. (Publication XIX) 1942. 243 pages. $5.00

Prayer: The Compulsive Word. Gladys A. Reichard. (Monograph VII) 1944. 121 pages, figures, bibliography. $2.50

Changing Configurations in the Social Organization of a Blackfoot Tribe during the Reserve Period (The Blood of Alberta, Canada). Esther S. Goldfrank. (Monograph VIII, bound with IX) 1945. 81 pages, plates, bibliography. $2.50

Observations on Northern Blackfoot Kinship. L. M. Hanks, Jr., and Jane Richardson. (Monograph IX, bound with VIII) 1945. 37 pages, figures. $2.50

Map of North American Indian Languages. Compiled and drawn by C. F. Voegelin and E. W. Voegelin. (Publication XX) 1945. Wall size, color. $2.00

The Influence of Islam on a Sudanese Religion. Joseph Greenberg. (Monograph X) 1946. 83 pages, figures, map, bibliography. $2.50

Alaskan Eskimo Ceremonialism. Margaret Lantis. (Monograph XI) 1947. 143 pages, maps, bibliography. $2.75

Economics of the Mount Hagen Tribes, New Guinea. Abraham L. Gitlow. (Monograph XII) 1947. 122 pages, plates, figures, maps, bibliography. $2.75

Ceremonial Patterns in the Greater Southwest. Ruth M. Underhill. (Monograph XIII, bound with XIV) 1948. 74 pages, bibliography, index. $2.50

Factionalism in Isleta Pueblo. David H. French. (Monograph XIV, bound with XIII) 1948. 54 pages, bibliography. $2.50

The Negro in Northern Brazil: A Study in Acculturation. Octavio da Costa Eduardo. (Monograph XV) 1948. 139 pages, map, bibliography. $2.75

Bali: Rangda and Barong. Jane Belo. (Monograph XVI) 1949. 71 pages, plates, figures, bibliography. $2.75

The Rubber-Ball Games of the Americas. Theodore Stern. (Monograph XVII) 1950. 129 pages, plate, maps, bibliography. $2.50

Fighting with Property: A Study of Kwakiutl Potlatching and Warfare 1792-1930. Helen Codere. With Tribal and Linguistic Map of Vancouver Island and Adjacent Territory, drawn and compiled by Vincent F. Kotschar. (Monograph XVIII) 1950. 143 pages, figures, maps, charts, bibliography. $3.00

The Cheyenne in Plains Indian Trade Relations 1795-1840. Joseph Jablow. (Monograph XIX) 1951. 110 pages, maps, bibliography, index. $2.50

The Tsimshian: Their Arts and Music. The Tsimshian and Their Neighbors, by Viola E. Garfield; Tsimshian Sculpture, by Paul S. Wingert; Tsimshian Songs, by Marius Barbeau. (Publication XVIII) 1951. 302 pages, plates, figures, maps, music, bibliography, index. $6.00

Navaho Grammar. Gladys A. Reichard. (Publication XXI) 1951. 407 pages, bibliography. $7.00

Buzios Island: A Caiçara Community in Southern Brazil. Emilio Willems in cooperation with Gioconda Mussolini. (Monograph XX) 1952. 124 pages, figures, maps, bibliography. $2.75

Chichicastenango: A Guatemalan Village. Ruth Bunzel. (Publication XXII) 1952. 464 pages, figures, bibliography. $7.00

Changing Military Patterns on the Great Plains (17th Century through Early 19th Century). Frank Raymond Secoy. (Monograph XXI) 1953. 120 pages, maps, bibliography. $2.75

Bali: Temple Festival. Jane Belo. (Monograph XXII) 1953. 78 pages, plates, chart, bibliography. $2.75

Hungarian and Vogul Mythology. Géza Róheim. With appendixes by John Lotz. (Monograph XXIII) 1954. 96 pages, map, bibliography. $2.75

The Trumai Indians of Central Brazil. Robert F. Murphy and Buell Quain. (Monograph XXIV) 1955. 120 pages, plates, map, bibliography. $2.75

The Deeply Rooted: A Study of a Drents Community in the Netherlands. John Y. Keur and Dorothy L. Keur. (Monograph XXV) 1955. 208 pages, plates, maps, bibliography. $3.00

The Tlingit Indians: Results of a Trip to the Northwest Coast of America and the Bering Straits. Aurel Krause. Translated by Erna Gunther. 1956. 320 pages, plates, figures, map, bibliography, index. $4.50

Village and Plantation Life in Northeastern Brazil. Harry William Hutchinson. 1957. 209 pages, plates, maps, charts, bibliography, index. $4.50

Malaya. Norton Ginsburg and Chester F. Roberts, Jr. 1958. 547 pages, maps, charts, bibliography, index. $6.00